Java P2P

Robert Flenner, Michael Abbott, Toufic Boubez, Frank Cohen,
Navaneeth Krishnan, Alan Moffet, Rajam Ramamurti,
Bilal Siddiqui, Frank Sommers

Unleashed

Java P2P Unleashed

Copyright © 2003 by Sams Publishing

International Standard Book Number: 0-672-32399-0

Library of Congress Catalog Card Number: 2002100053

Printed in the United States of America

First Printing: August 2002

05   04   03   02   4   3   2   1

Trademarks

Warning and Disclaimer

EXECUTIVE EDITOR
Michael Stephens

ACQUISITIONS EDITOR
Todd Green

DEVELOPMENT EDITOR
Tiffany Taylor

MANAGING EDITOR
Charlotte Clapp

PROJECT EDITOR
George E. Nedeff

COPY EDITORS
Seth Kerney
Lindsey Rue

INDEXER
Heather McNeill

PROOFREADER
Linda Seifert

TECHNICAL EDITORS
Earl Bingham
Frank Cohen
Hang T. Lau
Alan Moffet

TEAM COORDINATOR
Lynne Williams

MULTIMEDIA DEVELOPER
Dan Scherf

INTERIOR DESIGNER
Gary Adair

COVER DESIGNER
Aren Howell

PAGE LAYOUT
Julie Parks

Contents at a Glance

Contents

Part A   Appendix   673

About the Lead Author

Robert Flenner is an independent Java software developer based in Texas. He contributed to *Professional Jini* (Wrox) and *Professional Java eCommerce* (Wrox). Robert is a regular contributor to the O'Reilly ONJava Web site, where he is currently publishing a series of articles related to Jini and JavaSpaces. He has been involved in managing, architecting, and developing information systems for 17 years. His most recent book is *Jini and JavaSpaces Application Development* (Sams), published in December 2001.

Contributing Authors

Michael Abbott has more than 10 years of distributed computing experience, has been published in several peer-reviewed journals, and speaks regularly on XML and distributed transaction management. Mike founded METAmorphosis, a company focusing on managing distribution transactions across heterogeneous databases, and is currently working with code. Mike is very involved in the computing community—he participates on a JSR Expert Group at Sun, participates on a technical committee at OASIS, is currently the president of the BEA User Group in Silicon Valley, and has chaired the XML Sig for the Software Development Forum for the past two years.

Mike was most recently the CTO and Executive-Vice President of Electron Economy, a supply chain software company, prior to its acquisition by Viewlocity. During his tenure there, Electron Economy was named to Upside's Top 100 companies of 2000 and filed four technical patents. Mike also serves on the board of directors for Innogenex, and on the strategic advisory board to SchemaLogic. He holds a B.S. degree in biochemistry with a focus in computer science from California Polytechnic State University, and has completed Ph.D. work at the University of Washington.

Toufic Boubez is the Chief Technology Officer of Layer 7 Technologies, specializing in Web services security. While at IBM, he was a senior technologist in the Emerging Technologies group and the chief architect of IBM's Web services initiative, as well as the architect of the first iterations of the IBM Web Services Toolkit. He was also IBM's technical representative to UDDI, and a coauthor of the UDDI V1 API specification. Toufic represented IBM on other standards bodies, such as the UN/CEFACT/OASIS ebXML initiative, and helped drive IBM's early XML and Web services strategy. He has acted as technical chair for the XML Web Services One Conference, and technical chair for various tracks.

Toufic has more than 15 years of experience in IT and has presented and published papers in the areas of Web services, XML, software agents, machine learning, object technology, B2B, business modeling, simulation, neural networks, wavelet analysis, and distributed computing. He is the coauthor of *Building Web Services with Java* (Sams).

Frank Cohen is a software entrepreneur who has contributed to the worldwide success of personal computers since 1975. He has written operating systems for microcomputers, helped establish video games as an industry, helped establish the Norton Utilities franchise, lead Apple's efforts into middleware and Internet technologies, and is currently serving as principal architect for the Sun Community Server, Inclusion.net, and TuneUp.com. Frank is principal maintainer for the open-source TestMaker project and is CEO for PushToTest, a scalability and performance testing solutions company. Previously, Frank authored *Testing Web Services* (Osborne McGraw-Hill, 2002) and contributed to *Java Web Services Unleashed* (Sams, 2002). You can reach Frank at fcohen@pushtotest.com.

Navaneeth Krishnan works for Sun Microsystems's Sun ONE Identity Server group in Bangalore, India. He has extensive experience in designing and developing J2EE-based application frameworks and solutions. His current focus is on user identity management, Web services and peer-to-peer technologies. He has been involved in JXTA since mid-2001, and strongly believes that it has the potential to make a significant impact in the area of peer-to-peer computing.

He spends his spare time writing articles, contributing to books, and exploring the endless possibilities created by emerging technologies. Previously, he contributed to *JXTA: Java P2P Programming* (Sams).

Alan Moffet has over 20 years of development (C++, Java, Smalltalk, XML) and management experience with companies such as Northern Telecom (Texas). He is currently an independent consultant whose interests are in distributed systems, systems architecture, components and objects, and software engineering. He specializes in the application of emerging technologies and improving organizational development capacity.

Rajam Ramamurti is a designer and developer who specializes in creating documentation for a variety of technologies, including J2EE, EJB, XML, and C++. Clients have included Gene Logic, Kanisa, Netscape, Oracle, and Progress Software, for whom she conducted training sessions on EJB architecture. She holds a master's degree in linguistics from the University of Pennsylvania.

Bilal Siddiqui is an electronics engineer, an XML consultant, and the co-founder of WaxSys, a company focused on simplifying e-business. After graduating with a degree in electronics engineering from the University of Engineering and Technology, Lahore, in 1995, he began designing software solutions for industrial control systems. Later he turned to XML, and used his experience programming in C++ to build Web- and WAP-based XML processing tools, server-side parsing solutions, and service applications. He is a technology evangelist and a frequently published technical author.

Frank Sommers is CEO and founder of Autospaces, a company focused on bringing Jini technology and Web services to the automotive software market. He has been developing Java-based software since attending Sun Microsystems' first Java conference in November, 1995. Frank's interests include parallel and distributed computing, the discovery and representation of knowledge in databases, and the philosophical foundations of computing.

We Want to Hear from You!

As the reader of this book, *you* are our most important critic and commentator. We value your opinion and want to know what we're doing right, what we could do better, what areas you'd like to see us publish in, and any other words of wisdom you're willing to pass our way.

As an executive editor for Sams Publishing, I welcome your comments. You can email or write me directly to let me know what you did or didn't like about this book—as well as what we can do to make our books better.

Please note that I cannot help you with technical problems related to the *topic* of this book. We do have a User Services group, however, where I will forward specific technical questions related to the book.

When you write, please be sure to include this book's title and author as well as your name, email address, and phone number. I will carefully review your comments and share them with the author and editors who worked on the book.

Email: feedback@samspublishing.com
Mail: Michael Stephens
       Sams Publishing
       201 West 103rd Street
       Indianapolis, IN 46290 USA

For more information about this book or another Sams Publishing title, visit our Web site at www.samspublishing.com. Type the ISBN (excluding hyphens) or the title of a book in the Search field to find the page you're looking for.

Introduction

This book's in-depth coverage of peer-to-peer (P2P) computing is written for the professional Java developer who needs to learn the concepts, programming, and practical application of Java in P2P environments. Although the Java language has been designed to be relatively easy to learn and use, the platform is extensive and cannot be fully addressed here. Readers who would like to learn more about Java can benefit from these books:

- *Sams Teach Yourself Java 2 in 21 Days, Third Edition* by Laura Lemay and Rogers Cadenhead (Sams)
- *Java How to Program, Fourth Edition* by Harvey M. Deitel and Paul J. Deitel (Prentice-Hall)
- *Special Edition Using Java 2 Standard Edition* by Chuck Cavaness, Geoff Friesen and Brian Keeton (Que)

How This Book Is Organized

Java P2P Unleashed is divided into four parts.

Part I—P2P Explained

The first part of *Java P2P Unleashed* describes P2P systems and highlights the business ramifications and implementation issues surrounding P2P. It provides an overview to common P2P architectures, networks, and applications. It compares and contrasts P2P with existing and emerging technologies, such as Web services, JXTA, Jini, RMI, and CORBA.

Part II—P2P Systems and Architecture

Part 2 builds on P2P fundamentals and provides in-depth coverage of P2P system topics. Each chapter is dedicated to a specific P2P system requirement that is fundamental to designing and building mature P2P applications.

Topics covered include the following:

- Discovery—Designing and building P2P dynamic networks.
- Transports—The common transports and transport protocols in use in P2P networks.
- Metadata—The proper definition and use of metadata in emerging P2P ontologies.

- Data format and interchange—Common data formats and standards in P2P content definition.
- System performance—Performance requirements and their implications to robust P2P systems.
- Integration and interoperability—Using P2P with existing technologies and legacy systems.
- Security—Implementing security in a complex mesh of decentralized interconnected nodes.

A case is made for Java providing a compelling platform to address the requirements of P2P.

Part III—Building Distributed Systems Using Java

The third part of *Java P2P Unleashed* provides detailed coverage on hot topics and technologies in distributed computing. Programming examples are used to complement the technology descriptions.

Each Java P2P technology is approached from a P2P perspective, focusing on implementation concerns Java developers will face while using them.

Technologies include the following:

- J2EE/J2SE/J2ME—Developing P2P applications using JMS, JAXP, JAXB, JAXR, and small devices and surrogates.
- The Web services architecture—Understanding the components of Web services such as XML, SOAP, UDDI, and WSDL.
- Jini and JavaSpaces—Using Java network technology to provide a unifying framework for service discovery in P2P hybrid architectures. The role of multicast and unicast messaging is explained and explored.
- JXTA and XML—Standardizing P2P interchange formats using XML. This section describes the JXTA core, services, and common applications being built using the JXTA standard.

Part IV—Sample Applications

The final part provides detailed examples of P2P applications. Each example demonstrates programming techniques to address common problems encountered in building robust P2P applications:

- Building a personal portal—This sample application demonstrates file sharing and how to publish content over the Web using P2P shared spaces (JavaSpaces) and XML Dublin Core Metadata definitions.

- The P2P Dashboard—The P2P Dashboard program demonstrates techniques to create communities of peers and groups and that can detect peer presence. This program also illustrates the concepts of monitoring and the configuration of shared space.

- Using SOAP with P2P—We'll explore the idea of integrating Web services with P2P through service gateways. We'll consider what is common in these two technologies, in what manner they compete, and how they can cooperate with each other. Taking JXTA as a sample P2P network, you will develop a service gateway application that can work for the benefit of JXTA peers.

- The P2P game—The P2P game is a peer-to-peer game that allows players to join and leave the game based on obtaining and passing a "Get Out Of Jail" token that is circulated among players. This game demonstrates the techniques to form a community of peers and pass messages among the peers of the community.

- Distance learning—We'll use a sample program to illustrate the mapping of P2P protocols to software agents, and explore alternative communication techniques.

- Future directions—We'll outline and present important P2P trends, and project the future direction of P2P and related technologies.

Source Code

All source code and examples presented in this book are available at http://www.samspublishing.com. From the home page, type this book's ISBN (0672323990) into the search window, and click Search to access information about the book and a direct link to the source code.

Introducing P2P

PART

I

In This Part

What Is P2P?

by Robert Flenner and Frank Cohen

IN THIS CHAPTER

Java software developers are at the vanguard of efforts to deploy interoperable software applications to the scale of the Internet. Although these applications may include file sharing, instant messaging, business workflow, and more, they have a common need for application software running in one Java virtual machine to communicate, share resources, and use functions available in other Java virtual machines. Java developers have Remote Method Invocation (RMI) technology from Sun in which the remote service is guaranteed to be always present. And now JXTA technology enables Java developers to build loosely coupled interoperating systems that are wildly scalable and efficient. This chapter covers the important issues of history, business benefits, architecture, and implementation details that every Java developer needs to understand to build and deploy interoperable software applications.

A Brief History

Peer-to-peer computing hit the front page headlines of technical Web sites in early 2000. It came on the scene as a new paradigm in network computing, a new technology for connecting people, and effectively utilizing untapped resources anywhere on the Internet and the Web.

P2P boasted of a network of equals, in which the traditional client/server partitioning of functionality and communication was replaced. The new paradigm of *servents* (a term formed from *server* + *clients*), partners in computing opportunity, was upon us. A number of factors unfolding in computing technology were driving this trend. P2P was changing the balance of power, and giving rise once again to the "power to the people" mantra of the 60s. Only this time, rather than protesting for personal individuality, the protest was for machine and silicon equality. A new generation of protesters took to the digital highways and soon caught the attention of the world.

The key factors changing the balance of power included the increased availability of inexpensive computing power, bandwidth, and storage. This, coupled with the explosion of content and subscribers on the Internet, started the next wave of the digital revolution.

The widespread adoption of Internet-based protocols enabled P2P champions to develop applications over a global network, a network never before seen in this light. Previous impediments to connectivity had been removed, and what shone through was a wealth of computing power, with access to a massive amount of content.

Where the content resided was no longer an issue. It resided everywhere, within servers, within clients, within the fabric of the network itself. This liberal dissemination of data coupled with unlimited total access raised eyebrows.

Projections of digital asset ownership infringement and copyright abuse quickly became a reality. Users of Napster, the popular MP3 file sharing program, proliferated overnight. According to industry tracker Webnoize (www.webnoize.com), the Napster user base was estimated at 1.6 million users in February 2001. The exchange of MP3 files that month alone reached 2.7 billion, and control of content ownership was seen by the media as spinning out of control.

Needless to say, the U.S. courts blazed with a battle that resembled Samson versus Goliath. Here was a small dot-com startup taking on media giants and the corporate establishment.

Proponents of P2P lined up to proclaim that freedom and liberty itself were under attack. We were witnessing firsthand as technology disrupted the status quo and brought into question the very laws that govern us. The battle being fought in the courtroom would determine the future of our society, and more importantly, P2P technology!

And then the dust settled.

The court ruled against Napster, and it suspended file sharing in July 2001.

Back to the Future

So, does this close the chapter on P2P? Hardly. P2P is alive and well, and having a significant impact on the design and development of system architectures and commercial applications. It is having a profound impact on the Internet and the Web as we build the next generation of network-centric applications.

You will find that there is no universal agreement on what defines a P2P system. However, there are system characteristics that have surfaced, and a common nomenclature is being used to identify and describe P2P systems.

It has become common practice to express the relationship between two computing entities as *something-2-something*. For example, B2B is defined as business-to-business; B2C is defined as business-to-consumer; and A2A is defined as application-to-application—the list continues to grow. These computing entities pose no problem of definition. *Business* is well understood, as is *consumer* and *application*; but what about *peer*?

The dictionary defines a peer as "a person who has equal standing with another or others, as in rank, class, or age." What stands out in this definition is the equality relationship: one person equal to another person in an important characteristic, such as rank, class, or age. Often these characteristics equate to the status or control an individual possesses within a community or society.

So what you extrapolate from this definition is the notion of equality between computing entities. Fundamental to P2P is node equality, in which a node is defined as any processing entity that exists as a particular and discrete unit. See Figure 1.1.

FIGURE 1.1

Peers represent liberated entities on a network of equals on which anyone can speak and listen.

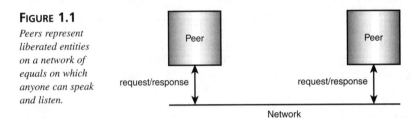

If a person refers to characteristics such as rank, class, or age, what are the characteristics of a peer? What characteristics are we measuring to be equal?

The simple answer is functionality. Peers are assumed to possess an equal capability in functions or services that they provide. This is contrary to traditional client/server models, in which the server possesses greater functionality and control than the client.

Napster was not pure P2P. All nodes did not possess equal processing capabilities. For instance, MP3 files were indexed on a central server; only the files remained on and were accessed from peer components. We will have more to say about mixed models such as this in a moment.

What made Napster and other P2P applications interesting is the ease with which large networks of cooperating nodes could be assembled, and that these nodes lived on the edge of the network. The nodes were common PCs that dynamically assembled to form a distributed file system. The network was constantly changing. The nodes of the network were transient by nature. They would enter and leave the network at will. This is not the traditional approach to network organization, and is atypical of filesystems.

Peer-To-Peer Application Hall of Fame

Consider the different types of applications a user with a desktop computer may expect to use today. In addition to a Web browser and "office" productivity suite, desktop users expect functions for the following:

- Managing and sharing information—Files, documents, photos, music, videos, and movies all want to be shared with business partners, friends, and colleagues. More advanced sharing enables one machine to act as a general task manager by collecting and aggregating results—for example, Google.com is an example of distributed task-managing system. Gnutella is an example of a personal P2P file-sharing system.

- Collaboration—Individual users find that address book, scheduler, chat and email software improves their productivity. Connecting the desktop productivity software together enables collaborative e-business communities to form for flexible, productive, and efficient working teams. For example, Java developers use OpenProjects.net to collaborate. On a broader scale, hundreds of thousands use instant messaging, which may be the most popular P2P application to date.

- Enterprise resource management—Coordinating workflow processes within an organization leverages the existing infrastructure of networked desktop computer systems. For example, Groove enables an aerospace manufacturer to post job order requests to partner companies and route the completed requests from one department to the next.

- Distributed computation—A natural extension of the Internet's philosophy of robustness through decentralization is to design peer-to-peer systems that send computing tasks to millions of servers, each one possibly also being a desktop computer.

Although P2P is still in the "pioneering" stage, P2P applications have emerged to satisfy the needs of users for all of these functions. As the benefits of P2P are better understood, it's likely that many more applications will be built using P2P technologies.

Motivation to Adopt P2P

Three primary business and technology issues are driving the adoption of P2P:

- Decentralization—Businesses realize greater efficiency and profits by attaining a flexible state. Consequently, business leaders have been decentralizing for decades. We have gone from mainframes, to a client/server model, to Internet computing, and now to P2P. The trend is undeniably decentralized and distributed.

- Cost and efficiency—Hardware and software will continue to be inexpensive and powerful. New systems that increase the efficiency or utilization of hardware or software present a compelling case for making the investment. P2P additionally has the capability to exploit resources that in the past went unrecognized.

- Pervasive computing—Imagine information systems everywhere: computer chips in clothing, appliances, automobiles, devices, anything you can think of. Not only are they everywhere, but they are connected. The market for network-connected devices continues to grow, and P2P systems are being designed to support the device market.

As enterprises advance their e-commerce efforts, they are increasingly recognizing the need to couple transaction flows and communication flows. Similarly, they are also recognizing the natural tendency for co-workers and their external counterparts to establish "communities" in order to perform both routine and special-purpose tasks. Growth in e-commerce should fuel more demand for collaborative commerce. P2P technology is a natural fit for this growing trend to establish distributed special-purpose communities.

Decentralization

Centralized systems have many advantages and are not disappearing. However, there are problems with centralized systems, as the next sections will show.

Eliminating Single Points of Failure

Centralized systems often suffer from single points of failure. These can occur as a result of a network problem, a hardware problem, or a malfunctioning application. It is expensive and sometimes impractical to build redundancy into every component of your system. When a centralized system fails, it brings business operations to a halt, resulting in costly downtime. P2P systems are proving to be resilient even in unstable environments.

Improving Scalability and Reducing Bottlenecks

Although centralized servers can process requests in parallel, every server has a characteristic threshold after which it slows to a crawl or crashes. Bottlenecks in centralized systems have often been addressed by the philosophy "buy bigger hardware." However, this is more of a stopgap measure than a long-term solution. Distribution of load across multiple machines (load balancing) is a popular solution to alleviate bottlenecks and scale systems. P2P systems are proving to be scalable.

Central Administration

Central administration can suffer from the lack of timely response to user requests. Users tend to be treated generically. The administrator must meet the needs of all users on the network, and therefore usually establishes broad settings like maximum storage limits and file access rights. Because it would require constant maintenance, granular attention is generally unavailable.

Location of Information

Decentralization can move resources closer to where they are accessed. This results in a number of benefits: Response time can be decreased, because network latency can be reduced or eliminated. Storage requirements can be partitioned and allocated to more closely resemble organizational use. Decentralization actually reflects the organizational reality that exists in corporations today.

Symmetric Versus Asymmetric Participation

Centralized systems suffer from one-way, or *unidirectional* communication. Most users connect to a central server, and push and pull data from that central server. The value of the network is decreased because of this unidirectional communication channel. Central servers often add no value to the communication. A more symmetric flow of information is established in P2P systems. This allows communication to flow from device to device, thus increasing the value of the network.

Removing Islands of Computation

Centralized systems tend to create information silos. These islands of computation are isolated and cut off from other systems and networks. Often, redundant information is housed in these silos that is neither current or correct.

Cost and Effective Resource Allocation

A client/server system is expensive. It requires client hardware and software, server hardware and software, a plethora of storage devices and software, and maintenance. P2P greatly increases the utilization of three valuable technology assets:

- Storage
- Bandwidth
- Computing resources

All of these are underutilized at this time, partly because of the traditional client/server computing model. Despite a decentralized Internet, the client/server model still dominates. Decentralized and mesh network topologies such as the SETI project will more effectively use resources that already exist.

Pervasive Computing and Edge Services

Non-PC devices such as PDAs, cell phones, life-enhancing appliances, and so on continue to proliferate. Interconnected devices are enabling a new generation of communication, information exchange, and pervasive computing.

Increased Connections

The number of connections is surging—the result of devices communicating directly with other devices, not through servers acting as intermediaries for devices. This increased connectivity will be supported by P2P-style architectures.

Enhanced connectivity provides the catalyst to promote *edge services*. Edge services reside on devices and common PCs across the Internet. Peer-to-peer networks make use of these resources. Edge services move data closer to the point at which it is actually consumed, acting as a network caching mechanism. This speeds up data access and better utilizes existing storage space, thereby saving money by eliminating the need for storage on servers.

With the right system design and architectural choices, these P2P applications have the ability to spread across the entire Internet and provide people with greater productivity and knowledge than ever before. Unfortunately, with the wrong architecture and design, the same P2P applications can fall apart at the seams.

Business and Implementation Issues

Every new technology goes through an experimental phase—the pluses and minuses of the technology are weighed against the costs and benefits. P2P is no different.

Three main challenges for P2P stand out:

- Overcoming issues of security and trust
- Lack of standards
- Enabling transactions

As has been highlighted, security is one area of strength for centralized systems. Control and lockdown of resources, users, and networks is at the core of centralized systems. It is often the very reason that centralized architecture is adopted.

Security in decentralized systems is very difficult. It has to be built into the architecture to be effective, and cannot be an afterthought to the design. Part of the appeal of P2P has been the lack of control, along with the freedom and anonymity that exists in P2P systems. However, this is not viable in commercial applications dealing with private information or monetary exchanges. These applications require traditional security assurances, regardless of the underlying architectural design.

Fortunately, Java has much to offer when building systems with strong security requirements. In addition, there are now commercial P2P applications that provide examples demonstrating encryption, public and private key usage, and the establishment of trust relationships over an untrusted network.

The next obstacle that will need to be overcome is the current lack of standards. For P2P to become viable as a foundation for building distributed systems, standards will be required. Standardization in any technology is difficult to achieve, especially with new technologies that have yet to mature.

There is promise in this area with Project JXTA and the widespread adoption of XML. P2P and Web services appear to be converging on XML messaging. Despite fundamental differences in architecture, with Web services biased toward client/server models and P2P biased toward decentralized models, many opportunities still exist to integrate and complement each architectural approach. As has been highlighted, many times mixed models are needed to adequately address application and system-specific requirements.

Another fundamental problem is with the transient nature of edge resources—sometimes they are available, and sometimes not. Reliability, bandwidth, and location are subject to change. Therefore, P2P applications must be able to accommodate these properties of edge resources.

Of course, to become widely adopted by businesses and corporations, P2P will have to offer transactions. Digital commerce requires some form of monetary exchange. Much of the press on P2P has perhaps made this more of a perception obstacle than a technical one, but it exists nonetheless. Transactions are difficult in distributed environments, and will require the other two key obstacles to be overcome—security and lack of standards.

P2P Architectures

What makes Gnutella and other P2P applications interesting is the ease with which large networks of cooperating nodes can be assembled, and that these nodes live on the edge of the network. The nodes are common PCs that dynamically assemble to form a distributed file system . The network is constantly changing—many nodes are behind firewalls and one-way Network Address Translation (NAT) routers; the computers may be turned off at night, and they enter and leave the network at will. This is antithetical to the network organization and typical filesystems found on business networks.

In a client/server model, the server controls and manages the relationship clients have with resources, such as databases, files, networks, and other clients. The server functions as a higher-level citizen within the computing community. It is given special privileges and functionality to control its subjects.

Node equality has a dramatic impact on the way we architect and build systems. What has been solved by traditional hierarchical systems is now unraveled, and up for debate and re-evaluation in the peer-to-peer world.

How do we identify and locate entities? Who controls access to resources? Although these questions are difficult to answer in any environment, they are at least well understood. In P2P systems, this is not the case. This is the new frontier of computing. The rules have not been defined, and the opportunity still exists to engage in design and development on the edge. P2P may be the first wave of delivering post Web-browser Internet content.

Interestingly, the definition of the verb tense of the word *peer* is "to look intently, searchingly, or with difficulty." This definition can be applied to the actions required by P2P nodes when you remove hierarchical relationships.

How do you search for peers and form groups of cooperating entities? The first generation of P2P applications grappled with the problems inherent in this question. As a result, they exposed the strengths and weaknesses of early P2P systems.

You can learn a lot about P2P by studying early systems like Napster, Gnutella, and Freenet. Applications such as these revealed common characteristics of P2P systems. P2P systems have a dynamic element that enables them to form or discover groups and communities. Early systems used this primarily for searching, or to solve a common problem.

P2P systems require virtual namespaces to augment current addressing technology. A virtual namespace provides a method for persistent identification, which would otherwise not be possible. For the moment, think of this as your email address that uniquely identifies you, regardless of what computer you use to access your mail.

Peers in a P2P system are considered equals in terms of functional capabilities. Equality means you no longer need an intermediary to help you participate in a network. If you're connected to the Internet, you can get involved.

Peers can appear anywhere on the network. They can be your PC, or the Palm Pilot that you hold in your hand. If you can connect it to the network, you can "peer" it.

Peers need not be permanent; they have a transient capability to appear and disappear on the network. Intermittent connectivity in many P2P systems is the norm rather than the exception. Early P2P systems were comprised of dial-up users who established connectivity, joined the network, and then disconnected and left the network. P2P systems had to account for this type of membership.

Peers have a wide array of processing, bandwidth, and storage capabilities. While they are all equal, some are more equal than others. A laptop computer can connect to the Internet through a dial-up connection and become a peer. A Sun Enterprise 10000 with fiber optic pipes can also become a peer on the same network. Functionally, in the P2P system they are equal. However, their performance capabilities are quite different.

P2P is changing the way we build systems that exploit the global network, and the characteristics of this evolution will teach us many lessons.

How P2P Forms Dynamic Networks

Dynamic networks are fundamental to P2P systems. The Internet is a dynamic network with a number of static properties. For example, each machine that connects to the Internet is assigned a unique IP address.

IPv4, the predominant protocol today, uses 32-bit addresses. Values are represented in decimal notation separated by dots; for example, `172.16.1.2`.

This configuration limits the possible addresses that are available. The proliferation of user machines and devices requiring IP addresses has gone beyond the original creators' vision. We are running out of addresses.

The IPv6 protocol has been defined to extend the range of possible addresses, and to be backward compatible with IPv4. IPv6 uses 128-bit addresses. Values are represented as hexadecimal numbers separated by colons; for example, `FEDC: B978:7654:3210:F93A: 8767:54C3:6543`. IPv6 will support 10^{12} (1 trillion) machines and 10^9 (1 billion) individual networks. However, how soon IPv6 will be widely available is still not clear.

Because humans remember names more easily that numbers, the Internet provides a way for us to use names to identify machines. The Domain Name Service provides the mechanism that helps users identify or map a machine name to an IP address. As a result, we can use `http://java.sun.com` rather than `http://192.18.97.71/`.

Although you can use IP and DNS to identify and find certain machines on the network, there still exist challenges for P2P systems. The limited number of IP addresses available using IPv4 has resulted in additional identification mechanisms. NAT makes it possible to assign a pool of reserved IP addresses to machines on a local network. When connecting to the Internet, the machines share a "public" IP address. Because the reserved pool has been set aside for use in private networks, they will never appear as public addresses. Consequently, they can be reused. Although these mechanisms do wonders to conserve addresses, they make discovering real machine addresses difficult, especially in dynamic environments. The next-generation Internet, which will use IPv6, is designed to address this problem, but it's also likely years in the future. In the meantime, dynamic IP assignment on the Internet is still common, and creates an inherent identification problem.

How do you recognize a peer that no longer has the same identity? Peer-to-peer networks must be able to uniquely identify peers and resources that are available. As a result, P2P systems have had to define their own naming schemes independent of IP addresses or DNS. They have had to create virtual namespaces, enabling users to have persistent identities on their systems.

Rather than being predefined or preconfigured such as in DNS, the nodes within the network "find" or "discover" each other using IP and DNS as a navigational aid to build a dynamic or virtual network. Dynamic network formation is typical of P2P networks. Chapter 5, "System Topics Explained," covers discovery in great depth.

Discovery

How peers and resources of the P2P system are discovered has generated a substantial amount of press and dialogue. To date, it has been the elusive measure of success for peer-to-peer systems.

You can think of discovery on two levels. First, the discovery process is associated with finding a peer. In this case, a peer refers to a computing entity that is capable of understanding the protocol of the messages being exchanged. It is an entity that "speaks" the same language—it understands the semantics of the dialogue. Peer discovery is required to find a service or help divide and conquer many problems associated with information processing. If we didn't understand what we were exchanging, we couldn't progress beyond digital babble.

The second level of discovery is associated with finding resources of interest. The early P2P applications dealt with file sharing and searching. In contrast to popular search engines, P2P applications define new techniques to discover files and information on the Internet.

The massive amount of information available on the Internet and its exponential growth is outpacing traditional information indexing techniques. In addition, the delay between content availability and content discovery continues to grow despite parallelism in popular search engines. P2P resource discovery provides a more real-time solution to information searching. However, the discovery techniques and protocols required have come at a price.

The Gnutella story has been well documented. A popular file sharing and search program, Gnutella uses an unconventional broadcast mechanism to discover peers, as illustrated in Figure 1.2. The broadcast technique grows exponentially—the more users, the more broadcasts. When the size of the user base grew too quickly, the system came crashing to a halt, flooding networks with Gnutella requests. The success of the software highlighted the limitations of its discovery architecture.

FIGURE 1.2

Gnutella discovery quickly ran into the "broadcast storm" problem once the network grew beyond initial expectations.

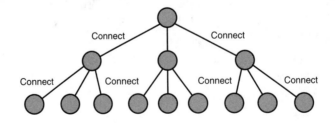

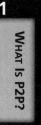

An effective discovery mechanism is critical to the successful design and deployment of a peer-based network. To be effective, a discovery mechanism must be efficient in different execution environments. It should be efficient in discovering peers and resources regardless of the size of the network. It should also be resilient enough to ward off attacks and security breaches that would otherwise jeopardize the viability of the technology.

Centralized methods of discovery often break down when applied to large peer-based networks. They often fail to scale or present single points of failure in the architecture.

There are a number of decentralized discovery methods in use that use a variety of designs and architectures. All of these methods have various strengths that make them attractive for certain circumstances. However, they all have tradeoffs in large peer-based networks.

Simple Broadcast

Simple broadcast sends a request to every participant within the network segment or radius. When used for discovery, it can reach a large number of potential peers or find a large number of resources. The drawback to this approach is that as the user base grows linearly, the number of requests grows exponentially.

This approach can result in huge bandwidth requirements. At some point, the network will be saturated with requests and trigger timeouts and re-transmissions, which just aggravates the already dire situation. There are also security and denial-of-service implications. A malicious peer can start flooding the network with a number of requests disproportionate to the true size of the user base. This can interrupt the network and reduce its effectiveness. Also, simple broadcast is only viable in small networks.

Selective Broadcast

A variation on simple broadcast is *selective broadcast*. Instead of sending a request to every peer on the network, peers are selected based on heuristics such as quality of service, content availability, or trust relationships. However, this type of broadcast requires that you maintain historical information on peer interactions.

Discovery requests are sent to selected peers, and the response is evaluated against the criteria that you have defined for peer connections. For instance, you might only send discovery requests to peers that support a certain minimum bandwidth requirement. Or you might send requests for resources only to peers likely to have that content. Of course, the more you need to know about the participants, the less dynamic the system can become. This can quickly eliminate the benefits of P2P if fixed and static relationships are not mitigated through some mechanism.

Security is still a concern with selective broadcast. It is important that each one of the peers be reputable for this operation to be effective.

Adaptive Broadcast

Like selective broadcast, *adaptive broadcast* tries to minimize network utilization while maximizing connectivity to the network. Selection criteria can be augmented with knowledge of your computing environment. For instance, you can set the amount of memory or bandwidth you will consume during discovery operations. You can limit the growth of discovery and searching by predefining a resource tolerance level that if exceeded will begin to curtail the process. This will ensure that excessive resources are not being consumed because of a malfunctioning element, a misguided peer, or a malicious attack. Adaptive broadcast requires monitoring resources, such as peer identity, message queue size, port usage, and message size and frequency. Adaptive broadcast can reduce the threat of some security breaches, but not all.

Resource Indexing

Finding resources is closely tied to finding peers. However, the difference is that peers have intelligence; they are processes capable of engaging in digital conversations through a programming interface. A resource is much more static, and only requires identity. Discovering resources can be done using centralized and decentralized indexing. *Centralized indexes* provide good performance, at a cost. The bandwidth and hardware requirements of large peer networks can be expensive. Centralized indexes hit the scalability wall at some point, regardless of the amount of software and hardware provided. *Decentralized index* systems attempt to overcome the scalability limitations of centralized systems. To improve performance, every document or file stored within the system is given a unique ID. This ID is used to identify and locate a resource. IDs easily map to resources. This approach is used by FreeNet. The drawback to this approach is that searches have to be exact. Every resource has a single and unique identifier.

Another problem with decentralized indexing systems is keeping cached information consistent. Indexes can quickly become out of sync. Peer networks are much more volatile, in terms of peers joining and leaving the network, as well as the resources contained within the index. The overhead in keeping everything up to date and efficiently distributed is a major detriment to scalability.

Because peer networks are so volatile, knowing when a peer is online is required to build efficient and user-centric distributed systems. P2P systems use the term *presence*, and define it as the ability to tell when a peer or resource is online. The degree to which this situation affects your environment is application-dependent; however, you must understand the implications.

Node Autonomy

P2P systems are highly decentralized and distributed. The benefits of distribution are well-known. You generally distribute processing when you need to scale your systems to support increased demand for resources. You also distribute for geographic reasons, to move resources and processes closer to their access point. Other reasons to distribute are to provide better fault resistance and network resilience, and to enable the sharing of resources and promote collaboration.

Decentralization gives rise to *node autonomy*, and in a peer-to-peer system, peers are highly autonomous. Peers are independent and self-governing. As mentioned, in a client/server model, the server controls and manages the relationship clients have with resources, such as databases, files, networks and other clients. This has many advantages in the operation, administration, and management of a computing environment. One of the advantages of centralization is central administration and monitoring. Knowing where resources are and how they are behaving is a tremendous advantage. Resources can be secured and administered from a central location. Functionality can be deployed to complement the physical structure of the network topology. For instance, servers can act as gatekeepers to sensitive technology assets.

With decentralization comes a number of significant challenges: The management of the network is much more difficult. In a distributed environment, failures are not always detected immediately. Worse yet, partial failures allow for results and side effects that networks and applications are not prepared to deal with. Response time and latency issues introduced as a result of remote communication can be unpredictable. The network can have good days and bad days. Peer-to-peer interaction can become unstable as error paths and timeouts get triggered excessively. Synchronization often strains available bandwidth.

Any solution that is based on distribution should be able to eliminate or mitigate these issues. P2P systems are built under the assumption that services are distributed over a network, and that the network is unreliable. How P2P systems cope with unreliable networks differentiates one system from another.

Peer of Equals

Peers in a peer-to-peer system have the capability to provide services and consume services. There is no separation of client versus server roles. Any peer is capable of providing a service or finding a peer that can provide the service requested. A peer can be considered a client when it is requesting a service, and can be considered a server when it is providing a service.

Peers are often used in systems that require a high level of *parallelism*. Parallelism is not new to computing. In fact, much of what we do in computing is done in parallel. Multiprocessor machines and operating systems rely on the capability to execute tasks in parallel. Threads of control enable us to partition a process into separate tasks. However, to date, parallelism has not been the norm in application development. While applications are designed to be multithreaded, this generally has involved controlling different tasks required of a process, such as reading from a slow device or waiting for a network response. We have not defined many applications that run the same tasks in parallel, such as searching a large database, or filtering large amounts of information concurrently.

Parallelism can provide us with a divide-and-conquer approach to many repetitive tasks. The SETI@Home project demonstrated that personal computers could be harnessed together across the Internet to provide extraordinary computing power. The Search for Extraterrestrial Intelligence project examines radio signals received from outer space in an attempt to detect intelligent life. It takes a vast amount of computing power to analyze the amount of data that is captured and the computations involved. People volunteered for the project by downloading a screensaver from the SETI Web site. The screensaver was capable of requesting work units that were designed to segment the mass amount of radio signals received. In the first week after the project launched, more than 200,000 people downloaded and ran the software. This number grew to more than 2,400,000 by the end of 2000. The processing power available as a result of this network outpaced the ASCI White developed by IBM, the fastest supercomputer built at the time. P2P systems are designed to meet this growing trend in divide-and-conquer strategies.

The SETI project is typical of system architectures that require a certain degree of centralization or coordination. Networks can be classified by their topology, which is the basic arrangement of nodes on the network. Different types of network configurations exist for network designers to choose from.

A decentralized topology is often augmented with a centralized component, which creates a *mixed model*, or hybrid architecture. With Napster, it's the centralized file index component that's capable of identifying and locating files. With SETI, it's the centralized task dispatcher that allocates work units.

Supporting Mixed Models

Many P2P technologies are now adopting a network-based computing style that supports a mixed model. The predominant decentralized model is augmented with centralized control nodes at key points. The architectures define central control points for improving important performance characteristics of P2P systems, such as discovery and content management. Hybrid architectures can also enhance system reliability and improve the fault tolerance of systems.

Let's review network topologies in order to understand the implications for P2P systems. This will also serve to highlight that there are many alternatives and design options to building P2P systems—one size does not fit all. Nelson Minar of MIT and co-founder of Popular Power, recommends we look at topologies from a logical perspective, rather than physical. In other words, use these patterns as a descriptive technique for information flow, rather than for physical cabling.

Five common topologies will be explained here:

- Star
- Bus
- Ring
- Hierarchical
- Mesh

Star Topology

The star network connects each device or node to a central point of control. All traffic in the network flows through this central point. A star network is usually easier to troubleshoot than most topologies. Figure 1.3 shows a typical configuration for client/server systems.

FIGURE 1.3

A star network topology has a central point of communication control.

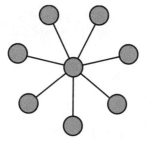

The Napster file index resembled a star topology. Of course, having a central access or control point exposes a potential single point of failure, which might have catastrophic consequences in a P2P network.

Bus Topology

A bus topology connects all devices or nodes to the same physical medium. There is no central control point, but rather a common backbone. The backbone is used to interconnect devices on the network, as seen in Figure 1.4.

FIGURE 1.4

A bus network topology has no central point of communication control. Each node inspects the message to determine whether it's the intended destination.

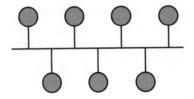

The bus topology does not have a central control point problem; however, a problem in the message bus can affect the entire network.

Ring Topology

In a ring topology, each device or node is connected to two other nodes, forming a loop, as in Figure 1.5. Data is sent from node to node around the loop in the same direction until it reaches its destination. Rings tend to have a predictable response time, because the distance a request must travel is consistent.

FIGURE 1.5

A ring network topology has no central point of communication control. Messages pass from one node to the next until the receiver is found.

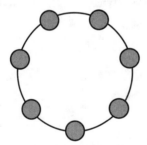

Ring networks still suffer from the problem of a single node malfunction disrupting the entire network.

Hierarchical Topology

A hierarchical network like the one shown in Figure 1.6 is similar to a cascading star topology. In other words, many nodes are connected to single nodes that in turn connected to other single nodes. These networks form parent–child relationships or resemble inverted trees.

FIGURE 1.6

A hierarchical network topology resembles a tree. The nodes above each node act as a central point of control for nodes directly below. This resembles the DNS structure of an inverted tree.

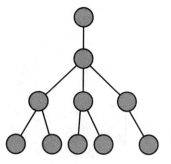

Mesh Topology

A mesh topology such as the one seen in Figure 1.7 requires all network devices or nodes to have dedicated paths to all other devices on that network.

FIGURE 1.7

A mesh network topology resembles the Internet routing topology.

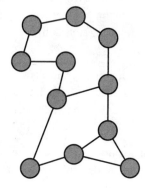

These networks typically exhibit resilience because more than one pathway exists between nodes. However, the fault tolerance is dependent on the integrity of the pathways.

Gnutella is probably the most "pure" mesh system used in practice today, states Minar, with only a small centralized function to bootstrap a new host. Many other file sharing systems are decentralized, such as Freenet.

Mixed Models

Most of the systems that we will investigate are far more complex than the simple topologies referenced in this section. However, systems are often composed of multiple topologies that complement and extend one or more network patterns. In Napster for example, there is a centralized file index node, but the file transfer or exchange resembles the point-to-point network of a meshed topology (see Figure 1.8).

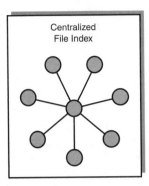 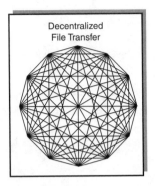

In addition, you can begin to map these patterns to key components or services in your P2P architecture. For instance, to build in fault tolerance and redundancy in your centralized file index, you can implement a ring topology. Each node in the ring serves as an access point to the index structure. If you lose connectivity to one index node, another node is there to service your request. This is a common failover technique. This works well for simple search applications; however, supporting transactional systems can involve a significant amount of complexity.

Minar states that "there are many possibilities in combining various kinds of architectures. Topology is a useful simplifying tool in understanding the architecture of distributed systems," in his article on distributed systems at `www.openp2p.com/pub/a/p2p/2001/12/14/topologies_one.html`.

Mapping key services into one or more communication models can highlight service constraints, vulnerabilities, and weaknesses in system design. The different topologies can be used as an evaluation aid in determining those strengths and weaknesses. Key measures to consider when building P2P systems include extensibility, information coherence, and fault tolerance.

JXTA and XML

As a Java developer with the task of building a new interoperating system, you need to consider several issues to deliver an excellent design that will scale up to support the system's future users. In the age of open source technology, Java developers rarely, if ever, need to start from scratch. The same is true with P2P technology.

Bill Joy and Mike Clary at Sun Microsystems realized the problem with early P2P technology: Most early P2P technology is proprietary and incompatible in nature. The early works seemed to be completely enamored with the possibility of interoperability on as grand a scale as the Internet can provide, but they omit the ingredients of a mature, stable platform that developers can reuse for years to come. The result is a set of early P2P technology that forms closed communities and is incapable of having one P2P application leverage the services of another P2P application.

Joy and Clary's work resulted in Project JXTA (pronounced *juxta*, short for *juxtapose*.) JXTA is available at `http://www.JXTA.org`. JXTA addresses the wider software development community's need for a common P2P language. JXTA is not a programming language; it provides a set of protocols that support interoperability among peers in a P2P environment. Although JXTA ships with a Java reference implementation, JXTA applications can be developed in any language, and can interoperate with other Project JXTA applications, regardless of their implementation language and underlying operating system, including .NET.

JXTA defines three layers. The bottom layer addresses the communication and routing and P2P connection management. The middle layer handles higher-level concepts, such as indexing, searching, and file sharing. The top layer provides protocols that the applications use to manage the middle-layer services and lower-layer "plumbing" to build full-featured P2P applications. The top layer is where typical applications, such as instant messaging, network services, and P2P collaboration environments are defined. In JXTA, all protocols are defined as XML messages sent between two peers. JXTA messages define the protocols used to discover and connect peers and to access network services offered by peers and peer groups.

Each JXTA message has a standard format, and may include optional data fields. So, JXTA standardizes the messages exchanged between peers by defining standard XML data streams used to invoke common functions or features of P2P services.

Messages are sent between logical destinations (endpoints) identified by a URI. The transport must be capable of sending and receiving datagram-style messages. Endpoints are mapped into physical addresses by the messaging layer at runtime.

The JXTA specification defines the following XML-encoded protocols:

- The Peer Discovery Protocol enables a peer to find advertisements on JXTA resources, such as other peers or peer groups.

- The Peer Resolver Protocol enables a peer to send and receive generic queries to find or search for information.

- The Peer Information Protocol enables a peer to learn about other peers' capabilities and status.

- The Peer Membership Protocol enables a peer to obtain group membership requirements, such as an understanding of the necessary credentials required to join a peer group.

- The Pipe Binding Protocol enables a peer to bind a pipe advertisement to a pipe endpoint. A pipe can be thought of as a named message queue. You can create, open, close, delete, send, and receive messages using the named queue/pipe.

- The Peer Endpoint Protocol enables a peer to query a peer router for available routes to send a message to a destination peer.

JXTA makes two significant contributions to P2P technology. First, JXTA provides huge validation for building all future P2P technology with XML. JXTA protocols use self-describing XML definitions to move messages and manage the environment.

Second, by providing a flexible and quality reference implementation, JXTA takes the Java development communities' focus away from basic P2P coding and on to solving P2P problems. P2P applications have matured, and are looking to increase interoperability among peers by defining standard protocols. P2P technologies will become more integrated into the network infrastructure so that more applications can utilize peer-computing services.

> **Note**
>
> JXTA is discussed further in Chapter 16, "JXTA and XML," and in Chapter 17, "The JXTA Shell."

A Future That Includes Web Services

This chapter demonstrates how happy desktop computer users can benefit from P2P technology for chat, messaging, and file sharing. Many of these applications provide an integrated experience. For example, many file sharing applications include chat and messaging. These applications show the enormous potential for building complex applications integrating data and functions from a variety of sources into one useful tool. Integration like this extends beyond P2P technology.

The vision behind Web services is very compatible to P2P technology. Web services enable developers to build loosely coupled, self-describing, highly scalable systems that provide interoperability between software on different platforms. Sound familiar?

Software developers working on traditional client/server and Web applications are challenged with the same issues: scalability, interoperability, performance, and maintenance. P2P technology is beginning to look very attractive as a tool for designing high performance, scalable, server-based systems.

P2P applications provide an integration model for Web services that works alongside the Simple Object Access Protocol (SOAP). Even with the use of SOAP, Web applications are typically designed to include a Web server and a browser client. Web applications usually result in centralized data centers and spread-out populations of clients. Centralized repositories have their place, but so do decentralized implementations, where the services provided at the edge of the network power an application. Imagine a stock trading application in which the trades are handled by a centralized server using SOAP, and the stock charting and history functions come from a network of information sources using P2P.

The software industry is headed toward larger interoperability, and P2P has already found a viable place. Device management, service monitoring, and resource management applications are being developed to support and complement current network management protocols, and e-commerce applications are being defined using P2P as a technology enabler, including the following:

- Online auctions
- Pricing and payment models
- Trading hubs and e-commerce communities
- Customer care
- Services for mobile users
- Service personalization

Although this chapter presents a good starting point, there are issues that you will need to understand to determine the applicability of P2P in your system selection and development.

Note

Web services are discussed in more detail in Chapter 11, "Web Services Explained."

Summary

In an environment in which the Internet is a network with millions of users that has moved beyond government and educational use into the very social and business fabric of our lives, P2P technology is an important tool for Java developers wanting to take advance of the Internet to develop next-generation applications. P2P is making huge contributions to new areas of communication, collaboration, and community.

In the next chapter, we'll explore the benefits of Java as a platform on which to build P2P applications.

A Case for Java and P2P

This chapter provides an overview of Java and the features of the language and platform that can be used to develop P2P applications. An emphasis is placed on Java as an enabling platform. The marriage of functional equivalence (peers) to platform independence (Java) demonstrates and explains the natural fit.

Java Language Benefits

For most readers of this book, the benefits of the Java programming language are well-known. Java is an extremely popular and mature language that has a proven track record.

Java is an object-oriented language. Java was designed to be object-oriented from the start. Java is also simple. It has taken many of the benefits of other object-based languages like C++, but removed the complexity. Most programmers find learning Java relatively easy compared with other programming languages in general.

Java provides a large collection of classes that are packaged and segmented into manageable "knowledge chunks." For instance, there is a package that deals with networking, and a package that deals specifically with I/O, and packages used to build visual components. You can specialize or focus your talent and energy on specific aspects of programming. The power of prebuilt frameworks delivered in packages truly accelerates the development and learning process. This is especially important in P2P, which is changing and adapting to many different environments. By its nature, P2P implies many active participants with many different motivations. As a result, it is very dynamic and will require programming languages and tools that can keep pace with its growth and development.

Java is an interpreted language, which is the direction most multipurpose languages will take in the future. This is because the power of interpretation and the benefits gained by eliminating the link-phase in most other languages far outweigh the additional processing time required for interpretation. The virtual machine that performs the runtime interpretation also abstracts the differences between system hardware and operating systems so that Java becomes platform-neutral. You can run your P2P application on Windows, Linux, Sun, Unix, you name it—anywhere there is a Java virtual machine defined. Of course, realize that there are areas where performance and squeezing out every millisecond of computing cycles is important. But this is the exception, not the rule. The computing power on your desk today far outweighs what most users even require.

Platform Independence

Java is compiled into bytecodes. The Java virtual machine (JVM) interprets the bytecode before execution on a specific operating system. So, unlike most applications that must be ported to each operating system, Java only requires the JVM to be available on a specific platform. The application can run anywhere. You have already seen how P2P does not try to differentiate between client and server roles. This is known as *functional equivalence*, and it is an important aspect of P2P architecture. Using Java now provides platform independence coupled with functional equivalence. This is a powerful combination in developing applications that are both portable and dynamic.

The Distributed Nature of Java

The interpretive nature of Java allows classes to be dynamically loaded into the JVM at runtime. Classes can be obtained locally or downloaded from the Internet, providing developers with a single component model that makes programming distributed applications simple. You can easily obtain information about the classes that are executing at runtime through reflection. *Reflection* allows you to look inside the class definition and determine the fields and methods of the class definition. You can exploit the capabilities of a class without having full knowledge of the class composition using reflection. This capability, coupled with the distributed nature of the language, makes a powerful combination.

The distributed nature of the language is further exemplified by the extensive support of networking in the java.net package. Internet capability was not an afterthought of the Java language; rather it is fundamental to the organization and class definitions of the Java packages. For example, the URL class provides an abstraction of a uniform resource locator. By constructing a URL class, you can easily open a connection to an Internet-accessible resource and download and display the contents. It also provides you with easy access to the HTTP protocol. This capability, coupled with reflection, provides a distributed and dynamic programming environment for P2P applications, while maintaining simplicity.

Remote Method Invocation

Remote Method Invocation (RMI) is a feature of the core Java API. RMI enables method invocation on objects running in separate virtual machines, and even on virtual machines that happen to be on another server in another network. RMI is yet another feature that makes Java suitable for building distributed applications. RMI uses Java serialization to transport objects across a network by writing byte streams that include the necessary information to materialize/unmarshal an object in a remote VM. Not only is the object's data transported, but also the behavior the object implements. This provides a powerful platform for mobile agents that move and migrate across machine and network boundaries. RMI can be used to provide the underpinnings of P2P mobile agents. RMI will be discussed in more detail in Chapter 14, "Jini and JavaSpaces."

Multithread Support

Java provides built-in language support for threads. Threads allow multiple lightweight processes to execute in parallel. At least they appear to be executing in parallel, even on single-processor machines. For example, many P2P programs have the capability to download files while simultaneously playing audio or video clips. The application must be written to support multiple paths of execution simultaneously. Multithreaded applications provide this type of support. Java provides an easy-to-use API that supports threads because it is built into the Java language.

Building applications that are more robust and resilient against network failures requires multithreaded programming. P2P applications often use unstable networks to provide their core functions. Java provides thread support as the alternative to nonblocking, asynchronous I/O, which is used heavily in networking applications written in other languages, such C and C++. These languages must use low-level notification and complex interrupt constructs to provide a similar functionality to what is easily written in Java.

Language Reliability and Maturity

Java has qualities inherent in robust object-oriented languages.

Java is a strongly typed language. *Strong typing* provides extensive checking for type mismatches that can occur during the development (compilation) and runtime phases of program execution.

Java provides extensive exception handling and requires exceptions to be handled in application code using try-catch blocks. try-catch blocks and exceptions make it easier for programmers to structure code to recover from errors. This is especially important in P2P applications that rely heavily on the network and I/O operations. These operations are especially vulnerable to exceptions, and therefore require more sophisticated error-handling procedures.

Java supports the use of abstract classes and interface definitions. Abstract classes enable you to defer method implementations while still defining method signatures. This is a common idiom in object-oriented programming. It is one of the techniques used to enable polymorphism.

Java also supports interfaces. Interfaces enable you to extend the notion of abstract classes. All the methods defined in an interface are fundamentally abstract. In other words, a concrete class must implement the interface to provide the functionality defined by the methods.

Interface definition enables you to define the methods and method signatures of a class without providing the concrete implementation. Two P2P applications can be written to the same Java interface, and yet have vastly different implementations. One implementation might be focused on speed of execution, while another might provide more reliability. Java interfaces provide an alternative to defining standard interfaces using data-oriented approaches, such as with XML or EDI.

Security

Because Java has been designed to support distributed applications from the ground up, security is an important part of the platform. As you learned earlier, Java makes it possible to load and run classes obtained from network sources or to invoke methods remotely. Naturally, Java protects systems from potentially executing untrusted code, or permitting someone from using resources without permission. Java provides sophisticated and flexible protection of information, systems, and services. P2P applications using Java will benefit from the built-in protection that it offers.

The Java Virtual Machine

It is difficult to understand how Java security works without having a high-level understanding of the Java virtual machine.

From a security perspective, the JVM provides the sandbox that ensures code runs in a protected space and has limited access to system resources. The key components in the JVM security framework are as follows:

- Class loader
- Class file verifier
- Security manager

The Class Loader

The class loader is used by the JVM to locate and load into memory the classes necessary to execute a Java program. Not all class files that are needed come from the local filesystem. For instance, RMI loads classes on demand over the network.

Classes can be divided into two categories: trusted and untrusted, as seen in Figure 2.1.

FIGURE 2.1

Security in the Java virtual machine.

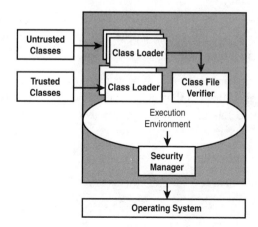

Trusted classes are those classes that are assumed to be safe. In Java 2, these were restricted to only the Java Runtime Environment (JRE) classes. These are the classes that are found in the boot classpath.

Untrusted classes are all classes that fall outside the boot classpath. This includes the files that are downloaded over the network. The class file verifier verifies these files.

The Class File Verifier

To ensure that a file meets certain criteria, the class loader invokes the class file verifier. The class file verifier performs a series of checks:

- File integrity check—Ensures that a file has the appropriate signature and length.
- Class integrity check—Ensures that all classes, methods, and fields have legal names and signatures.
- Bytecode integrity check—The runtime behavior of the bytecodes is examined and verified.
- Runtime integrity check—Extends the bytecode integrity check to look for code that is actually executed. This is to ensure that code that is never executed does not have to go through the entire verification process unnecessarily.

Other programming languages do not have this level of security built in. This is especially important for P2P applications, because they run in trusted and untrusted environments. One of the strengths of P2P is the ease with which you can discover services or resources in environments that you have little knowledge of. Despite this strength, adequate security must be in place to counter security threats. If the security is built into the language, the development and potential errors that can be introduced in the security architecture are minimized.

The Security Manager

The security manager is responsible for the runtime restrictions that are imposed on code after the code has gone through the verification process. The security manager enforces restrictions based on security policy statements.

The security manager enables an application to determine what operation is being attempted, and whether it is enabled in the current security context. The application can then allow or disallow the operation, depending on whether an application has permission to access a controlled resource.

Permissions fall into these categories:

- File—An application can access the file system to read, write, or delete files or directories, or to execute a file.

- Socket—An application can make or accept a connection using sockets.
- Net—An application can specify an authenticator to handle HTTP authentication, obtain a password from an authenticator, or change the default stream handler for a class that manages URL.
- Security—An application can get security policy information or set security policies, manage security providers, or manage identities.
- Runtime—An application can manage runtime elements, such as replacing the default security manager, create class loaders, or manage threads.
- Property—An application can set or get properties available through the Java virtual machine.
- Abstract Windowing Toolkit (AWT)—An application can access the system clipboard or listen to events from the AWT graphical subsystem.
- Reflection—An application can use reflection to access method or fields within a class.
- Serializable—An application can extend the classes used to serialize or deserialize classes, or perform substitutions of serialized objects.

As you can see, Java provides significant control over many important aspects of the system.

Configuring Basic Security with Policy Files

To configure security in Java-based systems, you define a policy file and associate the file with a process at startup:

```
java -Djava.security.policy=/usr/policy [rest of command]
```

The `-Djava.security.policy` property designates the location and name of the policy file to associate with the command process.

Policy Files

Permissions are managed in a text file. The default policy file is named `java.policy`, and it's located in your `user.home` directory. You can determine your system locations, such as `user.home`, by compiling and running the following short program:

```
class ListProperties
{
  public static void main(String args[])
  {
    System.out.println("sun.boot.class.path = " + System.getProperty
➥("sun.boot.class.path"));
    System.out.println("java.class.path = " + System.getProperty
➥("java.class.path"));
```

```
    System.out.println("user.home = " + System.getProperty("user.home"));
    System.out.println("java.ext.dirs = " + System.getProperty
➡("java.ext.dirs"));
  }
}
```

A policy file contains a list of entries or directives:

```
grant [signedBy signers] [,codebase URL] {
  permission permission_class [target][,action][,signedBy signers];
  permission …
};
```

The parts of this code are as follows:

- *signers* is replaced with the name of the entity or entities that have signed the code.
- *URL* is replaced by the URL address of the location from where the code originated.
- *permission_class* is the class type of the permission, such as `java.net.SocketPermission` or `java.io.FilePermission`.
- *target* is the target identifier of the permission; for instance, the socket number or filename.
- *action* is the permitted action of the permission, such as connect, listen, read, write, and so on.

If *signers* is omitted, then code coming from any signer will be granted the permission. Likewise, a missing *URL* will grant the permission to code coming from any location. The permission class `AllPermission` implies that all permissions are granted. As you can see, the policy file we've been using in the examples grants all permissions to any code from anywhere. This is clearly not desirable in a production environment.

Protection Domains

A protection domain is a set of permission entries associated with a code source. The code source includes the URL where the code originated, and optionally the certificates of the entities that have signed the code. Every Java class is uniquely associated with a code source. When an untrusted class is loaded, it is mapped to a protection domain based upon its code source and any signers it might have, as seen in Figure 2.2.

The `grant` entries in the policy file describe the permissions granted to the code source. Classes that have the same permissions but are from different code sources belong to different protection domains.

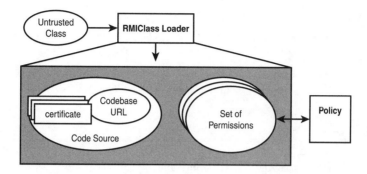

FIGURE 2.2

The protection domain of an untrusted class.

For example, to only grant permission to code signed from a specific user from a specific location, the following code would be used:

```
grant signedBy "rflenner" codebase "http://www.jworkplace.org" {
  permission permission_class [target][,action][,signedBy signers];
  permission …
};
```

This could represent a very restrictive policy, because it specifies both signed user code and code origination for the permission given.

To grant only permission to code signed from a specific user from any location, you would use this:

```
grant signedBy "rflenner" {
  permission permission_class [target][,action][,signedBy signers];
  permission …
};
```

To grant only permission from a specific location to any code, you would use this:

```
grant codebase "file:${java.class.path}" {
  permission permission_class [target][,action];
  permission …
};
```

In this last example, you are specifying the local file system classpath as the location.

Platform-Specific Benefits

Sun provides different development platforms for different development problems—one size does not fit all. Today we have three distinct Java development environments directed toward different processing requirements.

- The Java 2 Standard Edition (J2SE) provides the middle ground solution to capture client development directed at the traditional PC and workgroup environments.

- The Java 2 Enterprise Edition (J2EE) represents the high-end development environment required to support scalable solutions in business-to-business (B2B) and electronic commerce.
- The Java 2 Micro Edition (J2ME) now represents the attack on the device market, specifically aimed at resource-constrained devices.

J2SE

As of this writing, the current release of the Java 2 Standard Edition (J2SE) is version 1.4. You can download the release from `java.sun.com/j2se/`.

The J2SE provides the packages and APIs necessary to build client- and server-side applications targeted at traditional PC and workgroup environments.

Primary support includes the following:

- Java Applets
- JavaBeans Component API
- Java Networking
- Java Utilities
- Java Threads
- Java Media
- Java Foundation Classes/Swing
- Security
- Java Database Connectivity (JDBC)
- RMI/IIOP

P2P applications can utilize any of these programming APIs and supporting packages to speed up and ease development. Of special significance to P2P are Java networking, Java utilities, Java threads, Java foundation classes and security.

Java Networking

Java provides a tremendous amount of support for building networked applications. The `java.net` package contains a number of classes that greatly simplify the complexity of sending and receiving information across the network.

Using Java's `java.net.URL` class, you can establish connections with, and write or read content to or from, Internet resources without having to know much about sockets or specific protocols such as HTTP. Programmers can use the `java.net.Socket` class to make point-to-point connections using TCP, or `java.net.DatagramSocket` for UDP connections. `java.net.ServerSocket` makes it possible to construct sockets that accept and manage incoming connections, making it simple to write servers.

Dynamic discovery of peers and resources is a cornerstone of the P2P architecture. Java supports not only point-to-point unicast sockets, but also multicast sockets that can be used to discover peers on subnets. This, combined with directed unicast to relay or rendezvous peers, provides a powerful combination for building dynamic networks of cooperating peers.

The multicast sender shown in Listing 2.1 provides a simple example of how to send a datagram using multicast.

LISTING 2.1 MulticastSender Class

```java
import java.net.*;

public class MulticastSender {

    public static void main(String args[]) {
        int port = 1234;
        String address = "224.0.0.1";
        String data = "Hello Multicast";

        try {
            InetAddress ip = InetAddress.getByName(address);
            DatagramPacket packet =
                new DatagramPacket(data.getBytes(), data.length(), ip, port);
            MulticastSocket ms = new MulticastSocket();
            ms.send(packet);
            ms.close();
        } catch (Exception e) {
            e.printStackTrace();
        }

    }
}
```

A multicast listener is shown in Listing 2.2:

LISTING 2.2 MulticastListener Class

```java
import java.net.*;

public class MulticastListener {

  public static void main(String args[]) {
    int port = 1234;
```

LISTING 2.2   continued

```
    String address = "224.0.0.1";
    byte[] data = new byte[256];

    try {
      InetAddress ip = InetAddress.getByName(address);
      MulticastSocket ms = new MulticastSocket(port);
      ms.joinGroup(ip);
      DatagramPacket packet = new DatagramPacket(data, data.length);
      ms.receive(packet);
      String message =
        new String(packet.getData(), 0, packet.getLength());
      System.out.println(message);
      ms.close();
    } catch (Exception e) {
      e.printStackTrace();
    }

  }
}
```

Running one or more listeners followed by a sender results in the message "Hello Multicast" being sent to each listener. Although there may be some details in the code that you might not be acquainted with, you can see how easy it is to construct an application that makes use of multicast. Building applications using sockets or URLS is just as simple.

Java Utilities

Collections are of special importance to P2P developers. A *collection* is an object that represents a group of objects, known as elements. The Java collections framework provides a consistent approach to using and manipulating sets or groups of objects. Using collections allows you to avoid implementation-specific details by providing access through a generic container interface. In other words, the specific implementation of the collection can change without having to modify the interface. This enables you to change representations of the underlying data structure if access patterns indicate performance gains are possible by using one structure over another.

Collections have different properties; for instance, some collections allow duplicates, whereas others do not. Some collections support the sequencing or ordering of elements, whereas others might appear at random.

The root interface in the collection hierarchy is represented by the java.util.Collection interface. The Set and List interfaces provide two of the most popular descendent interfaces.

Developers in other languages like C++ often combine third-party products that supply collection frameworks. Of course, this usually means yet another set of classes and templates to learn, all of which are unique to a vendor's API. The Java platform, however, includes a collections framework. The primary advantages of a collections framework are that it

- Reduces programming effort—The proper use of collections can dramatically decrease the amount of code that must be written and maintained.

- Increases performance and flexibility—In most cases, the performance provided by the generic collection classes will outperform custom collection classes. In addition, different interfaces provide different performance tradeoffs. It is important to understand the implementation details of each interface so you can tune your program to the appropriate data structure.

- Provides interoperability—Collections can be passed between programs using a common language.

- Reduces the learning curve—Collections reuse many of the same method calls, which helps to minimize the time required to learn a collection's unique APIs.

- Reduces the development effort—This reduces the time and effort required to design, code, and test most projects.

- Reduces programming errors and promotes reuse—This provides a standard interface for collections and algorithms to manipulate them. It also uses tested framework code instead of ad hoc project code.

The Java collections framework consists of

- Collection interfaces—These interfaces represent different types of collections, such as sets, lists, and maps. These interfaces form the basis of the framework.

- Collection implementations—These classes represent the implementations of the collection framework interfaces.

- Wrapper implementations—Wrappers such as `java.util.Collections` augment primary collection functionality by adding polymorphic manipulation, collection transformation, and synchronization. Synchronization is especially important in multithreaded applications, where modification of data can occur in multiple threads.

- Abstract implementations—Partial implementations help to reduce the customization coding effort required to implement a primary collection interface.

Java Threads

Java's support for threads makes it a strong candidate for the multiprocessing capabilities required of peers in P2P networks. From a network perspective, this includes—but is not limited to—discovery and search. Both of these operations can take an inordinate amount of time when using slow network connections, or when the search horizon is extremely large.

Java threads provide an easy approach to providing multiple streams of execution within a process. So, while discovery or a Web search is being initiated, other processes such as supporting a user interface or establishing connections to multiple peers can proceed without being blocked by slow synchronous activities.

The Monitor class (shown in Listing 2.3) provides an example of extending the Java Thread class. Monitor is a thread that runs, waits a specified amount of time, then runs again. This example simply prints out the system time. However, it could be used to invoke a heartbeat process that periodically examines network utilization, file system capacity, or the number of concurrent connections to provide adaptive behavior in P2P networks.

LISTING 2.3 Monitor Class

```java
public class Monitor extends Thread {

    private volatile Thread listener;
    private int frequency;

    public Monitor(int frequency) {
        this.frequency = frequency*1000;
    }

    public void run() {
        listener = Thread.currentThread();

        while(listener != null) {
            // do something useful!
            System.out.println(System.currentTimeMillis());
            Thread.sleep(frequency);
        }
    }

    public void stopMonitor() {
        listener = null;
    }
}
```

A using application would start Monitor with the following code fragment:

```
Monitor monitor = new Monitor(60);
monitor.start()
```

Java Foundation Classes

Swing, along with AWT, provides support for the visual components of your P2P application. Swing provides support for all the usual visual widgets in graphical user interfaces, such as buttons, tables, trees, lists, and so on. In addition, it provides support for features that might be useful to P2P clients, such as browsing Web sites and documents.

Listing 2.4 shows the ease with which you can create a simple document browser using a Swing JEditorPane and the java.net.URL class.

LISTING 2.4   URLViewer Class

```
import java.awt.*;
import java.net.*;
import javax.swing.*;

public class URLViewer extends JFrame {

  private URL url;
  private JEditorPane webView;

  public static void main(String[] args) {
    URLViewer viewer =
      new URLViewer("http://www.pearsonptg.com/book_detail/
➡0,3771,0672323990,00.html");
  }

  public URLViewer(String address) {
    super("URLViewer");

    webView = new JEditorPane();
    webView.setEditable(false);
    webView.setPreferredSize(new Dimension(400, 400));

    JScrollPane scrollPane = new JScrollPane(webView);
    getContentPane().add(scrollPane, BorderLayout.CENTER);
    pack();

    try {
      url = new URL(address);
      webView.setPage(url);
      setVisible(true);
    } catch (Exception e) {
      e.printStackTrace();
    }
  }
}
```

`JEditorPane` encapsulates the functionality required to display HTML. Besides that, the code only makes use of one other Swing component, `JScrollPane`, to make it possible for the user to scroll the contents.

> **Note**
>
> `JEditorPane` is currently limited to supporting HTML 3.2. Consequently, some sites that you may browse might not display correctly. As a note, `JEditorPane` is also capable of displaying plain text and RTF.

Swing has an extensive set of packages that rival any GUI library on the market. Performance continues to be an area where improvements are being made.

Security

Robust network security will continue to gain importance in P2P architecture. Network security is commonly defined as the protection of information, systems, and services against manipulation, mistakes, and disasters. It is comprised of authentication, authorization, integrity, confidentiality, and nonrepudiation.

- Authentication is the most common type of network security. It generally involves a user or process demonstrating some form of evidence to prove *identity*. Such evidence might be information only the user would likely know (a password), or it might be information only the user could produce (signed data using a private key).

- Authorization involves the capability to enforce access controls upon an authenticated user. This is commonly implemented using an access control policy associating user access rights to system resources, such as databases, files, and processes.

- Integrity means ensuring that messages are delivered correctly, and that messages in transit have not been tampered with maliciously.

- Confidentiality and privacy ensure that data cannot be seen or disclosed over the network by outside parties. *Encryption* is a procedure used to convert text into code in order to prevent any but the intended recipient from reading that data. It can be used to ensure the confidentiality of data, the authentication of the data sender, or the integrity of the data sent.

- Finally, nonrepudiation guarantees that a sender cannot deny having sent a particular message.

Chapter 10, "P2P Security," discusses these topics in more detail, and provides a look at how Java can be used to build secure P2P applications.

Network security in Java is based on three primary components: Java Secure Sockets Extension support, the Java Authentication and Authorization Service, and Java cryptography extensions.

Secure Sockets Layer

The Secure Socket Layer (SSL) protocol provides encryption, authentication, and integrity of data by introducing a protocol layer above TCP/IP, and defining a handshake process that ensures communicating peers are authenticated. All data in transit is encrypted to ensure confidentiality. The Java Secure Sockets Extension (JSSE) supports SSL 3.0 and its successor, Transport Layer Security (TLS) 1.0. P2P applications can use JSSE to protect their network communication.

The JSSE was an optional package (extension) prior to JDK 1.4, and was a separate download from the core distribution. As of JDK 1.4, JSSE has been integrated into the core platform.

Java Authentication and Authorization Service (JAAS)

The Java Authentication and Authorization Service (JAAS) provides a framework and standard API for authenticating and authorizing users in Java-based applications. Java applications can now provide code-centric access control, user-centric access control, or a combination of both.

JAAS provides a means to validate users, and can make certain that a user is able to perform an action by using existing frameworks such as Kerberos, and it integrates those frameworks into standard Java security mechanisms. JAAS performs authentication using "pluggable" authentication technologies, making it possible to construct applications that are portable, in spite of the potentially different authentication mechanisms that may be required at deployment. It also relieves applications from managing identities and the low-level details of authentication themselves—they can let Unix or Windows NT provide the facilities.

Like JSSE, JAAS was an optional package prior to JDK 1.4. It is now a part of the basic services.

Java Cryptography Extensions

Java's cryptography extensions (JCE) provide most of the building blocks for secure applications. Fundamentally, JCE supports encryption and decryption, message authentication and key generation, and management. These services form the foundation for protecting information exchanged between parties.

Like other Java frameworks, JCE uses "pluggable" modules, making it possible to implement solutions independent of the underlying technology. The standard provider implements many useful and popular algorithms such as DES (FIPS PUB 46-1) and Triple DES. Although the standard provider is usually sufficient, providers that implement other algorithms, like the new federal standard for encryption AES, or cryptographic services can be obtained from companies such as RSA Security.

JCE was also an optional package prior to JDK 1.4 that is now a part of the standard JDK.

J2EE

As of this writing, the current release of the Java 2 Enterprise Edition (J2EE) is version 1.3.1. You can download it from `http://java.sun.com/j2ee/`.

The J2EE provides the packages and APIs necessary to build scalable high-end solutions in business-to-business (B2B) and electronic commerce.

Primary support includes the following:

- JDBC
- Enterprise JavaBeans
- JavaServer Pages and Servlets
- Java Messaging Service
- JavaMail
- Java Transaction Architecture (JTA)/Java Transaction Services (JTA)
- JNDI

P2P applications can utilize any of these programming APIs and supporting packages to build enterprise-level applications. As P2P applications mature, it's likely that these technologies will begin to interoperate, and might eventually integrate. Because J2EE provides a mature foundation for enterprise applications that is widely implemented, Appendix A provides an overview that should be useful to P2P programmers in understanding the breadth and architecture of the platform. Of the several standards that make up J2EE, JMS is particularly significant to P2P.

Java Messaging Service

The Java Messaging Service (JMS) provides a common way for Java clients to create, send, receive, and read messages. J2EE provides JMS as the interface to message-oriented middleware. JMS tries to standardize the interface to messaging systems.

JMS supports two models of communication:

- Point-to-point—Involves a single requestor sending a message to a single responder.
- Publish/subscribe—Enables a single requestor to send a message to an unknown number of responders, also known as subscribers.

Message addressing is based on the concept of *topics*, or names that identify message queues. Typically, JMS is implemented in an enterprise that has control over queue identity and can configure clients with the necessary information to find and access these resources. In this respect, P2P is more dynamic. Peers discover resources dynamically.

However, P2P and JMS both present compelling integration possibilities. For instance, a P2P application might subscribe to a known enterprise JMS topic, and receive notification of events in the enterprise that are of special significance to the P2P application. The P2P application could then act as a gateway to the P2P network. This provides a more secure interface to the external world from the enterprise, and still offers the advantages of dynamic discovery. The P2P peer and the JMS system are able to secure their identity and information to the desired level. This could include Java authentication and authorization services.

The P2P client acts as a rendezvous point for information housed in the enterprise messaging system. The messaging system only publishes information to the "P2P topic" that it wants the peer network to know. Trading markets and quoting applications might use this technique to increase access to commodities and securities yet still maintain control over the publication process.

Chapter 12, "Messaging and Java APIs for XML," explains JMS further and provides an example of how to use JMS.

J2ME

The Java 2 platform, Micro Edition (J2ME) is a more recent Java application environment. It is a framework for the deployment and use of Java technology in the post-PC world. J2ME software is configured for a variety of market segments.

J2ME is targeted at the device market, specifically at resource-constrained devices. It features a highly optimized runtime environment designed to efficiently use the available resources and provide the best possible performance. P2P applications have an opportunity to connect these devices to one another and to more capable peers. J2ME can help significantly.

Primary support includes the following:

- Personal Java API (MIDP/CDC)
- Embedded Java (CLDC)

The J2ME architecture is designed to be modular, using two fundamental elements: configurations and profiles. Together, they deliver a specification for consumer electronics and embedded device manufacturers to implement on their products.

Configurations and Profiles

A *configuration* is a virtual machine and a minimal set of basic class libraries and APIs. It specifies a generalized runtime environment for consumer electronic and embedded devices, and acts as the Java platform on the device.

A *profile* is an industry-defined specification of the Java APIs used by manufacturers and developers to address specific types of devices. A profile is built on top of and utilizes the underlying configuration necessary to provide a complete runtime environment for a specific kind of device. Profiles specify both the APIs and the configuration. An application written to the specification can execute in the specified Java technology environment without the addition of other Java classes (see Figure 2.3).

FIGURE 2.3

A configuration and profile provide the building blocks to J2ME.

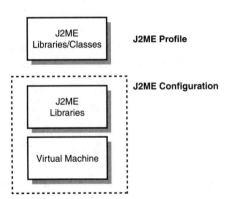

Two configurations make up current J2ME technology:

- Connected Limited Device Configuration (CLDC)
- Connected Device Configuration (CDC)

Connected Limited Device Configuration

The Connected Limited Device Configuration (CLDC) was developed for devices with a small amount of memory. It is used in small, resource-constrained devices, each with memory in the range of 160–512KB. This provides the minimal functionality needed to minimize the memory footprint for memory-constrained devices. These devices usually contain 16- or 32-bit processors, and a minimum total memory footprint of 128KB. The Mobile Information Device Profile (MIDP) is used with CLDC. It is targeted at devices such as cell phones (see Figure 2.4).

The CLDC is composed of the K virtual machine (KVM) and basic class libraries that can be used on a variety of devices. The KVM is a portable virtual machine designed for small-memory, limited-resource, network-connected devices. Newer, 32-bit devices with between 512KB and 1MB of memory can take advantage of the CLDC HotSpot virtual machine, which offers increased performance.

FIGURE 2.4

CLDC and MIDP targeting the "weak" device market.

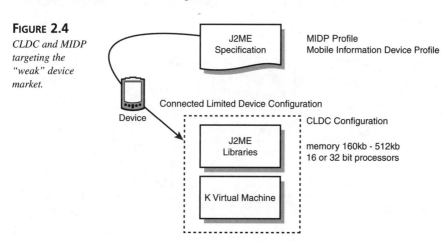

Connected Device Configuration

The Connected Device Configuration (CDC) was developed for devices with relatively large amounts of memory—two megabytes or more of total memory available for the Java platform. These devices typically require the full features and functionalities of the Java virtual machine. Target devices for CDC contain connectivity to a network with a wireless, intermittent connection and limited bandwidth (9600bps or less). Some devices that might be supported by CDC include residential gateways, next-generation smart phones, two-way pagers, Personal Digital Assistants (PDAs), home appliances, point-of-sale terminals, and automobile navigation systems. Currently, CDC has a profile called the Foundation Profile. The CDC is a superset of CLDC, and therefore a CLDC-compliant profile is upwardly compatible with CDC.

The Foundation Profile

The Foundation Profile is a set of Java APIs that, together with the CDC, provides a complete J2ME application runtime environment targeted at consumer electronics and embedded devices. The C virtual machine (CVM) in the CDC is the engine for the Foundation Profile libraries. The CVM is a full-featured virtual machine designed for devices needing the functionality of the Java 2 virtual machine feature set, but with a smaller footprint (see Figure 2.5).

In general, the Foundation Profile contains the complete basic Java packages from J2SE technology, except that the GUI dependencies on `java.awt` are removed. The CVM supports version 1.3 of the Java 2 Platform, and includes security, weak references, JNI, RMI, and JVMDI.

FIGURE 2.5

CDC and Foundation Profile targeting the "strong" device market.

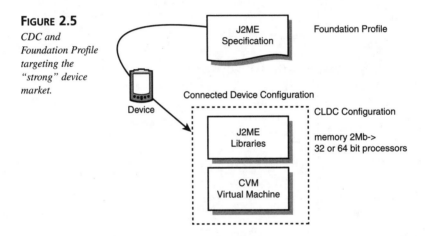

The J2ME architecture is changing rapidly. To find the latest information, you might want to visit the Sun Microsystems site at `http://java.sun.com/j2me/`.

The documentation and API specifications for the following releases can be downloaded from the Sun Web site at `java.sun.com/products`.

- The CDC release: `java.sun.com/products/cdc`
- The CVM release: `java.sun.com/products/cdc/cvm`
- The Foundation Profile release: `java.sun.com/products/foundation`

XML

As you will learn throughout the book, XML is a key component in P2P architecture. It is rapidly becoming the encoding standard for message exchange on the Web.

Java provides robust support for XML that goes far beyond simple message parsing. There are now a number of optional packages available to minimize your development requirements for processing XML-based message exchanges in B2B and Web services.

The JAX Pack

The Java XML Pack, also known as the JAX Pack, is a suite of Java technologies for XML. The Java XML Pack attempts to address the need for Java processing across standards for XML—such as SAX, DOM, XSLT, SOAP, UDDI, ebXML, and WSDL. It provides a single bundle of packages to jumpstart the Java processing of relevant XML technologies. In addition to the overview here, the JAX pack will be explored some more in Chapter 12, "Messaging and Java APIs for XML."

Java API for XML Processing

The Java API for XML Processing (JAXP) provides support for popular XML document-processing standards such as SAX, DOM, and XSLT. JAXP enables you to use any XML-compliant parser from within your application while standardizing the interface between implementations. It does this with what is called a *pluggability layer,* which enables you to plug in an implementation of the SAX, DOM, or XSL APIs.

The JAXP 1.1 reference implementation provides the Xalan XSLT processor and the Crimson parser, which was developed jointly between Sun and the Apache Software Foundation.

SAX is an event-driven XML parser. In other words, SAX triggers notifications to using applications when it recognizes an element in an XML document. SAX is used when you want to read XML data and parse it to find and process elements quickly.

DOM permits you to create an object model of an XML document. It enables you to not only read and parse the document, but also manipulate its contents. DOM creates an in-memory representation of the XML document. Each element is represented as a node that can be traversed and used to add and remove content from the document.

XSL allows you to transform an XML document from one XML representation to another. Besides normal conversions such as XML to HTML, XSL transformations can be used to bridge proprietary XML formats to industry-standard protocols and representations. These bridges open up possibilities for enabling P2P XML data to interoperate with industry standards such as ebXML.

Java Architecture for XML Binding

The Java Architecture for XML Binding (JAXB) maps XML elements to classes in the Java programming language. Like DOM, JAXB enables access to XML data in memory, but generally requires a smaller memory footprint. JAXB does not build in tree manipulation capabilities such as those supported by DOM. JAXB requires a schema or document type definition (DTD) to be defined for the XML document. It generates the Java classes based on the DTD definition and a JAXB defined schema that you must construct. You can use JAXB to create Java objects and convert data between different types.

Java API for XML Messaging

The Java API for XML Messaging (JAXM) implements SOAP messaging with attachments. It extends SOAP to provide a foundation for message profiles. A message profile is an implementation of a standard, such as the ebXML Transportation, Routing, and Packaging Message Handling Service. JAXM supports simple point-to-point SOAP messages, as well as message providers. Message providers enable asynchronous messaging between a SOAP requestor and a SOAP responder by introducing a level of indirection between the source and destination. A message provider can be an implementation of JMS.

A standalone client is limited to using a point-to-point connection that goes directly from the sender to the recipient.

To use a messaging provider, an application must obtain a connection to a messaging provider rather than to a specified recipient. You can get a provider connection by using a naming service. Once you have a connection, you can populate a standard SOAP message header and request. You can also customize message content using message factories.

JAXP also supports attachments. Any data can be used in an attachment, even non-XML data. This is another possible bridge between P2P and XML-based messaging systems. P2P applications can use the attachment specification to transfer data such as images, audio, and video files using SOAP-defined exchanges.

Java API for XML Registries

The Java API for XML Registries (JAXR) provides a standard Java API for interacting with XML registries such as UDDI and ebXML Registry/Repository.

Business registries provide the advertising capabilities for businesses on the Internet. They are often compared to the electronic "yellow pages" for business service publication. They contain a listing of the products and services that a business wants to promote electronically.

JAXR provides a Java interface to using business registries that are based on open standards or industry consortium-led specifications, such as UDDI.

Businesses can register themselves with a registry or discover other businesses with which they might want to do business. A business supplies its name, a description, and some classification concepts to facilitate searches. Standards groups have developed DTDs for particular kinds of XML documents. Because the DTD is stored in a standard business registry, both parties can use JAXR to access it.

A business can use JAXR to search a registry for other businesses. JAXR also supports using an SQL query to search a registry. Registries have become an important component of Web services because they enable businesses to collaborate with each other dynamically in a loosely coupled way.

JAXR enables enterprises to access standard business registries from the Java programming language.

Java API for XML-Based RPC

The Java API for XML-based RPC (JAX-RPC) supports XML-based remote procedure call (RPC) functionality conforming to the SOAP 1.1 specification.

The Java programming language already has two other APIs for making remote procedure calls: Java IDL and Remote Method Invocation (RMI). All three have an API for marshaling and unmarshaling arguments, and for transmitting and receiving procedure calls. The difference is that JAX-RPC is based on XML, and is geared to Web services. Java IDL is based on the Common Object Request Broker Architecture (CORBA) and uses the Object Management Group's Interface Definition Language (OMG IDL). RMI is based on RPC, where both the method calls and the methods being invoked are in the Java programming language—although with RMI over IIOP, the methods being invoked might be in another language.

All varieties of RPC are fairly complex, involving the mapping and reverse mapping of data types and the marshaling and unmarshaling of arguments. However, these take place behind the scenes and are not visible to the user. JAX-RPC continues this model, which means that a client using XML-based RPC from the Java programming language is not required to work with XML or do any mapping directly.

Although JAX-RPC implements a remote procedure call as a request-response SOAP message, a user of JAX-RPC is shielded from this level of detail. So, underneath the covers, JAX-RPC is actually a specialized form of SOAP messaging. In contrast, JAXM is a more robust form of SOAP messaging. This is especially true if a higher-level protocol such as ebXML is layered on top of SOAP.

The following list includes features that JAXM can provide and that RPC, including JAX-RPC, does not generally provide:

- Asynchronous messaging
- Routing of a message to more than one party
- Reliable messaging with features such as guaranteed delivery

The Power of Equivalence and Independence

Java's platform independence complements the distributed nature of P2P. Together these technologies can change many of the limitations or constraints in current application deployment. Java enables you to deploy code on the platform that makes the most sense for your requirements. P2P eliminates or reduces the client/server partitioning of functionality and promotes distribution to edge resources. The new device market can leverage many of the Java and P2P features to provide personal services in new and exciting ways.

Summary

Some unique benefits of Java in P2P environments include the following:

- Portable code
- Network-oriented
- Interpretive language/reflection or runtime discovery
- Mobile code/mobile agents
- Built-in robustness/multithreaded
- Built-in security

Today we have three distinct Java development environments directed toward different processing requirements.

- J2EE provides support for scalable solutions for B2B and electronic commerce.
- J2SE provides the middle ground solution, and is directed toward the traditional PC and workgroup environments.
- J2ME is specifically aimed at resource-constrained devices.

P2P applications can utilize many of the programming APIs and supporting packages provided in the Java distributions to accelerate and ease development.

Key J2SE features for P2P are Java networking, Java utilities, Java threads, Java foundation classes, and security.

Key J2EE features include JMS, interoperability, and the JAX Pack.

Key J2ME features include support for resource-constrained devices, the Personal Java API (MIDP/CDC), and Embedded Java (CLDC).

Java also provides a rich set of APIs for working with XML and XML-based messaging or remote procedure calls.

In the next chapter, we'll look at some specific P2P products and areas of development to demonstrate the exciting world of P2P. It will give you a feel for what has been done, and more importantly, what is possible.

P2P Application Types

by Robert Flenner and Frank Cohen

Chapter 1 introduced the wide world of P2P. It might have appeared that the definition of P2P is problematic—well, it is! P2P can be so broad in scope and definition that getting one's arms around P2P can be an enormous task. P2P came about as an answer to user needs for Internet-enabled application software. The Internet is always evolving and offering up new technologies, techniques, and user behavior every day. P2P is evolving along with the Internet, so fixed definitions do not usually last long.

Each new advance in Internet technology can either help Java developers working on Internet applications, or become a huge headache. For example, there was a time when Network Address Translation (NAT) routers were banned from networks. As you will see later in this chapter, they are now used widely, and a Java developer building a P2P application needs a solution to the unique one-way routing provided by a NAT router.

An easy way to get your arms around a P2P definition is to look at the functions delivered by the most notable P2P applications, including the following:

- Instant messaging
- Managing and sharing information
- Collaboration

What started out as simple file sharing, such as exchanging music files, has grown to include a wide array of applications and services. These are grouped under the umbrella term *distributed P2P services*. These include network and infrastructure software to enable

- Distributed processing (grid computing)
- Distributed storage
- Distributed network services

Although many of these applications began as ways to distribute stolen copyrighted music and video files, P2P has reached a level of maturity that is no longer confined to personal, casual use, but rather to build e-market hubs, corporate infrastructure, and Internet-enabled applications. In addition, single-function P2P applications are giving way to multifunction service-based architectures. For instance, it is common to aggregate instant messaging, file sharing, and content management to build distributed collaborative P2P applications.

Next we will look in depth at these applications and the technology that enables them.

Instant Messaging

Although Web publishing and browsing is the killer application for the Internet, instant messaging is the killer application for P2P. Instant messaging (IM) enables online users to communicate immediately and in real-time, one-to-one or in a group. It has become popular on the Internet among young adults, and is gaining popularity in business settings, too. For example, even IBM's Lotus group offers an IM product for business use. IM has gained recognition as a useful application, and most major Internet players offer IM services—AOL, Microsoft, and Yahoo! all offer IM functionality. New players are promoting niche products for e-commerce and supply chain management. There has been some market consolidation as lesser offerings have been eliminated, but there is still tremendous growth and opportunity.

With IM, users activate a special piece of client software that communicates with a central server and registers the user as being online. This user registration is mapped to an *identity*, such as a nickname or screen name. The user is then able to invite others to a conversation, or can be invited. IM servers communicate using an IM server protocol that enables messages to be relayed across the Internet. This interconnected IM network forms an IM cloud, or backbone, as seen in Figure 3.1. Most servers support a proprietary protocol, which has made it difficult for IM users to communicate across multiple IM systems.

FIGURE 3.1

Traditional instant messaging systems enable users to exchange messages through a proprietary IM cloud.

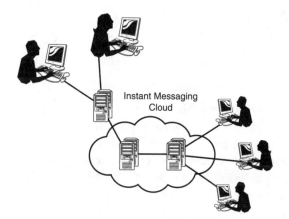

Instant Messaging Cloud

Unlike email, in which a message is stored and delivered once the user has connected to an email server, IM systems provide immediate end user delivery. If the user is not available, the message can be saved until the user comes online, or it simply may be discarded. To avoid this uncertainty in delivery, IM systems provide a "buddy list" or roster

3

P2P APPLICATION TYPES

that provides a mechanism to identify a user and determine the user's online status: for example, online, offline, or unavailable.

If the user is online, you can send text messages that are immediately delivered to the user. This promotes a two-way conversational style of communication with minimal delay. Tight integration between clients and servers enables instant messaging services to provide varying levels of security, online status, and reliable messaging, as seen in Figure 3.2. The client protocol defines the message structure necessary to communicate short text messages. The server protocol defines the higher-level services, such as routing, presence, and security.

FIGURE 3.2

Instant messaging systems define a client and a server protocol.

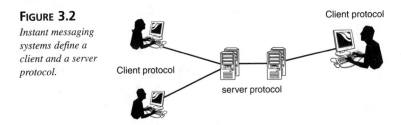

Applications of presence (online status) and instant messaging currently use independent, nonstandard, and non-interoperable protocols developed by various vendors.

Technology

Under the covers, IM systems provide identity, presence, and security using IM protocols.

Identity

Fundamental to the operation of any IM system is the need to uniquely identify users. IM identity is modeled much like email identity. For instance, your email address might be myName@domain.com. Similarly, your instant messaging address might be identified by myName@imdomain.com. IM systems support name aliases to simplify usage, so myName@imdomain.com can be aliased to p2pgeek. The server or client maintains a mapping between addresses and aliases to make the system more user friendly.

Presence

Presence is the online state of a user or application. Presence is a concept important to conversations, because it enables participants to enter or leave a conversation, and make other participants aware of their status.

A presence service provides a means for finding, retrieving, and subscribing to changes in the presence information of other users. This is especially important with instant messaging systems. Presence determines whether a specific user is online and available, whereas identity uniquely identifies that user within the specific IM domain.

Presence services are becoming more sophisticated, and are not limited to simple online/offline state information. Contextual information can be maintained to convey location, activity, and application-specific data. Presence information provides the context necessary to support P2P conversations. In addition, sophisticated presence services can provide status, identity, and location information to enable application-to-application communication.

Buddy lists are part of IM presence technology. A buddy list, also called a roster, defines a list of members of your messaging group or community. Members of your roster may be colleagues, friends, or associates that you communicate with regularly. They ultimately are peers that you trust.

Interoperability

IM is all about dynamically and rapidly grouping users and applications together to form working teams. It is counterintuitive that IM service providers would cause their IM protocols to be closed and proprietary.

The popularity of instant messaging and the growth in instant messaging systems has resulted in an increased demand for IM interoperability. Most instant messaging systems work only if the sender and receiver are using the same instant messaging software.

The protocols defined to exchange information, such as presence, messages, and identity are proprietary to the vendor. Software developers have resorted to building gateways or multi-headed clients to integrate disparate systems. However, the complexity and maintainability of the client can be limiting. Figure 3.3 illustrates communication with the Internet Relay Chat (IRC), AOL Instant Messenger (AIM), and MSN systems.

FIGURE 3.3

Multi-headed clients enable a user to communicate with multiple IM systems.

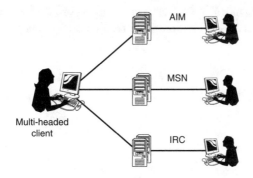

Multi-headed client

AIM

MSN

IRC

Of course, this solution puts a heavy burden on the client software. The software must be able to interoperate with different messaging structures, presence and identity identification, and different feature sets and security models offered by IM providers. There are also legal ramifications to usage, spam implications, and resource sharing that must be considered.

An approach being promoted by some of the larger IM providers is to provide a mechanism for the services themselves to interoperate. This is similar to how email works today. The interaction between instant messaging clients and associated servers remains the same. However, servers communicate with other servers to exchange presence information, messages, or other data, as in Figure 3.4. This approach preserves existing IM models. In addition, it helps protect investment by the larger participants in established IM communities. Clients "speak" a proprietary protocol, but IM servers use a standard open protocol. Servers must mediate message and protocol disparities and serve as a gateway to other IM systems.

FIGURE 3.4

Interoperability is achieved at the service level.

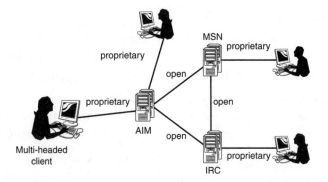

The Internet Engineering Task Force (IETF) (`www.ietf.org`) is developing what will likely become the standard protocol for instant messaging, called the Instant Messaging and Presence Protocol (IMPP). The goal of the IMPP Working Group is to define a standard protocol, so that independently developed applications of instant messaging and/or presence can interoperate across the Internet. The requirements being addressed include the following:

- Namespace and administration
- Scalability and performance
- Access control
- Network topology

- Message encryption and authentication
- Internationalization

For more information, go to `www.imppwg.org`. Standardization work is progressing, but adoption has been slow as vendors try to secure a dominant position with their current product offering.

Security

Instant messaging does not define a mechanism for secure communication. However, many commercial IM vendors have incorporated Public Key Infrastructure (PKI) digital certificates to add security and privacy to IM communication. IBM Lotus Sametime, for example, moves IM protocols over Secure Sockets Layer (SSL) connections. Messages, connection information, and identity are maintained on servers administered and controlled by the provider of the IM service. Most services provide a certain level of encryption, but there have been numerous security breaches on IM systems. This is one area that is changing, as new P2P entrants attempt to differentiate their product offerings through enhanced security.

Products

Because instant messaging has become so popular, it is not surprising that there is an abundance of IM providers. Today, many P2P applications are including an instant messaging component. It is envisioned that as businesses link their manufacturing, distribution, and sales processes, more reliance on IM features will be the result. Many Web sites already use IM as a key component in their customer relationship management (CRM) strategy.

IRC

Internet Relay Chat (IRC, `www.irc.org`), is often cited as the original chat medium on the Internet. It is the forefather to many of the IM protocols that have been developed. The IRC protocol was designed for use with text-based conferencing. The IRC protocol is based on the client-server model. A server forms a central point for clients (or other servers) to connect to, and performs the required message delivery, multiplexing, and IM functions.

Over the years, IRC has been expanded and changed to resolve scalability problems. For example, while the original IRC protocol required a single central server, today's IRC enables federations of interconnected servers to pass IM messages. OpenProjects.net (`www.openprojects.net`) provides a backbone of IRC servers that developers and users working on open-source projects use. IRC continues to evolve.

AIM

AOL Instant Messenger (AIM) is one of the most popular instant messaging programs. With 30 million users and 2.3 billion AIM messages passed every month according to Juniper Media Matrix, AOL has the largest single installed user-base on the Internet. AIM is so large that AOL had to pledge to provide interoperability with other IM networks as a prerequisite to the Time-AOL merger. AIM is the best example of open standards and interoperability colliding with capitalism. Attempts to open the AIM network have clashed with AOL's modification of the protocol to remain incompatible. Even today, AOL has shown how slow it can be to open its network.

AIM technology is designed around a system of interoperating servers to route IM messages, provide presence service and security. AIM uses the AOL directory service for authentication and provides client software on several platforms.

Jabber

Jabber (www.jabber.org) is an open source instant messaging platform being developed by the open source community. One of the features that distinguishes the Jabber system from existing instant messaging services is its open XML protocol. The Jabber protocol has been submitted as an IETF Request For Comments (RFC).

Jabber is attempting to build the interoperable protocol that all IM vendors will support. This would enable the interoperability that is envisioned by the IM community. In the meantime, the Jabber architecture is built on pluggable transport modules that communicate with specific IM systems, as seen in Figure 3.5.

The idea is that you use the Jabber XML protocol (XMPP) from the client to the Jabber server, and the server loads an IM-specific transport module to interoperate with the proprietary IM system.

Jabber's XML protocol contains three top-level XML elements:

```
<message/>
<presence/>
<iq/> (info/query)
```

Each of these elements can contain additional attributes and namespace definitions that are part of the Jabber protocol. Jabber sessions are maintained through the exchange of XML streams, one from the client to the server, and one from the server to the client. All `<message/>`, `<presence/>`, and `<iq/>` elements are sent within the context of these XML streams. Here is an example from the Jabber specification:

```
SEND:<stream:stream
SEND:to='jabber.org'
SEND:xmlns='jabber:client'
```

```
SEND:xmlns:stream='http://etherx.jabber.org/streams'>
RECV:<stream:stream
RECV:xmlns:stream='http://etherx.jabber.org/streams'
RECV:id='39ABA7D2'
RECV:xmlns='jabber:client'
RECV:from='jabber.org'>
(XML for user session goes here) *
SEND:</stream:stream>
RECV:</stream:stream>
```

FIGURE 3.5

The Jabber architecture from www.jabber.com.

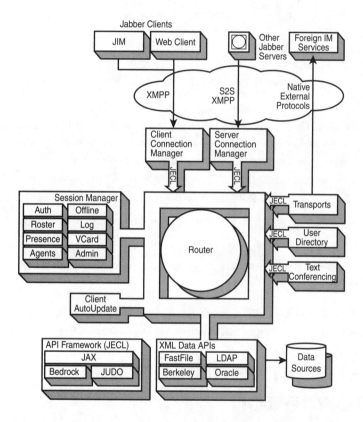

The Jabber protocol is designed to facilitate writing Jabber client code and conducting tests. Details on Jabber can be found at www.jabber.com. There you can download an applet that enables you to register with a Jabber server, as seen in Figure 3.6.

The Jabber architecture resembles email. A Jabber client is connected to a Jabber server. Like an email server, the Jabber server is responsible for the delivery and receipt of the client's messages. However, Jabber servers will attempt to deliver the messages immediately, thereby supporting instant messaging and conversational capabilities. The Jabber server will queue messages when a peer is unavailable or offline.

FIGURE 3.6

A Jabber client from www.jabber.com.

The peer-to-peer comparisons of Jabber are more appropriately realized with the relationship between Jabber servers. Every Jabber server is a peer to every other Jabber server. Jabber servers use a number of mechanisms to improve the integrity and security of the system. For instance, hostname dialback independently contacts the sending server to validate incoming data to prevent spoofing.

There are a number of Jabber clients available. Examples include the following:

- WinJab for Windows—winjab.sourceforge.net
- Jabbernaut for MacOS—www.jabbernaut.com
- Gabber for Linux—gabber.sourceforge.net

You can find a list of public servers and their current status at http://www.jabberview.com/. For more information, visit www.jabber.org.

Managing and Sharing Information

The next category of P2P services distributes the management and sharing of computer resources to a group of peers across the network. A number of subcategories are included:

- File sharing
- Resource sharing
- Distributed search engines

File sharing applications such as Gnutella and Freenet form ad hoc P2P communities. These applications share files without requiring centralized coordination or control. Resource sharing applications are a form of distributed computing that use of the cumulative power of dynamically networked peers to tackle tasks previously possible only on supercomputers. For example, the SETI project referenced in the first chapter is one example of resource sharing.

Finally, distributed search engines are a P2P technology that address the problems inherent in the large size of the information space. Distributed search engines push the computing functions needed to build an index of search results toward the edge of the network where peers live. Distributed search engines use a divide-and-conquer strategy to locate information and perform these searches in real time.

Technology

While the P2P applications presented in this chapter go a long way toward explaining the definition of P2P, P2P file and resource sharing requires knowledge of access control, searching algorithms, metadata, and system performance techniques such as caching, clustering, and synchronization, which we'll examine next.

Access Control

Early P2P applications favored open access over security. Now that 30 million users are chatting away on the America Online network alone, a significant percentage are using chat at work. Controlling access to chat conversations is a significant risk to businesses that now depend on chat.

P2P file sharing applications are commonly found in businesses today, and pose a large risk. A typical P2P file sharing application involves four steps:

1. Download and install the client.
2. Launch the client.
3. Designate a folder on your hard drive to share.
4. Search and download files from the peer(s) hard drive.

As you can see, the potential for security breaches is enormous. First, can the downloaded application be trusted? What assurance do you have that once installed, the application is not scanning your hard drive and sending information to an undisclosed destination—or that the program is not deleting files or otherwise performing a malicious activity? Unless the source is trustworthy, you have no assurance at all; and even then, malfunctioning programs can do damage unintentionally.

Despite the security hazards, P2P file sharing ranks number two in usage according to industry analysts. The reward of getting that hot MP3 file for free has outweighed security concerns for many individuals. However, for business adoption and the growth of distributed content networks (DCN), access control must improve. Improved network security will be required. Authentication and authorization services will be required to prove identity and associated permissions. Confidentiality and privacy will be required to ensure that data cannot be seen or disclosed over the network by outside parties. Message integrity is needed to protect data in transit.

Searching and Locating

P2P search engines are becoming more popular because they enable a search to be run in parallel using resources that heretofore have been untapped. Finding relevant information is more important and more difficult because of four important business trends:

- Information hypergrowth—Businesses continue to create huge amounts of information, and have turned to the Internet to serve as a global repository.

- Information silos—Businesses often create organizational, technical, or functional boundaries around their information, making it difficult to access openly.

- Unstructured content—Although EDI- and XML-defined content continues to grow, a tremendous number of ad hoc data structures are still used to store information.

- The growing need to collaborate—Internally and externally, businesses are becoming more interconnected. The need to collaborate continues to grow, and requires access to decentralized and relevant information.

A new breed of P2P applications is dealing with searching and locating information in new and innovative ways. Two important trends in computing are radically improving search capabilities in P2P applications:

- Parallelism—The capability to divide the search process into coordinated tasks.

- Metadata—Data that describes information to enable humans, and especially computers, to process that information more intelligently.

As a result, distributed searching has a number of benefits:

- Increased efficiency—Distributed searching eliminates the need to centralize and normalize the data.

- Increased accuracy—Content owners can continually update their information, even as others are searching it. Users see only the most current and accurate information.

- Simple maintenance—IT organizations don't have to maintain and update multiple sources of departmental information. The responsibility remains with the information owners.

Caching, Clusters, and Synchronization

The origins of P2P technology go back to a time when the scale of potential users of a software application grew from hundreds to thousands. P2P technology distributed the computing power of an application to the peers to avoid scalability bottlenecks imposed by a client/server architecture. Although P2P architecture worked for the jump to thousands of users, many P2P technologies today enable millions of users. Scaling up to millions of users required innovations in caching, cluster, and synchronization technology.

P2P caching technology largely drew from caching techniques developed for client/server systems, including the following:

- Replication—All peers eventually get a copy of every change in a P2P network. Each peer is programmed to forward a copy of a data change in a token. The token gives each new peer a unique identifier to the data and a validity date. The peer records the changed data if the validity date is more recent than the data it holds. Replication works best for applications that are not tied to a certain state. For example, whereas real estate listings don't change frequently and are not required to always be accurate, airline reservation systems would likely not work well in replicated systems.

- First-In First-Out (FIFO)—Each peer in a network is part of a hierarchy of peers that share data updates. New data filters into the P2P network and replaces existing data. The downside to FIFO is the overhead needed to coordinate the hierarchy of peers.

- Hybrid centralized/peer—Each peer holds its own copy of data, but looks to a centralized database to identify when data updates are available. The peer then finds the updates in other peers.

- Lossy data techniques—Each peer holds it own copy of data and shares data updates with the peers it immediately knows about. The downside to this is that data might not make it to all nodes in the P2P network.

Blindly implementing P2P architectures will not improve the efficiency of your network. Caching must be used to ensure that data is not accessed unnecessarily. The network must be aware of information location to avoid redundant network transport, or movement of data. However, highly volatile data has the overhead of synchronization to ensure that only the most recent information is available to users and applications, as stated previously. Intelligent caching can be difficult when used with highly volatile data.

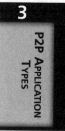

Clustering provides a mechanism to increase the throughput and availability of computing resources. By linking peers to form clusters, you can build more scalable solutions and redundancy into your network and applications. P2P clusters can form dynamically. This can minimize the amount of human intervention and administration required to operate and maintain networks.

All these techniques imply more intelligent software—software that is more "aware" of its environment.

Products

Like instant messaging, the popularity of file and resource sharing has created a large market for products.

Gnutella

As mentioned in Chapter 1, "What Is P2P?," Gnutella is a popular file sharing and searching protocol that operates with edge devices in a decentralized environment. In the Gnutella network, each peer acts as a point of rendezvous and a router, using TCP for message transport, and HTTP for file transfer.

Searches on the network are propagated by a peer to all its known peer neighbors who propagate the query to other peers. Content on the Gnutella network is advertised through an IP address, a port number, an index number identifying the file on the host peer, and file details such as name and size. Additional information on the current status of Gnutella can be found at http://www.gnutellanews.com/.

The Gnutella client LimeWire, (http://www.limewire.com/) is a software package that enables individuals to search for and share computer files over the Internet. LimeWire is compatible with the Gnutella file sharing protocol, and can connect with any peer running Gnutella-compatible software.

At startup, the LimeWire client connects via the Internet to the LimeWire gateway. The LimeWire gateway is an intelligent Gnutella router. LimeWire is written in Java, and will run on any machine with an Internet connection and the capability to run Java.

In the sample search request seen in Figure 3.7, a request for Eric Clapton audio files was submitted through the LimeWire client. The network responded with 178 matches! The application displays the type of file, the peer connection speed, the size of the file, and the IP address of the download location. You can select the MP3 file, download it to your local hard drive, and launch the included MP3 player.

FIGURE 3.7
LimeWire is a Gnutella client that promotes distributed searching and file sharing.

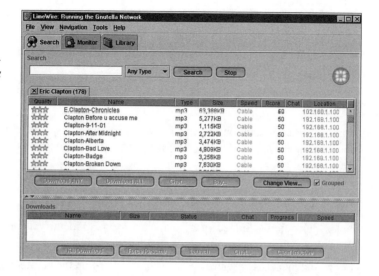

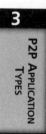

NextPage

NextPage bridges the consumer-oriented Internet architectures with corporate intranets and extranets. The company is adopting a P2P strategy with its server-oriented architecture. NextPage's NXT-3 Content Networking platform enables users to "manage, access, and exchange content across distributed servers on intranets and via the Internet." The platform indexes and connects content across organizational boundaries, allowing you to search and locate content from multiple locations without having to know where it physically resides.

NextPage offers an extensive array of search functions including keyword, Boolean, phrase, ranked, wildcard, and so on. For more information, go to www.nextpage.com.

Collaboration

P2P has extended Groupware to now include the Internet at large. This is having a radical impact on collaboration. Individuals and businesses no longer are bound by specific tools within a community or geographic region. Common interests and objectives are the driving force. The tools to support the formation and integration of decentralized communication and ad hoc group formation already exist. For example, the popularity of AOL Instant Messenger and ICQ have demonstrated that real-time communication is a viable and often preferred way to communicate. Products such as Napster and FreeNet have proven that decentralized file sharing is possible.

Collaboration is the next step. Collaboration increases productivity, and enables teams in different geographic areas to work together. As with file sharing, it can decrease network traffic by reducing email, and decreases server storage requirements by using edge devices to store projects and information locally.

Technology

Understanding P2P collaboration requires knowledge of shared spaces, content management, knowledge management, and workflow.

Shared Spaces

Shared spaces form the backbone to P2P collaborative applications:

- Rendezvous points—Shared spaces enable to peers to identify a common network accessible meeting place.
- Identity and presence services—Shared spaces become the common point for searching, retrieving, and updating identity and online status.
- Group membership—Shared spaces form the basis for defining a group or community of peers connected by a common interest or goal. Group membership in a shared space is controlled by the group, rather than by a central administrator.

Content Management

Inherent in P2P collaboration is content management. Content management systems (CMS) collect, manage, and publish the informational assets of an individual or organization. This involves securing, accessing, versioning, and storing content throughout its lifecycle. Structured data, such as XML-defined metadata, can be used to complement, organize, and describe the informational assets in a CMS. Content management systems are used extensively in Web publishing and content syndication environments.

Most CMS vendors have developed client-server models of content management. A centralized server controls access to the content system. These systems tend to use traditional technologies such as relational databases to store and index the information. P2P content management systems use *shared spaces*, which tend to be more object-oriented. Collaboration is achieved by enabling members of a shared space to exchange, version, and store documents in shared content repositories.

Workflow

More sophisticated collaborative applications provide some level of workflow. *Workflow management* is the automated coordination and control of work processes. A *work process* is a collection of activities, typically stretching across and beyond organizational boundaries. Activities might include direct interactions with a user or workflow partici-pant, or interactions via computer.

Workflow will become more popular as collaborative applications control more complex tasks. This will especially be significant when automated tasks are combined with man-ual processes. A driver for this type of environment is e-commerce, because you must be able to integrate Web-enabled business transactions into your back end systems to be successful. P2P architectures fit nicely into the distributed and decentralized environment of next generation-workflow management systems.

Knowledge Management

Finally, knowledge management (KM) is required to build more intelligent collaborative applications. KM focuses on the informational assets that provide the most value to the organization. KM includes the processes that facilitate the capturing, sharing, and updat-ing of knowledge to enhance the performance and value of the organization Generating value from such assets involves sharing them among employees, departments and even with other companies in an effort to devise best practices. It goes beyond content man-agement, which is more technical in nature, to the basic social aspects of collaboration.

Products

Collaboration software is combining single-function P2P applications, like instant messaging and file sharing, into coherent platforms for implementing distributed applications.

Groove

Groove Networks (www.groove.net) is the brainchild of Ray Ozzie, inventor of Lotus Notes. Groove is Ray's rethinking of the Lotus Notes architecture. Notes slightly gained popularity before the Web became very popular in the 1990s. Groove attempts to over-come Notes' Internet limitations by delivering a P2P platform to developing and deploy-ing secure enterprise applications.

At first, Groove Networks positioned Groove as a P2P collaborative platform. Recent moves to align itself with Microsoft have shown some promising uses of P2P technology in Windows environments. Although nothing has been publicly discussed at the time of this book's writing, Groove is definitely worth keeping an eye on.

Already Groove has found a home in enterprises, government, small businesses, and individuals (see Figure 3.8). It offers instant collaboration, shared spaces, Web connectiv-ity, and a host of add-on applications.

FIGURE 3.8

Groove promotes secure peer-to-peer collaboration using public and private networks.

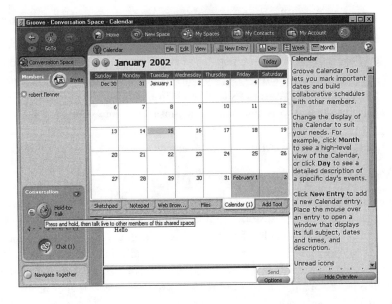

Developers can integrate Groove into their existing systems. Groove and other competing products not only provide the capability to access data on traditional corporate networks, but also in nontraditional devices such as PDAs and a range of handheld devices.

Other Collaborative Solutions

Collaboration has become very popular, and the following represents only a partial list of notable offerings:

- Ikimbo, Inc. (www.ikimbo.com) provides instant messaging, instant conferencing, presence detection, identity, message inbox, file transfer, and wireless devices, through their Omniprise product. It is a Java-based solution.

- Consilient, Inc. (www.consilient.com) provides a framework for the development and management of iterative business processes that flow within and between enterprises.

Distributed Services

Corporations increasingly see e-commerce, or collaborative commerce as it is often called, as a strategic tool. According to consulting firm Deloitte and Touche, corporations list the top goals of collaborative commerce as

- Reducing the cost of operations
- Gaining competitive advantage
- Increasing customer loyalty and retention

Collaborative commerce is being built on distributed services. Initially the focus is on Web services; however, complementary P2P technologies might turn out to be the enabler that Web services need to fulfill corporate expectations.

Technology

Distributed P2P services for collaborative commerce fall in three categories; distributed data services, distributed computing, and distributed network services.

Distributed Data Services

A study from IT industry researcher Gartner concluded that large enterprises can create competitive advantages using P2P by developing P2P content networking solutions based on what it calls the "data-centered P2P model." Gartner expects that by 2003 "30% of corporations will have at least experimented with data-centered P2P applications" (http://marketplacena.gartner.com/010022501oth-NextPage.PDF).

Distributed data services move data closer to usage using multiple nodes and sophisticated routing algorithms.

Peer-based storage has distinct advantages:

- Edge devices are plentiful and under-used.
- Users are more mobile, and must access information from multiple locations.
- Centralization has proven costly and prohibitive beyond a certain level of scalability.
- Mobile users are demanding faster access to content.
- Service providers are searching for cheaper solutions.

There are a number of complexities to implementing successful distributed content networks.

Distributed content networks require intelligent caching over a widely dispersed cluster of nodes. Some distributed content networks use *predictive seeding* to preconfigure the location of data based on usage patterns and known heuristics.

Multisourcing permits a content network to map multiple communication paths to a cluster and/or data store. This is often accomplished through intelligent routing. Security (encryption) is required to ensure integrity of data in transit.

Presence and bandwidth matching guarantees that nodes are available, and that they map performance capabilities appropriately. Content delivery networks automatically detect which peer servers are available on the network to serve the file segments with the greatest overall efficiency.

Distributed Computing

Distributed computing (also referred to as grid computing) attempts to use the idle processing cycles of the PCs on your network. It makes these commodity devices available to work on computationally intensive problems that would otherwise require a supercomputer or workstation/server cluster to solve.

There are usually three fundamental components to the architecture:

- The Network Manager manages client resources, and controls which applications are run on the client machines.
- The Job Manager permits application users to submit work and monitors the progress of this work, and retrieves results.
- The Client manages the running of applications on a client machine.

Distributed computing should continue to gain in popularity as more sophisticated problems surface, such as in genetics and bioinformatics.

Distributed Network Services

The attractiveness of distributed network services lies in their capability to localize traffic, lowering bandwidth expenditures and improving response times. By serving and fulfilling as many requests for data from devices on the LAN, enterprises and ISPs can cut costs and improve performance dramatically.

Bandwidth management technologies give network administrators at Internet service providers or corporate enterprises the capability to set and enforce policies to control network traffic, ensuring that networks deliver predictable performance for mission-critical applications. Bandwidth management systems can prioritize mission-critical traffic, as well as guarantee minimum bandwidth for the most critical, revenue-generating traffic (for example, voice, transaction-based applications).

Webcasting continues to grow, and bandwidth demands continue to increase. Distributed P2P network services automatically scale to use the available bandwidth and computer resources of new participants who request the stream. This is a more economical model for usage in high bandwidth-intensive applications that require infrequent activation.

Load balancing/traffic management products process network traffic streams, switching and otherwise responding to incoming requests by directing these requests to specific server clusters based on a set of predefined rules. These products usually have the capability to test the servers they are connected to for correct operation, and reroute data traffic around a server should it fail. Most of these devices also have the capacity to recognize the requester or the data being requested, and prioritize the request or the response accordingly. The capability of the load balancer/traffic manager to consider the source of the message or the relative load on each of several replicated servers and then direct the message to the most appropriate server increases efficiency and uptime.

The next generation of network services and technologies will continue to offer advantages in caching, load balancing, and bandwidth management. What distinguishes these next-generation services and technologies is their emphasis on further pushing the distribution mantra.

Distributed Networking Products

- Avaki (www.avaki.com) provides a high-level grid protocol that it's adapting to run on top of the XML/SOAP Web Services standard.

- Parabon Computation, Inc. (www.parabon.com) provides grid computing capabilities over the Internet using a Java-based framework.

- United Devices, Inc. (www.ud.com) provides a grid computing platform for corporations and research, along with a global Internet-enabled platform for large-scale distributed computing tasks.

- Porivo Technologies, Inc. (www.porivo.com) provides a service that measures the end-to-end performance of Web applications from the customers' perspective using a network of distributed PCs.

- vTrails, Ltd. (www.vtrails.com) offers a media delivery solution that leverages the power of peer-to-peer networking, smart routing, and edge network capabilities.

- The Cytaq Distributed ResourceNetwork Network (www.cytaq.com) is a network of resource routers linking and integrating varied information resources of an enterprise, such as applications, databases, and so on. The resource routers are small-footprint, Java software services. Multiple information resources can be linked to one resource router and vice versa.

3

P2P APPLICATION
TYPES

Summary

P2P is leveraging the computing, storage, and network resources on the edge of the network. P2P causes us to rethink our assumptions about connectivity, collaboration, and network infrastructure. What started out as simple file sharing has grown to include a wide array of applications and services:

- Collaboration is the communication side of P2P, with multichannel collaborative applications, content management, and instant messaging capabilities.
- Distributed services blend the features of grid computing and P2P communication to facilitate access to content located on user machines. Distributed services are used with collaborative groupware applications to provide a shared distributed workspace, and as a complement to centralized information portals.

Future Internet platforms and desktop applications will resemble P2P systems such as Jabber and Groove. In addition, corporate infrastructures might be extended to the global network using P2P distributed services. A fascinating view of this environment is already emerging.

This chapter showed a variety of P2P applications and the architectural issues that needed to be resolved to build them. Many of these applications make use of the Java technologies introduced next in Chapter 4, "P2P As a Framework for Distributed Computing."

P2P As a Framework for Distributed Computing

by Robert Flenner

IN THIS CHAPTER

This chapter compares and contrasts P2P systems with traditional systems and emerging technologies, including JXTA, Web services, and Jini/JavaSpaces network technology. We'll present each technology in the context of the essential P2P characteristics described in Chapter 1, "What Is P2P?"

P2P Common Functions and Characteristics

Early P2P applications were single-function, formed groups of peers from ordinary PCs, and peer group membership changed frequently or erratically. Chapter 3, "P2P Application Types" introduced multifunction applications and the commercialization and adoption of P2P in the corporate environment.

Now we can compare and contrast P2P with existing and emerging systems. Comparing these systems to P2P requires examining network formation, functional partitioning, models of communication, and the supported standards.

Dynamic Networks

Dynamic networks are an essential characteristic of P2P. Dynamic networks are enabled by

- Discovery—A dynamic approach to searching and locating an identity within a broadcast horizon
- Identity—A unique identifier for a peer or resource within a domain
- Presence—The online status of a peer or resource based on identity
- Domain space—A virtual space (network) bound by discovery

Edge devices are the building blocks of dynamic networks. They collaborate to form a virtual space of connected devices. Recent models of P2P are extending participation to include server-to-server and server-to-edge devices.

Equality and Autonomy

In addition to the dynamics of the network, you must look at the partitioning of the functionality. You need to identify whether there are central control points, and if so, what they control. You should also identify access control to resources, such as databases, files, networks and other clients.

In addition, you need to determine whether centralized administration of the system is required. You must also determine how the system and network is monitored for faults, availability, intrusions, and so on.

What are the security implications with the model implemented? It might provide limited or no security, or be highly secure in relation to the functionality provided.

You should consider centralization versus decentralization depending on the technology. Mixed models are composed of centralized and decentralized nodes (peers) that are connected at pivotal control points. For instance, a central node might be used as a file index, or provide presence and identity services.

Finally, look at the standards supported by the technology. Is P2P trying to provide a service that has already been standardized? Is there an overlap or fit with existing systems?

Comparing Traditional Systems

Now that we understand the basic building blocks of P2P networks, and have defined criteria for comparison, we can take a closer look at important distributed systems.

Usenet News and NNTP

Usenet News was based on the Unix-to-Unix copy protocol (UUCP), and was developed in the late 70s. It automates machine-to-machine file distribution and topic-based classification for posting messages between systems. Usenet was designed as a decentralized system with loose control over the topology and the reliability of the network. This lack of central control and network reliability compares favorably to the P2P model.

Today, Usenet uses the Network News Transport Protocol (NNTP) to coordinate the exchange of messages between newsgroups. Newsgroup articles are distributed via *news servers*, which contain databases of articles, and are operated by Internet service providers, universities, and public companies.

A newsgroup article is posted to a designated news server. The news server then sends copies of the article to its peers that have agreed to exchange articles. Those servers in turn send copies to their peers. Eventually, every server that carries the newsgroup has a copy. This sounds familiar to P2P propagation techniques, and to the communication patterns of products like Jabber.

However, there is no concept of discovery in the protocol. Servers are configured to receive articles from specific peers and send articles to specific peers based on newsgroups. In effect, the peer network is static and known in advance. Articles are replicated in many places on the network, and the timely delivery of any one article to a site is not guaranteed.

Since NNTP is similar in many respects to existing peer-to-peer applications, it's interesting to examine how NNTP manages the propagation of content in some detail.

Loop control is handled by a trace list and a list of the Message-IDs of received messages. Using these controls, a server can reject a message that it has already seen. The Path header shows the sites that the article has traveled through, between the originating server and the current server. This is similar to the technique used by router peers in P2P networks. If the receiving server appears in the Path line, the sending server does not try to send the article, because it knows that the receiving server has already received a copy.

The Message-ID header contains an identifying code that is unique for every article. Before transmitting the article, the sending server queries the receiving server to determine whether it already has the article or requires it to be transmitted.

Usenet News standardizes two variants of the NNTP protocols—one for communication between peer servers, and one for communication between a client and a server.

Information about a user of Usenet News is stored on the client. The server might not even know the identity of the clients using it. News clients keep state information to connected news servers. If the servers are not carefully synchronized, clients can lose important session information.

Usenet News does not support closed groups easily. When you post an article, it can literally go around the world!

The decentralized model is the primary reason for the P2P comparison. Identity, presence, and virtual spaces are not well defined. Control is based on administrative parameters, and there is a definite distinction between client and server roles. In addition, security can be an issue because access controls are minimal.

Email

As opposed to news, which provides public communication, email provides private communication. Email messages are addressed to specific individuals or groups. The primary components of an email system are

- Mailbox—Typically a file or directory where messages are stored.
- User agent—An application run directly by a user to interface with a transfer agent. This is probably the most recognized component of the system.
- Transfer agent—The component that is used to transfer messages between machines. Transfer agents in effect resemble communicating peers from a functional perspective. They form a chain of responsibility for transferring email between cooperating agents.
- Delivery agent—The delivery agent is responsible for adding the message to the user's mailbox. The transfer agent recognizes the destination address, and passes the message to the delivery agent for delivery.

Each message consists of two parts. The headers indicate the message's author, recipient, subject, the time and date of its creation, and so on. The body contains the actual information/message from the sender.

Transfer agents communicate using a transfer protocol. There are many in existence, but the most common is SMTP (Simple Mail Transfer Protocol). Mail routing uses the Domain Name System (DNS). Mail eXchanger (MX) records are maintained by domain name servers to tell mail transfer agents (MTAs) where to route mail messages. These MX records vary depending on the domain. An MX record has three parts: your domain name, the name of the machine that will accept mail for the domain, and a preference value. The preference value lets you designate the order in which multiple mail servers will be accessed to accept mail deliveries. This provides a form of fault tolerance for your domain.

The routing functionality of Internet email is based on DNS. The concept of dynamic discovery is not applicable in the email network. The comparisons to P2P arise from email servers being decentralized. However, email is actually based on the hierarchical structure of DNS. Email does have the concept of identity. In effect, your email address is your unique identity within a specific domain.

User agents are the client component of an email system. In this respect, email has a traditional client/server partitioning of functionality. Transfer agents could be considered peers. SMTP is well understood, and provides a standard protocol to enable message transfer.

Integration is occurring between instant messaging products and email. Expect this trend to continue.

Domain Name Service (DNS)

As explained in Chapter 1, the Domain Name System (DNS) is a distributed Internet directory service. DNS is used to translate between domain names and IP addresses, and to control Internet email delivery. The Internet relies on DNS to organize and control distributed resource lookup and decentralized email delivery. Without DNS, the Internet, and more specifically the Web, would not be possible.

DNS consists of 13 root servers in various worldwide locations that contain replicated information. These servers maintain information about *top-level domains*, such as where to find other DNS servers that have more specific information about domains such as those represented by `.com` or `.edu`. These servers are then used to find other DNS servers representing subdomains that are responsible for identifying the address of a specific host. Although DNS is comprised of thousands of machines distributed globally, it acts as a single directory with servers communicating to servers to provide address resolution.

4

P2P AS A
FRAMEWORK

The DNS directory contains billions of *resource records* that are split into millions of files called *zones*. There are two types of DNS servers, authoritative and caching. Authoritative servers are responsible for maintaining information on specific zones. Caching servers use authoritative servers to query for specific DNS zone information. This helps to improve the scalability, efficiency, and response time of the DNS system in general. Like DNS, P2P networks are developing rendezvous peers that are used to query and cache information for peer discovery. In this respect, a rendezvous peer could be considered authoritative or caching depending on its implementation.

DNS is a massively distributed and decentralized database. Its role as an underpinning for the Internet cannot be over-emphasized. It provides the identification and hierarchy to address and access resources across the Internet. P2P systems are augmenting DNS capabilities to support, higher-level routing, edge devices, and enabling firewall penetration.

In the next few sections, we will compare and contrast P2P to the new entrants in distributed processing. We'll see how these technologies—Web services, Jini/JavaSpaces, and JXTA—relate to P2P.

Web Services Overview

If you haven't heard about Web services, you probably haven't been on the planet for long. All the major vendors and industry analysts are promoting Web services as the "next big thing." Let's examine what has created all the attention and attraction. (Web services concepts are discussed in more detail in Chapter 11, "Web Services Explained.")

Web Services Defined

A *Web service* is a collection of functions packaged and published to a network for use by other programs and users. Web services result from software components being assembled and discovered by service providers and service consumers. However, the discovery process is not as dynamic as P2P. It typically involves a well-known address or directory service. The intent of Web services is to provide a level of integration standardization in making products and services available worldwide. The definition takes on more substance when combined with the technologies defining it.

Web services promote the following standards:

- SOAP (Simple Object Access Protocol)—A standard message exchange protocol
- WSDL (Web Service Definition Language)—A standard service definition protocol
- UDDI (Universal Description, Discovery and Integration)—A standard service discovery protocol

The W3C (www.w3c.org) and members of key organizations such as IBM and Microsoft envision an end-to-end view to Web service definition. This can be demonstrated as three complementary architectural stacks, seen in Figure 4.1. The wire stack provides the "on-the-wire" view of the supporting message exchange. The description stack enables business requirements to be mapped to technical specifications. The discovery stack provides the advertisement and categorization services necessary for business entities to publish and find service definitions.

FIGURE 4.1

The architectural stacks of Web services.

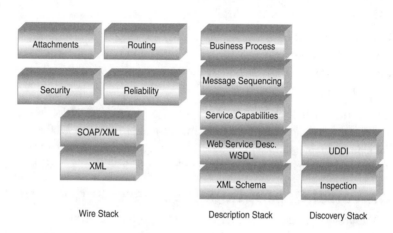

Simple Object Access Protocol

SOAP is used to enable interoperability between vendor implementations. SOAP is a lightweight protocol that uses XML to encode remote procedure calls between distributed systems. This XML-based protocol consists of three parts:

- The SOAP envelope in effect defines the SOAP message. It contains an optional SOAP header and a mandatory SOAP body.

- The SOAP header may contain additional processing instructions used to process the body of the message and information relevant to intermediaries.

- The SOAP body is the actual information needed by the recipient of the request to process and return a response.

SOAP can use HTTP as a transport protocol. By using HTTP, SOAP has access to most Web-based implementations today. This enables access to a vast array of resources, even through firewalls, if the Web-based implementation is SOAP-compliant.

SOAP provides a standard protocol for distributed communication. P2P applications have not defined this level of interoperability. As you will see, JXTA is attempting to provide a standard XML-based protocol to fill that gap. It is likely that bridges between SOAP- and P2P-based protocols will be developed to promote interoperability. This will be required for P2P to gain popularity in business environments using Web services.

Web Service Definition Language

WSDL is an XML language for describing Web services. Fundamental to the definition are network endpoints (ports), messages, and the operations that are performed on those messages.

It is important to recognize that Web services are being defined to support different technology platforms, operating systems, and programming languages. Thus, the Microsoft .NET initiative using non-Java-based implementations should integrate with IBM Java-based implementations.

Information about Web services, including URLs and WSDL documents, is published and therefore found in a registry such as the one provided by UDDI, which will be discussed in a moment. So, unlike P2P, which might require broadcast techniques to discover services, the UDDI registries will be available at well known locations.

Universal Description, Discovery, and Integration

UDDI provides a mechanism for publishing and finding service descriptions that support both business and technical information. Although the service information contained in UDDI complements the WSDL information, UDDI does not mandate WSDL. UDDI is attempting to be more generic in supporting any number of service description mechanisms.

The UDDI defines three primary components:

- A registry for service providers to publish services and products offered
- A service broker that maintains the registry
- A service requestor that uses the broker to find products and services

The service provider implements the Web service. This is typically the owner of the business process.

The service requestor is the entity invoking or initiating interaction with a Web service. Service requestors can search by industry code, products and services offered, and geographic location.

The service registry is where the service descriptions are published by service providers and then discovered by service requestors. Service descriptions are used by service requestors during service development and during execution.

It is projected that public and private UDDI nodes will be defined. Several companies, including Hewlett-Packard, IBM, and Microsoft, operate replicated registeries that form the public nodes of the UDDI network.

Private nodes between partner systems and within large corporations might also surface. For example, e-marketplace UDDI nodes for finding Web services and for doing business within a particular e-marketplace or industry; portal UDDI nodes supporting transactional Web presence and for restricting access and monitoring usage; internal integration nodes to bridge Web presence with back end service delivery.

The overall architecture is still in flux, and the pace of change presents a challenge to early adopters. There are divisions even within the Web services architecture, as competitors try to differentiate their tools and solutions.

P2P Applicability

Web services have created a standard way of describing a service through WSDL. Web services also utilize SOAP as a standard way to exchange messages in an object-oriented fashion. As P2P systems mature and interoperability becomes more important, standards for describing and interfacing with P2P services will be needed. Web services present a viable and complementary platform.

There appears to be some synergy between Web services and P2P. Web services might leverage the decentralized techniques of P2P to introduce more network resilience, whereas peers can mature their service descriptions using XML-defined Web service definitions.

Jini and JavaSpaces Overview

4

P2P As A
FRAMEWORK

Sun Microsystems' Jini promotes a Java-based interface to network services. The architecture is based on distributed services that are capable of discovery using restricted multicast and directed unicast messaging. (Jini and JavaSpaces concepts are discussed in more detail in Chapter 14, "Jini and JavaSpaces," and Chapter 15, "P2P Jini and JavaSpaces.")

Jini Defined

The notion of a service is fundamental to Jini. Jini services are usually manifested as Java objects that expose an interface that conforms to the Jini specification. The type of the service determines the interfaces that make up that service. Jini services advertise their operations by registering an object with a Jini-compliant lookup service. Service registration is at the core of building the Jini network community.

RMI and Mobile Code

A primary difference between Jini and other solutions is its capability to move code around the network. Because it uses RMI and object serialization, it is able to download code on demand. There is no human intervention required in the process. This has some distinct advantages over other systems being defined. The client of a service does not need the software installed prior to running the application. As long as the client can attain the interface to the service, it can execute the code. Software agent technology, especially mobile agents, can benefit from the framework Jini has established.

Lookup and Discovery

Every Jini community must have at least one registry or lookup service available. The lookup service (LUS) for Jini can be compared to:

- The registry in RMI (Remote Method Invocation)
- The Name Server in DNS
- The COS Naming Service in CORBA
- The UDDI in Web services

Each of these systems provides a mechanism for resolving a name to an information processing location. Each system takes a different approach and extends the functionality in different ways. For instance, RMI maps a name (`String`) to an object. DNS maps host names to IP addresses, and UDDI provides a directory to register a Web service.

The lookup service enables service-using entities to register and find services that meet specific criteria. The lookup service provides functions similar to a yellow page service. To Jini, the lookup service is just another service on the network, albeit an important one. The lookup service is what in effect bootstraps the Jini network. Services register with the lookup service, and applications find services of interest using the lookup service. After a service is found, an application can invoke the methods that the service exposes through its public interface.

Leasing

One of the concepts introduced in Jini is the concept of *resource leasing*, or time-based resource allocation. The leasing of resources has direct implications on the programming model used and the services that must be implemented to support a Jini network. Leasing implies that nothing is permanent in the Jini system. You must renew leases and renew interest in resources in order for them to remain active and available. Otherwise, they will be purged from the network by their removal from the lookup service. Imagine how much friendlier the Web would be if bad or invalid links were just magically purged or disappeared!

There is a lease renewal service defined as a helper service in the Jini framework that renews interest in resources for you. This is another service that enables disconnected clients and minimizes the amount of development work required by developers that use the Jini model.

JavaSpaces Defined

JavaSpaces is an example of a Jini service that runs on the Jini network and is closely tied to the Jini architecture. JavaSpaces was heavily influenced by the concept of a *tuple space*, which was first described in 1982 in a programming language called Linda. The concept is based on a shared-memory. Communication between distributed processes is provided through this shared-memory. Any number of processes can communicate without requiring prior knowledge of process location or how many processes might actually be "listening." Programs read, write, and take tuples from this shared workspace.

Peer-to-peer systems have already demonstrated the need for a distributed network of loosely coupled collaborating processes. These processes require identity, task management, and coordination. JavaSpaces provides a lightweight implementation of persistence that can aid in implementing a collective memory.

Distributed Storage

With JavaSpaces, distributed processes communicate by reading and writing entries into a space. The JavaSpace API provides an event notification mechanism, which enables processes to register for notification, when a specific object is written to a space. A space is defined by JavaSpaces as a shared, network-accessible repository for objects. This shared repository can persist objects written to a space beyond the lifetime of the process that created them. Spaces provide reliable storage for objects and support leases.

Objects in a space are located via *associative lookup,* as opposed to more traditional keys or identifiers. When you read or take an object from a space, a local copy of the object is created. As with any other local object, you can modify its public fields and invoke its methods.

In addition, JavaSpaces supports transactions for single operations, such as writing an object to a single space, as well as multiple operations over one or more spaces. JavaSpaces' strength lies in its capability to simplify the programming required to coordinate distributed communication and parallel processing.

Devices and Services

As mentioned previously, Jini is based on services that are available on a network. Jini blurs the distinction between hardware and software. This might have contributed to the

4

P2P AS A
FRAMEWORK

initial "technology for intelligent devices" mantra that was echoed so strongly in most publications defining Jini. But at the core, Jini is about services. It is about delivering services regardless of the platform. Whether the code is burnt into a device or deployed on a farm of servers is not the issue. The intent is that services are not limited to traditional platforms. The Jini design recognizes the emergence of devices as the next logical platform for executing networked application code.

P2P Applicability

Dynamic discovery enables peers and services to find each other. It allows for the quick formation of groups and communities sharing a common interest. However, speed of assembly must be tempered with network integrity. Jini uses a combination of unicast and multicast protocols to dynamically discover services on the network. There is the notion of a well-behaved service that implements these protocols in a specific manner. The intent is to ensure broadcast storms do not occur, and that there is a higher level of resiliency in the network.

Resource conservation will be required in any system that needs to scale dynamically. Whether it is enforced explicitly in the API and/or implicitly through rules of engagement remains unknown. Applications that use broadcast techniques to discover peers can contribute to serious network congestion when traffic does not get distributed appropriately. There is no clear winner is this space. However, the key components of the Jini framework are dynamic service discovery and the controlled formation of communities.

Jini is Java-based. Interfaces define the services and the protocols in the Jini network. Jini does not support the notion of XML being fundamental to the process of defining and accessing services on the network. In terms of the other solutions, Jini appears to be the maverick.

Jini relies on the richness of type semantics. There is also the belief that these type definitions and the ease with which they support subtyping (inheritance) resembles the way we build systems. Systems can evolve as the technology evolves. The other approaches rely on XML definitions or APIs that limit the systems' adaptability to change.

JavaSpaces provides a collective memory, which could provide rendezvous peers capable of supporting identity and presence services. JavaSpaces clusters could also be used to scale systems and provide fault resiliency.

JXTA Overview

As opposed to the other technologies described in this chapter, JXTA is being developed to directly support and promote P2P. Project JXTA is a Sun Microsystems initiative, defined as an open source project to provide standard protocols for P2P applications and services. The JXTA platform defines a set of XML protocols designed to address the common functionality required to enable peers to form dynamic networks, independent of the operating system, development language, and network transport. It is an outgrowth of the recognition that P2P applications need a level of standardization to promote interoperability and attain widespread adoption. (JXTA concepts are discussed in more detail in Chapter 16, "JXTA and XML," and Chapter 17, The JXTA Shell.")

JXTA Defined

JXTA describes a typical P2P application using three layers; a core layer, a services layer, and an application layer (see Figure 4.4).

FIGURE 4.4
JXTA defines a three-layer architecture applicable to most P2P systems.

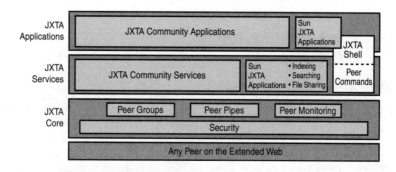

The core layer includes protocols and building blocks to enable P2P networking, including discovery, transport, security, and the creation of peers and peer groups. The elements of this layer are shared by all P2P solutions.

The services layer provides hooks for supporting generic services that are used in many P2P applications, but not necessarily all P2P applications. These include searching for resources, sharing files, and peer authentication.

The application layer is intended to support the types of applications that were highlighted in Chapter 3, such as file sharing, distributed storage, and instant messaging. These applications can be "vertical," or they can interoperate with other distributed applications developed to the JXTA core.

In addition to the layered architecture JXTA defines:

- Protocols—A standard format for representing and exchanging messages between peers. Each protocol is defined by one or more messages exchanged among participants of the protocol.

- Messages—A datagram consisting of an envelope and a stack of protocol headers with bodies. Each message has a predefined format. The format of the message is designed to support multiple transport standards. For instance, logical source and destination endpoints are defined in the form, or a URI. Endpoints are mapped to physical addresses using a messaging layer. Each protocol body can contain a variable number of bytes and credentials used to identify the sender to the receiver. The exact format and content of the credentials are not specified.

- Pipes—These simply represent communication channels for sending and receiving messages. Pipes are asynchronous and unidirectional, and a single pipe can be bound to one or more peer endpoints. JXTA defines a rather abstract definition of a pipe to enable a wide array of unicast and multicast communication implementations.

- Advertisements—An XML-structured document that names, describes, and publishes the existence of a resource, such as a peer, a peer group, a pipe, or a service.

- Peer groups—A collection of peers that share a common set of protocols.

Dynamic Networks

JXTA does not mandate a specific discovery implementation. It can be centralized, decentralized, or a hybrid model. However, the Java supplied examples do use a combination of directed unicast and multicast messaging.

The Peer Discovery Protocol (PDP) defines a low-level protocol for requesting advertisements from other peers, and responding to other peers' requests for advertisements. All resources in JXTA, peers, peer groups, pipes, and so on are represented as advertisements. Higher-level protocols can be built on top of PDP to provide specific discovery mechanisms.

The organization of information into advertisements simplifies the protocols required to make P2P work.

Identity and Presence

In traditional P2P networks, the identification of peers and resources uses network- or system-dependent identifiers. This could take the form of an IP address or a filename. JXTA attempts to be independent of the operating system or network transport. In a JXTA-compliant P2P network, any device should be able to participate, regardless of their operating system or network transport.

JXTA uses UUIDs to refer to peers, advertisements, services, and so on. A UUID is guaranteed to be unique only within a local domain. It is used as an internal identifier.

The UUID becomes significant if it is bound to other information, such as a name or a network address.

It is anticipated that naming and binding services will be developed for the JXTA platform. Identity and presence services are not yet defined for JXTA, but are in development.

Security

JXTA is independent of specific security approaches; however, Version 1.0 defines a limited set of security primitives to support JXTA services and applications. These include password-based login, an authentication framework, simple access control, encryption, and limited transport security modeled after TLS/SSL.

The JXTA demonstration services, called InstantP2P and CMS (content management service), make use of additional security features provided by the underlying Java platform.

Standardizing P2P Protocols

As mentioned previously, JXTA is primarily focused with standardizing the protocols used by P2P applications and services to interoperate. XML has been chosen for the initial encoding. The benefits of XML are well documented.

The six main protocols provided by JXTA (per the specification) are a part of the core layer. Each protocol is independent from the others.

- Peer Discovery Protocol—This is the default discovery protocol. It enables a peer to find advertisements on JXTA resources.

- Peer Resolver Protocol—A query/response protocol that is used in conjunction with PDP to find or search for peers, peer groups, pipes, and other information.

- Peer Information Protocol—Enables a peer to inquire about other peers' capabilities and status.

- Rendezvous Protocol—Enables a peer to subscribe to a message propagation service.

- Pipe Binding Protocol—Enables a peer to establish a communication channel between one or more peers.

- Endpoint Routing Protocol—Enables a peer to query a router for available routes for sending a message to a destination peer.

All these protocols are implemented using a common messaging layer. This messaging layer is what binds the JXTA protocols to various network transports.

4

P2P As A
FRAMEWORK

JXTA provides a far more abstract language for peer communication than previous P2P protocols, enabling a wider variety of services, devices, and network transports to be used in P2P networks. The employment of XML provides a standards-based format for structured data that is well understood, well supported, and easily adapted to a variety of transports.

Summary

Decentralized systems that exhibit limited peer-to-peer characteristics have been available for years. However, they do not promote dynamic discovery or support for edge devices. The concepts of identity, presence, and virtual spaces have not been as significant in traditional systems. Client and server roles still dominate these architectures, and casting these servers as peers misses the importance of key P2P characteristics.

It is envisioned that as businesses link their manufacturing, distribution, and sales processes, more reliance on P2P IM features will result. This might be another convergence point for Web services and P2P.

Resource conservation will be required in any system that needs to scale dynamically. Applications that use broadcast techniques to discover peers can contribute to serious network congestion when traffic is not distributed appropriately. Two of the key components of the Jini framework are dynamic service discovery and the controlled formation of communities. Jini might provide opportunities in service discovery for enterprise P2P systems.

JavaSpaces implements a distributed-shared memory, which could provide rendezvous peers capable of supporting identity and presence services. JavaSpaces clusters could also be used to scale systems and provide fault resiliency.

Finally, JXTA is attempting to standardize P2P protocols to enable interoperability. It is envisioned that JXTA will leverage Web service definitions in WSDL, SOAP, and UDDI to integrate with legacy systems. All of this points to convergence: Internet-based technologies supplanting and complementing traditional architectures.

P2P Systems and Architecture

PART II

System Topics Explained

by Robert Flenner

IN THIS CHAPTER

CHAPTER 5

This chapter provides an overview and roadmap to key P2P architectural topics as defined and discussed in subsequent chapters. The topics discussed provide a bridge between common system problems, unique P2P issues, and Java-based solutions.

Transport

In P2P systems, the *transport* refers to how messages are exchanged between peers. Peers must have some mechanism to transmit data over the network. There are a number of low-level activities that must be managed in order to ensure orderly communication, and low-level network programming can be difficult.

Fortunately, Java reduces the learning curve. As discussed earlier, the underlying details of network programming have been hidden by the Java programming API. This is both a blessing and, for some, a curse. The programming model is similar to the file programming model. So if you are experienced with file streams on local systems, reading and writing to remote systems should be familiar. In addition, Java's built-in multithreading capabilities ease the development of building applications that must handle concurrent multiple connections. Concurrent multiple connections are important to enabling peer group formation.

Chapter 6, "P2P Dynamic Networks," discusses the components and functions common to P2P networks. The transport is a critical component because of the impact dynamic discovery has on the performance of the overall system, and the frequency with which peers exchange data over the network. Placing the transport in context will help clarify the issues.

Models of Communication

The OSI reference model and the Department of Defense (DoD) Four-Layer model, illustrated in Figure 5.1, define and describe network communication services and protocols. They have become the standard reference models for application-to-application (A2A) communication.

The DoD model is the basis for the Internet protocols that are commonly used today. The model defines four layers:

- The network access layer is responsible for the physical transmission of data over a specific hardware media. The protocols at this layer were not explicitly defined by the model creators to enable access to a wide array of hardware media. Some of the protocols common to this layer include Ethernet, Token Ring, X.25, and Frame Relay.

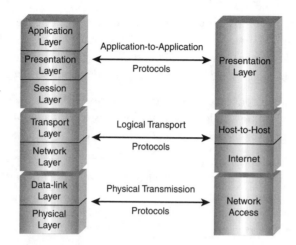

FIGURE 5.1

The OSI reference model and DoD model are used to describe the layers of communication in networked applications. The DoD model is referenced as the model of the Internet.

- The Internet layer is responsible for routing and providing a single interface to higher-layer protocols. The IP layer has logical routing intelligence, while the network layer has physical point-to-point responsibility. The popular "ping" of ICMP resides in this layer.

- The host-to-host layer abstracts the complexities of the network from applications. It handles connection rendezvous, flow control, retransmission of lost data, and other generic data flow management. The Transmission Control Protocol (TCP) and User Datagram Protocol (UDP) are most often cited as the workhorses of this layer.

- The process layer contains protocols that implement user-level functions. These include telnet for remote access, FTP for file transfer, NFS for file sharing, and SMTP for mail delivery. These protocols implement the set of functions most readily known to users of distributed applications.

From a P2P perspective, the most noteworthy layers are the host-to-host and process layers of the model. More specifically, at the host-to-host layer you are concerned with the two workhorse protocols, TCP and UDP, while the focus of the process layer is on HTTP, SMTP, and new P2P entrants such as XML-defined JXTA.

Discovery Implications

Peer discovery requires that you make a number of transport design decisions. For instance, do you use connection-oriented (TCP) or connectionless-oriented (UDP) communication to discover peers?

TCP creates a virtual circuit that remains open and connected during the life of the session, and guarantees a certain level of reliability during the exchange—and thus the discovery process. This connection-oriented transport generally has additional overhead because of the number of packets that must be exchanged and acknowledged.

The alternative is to use a connectionless transport such as UDP, which does not guarantee packet delivery. In addition, it does not maintain a session for communication. This has the tradeoff of speed versus reliability and performance.

Although most broadcast and multicast styles of discovery use connectionless communication, there are examples of connection-oriented transports, such as Gnutella, that use TCP-based broadcasting.

Virtual Namespaces

As mentioned before, dynamic networks are an essential characteristic of P2P. Dynamic networks are enabled by discovery, identity, presence, and a virtual space (network) bound by the discovery horizon.

Java uses the `InetAddress` class to represent an Internet network address. This class supports the `getByName` method, which retrieves the IP address of a list given its name. `InetAddress` makes it easy to map a host name to its address using the local and network naming services available, including DNS and NIS. The `InetAddress` contains two fields: the host name and the IP address.

Virtual namespaces extend addressing beyond IP addresses, and might actually map a machine address to another domain-specific representation. As mentioned in Chapter 3, "P2P Application Types," identity and presence services are not dependent on IP addresses. They might map an identity to an IP address at runtime, but this mapping is required to address routing issues more than for identification. Namespaces are important because they help to establish a context for higher-level communication. This context is required if peer applications are to interoperate.

Routing

Routing of P2P traffic occurs on the network and application levels. From a network perspective, routing refers to the path the network chooses to transport a message. This usually involves charting a course over a number of intermediate routing hops. Network and subnet portions of the IP are used to determine route source and destination. The actual path the message traverses between these endpoints is dependent on the routing protocol. Different routing protocols are used to improve efficiency and optimize network usage.

P2P addresses higher-layer (application) routing issues, which might affect (overlay) network layer routing. For instance, alternate routing often involves establishing paths between edge devices that would not normally be possible. In P2P networks, the path between the nodes emerges through the information sharing patterns, rather than being enforced by static configurations. Firewalls and NAT (Network Address Translation) devices are often used to block transmissions or constrain point-to-point communication. P2P networks have come up with novel ways of addressing these constraints and restrictions.

NAT devices enable nodes in a private network address domain to access the Internet when an insufficient number of unique public network addresses are available. They are also used to hide the identity of individual nodes from the network at large. Firewalls provide security by limiting network traffic allowed from the Internet to and from a private network. Firewalls employ three basic techniques:

- Packet filtering—Packet filtering involves examining network traffic passing through and selectively passing or dropping packets.

- Proxy servers—Proxy servers examine and filter packets, but also act as a relay between hosts behind the firewall and the external network domain. In this regard, they perform address translation functions similar to a NAT device. External systems only see the proxy server address.

- Stateful-inspection—Stateful-inspection methods monitor communication protocol and application-level state changes. An application context is built from the state changes to enable more intelligent inspection decisions based on the type and location of packets that should be exchanged in conjunction with the security policies in effect.

Most firewall and NAT configurations do not permit bidirectional communication between two peers separated by NAT devices and/or firewall(s). Solutions permitting outbound connectivity are usually more mature than solutions enabling inbound connectivity. This is because externally-initiated communication is assumed to be untrustworthy, and is not as predominant in client/server computing.

NAT devices and firewalls also typically limit communication so that only responses to requests that originated behind the devices are allowed back in. This blocks communications from hosts outside the protected domain to those hosts inside the domain. Often, certain ports/services are closed down completely and access is denied.

These restrictions reduce the utility of peer-to-peer networks by prohibiting public nodes from initiating communication to blocked nodes, and by preventing direct communication between pairs of blocked nodes. This has a dramatic impact on impeding the

5

SYSTEM TOPICS
EXPLAINED

formation of a P2P network. If you are behind a firewall, special configuration will be required to enable participation.

The Peer-to-Peer Working Group (`www.peer-to-peerwg.org`) has identified three primary techniques for overcoming firewall and NAT translation routing restrictions:

- The node behind a NAT device or firewall initiates communication with a node that is publicly addressable. Examples of this include Napster and Gnutella.

- Using a rendezvous server to provide a repository for advertisement information, such as that used by JXTA to support discovery.

- Using a publicly visible node to act as a relay, or router, for blocked nodes (for example, JXTA).

These solutions rely on a third-party host, running special software that can help nodes behind firewalls detect what kind of connectivity they have and help broker connections with other nodes. The following brokering techniques (see Figure 5.2) are often used:

- Reverse the connection—Whenever Node A wants to communicate with Node B, if Node B cannot receive connections, you would use a third party to tell Node B to initiate a connection to Node A. (This assumes Node B can initiate a connection to Node A.)

- UDP requests—The NAT device can allow UDP to "open up" a hole that allows incoming traffic and routes it to the machine that originally sent it. Node A, behind a NAT device, sends UDP packets to a third party. Then the third party tells Node B where to send packets to Node A. Reversal only works when one of the communicating nodes is behind a NAT device, while this solution works even if both Nodes A and B are behind NAT devices.

- Push requests—With this solution, intermediaries receive requests from clients that are unable to establish direct communication. The intermediary forwards the request to the intended target. The model is based on "pushing" the request to the intended recipient, who then establishes a connection with the push originator. This is similar to the Gnutella network solution, in which no central or special purpose servers need to be defined.

Overlay networks are an area of rapid development and change. Expect this to continue to evolve as peer-to-peer technologies become more prevalent in government, university, and corporate settings.

FIGURE 5.2

Three common models of peer-to-peer routing around and through firewalls and NAT devices.

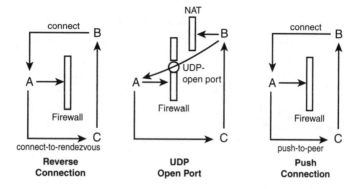

Protocols

A *protocol* is simply an agreed-upon set of standards that enables two or more software components to communicate. There are low-level protocols such as TCP and UDP, and high-level protocols such as HTTP, FTP, and SMTP.

Protocol *layering* is a common technique for simplifying network design and promoting extensibility. Protocol layering allows common functions to be defined, and the responsibility for implementing those functions mapped to a specific layer of the model or architecture. A layered approach is considered better practice than implementing a large "brick" of code that is difficult to understand. Layered architectures promote reuse, exchangeability, incremental development, and offer the advantage of localizing changes to specific layers. As the network evolves, layers can be replaced or exchanged without re-engineering the entire communication architecture.

Chapter 7, "Transports and Protocols," explores the protocol and service maze that exists in current P2P applications.

As Project JXTA has pointed out, there is a need for standards to promote interoperability in common P2P functions. However, it should be noted that JXTA does not define a specific transport binding. For instance, JXTA does not dictate or assume TCP/IP as the underlying network transport because the goal of the JXTA project is to promote interoperability with a minimal amount of constraints and assumptions about hardware, software, and the network environment.

The JXTA protocols are composed of six protocols that work together to enable the discovery, organization, monitoring, and communication between peers (see Table 5.1).

TABLE 5.1   JXTA Protocols

JXTA Protocol	Discovery	Organization	Monitoring	Communication
Peer Discovery Protocol (PDP)	Fundamental peer advertisement support			
Peer Endpoint Protocol (PEP)	Enables route discovery, enables firewall and NAT routing			
Peer Resolver Protocol (PRP)				Basic query / response(s) protocol
Pipe Binding Protocol (PBP)				Binds two or more endpoints of a pipe
Rendezvous Protocol (RVP)		Enables peer groups and provides message propagation, used by PRP and PBP		
Peer Information Protocol (PIP)			Provides status information such as state, uptime, and peer capabilities	

All of these protocols are implemented using a common messaging layer. It is the messaging layer that binds the JXTA protocols to various network transports.

Each of the JXTA protocols is independent of the others, and a peer is not required to implement all protocols. A peer just needs to implement the protocols that it needs to use. Per the specification:

> The JXTA protocols do not require periodic messages of any kind at any level to be sent within the network. For example, JXTA does not require periodic polling, link status sensing, or neighbor detection messages, and does not rely on these functions from any underlying network transport in the network. This entirely on-demand behavior of the JXTA protocols and lack of periodic activity allows the number of overhead messages caused by JXTA to scale all the way down to zero,

when all peers are stationary with respect to each other and all routes needed for current communication have already been discovered.

However, it should be noted that many important services supporting P2P have yet to be defined. For instance, as of this writing, presence and identity services for JXTA do not exist. The degree with which implementations of the protocol will be able to work without a "digital heartbeat" has yet to be determined.

Metadata

Much has been written about the importance of metadata and the significance it is having on describing information. *Metadata* is information about information. It makes understanding content easier for humans and—perhaps more importantly—machines. It helps in organizing and improving the semantics of the information we so often search, exchange, and accumulate. Part of its appeal is in the simplicity with which it can be represented. For instance, things like title, author, subject, and date represent descriptive information (metadata) about a document or publication that might appear on a Web site. Search engines capable of interpreting and automatically generating metadata are already at a distinct advantage. The effectiveness and relevance of search results can be radically improved by using metadata. It's akin to a semantic map for content.

The Web contains a wealth of knowledge—and unfortunately a wealth of worthless, outdated information rubble. Sifting through the rubble to find relevant information is difficult, even for the experienced "search-ologist." Using metadata effectively enables a search engine to use more than simple keyword matching, or pattern recognition and repetition techniques. Metadata can be used to improve search effectiveness by associating descriptive information with each searchable item. For instance, rather than searching by simple filenames associated with audio, video, or document files, metadata provides a means to classify, categorize, and build rich ontologies.

Music file metadata might be used to categorize by title, recording artist, length, and bit rate of encoding:

```
<title>
<album>
<artist>
<length>
<bitRate>
```

Video file metadata might include video title, director, and technical specifications:

```
<title>
<director>
<resolution>
<colorDepth>
<codec>
```

Document file metadata could include the author, title of the document, and the version requested:

```
<author>
<title>
<version>
```

If all this metadata is searchable, it greatly increases the search accuracy of search engines. P2P applications are using metadata to automatically arrange imported files into a personalized media library. They are being used to improve the cataloging capabilities of exchanged information, such as documents, emails, meeting notes, and so on.

P2P applications are even using XML to describe P2P services. In fact, like Web services, a whole new area of service description and message routing is being built on XML and XML metadata. All aspects of JXTA are being built on XML to structure data as advertisements, messages, and protocols. Jabber is being built as an XML router that relies heavily on XML namespaces to provide extensibility, as seen in Figure 5.3.

FIGURE 5.3

Jabber is defining an XML-based backbone that goes beyond integrating proprietary IM systems. Jabber is promoting XML routing as an integration technology.

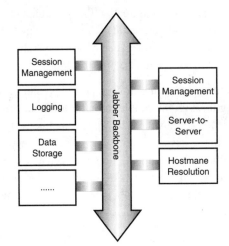

The Role of XML

XML has become the description language of choice for most metadata enthusiasts. XML is a good choice for representing data for a number of reasons:

- XML is a simple markup language based on an existing standard (SGML), and is a natural extension to HTML.
- Its text-based encoding makes it easily processed by programming languages. Java specifically has defined an entire set of packages related to parsing, formatting, messaging, and binding objects to XML.

- XML is capable of being edited by simple text editors, and there is an abundance of tools and resources available to support its adoption.

- XML is capable of expressing complex hierarchical relationships and links between documents and objects.

- XML is extensible and open, enabling authors to define their own set of markup tags to define and structure data.

- XML is widely adopted, and is a standard supported by the World Wide Web Consortium (`www.w3.org`).

The importance of XML and XML-defined metadata will continue to grow. Chapter 8, "P2P Data Formats and Interchange" will take a more in-depth look at how metadata is being used in P2P applications.

Data Formats

Before peers can exchange data across the network, peers have a fundamental choice to make. They can exchange data in binary, ASCII, or structured data such as XML. The choice is an important one. How will you encode the information that is passed between peers, between services, and between components?

There are low-level issues, such as how different computer architectures represent and store integers and floating point numbers. In some systems, called *big-endian* architectures, the most significant part of the integer is stored in the first byte of a two-byte integer. On *little-endian* architectures, the convention is reversed.

Fortunately, if you are using Java, this distinction is not an issue you need to address directly. The Java virtual machine for a specific architecture provides a consistent low-level data representation. However, you will see references to little-endian and big-endian architecture as you delve into cross-platform interoperability. Care must be taken to encode information in a platform-neutral representation. As a result, text-based protocols tend to be the norm on the Internet. Most common protocols convert numbers to text, and use the resulting text representation in the data transfer. Of course, this results in larger messages, or *heavy* protocols on the wire. Despite this drawback, many systems are moving from traditional RPC mechanisms to text-based protocols.

There are instances where the data being exchanged can't be easily converted to text, such as music files or video files. In these cases, many systems are still converting the data from binary into ASCII representations for ease of use.

Chapter 8 will take a more in-depth look at data formats being used in P2P applications.

Integration and Interoperability

We have already discussed the trend toward multifunction service-oriented P2P systems. These systems recognize the need for open architectures. Rather than defining a closed API that performs a specific function, P2P open frameworks are emerging that provide *hooks*, or published interfaces to provide extension and interoperability. This will be especially important if P2P is to become an important component in defining the architecture of a virtual corporation, as illustrated in Figure 5.4.

FIGURE 5.4

The virtual corporation requires three successive steps of integration: internal employees must be connected; external suppliers and partners must be connected with your internal systems; and both internal and external entities must be able to collaborate.

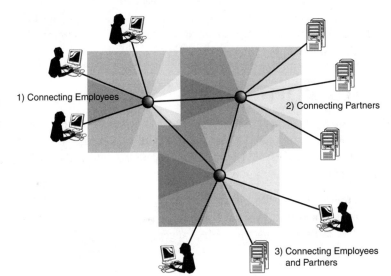

1) Connecting Employees

2) Connecting Partners

3) Connecting Employees and Partners

Virtual corporations integrate their systems—employees, customers, and partners—into a mesh-like topology. This is a much deeper level of integration, both internally and externally, than is common in most corporations today. However, as supply chain management continues to leverage public networks, the opportunity for this level of integration becomes viable. Virtual corporations also exhibit a much more dynamic relationship with their suppliers and partner systems. Business relationships come and go more frequently, and it must be possible for the systems that support this activity to keep pace.

Web services and P2P techniques that embrace XML can provide the basis of a solution. XML provides a common data format, and enables alternative middleware choices. This is an important attribute, because most large systems have invested significantly in middleware technology. Replacing middleware is never an easy undertaking. Often the middleware implemented is an extension of the current platform selection, and requires a specific transport implementation. XML can be used with a wide array of transports, including those being popularized by Web services and P2P networks.

These technologies are providing a unifying framework for service-oriented architectures. Intersystem processing and integration is not new. Other technologies, such as CORBA, EJB, and DCOM, have built solid frameworks for cross-system integration. However, these technologies often function best when used within the domain of large business systems, where the control of software selection is unified. When used to integrate intersystem processes, they often don't achieve the level required for virtual corporations because they assume a certain level of technology homogeneity.

Combining the dynamics of P2P group formation with the integration potential of Web services will have far-reaching implications. A technology solution to enable the virtual corporation might finally be at hand.

J2EE and Java Messaging Service

Java Messaging Service (JMS) is the J2EE-based messaging service. Messaging services continue to grow in importance because of their capability to loosely couple distributed systems. JMS attempts to standardize the messaging providers interface using Java. It supports popular messaging paradigms such as publish and subscribe. Subscribers register their interest in a topic or a pattern of events, then asynchronously receive events matching their interest, regardless of the event's publisher. Subscribers can come and go as processing mandates and the number of subscribers can change dynamically. Topic-based publish-subscribe communication is similar to group-based communication (shown in Figure 5.5); subscribing is equivalent to becoming a member of a group. Of course, building a system that can scale to support a large network in light of system failures on public networks is still a challenge. JMS will be described in more detail in Chapter 12, "Messaging and Java APIs for XML."

FIGURE 5.5

JMS topics can provide a bridge to JXTA peer groups. Both provide a level of publish and subscribe event notifications.

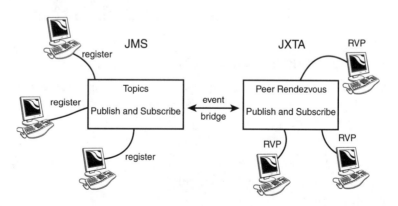

A sample implementation of JMS-to-P2P integration is Hive (www.alberg.com). Hive provides a JMS-based framework that enables non-JXTA clients such as browsers to interact with a JXTA client. In the Hive framework, servlets register as a topic in a JMS server. Web site activity triggers events that are published by the JMS server. Any interested entity can receive these events based on topic registration. In effect, topic queues map to state changes during Web site usage, such as when you complete a form.

Illustrated in Figure 5.6, Hive uses JMS as a standard layer over the JXTA Peer-to-Peer Platform.

FIGURE 5.6

Hive is a sample framework that uses JMS and JXTA to integrate P2P into the enterprise.

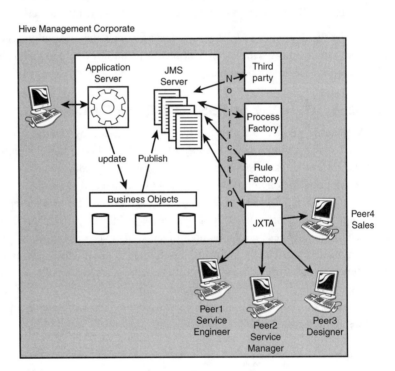

Web Services and SOAP-RP

As stated, Web services are not dependent on any specific infrastructure or middleware. The adoption of Web services will remove one of the obstacles to the integration of the virtual corporation by providing a common language to describe the interactions between cooperating entities, without forcing all parties to a specific middleware implementation.

Figure 5.7 shows how a client and a Web service provider can interoperate. It also extends the traditional triangle to integrate with JXTA services. The steps required include the following:

1. The service provider registers itself and the services it provides. In this case, the service provides connection to a number of JXTA services.

2. Clients that use this service query the UDDI registry to identify entities providing the required service and then download the service definition in WSDL.

3. The client can then connect to the service provider and exchange the appropriate SOAP messages.

We have extended the Web service to integrate with JXTA by translating SOAP-XML to JXTA-XML-compliant messages, and by using SOAP-RP.

FIGURE 5.7

SOAP-RP provides an enhancement to the routing capabilities of SOAP. It enables the specification of routing paths.

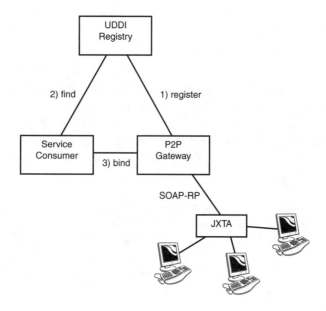

SOAP-RP provides an enhancement to the SOAP protocol to extend its routing capabilities. SOAP-RP enables intermediary nodes to be specifically identified over a route path. This would be necessary to gain access to overlay networks. The simple routing of SOAP over HTTP is unable to accomplish this.

CORBA and SCOAP

The Object Management Group's (www.omg.org) *Common Object Request Broker Architecture (CORBA)* defines the programming interfaces to an object request broker (ORB). An ORB supports the communication between distributed objects. Much like RPC, objects make invocation requests on other objects regardless of network location. The ORB goes further to abstract network communication and programming languages required for object-to-object interaction. CORBA is yet another attempt to make distributed systems interoperate and integrate. CORBA gained modest acceptance during the 90s as specific industry groups, such as telecommunications, began to adopt the technology as the integration "glue" for the growing number of disparate systems that required some level of interoperation.

The Object Management Group's *Interface Definition Language (IDL)* provides a standardized way to define the interfaces to CORBA objects. IDL is often cited as defining the contract that exists between cooperating objects. IDL separates the interface from the implementation, thus giving implementors flexibility performance, optimizations, and extended features of service implementations. The mapping of IDL to specific languages provides flexibility in language and platform selection, and helps to avoid a "one-way" mentality to service implementation.

Not wanting to be left out of the Web services craze, OMG is positioning its CORBA support. An IDL mapping called the Simple CORBA Object Access Protocol (SCOAP) is being defined to support the SOAP protocol. This will enable SOAP clients to communicate with CORBA services and SOAP servers using CORBA (see Figure 5.8). This will also promote ORB interoperability over the Internet by tunneling IIOP over SOAP/HTTP headers. IIOP (OMG's Internet Inter-ORB Protocol) defines an interoperability protocol for ORBs using TCP/IP.

FIGURE 5.8

The SCOAP protocol enables CORBA to integrate with Web services. The common element with P2P appears to be XML and HTTP. The CORBA event service already supports the publish/subscribe style of notifications.

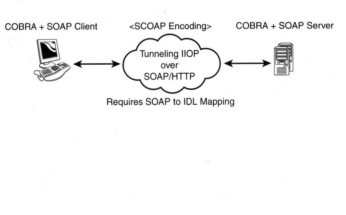

This effort once again points to the convergence occurring with architectures based on XML messaging using HTTP.

Jini and JavaSpaces

Jini does not make XML or HTTP fundamental to its integration model. It is based on Java-defined interfaces. You are more likely to use Jini and JavaSpaces if you are developing in a Java language-based environment. This is not a strict requirement, but more of a practical one.

That said, the Jini services provide an optional path to service integration. Fundamentally, Jini is about services, and the ad hoc formation of services enabled through a lookup service using multicast or unicast messaging. This maps well to the environment of P2P peer groups.

JavaSpaces is especially well suited to providing the foundation for rendezvous peers. The JavaSpaces service provides a simple programming API that enables distributed applications to share and persist communication. The service also supports distributed transactions using the Jini transaction service. This could play a critical role in enabling distributed transactions between partners in the virtual corporation.

The use of Remote Method Invocation (RMI) as an underpinning in the architecture provides code movement over the network. In other words, it is the only architecture presented that is based on the concept of code mobility. This has two important implications:

- Administration can be minimized and simplified through dynamic updates.
- As agent software becomes more prevalent on the Internet, code mobility (RMI) can provide a framework for mobile agents.

There are a number of concepts, such as leasing, that map well to the unstable environment of the Internet, and thus P2P systems in general. We will discuss JINI and Javaspaces in Chapters 14 and 15.

Security

Chapter 10, "P2P Security," discusses traditional network security in distributed systems and highlights new P2P issues.

Traditional Requirements

Traditionally, security is defined as the protection of information, systems, and services against manipulation, mistakes, and disasters. Network security is comprised of authentication, authorization, integrity, confidentiality, and nonrepudiation.

The Elements of Network Security

Authentication is the most common type of network security. It generally involves a user or process demonstrating some form of evidence to prove *identity*. Such evidence might be information only the user would likely know (a password), or it might be information only the user could produce (signed data using a private key).

Authorization involves the capability to enforce access controls upon an authenticated user. This is commonly implemented as an access control policy that provides an association between a user's access rights and system resources, such as databases, files, and processes.

Integrity ensures that messages are delivered correctly, and that messages in transit have not been tampered with maliciously.

Confidentiality and privacy ensure that data cannot be seen or disclosed over the network by outside parties. Encryption is a procedure used to convert text into code to prevent anyone but the intended recipient from reading that data. It can be used to ensure the confidentiality of data, the authentication of the data sender, or the integrity of the data sent.

Finally, nonrepudiation guarantees that a sender cannot deny having sent a particular message.

P2P requires the same level of security as traditional distributed systems. In addition, P2P highlights a number of security-related topics such as anonymity, trust, and accountability.

Anonymity

Anonymity relates to privacy. It ensures that someone can publish a document without having the system or an individual trace its origin. In other words, the author can remain anonymous. Anonymity can extend beyond the author to include the publisher, the reader, or the physical hardware and network supporting the system. Ensuring anonymity can be a difficult requirement to meet in distributed systems.

A number of techniques have been implemented to guarantee anonymity. Proxy servers or gateway servers can manipulate IP addresses to mask the real IP address of the publisher. An individual file can be split into multiple components and stored on multiple servers. Only encrypted keys can rebuild the original file. Keys are held by trusted members.

Trust

Trust is an important concept in computers. We often are more trustworthy on the Internet than we might like to believe. How often have you downloaded a file without checking the integrity or reliability of the source?

Trust implies confidence with the individual or system of interaction. You assume that malicious behavior will not occur with members or machines in the community. Of course, in the real world this is not always the case. Systems must be designed to ensure that less trustworthy components are identified and quickly removed. You cannot guarantee the content of a file or message exchange, but you must be able to identify and hold accountable some entity for disruptive or malicious behavior. As you can see, trust and anonymity can have conflicting goals.

To improve trust, downloaded files can be secured with *message-digest* functions. A message-digest function takes a variable length input message/file and produces fixed-length output. The same input will always produce the same output. Message digest functions are used to detect file tampering. This raises the level of trust that the downloaded file has not been altered.

Often *digital signatures* are used to identify the author of a file. An author can digitally sign a file to provide proof that the file indeed is from the author. Digital signatures involve encrypting information using two keys—a private key and a public key. The author uses the private key to create a signature on the file. The public key is used by the receiver to verify the signed data is from the author.

Digital certificates improve our ability to trust information by providing a process to ensure the private/public key pair is legitimate and registered with a third-party authority. Digital certificates are issued by companies called *certifying authorities (CAs)*. An individual or corporation must apply for a digital certificate with the proper credentials, usually requiring a fee.

Pretty Good Privacy (PGP) is software (`www.mit.edu/network/pgp.html`) that automates encrypting files and email using digital certificates. It enables certificates to be generated without CA involvement. Individuals can certify each others' certificates. Although this might not seem secure, the idea is that you can trust an individual that has signed for another individual. In effect, intermediaries begin to act as certifying authorities. If you trust the person who has certified a peer, then you trust the peer. It's kind of like transitive trust. This is actually being termed the "web-of-trust" in P2P systems.

Most P2P offerings to date that are PGP-based typically require all members of the community to share the same key. Shared keys in a P2P system create a security loophole, as when one member is removed from the community, all peers and all the content they share must be re-encrypted.

Accountability

Accountability refers to the concept of making users accountable for the resources they consume. For instance, most systems require a user to have an account, which in turn provides the user with access to certain resources and services offered by the system. The account provides the identification to track the use of resources. Of course, this is not a problem in centralized systems, in which all access goes through a central point of control. However, distributed P2P systems can present a number of challenges, and are more vulnerable to attack. For instance, without an identity service, user identification can be difficult if not impossible to implement. Network maps might only contain IP addresses, and these are often changing and transient for edge devices. In addition, many unknown intermediaries might be involved in a transaction or exchange, complicating most electronic payment systems.

One approach to accountability is the *pessimistic model*. A system based on this model minimizes the resources available, such as bandwidth, disk space, and message transfer to all participants in the P2P system. It is a simple risk-versus-reward model.

A second approach can be referred to as the *optimistic model*. This model assumes resource allocation is proportional to the degree of trust. The more trustworthy a member of the community, the more resources available for consumption. This model requires a reputation system, which collects history on the identification and usage patterns of a peer member.

Performance

There is a wide range of performance implications that must be considered when designing P2P applications:

- Broadcast, multicast, or unicast messaging for discovery
- Indexing versus flooding for searches
- Variable-length versus block-oriented data storage and transfer
- Message-passing versus RPC versus other communication patterns
- Bandwidth and scalability constraints
- Fault tolerance and network reliability
- Load balancing and distribution
- Replication and redundancy of information
- Security, public or private keys, encryption

In the next chapter and in the remainder of the book, we will highlight areas in which performance considerations are especially important, and in which a P2P solution might not be the best choice.

Summary

This chapter has pointed out a number of important issues that need to be addressed when designing and building P2P applications and services:

- Transport selection and routing
- Protocols and service-oriented architectures
- Data formats and payloads
- Metadata definition
- The role of XML
- Integration technologies, Web services, CORBA, Jini and JavaSpaces
- Standards such as JXTA
- Security and new security considerations
- Overall performance and scalability of P2P systems

Peer-to-peer principles map well to some of the problems faced in current systems and the extension of systems into the virtual corporation. However, P2P is not a single architecture, and still requires significant development to mature.

JXTA offers promise to promoting P2P interoperability on a larger scale. XML is beginning to gain acceptance as a general data format, with HTTP the preferred transport.

Armed with this background, let's start the journey of developing solutions to the issues and problems inherent in P2P development.

P2P Dynamic Networks

by Robert Flenner and Frank Cohen

In This Chapter

Techniques for peers to discover and use each other's functions are perhaps the greatest distinction between P2P technology and client/server Web technology. P2P technology expects peers to live at the edge of a network, and to require a variety of techniques to interoperate. On the other hand, client/server Web technology requires the network to know where to find resources before the request is made. P2P uses a group of methods known collectively as discovery.

Discovery

Discovery answers the big questions about a network:

- What peers exist on the network?
- How are the peers organized around their capabilities?
- What uniquely identifies a peer?
- How does a peer exchange data with another peer?

P2P is forced to identify answers to these questions. Unfortunately for the Java developer, not all P2P technologies are successful. Worse yet, some P2P technologies are closed and proprietary, or they hard-code implementations into one solution that would otherwise use open technology.

Although many P2P techniques exist to build peers, three types of peers have emerged as popular designs:

- Simple peer
- Rendezvous peers
- Router peers

A *simple peer* is designed to be an endpoint that offers functions and data to peers making requests. Simple peers have the least responsibility of all three peer types. They usually reside outside a general network, and possibly behind a firewall or Network Address Translation (NAT) router. Simple peers are not expected to handle communication on behalf of other peers, or to serve information that they don't directly consume themselves.

Rendezvous peers provide a dating service in which peers discover other peers and peer resources like data and functions. All three types of peers issue discovery queries to rendezvous peers, but the rendezvous peer is also usually a cache of previous requests. When a rendezvous peer lives behind a firewall, it must have the ability to communicate through the firewall to other peers.

Router peers provide a mechanism for peers to communicate through firewalls and NAT routers. A router peer tunnels peer requests across a network. The information needed to use a router peer is enough to replace the need for a Dynamic Naming Service (DNS) and supports dynamic IP addressing.

Let's look at a simple example of the three peers in action. Imagine using a P2P client that looks for magazine articles on human genomics. The user initiates a search for the articles with a simple peer. The peer sends a discovery query to all its known simple peers and rendezvous peers. The rendezvous peers that receive the query look to see whether they have data the simple peer is looking for. If so, the rendezvous peer might return a discovery response message containing advertisements from other peers that are stored in its cache. The rendezvous peer will also likely send along the same query to its list of known peers.

Although we have described three different types of peers, in real-world P2P applications each peer might include a combination of the functions described in simple, rendezvous, and router peers. Let's look at how peers discover data, functions, and services using a variety of P2P techniques.

Router Peers and Dynamic Networks

P2P technology expects to find a network filled with firewalls, dynamic addresses, and changing peer locations. P2P provides a loose coupling of peers, so the P2P network remains functional even when parts of the real network break. Three P2P discovery techniques have become popular in this environment:

- Broadcast—Sends a discovery request to every network node that is reachable
- Selective broadcast—Sends a discovery request to every network node based on established heuristics
- Adaptive broadcast—Sends a discovery request to every network node based on heuristics and rules

These techniques will be joined, modified, and abandoned over time as new ways to dynamically form a network are identified. The following are some of the areas of study from which P2P technology innovations might spring:

- Transport—How do transport services such as broadcast, multicast, and unicast messaging relate to discovery?
- Radius—How is the discovery horizon established and maintained?
- Frequency of broadcast—How often should discovery messages be broadcast to populate the network?

- Discovery protocol—What information should be defined in a discovery protocol?
- Discovery roles—Do all peers participate equally in the discovery process? Do all peers have the same broadcast role?

Broadcasts

Traditionally, broadcast messages have been sent by devices that deal with network routing or data packet exchange at a low level, such as routers. Broadcast messages on IP networks contain a special address reserved for broadcasting. The network and host part of the address is set to ones (hex: —FFFFFFFF). This indicates to the network layer that the packet is addressed to every device on the subnet, as seen in Figure 6.1.

FIGURE 6.1

Broadcasts try to reach all nodes on the subnet.

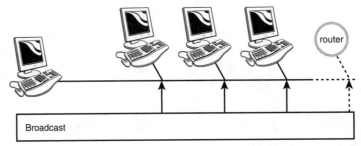

Broadcast

Message sent to every reachable (subnet) listener

In a P2P context, broadcasting might sound like TCP/IP multicasting, but it isn't. P2P technology plays mostly in the application layer of a software application. The actual method for moving a broadcast message across the Internet might use multicasting or a number of other techniques that we will explore next.

Transport—Multicast Versus Unicast Messaging

Multicast messaging is often compared to radio or TV broadcasts, in the sense that only those who have tuned their receivers to a particular frequency receive the information. Only the channels selected are heard. The sender sends the information without knowledge of the number of receivers.

In contrast, when you send a packet and there is only one sender and one recipient, this is referred to as *unicast*. A unicast transmission is by definition point-to-point. Unicast can be used to send identical information to many different destinations; however, this involves replicating data, and is not the most efficient transport.

Multicast addresses are in the Class D 224–239 range. Multicast messaging uses this range of addresses to define multicast groups, as shown in Table 6.1.

TABLE 6.1 IPv4 Address Classifications

IP Address Classification	Address Range
Class A	0.0.0.0–127.255.255.255
Class B	128.0.0.0–191.255.255.255
Class C	192.0.0.0–223.255.255.255
Multicast (Class D)	224.0.0.0–239.255.255.255
Reserved	240.0.0.0–247.255.255.255

Note

You can find all the reserved multicast addresses at http://www.iana.org/assignments/multicast-addresses.

Multicasting has produced mixed results in applications that require a number of machines in a distributed group to receive the same data, such as conferencing, group mail, news distribution, and network management. Multicasting suffers from the lack of a control protocol, which makes it unsuitable for large, reliable, and sustained transmissions. Multicasting appears to be well-suited to P2P because peers on a P2P network do not require the synchronization of data among the peers, as multicasting often fails to deliver 100% of its data to everyone listening to the multicast. Figure 6.2 shows multicasting being used in P2P networks for discovery.

FIGURE 6.2

Multicasting goes beyond simple subnet penetration, but it requires that receivers listen on a specific "channel." The underlying network supports the transport services.

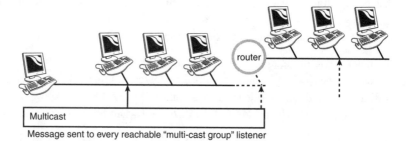

Multicast advantages include the following:

- Decreased network utilization—Reduces the number of messages required by elim-inating redundant packets and decreasing the number of point-to-point connections that must be established.

- Resource discovery—Discovery and multicasting assume a sender is transmitting to an unknown number of peers without knowledge of their location.

- Dynamic participation—Multicasting provides flexibility in joining and leaving a group. This membership flexibility supports the transient behavior of peers.

- Multimedia support—Multimedia transmission continues to increase in popularity and consumes a significant amount of bandwidth. This is one area where network optimization is of paramount importance. Multicasting can be used to transmit multimedia data to receiving stations that compress the transmission and then deliver it to destination nodes, rather than using point-to-point connections for all destinations.

Unfortunately, multicasting is not implemented everywhere. Hardware, specifically routers, often block multicast traffic from penetrating corporate networks or traversing ISP providers. Firewalls and NAT devices often block not only multicast traffic, but con-strain traffic in general to well-controlled choke points (ports). As a result, additional means of discovery are generally required in scalable P2P networks.

Radius of Broadcast

Broadcast packets need to have a mechanism to avoid bouncing around the network for-ever. This can happen when there is invalid addressing or routing information delivered with a packet. The time-to-live (TTL) parameter (an 8-bit field in an IP packet header), has been defined to address this issue. It ensures that packets cannot traverse the network endlessly. Each packet has a TTL value, which is a counter that is decremented every time the packet passes through a hop; for instance, a router between networks.

In the example in Figure 6.3, the TTL parameter is set to 4, and the broadcast request needs to make five hops (pass through five routers) to make it to the nearest peer. Peer-2 will never "hear" the broadcast request, and Peer-1 will never "know" about Peer-2 through this route. The packet will be discarded when the TTL count reaches zero.

When a peer receives a request, it looks at the TTL value. If the value is greater than 1, it decrements the value and transfers the request to the destination address or the next hop. If the value is 1 or less, it discards the message. In this respect, the P2P network is pro-viding a layer of control that "overlays" the network layer.

FIGURE 6.3

*Time-to-live para-
meters define the
extent to which a
packet can travel
across the net-
work. Routers typ-
ically decrement
the TTL value of
the packet as it
passes through the
router. When it
reaches zero, the
packet is
discarded.*

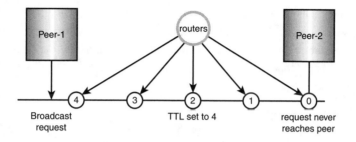

Frequency of Broadcast

Most systems that use broadcast techniques place some control on the frequency of the broadcast. For instance, when a peer activates, it sends a discovery message on the local subnet and waits a predetermined time before sending another discovery request. If no response is returned within that time interval, a subsequent request will be sent. In effect, the peer has started to poll the network. If responses are returned, the peer builds a map, or *view* of the peer network. This is important, because the peer view is probably very different from the physical view. The map reflects the peers that responded to the discovery request.

As peers enter and leave the network, they must be able to update their view. One approach is to go into a *heartbeat* mode of polling. The peer periodically sends a discovery request. As responses are received, the map is updated. During the polling process, some peers might no longer be available. In Java fashion, these peers are eventually removed when the Java garbage collector destroys the object holding the instantiated map. New peers that respond will be added to the map. A simple ping map contains the list of peers that have responded to discovery requests. The ping map can be as simple as a list of active IP addresses, as in Table 6.2.

TABLE 6.2   Ping Map

IP Addresses
172.16.1.3
172.16.1.4
12.239.129.4
...

The ping map, which might also be viewed as a peer routing table, is built from scratch each time the peer activates. In this model, the peer does not implement the notion of memory. In other words, each time the peer activates, it invokes the discovery process and collects a new image of the peer network. This approach is unable to deal with many of the problems inherent with P2P networks. For instance:

- Dynamic IP assignment—History of peer interaction is limited to current IP assignment.
- Size and scale of network—Every peer maintaining maps of connections cannot scale.
- Reputation and trust issues—No history of past peer interactions is possible.
- Equitable resource allocation—No controls are placed on resource utilization.
- Security in general.

The identity of the peer is directly mapped (implicitly) to the IP address. If a peer changes its IP address, it is considered a new member of the network. A history of prior interactions is not possible.

The ping map can be extended to include the notion of *identity*, which resolves some of the problems. Persistence or memory of the peer network becomes more viable and attractive with identity. This approach requires each peer to have a unique ID. Once generated, the ID is fixed for the lifetime of the peer. When a discovery request is received, the responding peer returns its IP address (which might be different) and its unique ID (which never changes). This assumes that peers have a consistent method to generate unique IDs (see Table 6.3). ID collision occurs if two peers generate the same ID. Inconsistent ID representation (integer, String, UUID, and so on) causes identification problems throughout the network. Clearly, there are control mechanisms required even when using this simple approach.

TABLE 6.3 Ping Map with Peer Identity

IP Address:Port	Unique ID
172.16.1.3:	ABCD-3456-2345-DEFA
172.16.1.4:	DECF-5432-5643-EFDA
12.239.129.4:	DCDD-1324-7654-DEAC
...	...

Selective Broadcast

Instead of sending a discovery request to every peer on the network, peers are selected based on heuristics such as quality of service, content availability, or trust relationships.

Trust relationships are commonly used when a specific peer(s) acts as a relay or router to the peer network. Usually the trusting peer is seeded with the IP address of the trusted peer. This is the technique used by JXTA routing and rendezvous peers. The trusted peer has some knowledge of the network and is publicly available.

Selective broadcast requires that you maintain historical information on peer interactions, peer roles, peer identity, and so on. It begins to extend the ping and identity map concept to include the following:

- Peer discovery roles—Peers have special roles to enable discovery. All peers are "not" equal.

- Past performance metadata—A historical record of peer performance is maintained. This includes availability metrics, as well as environmental metadata.

- Environmental metadata—Includes additional information on the peers' capabilities, such as bandwidth, disk space, and processing power (see Table 6.4).

Selective broadcast systems are much more scalable than simple broadcast networks. Instead of sending a request to all peers, it is selectively forwarded to specific peers who have a higher probability of being able to locate other peers or resources.

Each peer must contain or have access to information used to route or direct requests received. Although this might be appropriate from relatively small networks, in larger networks this overhead can quickly grow to levels that are unsupportable.

TABLE 6.4 Ping Map with Peer Identity and Metadata

IP Address:Port	Unique ID	Metadata
172.16.1.3:	ABCD-3456-2345-DEFA	Dial-up, # of concurrent connections
172.16.1.4:	DECF-5432-5643-EFDA	DSL, # of concurrent connections
12.239.129.4:	DCDD-1324-7654-DEAC	T1, # of concurrent connections
...	...	...

Adaptive Broadcast

As mentioned in Chapter 1, "What Is P2P?," adaptive broadcast tries to minimize network utilization while maximizing connectivity to the network. You can limit the growth of discovery and searching by predefining a resource tolerance level that, if exceeded, will begin to curtail the process. This will ensure that excessive resources are not being consumed because of a malfunctioning element, a misguided peer, or a malicious attack. Adaptive broadcast requires monitoring resources such as peer identity, queue size, port usage, and message frequency.

Rules can be used to complement metadata to build sophisticated discovery techniques (See Table 6.5).

TABLE 6.5   Ping Map with Peer Identity, Metadata, and Rules

IP Address:Port	Unique ID	Metadata	Rules
172.16.1.3:	ABCD-3456-2345-DEFA	Dial-up, # of concurrent connections	Congestion -> Throttle Connections -> Accept
172.16.1.4:	DECF-5432-5643-EFDA	DSL, # of concurrent connections	Congestion -> Throttle Connections -> Accept
12.239.129.4:	DCDD-1324-7654-DEAC	T1, # of concurrent connections	Congestion -> Throttle Connections -> Accept
...	...	...	...

The ALPINE Network implements a form of adaptive broadcast in its adaptive social discovery protocol. It's based on the ALPINE-defined datagram protocol DTCP. See www.cubicmetercrystal.com/alpine/overview.html for more information on ALPINE networks and protocols.

Identity and Presence

As discussed in Chapter 3, "P2P Application Types," users of instant messaging (IM) systems must be uniquely identified. How a user is identified is fundamental to the operation of the system.

Identity has also proven fundamental to discovery and P2P systems in general. Our simple ping map example was unable to satisfy the critical requirements of P2P networks. It had no way to resolve the dynamic and transient nature of peer participation.

Peers and resources need to be uniquely identifiable. This identity must not be limited to current session or current IP address identification. It must persist to enable contextual information and historical interactions to be stored and subsequently restored. In effect, it is required to accumulate the knowledge necessary to support sophisticated P2P networks. Presence information tied to identity can be used to ensure that peer maps are consistent and represent the current state of the network. Knowing when a peer is online is required for building efficient, distributed, and user-centric systems.

Virtual Spaces

Broadcast messages require senders and receivers to agree on the semantics of the exchange (protocol) to create groups of collaborating nodes. The formation of a group of nodes creates a virtual space that shares a common context. Even at the base level of discovery, there is a significant amount of cooperation and collaboration involved. This is before any real work, such as transferring files, messages, transactions, and so on has even been initiated. A virtual space implies more than simple connectivity.

Another way of looking at virtual spaces involves JXTA. Before JXTA, a Java developer's choices for P2P technology were limited. If you were developing a file sharing application, the likely choice would have been the Gnutella protocol; for instant messaging, it would have been ICQ. The protocols' incompabilities divided the network into groups of applications based on protocols. With JXTA, the protocols are mixed-and-matched freely.

A natural result of JXTA mixing-and-matching protocols in P2P applications is found in peer groups. Peer groups are formed by combining groups of peers to serve a common interest or goal defined by the application the peers were built to solve. Peer groups provide services that are not available to other peers in the P2P network.

The J2SE implementation of JXTA organizes peer groups hierarchically. At the root is the NetPeerGroup, of which all peers are members by default (see Figure 6.4). On a local network, the NetPeerGroup provides peers with global connectivity according to the restrictions imposed by network administrators.

The common services shared by the members of the NetPeerGroup include the following:

- Discovery service
- Membership service
- Resolver service
- Endpoint service
- Pipe service
- Peer Info service

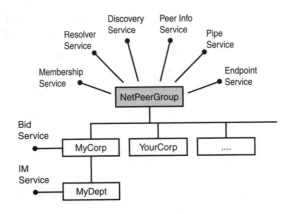

FIGURE 6.4

JXTA provides a view of a virtual space as a collection of common services shared by a group of peers.

Peers self-organize into peer groups, each identified by a unique peer group ID. So, it is the peer group ID that uniquely identifies the virtual space in the JXTA protocol.

Discovery, identity, and namespaces are the building blocks of a virtual space. Discovery determines the horizon or scope of membership. Identity uniquely defines the membership, and namespaces supply the context for membership.

In the computing disciplines, the term *namespace* conventionally refers to a *set* of names; that is, a collection containing no duplicates. In the context of P2P, a virtual namespace augments current addressing technology. It provides the context to support consistent identification and service composition.

You can define context as any information that can be used to characterize the situation of an entity or an action. Formal context definition is critical to enabling richer integration between distributed systems. Our software must be more intelligent and adaptive to the environment. For software to be adaptive, it must be able to "reason" and make assertions based on situational analysis. A virtual space provides the context. Members share a common protocol and metadata definition. P2P will help provide identity, presence, and context within the virtual spaces of cyberspace.

Discovery Implementations

This section discusses some P2P implementations of discovery.

Gnutella Discovery

Gnutella uses a broadcast-messaging protocol for peer discovery. The Gnutella net has no hierarchy. Every peer is both a client and a server (servent). Each Gnutella peer knows about the peers to which it is directly connected. All other peers are invisible, unless they announce themselves by answering to a broadcast request or a query.

After making the initial connection to a peer, you must *handshake*. Currently, the handshake is very simple. The connecting peer sends

```
GNUTELLA CONNECT/0.4\n\n
```

The accepting peer responds with

```
GNUTELLA OK\n\n
```

A Gnutella network is cyclic, in that loopback messages are possible. All messages have a unique ID (GUID). Gnutella peers check the message ID and if they have received the message before, they discard the request. If they have not seen the message, they route it to the peers to which they are directly connected.

JXTA Discovery

Per the specification, "JXTA does not mandate exactly how discovery is done. It can be completely decentralized, completely centralized, or a hybrid of the two." JXTA enables discovery by providing a discovery service, which provides a mechanism in JXTA for discovering advertisements. The Peer Discovery Protocol (PDP) defines a protocol for requesting advertisements from other peers, and responding to other peers' requests for advertisements.

Technically, *advertising* means sending an advertisement to everyone on the network. An advertisement is an identifier for any network resource that a using entity might need. A JXTA advertisement is platform-independent, and is typically represented by an XML document.

In JXTA, you can control the scope of discovery by specifying a threshold. The *threshold* is an upper limit of the number of advertisements that the requesting peer specifies. The responding peers cannot exceed this limit. Each PeerGroup has an instance of a DiscoveryService, so the scope of the discovery is limited to the group.

JXTA discovery mechanisms include local broadcast, peer invitation, message cascading, and discovery using rendezvous peers.

Rendezvous peers help an isolated peer by quickly seeding it with network information. Rendezvous peers provide peers with two possible ways of locating peers and other advertisements:

- Propagation—A rendezvous peer will pass the discovery request to other peers on the network it knows about, including other rendezvous peers that will also propagate the request to other peers, a process illustrated in Figure 6.5.

- Cached advertisements—A rendezvous peer can use cached advertisements to reduce network traffic, and can use cached advertisements to respond to a peer's discovery queries.

FIGURE 6.5

Rendezvous peers provide "fan-out" capabilities by propagating discovery requests from peers initiating discovery.

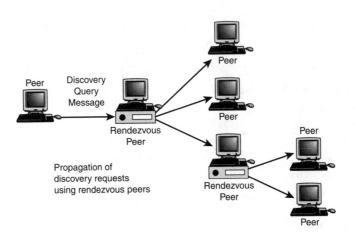

Relay peers also have a special role in JXTA discovery. These are peers that are capable of forwarding requests to rendezvous peers and other relay peers. They are used to provide connectivity, or a *bridge*, from behind a firewall or NAT device to the peer network. Any peer can query a peer relay for route information, and any peer in a peer group may become a relay. Peer relays typically cache route information. Route information includes the peer ID of the source, the peer ID of the destination, a TTL for the route, and an ordered sequence of gateway peer IDs (see Figure 6.6).

FIGURE 6.6

Relay peers can be used to circumvent firewalls and NAT devices. Typically, these IP addresses (relay and rendezvous) will be configured in the PlatformConfig *file of the JXTA platform.*

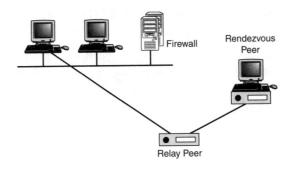

When a peer sends its advertisement to another peer, it can expect the other peer to reply by sending its advertisement back. This way, both peers will have the other party's advertisement.

Advertisements are stored in a persistent local cache (the cm directory). When a peer activates, the same cache is referenced. A JXTA peer can use the getLocalAdvertisements method to retrieve advertisements that are in its local cache. If it wants to discover other advertisements, it uses getRemoteAdvertisements to send a DiscoveryQuery message to other peers. `DiscoveryQuery` messages can be sent to a specific peer, or propagated to the JXTA network.

In the J2SE platform binding, `DiscoveryQuery` messages not intended for a specific peer are propagated on the local subnet utilizing IP multicast, and they're also propagated to the configured rendezvous peers. A peer includes its own advertisement in the `DiscoveryQuery` message, performing an announcement or automatic discovery mechanism. Only peers in the same peer group will respond to a `DiscoveryRequest` message.

Discovery Protocol

The information that should be defined in the discovery protocol depends on various factors. If all your problems could be solved with the ping/identity map, the resulting protocol would be simplistic. However, there are many additional considerations, such as routing impediments, network connectivity, security, presence, and so on. As a result, protocols must be more complex than simple ping requests.

JXTA defines two protocols specific to discovery:

- Peer Discovery Protocol—This protocol enables a peer to find advertisements on other peers, and can be used to find any of the peer, peer group, or resource advertisements.

- Peer Endpoint Protocol—This protocol enables a peer to query a peer router for available routes to send a message to a destination peer. This is used in a case where NAT or firewall impediments block peers from communicating directly. Peer routers respond to queries with available route information. Any peer can decide to become a peer router by implementing the Peer Endpoint Protocol.

The organization of information into advertisements simplifies the JXTA protocols required to make P2P work. The format of the advertisements themselves dictates the structure and representation of the protocol data.

Routing

Routing is a broad topic. An entire book (in fact, many) could be devoted to the subject of Internet routing. P2P introduces application-level routing that overlays network routing. This is the area we will focus on.

Overlay Networks

A P2P network forms a self-organizing overlay network on the Internet. Any Internet-connected host that runs P2P software and has proper credentials can participate in the overlay network. Each P2P node typically has a unique ID.

The P2P software builds a routing table that attempts to organize the overlay network to increase efficiency and resiliency. The sophistication of locality metrics, and the location, or *path diversity*, improves the performance of the overlay network.

Locality

Locality is based on a proximity metric. In other words, efficiency can be gained if you know the "distance" between any pair of nodes. This distance value represents the number of hops required to get from point A to point B. Or, it might represent the latency, or time delay between points. How it is computed or determined is implementation-specific.

The most simplistic routing implementation ignores locality considerations altogether. Every peer in the routing table is considered equal. Any peer can be used to transfer a discovery or search request. Message propagation ensures that as many peers as possible are queried. In this scenario, you typically limit the number of peers (connections) in the routing table. In addition, you must implement a loopback mechanism to drop message requests you have already received. A unique message ID is stored for each message to determine redundant requests. This is the routing technique employed in most flooding broadcast systems.

A more sophisticated approach recognizes the distance metric. The function that determines distance is critical to the overlay network's effectiveness. Peers that are determined to be close will receive preferential routing. However, that has to be balanced to ensure diversity in the routing table population.

Diversity

Diversity is based on a distribution metric. The goal of the distribution metric is to ensure that discovery requests are appropriately partitioned. Unlike locality, which optimizes distance, diversity optimizes geographic distribution.

The uniform distribution of peers such as relays and rendezvous points improves the scalability of the virtual space by reducing or eliminating a large number of discovery requests. This requires a function that is capable of computing a distribution metric when given a unique value, such as an IP address, or the preconfiguration of pivot points in the network. A *pivot point* provides a route from one major network segment to another.

The uniform distribution of peers ensures an even population of the virtual space (network), and reduces the size requirements of the routing table. Each node within the routing table can refer to one of potentially many nodes within a geographic distribution.

Node Redundancy

Finally, redundancy ensures that pivot points in the routing map, such as those that implement diversity, are replicated and redundant. This is to ensure that no single point of failure exists in the overall virtual space.

Flat Network Model

In a flat overlay network, each peer processes and propagates requests they receive to other peers to ensure the broad distribution of requests, as shown in Figure 6.7. As mentioned previously, network traffic will grow exponentially given a linear increase in peers or queries within the network.

FIGURE 6.7

A flat overlay network model will broadcast requests to every reachable peer. This model grows exponentially as the network grows linearly. Bandwidth saturation quickly becomes an issue. This model is only applicable for small work groups.

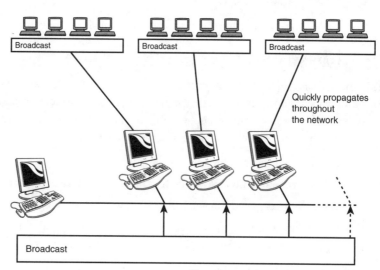

Simple broadcast is only viable in small networks.

Hierarchical Network Model

A hierarchical overlay network will reduce network traffic by organizing peers into a group hierarchy. Peers are only capable of discovery within their own group, or peers only communicate with peers that possess certain operational characteristics. For instance, hierarchical organization can result from differentiating high-bandwidth, dedicated peers from slower, less powerful ones. Hierarchies can be built from metadata that defines network intelligence and peer capabilities. Such metadata can include the following:

- Equate resource consumption to the level of network participation. Discovery and search requests are discarded from noncontributing (sharing) peers.

- Avoid expensive protocol operations such as unnecessary broadcast replies with intelligent forwarding to intended destinations.

- Implement connection profiles to favor higher-bandwidth connections over slower modem connections.

- Allow high-bandwidth broadband users to act as proxies for slower modem users.

- Collect peer performance and measurement metrics.

Performance

In this final section, we will look at discovery performance implications.

Bandwidth and Scalability

This chapter has emphasized that uncontrolled discovery (broadcast) is only appropriate for small work groups. Balancing geographic reach while limiting excessive bandwidth consumption is a critical requirement of any scalable P2P network. There are a number of solutions that can be applied to optimize the discovery process:

- Use diversity to reach a broader range of the virtual space more efficiently.

- Minimize routing table size by seeding the table with special-purpose peers.

- Throttle discovery requests and minimize heartbeat polling.

- Segment the routing table by operational and environmental metadata.

- Constrain total bandwidth allocated to discovery processing.

- Monitor peer consumption, including bandwidth used by incoming packets, peak bandwidth used, and a quality value associated with the responses received.

Searching

The quality value of the response received can be used to determine future query and discovery scenarios. If you record the quality of a peer response, you can begin to maintain a search priority matrix by topic or category. Peers with high values for a given category will be queried first. You'll query lower-grade peers only if the higher-quality peers fail.

One outcome of this technique is that you may organize peers into *peer clusters*, or groups of peers capable of satisfying discovery requests by type or class of information. Additionally, peer clusters often have the overall effect of limiting the number of packets used, and thus the network bandwidth required to search for a desired response.

Transport

As this chapter has highlighted, discovery and searching have huge implications on network bandwidth requirements. Most implementations currently reside on either TCP (to improve reliability), or UDP (to improve performance). In addition, the topology of the discovery network is critical to understanding bandwidth and performance requirements.

A decentralized discovery topology relies on peers to propagate discovery requests across the network. Defining special discovery roles is minimized, and the failure of any one node does not necessitate widespread network failure. Often, UDP can be used because of the inherent redundancy built into the discovery (mesh) topology.

Contrasted with a decentralized topology is a centralized discovery platform. Some would argue that centralized discovery, or *super nodes*, are in direct contradiction to basic P2P network formation. However, in corporate environments, where large enterprise systems are needed for scalability, administration, and security, centralized servers using TCP might be appropriate.

The emerging middle ground (hybrids) uses a combination of centralized and decentralized discovery processing. Special broadcast roles, such as rendezvous and relay peers, effectively bridge the network to minimize the number of concurrent connections that must be supported.

Fault Tolerance

Providing an adequate level of fault tolerance in P2P networks will be critical to their widespread adoption.

Redundancy

P2P technology solves problems inherent in a dynamic network, including dynamically assigned addresses, routing changes, and firewalls. Redundancy is key to reducing failure points and providing extra value for a P2P network.

Load Balancing

Techniques such as round-robin processing, workload queries, and node diversity (geographic distribution) are required to scale P2P networks. This should be implemented without requiring any global coordination.

Storage

Data caching of routes, peer groups, and peers will radically improve performance. Subsequent lookup requests whose paths intersect can be served the cached copy. Initialization of peers from cached information can quickly transfer a large amount of virtual space knowledge from one peer to another.

Distributed caching offloads the peers that hold the primary replicas of data, and minimizes delays and network traffic by dynamically caching copies near interested clients.

Communication

A key design issue is how to efficiently and dynamically maintain the routing table in the presence of peer failures, peer recoveries, and new peer arrivals. Special broadcast peers can periodically exchange keep-alive messages. If a peer is unresponsive for a period, it is presumed failed. All members of the failed peer's group are notified and update their group membership.

Routing table entries that refer to failed peers can be repaired lazily; in other words only when explicitly requested or addressed to do so.

Applications can perform efficient multicast on subnets to repair or recover from localized damage or failures.

Summary

Discovery is the process of locating peers and resources in a P2P network. Discovery is based on three messaging techniques: broadcast, selective broadcast, and adaptive broadcast.

Broadcast, multicast, and replicated unicast all represent viable discovery transport services when used appropriately. Flooding broadcast techniques are only applicable for small work groups. A combination of constrained multicast and targeted unicast is gaining in popularity. It provides the necessary balance between connectivity and bandwidth consumption.

The TTL parameter is a technique used to limit the broadcast horizon in P2P networks. TTL is also used in the network layer to control packet routing in general.

Heartbeat polling in large P2P networks should be minimized, if not eliminated. The frequency of broadcast requests should be monitored. Controls and rules placed on bandwidth consumption can help to mitigate network problems, resource allocation, and security breaches.

Discovery protocols are maturing and becoming more complex. Metadata is providing an important element to extending protocol definition and enabling a more robust network.

Special-purpose discovery roles, such as relays and rendezvous points, provide a number of attractive alternatives for scaling a P2P network.

CHAPTER 7

Transports and Protocols

by Navaneeth Krishnan

Regardless of the kind of application you are building, there are many critical design decisions that you need to take during the very early stages of its development. If you are an application architect, there will be many a situation where you will have to choose from seemingly equal but drastically different alternatives. In such cases, you need to be familiar with all the options available to you to be assured of choosing the right one that suits your requirement.

The intent of this chapter is to take a look at the various transport protocols that you can use to build your P2P application. Choosing the right transport protocol might not necessarily dictate the success of your application, but it will be a very important factor.

What Is a Protocol?

A *protocol* can be defined as an agreed-upon, well-defined set of conventions for information exchange between two networked entities. Any two entities can meaningfully interact with each other only if they can communicate using the same protocol.

There are a variety of protocols to choose from when you are developing an application. You might even decide to write your own protocol, if circumstances necessitate it. In the subsequent sections, we'll explore some of the more popular protocols that are used today, namely HTTP, SMTP and SOAP. We'll also take a fairly detailed look at BEEP, a new protocol that seems to hold a lot of promise for future P2P applications.

HTTP

Hypertext Transfer Protocol (HTTP) is undoubtedly one of the most popular protocols today. HTTP is the underlying protocol on which the World Wide Web is built. HTTP is internally built on TCP/IP, a combination of two lower-level protocols (Transmission Control Protocol and Internet Protocol.

HTTP is used to deliver files, images, sounds, or any other kind of data (collectively known as resources) over the Internet. URLs (Uniform Resource Locators) serve as global addresses to identify these resources. HTTP generally uses port 80 for its operation.

This is how HTTP works:

1. An HTTP client opens a HTTP connection to the server whose services are required.
2. The client sends an *HTTP request* to the server. Requests are generally to access resources.

3. The server sends an *HTTP response* back to the client. The response might contain the requested resource or any other information to be sent back to the client.

4. The connection is then closed.

It is also possible to send multiple requests and responses over the same TCP/IP connection. In such cases, the requests and responses are said to be *pipelined*.

> **Note**
>
> Pipelining was made possible only after HTTP 1.1, prior to which every request/response used to necessitate a new TCP/IP connection and was therefore inefficient.

HTTP requests and responses share a similar format. Both these messages consist of

1. An initial line

2. Zero or more header lines

3. A blank line or CRLF (Carriage Return/Line Feed)

4. An optional message body containing data

HTTP is a stateless protocol, as no state information is stored between two successive message transfers. The beauty of the protocol is its simplicity. The protocol defines just a few basic operations that a client can invoke on a server (GET and POST are the most commonly used ones), yet it has been extended to make possible thousands of complex interactions taking place on the Internet today..

HTTP for P2P

A large number of P2P applications use HTTP as an underlying transport mechanism. The ubiquitous nature of HTTP is the most important reason for this. Being the most extensively used protocol on the World Wide Web, any application that uses HTTP can be sure to appeal to a large base of users. HTTP is also the safest bet when you expect your application to be used in a variety of environments. The reason for this is that many environments, especially corporate environments, have firewalls that restrict network traffic coming in and going out their domain. These firewalls normally permit HTTP traffic to pass through because HTTP traffic generally caters to Web users who surf the Internet.

This is the also the reason why many popular instant messaging and file sharing applications use HTTP underneath. Often, these applications avoid violations of corporate policies as well as copyright laws. HTTP acts as a convenient means by which such applications can act in a stealth mode.

Therefore, if you decide to use HTTP applications, you need to evaluate the intent of your application. Is it meant to help anonymity and stealth? If the answer is yes, then HTTP is your best bet. Is it meant to be an enterprise application? If so, then why do you really need HTTP? Isn't it much better to use your customized protocol and let the network administrator configure the network for its use?

SMTP

Simple Mail Transfer Protocol (SMTP) is defined in RFC 821. It is the most commonly used protocol for sending email. Even though email is not truly peer-to-peer, SMTP can be used as a protocol over which peer-to-peer applications can be built.

Email offers an asynchronous communication path between any two entities. For instance, User A can log in to her server and send an email to User B without knowing if User B is online at that time. Similarly, User B can at any time retrieve all messages sent to her from her email server, and if needed, send a message to User A.

> **Note**
>
> Even though SMTP provided a strong and reliable framework for sending email, there was a strong need for the capability to add new functionality. This led to Extended SMTP (ESMTP), defined by RFC 1425. ESMTP defines how extensions can be integrated into the basic SMTP protocol, instead of redefining a completely new protocol. It enhances SMTP by providing a framework in which all future extensions can be built in a consistent way.

This fundamentally asynchronous path offered by email can be used as an effective channel for P2P application communication.

However, this might not be feasible in a real-world scenario. It might be possible, so use SMTP in applications where communications are infrequent and response time is not critical.

SOAP

Simple Object Access Protocol (SOAP) is a simple, extensible mechanism for decentralized information exchange using XML. It can be used to access remote services in a platform-independent, protocol-independent, programming language-independent manner, and is fast becoming a de facto standard for Web Services.

Systems using SOAP interact with each other by sending and receiving SOAP messages. SOAP consists of

- An envelope that defines the contents of a SOAP message, who has to process it, and whether it is mandatory or optional.

- A serialization mechanism that can be used to exchange application data types.

- A convention that can be used for remote procedure calls.

SOAP does not depend upon any network protocol. SOAP data is sent as XML text to enable a standard data representation that can be interpreted by any standard XML parser. Hence SOAP messages can be exchanged via any convenient protocol such as HTTP, SMTP, or FTP. However, HTTP is still the most commonly used protocol today.

Chapter 11, "Web Services Explained," will cover SOAP in detail. It will also show you how to process SOAP requests and responses using Simple APIs for XML (SAX).

SOAP is a very good candidate on which to develop your application because of its extensible and independent nature. However, because SOAP uses XML extensively, applications using SOAP as a transport might be slower than similar ones using HTTP or TCP/IP directly. This is because all data structures will have to be converted into plain text before generating the XML message. At the receiving end, the XML message will have to be parsed to re-create the data structures. This will consume quite a bit of processing power. For the same reason, SOAP might not be suitable if you are developing applications for small devices with constrained environments, such as PDAs and mobile phones.

BEEP

Blocks Extensible Exchange Protocol (BEEP, formerly known as BXXP) is a relatively new protocol, and is rapidly gaining industry attention. It would be an understatement to think of BEEP as a mere application protocol. It is a protocol that can act as a framework over which other protocols can be built upon.

RFC 3080 discusses the BEEP Core, and RFC 3081 explains mapping the Core on TCP.

BEEP Jargon

Before getting into the details of the BEEP protocol, let us first define some important terms that you will come across:

- Peer—Any BEEP-enabled endpoint in a network is called a *peer*. Typical to any peer-to-peer protocol, BEEP makes no assumptions about the endpoint. A peer can act as a client in some cases, and as a server in others.

7

TRANSPORTS AND
PROTOCOLS

- Initiator/listener—It does not make sense to use the terms "client" or "server" in a peer-to-peer environment, in which such roles change dynamically. Yet at a per-request level, there is always an entity that initiates a communication, and an entity that listens to initiated communications. BEEP always refers to entities as *initiators* and *listeners*. The initiator performs a client role, and the listener performs a server role. Of course, these roles are not static. A peer that is an initiator for one request could be a listener to the following request.

- Session—A *session* denotes a single connection between two peers. A session is mapped to the underlying transport service that the BEEP framework is built upon. In the case of TCP, a BEEP session is mapped to a single TCP connection (see RFC 3081).

- Channels—All data exchanges between communicating peers occurs through *channels*. A session can be therefore divided into multiple channels. Because all channels use the same session and hence the same connection, channels are created by multiplexing a single connection.

- Profile—A *profile* defines the syntax of valid messages that can be exchanged within a channel. Each channel is associated with a profile.

How BEEP Works

As with most network protocols, BEEP communication starts with a listener, listening for connections. The initiator initiates a session (connection) with the listener.

All data exchanges can only take place through BEEP channels. However, during the initial communication between the initiator and the listener, each one has no idea about the channels and profiles supported by the other. For this reason, a special channel called the *management channel* (also called *channel zero*) exists. The management channel supports a well-known profile called the *channel management profile*. Channel zero helps the peers advertise to each other about the various profiles that they support. It also helps the peers create new channels based on one of these mutually supported profiles.

Once new channels are created, the entities can communicate with each other using messages adhering to the profile that they support. Multiple channels can be in use simultaneously.

There are two types of channels:

- Initial tuning channels—Present only during the initialization process. Their main aim is to provide the initialization services before any actual communication starts. These channels become inactive after the initialization phase. Only one tuning channel can exist in a session at a time. For instance, there could be an initial tuning channel that authenticates the initiator and listener to each other.

- Continuous channels—These carry the actual data being exchanged. They are typically activated after the initialization phase is over. A session can have multiple simultaneous continuous channels.

Once the data exchange between the initiator and the listener is complete, channel zero is again used to close all the open channels.

Using the BEEP Java Binding

BEEP has been implemented in various programming languages like Java, C, TCL, Python, Ruby etc. In order to illustrate how BEEP works, let us use the BEEP Java Binding. The BEEP Java binding is available from `beepcore.org`. It is the reference implementation of RFC 3080 and 3081.

We will develop an example of a simple message exchange using the BEEP protocol. You'll first need to install the BEEP Java binding, which can be found at `www.beepcore.org`.

Note that to successfully install the binding you also need

- Xerces, or any other XML parser that supports the `javax.xml.parsers`, `org.w3c.dom`, and `org.sax.xml` interfaces.
- The optional JSSE library from Sun Microsystems. However, if you are using JDK 1.4 or above, you won't need this. The library has been integrated along with the core Java classes from this release.

The `HelloListener` Class

The `HelloListener` class is a simple BEEP listening peer. It simply listens for any incoming BEEP session. Once a session and a channel are established, it receives whatever message the initiator sends. It also sends back a reply for this message and exits. The `HelloListener` class can be seen in Listing 7.1.

LISTING 7.1 The `HelloListener` Class

```
import org.beepcore.beep.core.*;
import org.beepcore.beep.profile.Profile;
import org.beepcore.beep.profile.ProfileConfiguration;
import org.beepcore.beep.profile.echo.EchoProfile;
import org.beepcore.beep.transport.tcp.AutomatedTCPSessionCreator;
import org.beepcore.beep.transport.tcp.TCPSession;
import java.io.BufferedReader;
import java.io.InputStreamReader;
```

LISTING 7.1   continued

```
/**
 * This is a BEEP Peer which listens for an incoming
 * request. The port and profile string are defined
 * by the constants. The peer also send back a response to the
 * initiator of the message that it receives.
 */
public class HelloListener{

    // Port number that is used
    public  static final int    PORT           = 8888;

    // This string is a URI that represents the profile.
    public  static final String PROFILE_STRING = "http://testdomain.com/test";

    // private variable to check if the application can exit
    private static boolean      exit           = false;

    /**
     * The main method creates an instance of the HelloListener.
     * The listener is made to listen for incoming messages.
     */
    public static void main(String args[]) throws Exception{
        // Create a new HelloListener object and listen
        // for any initiator
        new HelloListener().listenForInitiator();
    }

    /**
     * The method listens for a TCP Session to be initiated by
     * the initiator. Once a session is obtained the method exits
     * after a sleep interval.
     *
     */
    public void listenForInitiator() {

        log("Starting to Listen on port "+PORT);
        // create a new ProfileRegistry
        ProfileRegistry registry = new ProfileRegistry();
        // Add a StartChannelListener to the registry.
        // This listener will contain logic to manage
        // starting and stopping of channels.
        // In this case we use the HelloProfile to
        // get an instance of the HelloChannelListener.
        try{
            registry.addStartChannelListener(PROFILE_STRING,
                new HelloProfile().init(PROFILE_STRING,null),null);
        } catch(BEEPException beepException){
            // This means that creating a profile failed
            // The listener should be exited
```

LISTING 7.1 continued

```java
      exit = true;
    }
    // continue till the exit flag is true.
    while(!exit){
      try{
        // Get a TCPSession.
        // This is a blocking call.
        TCPSession session =
          AutomatedTCPSessionCreator.listen(PORT,registry);
        // sleep for a small delay.
        // This ensures consistency of output.
        Thread.sleep(2000);
      } catch(BEEPException beepException){
        // This means that the application is not
        // able to listen properly
        // Try to abort.
        log("Unable to listen Message is : "+
            beepException.getMessage());
        exit = true;
      } catch(InterruptedException excp){
        // No OP
      }
    }
    log("Exiting ...");
}

/**
 * A simple Beep profile  which implements the
 * <code>Profile</code> interface.
 *
 */
class HelloProfile implements Profile{

  /**
   * Initializes the profile and returns an appropriate
   * <code>StartChannelListener</code>.
   *
   */
  public StartChannelListener init(String uri, ProfileConfiguration config)
                         throws BEEPException{
    return new HelloChannelListener();
  }
}

  /**
   * A Listener implementing the <code>StartChannelListener</code>
   * interface.It contains logic for managing the start and stop
   * events in a given channel.
   */
```

LISTING 7.1   continued

```
class HelloChannelListener implements StartChannelListener{

  /**
   * Callback method that determines if a profile can be advertised.
   * If there are any prerequisites for a profile, they must be checked
   * here.Only
   *
   */
  public boolean advertiseProfile(Session session)
                  throws BEEPException{
    return true;
  }

  /**
   * Called when a new channel is started.
   *
   */
  public void startChannel(Channel channel,
                      java.lang.String encoding,
                      java.lang.String data)
                      throws StartChannelException{
    //create a new data listener for this channel.
      channel.setDataListener(new HelloDataListener());
  }

  /**
   * Called before a channel is closed.
   */
  public void closeChannel(Channel channel)
               throws CloseChannelException{

    // reset the data listener
    channel.setDataListener(null);
    // reset the application context
    channel.setAppData(null);
  }
}

  /**
   * A Message listener which gets notified whenever
   * any message is received. It implements the
   * <code>MessageListener</code> interface.
   */
class HelloDataListener implements MessageListener{

  /**
   * Receives a BEEP message.
   */
```

LISTING 7.1   continued

```
        public void receiveMSG(Message message) throws BEEPError,
                                           AbortChannelException{
     try{
        // Get a data stream from the message.
        DataStream stream = message.getDataStream();
        // Create a buffered reader for reading the data.
        BufferedReader reader =
          new BufferedReader(new InputStreamReader
            (stream.getInputStream()));
        // Print the recieved message to console.
        log("Message from initiator => "+reader.readLine());
        // Close the reader
        reader.close();
        // Send a reply to the initiator of the message
        log("Sending a reply to initiator ...");
        message.sendRPY(new StringDataStream("Hello Initiator !"));
        // exit the application
        exit = true;
     } catch(java.io.IOException excp ){
        log("Message from Exception : "+excp.getMessage());
        throw new AbortChannelException(excp.getMessage());
     } catch(BEEPException beepExcp){
        log("Message from Exception : "+beepExcp.getMessage());
        throw new AbortChannelException(beepExcp.getMessage());
     }
    }
  }

  // private method to log messages to console
  private static void log(String message){
    System.out.println(message);
  }
}
```

The `AutomatedTCPSessionCreator` is used by `HelloListener` to create a TCP-based BEEP session. This is done by the static `listen(port,registry)` method. This is a blocking call, and will do so until a `TCPSession` is created. The registry required by this method is `ProfileRegistry`, a class that contains a list of listeners (implementations of the `StartChannelListener` interface) that need to be notified when a new channel is started in this session.

We have also created a simple profile called `HelloProfile`. This profile also has its own `StartChannelListener` called `HelloChannelListener`. Obviously, even before we start to listen for a session, we need to add the `HelloChannelListener` to the `ProfileRegistry` so that it is notified of all channel management events.

Although the `HelloChannelListener` is aware of all channel management events (the starting of a new channel, the closing of an existing channel, and so on), it is unaware of any incoming messages through this channel. For this purpose, we need a `MessageListener`.

We have a `HelloDataListener`, an implementation of `MessageListener` that we use in this example. This listener's `receiveMSG` method is invoked on the receipt of any message. Whenever a new channel is started, the `HelloChannelListener` sets up a new `MessageListener` to receive all messages sent through the channel. Invoking the `setDataListener` method of the `Channel` object by passing a new instance of the `HelloDataListener` as an input achieves this.

The `HelloDataListener` listens to all incoming messages and prints the content of each message to the console. It also sends back a reply to the initiator of the message. This is achieved by the `sendRPY` method of the `Message` object.

The `HelloInitiator` Class

The `HelloInitiator` represents an initiating BEEP peer. It tries to open a session with the `HelloListener`. The `HelloInitiator` is listed in Listing 7.2.

LISTING 7.2   The HelloInitiator Class

```
import org.beepcore.beep.core.*;
import org.beepcore.beep.lib.NullReplyListener;
import org.beepcore.beep.transport.tcp.AutomatedTCPSessionCreator;
import org.beepcore.beep.transport.tcp.TCPSession;

import java.io.BufferedReader;
import java.io.InputStreamReader;

/**
 * This is a BEEP Peer which initiates a session with the listener peer.
 * The host name of the listener peer is contained in the HOST variable.
 * Currently it points to the same host as the initiator. This can be
 * changed to point to any host.
 *
 */
public class HelloInitiator{

  /**
   * Host name of the listener
   */
  public static final String HOST           = "localhost";

  /**
   * The main method creates an instance of the
```

LISTING 7.2   continued

```
 * <code>HelloListener</code>
 * The initiator is made to connect to the listener and send a
 * message. It exits after a small sleep interval.
 *
 */
public static void main(String args[]){

  try{
    // initiate a connection to the listener running on HOST
    TCPSession session =
      AutomatedTCPSessionCreator.initiate(HOST,HelloListener.PORT,
                                          new ProfileRegistry());
    // Start a new Channel with a profile as by
    // the PROFILE_STRING uri.
    Channel channel = session.startChannel(HelloListener.PROFILE_STRING);
    // Create  a new StringDataStream
        DataStream messageData = new StringDataStream("Hello Listener !!");
    // send the message
        channel.sendMSG(messageData,new HelloReplyListener());
    // sleep for a small delay and exit.
    Thread.sleep(2000);
  } catch(BEEPException beepException){
    log("Unable to send a successful Message. Reason is : "+
        beepException.getMessage());
  } catch(InterruptedException excp){
    // NO OP
  }
}

/**
 * A listener implementing the <code>ReplyListener</code> interface.
 * A reply listener can be used per message sent.
 *
 */
static class HelloReplyListener implements ReplyListener{

  /**
   * Called when a reply is received .
   *
   */
  public void receiveRPY(Message message) {

    try{
      // Get a data stream from the message.
      DataStream stream = message.getDataStream();
      // Create a buffered reader for reading the data.
      BufferedReader reader =
        new BufferedReader(new InputStreamReader
          (stream.getInputStream()));
```

LISTING 7.2 continued

```
        // Print the recieved message to console.
        log("Message from listener => "+reader.readLine());
        // Close the reader
        reader.close();
          ((FrameDataStream)message.getDataStream()).close();
      } catch(Exception excp ){
        log("Message from Exception : "+excp.getMessage());
      }
    }

    /**
     * Called when the underlying a reply of type ERR is received.
     * Not used in this example.
     *
     */
    public void receiveERR(Message message) {

        ((FrameDataStream)message.getDataStream()).close();
    }

    /**
     * Called when the underlying a reply of type ANS is received.
     * Not used in this example.
     *
     */
    public void receiveANS(Message message) {
        ((FrameDataStream)message.getDataStream()).close();
    }

    /**
     * Called when the underlying a reply of type NUL is received.
     * Not used in this example.
     *
     */
    public void receiveNUL(Message message){
    }
  }

  // private method to log messages to console
  private static void log(String message){
    System.out.println(message);
  }

}
```

The `HelloInitiator` also uses the `AutomatedTCPSessionCreator` class to initiate a session. This is achieved by using the `initiate` method. Once a session is initiated, it starts a new channel, with the given URI representing the profile. This is denoted by the constant `PROFILE_STRING`. It is important for both the `HelloListener` and the `HelloInitiator` to use the same URI, which serves as an identifier to the profile.

Once a channel is set up, the `HelloInitiator` sends a simple string message to the listening peer. This is done by the `sendMSG` method of the channel object.

Now every message that is sent to a listening peer can have a corresponding reply. The sender is free to delegate a listener for receiving the reply. All such listeners have to implement the `ReplyListener` interface. The `HelloInitiator` uses the `HelloReplyListener` as a listener to the reply it receives from the `HelloListener`.

APEX

Application Exchange (APEX) is an application protocol defined on top of BEEP. In simple terms, it is a BEEP profile. It provides services such as an access service that can be used to manage access information at endpoints, a presence management service, a report service, and so on.

APEX uses a mesh of interconnecting relays to transfer data from one APEX endpoint to another. All communications are sent to the mesh, which is responsible for sending the messages to the appropriate endpoint, regardless of the location to which it is connected. At the time of this writing, no implementation of APEX exists.

The Future of BEEP

BEEP holds a lot of promise to act as a base protocol upon which to build the application protocols of the future. A lot of work is already going in this direction. Many interesting BEEP profiles are currently being defined, including the following:

- Intrusion Detection Exchange Profile (IDXP)
- Tunnel Profile
- Common Presence and Instant Messaging Profile (CPIM)

Many applications have started looking seriously into BEEP. For instance, the JXTA reference binding uses BEEP as one of the supported communication protocols.

However, BEEP may not be appropriate for all cases. For example:

- If an application uses an already existing and widely deployed protocol, it would make little sense in rewriting it to use BEEP.
- BEEP does not make sense when the underlying communication protocol is multicast- or broadcast-based.
- If the amount of data exchanged is very small, BEEP becomes an overhead.

Using a Custom Protocol

Until now we have seen just a few popular protocols that can be used for P2P application development. But there are many more options. You could even choose to write your own protocol for your application.

This might be advantageous for many reasons:

- You might have the flexibility to incorporate the features that you need at the protocol level.
- You might also be able to optimize the protocol to suit your requirements, thus increasing the efficiency and performance of your system.
- You might not find any existing protocol suitable for the application that you are building.

However, you might need to seriously reconsider writing your own protocol if interoperability is or might become one of your requirements. By writing your own protocol, you'll need to put in a lot of effort and resources. You don't want to "re-invent the wheel."

Summary

This chapter explored the protocol maze that exists in current P2P applications. We had a quick look at some of today's popular protocols. We have also given you some insight about BEEP, a fairly new protocol that is currently gaining influence.

CHAPTER 8

P2P Data Formats and Interchange

by Michael Abbott

IN THIS CHAPTER

The World Wide Web (WWW) is evolving from a platform that delivers information to people into a platform for distributing information among different network hosts. One critical component of the WWW that is inhibiting this transformation is the weak support for metadata and information exchange semantics. Indeed, many Web sites use the <TITLE> or <META> tags embedded in Hypertext Markup Language (HTML) to describe the content of the page, but this approach is awkward at best, and the semantics of the tags are rarely supported. This lack of metadata infrastructure for WWW documents increases the difficulty of searching for content, and has driven the creation of companies like Google to address some of these problems.

In the P2P domain, the issue is of great importance, as the capability to discover other peers with a particular piece of knowledge or content is critical to P2P infrastructure. To address this challenge, the WWW Consortium's (W3C) metadata vision is captured within the concept of a Semantic Web, wherein all content on the Web has metadata that describes it. There is no way to enumerate all the metadata tags that could possibly exist, so solutions such as the Resource Description Framework (RDF) have been adopted to address the Semantic Web challenge. This chapter will explore the role of metadata in various computing architectures, including *n*-tier and P2P frameworks now and moving forward.

Current Representations of Metadata

If you examine the vast world of information, you'll find that many examples of metadata management exist, particularly in the storage space. Relational databases manage how data is represented, stored, and retrieved using metadata. Beyond the enterprise, you discover that a majority of content exchanged is either structured in text files with delimiters, or not structured at all. These semistructured text files typically have no metadata associated with them, but rather rely on the sender and recipient implicitly understanding the contents and semantics of the files. As we will discuss in Chapter 9, "Integration and Interoperability," EDI fundamentally works on the notion that the sender and the receiver explicitly use a certain structure based on a template for the data.

On the other hand, if you look at a text document without structure, there is no mechanism by which the context or concepts of the information can be inferred. This had led to the use of linguistic and heuristic techniques to build metadata from raw content; several companies have built products that apply these techniques to unstructured text. But what is needed is a nonproprietary ASCII (or ASCII-friendly) "meta language" to assign descriptions of each element or attribute. This language is XML.

The P2P Dilemma

As we have discussed, the WWW today provides an immense amount of readily available online information that lacks metadata describing its content. Traditionally, the WWW browser has been the single interface for accessing content on the Web. This interface, built around the concept of the hyperlink, gave rise to most of the content on the Web today.

With P2P architectures, there might be content on the Web with no browser-friendly link, and thus only accessible via a unique interface. A prime example of this would be Napster, which is a network that primarily shares music files encoded in MP3 format. To view or access files on this network, a proprietary client application is required; the only semantic link between content comes from a centralized server that provides content location. There is no fundamental link relating different content in the network; only peers that act as both server and client depending on their current dynamic roles. How does a peer in one group discover content from a peer in a different network?

The issue of building additional infrastructure to connect and share content compounds the difficulty in building a metadata solution to address the heterogeneity of interconnected networks and the content transferred over them. In the P2P domain, how can we learn from our experience with the WWW to prevent history from repeating itself? How can we solve the metadata problem before P2P content and networks are too pervasive for a solution?

Metadata and Information

The notion of metadata initially emerged in the sciences: How do we coherently organize information in a manner that scales well as the amount of information grows geometrically? Metadata is not a complex concept, really; it is just "data about data."

Ontologies are a methodology for defining metadata standards for a particular domain. For example, biologists more than a hundred years ago defined an ontology by which to organize various living organisms in a comprehensive and understandable manner. Ontologies help establish consensual terminologies that make sense to both sites, thus allowing distinct peers to interact in a common vernacular.

Metadata plays the largest role in areas where there is a complex or large set of information that requires both searching and indexing. Yahoo! was founded on the concept of building a structure to manage information on the WWW to address this very problem. In the public sector, researchers have spent a great deal of time working on solving this complex problem. One of the larger efforts is the Dublin Core Metadata Initiative. Founded in 1994, the effort uses a minimal set of metadata constructs (15 elements) to simplify the discovery of information on the Web. Later in this chapter, we will be exploring this initiative in greater detail. Although work has been done in the area of metadata modeling, and definition in domains such as library science, our present concern is how to apply metadata research to P2P architectures to avoid the current challenges of finding content on the WWW.

World Wide Web, P2P, and Metadata

To reiterate, content on the WWW is difficult to locate because of the lack of support for metadata. Although there is some lightweight support (mainly the `<META>` tag), the WWW infrastructure doesn't provide much help. Search engines do not require metadata information when registering a site, although if provided it can aid indexing and searching. Domain registrars do require a name for an Internet domain, but the name need not be related to the content found within.

If we return to the example of Napster, where all content is shared and the names or labels of the shared entities themselves provide search criteria, the demand for metadata is low. Yet as we look to P2P frameworks such as JXTA, where many different content types can be exchanged, the need for comprehensive metadata will only increase. Otherwise, we will end up with millions of nodes providing services and content that will not be leveraged because of poor discovery mechanisms. Sound familiar? It should.

HTML and Metadata

The `<TITLE>` tag is the mainstay of metadata for the WWW world. As someone who spent time providing solutions for search engine ranking optimization, I can confidently say that this tag very rarely describes the content of the page accurately. The `<META>` tag was intended to address this problem, but it's too simplistic and inflexible (no child elements, for example). So although you could tag metadata for files relating to subjects from health to finances, there is no way to build an ontology within which to define the appropriate content.

XML and Metadata

At IBM in 1974, Charles Goldfarb created the Standard Generalized Markup Language (SGML) to automate document processing in general. SGML is an international standard for the description of marked-up electronic text. In 1989 Tim Berners-Lee and Robert Caillau at CERN used SGML to develop a flexible hypertext document markup language that they called HTML. Later, members of the W3C designed a new markup language designed specifically for the Web called XML, also a subset of SGML.

Because it leverages the powerful features of SGML and omits the more obscure features, XML is a simple and general syntax for describing hierarchical data that is explained in greater detail in Chapter 3, "P2P Application Types." The SGML Editorial Board under the W3C officially developed XML in 1996. The original specification sets out the following goals:

- It shall be straightforward to use XML over the Internet.
- XML shall support a wide variety of applications.
- XML shall be compatible with SGML.
- It shall be easy to write programs that process XML documents.
- The number of optional features in XML is to be kept to an absolute minimum, ideally zero.
- XML documents should be human-legible and reasonably clear.
- The XML design should be prepared quickly.
- The design of XML shall be formal and concise.
- XML documents shall be easy to create.

XML namespaces separate application-defined XML data from the special instructions and information used by XML extensions. These features make XML very useful in expressing metadata.

The Semantic Web—A Historical Perspective

To reflect back on the beginning of this chapter, we discussed the W3C's vision of a Semantic Web. Layering a Web of metadata over the existing WWW would result in a comprehensive and coherent ontology of content and information. Today, hyperlinks do indeed link pages across the WWW, but with no apparent context. In an effort to learn from the past for the benefit of the next generation of P2P frameworks, let's review some of these concepts.

An early effort to address some of the concepts of a Semantic Web was the Platform for Internet Content Selection (PICS). One of the driving forces for this movement was to facilitate a wide range of filtering and rating services and content.

The implementation used a simple metadata label like the following, which could capture a classification and rating:

```
HTTP/1.0 200 OK
Date: Thu, 30 Jun 1995 17:51:47 GMT
Last-modified: Thursday, 29-Jun-95 17:51:47 GMT
Protocol: {PICS-1.1 {headers PICS-Label}}
```

```
PICS-Label:
 (PICS-1.1 "http://www.gcf.org/v2.5" labels
on "1994.11.05T08:15-0500"
exp "1995.12.31T23:59-0000"
for "http://www.greatdocs.com/foo.html"
by "George Sanderson, Jr."
ratings (suds 0.5 density 0 color/hue 1))
Content-type: text/html
...contents of foo.html...
```

Once a label was created, the developer would distribute it along with the document(s) in one of several ways. The recommended method, if your HTTP server allowed it, was to insert an extra HTTP header that preceded the contents of documents sent to Web browsers. The correct format as documented in the specifications was to include the two headers Protocol and PICS-Label, as seen in the previous example. The other method was to embed the label directly in the HTML, as follows:

```
<HTML><head>
<META http-equiv="PICS-Label" content='
(PICS-1.1 "http://www.gcf.org/v2.5"
   labels on "1994.11.05T08:15-0500"
         until "1995.12.31T23:59-0000"
           for  http://www.greatdocs.com/foo.html
     ratings (suds 0.5 density 0 color/hue 1))
 '>
 </head>…
 </HTML>
```

PICS defined a detailed set of classifications and ratings, but they were tightly coupled to specific applications. Although one of its goals was to enable different groups to create their own content rating vernacular, it lacked namespaces, which prevented a label to reference or borrow from multiple independent vocabularies. Because of this and other issues, the group decided to preserve the work that they had done in the areas of vocabularies and security in the protocol and lead the formation of the Resource Description Framework (RDF). For more information on PICS see http://www.w3.org/PICS/.

RDF is a data model and XML syntax for type description that enables definition of the relationship between two hyperlinked resources. RDF leverages the vocabulary and query protocols from PICS to relate unique resources via unique identifiers. The unique identifier in RDF is a key notion for the world of metadata. Using unique identifiers and specific means of describing them solves some of the challenges that PICS was unable to accomplish. RDF deployments use a common semantic set to identify all elements as resources, regardless of their origin, and uses *Uniform Resource Identifiers (URIs)*. In the WWW, the Uniform Resource Locator (URL) is a type of URI that describes the location and retrieval of a resource. The URI is more generic and could identify a resource that is not retrievable.

Beyond the world of resources lies the notion of *properties*. Also a URI, the property describes the elements of a resource, as well as its relationships with other resources. Like resources, properties can take a plurality of definitions and meanings, which provides immense flexibility. By explicitly separating the data from the meaning of the data, RDF provides a consistent layer of abstraction that is defined by the developer, rather than by a standards body.

In RDF, the *Resource Description Framework Schema (RDFS)* language models class and property hierarchies, as well as other primitives from the RDF model. Figure 8.1 displays RDF semantics and relationships. RDFS defines a schema that RDF documents can be checked against for consistency. RDFS support for modeling ontological concepts and relations is quite basic, and has been placed on the low end of expressiveness. RDFS does not attempt to provide the answer to all knowledge representation problems, but rather an extensible core language. This model for managing content and resources for the Web can be applied to P2P, as the challenges and issues are quite similar. For example, we can imagine that if the content being exchanged leveraged RDF, searching and discovery of content across a P2P landscape would be significantly more effective.

FIGURE 8.1
The RDF model.

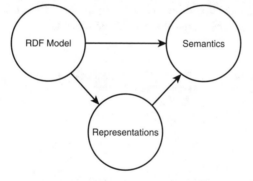

Dublin Core Metadata Initiative

As we discussed earlier, in the mid-1990s a team set out to define a set of elements that could describe any resource available online to pick up where PICS left off. By focusing on normalizing the requirements between many resources, the group intentionally avoided trying to define the semantics for specific instances. The group eventually defined 15 core metadata elements. The following is a typical example of Dublin Core metadata in HTML; <META> tags encapsulate elements from the Dublin Core:

```
<html>
  <head>
    <title>John's Book Page</title>
    <meta name="description" content="This book is about...">
    <meta name="subject" content="Computing ">
    <meta name="creator" content="John Smith ">
    <meta name="date" content="2002-01-22T00:10:00+00:00">
    <meta name="type" content="html">
    <meta name="language" content="en-us">
```

Because in HTML there is native control of the names of the elements with a <META> tag, there is the potential for ambiguity. With the Dublin Core, we can also use XML namespaces to enable the mixing of descriptive elements that are defined by individual groups without dealing with name or label issues. As each piece of data is linked to a URI, a context and definition is provided by that particular entity.

In the following example using RDF, you can see that the Dublin Core elements have a prefix of dc:, which is associated with the http://purl.org/dc/elements/1.1 namespace as indicated in the header section of the XML document:

```
<?xml version="1.0" encoding="iso-8859-1"?>
<rdf:RDF
  xmlns:rdf="http://www.w3.org/1999/02/22-rdf-syntax-ns#"
  xmlns:dc="http://purl.org/dc/elements/1.1/"
  xmlns="http://purl.org/rss/1.0/"
>
...
  <item rdf:about="http://www.foo.com/.../metadata.html">
    <title>Book</title>
    <link>http://www.foo.com/.../book.html </link>
    <dc:description>This book is about...</dc:description>
    <dc:subject>computing </dc:subject>
    <dc:creator>John Smith </dc:creator>
    <dc:date>2002-01-22T10:34:00+00:00</dc:date>
    <dc:type>book</dc:type>
    <dc:language>en-us</dc:language>
    <dc:format>text/html</dc:format>
    ...
  </item>
```

The <dc:subject> tag equates with the subject element in the dc namespace as defined at the URI http://purl.org/dc/elements/1.1. As a result, namespaces enable you to incorporate additional semantics for specific resources from a generic framework provided by the Dublin Core Metadata Initiative.

In leveraging the Dublin Core, a document does not need to incorporate all 15 elements that it defines. However, it is obvious that the more tags that are embedded in the document, the better defined the metadata. For P2P frameworks, this might result in a decrease in network resources usage, as fewer results might be returned for a specific peer's query.

Other Standards

Ontology Interchange Language (OIL) is a representation and inference layer for ontologies to represent semantics of information on the WWW. OIL synthesizes work from three different communities to provide a general-purpose markup language for the Semantic Web. These areas include the following:

- Frame-based systems—A model of using classes and properties (modeling primitives)
- Description logics—Describing knowledge as concepts (semantics)
- XML and RDF Web standards—Syntax

OIL is an early ontology representation language that is grounded in W3C standards such as RDF and XML. For more information, see `http://www.ontoknowledge.org/oil`.

The DARPA Agent Markup Language (DAML) is another emerging standing that extends RDF, XML, and OIL. By including support for bounded lists, class expressions, equivalence, and formal semantics, many architects are looking to DAML so solve complex metadata problems. For more information on DAML see `http://www.daml.org`.

Java and RDF: HP's Jena Toolkit

Jena is a Java API for manipulating RDF models that has been released into the open source community by HP Labs. Their vision of standardized representations for data (RDF) and the conceptual structures behind that data (RDFS, DAML) has been realized in the publication of Jena, an open source toolkit that implements these standards (`http://www.hpl.hp.com/semWeb/download.html`). The toolkit provides:

- Statement-centric methods for manipulating an RDF model
- Resource-centric methods for manipulating an RDF model as a set of resources with properties
- Cascading method calls for more convenient programming
- Built-in support for RDF containers
- Enhanced resources—The application can extend the behavior of resources

- Integrated parsers

To illustrate the Jena API, Listing 8.1 is a class to create, iterate over, and write out an RDF model. This example illustrates a small model, which stores information on how a person rates a book.

LISTING 8.1 Sample from HP Jena Toolkit

```
import com.hp.hpl.mesa.rdf.jena.mem.ModelMem;
import com.hp.hpl.mesa.rdf.jena.model.*;
import com.hp.hpl.mesa.rdf.jena.vocabulary.*;

import java.io.FileOutputStream;
import java.io.PrintWriter;

public class RDFGenerator extends Object {

    public static void main (String args[]) {

        // some definitions
        String personURI   = "http://somewhere/JohnSmith";
        String givenName   = "John";
        String familyName  = "Smith";
        String fullName    = givenName + " " + familyName;

        try {
            // create an empty graph
            Model model = new ModelMem();

            // create the resource
            //    and add the properties cascading style
            Resource johnSmith
              = model.createResource(personURI)
                      .addProperty(VCARD.FN, fullName)
                      .addProperty(VCARD.N,
                              model.createResource()
                                    .addProperty(VCARD.Given, givenName)
                                    .addProperty(VCARD.Family, familyName));

            // now write the model in XML form to a file
            model.write(new PrintWriter(System.out));

        } catch (Exception e) {
            System.out.println("Failed: " + e);
        }
    }
}
```

The output from the above code generates the following RDF code:

```
<rdf:RDF
  xmlns:rdf='http://www.w3.org/1999/02/22-rdf-syntax-ns#'
  xmlns:vcard='http://www.w3.org/2001/vcard-rdf/3.0#'
 >
  <rdf:Description rdf:about='http://somewhere/JohnSmith'>
    <vcard:FN>John Smith</vcard:FN>
    <vcard:N rdf:resource='#A0'/>
  </rdf:Description>
  <rdf:Description rdf:about='#A0'>
    <vcard:Given>John</vcard:Given>
    <vcard:Family>Smith</vcard:Family>
  </rdf:Description>
</rdf:RDF>
```

The RDF specifications specify how to represent RDF as XML, and we can see that representation above. Let's examine the RDF output a bit closer, and initially look at the `<rdf:RDF>` element. This element is optional, and defines the two namespaces used in the document. The `<rdf:Description>` element describes the resource whose URI is `'http://somewhere/JohnSmith'`. If the `rdf:about` attribute were missing, this element would represent a blank node. The `<vcard:FN>` element describes a property of the resource and the property name is the FN in the `vcard` namespace. RDF converts this to a URI reference by concatenating the URI reference for the namespace prefix and `FN`, the local name part of the name. In this example, this gives a URI reference of `'http://www.w3.org/2001/vcard-rdf/3.0#FN'`. More detail can be found at `www.w3.org/TR/rdf-primer` in regards to the XML representation of RDF.

XML and Metadata in P2P Systems: Applications

Now that we have reviewed the basics of XML and metadata, the application areas that are beneficial for P2P frameworks may seem evident. Core areas for leveraging XML and metadata in P2P systems include messaging, content management, data storage, and software distribution.

Messaging

Although messaging is nothing more than communication between peers, XML offers a platform-neutral format for sending short structured messages between peers for communication or exchanging content. The use of XML messages allows for many different kinds of peers to discover, participate, and communicate with each other. Many P2P frameworks like Napster and Gnutella have their own protocols for communication. If these two frameworks need to exchange data, using XML in the underlying protocol for each will solve this integration issue quite easily, provided there is a "translation," using XSLT or something like it. Thus, different applications that work on different platforms and talk different message dialects can interact and exchange information by using this stylesheet to convert between disparate formats. The mapping requirements in order to build these stylesheets require an understanding of both protocols' message formats and vocabularies, but once achieved, they provide a powerful message exchange medium. XML can also be leveraged at the messaging layer to broadcast metadata to a peer group. This example is embodied in JXTA by advertisements that can be represented in XML.

Content Management

Enterprises often manage data within their environments via either a centralized portal or replicated servers. *Web portals* are centralized hubs that present data for companies and their respective suppliers or partners in a single user interface; in order to share data, participants must somehow get it onto the portal. This cumbersome approach not only requires significant maintenance, but is also disruptive to work processes that require data to remain in its original locations. *Replicated servers* is a system wherein each corporation or department uses its own server for storing information; periodically, each server must synchronize with or replicate its data to each of the other servers. This has a disadvantage for the user who wants to see recent data; he might not be looking at the most up-to-date information because of the synchronization schedules or because of network partitioning or other connectivity issues.

By moving to a P2P framework, decentralized access to content in its native format becomes a reality. As the content can remain on the respective servers, more granular control of the information can be applied. To construct such a framework, a robust technology foundation and an effective search engine construct is required in order to discover the information, and then subsequently orchestrate how the information is accessed. The initial stage of discovery is a key area for the role of metadata in P2P frameworks.

XML As Data Sources

In most IT environments, data is stored in one of two ways. The first method uses custom or unstructured data formats. A second approach uses a relational database to store the information and manage the relationships between the data records. Because true P2P systems have no central server for managing information between peers, efficiently distributing and storing application data for peer access is not a trivial task. Data often has to reside locally on the peer for processing; XML provides for a simple and lightweight interchange format suitable for network transmission.

XML As P2P Application Deployment Model

As the number of peers in a P2P network expands, the issues with application deployment dramatically increase. One XML-based solution to this problem is the *Open Software Description Model (OSD)*. OSD files enable system architects to define the application components required for peer applications, along with the locations to download these components and any component dependencies. Each peer can verify that it has the most recent software components and automatically download upgrades if needed. The goal of the OSD format is to provide an XML-based vocabulary for describing software packages and their interdependencies, whether it is peer initiated (*pulled*), or automated (*pushed*). Using an XML data model, the markup tags in the OSD vocabulary are represented as elements of a tree. Effectively integrating OSD files into a P2P deployment strategy shifts the burden of software upgrades from the user to the P2P application itself.

Searching Across Peers

In the current P2P world, systems have provided for simple keyword searches but not much more. Gnutella's Infrasearch, for example, enables multiple term definition and processing. Thus, you can search for multiple terms concurrently across a space to locate a match. The Infrasearch model enables simple searches to be executed without significant capabilities to place constraints on the search field. Although Freenet has the capability to couple a metadata file to a piece of content within its P2P network, it does not currently enable searching across a document. The structure of the information in the document is also left up to the user, which often means reverting to the <META> tag issue in HTML.

P2P applications have successfully defined search mechanisms for special cases such as file exchange, which we have discussed using Napster as an example. However, retrieving "all songs by Sting" does not require complex query languages or complex metadata, so special purpose formats for these P2P applications have been sufficient. By concentrating on domain-specific formats, current P2P implementations appear to be fragmenting into niche markets instead of developing unifying mechanisms for future P2P applications.

Edutella

The Edutella open source project (http://edutella.jxta.org/) is attempting to address some of the shortcomings of current P2P applications by building on the W3C RDF metadata standard. The project is an effort to deploy an RDF-based metadata infrastructure for P2P-networks based on the recently announced JXTA framework. The initial services that this framework will be providing include the following:

- Query service—Standardized query and retrieval of RDF metadata.
- Replication service—Provide data persistence/availability and workload balancing while maintaining data integrity and consistency.
- Mapping service—Translate between different metadata vocabularies to enable interoperability between different peers.
- Annotation service—Annotate materials stored anywhere in the Edutella Network.

The first application is a P2P network for the exchange of educational resources between German universities, Swedish universities, Stanford University, and others. By linking heterogeneous educational resources across this academic framework, the project aims to enable a user to easily discover content simply and efficiently.

Edutella's generic framework of unique ontologies for different domains that still interrelate will certainly be the winning solution to the metadata challenge in the P2P world.

Summary

Although the client/server model of the WWW can survive with weak support for metadata, P2P architecture must have a mature metadata model to succeed. To date, P2P frameworks have developed their own metadata model that is typically domain-specific, already leading to fragmentation. Efforts like the Edutella project are working toward building a common data model, leveraging standards such as XML, RDF and DAML to solve this problem. The key metadata and P2P framework issues are

- Describe resources clearly and concisely using a standardized model (such as RDF).
- Define the unique ontology for the domain with standards in mind (DAML, OIL).
- Don't let history repeat itself—HTML and the WWW can give us insight into the challenges to be faced if the metadata problem is not addressed.

Integration and Interoperability

by Michael Abbott

IN THIS CHAPTER

Integration means different things in different contexts. In software engineering, for example, integration typically refers to the act of taking modules that have been developed separately (often in isolation from each other) and making them work together as a system—or at least attempting to.

Integration in the context of networked or distributed systems (and hence P2P systems) is fundamentally about communication. The need to tie or link systems to each other so that each can use the other's services and functionality or pass messages to each other drives much of today's IT work. Many of the most interesting problems in distributed systems arise from the need to integrate disparate systems, and many of the most innovative architectures and system design paradigms come from creative solutions to difficult integration problems.

Some of the things that make integration difficult and interesting include the following:

- The systems that need to be integrated are typically heterogeneous; that is, they run on different platforms (different hardware and/or different operating systems).

- Different network languages (protocols or transports) might need to be used. For example, an application that only understands HTTP might need to be linked or integrated to a system that only understands FTP. One of these applications must learn to speak the other's language, otherwise a proxy or intermediary must be used between the two applications to translate.

- Multiple businesses or vendors might be involved. In addition to the complicated matters of platform and network transport that must be dealt with, each organization might have their own integration methodology and preferred set of tools or vendors (not to mention financial or organizational agendas). Integration is sometimes a social engineering problem.

In this chapter, we provide an overview of and commentary on common integration technologies and issues, and how they relate to P2P.

From Sockets to Distributed Objects: Integration Transports

Once upon a time, if a programmer wanted one program to talk to another across a network, the choices were limited. The most common way to accomplish this used to be communication endpoint mechanisms called *sockets*, sometimes called *TCP sockets* or *BSD sockets*. The metaphor is straightforward: a socket exists on each end, and you plug each end of your (virtual) communication circuit into one of the sockets, and then the two sockets talk to each other. Sockets are still one of the most efficient and frequently used communication mechanisms, and are often considered to be fairly low-level programming constructs. Most higher-level or simpler communication APIs, regardless of programming language, are built on top of sockets. This includes many Java networking APIs.

With distributed communication, as with most other engineering challenges, there is more than one way to do it. Over the last few years there has been a change in how programmers think about network communication, a shift that parallels the shift in programming methodologies from structured or imperative languages like C, Pascal, and COBOL to object-oriented languages like C++, Smalltalk, and Java. Now, network programmers are just as likely to think about "distributed objects" or "remote service interfaces" as they are to think about sockets. It is sometimes nice to be able to treat an object or service that is "somewhere out there" on the Internet as if it were part of your program, running on the same computer (if only things were truly that simple). CORBA, Java RMI, DCOM, Web services, and now P2P each provide different ways to think about distributed communication.

The hows and whys of network communication are of very real importance in integration. There are different styles of communication, each with its own set of advantages, disadvantages, and caveats. Sometimes the choice of what communication style to use will be made for you by virtue of the systems or applications that are to be integrated.

Distributed Object Protocols: Object-Oriented Communication

Distributed object protocols extend object-oriented programming ideas to network programming. With distributed objects, an object running in a process space in a remote location—on a different computer across the network—appears as if it were running locally. Methods or functions can be called on the remote object, treating it no differently than if it truly were local. (This is not the whole truth, as we'll discuss later in this chapter.)

The location transparency achieved with distributed objects is intended to simplify life for the network programmer. Often this is the case—distributed objects represent significant "syntactic sugar" to the programmer; that is, network communication can be achieved with significantly less work on the part of the programmer. However, there is often performance overhead associated with distributed object protocols, and sometimes the infrastructure and configuration required to achieve location transparency of objects is more trouble than it's worth. We'll discuss some distributed object protocols—specifically CORBA, Java RMI, DCOM, and Web services—in a bit more detail later in this chapter.

Distributed object systems generally share some basic ideas. There is usually some notion of a proxy, or *stub* that the client of a remote object uses to invoke method calls on that object. There is also the notion of a server-side proxy, sometimes called a *skeleton*, that is the corresponding server-side proxy for the client. Method arguments or parameters are collected and transformed into a form suitable for sending over the wire, a process called *marshalling*. You can think of marshalling as a kind of "dehydrating" process. At the server side, the method arguments are "rehydrated," or demarshalled back into the proper form for handling by the remote object. In CORBA and Java RMI, the client stub is called the stub or proxy, and the server stub is called the skeleton. In DCOM, the client stub is the proxy and the server stub is the stub.

When you're building network-aware applications in Java, it's natural to consider distributed object protocols like Java RMI for communication.

Java is an object-oriented programming language, and so depending on the requirements and constraints of the application, an object-oriented communication protocol might be desirable. P2P systems built in Java are no exception.

Integrate To...What?

It is interesting to consider just what the targets of integration are. What kinds of systems do new applications need to link or tie into, and what kind of information is passed between integrated applications and between peers?

Accounting systems built in the 1970s might need to be WWW-enabled. New human resources (HR) or customer relationship management (CRM) applications written in Java might need to communicate with an insurance company's Oracle-based database systems. There is a wide range of hardware, operating systems, and programming languages out there, and each type might need to talk to another.

Legacy Systems (Run the World)

The term *legacy systems* is at the same time useful and a bit unfortunate. Many people associate the word "legacy" with old, slow, awkward, proprietary information systems held together with spit and rubber bands. There is perhaps some truth to this, but here's a secret—legacy systems, including mainframe computers, run the world. In some ways there is no such thing as legacy systems, just older or newer information systems. The now ubiquitous PC-based Linux or Windows servers running Java application servers are a very recent addition to the computing world.

Many integration efforts focus on proprietary or custom computer systems. They might have difficult or unsupported programming interfaces—actually, if a programming interface exists at all, that's a bonus, and if a network-programming interface exists, it's cause for celebration! Many might have been developed internally by the organization that uses them, or were perhaps cobbled together in COBOL or Fortran. Documentation may or may not exist. This is just as true for applications built yesterday as for systems built 20 years ago.

Building communication bridges or adapters to such systems is one of the more interesting parts of integration efforts. Communicating with legacy applications runs the spectrum from using the file system itself to pass information, to actually being able to use more recent, Internet-oriented transports like TCP sockets or HTTP, to using email to pass messages, or even using nice Java network APIs like JMS or RMI.

The Problem of Syntax and Semantics

A significant problem when linking disparate systems is that of data or interchange formats. As mentioned later in our discussion of EDI, there simply isn't a single standard. This means that integrating two applications might require not only building adapters or bridges for network protocols, but also building data translation or transformation components. The rapidly increasing use of XML will also help this situation, but syntax or format alone is unfortunately not the only problem.

When a native Language 1 speaker communicates with a native Language 2 speaker, each might be able to translate words literally so that the other can understand what is being said, but the meaning might not translate without some added contextual information. A concept in one language and culture might not even exist in the other. In other words, there might be a conceptual gap that syntax alone cannot bridge. This semantic gap is a more serious problem than, say, the problem of translating between nice human-readable XML and nasty machine-readable binary data.

In these situations, often the only way to solve the problem is to get enough information from experts in the different systems or applications to be able to bridge that gap in a reproducible manner. After all, the solution must be able to be carried out by a computer. This again is where integration can be a social engineering endeavor. Negotiation and compromise are integration tools.

9

INTEGRATION AND
INTEROPERABILITY

Common Integration Protocols and Systems

Various protocols and standards have emerged over the past several decades in computing to address the challenges of distributed computing. From EDI to SOAP, we will review how various technologies work, and you will be able to see how certain advances with standards and implementation languages have shaped this evolution. In Chapters 3 and 4, we began an early study of RMI and CORBA, and in this chapter we will expand our analysis of integration to include other approaches as well. We will then discuss how these protocols are being used in the P2P domain in some cases.

The Sturdy Veteran: EDI

Electronic Data Interchange (EDI) is commonly defined as direct computer-to-computer transfer of business information. This information can include purchase orders, invoices, planning messages, shipping and receiving notices, payments, scheduling messages, and so on. EDI is a venerable technology (it's about 30 years old); it could be considered the first and most important (and maybe the most successful) integration technology. EDI is widely used in nearly every industry, up to and including health care and insurance, across the globe. The format and rules for EDI documents or transactions are governed by standards: ANSI X.12, used mainly in North America, and UN/EDIFACT, used worldwide.

EDI came into use at a time when every byte sent across the network mattered—because each was expensive. The documents that make up EDI transactions were thus made to be compact, concise, and machine-friendly. It is not pleasant to read an EDI document, but it was not really the intention that someone read them. In practice, it is sometimes necessary to trace problems in EDI documents, and that might mean reading and understanding "raw" EDI.

EDI was intended to solve a number of the problems with "human integration"; that is, the exchange of business information and transactions via mail, fax, and phone. And for the most part, it has been very successful—after thirty years, it is still in widespread use, while many companies promising "modern EDI" or "Internet EDI" technologies have tried and failed.

One of EDI's main strengths is also (strangely enough) one of its biggest problems. EDI documents and protocols (how the documents are exchanged) must adhere to a common standard. Standard formats and protocols are a good thing. Therein lies the EDI problem: It is the non-standard standard. Each pair of organizations that shares data via EDI does things a little differently. For example, a pair of trading partners might decide that the first address in an EDI purchase order will be used for the billing address, and the second will be used for the shipping address. This is a private agreement that may or may not adhere to recommendations for how that EDI document should be used. This is fine, but when a third trading partner comes into the picture, that same agreement must be negotiated yet again, perhaps with compromises made for the needs of the new partner.

This is not a unique occurrence—it's common practice. This is why EDI works well once all the bugs are worked out of the process, but getting to that point is…well, let's just say we're back to the social engineering problem. This problem has represented a wealth of opportunity for products and services focused around EDI data translation and communication—this is integration at its roots.

EDI predates widespread usage of the Internet, and companies needed to get these electronic documents to each other somehow. There were some options, which in fact are still active and viable transports, although the use of the Internet has for reasons of availability and cost since become one of the preferred EDI transport mechanisms.

Value Added Networks (VANs) are companies that provide communications services for EDI customers: message store-and-forwarding, electronic mail boxes, and so on are typically offered. VANs are essentially "EDI ISPs." Leased lines are another common method of connecting EDI business partners. A leased line is a dedicated telephone line or cable leased directly from a telephone or telecommunications company. Leased lines provide dedicated, reliable bandwidth for communications. Leased lines are generally not subject to the kinds of outages that sometimes plague ISPs.

XML-ified/HTTP-ified EDI: Is This Web Services?

As mentioned previously, EDI is not pleasant to read. The document formats make sense, but they were designed to be concise, machine-readable, and easily parsed. When integrating newer, WWW-enabled applications to EDI systems, it is tempting to simply "XML-ify" the EDI document formats you want to send and receive. In such cases, the XML version of an EDI document will be received from another application—perhaps through a WWW server, generated from an HTML form via CGI or Java Servlets, or JSP.

This is not necessarily a bad thing, but this type of interoperation is not really Web services in action. Often what happens is that once the XML is received and is parsed, a true EDI document (that is, non-XML) will be created and used for processing. Actually, this might be a good way to introduce new ideas and technologies to an integration partner that is used to doing things one way (in this case EDI) and only that way. Integrating with EDI can require a good dose of social engineering; as much time might be spent negotiating with and educating trading partners as is spent in the actual technical work.

Java RMI

Java Remote Method Invocation (RMI) is a way of invoking methods on Java objects in a different or remote process space, as we learned in Chapter 2. RMI is a distributed object system that enables networked or distributed applications to be built in Java quickly and relatively easily, and (mostly) enables programmers to use the same semantics they are used to with local or nondistributed applications. RMI handles all the nasty parts of dealing with network communication, enabling the programmer to just deal with the problems at hand. RMI is a Java-only technology; if one needs to integrate Java applications with non-Java applications, RMI alone will not do the job.

As in most distributed object schemes, the RMI networking subsystem uses stubs and skeletons to proxy clients and servers for each other. In RMI, each stub represents an actual object. This means that object reference semantics can extend between JVMs, permitting distributed garbage collection and leasing to take place. These very interesting topics are beyond the scope of this chapter, but they are recommended reading.

Also as with other distributed object systems, RMI has the notion of remote interfaces, which are the sets of method signatures used to interact with remote objects. RMI also has a built-in lookup service and a naming service, but no automated discovery mechanism as in Jini and other service-oriented architectures.

RMI has a feature that enables some exciting and otherwise very difficult things to be done: Object and class definitions can be passed across the network via RMI, essentially allowing code itself to be mobile. You can actually make your applications send and receive new types of objects, which enable things like dynamic library updates and mobile agent-like behavior.

However, you need to be aware of what kind of object you're passing in a remote method call: a remote-capable object (an object that objects in other JVMs can invoke remote methods on), or a local object that is accessible only within the same JVM. The semantics make a difference here; a local object will be passed *by copy*—this means that a copy of the local object will be created, and marshalled for sending to the remote server. In the remote JVM, the copy might be acted upon, but nothing that happens there will directly affect the original in the local JVM. When passing a remote-capable object, the remote representation of the object is actually being passed—that is, the stub. The methods accessible on the remote object are RMI remote methods, thus changes made to it in the remote JVM will possibly (depending on the way that object works) affect the object in the originating JVM. This is often the desired behavior.

Let's see a very simple example of Java mobile agents that illustrates what happens when an object is passed by copy in RMI. Agents are simple objects with a humble role in life: Select a RemoteAgentServer in its itinerary (the Agent's itinerary is a list of IP addresses or hostnames of RemoteAgentServers), get a remote handle or reference to that RemoteAgentServer, and send itself to the selected RemoteAgentServer. A RemoteAgentServer, on the other hand, maintains a list of Agents that have visited it, and when an Agent visits it, it adds the new Agent to its list and simply prints the list of hosts that Agent has visited.

Here is the RemoteAgentServer's rather simple interface:

```
public interface RemoteAgentServer extends java.rmi.Remote {
    public void accept(Agent remoteAgent) throws java.rmi.RemoteException;
}
```

The RemoteAgentServer has a single method: accept(), which takes an Agent object as a parameter. Here is the code for the accept() method in the RemoteAgentServerImpl, the concrete class that actually implements the RemoteAgentServer interface:

```
public void accept(Agent remoteAgent) {
    agentsAccepted.addElement(remoteAgent.getAgentName());
    remoteAgent.go();
    ArrayList hostsVisited = remoteAgent.getHostsVisited();
    for (int i = 0; i < hostsVisited.size(); i++) {
      System.out.println("Host "+ (i+1)
         +":"hostsVisited.get(i));
    }
  } // accept()
```

Simple, eh? The RemoteAgentServerImpl simply adds the Agent to its list and calls go() (which sends the Agent on its way to the next host on its itinerary) on the Agent, then prints the hosts that the Agent has visited. Here is the Agent's go() method:

```
public void go() {
    String nextHost = itinerary.get(0);
    hostsVisited.add(nextHost);
    itinerary.remove(0);
    try {
        /* get the remote reference to the next server;
         * this would be a good place for error handling.*/
➥RemoteAgentServer agentServer =  (RemoteAgentServer)
➥Naming.lookup("rmi://" + nextHost +"/RemoteAgentServer");
        /* send myself to the next RemoteAgentServer! */
➥agentServer.accept(this);
    } catch (Exception e) {
      e.printStackTrace();
    }
  } // go()
```

This is nearly as simple as the RemoteAgentServer's accept() method.

We see the Agent do a bit of bookkeeping with its itinerary, and then access the next RemoteAgentServer in its itinerary via RMI's naming service. (Usage of RMI's naming service is an interesting topic in its own right, but is not detailed here.) The interesting part is the call to accept(), where we see that the Agent passes itself as a parameter using Java's `this` keyword. `accept()` is a remote method; however, `Agent` objects are not RMI remote objects. Thus a *copy* of the `Agent` is passed to the `RemoteAgentServer` (which is why the `Agent` does its bookkeeping before it calls `accept()`). If the `RemoteAgentServer` actually did some manipulation or modification, the `Agent` at the originating host would not be changed.

RMI is a nice Java-only distributed object technology that is part of the core of the Java platform. It's always available to the Java programmer, and enables distributed applications to be built quickly and easily. But, as with anything else, it's not a silver bullet. There are JVM and code versioning issues that sometimes must be taken into account, and there is also the problem of making RMI-based applications work across firewalls. As in other networking technologies, RMI has advantages, disadvantages, and caveats that must be understood in order to use it effectively. Builders of Java P2P systems, for example, might use RMI to get the network communication job done, but would need to create their own peer discovery system, as RMI does not have this facility.

CORBA

CORBA, the Common Object Request Broker Architecture (quite an acronym), is an open and vendor-independent architecture and infrastructure that enables language-neutral network communication, as we learned in an introductory manner in Chapter 5. Basically, CORBA is the granddaddy of middleware platforms. CORBA is a distributed object scheme that uses Interface Definition Language (IDL), a kind of "language proxy," to specify how remote objects should interact with each other. The Object Management Group (OMG) is a consortium of companies that oversees CORBA specifications and compliance (in addition to other interoperation initiatives or specifications, such as UML).

CORBA has been used for years with varying levels of success—many of CORBA's ideas have influenced more modern or recent distributed object systems, such as Java RMI. For example, using a client and server proxy scheme (stubs and skeletons) is a concept used in CORBA. Remote method invocations and the marshalling/demarshalling of method arguments is specified in CORBA.

The key to the CORBA architecture is the ORB—the Object Request Broker. The ORB is essentially an "object bus" through which remote CORBA clients interact with each other. Acting as a central controller, the ORB is responsible for locating a remote CORBA object's actual implementation, and brokering remote method calls between it and its clients.

IDL enables inter-language unification (a fancy way to say you're probably able to use your preferred language for CORBA). CORBA interfaces are described in IDL, and each language mapping translates the concepts laid out in IDL for a particular interface or service. IDL compilers for each language are mapped to take IDL and produce language-specific constructs code that is then compiled, linked, and so on, depending on the language you're using.

Here's the classic Hello World, CORBA style, done in IDL:

```
module HelloWorld {
    interface HiThere {
        string helloWorld();
    };
};
```

A CORBA module declaration maps to a Java package—thus, this example would correspond to the Java package `HelloWorld`. The interface defined would correspond to the Java interface `HelloWorld.HiThere` (fully qualified, with the package name). The `HiThere` interface has a single (remote!) method, `helloWorld()`, which returns a `string` (a `String` in Java), and does not raise or throw any exceptions.

The following is a list (not necessarily comprehensive) of languages with IDL mappings:

- Java
- C
- C++
- Ada
- COBOL
- SmallTalk
- Python

CORBA Services and Facilities

CORBA Services (COS) are a major part of CORBA's infrastructure and specification. They are a set of distributed object services built on top of the CORBA ORB to support the integration and interoperation of CORBA objects. CORBA Services are considered fundamental to constructing distributed applications with CORBA, and are thus viewed as independent of specific application semantics or domains. Some examples of CORBA Services include the following:

- Naming Service—Provides context-oriented namespace services; similar naming/namespace facilities are a common characteristic of distributed object architectures.
- Property Service—Provides a service-based approach to dealing with configuration

or property information. It provides the capability to associate values with objects and create and/or manipulate sets of name-value pairs or name-value-mode tuples.

- Event Service—Provides a channel or route for events or event-related data to be sent between event "producers" and event "consumers."

- Time Service—Permits a CORBA object to obtain the "current time," along with an error estimation that might be associated with it.

- (Object) Query Service—Provides query operations on collections of objects. This includes not only read-only queries, but also general manipulative operations such as insertion, deletion, and updating collections of objects.

The CORBA Facilities, or *Common Facilities*, are a group of services intended for common use by any CORBA objects or applications, but are not considered to be as fundamental to CORBA as COS.

P2P developers or architects might see CORBA as a solution for the hybrid-P2P models (such as Napster) because of its discovery, transactional, and strong interoperability features. Because of the complexity of the specification and the loose definition of certain components of the ORB, CORBA has not gained significant traction in the enterprise model. It is unlikely that CORBA will be leveraged in a significant number of P2P architectures.

DCOM

DCOM, or Distributed COM, is Microsoft's distributed component or distributed object system (COM stands for Component Object Model). Often called "COM on the wire," DCOM supports remote objects by running on a protocol called the Object Remote Procedure Call (ORPC). The ORPC layer is built on top of DCE RPC (RPC is a venerable remote procedure call system) and interacts with COM's runtime services. As long as COM is available on a platform, DCOM can be used there as well.

DCOM is built on top of COM, which has gone through various incarnations as Dynamic Data Exchange, Object Linking and Embedding, COM itself, and ActiveX, or Internet-oriented COM. DCOM features the usual suspects. Stubs and skeletons are present, or in DCOM parlance, proxy on the client side, and stub on the server- or component-side. DCOM also features object activation, which is the capability for a new remote object or component to be created as the result of client calls, a very useful feature that both RMI and CORBA also provide.

Like CORBA, DCOM claims language neutrality, and in practice, for the Java practitioner there is several Java-COM bridges that permit interoperability between Java objects and COM/DCOM objects. C++, Visual Basic, Delphi, and COBOL among other languages also work with COM/DCOM. Heavily used on Microsoft's platforms, DCOM is also available for Unix and Linux, and for mainframe platforms as well.

P2P developers or architects might see DCOM more or less in the same category as CORBA, perhaps with less interoperability. Java developers might be less interested than others due on the one hand to the wealth of more Java-friendly tools available, and on the other hand to Microsoft's openly hostile attitude towards Java.

Web Services, XML-RPC, and SOAP

Web services, SOAP, and XML-RPC are the buzzwords du jour. Actually, they might represent a major shift in software applications and interoperability, something of more than a little interest to anyone concerned with integration. We briefly introduce Web services and SOAP in Chapter 4, and they are discussed in greater depth in Part III of this book, so we'll just skim over the top a bit here—integrators should at least be aware of the concepts and options available for Web services.

First some basics: What are Web services? They are self-contained, modular applications or services that can be described, located, and activated or invoked across the Internet. Some consider Web services to be another attempt at distributed objects. This school of thought sometimes considers CORBA, DCOM, RMI, and Enterprise JavaBeans failures because they're too heavyweight, tightly coupled, and platform-, language-, or company-centric.

Usually, when discussing Web services, we mean platform- and language-neutral, light-weight, XML-based applications that use HTTP for a network transport, and generally enable the publish/find/bind cycle. Service builders or providers *publish* service definitions or interface descriptions (using a neutral description format such as an XML dialect) to a service registry or brokerage. Service consumers or users *find* the services using the service registry. They then *bind* them, meaning they map requests for specific data or functionality to the service interface they found via the service registry or brokerage.

Web services can be viewed as the next step in an intelligent evolution of software architectures toward more modular, loosely coupled, technology-independent systems that are easy to build by composing discrete chunks of software...okay, maybe you've heard this one before. Perhaps it is another go at distributed objects. But for the first time, open and standards-based technology are driving the evolution; and considering the widespread adoption among such movers and shakers as Microsoft, IBM, Sun, Oracle, et. al., there is a good chance that much or most of the distributed application development over the next few years will use Web services. P2P systems are no exception—the publish/find/bind

9

INTEGRATION AND
INTEROPERABILITY

cycle is very useful for distributed peer computing systems.

XML-RPC is a remote procedure call technology that uses HTTP as the transport and XML as the encoding language. It's designed to be simple and lightweight, enabling programming language-independent method or function calls to be sent across the network.

From the XML-RPC specification at Userland's `www.xmlrpc.com`:

> XML-RPC is a Remote Procedure Calling protocol that works over the Internet.
>
> An XML-RPC message is an HTTP-POST request. The body of the request is in XML. A procedure executes on the server and the value it returns is also formatted in XML.
>
> Procedure parameters can be scalars, numbers, strings, dates, and so on; and can also be complex record and list structures.

SOAP is a more complex or comprehensive version of XML-RPC (okay, let the tar and feathering start—some people bristle when they hear that definition).

SOAP probably has the upper hand because it's the preferred Web services transport. XML-RPC represents a shorter path for the developer that wants to use a simple HTTP-based XML procedure call mechanism without dealing with the power or complexity of SOAP.

If we return our focus on P2P architectures, we can imagine a peer whereby it runs both as a client/server, depending upon the role that it is playing during a conversation with another peer. In this case, servers are now talking with other servers as peers, but in different roles. We can see how some of the classic distributed computing protocols and newer ones like SOAP can be applied to these new software architectures.

Other Systems

Beyond the approaches that we have reviewed, we must also recognize that the IT landscape is quickly changing as vendors attempt to solve many of the distributed computing problems. It's likely that other systems and standards will emerge that will bridge the gaps in interoperability.

Summary

In this chapter we surveyed a variety of technologies that are commonly used in the practice of integrating or linking different systems and applications together.

Integration is very much concerned with network or distributed communication, and so many of the technologies used are also used in building P2P systems.

P2P Security

by Alan Moffet and Robert Flenner

CHAPTER 10

With all the chatting and sharing going on, peer-to-peer computing sounds friendly, almost neighborly. Exchange some information? Borrow a few computing cycles? How about your credit card number? Obviously there are limits to what we want to be able to share, or whom we want to trust. We want to protect ourselves and the things we value, such as our property.

In this respect, peer-to-peer computing does not offer any challenges beyond those presented by ordinary networked computing. However, when thinking about how to implement the mechanisms for identifying, authenticating, and authorizing users across a widely distributed and often changing network, peer-to-peer systems have unique requirements that come with their own set of challenges.

In this chapter, we will examine the issues and technological solutions that are common to network computing as well as the additional considerations brought about by peer-to-peer computing.

Security Requirements

Security in computer systems consists broadly of the following:

- Establishing a base of things that we trust, which constitute little or no risk—those things that we do not have to worry about
- Taking precautions that protect us from either malicious or accidental acts
- A combination of these things

For example, on a personal computer at home, members of the family are allowed to use the computer—they can run software, open or modify documents, and may be allowed to change the configuration by modifying settings or installing new software. If there are children in the family, a set of restrictions may be applied to safeguard the system, the information, or the children themselves: they are given a set of programs they can run, they may not be allowed to install new software, or they may need to be supervised while surfing the Internet. If the computer is connected to the Internet, it is likely that the system is safeguarded by additional constraints, such as preventing external users from accessing the system at all through the use of a firewall.

In this example, as in many other scenarios, there are two significant components that work together to build secure systems—identity and availability. Being able to identify a user permits us to define what that user is allowed to do. We can make information or system resources available to users in a way that does not compromise security. Typically, this is performed by authorizing trusted identities to use system resources.

In networked systems, where the participants are often unknown to or separated from one another, authenticity and integrity make up a large part of the equation for a secure system. Authenticity proves the identity and origin of something, whereas integrity provides the assurance that it has not been altered.

In both cases, the issue of confidentiality is almost always important. *Confidentiality* ensures that information or resources are only revealed to approved parties.

Finally, as users or systems interact with one another, it often becomes necessary for them to prove that an act occurred or a commitment was made. *Nonrepudiation* is the property of a system that enables it to do this.

Modern computing systems include mechanisms to meet these needs. However, because the Internet is a system of independent, interconnected systems, for the most part security has been localized to the systems themselves or the intranets they are connected to. As they begin to work in a peer-to-peer fashion, the systems will have to work together to provide scaled-up secure services between themselves.

Network Identity

Identity is fundamental to the other components of security. *Identity* can be thought of as a collection of attributes that collectively represent a person or object uniquely. A significant amount of effort has been expended on technologies that store, validate, or verify identity.

Identity is important to many aspects of distributed computing. For the most part, it simply isn't possible to ignore the personal side of users. Users have preferences and rights, and their own credit card numbers—thereby having the capacity to enter into personal agreements with other users or organizations.

Although quite a bit of the Internet is "anonymous," more and more of it requires some knowledge of the user to provide customizable services, or to provide an environment that is secure.

> **Note**
>
> Because identity is so personal, it is the subject of considerable interest and debate. As you will learn later, privacy and anonymity are as important a security consideration as being able to identify a user.

10

P2P Security

In today's Internet, users must establish identities for each of the systems they interact with in a personal and often secure way. At the least, the identities consist of a user ID and a password, which is used to authenticate the user. Rather than having identities on each system that a user interacts with, a network identity can represent a user across an entire domain. The same identity will be useful to all the systems in the network.

Because of the dynamic nature of peer-to-peer systems, using identities is a particularly interesting problem. If identity is associated with the right to access a resource, it becomes necessary for every peer to understand how to validate an identity, and to associate it with the services a peer provides. Network identities can help reduce the burden a peer faces in managing and using identities or validating them. It's also possible to perform authorization at the network level, so that peers do not have to maintain lists of rights. You'll see how this can happen later in the chapter.

Several other challenges exist in connection with identity. For example, the attributes that are selected to represent something must be unique within the domain—searching for "Bubba Smith" in the state of Texas using Infospace.com yields 11 individuals. Without additional information, it's difficult to know which is the one you're looking for. On the other hand, the information that composes an identity should not be too revealing. Also, an identity is not a person or an object—it only represents one. It's possible to possess or create an identity that is not your own. In the rest of the chapter, we will learn how identity is used, managed, and protected.

Foundations of Security

As mentioned earlier in the chapter, secure systems require several components that work together to provide an environment that is safe. An environment that is safe is made up of elements that are trustworthy, combined with other things that protect us from dangerous objects or that we simply do not know much about. Such systems include policies that establish rules, and mechanisms that are used to implement the functions or services required by the policies.

The set of services that are commonly available to secure systems are

- Identification
- Authentication
- Authorization
- Integrity
- Confidentiality
- Nonrepudiation

- Monitoring/auditing
- Security management

In computer systems, many of the mechanisms used to establish secure systems are built on the foundations of cryptography.

Cryptography

Part of the larger mathematical discipline of cryptology (from the Greek *kryptos logos*, meaning "hidden word"), cryptography has become more than the science of hiding and recovering information. Cryptography extends to include many more aspects of communication, including most of the services mentioned previously. Ronald Rivest, co-creator of the RSA algorithms and a number of other important security products, said that "Cryptology is about communication in the presence of adversaries." Cryptography is the branch of cryptology that concerns itself with the enforcement of security. Its sibling, cryptanalysis, is dedicated to defeating cryptographic mechanisms.

The most common use of cryptography is for communicating privately or for protecting information by transforming data into a state that is useless without a function or key to return it to a meaningful state. Peer-to-peer systems have many uses for cryptography, such as hiding information exchanged between instant message peers. The process of transforming meaningful data, called plaintext, into useless ciphertext is called *encryption*. The reverse process is called *decryption*. Functions that perform encryption and decryption are sometimes known as *ciphers*.

> **Note**
>
> Interestingly enough, the word *cipher* has an ancient origin, with an associated meaning of "to be empty"—in the case of cryptography, that can be taken to mean "void of meaning."

Early schemes depended on the secrecy of cryptographic functions or their workings (*algorithms*) to protect information. More useful functions introduced *keys*, or additional data, into the mixture. These ciphers code and decode information, using one or more keys whose values contribute to the result. Cryptographic keys perform the same function that household keys do for doors—having the correct key provides access to the information. Most of us can recall having seen pictures of early padlocks with keys of simple design. These worked well when only a few people owned locks and keys. As more people acquired keys (or became proficient in bypassing the mechanisms of the locks), it became necessary to develop more sophisticated locks and keys. Similarly, cryptography has progressed from simple functions and keys to very sophisticated functions with complex keys.

Cryptosystems

In studying any cryptographic service, there are a number of identifiable elements that constitute a system that provides the service. A *cryptosystem* consists of the following:

- A set of cryptographic functions
- A set of keys (a *keyset*)
- The set of all possible plaintexts
- The set of all possible ciphertexts

Secret Key Cryptography

Secret key cryptography is also known as symmetric key cryptography, because the same key is used in both encrypting and decrypting operations. After the plaintext is encoded using the key, anyone who wants to decrypt the ciphertext must know the value of the key used to produce the ciphertext. Symmetric key algorithms use the key to combine with and permute the plaintext. They frequently are designed to work with operations that are performed quickly using hardware, such as the addition and exclusive—or operations. Cryptographers design functions that obscure information by doing things such as removing natural patterns while preserving the capability to recover the plaintext. Although it is beyond the scope of this book to get into the details of algorithms, you can be assured that you can find an algorithm resistant enough for your needs from among those that have been developed thus far.

The length of a key is often significant to producing ciphertext that is resistant to *cracking*, or the attempt to decipher encrypted text without possessing the key. If the algorithm is well designed, a *brute-force* attack may be required, wherein keys from the keyset are applied to the ciphertext until meaningful plaintext appears. Larger keysets generally make it more difficult to guess what key is the right one. This also makes it possible for more than one key to produce something that might be meaningful, yet different enough from the other results that it casts doubt on all of them.

The numbers of bits in a key determine the number of possible keys. A key that is composed of n bits will produce a keyspace of 2^n possible keys. In practice, such things as using words or phrases that are made up of characters from the western alphabet often reduce keyspaces. On average, you'll try half of the possible keys before finding the correct one. So, if a key has a length of 32 bits, it will take approximately 2 billion attempts to discover a key. Although this is daunting for a human, it's cyber-play for a computer. A current effort at `Distributed.net` is searching the keyspace for a 64-bit key for the RC5 algorithm at an average rate of 98,609,946 gigakeys/sec; using about 31,000

Internet-linked computers in a single day. The 32-bit key of our example will be found in fewer than one-hundredths of a second. At 5 million keys per second, even a single computer is a formidable challenger. Generally, key lengths of 128 bits or more, resulting in 2^{128} possible keys, are considered to be safe.

> ### Note
>
> "Safe" is a pretty relative term. Because cyber-thieves have to access encrypted data using algorithms and keys, the idea is to make it difficult or costly enough that the value of what is inside is negligible by the time they are able to access it. Most modern symmetric algorithms that use keys of 128 bits or greater are capable of protecting information for more than 40 years, assuming that advances in computing progress at about the same rate it has for the last decade.

DES, Triple-DES, CAST, RC4 and RC5, IDEA, and Blowfish are all examples of common symmetric algorithms. For many years, DES, or the Data Encryption Standard, defined the algorithm (called the Data Encryption Algorithm, or DEA) endorsed by the government for encryption of data, such as the information that accompanies electronic funds transfers. DEA uses a key that is effectively 56 bits in size. Advances in computing technology and cryptanalysis have rendered DEA ineffective for many of the applications it was originally intended for. In October 1999, the "approved symmetric algorithm of choice" became Triple-DES (TDES), and DES has been restricted to use in legacy systems. Triple-DES retains DEA, but requires the algorithm to be exercised with three keys, effectively expanding the available keyspace.

As early as 1997, the National Institute of Science and Technology (NIST) began searching for a successor to DES. The Advanced Encryption Standard (AES) specifies that a new symmetric algorithm, Rijndael (pronounced "Rhine Dale"), has been approved for use. Rijndael can use key lengths of 128, 192 or 256 bits, and has a sufficiently strong algorithm to provide security for another 20 years, or until the Advanced Encryption Standard is replaced.

> ### Tip
>
> Students of cryptography will likely find the other contenders for the "advanced encryption algorithm" and the mechanisms used to select the winner interesting. They are MARS, RC6, Serpent, and Twofish. See the "Additional Resources" section for pointers to where you can obtain additional information.

Secret key cryptography, then, continues to be useful for encryption and will be for many more years. All that one has to worry about is how to provide the secret key to the intended recipient of encoded information, while avoiding giving the key to somebody who shouldn't be "in the know." If a large number of people need to have a key, it is more likely that the key will be compromised. On the other hand, if we used a separate key for each recipient, there might be a lot of keys, and there will certainly be a number of ciphertexts that are all encoded versions of the same plaintext. This might also expose the information to clever cryptanalysts.

Public Key Cryptography

If there were a way that the secret key wasn't so, well, secret—then the problem of distributing keys would not be so difficult. Although this sounds strange, it is the basis for public key cryptography.

Public key cryptography makes use of pairs of keys. One of the keys is used with an encryption function and is made publicly available; the other is used with a decryption function and is kept private. With public key cryptosystems, data encoded using a public key can only be decoded with the corresponding private key. It isn't necessary to transfer any secrets to share information securely. Because the private key is never shared with anyone, it is not a "secret"—leading to the distinction between secret keys that are used with symmetric algorithms, and private keys that are part of public key cryptosystems.

Using public key cryptography, if Larry wanted to send a private message to Ellen, he would use Ellen's public key to encrypt the message. Larry may have received Ellen's public key directly from her, or from a public repository. Using her private key, Ellen is the only one who can decipher the message. Unlike secret key cryptography, Ellen and Larry do not have to share a key that is only known between them. Of course, if Ellen wanted to securely reply to Larry, she would have to use Larry's public key to encrypt her message to Larry. Because peer-to-peer systems often connect to other systems without prior arrangement, public key cryptography is particularly useful.

Public key cryptography relies on problems that are difficult to solve, or *hard problems*. With these problems, it may not matter if one understands the problem well or has a grasp of the mechanisms involved.

Most hard problems that are applied to securing information are computationally intensive. One example of a hard problem that is the basis for several cryptosystems is factoring large numbers. From your studies in math, you might recall that integers can be the multiplicative product of two or more integers. *Factoring* an integer results in identifying the smallest integers whose product is the original number. If the integer we are interested in is very large, and the factors of that number are very large themselves, it's difficult to identify the factors. Doing so requires the ability to determine whether an integer is a factor, and whether it is prime (divisible only by itself and one). Try, for example, to determine the factors of 4,405,829—it's prime, but it will take some manual effort to determine this, although it's relatively trivial to determine whether this small number is prime using a computer. Much larger numbers are significantly more difficult, even for a powerful computer. (Incidentally, 4,405,829 is the patent number awarded to RSA Security, which developed a popular cryptosystem around this particular hard problem.)

It's a lot easier to multiply together two large prime integers to obtain another integer than it is to determine what the original integers were from the result. Functions and their inverses that exhibit these properties are known as *one-way functions*. Formally, one-way functions are those functions in which it is significantly easier to compute a function in one direction than it is to compute the inverse function. When the ease of computing the inverse function is significantly increased with some additional knowledge, such as one of the original factors, a function is known as a *trapdoor one-way function*. The trapdoor provides an easy escape from the difficulty of the inverse function.

Public key cryptography makes use of keys that are mathematically related in such a way that knowing the public key does not make it easier to derive the private key—the relationship between them is the result of an application of a one-way function. At the same time, the algorithm used to encrypt a plaintext message using a public key is a trapdoor one-way function, in that the private key "unlocks" the trapdoor. Common public key cryptosystems include RSA, Rabin, ElGammal, LUC, and Elliptic Curve Cryptosystems (ECC).

If public key cryptography eliminates the need to distribute secret keys, you may be wondering why secret key cryptography hasn't been replaced. Public key cryptosystems are slower than their secret key counterparts, in part because of their computational complexity, and also because of their affinity with large numbers.

Because public key cryptosystems are more likely to be attacked by using approaches to solving hard problems rather than by brute force, they require keys that are longer than those used by secret key cryptosystems. For example, it's generally agreed that a key length of 1024 bits for RSA is sufficient for the moment.

Public key systems often work together with secret key systems—they're ideal for protecting the exchange of a secret key. In fact, public key systems evolved from work performed in connection with the design of secure transmission mechanisms for secret keys. Public key cryptosystems are used to create a *digital envelope* that encloses a secret key (called a *session key*) used for future communication. The combination of public key and secret key cryptosystems results in better performance by using the faster secret key cryptosystem to secure the bulk of the information.

10

P2P SECURITY

Digital Signatures

The usefulness of public key cryptosystems extends beyond their capability to secure information. They can also be used to "sign" data. For example, the functions used in the RSA public key cryptosystem permit it to be used "in reverse." In other words, the encoding function can also be used with the private key to produce ciphertext that is decipherable by the corresponding public key. Although this does not produce a very private message—anyone can use the public key to decrypt the content— it does produce a "signature" (the ciphertext) that is unique to the application of the private key to the plaintext.

A digital signature "affixed" to a document associates an identity with the document and asserts the content. Only the owner of the private key can sign the document, and if the document is changed, the ciphertext will also change. Once again, there is no need to share a private key. A person can encrypt a message or verify that a document has been signed by using only a public key. For example, if Ellen wanted to ensure the integrity of a message sent to Larry, she would use her private key to produce a signature, which is appended to the document. Using Ellen's public key, Larry can decrypt the signature to produce a copy of the original document. If the copy and the original document match, the document is authentic.

As mentioned earlier, RSA's public key cryptosystem is capable of encryption, decryption, and creating signatures. The ElGammal Signature Scheme (ESS) and its close relative the Digital Signal Algorithm (DSA) are specialists, producing only signatures. DSA is the United States national standard for digital signatures, known as the Digital Signature Standard (DSS).

Hashes

One problem with digital signatures is that they tend to be very large. In the case of RSA's functions, they are at least as large as the plaintext being signed. DSS produces signatures that are twice as large. While incredibly useful, the cryptosystems used to produce signatures are often slow, relying on algorithms that use complicated arithmetic operations.

Special cryptographic functions have been developed for the purpose of validating content. These functions do not require a key, and are not intended to produce ciphertext that can be decrypted to produce the original plaintext. *Hash* functions are one-way functions that have the following properties:

- They easily produce a fixed length output for input of arbitrary size.
- They produce an output that is unique for every possible input plaintext.

- It is computationally unfeasible to recover the content of the message used to produce the output.

Hash functions take input of any size and produce a *message digest* of a specific size. In most cases, the digest is at least 160 bits, the minimum size required for DSS. Message digests are used with digital signatures to ensure the integrity of a document. Being smaller, digests are easily signed. Because the digest accurately represents the original message, only the digest needs to be encrypted to insure that the document has not been tampered with. In this case, Larry would decrypt the signature with Ellen's public key to produce the original digest. Using the same digest algorithm that Ellen used, Larry would apply the algorithm to the received document and compare the resulting digest to the one obtained from Ellen's signature. If they match, the document has not been altered.

Examples of systems that produce digests are the Secure Hash Algorithm (SHA-1), produced by NIST and a part of the Secure Hash Specification (SHS), a nationally endorsed standard, and Message Digest Version 5 (MD5) from RSA Security. SHA produces a 160-bit message digest, and MD5 produces a 128-bit digest.

With the background presented in the chapter to this point, we are now ready to look at some of the cryptography services.

Identification

As mentioned earlier in the chapter, identity consists of the collective characteristics that make something distinct. To a computer, not much is needed—who we are often distills to a name. Identity is often abstracted from an individual or user to a role or context. For example, security policies frequently have differing rules for administrators or members of specific workgroups. In these cases, a system may or may not know any more information about an entity, other than the fact that it is acting in a role ("This user is a supervisor") or from a particular context ("This user is at a public computer"). In every case, a system that requires identity must distinguish objects through the process of identifying them.

Let's consider a few concepts that are important in identifying things.

Addresses

All computers that are connected to a network are named in some way so that you can communicate with them. They have addresses, the most common of which is an IP address. Using addresses, the designers of IP made it possible to establish a connection to a predetermined host. Similarly, the places where we persistently store things are named with volume labels or paths, so that we can consistently find and use something we "put away." Addresses and paths are frequently used as a part of an identity. They may also compose a whole identity. As mentioned earlier, peer-to-peer systems often work behind gateways or firewalls that implement network address translation (NAT) or obtain their IP addresses through DHCP, making addresses potentially unsuitable as long term identifiers. Of course, if the system has a fixed host name in the domain name system, the fully qualified address can be used.

Namespaces

A *namespace* is an available pool from which to draw on in naming something; it must be sufficiently large to be able to distinguish one thing from another. IPv4 addresses are made up of 32 bits, making 4 billion addresses available in that namespace. Amazingly, because IP addresses are distributed in blocks, it has become necessary to enlarge the namespace by increasing the size of an IPv6 address to 128 bits. The *Universally Unique Identifier (UUID)* is another 128-bit identifier that is commonly used for discriminating between software classes or interfaces. The size of these spaces makes it possible to catalog quite a few things for a considerable amount of time. The size of the domain of things that need to be distinct and whether the identifier needs to be indelible are both important factors in identification.

Central and Local Identification

Central authorities might regulate identifiers to guarantee uniqueness or some other quality of the identifier. Because it's important that no two computers have the same address, Regional Internet Registries (RIR) such as the American Registry for Internet Numbers (ARIN) issue IP addresses. Similarly, organizations that support instant messaging, such as AOL and Microsoft, regulate the names that users can adopt.

Names that make up part of the Domain Name System are a useful and interesting mixture of a combined effort between centralized and localized systems. Part of the name is registered with a central authority, and the rest of it is left for you to decide. The registering authority makes certain that the domain you are registering is not in use by anyone else.

For example, a company might register the domain `zzyxx.com`. After registering, the company is assured that the domain is unique. Then, the company can assign individual names for computers. A computer can now be named `mickey.zzyxx.com`. As long as there are no other computers named `mickey` in the domain, then that computer has a unique name. With a domain, you can build other addressing or naming schemes. A Universal Resource Identifier (URI) permits you to name or address any Web resource, be it a Web page or peer-to-peer service. Email addresses are used successfully to uniquely identify individuals from among the large number of users.

Additional Information

Although we have focused on names as an identifier, an identity often needs to include much more information than a label. An identity minimally consists of as much information as it takes to make one member of the domain distinct from another. Additional information such as the groups one belongs to or other attributes might be necessary for a system to perform its work. In most cases, a system possesses its own conception of what an identity is.

As mentioned earlier in the chapter, it can be useful to be able to share an identity between systems or domains. This is a *network identity*. A network identity can be more convenient for its users and reduce the complexity of applications, which do not have to store and manage identities for themselves. However, in implementing network identities, it is important to partition information that comprises an identity so that systems obtain only the information they require.

Authentication

Authentication is concerned with whether something is genuine. How can you be sure that something is what it claims to be? In connection with identity, how can you be sure that somebody is who he claims to be?

Users are often verified in the following ways:

- They know something that is unique to them, such as an identifier or a password.
- They possess something that positively identifies them, such as a key or a driver's license.
- Their identity is self-proving—an attribute or combination of attributes is enough to establish credibility. For example, a person's fingerprints are unique enough that additional proof isn't necessary.

Passwords

Most of us are familiar with having to provide a password in addition to a user-supplied identifier. The password is a secret that the user and the authenticating system both know about. If the user can successfully produce the secret when asked, the system can assume that the user is who he claims to be. To prevent discovery by eavesdropping, the password is exchanged after it has been encrypted by a one-way function. The password is stored, in hashed form, on the authenticating system to protect it from a possible attack on the database or file.

> **Note**
>
> The examples in this section illustrate communication between a system and a user. However, the principles equally apply to communication between users to other users, systems to other systems, and so on.

Challenge-Response

A variant of this approach called *challenge-response* uses shared secret keys. In this case, a user is issued a challenge by the authenticating system, to which the user must reply with a correct response. The challenging system sends data to the user that she must encrypt with her secret key and return. Using the same secret key, the authenticating system attempts to decrypt the returned ciphertext to produce the original plaintext. The secret key might be stored at the authenticating system or be exchanged at the beginning of a session.

Using public key cryptography eliminates the need to share a secret key. In this case, the user encrypts the challenge plaintext with his private key and the authenticating system uses his public key to validate the response. This protocol is an example of a mechanism that uses *zero knowledge proofs*. In performing the authentication, no additional information is revealed to the authenticating system. Zero knowledge proofs permit you to convince somebody about a fact without revealing information to them beyond that which they already know. Protocols based upon zero knowledge proofs are preferable to others. Thus, in the initial challenge-response example using a shared secret key, it will be better to use a stored key rather than to exchange one each session—because the authenticating system "learns" the user's secret key during the protocol. Sharing the secret key is more vulnerable to attack. If the authenticating entity is another user, he learns a secret password.

Trusted Third Parties

Often, a trusted third party can be inserted into an authentication scheme to increase security. Here, users communicate with the third party using one of the authentication protocols mentioned earlier. This results in both users being authenticated to the third party. This party then issues one or more session keys for use between the parties. Neither user learns anything about the other in the transaction, except that they are who they claim to be. Peer-to-peer systems can make particular use of trusted third parties or of tokens, as described in the next section. Using trusted third parties, a system can maintain a list of trusted peers that is much smaller than the list of all of the peers that might want to access its services. Any peer that wants to access a resource can simply obtain a session key from a "friend" of the system providing the resource. In this way, peer-to-peer systems can distribute the responsibility for authenticating users among themselves. Later in the chapter, you'll learn more about some systems that can provide the foundations for this kind of authentication.

Tokens

Users who want to authenticate themselves can also present a digital token to the system they want to authenticate with. Possession of the token is sufficient proof of identity, in the same way that having a hotel key with a magnetic stripe allows you to access your hotel room. However, after you've given a copy of the token to someone, how do you prevent him or her from using it? What if the token is stolen?

The token can be stamped with a *digital timestamp*—the expiration of which invalidates the token. The token can also be issued for use in connection with another object, such as a session key.

Although these techniques can help abate the possibility of misusing a token, they cannot do anything in the case where a token, and consequently an identity, is forged. Although the token proves that the sender is able to construct a token, you cannot be certain that something is not masquerading for another. A digital certificate can help alleviate this problem.

Digital Certificates

Digital certificates provide a way to associate an identity with a public key or other attributes that is certified by a trusted party, called a *certificate authority*. The most common certificates are those based on the International Telecommunications Union (ITU) standard X.509v3. Table 10.1 lists the contents of an X.509 certificate.

TABLE 10.1   Contents of an X.509 Certificate

Field	Description
X.509 Version	V1, V2 or V3
Serial Number	A number that uniquely identifies the certificate among those issued by the Certificate Authority
Signature Algorithm	The algorithm used by the Certificate Authority to sign the certificate

TABLE 10.1 continued

Field	Description
Issuer	The name of the Certificate Authority
Validity Period	The period for which the certificate is valid, composed of "Valid from" and "Valid to" fields that are made up of a date and a time
Subject	The name of the entity whose public key is being certified
Public Key	The public key of the entity
Issuer's Unique Identifier	A unique identifier representing the issuer (V2 and V3 only)
Subjects Unique Identifier	A unique identifier representing the subject (V2 and V3 only)
Extensions	Additional attributes (V3 only)
Signature	The signature of all the previous fields

As you can see, a certificate has a number of elements that are validated by the certificate authority and confirmed by its digital signature. To obtain a certificate, a user must apply to a certificate authority and prove she is who she claims to be. The certificate authority will then issue a certificate on behalf of the user, who is known as a *subject*. Because the certificate contains the subject's public key, the subject can encrypt data with her private key and send it, along with her certificate, to another party. The receiver can use the public key contained in the certificate to decrypt the data, with assurance that the data is truly from the subject.

Authorization

Deciding what users are permitted to do or what resources they are allowed to use are important functions of secure systems. Generally, the decision to provide access to services or resources is made by considering user requirements, or what the potential impact on other users of the system and to the system itself might be. For example, protection is often extended to files so that one user cannot destroy or modify another user's data. In another case, a user might be limited in the amount of disk space or network bandwidth so he does not monopolize the resource.

Authorization can be based on identity or the use of keys. As mentioned earlier in the chapter, identity may consist of an entity, a role or context, or a combination of these things. Two common mechanisms are useful in determining how much access to provide to resources. *Capability lists* associate a user or key with a set of access rights. An *access control list* links resources to a set of authorized users. After a system has authenticated a user (or a key, for that matter), it uses one of these lists in combination with a security policy to decide what constraints exist for the user in relation to the service. Although these lists are typically stored on the system that hosts the resources, a client can manage its own capability list. In this case, a client obtains a token or certificate from a system that provides a service, which entitles the bearer to use the service. These tokens or certificates are called *credentials*.

Peer-to-peer systems have unique requirements for identifying and authorizing entities. Storing identities on a peer for every possible user is impractical. It can result in large lists and a significant amount of redundant information between peers. Key- or credential-based systems are more useful. Centralized schemes can also be used effectively.

The problems of authenticating and authorizing users are frequently addressed by systems that are specialized to the tasks. In the next few sections, we will look at several that can be useful for peer-to-peer systems.

Kerberos

Kerberos was initially developed at the Massachusetts Institute of Technology as a component of a larger initiative to help link computing resources and services while providing a consistent user experience across workstations. It has since become widely adopted as a network authentication protocol for client server applications, and it uses secret key cryptography. Although Kerberos was initially developed for use with Unix systems, it has been incorporated into Microsoft Windows as an optional authentication mechanism. Kerberos enables clients to authenticate themselves to services. To prevent any confusion between clients of the Kerberos authentication service and clients of other services, the former are called *principals*. A few more additional terms should be defined before beginning the explanation of how Kerberos works:

- *Key*—Kerberos principals possess keys that are large numbers. For a user, the key is the result of applying a one-way function to her password.

- *Ticket*—A ticket is a Kerberos credential that includes the name of a principal, the name of the server, the client's network address, a lifetime for the ticket, and a session key.

- *Authenticator*—An authenticator is a credential that is used to make sure that the principal is who he claims to be. An authenticator is made up of the principal's name, his network address, and a timestamp.

Kerberos uses a trusted third party to authenticate clients. The Kerberos trusted third party knows the secret keys for all the principals that communicate with it. By default, it uses DES for any ciphering. Figure 10.1 illustrates the scenario used in the following example.

10

P2P SECURITY

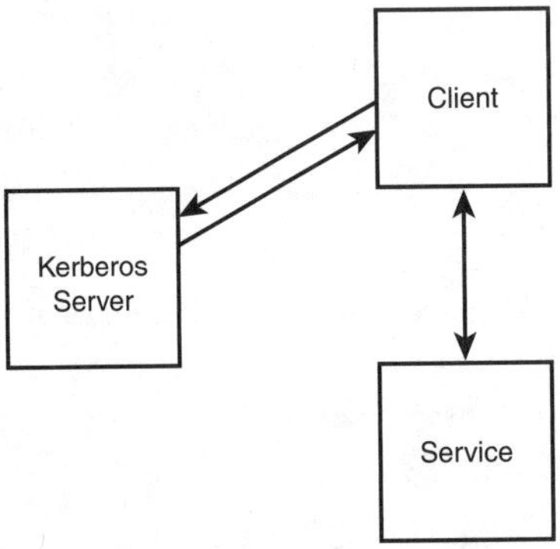

FIGURE 10.1

A simple Kerberos network topology.

Kerberos operations can be divided into three basic functions:

- Authenticating a principal (Authenticating Service Exchange)
- Obtaining a ticket to use a service (Ticket Granting Service Exchange)
- Applying to use the service (Client-Server Exchange)

Officially, these operations are the subprotocols whose names appear in parentheses here.

For example, suppose that Kyle, a principal who desires to use a service must first authenticate with the Key Distribution Center (KDC). Upon logging into his workstation, the Kerberos client takes the following steps:

1. It sends a message, which contains information about Kyle, including his username and the name of the service he wants to authenticate with to Kerberos. In this early stage, it is the Ticket Granting Service (TGS).

2. The TGS looks to see if Kyle is an authorized principal. Principals are added to the system by security administrators. If Kyle is an authorized principal, the Ticket Granting Service will return a session key encrypted with Kyle's secret key and a Ticket Granting Ticket (TGT) encrypted with the TGS' own secret key.

3. On receipt of this information, the Kerberos client will use the password Kyle provided at login to obtain the session key.

Now that Kyle has the necessary credentials to interact with Kerberos, he can authenticate himself to other services. Before contacting the services directly, however, he must obtain the credentials to interact with the service from the Ticket Granting Service. It's important to note that, from this point on, Kyle is usually unaware of the authentication going on—he does not have to login each time he accesses a service.

Upon determining that Kyle must be authenticated for a service, the process continues as follows:

4. The Kerberos client sends a message to the Ticket Granting Service containing the name of the service that Kyle wants to access, the Ticket Granting Ticket received earlier, and an authenticator, which is encrypted with the session key, also received earlier. As mentioned previously, the authenticator is a credential used to validate a ticket the client is presenting. It does this by decrypting the authenticator with the session key stored in the ticket. Successfully decrypting the authenticator means that the client who claims to own the ticket has the session key, and should be the rightful owner of the ticket.

5. If the ticket is good, the TGS issues a session key for use between Kyle's Kerberos client and the service he is trying to access. It also builds a ticket for the service (encrypted using the secret key of the target service), and returns both. The reply is encrypted using the session key from the TGT.

6. Kyle is now ready to redeem the ticket to the service. The Kerberos client constructs an authenticator for the ticket and dispatches the authenticator and ticket to the service, which validates the ticket, thereby receiving assurance that Kyle is who he claims to be.

Although the protocol may seem complex, it really distills to this: Kyle and the service both know and trust the Kerberos Ticket Granting Service, but do not have a permanent relationship between themselves. Kerberos makes it possible to introduce Kyle to the service ad hoc, and assure both Kyle and the service that they are genuine when they meet.

Kerberos does not intrinsically provide authorization. The Kerboros Ticket Granting Service does not make decisions about whether one principal is permitted to approach another. That decision is left to the principals who, with the information obtained from a ticket, can use local policy to decide.

Kerberos can partition authentication information into domains called *realms*, making it possible to scale-up, while ensuring manageability and permitting additional degrees of security. Principals can authenticate across realms if they are set up appropriately.

A complete specification for the operation of Kerberos version 5 can be found in RFC 1510, available from the Internet Engineering Task Force's Web site at http://www.ietf.org/rfc/rfc1510.txt?number=1510.

PKI

Earlier in the chapter, you learned about digital certificates. Throughout the rest of the chapter you will see that digital certificates and public key cryptography are incredibly useful—so useful that it would make sense that some trusted system for creating and revoking certificates, and for storing, finding and distributing them would be implemented. Being trusted entities, and because of the value of certificates, we expect that those systems will be very secure. The Public Key Infrastructure (PKI) is all this and much more. The most common PKI is based on the ITU's X.509 Public Key Infrastructure (PKIX) Standard. The components of the standard, as they apply to the Internet, have been documented in IETF RFCs. The list of RFCs appears in Table 10.2.

TABLE 10.2   Internet RFCs for X.509

RFC	Subject
RFC 2459	Profiles of X.509 v3 Public Key Certificates and X.509 v2 Certificate Revocation Lists (CRLs)
RFC 2510	PKIX Certificate Management Protocols
RFC 2559	Operational protocols
RFC 2585	Operational protocols
RFC 2560	Operational protocols
RFC 2527	Certificate Policy and Certification Practices Framework
DRAFTS ONLY	Time-stamping and data-certification services

These documents provide clear guidelines and standards for the instruments of PKI so that digital certificates and their keys are managed efficiently and securely, while remaining useful to their clients. Although we can't discuss the complete PKIX standard in a single chapter, we will take a moment to focus on certificates again.

As you'll recall from earlier in the chapter, a certificate authority binds a subject name to a public key and other attributes. It does this by signing the document with its private key after verifying that the object or person is what or who it claims to be, and making sure that it has possession of the private key linked to the public key in the certificate.

> **Note**
>
> http://www.pkiforum.com/resources/verisigncerts.html contains many interesting articles and alerts that pertain to stolen or forged certificates.

In addition to publishing digital certificates, certificate authorities also publish *Certificate Revocation Lists (CRLs)*. A CRL has several of the same elements used in a certificate: a version number, a signature algorithm identifier, the issuing certificate authority (CA) name, extensions, and a signature. In addition, it contains the date the list was issued and the date of the next anticipated update. Finally, it contains a set of serial numbers and revocation dates for invalidated certificates. Clients who receive a digital certificate are required to check with a CA to determine if the certificate appears on a CRL. Software that is certificate-aware often does this without notifying the user. To assist in efficiently locating CRLs, X.509v3 certificates have an extension, called the *issuing distribution point*, that identifies the location of one or more CRLs that might apply to the certificate.

CRLs help maintain the currency of certificates. In combination with certificates and the rest of the public key infrastructure, they make a great addition to the set of tools we have to create secure applications.

SAML

A promising standard is emerging in the form of the *Security Assertion Markup Language (SAML)*. SAML is being developed by representatives of more than 20 companies with the input of users, under the auspice of the Organization for the Advancement of Structured Information Standards (OASIS). SAML is an XML-based framework for exchanging security information in an interoperable way. SAML does not currently define the underlying mechanisms used to obtain information—instead it focuses on the protocols and vocabulary that clients and SAML authorities use to communicate with each other. SAML is independent of the underlying transport and other communication layers. Currently, a SOAP binding is defined so that SAML messages can be delivered using SOAP. In this case, SAML messages are mapped into the SOAP message body. Upcoming plans provide for a binding to raw HTTP.

SAML policies define the rules required to use SAML, with other frameworks or protocols to add or supplement security. Version 1.0 defines the WebBrowser Single Sign On (SSO) profile, in that an authenticated user within a particular domain can become authenticated in another domain without user interaction.

SAML clients and authorities communicate using a request-response protocol. However, SAML does not enforce client-server architecture. Authorities or "clients" can communicate with each other. Figure 10.2 illustrates a typical interaction.

FIGURE 10.2

Communication between a SAML requestor and authority.

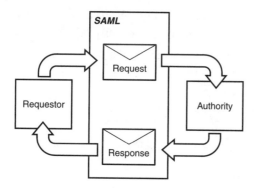

Messages have several common elements: They contain information about the source of the message, the subject, and specific conditions that apply to the included assertions.

SAML authorities make three kinds of *assertion statements* about a subject. As defined in the specification, they are as follows:

- Authentication—The specified subject was authenticated by a particular means at a particular time.
- Authorization Decision—A request to allow the specified subject to access the specified resource has been granted or denied.
- Attribute—The specified subject is associated with the supplied attributes.

Let's look at a request and a corresponding response. For this example, we will assume that Kalyn is attempting to log on to her workstation, and that a SAML-aware client is requesting authentication against the specified attributes. The following message illustrates the SAML request:

```
<samlp:Request MajorVersion="1" MinorVersion="0" RequestID="10.10.0.4.12345" >
  <samlp:AuthenticationQuery>
    <saml:Subject>
      <saml:NameIdentifier SecurityDomain="zzyxx.com" Name="kalyn"/>
    </saml:Subject>
    <saml:Atttribute AttributeName="userid" AttributeNameSpace=
➥http://www.zzyxx.com>
      <saml:AttributeValue>
        cinderella
      </saml:AttributeValue>
    <saml:Atttribute AttributeName="password" AttributeNameSpace=
➥http://www.zzyxx.com>
      <saml:AttributeValue>
        0qRRa400-loOA
      </saml:AttributeValue>
    </saml:Atttribute>
  </samlp:AuthenticationQuery>
</samlp:Request>
```

If the authority successfully authenticates Kalyn, given her user ID and password, it might return a response to a SAML client that looks like this:

```
<saml:Assertion MajorVersion="1" MinorVersion="0" AssertionID="10.10.0.4.12345"
Issuer="zzyxx.com" IssueInstant="2002-05-06T17:12:01Z">
  <saml:Conditions NotBefore="2002-05-06T17:12:00Z"
      NotAfter="2002-05-07T00:00:00Z"/>
  <saml:AuthenticationStatement AuthenticationMethod="password"
      AuthenticationInstant="2002-05-06T17:12:00Z">
    <saml:Subject>
      <saml:NameIdentifier SecurityDomain="zzyxx.com" Name="kalyn"/>
    </saml:Subject>
  </saml:AuthenticationStatement>
</saml:Assertion>
```

This response indicates that Kalyn has been successfully authenticated, with the condition that the authentication will expire at midnight.

This scenario can be expanded to demonstrate the additional power of SAML. Now imagine that Kalyn wants to purchase an extra pair of glass slippers from an online merchant. Navigating to that site with her Web browser, she is authenticated there also. Finding the slippers she wants, she places an order that indicates that she would like to pay using a direct withdrawal from her bank, which has arranged for a temporary loan to cover the cost of her pumpkin carriage, gown, and accessories. In the course of the order, Kalyn's bank is contacted by her own client (using SAML, of course) to obtain authorization to spend up to a predetermined amount that is included in the order forwarded to the online merchant. The merchant sends the slippers, and everyone lives happily ever after.

There are several efforts that are closely related to the development of SAML, including the work of the Liberty Alliance, which is working to promote an open interoperable standard for network identity. For pointers to useful information about SAML or work related to it, see the "Additional Resources" section of this chapter.

Microsoft .NET Passport

.NET Passport is Microsoft's authentication and authorization scheme for Web-based services. More than 200 million consumers rely on it to provide access to a number of services, including Hotmail, Microsoft Money and other Microsoft products, eBay, McAfee, Monster.com, Buy.com, Computer Discount Warehouse, and Starbucks. Although .NET Passport is proprietary, freely available SDKs are available for Microsoft Windows and the Solaris and Linux operating systems.

In designing the system, engineers at Microsoft decided that .NET Passport should be compatible with technologies that currently exist in Web browsers and servers. As a result, it uses HTTP redirects, cookies, JavaScript, and SSL.

.NET Passport users are required to sign up to use it. They provide personal information to Microsoft when they do so. The information stored by .NET Passport is listed in Table 10.3.

TABLE 10.3 Core Attributes for .NET Passport

Attribute Name	Description
Accessibility	Determines if accessibility features should be enabled
Bday Precision	Defines the precision of the Birthdate attribute (required)
Birthdate	The member's birth date

TABLE 10.3 continued

Attribute Name	Description
City	A GeoID that maps to the member's city
Country	An ISO 3166 country code for the member's country or region
FirstName	The member's first name
Flags	Various flags for indicating such things as whether the member's email address has been verified (required)
Gender	The member's gender
Lang Preference	The member's preferred language, as a LocaleID (LCID)
LastName	The member's last name
MemberIDHigh	The upper 32 bits of the Passport Unique ID (PUID) that is assigned when the member initially signs up for the service (required)
MemberIDLow	The lower 32 bits of the PUID (required)
MemberName	A complete sign-in name, including a domain. This attribute has been deprecated.
Nickname	The member's preferred name
Occupation	The occupation of the member
Preferred email	The member's email address
PostalCode	The member's postal code
ProfileVersion	The version of the core profile in use
Region	A GeoID that maps to the member's region within a county
TimeZone	The time zone that the member lives in
Wallet	Determines whether the member has opted to establish a .NET Passport wallet (required)

As you can see, there is potentially quite a bit of information available to systems that authenticate using .NET Passport. Another goal of .NET Passport is to provide Single Sign-In (SSI) capabilities to users, enabling them to login to any .NET Passport-enabled Web site and have access to additional .NET Passport-enabled sites without logging in again. Also, because a significant amount of a user's personal information is contained in his .NET Passport profile, the user also does not have to provide it to each site—it's available by default.

Now that you understand the scope of information that .NET Passport provides, we can examine how it works. Figure 10.3 illustrates the scenario for the following discussion.

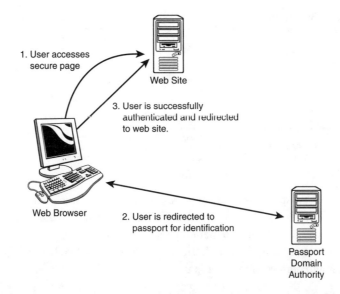

FIGURE **10.3**
The .NET Passport architecture.

1. User accesses secure page

Web Site

3. User is successfully authenticated and redirected to web site.

Web Browser

2. User is redirected to passport for identification

Passport Domain Authority

Users approach Web pages or services by using the HTTP protocol, along with the address of the resource. For the sake of this example, we will assume that a user is attempting to access a Web page using a browser. If the site requires authentication by the .NET Passport service, it will redirect the browser to a domain authority, where the user is presented with a sign-in page that is delivered over a secure connection. The request contains a site identifier for the site the user was redirected from, the URL to return to upon successful authentication, and information about the version of .NET Passport and the key used to encrypt the information returned. The user then enters her username and password, which is verified by the login server. If the user provides the correct username and password, the login server retrieves the user's PUID and profile. This information is incorporated into HTTP cookies that are returned when the browser is once again redirected to the return URL. Table 10.4 lists these cookies and the information they contain.

TABLE **10.4**   Contents of .NET Passport Cookies

Common Name	Label	Description and Contents
Ticket	MSPAuth	Contains the encrypted .NET Passport timestamps (last refresh and manual sign-in) and various flags
Profile	MSPProf	Contains the encrypted core profile attributes
Ticket Granting Cookie	MSPSec	Contains the PUID and password used for silent sign-in

TABLE 10.4   continued

Common Name	Label	Description and Contents
Visited Sites Cookie	MSPVis	Contains a list of the .NET Passport sites visited, using their site ID
Domain Cookie	MSPDom	Stores the last domain authority used when signing in to .NET Passport

These cookies are unavailable to the client, as they are created in the .NET Passport.com domain. They are for use by .NET Passport.

However, .NET Passport does provide access to the information contained in two of the cookies by adding them as encrypted query string parameters to the return URL. MSPAuth and MSPProf, which contain information about a user, are decrypted by Web server extensions to reveal the user's core attributes to the client. The client can then authenticate the user and permit him to access the Web page.

> **Note**
>
> Microsoft uses Triple-DES to perform encryption. As part of setting up a Web site that uses .NET Passport, the site administrators, and .NET Passport operators must decide on a password that is a shared secret. It is this password that is used to encrypt the cookies and query string parameters.

If the user has been authenticated once by .NET Passport, visits to other .NET Passport-enabled sites result in authentication that the user is unaware of. Upon accessing a second .NET Passport-enabled site, the client again redirects the browser to a domain authority. However, in this case, .NET Passport obtains the cookies it set previously, ultimately causing it to produce a redirection back to the referring site without requiring the user to log in again. The login server updates its own cookies and provides information about the user to the client again. Sites can force users to reauthenticate. Users log out of the system when their browser session is closed or when they explicitly command a logout. In the latter case, .NET Passport causes scripts to run at each .NET Passport site that has been visited, so that the site-specific cookies are deleted also.

In September 2001, Microsoft announced that .NET Passport would soon be able to interoperate with Kerberos v.5, thereby making .NET Passport less centralized. However, to realize the full benefit of a federated sign-in, users must authenticate through .NET

Passport. Also, Microsoft does not appear to have loosened its grip on the .NET Passport service itself—only Microsoft can operate one, and partners must pay to access the service at runtime. Additional information about .NET Passport is available at `http://www.passport.com`.

Integrity

Even if you can validate the origin of something, you often cannot be sure that it has not been altered. Several cryptographic functions help detect changes.

Digital signatures and digests can detect changes as small as a single bit in megabytes of data. Common practice is to use a hash function such as MD5 to produce a fingerprint of the data. The fingerprint is signed using a private key to create a digital signature. The data and signature are then delivered to the recipient, who uses the sender's public key to produce the original digest. Finally, MD5 produces the current fingerprint of the data and compares both fingerprints. A match indicates that the data is intact.

A second means of demonstrating the integrity of information is through the use of a Message Authentication Code (MAC). MAC functions perform the same task as hashes, but require a key. Functions that produce a MAC using a cryptographic hash algorithm in combination with a key are known as keyed hash-based Message Authentication Code (HMAC) functions. Using one of these function types, the sender will compute the MAC and send it and the data to the receiver. Using the secret key, the receiver simply computes the MAC for the received data and compares it with the sent MAC. Matching MACs provide assurance that the data is intact.

NIST's standard for the MAC algorithm is the Data Authentication Algorithm, which uses DES at its core. NIST's keyed hash-based Message Authentication Code algorithm preference is named HMAC. Other useful algorithms for insuring data integrity are HMACMD5 and HMACSHA1, based on the MD5 and SHA1 message digests, respectively.

Confidentiality

When people think of cryptography, confidentiality and privacy are probably the two things they think of first. Secret and public key cryptosystems help to hide information from others, or restrict access to a well-defined audience. By this time, you have a good grasp of how this is done. All that remains is to cover a few more technologies.

To promote the use of the Internet in e-commerce transactions, Netscape Communications developed the Secure Sockets Layer (SSL) protocol. SSL is used to transparently secure a communications channel by providing for the encryption and decryption of messages at the endpoints. SSL uses a combination of secret and public key technologies. The following list illustrates how SSL works:

1. A client that wants to communicate securely with a server initiates a handshaking protocol designed to select the cryptosystem and to exchange keys and authenticate the server.

2. The server submits its certificate to the client.

3. In response, the client verifies that the certificate has been issued (and is not revoked) by one of the trusted Certificate Authorities from a list that it stores locally. The client then generates a pre-master key, encrypts it with the server's public key and sends it to the server.

4. The server generates a master key and encrypts it with the server's private key and sends it to the client.

5. The client receives the master key.

6. Both the client and server generate a session key, which is used to encrypt future messages between them and to verify the integrity of those messages.

7. The server and client then send messages to each other indicating that future messages will be encrypted by the session key.

The client can be optionally authenticated with the server. Most Web browsers indicate that a secure connection is in use when a small key or lock icon appears on the frame somewhere.

> **Note**
>
> Although the terms *client* and *server* are used in the example, SSL can be used for peer-to-peer. In this case, the server is a peer that performs the protocol functions of the server-side of the connection.

When SSL Version 3 (SSLv3) was submitted as a protocol for Internet Standardization, the initial work to produce an Internet standard resulted in an evolution of SSL called Transport Layer Security (TLS). The basic high-level operation remains the same.

Many of the toolkits that are used to secure peer-to-peer communication depend on SSL or TLS. For example, JXTA depends on TLS. Because most of the work occurs behind the scenes in these technologies, peer-to-peer applications do not have to worry about adding much to their code to provide secure communication.

Nonrepudiation

Nonrepudiation consists of the acts or state of a system that enable it to prove something to the extent that it cannot be refuted. In most cases, it means that the system is capable of rebutting an attempt to deny knowledge of an act. Nonrepudiation involves most of the cryptographic services discussed so far:

- Identification and Authentication—Knowing who or what did something is an important nonrepudiation function for most systems. Minimally, names or identifiers must be persistent and unique. Having confidence that the user really is the person you think they are is important, also. Shared secret keys such as passwords enable the system to be confident that a client possesses a key. However, it cannot determine if the identity or key has been stolen. Certificates improve the situation by virtually eliminating the possibility that an identity is counterfeit, but still leave the possibility of a borrowed key. Increasing the quantity of knowledge or things that one or more users must provide makes the system even more robust. For example, a system can require a client to find somebody else willing to support the client's claim of identity—and make both provide credentials. Other more advanced techniques make use of features of the identify itself. Biometric-based authentication uses physiological or behavioral characteristics. Currently, biometric authentication is performed using fingerprint, iris, facial, or speech recognition.

- Authorization—By authorizing access to system resources, you fence them in. Fences can protect users from what is on the other side and vice versa. Passing through a gate in the fence, a user often registers an act or commitment. Passing around or over a fence usually indicates malicious intent. All these things are useful to systems that require nonrepudiation, particularly if you have to place something "at the scene of the crime."

- Integrity—It's important to ensure that information cannot be tampered with undetected. Identities, passwords, certificates, and data should not be modifiable by unauthorized entities. If integrity is lost, it must be restored, thereby limiting the effect of the loss. Systems that do not have internal integrity often cannot make irrefutable claims on others.

One particular example illustrates how protocols can be designed to support nonrepudiation. Figure 10.4 illustrates the example.

FIGURE 10.4

An example of a nonrepudiating protocol using a third party.

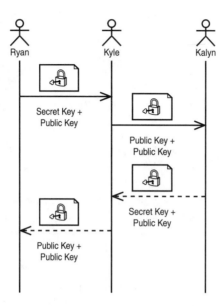

Suppose Ryan and Kalyn need to exchange the latest Nintendo cheats, and they want to be certain that each receives the message. They also want to be assured that they are only communicating with each other. They ask a trusted friend, Kyle, to help them. The process is as follows:

1. Ryan begins by signing his message with Kalyn's public key. After adding a time-stamp and a secret known only to Ryan and Kyle, he now signs the document with his own private key and sends it to Kyle.

2. Kyle decrypts the document with Ryan's public key and makes certain that the additional information provided is the secret they share.

3. Kyle adds a timestamp to the document (now stripped to the ciphertext intended for Kalyn), and encrypts it with his own private key. He sends the document to Kalyn.

4. When Kalyn receives the message, she uses Kyle's public key and her own private key to decrypt it.

5. After reading and memorizing it, she encrypts the message with her private key. She then adds a timestamp and the secret shared between her and Kyle and encrypts the document with Kyle's public key, returning it to Kyle when she is done.

6. Kyle decrypts the document with his private key, verifies the secret information, adds a timestamp, encrypts the document with his public key and sends it to Ryan.

7. Upon receipt, Ryan decrypts the document with Kyle and Kalyn's public keys and compares the document to the original. If they are the same, he can be certain that Kalyn received the document he sent.

With a large number of words, we have just rediscovered certified delivery by courier with return receipt for electronic documents.

In this example, the third party helps to ensure that the information is delivered only to the intended recipient because the sender and receiver are authenticated with the third party. In addition, the third party becomes also becomes a "witness" of the transactions to support nonrepudiation.

To support nonrepudiation, system and client events are written into a database of logs.

Nonrepudiation is a fairly advanced security concept that has not found its way into most of the relatively new peer-to-peer applications. However, as peer-to-peer makes its way into business usage, it will become an important service.

Privacy and Anonymity

Most of us have some things that we would rather keep to ourselves. The things that we conceal are private, and the rest we deem public. Although the things that we reveal are "open" to the public, we often still consider them to be a part of our being—something that we would like to retain ownership of, or control access to.

People can regain ownership and exercise a significant amount of control through managing their identity. Anonymity and pseudonymity permit them to reduce their identity to characteristics they hope to manage. At the same time, they often reconstruct their persona, demarcating new personal boundaries—including those that define privacy.

> **Note**
>
> Anonymity has an obviously negative effect on identity-based security and services, such as nonrepudiation and accountability. P2P applications can be built around activity-based security and services instead.

Computer systems are similar. There are walls about personal information, software and physical devices. In an open networked environment, some of the system is exposed to the public through physical or logical interfaces. We use security systems to choose what is accessible and to protect ourselves from the activities of others.

10

P2P SECURITY

As mentioned earlier, anonymity enables you to draw broad strokes around yourself, affording a great deal of protection by hiding your true name. Pseudonymity does the same thing, but offers the useful feature of being able to be consistently identified with a name. Pseudonymity is more flexible in that it allows for longer, more permanent relationships. However, pseudonymity is at a disadvantage to anonymity in that it is potentially traceable. Even so, users want even more control than the little that remains in the public realm. Suppose that a user who is known only as mm-man signs up for a daily news bulletin from the M&M fan club. He wants to be among the first to find out what color wins the worldwide vote and becomes the next official M&M color. Each day he receives interesting and useful news, including tips about exercises that he can perform at his desk to keep in shape. Then, one day he receives an unsolicited email from the Ab-Exerciser Company. Soon, he is getting emails from hundreds of companies, and some of them are offensive. mm-man would have appreciated it if the M&M fan club (or somebody else) would have treated his personal information with more care—as something that was private.

Several of the techniques outlined earlier in the chapter can be used to enhance user privacy in this application. For example, mm-man can work with a third-party system that rejects email that does not have a credential issued by mm-man. Thinking of the sender as a peer and mm-man as another, you can see how peer-to-peer systems can be designed to support user requirements for privacy and provide the security necessary to safeguard all concerned.

> **Note**
>
> For readers interested in a discussion about identity, anonymity, psuedonymity, and other "nymities," see "The Theory of Nymity" at http://www.geektimes.com/michael/culture/humor/items/Geekish/theoryOfNymity.html. Although it's meant to be humorous, there are some interesting thoughts.

Several interesting examples of peer-to-peer systems that provide anonymity exist. One is Publius, a system that is designed to publish documents that resist censorship, while providing full anonymity to the author or publisher. Publius consists of an arbitrary number of Web servers that have the Publius software installed. The servers are independently owned, and there are no restrictions placed on the administrators.

When a writer publishes a document, the Publius software generates a key that is used to encrypt the document. The key is then split into "shares" that are distributed with a copy of the encrypted document to all the Publius servers. Each server receives a complete copy of the document and one share. Only a few of the shares are required to reconstruct the key. The Publius software then constructs a special URL that encodes the location of the shares and encrypted files on the Publius servers. To get the document, the Publius client obtains and parses the URL, and randomly picks as many Publius servers as are required to reconstruct the key. It then downloads the shares from those servers, reconstructs the key, and finally downloads one copy of the document.

Publius is censor-resistant in part because documents are distributed across a number of systems. Publius does not require any information about the author, so it is an anonymous service. However, as it's independently administered, it's possible that the Web servers log IP addresses that can potentially link the writer to a document.

An *anonymizing proxy* gives additional protection to the writer. Anonymizing proxies work by accepting the address that a client wants to connect to, making the connection on behalf of the user, and relaying the response. The address that is logged at the Publius Web server is the proxy's address. Additional information about Publius can be obtained from `http://www.publius.com/`.

Trust

Secure systems try to take things that are untrusted and add to them so that users or systems can confidently and safely interact. If it were possible, they would eliminate trust altogether by providing an environment where nothing is uncertain or potentially harmful. Because this isn't possible, secure systems treat almost everything as though it were an adversary.

Message digest functions and digital signatures improve trust by making it possible to test the integrity of information or authenticate parties so that a system can respond appropriately if something is wrong. Although secure systems are on guard for most things, they do trust certificate authorities. It's helpful to understand how these systems use trust with digital certificates.

Because there are many certificate authorities, subjects that want to interact with each other using certificates might have difficulty if they trust different certificate authorities. Several trust models have been defined to resolve this issue.

In the X.509 trust model, certificate authorities are organized hierarchically. Figure 10.5 illustrates a hierarchy of certificate authorities.

The most trustworthy CA is known as the root CA. It issues certificates to the CAs that are subordinate to it. These CAs might also issue certificates (to subjects or other CAs), resulting in a *certification chain*. For a subject to validate its key to another, the subject must present its own certificate, along with the certificates for all the CAs in its certification chain, to the other party. That party will attempt to find a CA that it trusts at the proper level in the hierarchy. If it finds one, it will determine that the subject's key is valid. For example, A and B both trust the ROOT CA. B and C both trust CA2.

10

P2P Security

FIGURE 10.5

X.509 defines a hierarchical relationship in its trust model.

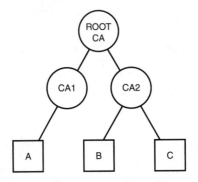

Hierarchical trust models sometimes do not model real-world relationships. X.509 provides for some flexibility in this regard by allowing CAs to *cross-certify*. Figure 10.6 illustrates a scenario in which a certificate authority, CA1, has cross-certified with another certificate authority, CA3. In this case, A and B can validate each other's keys more directly.

FIGURE 10.6

X.509 certificate authorities might cross-certify with each other.

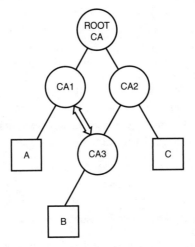

Although X.509 requires that only certificate authorities issue certificates, other models of trust permit ordinary users to create their own certificates; in effect becoming their own CA.

Two models of trust are common:

- Direct trust—In the direct trust model, a user trusts that another's key is valid because the user is certain that the key came from its source.

- Web of trust—The web of trust model comes from Phil Zimmermann, the designer of the popular Pretty Good Privacy (PGP) software. In this model, a key is valid if it has been "signed" by one or more PGP users that have validated the identity of the key owner.

Figure 10.7 shows a web of trust that includes four users.

Figure 10.7

The PGP web of trust model.

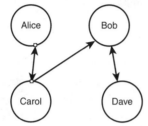

In this example, Carol and Alice signed each other's key when they met at a key-signing party, where Carol and Alice verified their identities. Carol had met Bob previously. At that time, Carol verified Bob's identity and signed Bob's key. However, Carol forgot her identification, so Bob did not sign Carol's key. In this web of trust, Alice and Bob can validate each other's keys, because Carol has validated both of their keys. Now that Alice trusts Bob, she can also trust Dave—because Bob and Dave trust each other.

A unique feature of the web of trust model is that, as other user's public keys are added to the *keyring* (a place where users store certificates), the keyring owner can assign a *trustworthiness level.* In our previous example, if Alice assigned Carol's public key (on Alice's own keyring) a trustworthiness level of untrusted, Alice cannot validate Bob's key. If more than one key were available to validate Bob's key, PGP would use the sum of the trustworthiness levels to determine if enough trust was present among all of them to validate the key.

PGP is used solely for the secure exchange of email, but the web of trust is an interesting trust model to developers of peer-to-peer software. The decentralized nature of the web of trust and its relative simplicity make this model potentially useful.

Note

PGP is extremely popular software used to secure email. It integrates rather nicely with most popular email programs. For more information, you can visit `http://web.mit.edu/network/pgp.html` or `http://www.pgpi.org/`.

10

P2P Security

Accountability

Although users benefit from anonymity, there is also a loss of accountability. The system can't attribute actions to anyone. If the system also lacks the capability to control the use of resources, users might take advantage of the system by consuming them unfairly. P2P systems can regain control of and make clients accountable for the use of system resources by using the micro payment and reputation models.

Micro Payment

Peer-to-peer systems can divide the resources among participants using the micro payment model. With this model, the consumers of the service make small payments of some kind to the producer for small units of work. By keeping the work units small, the producer minimizes the risk to itself. Payments continue with each transaction, until one of the parties is not satisfied, or until all the transactions have been completed.

Although the term *micro payment* seems to imply cash or something equivalent, it can be also be a *Proof of Work (POW)*. A POW is designed to slow the consumer down, to prevent the consumer from overwhelming the system or using more of the resource than it should. This model is suitable for use by identifiable and private clients.

Reputation

P2P systems can work with pseudonymous or public consumers over a longer period using a model built upon reputation. Consumers consult a reputation server to obtain information about potential producers. Using this information, the consumer offers work to the producer of choice. The producer consults a reputation server to discover the reputation of the consumer. Based on the reputation, the producer may reject or proceed with the transaction. Fewer resources are given to peers that have poorer reputations.

Although the prior example used a centralized reputation server, it is possible to use a system such as PGP's web of trust, or the X.509 Public Key Infrastructure.

> **Note**
>
> Accountability systems like these can also significantly reduce *freeloading,* or the tendency of people to take resources without giving anything back for them. A September 2000 study conducted by Xerox PARC concluded that 70% of Gnutella clients did not contribute to the shared content, causing overall system degradation.

Free Haven, a peer-to-peer document storage service, is an example of a system that provides accountability based on reputation in an anonymous environment. Free Haven's servers work together to publish documents by accepting contracts between themselves to store each other's data. A server broadcasts a positive referral about a peer when the peer successfully fills a contract for the server. Servers obtain additional storage space on other servers for better reputations. Documents are fragmented into *shares*, and shares are paired as *buddies*. Buddies are not stored together. Each share knows what server its buddy is on. A share periodically queries its buddy to see if it's still alive. It broadcasts a negative referral about a server if it notices that its buddy doesn't respond.

Software for Developing Secure P2P Applications

Developers who want to add security to peer-to-peer applications can choose from several toolkits that bundle many of the technologies outlined in this chapter:

The Intel Peer-to-Peer Trusted Library is an open source cross-platform solution for C++. It includes support for peer identification and authentication, secure storage, and networking. The library allows developers to work with digital certificates, digital signatures, digital envelopes, public key encryption, and symmetric key encryption. Additionally, it has useful classes to support multithreading and synchronization across platforms. More information can be found at its home on SourceForge—see `http://sourceforge.net/projects/ptptl`. Java programmers can use the security features found natively in the Java 2 Standard Edition platform version 1.4 (J2SE v1.4).

The Java Cryptography Extension (JCE) offers support for identification and authentication using digital certificates, digital signatures and message digests. It also includes functions for symmetric and public key encryption. Finally, it provides an implementation of the Internet Proposed Standard Generic Security Services Application Programming Interface Version 2 (GSS-API) for securely exchanging messages between applications on a per-message basis. The GSS-API is particularly interesting in that it provides support for a number of underlying security mechanisms, such as Kerberos, to provide end-to-end security, including client identity, rights, confidentiality, and data integrity. It can be especially useful for peer-to-peer applications because it provides a significant amount of functionality that can be applied to short sessions.

10

P2P SECURITY

> **Note**
>
> The GSS-API is also implemented in C and C++, Python, and other languages. See the "Additional Resources" section for a pointer to the specifications, including the language bindings.

The Java Secure Socket Extension (JSSE) enables secure Internet communications using SSL (Secure Sockets Layer) and TLS (Transport Layer Security).

The Java Authentication and Authorization Service (JAAS) enables services to authenticate and enforce access controls upon users. With JAAS, developers can leverage existing authentication and authorization services. Native support for Kerberos v.5 is included, and providers exist for authentication using Solaris, generic Unix, and Windows NT domains.

Using JAAS to Provide Authentication and Authorization

JAAS defines a number of core classes that are central to providing authentication and authorization. As mentioned earlier in this chapter, authentication confirms identity, and authorization provides access control. The JAAS core classes fall into three categories: common, authentication, and authorization.

The JAAS common classes are `Subject`, `Principal`, and classes associated with credentials.

A *subject* is any user of a computing service. This might be an actual person, or a running program or process. JAAS uses the subject to authorize access to resources.

A *principal* is a name associated with a subject. A subject might have one or more names associated with it. If you use multiple systems, it is likely that you have multiple logon identifiers. One system might require a unique ID, such as a username, and perhaps another system might require a social security number. The concept of a principal can be used to map multiple named associations to your identity, and help promote single sign-on environments.

A credential contains information used to authenticate a subject. The most common type of credential is a password. However, more secure credential representations exist, such as Kerberos tickets and public key certificates. JAAS also supports an extension mechanism that allows third-party credential implementations to be *plugged-in*. A subject's credentials are divided into two sets. One set contains the public credentials (public keys), and the other set contains the private credentials (passwords, private keys). Access to public credentials requires no special permissions, whereas access to private credentials is security-checked.

The authentication framework is based on Pluggable and Stackable Authentication Modules (PAM). The intent is to enable different vendors and administrators to plug in different authentication modules based on unique security policies.

The JAAS authentication classes are `LoginContext`, `LoginModule`, `CallbackHandler`, and `Callback`. These classes are central to JAAS authentication.

The `LoginContext` class shown in Listing 10.1 is an implementation of the PAM framework.

LISTING 10.1 `LoginContext` Class

```
public final class LoginContext {
    public LoginContext(String name) { }
    public LoginContext(String name, CallbackHandler callback) {}
    public LoginContext(String name, Subject subject) {}
    public LoginContext(String name, Subject subject,
➥CallbackHandler callback) {}
    public void login() { }              // two phase process
    public void logout() { }
    public Subject getSubject() { }    // get the authenticated Subject
}
```

The `name` parameter identifies a login configuration file used to identify one or more login modules.

If you are familiar with transactions, you will be familiar with the mechanics of authentication using pluggable authentication modules (see Listing 10.2).

LISTING 10.2 `LoginModule` Class

```
public interface LoginModule {
    boolean login();      // 1st authentication phase
    boolean commit();     // 2nd authentication phase
    boolean abort();
    boolean logout();
}
```

To guarantee that either all `LoginModules` succeed or none succeed, the `LoginContext` performs the authentication steps in two phases:

- Phase 1—In the first phase, the LoginContext invokes the LoginModules identified in the login configuration file. Each module is instructed to attempt authentication using whatever mechanism that LoginModule implements. If all the necessary LoginModules successfully pass this phase, the LoginContext enters Phase 2.

- Phase 2—In the second phase, the LoginContext invokes the LoginModules again, instructing each to formally commit the authentication process. As can be seen, this two-phase commit is similar to transaction processing. During this phase, each LoginModule associates authenticated principals and credentials with the subject.

If either the first phase or the second phase fails, the LoginContext invokes the abort method on each configured LoginModule. Each LoginModule then cleans up any login state information it had associated with the authentication attempt.

As described in Sun's JAAS documentation (http://java.sun.com/security/jaas/doc/api.html), the following steps are performed to authenticate a Subject:

1. The caller instantiates a LoginContext.
2. The LoginContext uses a login configuration (Configuration object) to load the LoginModules configured for the application.
3. The caller invokes the LoginContext's login method.
4. The login method invokes all the loaded LoginModules.
5. Each LoginModule tries to authenticate the Subject. After authentication is complete, the LoginModules associate relevant Principals and credentials with the Subject.
6. The LoginContext returns the authentication status to the application (pass or fail).
7. If authentication succeeds, the application retrieves the authenticated Subject from the LoginContext.

The following configuration file defines a single login module:

```
/** Login Configuration for JWorkPlace **/

JWorkPlace {
  org.jworkplace.login.WorkPlaceLoginModule required debug=true;
};
```

A login module can be associated with a service by setting the following property:

```
-Djava.security.auth.login.config==/usr/JiniServices/CMS/config/login.config
```

The LoginHandler class shown in Listing 10.3 creates a LoginContext, and implements the CallbackHandler interface. The CallbackHandler interface implements one method:

```
    void handle(Callback[] callbacks)
            throws java.io.IOException, UnsupportedCallbackException;
```

Security services make requests for different types of information by passing `Callbacks` to the `CallbackHandler`. The `CallbackHandler` implementation decides how to retrieve and display the information depending on the `Callbacks` passed to it. For example, if the service needs a username and password to authenticate a user, it uses a `NameCallback` and `PasswordCallback`. The `CallbackHandler` can then prompt for the appropriate information.

LISTING 10.3 LoginHandler Class

```
package org.jworkplace.login;

import java.io.*;
import java.util.*;
import java.security.Principal;
import javax.security.auth.*;
import javax.security.auth.callback.*;
import javax.security.auth.login.*;
import javax.security.auth.spi.*;
import com.sun.security.auth.*;

public class LoginHandler implements CallbackHandler {

  LoginContext lc;
  NameCallback nameCallback;
  PasswordCallback passwordCallback;
  int loginTries = 0;
  String user;
  char[] password;

  // create the LoginContext using the JWorkPlace configuration
  public LoginHandler() {
    try {
      lc = new LoginContext("JWorkPlace", new Subject(), this);
    } catch (LoginException le) {
      le.printStackTrace();
      System.exit(-1);
    }
  }

  // The Callback Interface
  // provides the types of callbacks used to interface with the LoginModule
  public void handle(Callback[] callbacks) throws IOException,
                    UnsupportedCallbackException {
    for (int i = 0; i < callbacks.length; i++) {
      if (callbacks[i] instanceof TextOutputCallback) {
        // display the message according to the specified type
```

LISTING 10.3 continued

```java
        TextOutputCallback toc = (TextOutputCallback)callbacks[i];
        switch (toc.getMessageType()) {
        case TextOutputCallback.INFORMATION:
          System.out.println(toc.getMessage());
          break;
        case TextOutputCallback.ERROR:
          System.out.println("Login error: " + toc.getMessage());
          break;
        case TextOutputCallback.WARNING:
          System.out.println("Login warning: " + toc.getMessage());
          break;
        default:
          throw new IOException("Unknown message type: " +
                    toc.getMessageType());
        }

      } else if (callbacks[i] instanceof NameCallback) {

        nameCallback = (NameCallback)callbacks[i];
        nameCallback.setName(user);

      } else if (callbacks[i] instanceof PasswordCallback) {

        passwordCallback = (PasswordCallback)callbacks[i];
        passwordCallback.setPassword(password);

      } else {
       throw new UnsupportedCallbackException
           (callbacks[i], "Unrecognized Callback");
      }
   }
 }

// user defined login method which simply counts the number of login attempts
// and sets the user and password which will be used in the callback above
 public boolean login(String user, char[] password)
 {
    if(loginTries > 2) {
     System.out.println("Sorry charlie...");
     return false;
    } else {
     this.user = user;
     this.password = password;
    }

    loginTries++;

    try {
     // attempt authentication on the LoginContext
```

LISTING 10.3   continued

```
        lc.login();

        // authentication succeeded
        return true;

    } catch (AccountExpiredException aee) {

        System.out.println("Your account has expired. " +
                "Please notify your administrator.");

    } catch (CredentialExpiredException cee) {

        System.out.println("Your credentials have expired.");

    } catch (FailedLoginException fle) {

        System.out.println("Authentication Failed");

    } catch (Exception e) {

        System.out.println("Unexpected Exception - unable to continue");
        e.printStackTrace();
    }
    // authentication did not succeed
    return false;
    }
}
```

The WorkPlacePrincipal class in Listing 10.4 implements the Principal interface.

LISTING 10.4   WorkPlacePrincipal Class

```
package org.jworkplace.login;
import java.security.Principal;

public class WorkPlacePrincipal implements Principal, java.io.Serializable {
  private String name;

  public WorkPlacePrincipal(String name) {
    if (name == null)
      throw new NullPointerException("illegal null input");
    this.name = name;
  }

  public String getName() {
    return name;
  }
```

LISTING 10.4   continued

```java
public String toString() {
  return("WorkPlacePrincipal: " + name);
}

public boolean equals(Object o) {
  if (o == null)
    return false;

  if (this == o)
    return true;

  if (!(o instanceof WorkPlacePrincipal))
    return false;
  WorkPlacePrincipal that = (WorkPlacePrincipal)o;

  if (this.getName().equals(that.getName()))
  return true;
  return false;
}

public int hashCode() {
  return name.hashCode();
}
}
```

To initialize a `LoginModule`, the `LoginContext` calls each configured `LoginModule`'s no-argument constructor:

```java
void initialize(Subject subject, CallbackHandler callbackHandler,
    Map sharedState, Map options);
```

The `WorkPlaceLoginModule` class in Listing 10.5 implements the `LoginModule` interface. The specific validation of the username and password is not shown, as you would provide your own specific implementation.

LISTING 10.5   WorkPlaceLoginModule Class

```java
package org.jworkplace.login;

import java.util.*;
import java.io.IOException;
import javax.security.auth.*;
import javax.security.auth.callback.*;
import javax.security.auth.login.*;
import javax.security.auth.spi.*;

public class WorkPlaceLoginModule implements LoginModule {
```

LISTING 10.5 continued

```
// initial state
private Subject subject;
private CallbackHandler callbackHandler;
private Map sharedState;
private Map options;

// configurable option
private boolean debug = false;

// the authentication status
private boolean succeeded = false;
private boolean commitSucceeded = false;

// username and password
private String username;
private char[] password;

private WorkPlacePrincipal userPrincipal;

// the initialize method is called by the LoginContext
public void initialize(Subject subject, CallbackHandler callbackHandler,
        Map sharedState, Map options) {

  this.subject = subject;
  this.callbackHandler = callbackHandler;
  this.sharedState = sharedState;
  this.options = options;

}

// this is the login method that is called by the LoginContext
public boolean login() throws LoginException {

  // prompt for a username and password
  if (callbackHandler == null)
    throw new LoginException("Error: no CallbackHandler available ");

  // Two Callback are created, one for the name and one for the password
  Callback[] callbacks = new Callback[2];
  callbacks[0] = new NameCallback("JWorkPlace username: ");
  callbacks[1] = new PasswordCallback("JWorkPlace password: ", false);

  try {
    // this is the callback to our LoginHandler
    callbackHandler.handle(callbacks);
    // get the username and password provided in the callback
    username = ((NameCallback)callbacks[0]).getName();
    char[] tmpPassword = ((PasswordCallback)callbacks[1]).getPassword();
    if (tmpPassword == null) {
```

10

P2P SECURITY

LISTING 10.5   continued

```
         // treat a NULL password as an empty password
         tmpPassword = new char[0];
      }
          password = new char[tmpPassword.length];
          System.arraycopy(tmpPassword, 0,
            password, 0, tmpPassword.length);
      ((PasswordCallback)callbacks[1]).clearPassword();

   } catch (java.io.IOException ioe) {
      throw new LoginException(ioe.toString());
   } catch (UnsupportedCallbackException uce) {
      throw new LoginException("Error: " + uce.getCallback().toString());
   }

      // verify the username/password
      // insert code to verify user / password here
      // Authentication succeeded
      succeeded = true;
      return true;

      // Authentication failed      succeeded = false;
      throw new FailedLoginException("Password Incorrect");

   }

   // the 2 phases of authentication - success commit
   public boolean commit() throws LoginException {
     if (succeeded == false) {
       return false;
     } else {
       // add a Principal (authenticated identity)
       // to the Subject

       // assume the user we authenticated is the WorkPlacePrincipal
       userPrincipal = new WorkPlacePrincipal(username);
       if (!subject.getPrincipals().contains(userPrincipal)) {
         subject.getPrincipals().add(userPrincipal);

     }
       // clean out state
       username = null;
       for (int i = 0; i < password.length; i++)
           password[i] = ' ';
       password = null;

       commitSucceeded = true;
       return true;
     }
   }
```

Listing 10.5 continued

```
  // the 2 phases of authentication - failure abort
public boolean abort() throws LoginException {
  if (succeeded == false) {
    return false;
  } else if (succeeded == true && commitSucceeded == false) {
    // login succeeded but overall authentication failed
    succeeded = false;
    username = null;
    if (password != null) {
      for (int i = 0; i < password.length; i++)
      password[i] = ' ';
      password = null;
    }
    userPrincipal = null;
  } else {
    // overall authentication succeeded and commit succeeded,
    // but someone else's commit failed
    logout();
  }
  return true;
}

public boolean logout() throws LoginException {
  subject.getPrincipals().remove(userPrincipal);
  succeeded = false;
  succeeded = commitSucceeded;
  username = null;
  if (password != null) {
    for (int i = 0; i < password.length; i++)
      password[i] = ' ';
    password = null;
  }
  userPrincipal = null;
  return true;
}
}
```

After successful authentication, JAAS provides the capability to enforce access controls on the principals associated with the authenticated subject. You will need to grant the necessary security permissions to your codebase. If you are using JDK 1.3, JAAS is not a part of the core distribution, and therefore requires a grant statement similar to the following:

```
/** Java 2 Access Control Policy for the JAAS Application **/

/* grant the JAAS core library AllPermission */
grant codebase "file:/usr/java/jdk1.3/jre/lib/ext/jaas.jar" {
```

```
    permission java.security.AllPermission;
};

/* grant the sample LoginModule AllPermission */
 grant codebase "file:/usr/JWorkPlace/lib/login.jar" {
   permission java.security.AllPermission;
};

grant codebase "file:/usr/JWorkPlace/lib/service.jar" {
   permission javax.security.auth.AuthPermission "createLoginContext";
   permission javax.security.auth.AuthPermission "doAs";
   permission java.util.PropertyPermission "java.home", "read";
   permission org.jworkplace.login.AccountPermission "createAccount";
};
```

A login policy can be associated with a service by setting the following property:

```
-Djava.security.policy==/usr/JiniServices/CMS/config/login.policy
```

The following policy extends the Java 2 codebase policy with `Subject`-based access control. This grant entry provides the necessary permissions to perform a sensitive operation (createAccount) to any `Subject` that has an associated `WorkPlacePrincipal`.

```
/** Subject-Based Access Control Policy for the JWorkPlace Application **/

grant codebase "file:/usr/JWorkPlace/lib/service.jar",
  Principal org.jworkplace.login.WorkPlacePrincipal * {
    permission org.jworkplace.login.AccountPermission "createAccount";
};
```

A login authorization policy can be associated with a service by setting the following property:

```
-Djava.security.auth.policy==/usr/JiniServices/CMS/config/login_jaas.policy
```

JAAS supplements the Java 2 security with architecture using the `Subject.doAs` method to dynamically associate an authenticated subject with the current `AccessControlContext`. The `AccessController` can base its decisions on both the executing code itself and the principals associated with the `Subject`.

The `WorkPlaceAction` class in Listing 10.6 implements the `PrivilegedAction` interface. The `PrivilegedAction` interface is implemented by classes that require access control checks. The `run` method is called by the `AccessController.doPrivileged` method after enabling privileges.

LISTING 10.6   WorkPlaceAction Class

```
package org.jworkplace.login;

import java.io.File;
import java.security.PrivilegedAction;

public class WorkPlaceAction implements PrivilegedAction {
  // run method defined in the PrivilegedAction interface
  public Object run() {
    // get the security manager and check if permission has been granted
    SecurityManager sm = System.getSecurityManager();
    sm.checkPermission(new AccountPermission("createAccount"));
    return null;
  }
}
```

Finally, the AccountPermission class shown in Listing 10.7 extends BasicPermission. BasicPermission provides a simple base class for creating new permission types. In this case, you create a new AccountPermission class that is checked in the WorkPlaceAction to verify that the thread of control associated with the current Subject has the necessary permission to create an account.

LISTING 10.7   AccountPermission Class

```
package org.jworkplace.login;
import java.security.BasicPermission;

public final class AccountPermission extends BasicPermission
                    implements java.io.Serializable
{

  public AccountPermission(String name) {
    this(name,null);
  }

  public AccountPermission(String name, String action) {
    super(name);
  }

}
```

10

P2P SECURITY

Additional Resources

- National Institute of Standards and Technology Computer Security Resource Center (http://csrc.nist.gov/publications/fips/index.html)

  Here you will find the recommendations of the United States government related to cryptographic standards and applications.

- AES Algorithm (Rijndael) Information (http://csrc.nist.gov/encryption/aes/rijndael/)

  The specification and a sample implementation of Rijndael in C is available here.

- The Block Cipher Rijndael (http://www.esat.kuleuven.ac.be/~rijmen/rijndael/)

  This is the original page for information about the Rijndael cipher. The page is not maintained at this time. However, having been selected as the standard, there is a considerable amount of information elsewhere.

- Source Code for AES Finalist Algorithms (http://csrc.nist.gov/encryption/aes/round2/r2algs-code.html)

  The source code for the candidates for the AES algorithm can be found at this Web site.

- MARS cipher (http://www.research.ibm.com/security/mars.html)

  Another contender for AES, documentation describing the algorithm is available here.

- RC6 Block Cipher (http://www.rsasecurity.com/rsalabs/rc6/index.html)

  This is the RSA Laboratories submission for the AES algorithm.

- SERPENT (http://www.cl.cam.ac.uk/~rja14/serpent.html)

  The runner-up in the competition for AES, the SERPENT algorithm and implementation is described in papers available at this site.

- Twofish symmetric algorithm (http://www.counterpane.com/twofish.html)

  A contender in the competition to select an algorithm for AES, Twofish is an impressive, unencumbered offering. Counterpane Labs' site provides information about its algorithm, which is unpatented, uncopyrighted, and free for use.

- The Kerberos Authentication Service v.5 (http://www.ietf.org/rfc/rfc1510.txt)

  This document provides an overview and specification for Kerberos v.5.

- Security Assertion Markup Language (SAML) (http://www.oasis-open.org/committees/security/)

This is the homepage for the SAML 1.0 Specification Set. From here you can also follow the proceedings as the standard is developed.

- XML Signature, XML Encryption and Canonicalization, and XKMS (`http://www.w3c.org`)

  These standards are important pieces of work that augment SAML to provide additional features.

- The Liberty Alliance (`http://www.projectliberty.org/`)

  The home page for the organization whose charter is to promote interoperability and open systems for network identification. The site is surprisingly bare at the moment, but should become useful shortly.

- Microsoft Passport Authentication Service (`http://www.passport.com/`)

  Information about signing up to become a .NET Passport member, as well as information for developers, can be found at this site.

- Transport Layer Security (`http://www.ietf.org/html.charters/tls-charter.html`)

  The IETF working group for TLS maintains its homepage here. Internet Drafts and Request for Comments for TLS and related technologies are available.

- PGP (`http://web.mit.edu/network/pgp.html`)

  This is the homepage for the free noncommercial version of PGP.

- Free Haven (`http://www.freehaven.net/`)

  Information about this interesting P2P project is provided at this Web page.

- *Free Riding on Gnutella*, E. Adar and B. Huberman, Xerox Palo Alto Research Center (`http://www.firstmonday.dk/issues/issue5_10/adar/`)

  This is an interesting look at Gnutella and usage patterns.

- Intel Peer-to-Peer Trusted Library (`http://sourceforge.net/projects/ptptl`)

  The library and source code for Win32 and Linux platforms is available at this project homepage.

- Java 2 Standard Edition platform version 1.4 (`http://java.sun.com/j2se/`)

  Sun's software development kits, documentation, and tutorials for the Java programming language can be found here.

- Generic Security Services Application Programming Interface Version 2 (`http://www.rfc-editor.org/rfc/rfc2078.txt`)

  This RFC defines GSS-API and serves as the base for the specifications related to the GSS-API. RFC 2744 defines the C bindings, and RFC 2583 defines the Java bindings.

10

P2P SECURITY

Summary

In this chapter we've covered the basics of secure systems, including the fundamental concepts and some of the mechanisms used to construct secure systems. Although peer-to-peer architecture is different in many respects from the traditional client-server architecture, the same principles of security apply, and many of the same mechanisms can be employed. Where peer-to-peer systems have differing requirements, the mechanisms can be adapted. In some cases, peer-to-peer requires a unique solution, particularly for those involving identity and anonymity.

With the information presented here, you should be able to make decisions about the technologies that can be integrated into peer-to-peer applications to make them secure. You have learned about some useful toolkits, including Intel's peer-to-peer library that can help you quickly secure your application. Java provides a suite of APIs that makes it possible to use almost any of the mechanisms explored in this chapter. Finally, you are also prepared to recognize the issues peculiar to peer-to-peer systems and explore security in more depth.

Building Distributed Systems Using Java

PART
III

IN THIS PART

Web Services Explained

by Toufic Boubez

IN THIS CHAPTER

The Web services concept has been gaining momentum in the past two years. Most major software companies have embraced the concept in one form or another. Some have even staked their future on it. Although the convergence toward a common understanding of what the term means has been slow, a clear definition of what Web services are is finally emerging. This is reminiscent of the early days of object-oriented programming (OOP); not until the concepts of inheritance, encapsulation, and polymorphism were well defined did OOP become accepted into the mainstream of development methodologies. This chapter defines Web services and provides an overview of the concepts, architectures, and standards that are involved.

Web Services and the Drive Toward Interoperability

It's always interesting to start a discussion on distributed computing with a quote attributed to Leslie Lamport: "A distributed system is one in which the failure of a computer you didn't even know existed can render your own computer unusable." Although Lamport said this several years ago, the concept still applies.

It is clear that interoperability has been one of the major themes in software engineering in general, and in Enterprise Application Integration (EAI) in particular, for the past decade.

Unfortunately, the seamless interoperability vision is still a dream. Brittleness in all current architectures is preventing software from achieving this vision. This brittleness comes from tightly coupled systems that generate dependencies at every level in the system. One of the most important lessons we learned as developers and architects is that systems need to be able to find resources—software or otherwise—automatically, when and as needed, without human intervention. This frees up business people to concentrate on their business and customers, not worrying about IT complexities, and frees up system developers to concentrate on enabling their business and their customers, not dealing with interoperability headaches by writing glue code and patching systems together. More than any technical consideration, this concept of implicit, seamless integration as a major business benefit is one of the main drivers for Web services. In other words, the time has come for just-in-time integration!

On the technical side, as a response to the demands of business, major shifts have taken place toward flexibility and interoperability, through open and widely accepted standards. The first major shift happened a long time ago with the advent of TCP/IP as an open platform for networking. This major step enabled such important and pervasive architectures as client/server computing. It took the advent of the Web for the next major shift, with HTML and HTTP providing the first truly universal open and portable user interface. Next, Java gave us truly open portable programming. Finally, XML brought with it open portable data exchange.

Integration

The next step in this evolution of open standards is the integration step. How do all these ingredients come together to facilitate the next evolution of e-business? We will see how and why the Web services concept is the answer to this question. As is becoming clear from the computing trends described in this book, distributed computing integration and interoperability is essential.

Enabling all these trends has been a realization that interoperability is really best served by a set of open standards that are accepted and agreed upon by all parties who want to interoperate. It can be argued that TCP/IP was one of the first significant enabling standards to make possible the current Internet as we know it. The Web revolution was enabled by HTML and HTTP, which was built on top of TCP/IP. HTML led us to the necessity of XML, and the original combination of XML and HTTP led to SOAP.

In the early days of the Object Orientation (OO), the general question was "What can Smalltalk (or C++, or Eiffel) do that I can't do with C?" It took some time to realize that this was the wrong question to ask. Not until the definitions of Object Orientation started being formulated (inheritance, encapsulation, polymorphism) and the corresponding benefits started being clarified did OO start to gain serious acceptance as a valid approach. The Web services concept finds itself at a similar stage in its development. In other words, "What can I do with Web services that I can't do with COM or CORBA or Jini?"

To get to an answer, we need to start articulating clear definitions of what constitutes a Web service and formulate the corresponding benefits of the approach. To this end, if we start thinking of software as a utility that is constantly available, we can start envisioning a system or an ecology of software components that live on the network, perform various tasks, conform to a set of declared interfaces, and can be found and invoked interchangeably as needed. This is essentially a fuzzy description of Web services.

For a clearer definition, we can say that a Web service is a *platform- and implementation-independent* functionality that can be

- Described using a known service description language;
- Published to a known registry;
- Discovered through a known standard mechanism;
- Invoked through a declared API; and
- Composed with other services.

While we're on the topic of definitions, one important point to keep in mind is that a Web service need not necessarily exist on the Web. This is an unfortunate historical naming issue. A Web service can live anywhere on the network, Internet, or an intranet. Another important point is that a Web service implementation and deployment platform is irrelevant. A service is available through its declared API and invocation mechanism. This set of definitions are the requirements that make Web services a system of loosely coupled services.

Web services intend to build on current accepted specifications such as XML and SOAP, while defining an additional set of specifications to complete the general Web services architecture.

Service-Oriented Architectures

Web services belong to a set of architectures called Service-Oriented Architectures (SOA). A SOA recognizes three simple roles—services requester, services provider, and services registry—and three simple operations—publish, find, and bind (see Figure 11.1). These roles and operations are self explanatory and can be performed by any entity at various times. For example, a networked calendar application might provide its calendaring capability as a service; at the same time, it might request the services of a networked messaging system to send an alert to a user.

FIGURE 11.1

Roles and operations in a SOA.

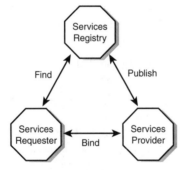

The Web Services Architecture: The Interoperability Stacks

Every architecture needs at least one stack of components (sometimes known as a *layered cake*). Web services incorporate several different technologies and standards that need to work together.

Software architects in general rely on architecture stacks to define how different technology components work together. Companies that are working on Web services technologies have agreed to define three Web services "interoperability" stacks, first proposed as the Web Services Framework at the W3C Workshop on Web services in April 2001. The three stacks help us make sense of the veritable alphabet soup of Web services-related acronyms. These stacks are as follows:

- Wire Stack—Represents the components that are necessary to transmit messages— including data and metadata—for service discovery and invocation

- Description Stack—Represents the components that are needed to describe and compose services

- Discovery Stack—Represents the components that are needed for static (design time) or dynamic (runtime) discovery and introspection of services

These stacks have evolved since they were first introduced, and they are still evolving. The stacks are not meant to specify in complete details all the components of an architecture, but to capture the required components for true interoperability, security, and other components, while specifying the current adopted de facto or ratified standards. The next three sections present the current prevailing view of the interoperability stacks. You will see several technologies mentioned in various parts of the stacks. The main technologies (XML, SOAP, WSDL, and UDDI) will be covered in later sections.

The Web Services Wire Stack

The Web Services Wire Stack (see Figure 11.2) represents the components that are needed to transmit a message among the three roles of a generalized SOA—in other words, all the components that are required to put data on the wire and ensure that it is retrieved at the other end securely by its intended recipient(s).

FIGURE 11.2
The Web Services Wire Stack.

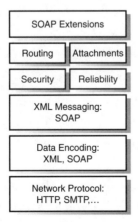

At the base of the stack is the network protocol, specifying that different protocols such as HTTP or SMTP can be substituted, increasing the potential for interoperability. This means that the same service can potentially be accessed through different means. The stack goes on to specify that XML should be the data encoding of the messages, and that Simple Object Access Protocol (SOAP) is the preferred messaging protocol. Keep in mind that although SOAP is specified in the Wire Stack, you can deploy Web services that are invoked with other messaging protocols, as long as you describe that protocol somewhere. (That's where WSDL and UDDI come in, as we'll see later.) Finally, the stack specifies that issues of security, reliability, routing, and additional attachments to messages are to be handled as extensions onto XML and SOAP.

The Description Stack

One of the most important aspects of deploying a service is the ability to describe it in a manner that will allow others to locate it, invoke it, and compose it with other services. The Description Stack defines the technologies that serve that purpose (see Figure 11.3). At the base of the stack is XML schema (see the section "XML" later in this chapter) because all description mechanisms are expressed in XML. Another important technology, Web Services Description Language (WSDL), a kind of Interface Definition Language (IDL), allows service interfaces and implementations to be described. Other technologies will allow descriptions of service capabilities and the orchestration of services into workflows.

FIGURE 11.3

The Web Services Description Stack.

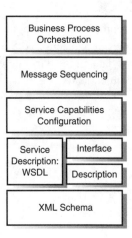

The Discovery Stack

Finally, the right service needs to be located to be used. Two aspects to discovery exist in the Web services architecture. The first aspect is the need for a well-known registry (or set of registries) that provide a search mechanism for services. The other aspect is the need for an introspection capability on services to make sure that the service being selected is the right one. The Discovery Stack (see Figure 11.4) specifies the technologies that enable service requesters to locate and introspect the services they will use.

FIGURE **11.4**
The Web Services
Discovery Stack.

The main discovery mechanism is Universal Description, Discovery, and Integration (UDDI), a set of replicated registries with a corresponding API for publishing and querying. As far as introspection mechanisms, the emerging standard seems to be Web Services Inspection Language (WSIL), also referred to as WS-Inspection. WSIL provides a mechanism that complements both WSDL from a description point of view and UDDI from a discovery point of view. It does this by providing a service with the capability of describing itself upon request. Because WSIL is still in the emerging state, we won't cover it in detail in this chapter.

The Principal Web Services Technologies

The Web services stacks make use of several technologies. In this section, we will cover what are considered to be the main components of today's Web services architectures, namely XML, SOAP, WSDL, and UDDI. Due to space consideration, the discussion will concentrate on the basic concepts, representations, data structures, and mechanisms, without going too deeply into arcane details that are better left to a specialized book.

XML

A section in a chapter in a book about P2P is probably not the best in-depth reference on XML. Although this book assumes that you are somewhat familiar with XML, this section does cover the main concepts of XML to give you a good basis for understanding the other topics covered. If you are comfortable with XML, you can skip this section.

Data and Document-Centric Languages

The concept of markup languages has been around for a long time (SGML and HTML are two major examples), but no simple yet flexible standard (that is, recognized by major players) was available to define and exchange data. Document-centric markup languages such as HTML are good at specifying the components of a document (such as titles, paragraphs, lists, and tables) without describing the data that is contained in that document. XML, on the other hand, is a data-centric markup language whose main purpose is to define the data that is contained in a document. Consider, for example, the two fragments shown next. First, look at an HTML fragment:

```
<table BORDER COLS=3 WIDTH="100%" >
   <tr BGCOLOR="#CCFFFF">
      <td>Book Title</td>
      <td>Author</td>
      <td>SKU</td>
   </tr>
   <tr>
      <td>Brain Surgery Explained</td>
      <td>John Smith</td>
      <td>154-455</td>
   </tr>
   <tr>
      <td>DIY Surgery</td>
      <td>Betty Mitchell</td>
      <td>154-323</td>
   </tr>
</table>
```

Next, look at an XML fragment:

```
<books>
   <book>
      <title>Brain Surgery Explained</title>
      <author>John Smith</author>
      <sku>154-544</sku>
   </book>
   <book>
      <title>DIY Surgery</title>
      <author>Betty Mitchell</author>
      <sku>154-323</sku>
   </book>
</books>
```

At this point, the distinction should be clear. Although the HTML code is good at telling an application such as a browser *how to display* the book data, it does nothing to tell the application *what* the data consists of. For example, a distinction isn't made between metadata (in this case, the first row, which describes the column headings) and data (the remaining two rows). By contrast, the XML code tells the application about the structure of the data and metadata, leaving decisions on what to do with the data to the application. (This includes how and what to display, and whether to display at all. As a matter of fact, the application could be an order-processing application that has nothing to do with displaying data.) That, in a nutshell, is one of the greatest advantages of XML.

Still considering the two code snippets, we can make another important observation: In the HTML code, the tags (such as `<td>` and `<tr>`) are predetermined and defined in the HTML language specification. Developers are not allowed to define their own tags. In the XML code shown, the developer defined the tags. (We will explore the definition mechanism later in this section.) Remember that the *X* in XML stands for *extensible*. This means that developers can define and extend their own tags and make up their own languages. That is the other great advantage of XML.

XML Instance Document Components

XML documents are of two types: instance documents and specification documents. Instance documents are often matched to a specification, which specifies the tags and their allowed occurrences within the document. We first cover the details of instance documents. (These are the documents that you will usually get to see.) Specification documents will be covered later.

Let us now look at a more complete XML listing (Listing 11.1) so that you can understand the components that form an XML document.

LISTING 11.1   Book Sellers XML Document

```xml
<?xml version="1.0" encoding="UTF-8"?>
<books>
   <book isbn="123456789">
      <title>Brain Surgery Explained</title>
      <author>
         <firstname>John</firstname>
         <lastname>Smith</lastname>
      </author>
      <retailer>
         <name>booksgalore</name>
         <sku>154-455</sku>
         <price>24.99</price>
      </retailer>
      <retailer>
         <name>seriousbooks</name>
         <sku>465-40-143</sku>
         <price>27.99</price>
      </retailer>
   </book>
   <book isbn="987654321">
      <title>DIY Surgery</title>
      <author>
         <firstname>Terry</firstname>
         <lastname>Mitchell</lastname>
      </author>
      <author>
```

LISTING **11.1** continued

```
        <firstname>Joe</firstname>
        <lastname>Mitchell</lastname>
    </author>
    <retailer>
        <name>seriousbooks</name>
        <sku>465-40-365</sku>
        <price>32.49</price>
    </retailer>
  </book>
</books>
```

This listing is an XML instance document. It consists mainly of two parts: the prologue and the body. The prologue is the following line:

```
<?xml version="1.0" encoding="UTF-8"?>
```

This line starts with the characters <?, which define what's called a *processing instruction*. Processing instructions are beyond the scope of this discussion; suffice it to say, most of the time what you'll use is the same line shown in Listing 11.1.

The rest of the document forms the body, and it consists of a hierarchy or tree of paired tags, starting with a root node—in this case, the node that is bracketed and defined by the paired tags <books> and </books>. A tree view of the body of the document is shown in Figure 11.5.

FIGURE **11.5**

Tree view of the books.xml *XML document.*

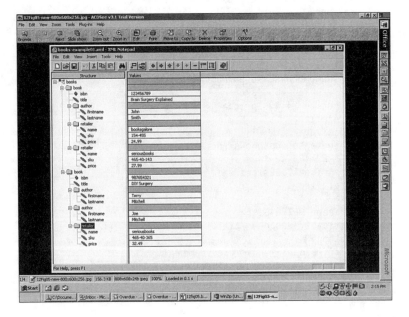

An XML document is, in essence, a collection of paired tags such as `<author>` and `</author>`, with data between the tag pairs. This data is either string data such as an author's name, or other sets of nested paired tags. Each set of these paired tags defines what's called an *element*. Unlike HTML, for example, XML element tags have to be completely nested, or ordered properly. For example, the following HTML syntax, with the bold and italic tags out of order, is acceptable:

```
<B><I>This is OK in HTML</B></I>
```

In XML, a similar syntax such as

```
<book><title>Web Services</book></title>
```

is not valid, but has to be properly ordered:

```
<book><title>Web Services</title></book>
```

A document in which all the tags are properly matched and nested and in which no syntax errors exist is called a *well-formed document*.

XML has different types of element tags, but the main three are illustrated in the listing:

- Elements that contain other nested elements—These elements are nodes within the document tree. An example is the `<book>` element, which contains the `<title>`, `<author>`, and `<retailer>` elements.

- Elements that contain string data—These are leaf nodes in the document tree. An example is the `<title>` element, which describes the title of a book in string form.

- Elements that are empty—These elements do not contain data outside of the element tag. Instead, they convey information just by their presence, or through the attributes they contain. As an example, instead of using `<price>27.99</price>`, we can use `<price value="27.99"/>`. Notice that the start and end tags are combined into one tag.

Now let's take a closer look at the `<book>` tag from the previous listing:

```
<book isbn="123456789">
```

The name-value pair (`isbn="123456789"`) before the closure of the angle bracket (`<`) is called an *attribute*. Start tags of XML elements can have attributes added within their angle brackets, and an attribute's value (the value part of the name-value pair) can only be a string.

If you're asking yourself at this point why attributes are needed or what attributes provide that can't be done with elements, give yourself some bonus points. Conceivably, we could have rewritten the majority of the elements in the `<books>` XML document as a set of empty elements, with data such as book titles or author names provided as strings within the attribute values. For various reasons, however, this is not a good idea. The debate over the usage of attributes has been raging in the XML community since the introduction of the XML specification, with no clear winners. The general rule of thumb is to use elements to convey content, and attributes to convey characteristics of that content, especially if those characteristics can be enumerated (such as a small set of colors). For example, when describing a book, the book title is considered content, and described in a `<title>` element. The book type, on the other hand (for example, "technical," "fiction," and so on) can be described in an attribute. Also keep in mind that elements are usually processed more efficiently by parsers and XML tools..

DTD, Schema, and Namespaces

Let us now consider the following example:

```
<?xml version="1.0" encoding="UTF-8"?>
<results>
    <book>
        <name>Our House</name>
        <autor>John Doe</autor>
        <author>Mary Public</author>
    </book>
</results>
```

This is a well-formed document (correct syntax, all the tags are properly paired, and so on), but did we intend to have two different elements, `<author>` and `<autor>`, in the document, or is that an error? Also, even though one would think of a book as having a title and an author as having a name, no `<title>` element is present. Instead, the element `<name>` seems to refer to the title of the book, not an author's name.

These two irregularities illustrate the point that writing well-formed XML documents is often not sufficient. These documents do not exist in a vacuum: They usually serve some purpose for exchanging data, and they are usually shared with other people or between applications. Therefore, they must have a shared meaning, a shared purpose, and a shared structure that can be validated. This validation is done through a *specification* document.

In the early days of XML, XML document structure and validation were specified through document type definition (DTD) documents. An example DTD for the `books.xml` document is relatively self explanatory and is shown in the following code:

```
<!ELEMENT books (book+)>
<!ELEMENT book (title , author+ , retailer+)>
<!ATTLIST book  isbn CDATA  #IMPLIED >
<!ELEMENT title (#PCDATA)>
<!ELEMENT author (firstname , lastname)>
<!ELEMENT retailer (name , sku , price)>
<!ELEMENT name (#PCDATA)>
<!ELEMENT sku (#PCDATA)>
```

```
<!ELEMENT firstname (#PCDATA)>
<!ELEMENT lastname (#PCDATA)>
<!ELEMENT price (#PCDATA)>
```

DTDs have some useful properties in that they allow the specification of the vocabulary and the grammar of an XML document (that is, they specify what tags are allowed and what their containment model is within the document). However, DTDs quickly proved to be too simple for interesting use of XML. Aside from their non-XML syntax, DTD documents had two major deficiencies: They did not allow the specification of the *type* of data allowed within the tags of an element; they did not allow the use of *namespaces*, an important and useful mechanism for reuse of XML elements.

To illustrate the need for namespaces, imagine a messaging system that handles messages from different organizations and wraps them in a `<message>` element, as shown in the following XML fragment:

```
<message>
   <sender>BooksGalore</sender>
   <receiver>dianadoe@hotmail.com</receiver>
   <body>
      <purchaseOrder ID="45933">
         <billTo>Diana Doe</billTo>
         <book isbn="123456789">
            <title>Brain Surgery Explained</title>
            <author>John Smith</author>
            <sku>154-544</sku>
         </book>
         <message>Book is on back order.</message>
      </purchaseOrder>
   </body>
</message>
```

This example illustrates two of the issues that are raised when different XML documents are composed into one, or when elements are reused. First, the element `<message>` exists in two different places, with two different meanings or contexts. The messaging system defines its own `<message>` element as a wrapper for the whole message, and the message sender uses its own `<message>` element to indicate messages to the receiver (such as when a book is on back order). This ambiguous use of an element can be confusing to the XML parser and to the application that is handling the document, and is called a *namespace collision*.

The other concept is that the `<book>` element is the same one used in examples throughout this section, and has been reused by the message sender. Does the sender in this case need to redefine the specification for the `<book>` element, or should there be a way that the sender can indicate that this is an element defined elsewhere? An associated issue is that the `<body>` element should be allowed to contain *any* type of XML tags that the sender requires. How can the designers of that specification handle this requirement without prior knowledge of the contents? How will the receiving application know when the `</message>` element is the root element for the message being delivered, or the containing element for the message to the customer?

The issue of namespaces has been familiar to software engineers for a long time and has been recently brought to the surface because of the important object-oriented concept of reuse.

It manifests itself, for example, in the use of package names to fully qualify class names in Java, thus enabling the use of classes from a variety of sources in the same application. Similar issues have been encountered in XML usage: What if it makes sense to use elements from different sources in the same XML document? As in the Java fully qualified class names, namespaces solve this problem by providing the ability to disambiguate elements that are spelled the same but have different contexts.

Using namespaces to qualify elements in the XML document shown in the previous example would result in a document similar to the one shown here:

```
<message>
    <sender>BooksGalore</sender>
    <receiver>dianadoe@hotmail.com</receiver>
    <body>
        <po:purchaseOrder ID="45933"
            xmlns:po="http://localhost:8080/xml/schemas/purchaseorder">
            <po:billTo>Diana Doe</po:billTo>
            <bk:book isbn="123456789"
                xmlns:bk="http://localhost:8080/xml/schemas/book">
                <bk:title>Brain Surgery Explained</bk:title>
                <bk:author>John Smith</bk:author>
                <bk:sku>154-544</bk:sku>
            </bk:book>
            <po:message>Book is on back order.</po:message>
        </po:purchaseOrder>
    </body>
</message>
```

You can include namespace declarations in different ways. As you see from the example, a namespace declaration can be included in the root element of the new namespace—in this case, one in the `<purchaseOrder>` element, which is the highest level in that hierarchy, and one in the `<book>` element, which is the root element of the next namespace. The syntax of the declaration is relatively simple and takes the form `xmlns:`*namespaceidentifier*`=`*URI*, as shown here:

```
<bk:book isbn="123456789"
    xmlns:bk="http://localhost:8080/xml/schemas/book">
```

In this declaration, the *namespaceidentifier* is bk; it is used as a prefix for all elements that belong to that namespace, such as <bk:book> and <bk:author>. The Uniform Resource Identifier (URI) uniquely identifies the namespace and usually tends to be a Uniform Resource Locator (URL), although this is *not* a requirement. URIs in general can be any uniquely identifying sequence of characters, and they do not identify the location of a resource (as opposed to URLs). Using URLs is generally easier than using URIs because URLs are usually uniquely identified. A namespace declaration is scoped by the element in which it appears so that elements outside of that scope do not belong to that namespace. In our example, the <po:message> element is within the scope of the xmlns:bk="http://localhost:8080/xml/schemas/book" declaration; in contrast, the <message> element is outside the scope. Therefore, <message> is from a different namespace—in this case, the *default* undeclared namespace of the main document.

Alternatively, all namespace declarations can be included in the root element of the document, as follows:

```
<message
    xmlns:po="http://localhost:8080/xml/schemas/purchaseorder"
    xmlns:bk="http://localhost:8080/xml/schemas/book">
    <sender>BooksGalore</sender>
    <receiver>dianadoe@hotmail.com</receiver>
    <body>
        <po:purchaseOrder ID="45933">
            <po:billTo>Diana Doe</po:billTo>
            <bk:book isbn="123456789">
                <bk:title>Brain Surgery Explained</bk:title>
                <bk:author>John Smith</bk:author>
                <bk:sku>154-544</bk:sku>
            </bk:book>
            <po:message>Book is on back order.</po:message>
        </po:purchaseOrder>
    </body>
</message>
```

What is the alternative to DTDs? The answer to this question was defined by the publication of the XML schema specification. The schema definition for the <books> example is shown in Listing 11.2.

LISTING 11.2 Book Sellers XML Schema

```
<?xml version="1.0" encoding="UTF-8"?>
<xsd:schema xmlns:xsd="http://www.w3.org/2001/XMLSchema"
    elementFormDefault="qualified">
    <xsd:element name="books">
        <xsd:complexType>
            <xsd:sequence>
                <xsd:element ref="book" maxOccurs="unbounded"/>
```

LISTING 11.2   continued

```
            </xsd:sequence>
         </xsd:complexType>
      </xsd:element>
      <xsd:element name="book">
         <xsd:complexType>
            <xsd:sequence>
               <xsd:element ref="title"/>
               <xsd:element ref="author" maxOccurs="unbounded"/>
               <xsd:element ref="retailer" maxOccurs="unbounded"/>
            </xsd:sequence>
            <xsd:attribute name="isbn" use="optional" type="xsd:string"/>
         </xsd:complexType>
      </xsd:element>
      <xsd:element name="title" type="xsd:string"/>
      <xsd:element name="author">
         <xsd:complexType>
            <xsd:sequence>
               <xsd:element ref="firstname"/>
               <xsd:element ref="lastname"/>
            </xsd:sequence>
         </xsd:complexType>
      </xsd:element>
      <xsd:element name="retailer">
         <xsd:complexType>
            <xsd:sequence>
               <xsd:element ref="name"/>
               <xsd:element ref="sku"/>
               <xsd:element ref="price"/>
            </xsd:sequence>
         </xsd:complexType>
      </xsd:element>
      <xsd:element name="name" type="xsd:string"/>
      <xsd:element name="sku" type="xsd:string"/>
      <xsd:element name="price" type="xsd:float"/>
      <xsd:element name="firstname" type="xsd:string"/>
      <xsd:element name="lastname" type="xsd:string"/>
</xsd:schema>
```

Notice, for example, that the content of the different elements is typed. For example, we can now make sure that the <price> element contains a float. Typing and namespaces are only two of the many new features of XML schemas. Schemas give XML developers enormous flexibility in designing their documents, allowing things such as inheritance and range restrictions, among others.

Having defined the schema for the <books> example, how would an instance document make use of that fact? Let us look at an instance of XML that uses the books.xsd schema (see Listing 11.3).

LISTING 11.3   Book Sellers XML Document Using XML Schema

```xml
<?xml version="1.0" encoding="UTF-8"?>
<books xmlns:xsi="http://www.w3.org/2001/XMLSchema-instance"
xsi:noNamespaceSchemaLocation="http://localhost:8080/xml/schemas/books.xsd">
   <book isbn="123456789">
      <title>Brain Surgery Explained</title>
      <author>
         <firstname>John</firstname>
         <lastname>Smith</lastname>
      </author>
      <retailer>
         <name>booksgalore</name>
         <sku>154-455</sku>
         <price>24.99</price>
      </retailer>
      <retailer>
         <name>seriousbooks</name>
         <sku>465-40-143</sku>
         <price>27.99</price>
      </retailer>
   </book>
   <book isbn="987654321">
      <title>DIY Surgery</title>
      <author>
         <firstname>Terry</firstname>
         <lastname>Mitchell</lastname>
      </author>
      <author>
         <firstname>Joe</firstname>
         <lastname>Mitchell</lastname>
      </author>
      <retailer>
         <name>seriousbooks</name>
         <sku>465-40-365</sku>
         <price>32.49</price>
      </retailer>
   </book>
</books>
```

SOAP

By now, I hope I've convinced you that XML is a great idea for data exchange and interoperability. The next logical step in the evolution of interoperability standards is whether XML can be used not only to define data, but also to define messages between applications. That leads us to take a closer look at SOAP.

The first paragraph in the W3C note of the SOAP 1.1 specification (http://www.w3.org/TR/SOAP/) gives a great summary of what SOAP is: "SOAP is a lightweight protocol for exchange of information in a decentralized, distributed environment. It is an XML-based protocol that consists of three parts: an envelope that defines a framework for describing what is in a message and how to process it, a set of encoding rules for expressing instances of application-defined datatypes, and a convention for representing remote procedure calls and responses. SOAP can potentially be used in combination with a variety of other protocols; however, the only bindings defined in this document describe how to use SOAP in combination with HTTP and HTTP Extension Framework."

Although the readability of the specification goes downhill from there, this section should provide you with enough of a background to be able to use SOAP effectively. In essence, SOAP is a simple, lightweight protocol that allows you to use XML to exchange data across networks. SOAP can be invoked over (but not restricted to) HTTP, thereby getting around traditional firewall issues. This section goes into more detail about SOAP and its components.

The Structure of a SOAP Message

If you think of sending a message over the networks as being analogous to sending a letter in the mail, then the SOAP model starts making sense. The top-level SOAP structure is the SOAP Envelope, which contains a SOAP Header and a SOAP Body. This envelope is carried by some transport mechanism, most commonly HTTP (although other protocols such as SMTP can be used). Listings 11.4 and 11.5 show a SOAP message embedded in an HTTP request and the SOAP response embedded in the HTTP response. (All examples in this section are generated using the Apache Axis implementation and tools found at http://xml.apache.org/axis/.)

LISTING 11.4   SOAP Message Within an HTTP Request

```
POST /axis/servlet/AxisServlet HTTP/1.0
Content-Length: 459
Host: localhost
Content-Type: text/xml; charset=utf-8
SOAPAction: "http://soapinterop.org/echoString"

<?xml version="1.0" encoding="UTF-8"?>
<SOAP-ENV:Envelope
   SOAP-ENV:encodingStyle="http://schemas.xmlsoap.org/soap/encoding/"
   xmlns:SOAP-ENV="http://schemas.xmlsoap.org/soap/envelope/"
   xmlns:xsd="http://www.w3.org/2001/XMLSchema"
   xmlns:xsi="http://www.w3.org/2001/XMLSchema-instance">
 <SOAP-ENV:Body>
  <ns1:echoString xmlns:ns1="http://soapinterop.org/">
   <arg0 xsi:type="xsd:string">Hello!</arg0>
  </ns1:echoString>
 </SOAP-ENV:Body>
</SOAP-ENV:Envelope>
```

LISTING 11.5 SOAP Message Within an HTTP Response

```
HTTP/1.1 200 OK
Content-Type: text/xml; charset=utf-8
Content-Length: 499
Date: Thu, 24 Jan 2002 19:26:30 GMT
Server: Apache Tomcat/4.0.1 (HTTP/1.1 Connector)

<?xml version="1.0" encoding="UTF-8"?>
<SOAP-ENV:Envelope
   SOAP-ENV:encodingStyle="http://schemas.xmlsoap.org/soap/encoding/"
   xmlns:SOAP-ENV="http://schemas.xmlsoap.org/soap/envelope/"
   xmlns:xsd="http://www.w3.org/2001/XMLSchema"
   xmlns:xsi="http://www.w3.org/2001/XMLSchema-instance">
 <SOAP-ENV:Body>
  <ns1:echoStringResponse xmlns:ns1="http://soapinterop.org/">
  <echoStringResult xsi:type="xsd:string">Hello!</echoStringResult>
  </ns1:echoStringResponse>
 </SOAP-ENV:Body>
</SOAP-ENV:Envelope>
```

Although simple, the previous two listings are representative of SOAP messages. A SOAP message is an XML document that consists of a root `<Envelope>` element, sometimes containing an optional `<Header>` element, and typically containing a `<Body>` element. The names are self explanatory.

Typically, you won't have to build SOAP messages by hand because development tools from various sources such as Apache, IBM, and Microsoft will automate the construction of the messages. You need to keep two important issues in mind, however. The first one is the conversion of Java types into XML payload for the SOAP messages. This is important because few interesting or realistic services would take simple types—such as strings and numbers—as parameters or return simple types as results. For example, this would be the case when a purchasing service takes as parameter a complex `PurchaseOrder` object and returns a complex `Receipt` object. The easiest method to accomplish this conversion is to implement your complex data types as JavaBeans, providing them with the usual setter and getter methods. Most deployment tools will then automatically perform the conversion from JavaBeans to XML. In the following example, we are providing a relatively simple `PurchaseOrder` class, with two instance variables, `isbn` and `quantity`:

```
package myExamples.purchase;
public class PurchaseOrder {

    private String isbn;
    private Integer quantity;

    public String getIsbn() { return isbn; }
```

```
    public Integer getQuantity() { return quantity; }

    public void setIsbn(String newIsbn) { isbn = newIsbn; }
    public void setQuantity(Integer newQ) { quantity = newQ; }
}
```

The details of the next step will depend on the tool you happen to be using, but you need to provide a mapping from the parameters to the Bean class for the serialization to occur properly. In the Apache Axis implementation, this can be done in the Web Service Deployment Descriptor (WSDD) file that you create for the service. In it, you include a <beanMapping> element that holds that information. In the following example, the Bean class (myExamples.purchase.PurchaseOrder) is provided as the mapping for the purchase order input parameter of the service:

```
<deployment xmlns="http://xml.apache.org/axis/wsdd/"
    xmlns:java="http://xml.apache.org/axis/wsdd/providers/java"
    xmlns:po="http://localhost/PurchaseService">
<service name="PurchaseService" provider="java:RPC">
  <parameter name="className" value="myExamples.purchase.PurchaseService"/>
  <parameter name="methodName" value="*"/>
  <beanMapping qname="po:PurchaseOrder"
    languageSpecificType="java:myExamples.purchase.PurchaseOrder"/>
 </service>
</deployment>
```

Let us now look at the SOAP message that invokes the service:

```
POST /axis/servlet/AxisServlet HTTP/1.0Content-Length: 704Host:
localhostContent-Type: text/xml; charset=utf-8SOAPAction:
"PurchaseService/processOrder"
<?xml version="1.0" encoding="UTF-8"?>
<SOAP-ENV:Envelope
   SOAP-ENV:encodingStyle="http://schemas.xmlsoap.org/soap/encoding/"
   xmlns:SOAP-ENV="http://schemas.xmlsoap.org/soap/envelope/"
   xmlns:xsd="http://www.w3.org/2001/XMLSchema"
   xmlns:xsi="http://www.w3.org/2001/XMLSchema-instance">
 <SOAP-ENV:Body>
  <ns1:processOrder xmlns:ns1="PurchaseService">
   <arg1 href="#id0"/>
  </ns1:processOrder>
  <multiRef id="id0" SOAP-ENC:root="0" xsi:type="ns2:PurchaseOrder"
      xmlns:SOAP-ENC="http://schemas.xmlsoap.org/soap/encoding/"
      xmlns:ns2="urn:PurchaseService">
   <quantity xsi:type="xsd:int">5</quantity>
   <isbn xsi:type="xsd:string">0-672-32181-5</ISBN>
  </multiRef>
 </SOAP-ENV:Body>
</SOAP-ENV:Envelope>
```

You will notice that the conversion from the `PurchaseOrder` object to XML was performed automatically, resulting in the two instance variables being incorporated as the `<quantity>` and `<isbn>` subelements of the `<arg1>` element.

WSDL

In any reusable component-programming model, properly using a component requires finding out what it does, how to invoke it, what parameters it will take, and what kinds of results it will return. This also applies to Web services, which can be thought of as reusable components that can be invoked over the network through a variety of transports.

You have seen that XML is an essential ingredient for interoperable data definition and exchange, and that SOAP, built on top of XML and HTTP, is a good way to exchange messages. The next requirement for a robust, loosely coupled, distributed services architecture is the service description mechanism so that service providers can describe their services and how to invoke them. In this area, the WSDL specification has emerged as the de facto standard. This section will cover the basic concepts of WSDL and give some examples, but keep in mind that all current Web services tools such as IBM's and Microsoft's can automate the generation of WSDL descriptions of the Web services you develop.

WSDL is closely related to the concept of an IDL, as shown in the following example. The WSDL design pattern is to define a set of abstract reusable types and components, and then physical implementations that make use of these abstract components. During the following discussion, we will refer to the example in Listing 11.6 to go over the details of WSDL. In this example, a book retailer is defining a Web service that allows customers to request the price of a book either by ISBN or by author name.

LISTING 11.6   WSDL Document for the `GetBookPrice` Service

```xml
<?xml version="1.0" encoding="UTF-8"?>
<definitions name="GetBookPrice"
   targetNamespace="http://localhost:8080/axis/BookPriceService.jws"
   xmlns:soap="http://schemas.xmlsoap.org/wsdl/soap/"
   xmlns:serviceNS="http://localhost:8080/axis/BookPriceService.jws"
   xmlns:xsd="http://www.w3.org/2001/XMLSchema"
   xmlns="http://schemas.xmlsoap.org/wsdl/">
   <types>
      <xsd:schema
         targetNamespace="http://localhost:8080/xml/schemas/bookprice.xsd"
         xmlns:xsd="http://www.w3.org/2000/10/XMLSchema">
         <xsd:element name="BookPriceByISBNRequest">
            <xsd:complexType>
               <xsd:all>
```

LISTING 11.6 continued

```xml
                    <xsd:element name="isbn" type="string"/>
                </xsd:all>
            </xsd:complexType>
        </xsd:element>
        <xsd:element name="BookPriceByAuthorRequest">
            <xsd:complexType>
                <xsd:all>
                    <xsd:element name="author" type="string"/>
                </xsd:all>
            </xsd:complexType>
        </xsd:element>
        <xsd:element name="BookPriceResponse">
            <xsd:complexType>
                <xsd:all>
                    <xsd:element name="price" type="double"/>
                </xsd:all>
            </xsd:complexType>
        </xsd:element>
    </xsd:schema>
<types>
<message name="GetBookPriceByISBNInput">
    <part name="body" element="bpxsd:ISBNBookPriceRequest"/>
</message>
<message name="GetBookPriceByAuthorInput">
    <part name="body" element="bpxsd:AuthorBookPriceRequest"/>
</message>
<message name="GetBookPriceOutput">
    <part name="body" element="bpxsd:BookPrice"/>
</message>
<portType name="BookPricePortType">
    <operation name="GetBookPriceByISBN">
        <input message="bp:GetBookPriceByISBNInput"/>
        <output message="bp:GetBookPriceOutput"/>
    </operation>
    <operation name="GetBookPriceByAuthor">
        <input message="bp:GetBookPriceByAuthorInput"/>
        <output message="bp:GetBookPriceOutput"/>
    </operation>
</portType>
<binding name="BookPriceSoapBinding" type="bp:BookPricePortType">
    <soap:binding
        style="document"
        transport="http://schemas.xmlsoap.org/soap/http"/>
    <operation name="GetBookPriceByISBN">
        <soap:operation soapAction="http://example.com/GetBookPriceByISBN"/>
        <input>
            <soap:body use="literal"/>
        </input>
        <output>
            <soap:body use="literal"/>
```

LISTING 11.6 continued

```
        </output>
    </operation>
    <operation name="GetBookPriceByAuthor">
        <soap:operation soapAction="http://example.com/GetBookPriceByAuthor"/>
        <input>
            <soap:body use="literal"/>
        </input>
        <output>
            <soap:body use="literal"/>
        </output>
    </operation>
</binding>
<service name="BookPriceService">
    <documentation>Get Book Prices</documentation>
    <port name="BookPricePort" binding="bp:BookPriceSoapBinding">
        <soap:address location="http://example.com/bookprice"/>
    </port>
</service>
</definitions>
```

The Java Implementation of the Web Service

First let us look at the Java implementation of the service, showing the two methods and their signatures. This is a simplistic example, where the bulk of the actual work in terms of calling various databases and finding a real answer is not shown. (Again, all Web services code shown has been deployed on the Apache Axis implementation.)

```
package samples.bookprice;
public class BookPriceService {
    public double getPriceByISBN(String isbn) {
    //perform some hard work and return an answer
        return 24.55;
    }

    public double getPriceBySKU(String sku) {
    //perform some hard work and return an answer
        return 24.55;
    }
}
```

Constructing the WSDL Document

Now let us start constructing the WSDL document that describes this service. A WSDL document is an XML instance document. Therefore, it starts with the XML definition you saw in the section "XML." The root element in a WSDL document is the <defini-tions> element. Aside from being a container for all the WSDL definitions, it also allows us to define the various namespaces to which we will need to refer:

```
<?xml version="1.0" encoding="UTF-8"?>
<definitions name="GetBookPrice"
   targetNamespace="http://localhost:8080/axis/BookPriceService.jws"
   xmlns:soap="http://schemas.xmlsoap.org/wsdl/soap/"
   xmlns:serviceNS="http://localhost:8080/axis/BookPriceService.jws"
   xmlns:xsd="http://www.w3.org/2001/XMLSchema"
   xmlns="http://schemas.xmlsoap.org/wsdl/">
```

Usually, the first section in a WSDL document is the <types> section. This section of the WSDL document is where you define data types such as parameters and return types that will be used in various messages. These data types will be referred to in the rest of the document. These type definitions follow the format of the XML schema definitions that we discussed in the XML section of this chapter, as shown on the second line of the following listing. Therefore, it is not necessary to define simple types such as strings and integers.

In this example, however, for the sake of illustration, we have defined three named data types: two string types for the input parameters (ISBN and Author name) and a double for the returned price. Another argument for defining even simple types in the <types> section is that these predefined names can be used throughout the document, and any future changes to the type are localized to this section. For example, having defined BookPriceResponse to be a double, we can then use it in several places. If the actual definition changes to float (due to a change in the implementation, for example), we only have to change the definition in the <types> section. (Good software engineering practices always apply, even to XML!)

```
<types>
   <xsd:schema
       targetNamespace="http://localhost:8080/xml/schemas/bookprice.xsd"
       xmlns:xsd="http://www.w3.org/2000/10/XMLSchema">
       <xsd:element name="BookPriceByISBNRequest">
          <xsd:complexType>
             <xsd:all>
                <xsd:element name="isbn" type="string"/>
             </xsd:all>
          </xsd:complexType>
       </xsd:element>
       <xsd:element name="BookPriceByAuthorRequest">
          <xsd:complexType>
             <xsd:all>
                <xsd:element name="author" type="string"/>
             </xsd:all>
          </xsd:complexType>
       </xsd:element>
       <xsd:element name="BookPriceResponse">
          <xsd:complexType>
             <xsd:all>
                <xsd:element name="price" type="double"/>
```

```
        </xsd:all>
      </xsd:complexType>
    </xsd:element>
  </xsd:schema>
<types>
```

Next we usually define a set of <message> elements. This is how the abstract definitions of the messages that will be used in various operations (such as input or output messages) are declared. Message definitions are typed and include the passed parameters, if any. Here, we have defined three abstract message types: two request (or input) messages and one response (or output) message:

```
<message name="GetBookPriceByISBNInput">
  <part name="body" element="bpxsd:ISBNBookPriceRequest"/>
</message>
<message name="GetBookPriceByAuthorInput">
  <part name="body" element="bpxsd:AuthorBookPriceRequest"/>
</message>
<message name="GetBookPriceOutput">
  <part name="body" element="bpxsd:BookPrice"/>
</message>
```

Next we can compose abstract operations from defined messages. An *operation* is an abstract definition that is analogous to a method signature declaration in Java. An operation will usually declare an input message and an output message. These operations are collected within a <portType> element. A portType is where the various abstract definitions are put to use. A portType assembles a set of operations that are to be supported by one *port*, or access point. Here, we have defined two different abstract operations: one to get the price of a book given the ISBN as an input parameter, and the other to get the price given the author name. Both operations use the same abstract message definition GetBookPriceOutput to return the book price:

```
<portType name="BookPricePortType">
  <operation name="GetBookPriceByISBN">
    <input message="bp:GetBookPriceByISBNInput"/>
    <output message="bp:GetBookPriceOutput"/>
  </operation>
  <operation name="GetBookPriceByAuthor">
    <input message="bp:GetBookPriceByAuthorInput"/>
    <output message="bp:GetBookPriceOutput"/>
  </operation>
</portType>
```

Finally, a <binding> element is where the abstract definitions within a portType are given a concrete correspondence to actual protocols. In this case, the retailer has decided to implement the operations that are defined within the BookPrice portType as SOAP over HTTP:

```xml
<binding name="BookPriceSoapBinding" type="bp:BookPricePortType">
  <soap:binding style="document" transport="http://schemas.xmlsoap.org/soap/
http"/>
  <operation name="GetBookPriceByISBN">
    <soap:operation soapAction="http://example.com/GetBookPriceByISBN"/>
    <input>
      <soap:body use="literal"/>
    </input>
    <output>
      <soap:body use="literal"/>
    </output>
  </operation>
  <operation name="GetBookPriceByAuthor">
    <soap:operation soapAction="http://example.com/GetBookPriceByAuthor"/>
    <input>
      <soap:body use="literal"/>
    </input>
    <output>
      <soap:body use="literal"/>
    </output>
  </operation>
</binding>
```

Notice that the binding definition has defined the implementation of the operations as SOAP over HTTP, but no address was given. This further decouples the definitions from the actual implementation, allowing the possibility of reusing these definitions in other WSDL documents.

The final required definition, that of an actual invocation address, is given in the `<port>` element within the `<service>` element. In WSDL terminology, a *service* is the highest-level definition; it consists of a bundling of one of more ports, which describe physical access points to the different operations provided by the service. In short, a port brings together a binding and an address for that binding. (Unfortunately, the WSDL terminology can sometimes be unnecessarily confusing, but it will start to make sense after you start using it.) In the following example, the address where the SOAP message should be sent is associated with the binding that was defined previously:

```xml
<service name="BookPriceService">
  <documentation>Get Book Prices</documentation>
  <port name="BookPricePort" binding="bp:BookPriceSoapBinding">
    <soap:address location="http://example.com/bookprice"/>
  </port>
</service>
```

Now, all the elements that are necessary to invoke the BookPrice service are in place. After the WSDL document is complete, it can be communicated to potential users, either directly (such as through email or FTP) or through discovery mechanisms, such as UDDI, which we will explore in the next section.

Invoking the Web Service

As a final example, let us examine the actual invocation of one of the services that is defined in our WSDL document. The SOAP invocation of the GetBookPriceByISBN is shown here:

```
POST /axis/BookPriceService.jws HTTP/1.0
Content-Length: 422
Host: localhost
Content-Type: text/xml; charset=utf-8
SOAPAction: "/getPriceByISBN"
<?xml version="1.0" encoding="UTF-8"?>
<SOAP-ENV:Envelope
   SOAP-ENV:encodingStyle="http://schemas.xmlsoap.org/soap/encoding/"
   xmlns:SOAP-ENV="http://schemas.xmlsoap.org/soap/envelope/"
   xmlns:xsd="http://www.w3.org/2001/XMLSchema"
   xmlns:xsi="http://www.w3.org/2001/XMLSchema-instance">
 <SOAP-ENV:Body>
  <getPriceByISBN>
   <op1 xsi:type="xsd:string">4578498</op1>
  </getPriceByISBN>
 </SOAP-ENV:Body>
</SOAP-ENV:Envelope>
```

The SOAP response from the Web service is as follows:

```
HTTP/1.1 200 OK
Content-Type: text/xml; charset=utf-8
Content-Length: 470
Date: Thu, 28 Feb 2002 03:16:20 GMT
Server: Apache Tomcat/4.0.1 (HTTP/1.1 Connector)

<?xml version="1.0" encoding="UTF-8"?>
<SOAP-ENV:Envelope
   SOAP-ENV:encodingStyle="http://schemas.xmlsoap.org/soap/encoding/"
   xmlns:SOAP-ENV="http://schemas.xmlsoap.org/soap/envelope/"
   xmlns:xsd="http://www.w3.org/2001/XMLSchema"
   xmlns:xsi="http://www.w3.org/2001/XMLSchema-instance">
 <SOAP-ENV:Body>
  <getPriceByISBNResponse>
   <getPriceByISBNResult xsi:type="xsd:double">24.55</getPriceByISBNResult>
  </getPriceByISBNResponse>
 </SOAP-ENV:Body>
</SOAP-ENV:Envelope>
```

UDDI

Having created and deployed a service and written its WSDL description, the last major step is allowing potential users to find it. We have used the component programming analogy before to explain the need for a description language such as WSDL. We can extend the analogy to the concept of a services registry.

It is clear that an object or component registry is an essential element in any component-programming framework, facilitating the discovery and use of components. Imagine, for example, trying to write Java code without having access to a browsable set of JavaDocs, or working in Smalltalk without having access to a class browser. If you consider the Web services concept as an evolution of component programming, it follows that for the purpose of service discovery, it is necessary to have access to registries of business and service descriptions that can be browsed and queried. This is the role that UDDI plays in the Web services world.

When the idea of Web services started gaining momentum within the IT community in early 2000, two things became clear: Web services registries were going to be essential for the concept to become practical, and registry standards would have to be endorsed by several, if not all, of the large software providers for any hope of adoption by the various industries. Thus, the UDDI initiative, the result of several months of collaboration between representatives from Ariba, IBM, and Microsoft starting in the spring of 2000, was born and formally announced on September 6, 2000, with support from several other companies. Currently, the UDDI project (`http://www.uddi.org`) involves a community of more than 300 companies.

The purpose of UDDI is to facilitate service discovery both at design time and dynamically at runtime. Consequently, the UDDI project runs a public online business (and services) registry, which first went live on May 2, 2001. This registry is referred to as the UDDI Business Registry. The UDDI Business Registry actually consists of replicated registries that are currently hosted by several companies, called the UDDI *Operators*. Registries that conform to the first UDDI specification (UDDI V1) are hosted by IBM and Microsoft, whereas registries that conform to the second specification, still in beta releases (UDDI V2 Beta), are hosted by Hewlett-Packard, IBM, Microsoft, and SAP. More registry Operators are expected to join the Operators group.

UDDI is more than a business and services registry, however. It also defines a set of data structures and an API specification for programmatically registering and finding businesses, services, bindings, and service types. The UDDI API specification provides a set of Publication APIs to register services, and Inquiry APIs to find services. In addition to providing a programmatic API, UDDI registry Operators provide a Web-based user interface for registering, managing, and finding businesses and services in the registry. These Web sites provide a subset of the programmatic API and are relatively self explanatory. As a matter of fact, the Web interface to UDDI is probably the easiest and fastest way to register your services and to locate services. As of this writing, only the UDDI V1 service is running in production mode. Consequently, although we will mention the addition brought by UDDI V2, this section will be primarily concerned with the usage model of UDDI V1. IBM has its UDDI Web site at `http://www.ibm.com/services/uddi` and

Microsoft's is at `http://uddi.microsoft.com`. Of course, all of the Operator nodes are accessible from `http://www.uddi.org`.

The UDDI Data Model

UDDI V1 has defined four core data structures: `businessEntity`, `businessService`, `bindingTemplate`, and `tModel`. UDDI V2 has added a fifth structure: the `publisherAssertion`. One of the important characteristics of these entities is that each has a unique identifier that can be used to locate it and refer to it. UDDI has adopted the use of Unique Universal Identifiers (UUIDs) for uniquely identifying the different entities. As we go into more detail about each structure, you will notice that each element has a `key` attribute. This key holds the UUID that is assigned by the operator at creation time. In the following discussion of the UDDI data model, please refer to Figure 11.6 as an example of how these structures are related. These data types are outlined next.

FIGURE 11.6

The five UDDI core data types.

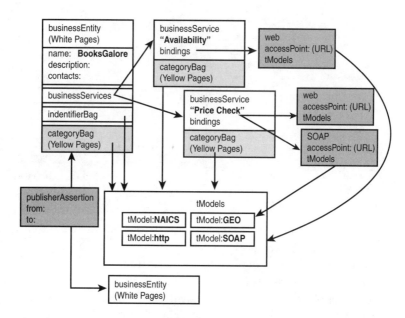

businessEntity

The `businessEntity` is where businesses (and organizations) register detailed information such as name, contact information, and business type about themselves. The `businessEntity` structure is shown in Figure 11.7. Aside from the usual self-explanatory elements such as `<name>` and `<contacts>`, you should pay special attention to two elements: `<categoryBag>` and `<identifierBag>`. As their name suggests, these elements are used to categorize and identify services.

FIGURE 11.7

The
`businessEntity`
structure.

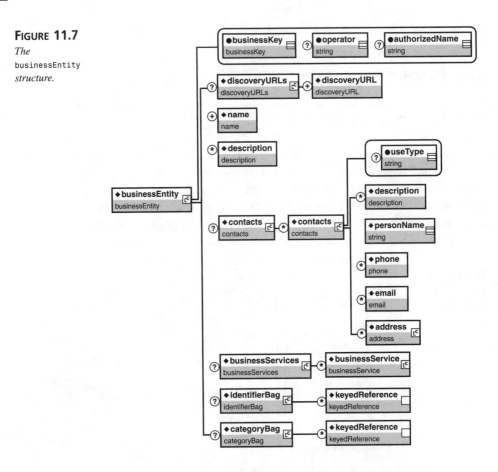

Although a full discussion of taxonomies is beyond the scope of this chapter, you can think of the `<categoryBag>` element as a way to fit a business or a service into one or more different categories in a taxonomy. As an example, one of the most common taxonomies is the one provided by Yahoo! to categorize Web sites. UDDI has established three canonical taxonomies: the North American Industry Classification System (NAICS), the Universal Standard Product and Services Code (USPSC), and a geographic location classification, the ISO 3166 Geographic Taxonomy. Although UDDI operators are free to offer more taxonomies at their sites, you have to be aware of the fact that this additional information is not replicated to the other UDDI registries, and it cannot be used in searches from other registries.

In addition to categorization, identification information such as the Dun & Bradstreet Data Universal Numbering System (DUNS) can be stored in the `identifierBag` elements. This greatly facilitates searching for businesses or organizations if their name is ambiguous.

businessService

A business or organization can register several services. This is reflected by the fact that the <businessEntity> element is the parent for the <businessServices> element, which is a container for the <businessService> elements. <businessService> elements allow users to register information about their services. The businessService structure is shown in Figure 11.8. Business services, like businessEntity entries, can also be categorized through <categoryBag> entries.

FIGURE 11.8
The businessService structure.

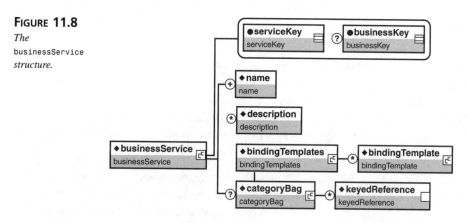

bindingTemplate

The bindingTemplate structure is where the rubber meets the road in completely defining a service and its invocation mechanism. In a sense, all of the other UDDI structures are there to allow users to finally get to a binding so that a service can be invoked. It closely corresponds to the concept of a binding as we saw it in WSDL. The bindingTemplate structure is shown in Figure 11.9.

FIGURE 11.9
The bindingTemplate structure.

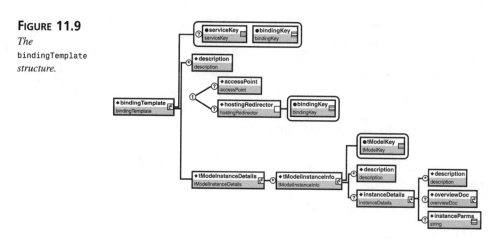

tModel

Several components are required to fully define a service. These include input parameters, an output format, a transport mechanism, a security mechanism, and so on. As we saw in the WSDL section, many of these details can be supplied in the service description document. WSDL documents contain reusable abstract definitions (such as the message declarations) and concrete implementation definitions (such as the port declaration). This type of abstraction of reusable definitions is a step in the right direction, but it needs to be extended beyond the boundaries of one particular service or even one particular organization.

The technology model (tModel) definitions were meant to hold such cross-entity abstractions. For example, if a book dealership trade organization were to define some standard service interfaces such as some of the ones we have already seen, they would register them as tModels in UDDI. This would relieve the various book dealers from having to redefine these interfaces in their service descriptions. Their UDDI service entries would just refer to the corresponding tModel for the abstractions and provide the remaining concrete part of the definitions.

As a side effect of their use as abstractions, tModels generally are used as references. By convention, the UDDI specification suggests two main uses for them. The primary use is in defining what is called a *technical fingerprint*. This refers to any technical specifications or prearranged agreements on how to conduct business. The other main use for tModels is in defining namespaces to be used in the `identifierBag` and `categoryBag` structures.

Another important use for tModels, however, is from a user's perspective when searching for services. A common scenario would be that a service requester wants to do business with service providers that implement certain interfaces. The requester would then query the UDDI registry for providers who use the corresponding tModels.

Based on the UDDI specification, a tModel could define just about anything. It consists of a key, a name, a description, and a URL (see Figure 11.10).

publisherAssertion

To the four core data types we've just described, UDDI V2 has added a fifth: the `publisherAssertion` structure (see Figure 11.11). This structure is used to declare business relationships between different business entities.

FIGURE 11.10
*The tModel
structure.*

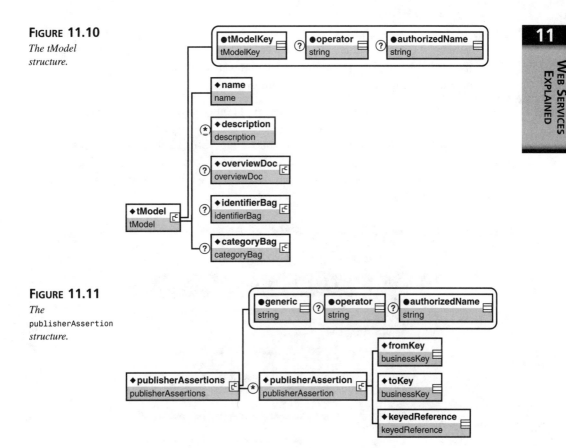

FIGURE 11.11
*The
publisherAssertion
structure.*

Using the UDDI Web Interface

As we mentioned earlier, the UDDI Web interface that the individual UDDI operators
provide is probably the fastest and easiest way to register your business and service
information into UDDI and to locate other businesses and services while you're designing applications that consume services. For this section, we will be using the IBM UDDI
Business Test Registry (accessible from `http://www.ibm.com/services/uddi`), which is
typical of the interfaces that the other registry operators provide.

UDDI offers two different types of operations: authenticated and non-authenticated. Non-
authenticated operations are generally search operations to locate businesses, services, or
implementation details. Authenticated operations are the ones that allow you to register,
edit, and delete businesses and services. To use the authenticated operations, you need to
register with an operator. After you are registered, you can edit your information only

from that operator's site, unless you require a transfer of custody to another operator. Keep in mind, however, that although you can edit your information through one operator only, the information will be replicated to all other operators so that anyone who is searching the Operator node can find your information.

After you are registered and logged in, the first option is to create a new business entry. We've created a new business named BooksGalore. After that step is out of the way, we can enter detailed information about the business. Figure 11.12 shows the options that are available to us. We can enter a business description, contact information, and a business locator. *Business locators* are how we can categorize the business, as discussed in the previous section.

FIGURE 11.12

Creating a new business entry at the UDDI Registry Web site.

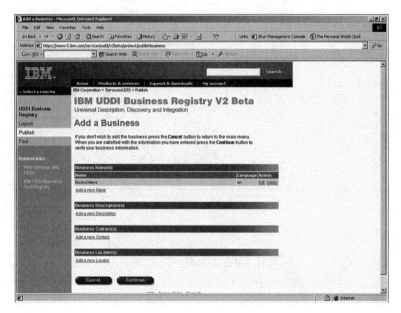

Figure 11.13 shows our options: NAICS, UNSPSC, and GCS-ISO 3166-1999. If we select the NAICS option, we can drill down the consecutive levels until we reach the desired level: Book Stores—451211 (see Figure 11.14).

The rest of the interface is relatively straightforward. We can enter contact information and a business description.

FIGURE 11.13

Selecting a type of locator for categorization.

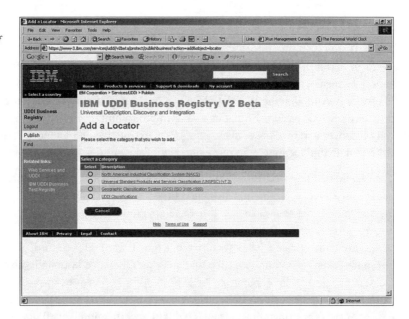

FIGURE 11.14

Selecting a NAICS category.

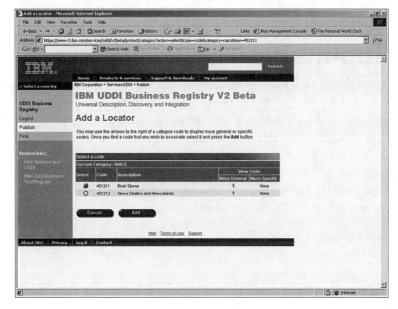

The UDDI API

The next step is to find information in the registry. Searching the registry usually takes the form of a drill-down pattern, where a particular service is first located through a variety of means, and then the particular binding documents for that service are retrieved to invoke it. Although the Web interface can be used to perform these functions, UDDI provides a SOAP-based API that can be used programmatically at runtime to dynamically discover and invoke services. The API is exhaustive and includes calls for creating, editing, deleting, locating, and retrieving any of the entities that are in the registry.

The creation/editing operations take the form of `save_entity`, where `entity` is `business`, `service`, `binding`, or `tModel`. In V2, `publisherAssertions` are set through the `set_publisherAssertions` call. Delete operations are performed through `delete_entity` calls. These operations, because they involve modifying data in the registries, are authenticated. They require the acquisition of a token through the `get_authToken` operation. After the token is used, it can be optionally discarded through the `discard_authToken` operation. As expected, find operations through `find_entity` calls. Details about business or service entries are retrieved through the various `get_entityDetail` operations. The UDDI API specification is well documented at the UDDI site.

Summary

Although it is hard to cover the full scope of Web services in one chapter, this chapter did cover the general topic of service-oriented architectures, with an emphasis on the main standard components of Web services architectures. We briefly covered the use of XML as the central data format in today's Web architectures. This led us to explore the use of XML in SOAP as a message format for Web services. The next step in fully specifying Web services was the description mechanism. Here, WSDL has become the de facto standard, and we saw how to generate WSDL descriptions for our services. Finally, we covered the UDDI discovery mechanism.

Messaging and Java APIs for XML

by Bilal Siddiqui

IN THIS CHAPTER

This chapter discusses several messaging and XML-related Java APIs that are used in developing P2P applications. We will discuss the architectural aspects, provide sample code to use each API, and develop sample projects.

Standard APIs to Third-Party Services

Peer-to-peer architecture is designed to be a network of peers that can discover other peers having common interests, exchange messages with them, and share resources. This interconnection of peers requires a basic mechanism for messaging. For example, consider the JXTA project, which is a set of open, generalized P2P protocols defined as XML messages that establish a layer on top of the Internet and non-IP network protocols. The JXTA set of protocols allows peers ranging from cell phones and wireless PDAs to PCs and servers to interact through messaging, independent of their network location and topology. The JXTA project has defined a layered architecture for this purpose. We will now discuss the logical requirements of any P2P architecture and list the set of APIs that Java offers for these requirements.

Two Basic Requirements of Any P2P Architecture

Any P2P system will require a mechanism to accomplish the following tasks:

- Peers should be able to send and receive messages to and from each other.
- Every peer should be able to process messages being exchanged. This includes the capability to author messages that a peer wants to send to other peers, and the capability to understand messages coming from other peers.

As an example, consider the following scenario. A peer wants to ask other peers if anyone knows the address of a discussion group on P2P issues. He will need to author a search query (message) and send it to the peers that he thinks are relevant and might answer his search query. Recipients of this search query will need to process the incoming message to understand what is required. Some of the peers who receive this search query might want to forward this message to other relevant peers.

This scenario clearly asks for the capability to perform the two previously defined tasks—each peer should be able to send and receive messages and process the messages coming in from other peers. These two requirements are very basic in nature, and any network that behaves in a P2P manner will address them.

How Java Handles Basic P2P Requirements

Sun has provided the Java Messaging Service (JMS), an API meant to cater for general messaging requirements. The JMS API defines a common set of interfaces and associated semantics that allow Java applications to communicate with other messaging implementations. JMS is a part of the J2EE specification, so all major J2EE-compliant application servers include JMS features. Independent JMS implementations are also available.

JMS provides a basic messaging framework in which you can create messaging sessions based on topics of your interest. The API does all the low-level tasks, such as

- Creating and maintaining topics for messages to be exchanged
- Maintaining a database of users and the interest of each user in different topics
- Network-related tasks such as the creation of listeners

You can build your messaging logic on top of JMS. Later in this chapter, we will describe the JMS architecture in detail. We will also build a sample messaging application based on JMS.

Processing of Messages

XML has become the de facto standard for almost all exchanges of structured information over the Internet. Naturally, XML is the favorite candidate to be used as the format of P2P messages. JXTA has defined several XML formats to provide various services. For example, the search service in JXTA defines XML structures (Document Type Definitions, or DTDs) to specify and respond to search requests.

All JXTA applications will need to process (author and understand) XML messages. Java has comprehensive support for XML processing. There are two Java-based APIs for XML processing:

- Java API for XML Processing (JAXP)
- Java API for XML Binding (JAXB)

JAXP and JAXB provide different approaches to address the same problem—XML processing. JAXP has implemented the four popular XML-related W3C specifications:

- Simple API for XML (SAX)
- Document Object Model (DOM)
- Extensible Stylesheet Language for Transformation (XSLT)
- XPath

SAX, DOM, and XSLT are ways to expose an XML file for processing. XPath helps in reaching specific parts of an XML document. We'll discuss details of JAXP later in this chapter and provide sample implementations of small projects related to SAX, DOM, XSLT and XPath.

JAXB is a recent addition to Java's capability of XML processing. In fact, JAXB specification is still under development, and only an early access release is yet available. JAXB enables the quick and easy generation of Java classes capable of processing any particular XML structure (DTDs).

JAXB can compile your DTD into one or more Java classes. Currently, only DTDs are supported, although support for XML schemas is anticipated in the coming versions. When Java classes are available for XML processing, your Java applications can use these classes. We will do a small JAXB project later in this chapter.

The Concept of XML Messaging

The Java API for XML Messaging (JAXM) combines the XML processing and messaging features in one API. It offers both a messaging framework similar to that of JMS, and a SOAP authoring mechanism. Therefore, the basic purpose of having JAXM is to provide for Java-based SOAP messaging. There are a number of ways we can accomplish SOAP messaging in Java. The last section of this chapter is focused on this topic.

JMS and the Importance of Messaging

In this section we will describe messaging architecture, illustrate its logical similarity with P2P architecture, and describe the Java Messaging Service (JMS). We will also discuss JMS providers (which are part of the J2EE platform), and put them to service.

What Is Messaging?

Messaging is a mechanism through which two or more entities (applications or software modules) can communicate with each other. Communicating entities operate independently of each other; that is, they are not bound to each other in any way. For example, if one entity sends a message to another entity, it will not wait for the response from the other side. This type of messaging is called *asynchronous* communication.

Messaging Versus Request-Response

Consider what happens when you use an Internet browser program such as Internet Explorer. The browser sends an HTTP *request* and receives an HTTP *response* from a Web server. The browser remains busy after issuing the HTTP request until it receives the response (normally an HTML file), although the browser does not have much to do other than waiting for the response. In this way the browser is bound to the Web server, at least for a while.

This is called *synchronous* communication, and it's the main difference between request-response and messaging models. With messaging, we have asynchronous communication that does not require waiting for response. Therefore, messaging entities remain independent of each other.

Telephonic conversation is a real-life example of synchronous communication between humans. On the other hand, the exchange of letters or emails is asynchronous in nature. The only difference between email and messaging is that messaging always takes place between software components and software applications. Unlike email, messaging never involves human interaction.

Messaging Clients and Messaging Providers

In the request-response model, we normally have clients and servers. Clients request and servers respond (serve). Servers are normally designed to serve a number of clients simultaneously, and therefore have more powerful computing capabilities compared to clients.

On the other hand, the messaging model has only clients and no servers. This gives rise to the equality of clients. Each client is supposed to a *peer* of every other client.

However, this does not mean that there is no requirement to handle administration issues, such as the following:

- Different messaging clients will be interested in messages related to different topics. For example, consider a messaging-based workflow solution for a company. The purchase manager (a messaging client) is interested in receiving messages related to new purchase requisition requests. The after-sales support manager (another messaging client) is interested in messages related to faulty equipment from customers. The messaging administration module will keep a record of these different topics and map the list of clients interested in different topics.

- If a message needs to be sent to a client who is currently offline, the messaging administration module will keep the message stored until the client is online again. The JMS API can ensure that a message is delivered once and only once. Lower levels of reliability are available for applications that can afford to miss messages, or to receive duplicate messages.

Management tasks such as these call for a management entity, called a *messaging provider*.

Messaging Clients as Peers in P2P

Messaging clients are logically similar to the concept of peers in P2P. A client acting as a peer can send messages for several purposes—for example, the discovery of other peers, searching for information, and so on.

Imagine a messaging application in which clients follow the XML formats of JXTA. This messaging application will become very similar to a JXTA-based P2P application. This similarity emphasizes the role of messaging in P2P applications.

Role of Messaging Providers in P2P

JXTA calls for an architecture in which messages sent by peers can be forwarded to other peers and so on, until they reach the required destination peer.

An example of this type of messaging is the JXTA search specification. If a JXTA peer wants to search for a specific bit of information, it will send an XML message to the relevant peers. The peers receiving this message might in turn forward this search request to other relevant peers. This way, the search message has the chance of eventually reaching a peer that has the requested information.

This type of architecture can be realized through messaging. You will need to build a messaging provider application that can also act as messaging client to other messaging providers. In this way, it can forward specific messages from its clients to other providers, who will in turn forward the message to their clients and other providers.

Message-Oriented Middleware (MOM)

Based on the concepts of messaging discussed previously, proprietary implementations are available from different vendors. Some examples of proprietary messaging frameworks are the following:

- MQSeries from IBM
- SonicMQ from Progress
- FiranoMQ from Firano

These messaging frameworks are called message-oriented middleware (MOM).

Sun released the specification of JMS, which eventually became a part of the J2EE specification. The reference implementation of JMS is now included in J2EE SDK v1.3.

Java Messaging Service

JMS aims to provide access to vendor-specific MOM implementations through a standard Java API. JMS allows you to have proprietary implementations of JMS administrative objects. This means that vendors are free to implement administrative objects in any manner they want. (JMS manages these objects administratively rather than programmatically. Therefore, they are called *administered objects*. Administered objects are meant to administrate topics and connections as described previously in the section "Messaging Clients and Messaging Providers.") The only restriction is at the API level. JMS providers talk to JMS clients according to the API; JMS clients will access JMS providers to get messaging services.

The interaction between JMS clients, the JMS provider, and administered objects is shown in Figure 12.1.

FIGURE 12.1

The JMS architecture.

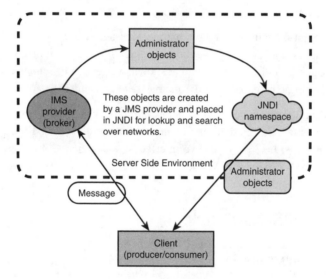

Figure 12.1 shows four components: JMS clients, the JMS provider, administered objects, and the JNDI (Java Naming and Directory Interface) namespace. These components work as follows:

- JMS clients—Clients can be of two types: message *producers* and message *consumers*. Producers have the role of producing messages that consumers will receive. Any messaging peer (client) can assume either or both roles in the messaging architecture.

- JMS provider—This is actually the JMS implementation that provides a communication framework to all messaging clients. The provider plays the role of a broker that keeps information about what topics are available for messaging and which clients are interested in a particular topic. Because JMS is part of the J2EE v1.3 specification, all J2EE v1.3 platform implementations have a built-in JMS provider.
- The JMS provider creates administered objects and places (stores) them in a JNDI namespace. JNDI provides a standard interface for distributed Java applications to store files and look them up later. JMS clients will use JNDI methods to look up and check what topics are available.

JMS allows two messaging domains: publishing/subscribing and point-to-point. The publishing/subscribing domain is a topic-based messaging mechanism in which message producers publish their messages on a topic. Message consumers subscribe to the topics in order to consume (receive) messages. Every message will be delivered to all subscribers of the topic.

The point-to-point domain is based on queues. Message senders will send their messages to message queues. Each message queue is destined for one consumer. Consumers will receive messages from their queues and acknowledge receipt to senders. In this way, each message will be received by only one message consumer.

Both queues and topics are referred to as *destinations*. A JMS-administered object is supposed to administrate destinations and connections to destinations. To provide connections to destinations, JMS provides two interfaces: `QueueConnectionFactory` and `TopicConnectionFactory`. A JSM client will use either of the two connection factories to connect to a JMS provider.

Putting JMS to Work

We will now discuss the architecture of a complete messaging system based on JMS. While designing a JMS messaging system, you will need to address the following issues:

- Configure a JMS provider. You will normally not implement a JMS provider yourself. Many implementations are already available as a part of J2EE application servers. You will only need to configure it according to your application.
- Use JMS-client API in your messaging logic.

Let's see how you will accomplish these tasks by taking a simple messaging application as a design example.

A JMS-Based Messaging Application

We will now demonstrate the design and implementation of a simple messaging application that is very similar to the concept of P2P. The architecture of our application is shown in Figure 12.2.

FIGURE 12.2

Four instances of a JMS-based messaging application.

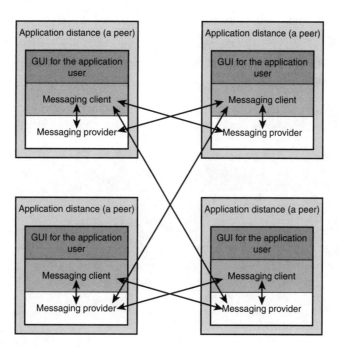

We have shown four instances of our application running simultaneously. Each instance will act as a peer. Theoretically, there can be any number of simultaneous instances of this application, but for the sake of simplicity and clarity we'll discuss only four instances. Think of each instance as a peer in our messaging system.

Another simplification that we have assumed is that the messaging peers have already discovered each other—that is, all four peers know the addresses of the other peers. Therefore, they can send and receive messages to each other.

Each messaging peer has three modules:

- The messaging client is capable of sending and receiving messages to and from other peers (application instances).

- The messaging provider listens to the messages sent from other peers and forwards them to peers that are interested in receiving messages related to particular topics.

- The GUI, seen in Figure 12.3, contains the following components:

    - A drop-down list to select which peer to contact
    - A set of radio buttons to specify whether you want to send a message or start listening to incoming messages
    - A drop-down list to select a topic of interest
    - A button to send messages
    - A button to start listening for incoming messages
    - A text area to display messages

Using the GUI, each peer can send a message to any other peer. Each peer can also register itself with any other peer to receive messages related to any particular topic.

FIGURE 12.3

The GUI for our messaging application.

Let's see how our messaging application works. We'll need to perform the following steps detailed in the following sections.

Configuring the Provider

In this application we have used Sun's J2EE SDK v1.3 that includes a JMS provider implementation, so you will need a running J2EE server. Once the server is running, use the following command to create a topic connection factory (an administrator object):

```
j2eeadmin -addJmsFactory MyTopicConnectionFactory topic
```

Even if you don't do this, the application will run using the default topic connection factory.

Then use the following commands to create topics (also administered objects):

```
j2eeadmin -addJmsDestination Topic1 topic
j2eeadmin -addJmsDestination Topic2 topic
```

This will create two topics on the JMS provider, which is now set. You will need to configure the provider for every instance of this application.

Logic for the Messaging Client

We have written two classes for our messaging client: MessageConsumer (Listing 12.1) and MessageProducer (Listing 12.2). MessageConsumer.java implements a JMS client that consumes JMS messages, and MessageProducer.java implements a JMS client that produces JMS messages.

LISTING 12.1 MessageConsumer.java

```java
import javax.swing.*;
import javax.jms.*;
import javax.naming.*;
import java.io.*;
import java.util.*;

public class MessageConsumer {

        // We would like to keep a reference of TopicConnection
        // and TopicSession so that we can destroy it at the end.
        private TopicConnection              topicConnection = null;
        private TopicSession                 topicSession = null;

        // This Subscriber will listen for incoming messages.
        private TopicSubscriber              topicSubscriber = null;
        // This listener will receive the incoming messages.
        private TextListener                 topicListener = null;
        // The TextArea to display the messages.
        private JTextArea                    textArea = null;
        // Names of machines over the network.
        // These machines will have JMS Providers running.
        // In real applications, names of machines should come
        // from the GUI.
        private final String COMPUTER1 = "computer6";
        private final String COMPUTER2 = "computer13";
        private final String COMPUTER3 = "computer14";
        private final String COMPUTER4 = "computer15";

        // Connect to the JMS Provider and start listening.
        public void connectToProvider (String topicName, String jmsProvider) {
                // We will get a reference of System properties.
                // We will add the Properties related to JMS functionality.
                Properties env = System.getProperties();
```

LISTING 12.1 continued

```
          env.put("com.sun.jms.internal.java.naming.factory.initial",
→              "com.sun.enterprise.naming.SerialInitContextFactory");
          // Port number where the Naming service of
          // remote JMS Provider is listening.
          env.put("rg.omg.CORBA.ORBInitialPort","1050");

          try {
                  // Set the network address of target machine
                  // where JMS Provider is running.
                  if (jmsProvider.equals("Server1"))
                          env.put("org.omg.CORBA.ORBInitialHost",COMPUTER1);
                  else if (jmsProvider.equals("Server2"))
                          env.put("org.omg.CORBA.ORBInitialHost",COMPUTER2);
                  else if (jmsProvider.equals("Server3"))
                          env.put("org.omg.CORBA.ORBInitialHost",COMPUTER3);
                  else if (jmsProvider.equals("Server4"))
                          env.put("org.omg.CORBA.ORBInitialHost",COMPUTER4);
                  // Get an object of JNDI InitialContext
                  // from given JMS Provider.
                  Context jndiContext = new InitialContext(env);
                  // Get JMS Administrator Objects
                  TopicConnectionFactory topicConnectionFactory =
→         (TopicConnectionFactory)
→                 jndiContext.lookup("TopicConnectionFactory");
                  Topic topic = (Topic)
→                 jndiContext.lookup(topicName);
                  // Establish the connection.
                  topicConnection =
→         topicConnectionFactory.createTopicConnection();
                  // Create the session.
                  topicSession =
→             topicConnection.createTopicSession
→             (false, Session.AUTO_ACKNOWLEDGE);
                  // Create the subscriber for the topic of interest.
                  // Specify a TextListener object (inner class)
                  // who will receive messages.
                  topicSubscriber = topicSession.createSubscriber(topic);
                  topicListener = new TextListener();
                  topicSubscriber.setMessageListener(topicListener);
                  textArea.setText("starting the listener for messages");
                  // We are all set, Start listening.
                  topicConnection.start();
          } catch (NamingException e) {
                  textArea.append (
→                         "JNDI lookup failed: "+
→                         e.toString());
          } catch (JMSException e) {
                  textArea.append("JMS Exception occurred: " + e.toString());
          }
  } // connectToProvider()
```

LISTING 12.1   continued

```
        // Stop Listening for messages and close the Connection.
        public void stopListening() {
            if (topicConnection != null) {
                try {
                            topicSubscriber.close();
                            topicSession.close();
                            topicConnection.close();
                            textArea.setText("\nStoped Listining" );
                } catch (JMSException e) {
                            textArea.setText("\nException in listing" );
                    }
            }
        } // stopListening()

        public void setDisplayArea (JTextArea textArea) {
                this.textArea = textArea;
        }// setDisplayArea


        // Inner class to receive messages.
        private class TextListener implements MessageListener {
            public void onMessage(Message message) {
                TextMessage msg = null;
                try {
                        // Our application can only handle Text Messages.
                        if (message instanceof TextMessage) {
                                msg = (TextMessage) message;
                                textArea.append(
                                    "\n\n The Message is Received: \n\t"
                                    + msg.getText());
                        } else {
                                 textArea.append(
                                    "\n Message of wrong type: " +
                                    message.getClass().getName());
                        }//else
                } catch (JMSException e) {
                                textArea.append("JMSException in onMessage(): "
                                        + e.toString());
                } catch (Throwable te) {
                        textArea.append("Exception in onMessage():"
                                        + te.getMessage());
                }//catch
            } // onMessage()
        } // TextListener class
}// Message Consumer class
```

LISTING 12.2 MessageProducer.java

```java
import javax.jms.*;
import javax.naming.*;
import java.util.*;

public class MessageProducer {
        // We would like to keep a reference of TopicConnection, Session
        // and TopicPublisher so that we can destroy it at the end.
        private TopicConnection        topicConnection = null;
        private TopicPublisher topicPublisher = null;
        private TopicSession topicSession = null;

        // Names of machines over the network.
        // These machines will have JMS Providers running.
        // In real applications, names of machines should come
        // from the GUI.
        private final String COMPUTER1 = "computer6";
        private final String COMPUTER2 = "computer13";
        private final String COMPUTER3 = "computer14";
        private final String COMPUTER4 = "computer15";


        // Connect to the JMS Provider and send the message.
        public String connectToProvider (String topicName,
                            String jmsProvider ,String msg ) {
            // We will get a reference of System properties.
            // We will add the Properties related to JMS functionality.
            Properties env = System.getProperties();
            env.put("com.sun.jms.internal.java.naming.factory.initial",
                "com.sun.enterprise.naming.SerialInitContextFactory");
            // Port number where the Naming service of
            // remote JMS Provider is listening.
            env.put("rg.omg.CORBA.ORBInitialPort","1050");

            try {
                    // Set the network address of target machine
                    // where JMS Provider is running.
                    if (jmsProvider.equals("Server1"))
                            env.put("org.omg.CORBA.ORBInitialHost",COMPUTER1);
                    else if (jmsProvider.equals("Server2"))
                            env.put("org.omg.CORBA.ORBInitialHost",COMPUTER2);
                    else if (jmsProvider.equals("Server3"))
                            env.put("org.omg.CORBA.ORBInitialHost",COMPUTER3);
                    else if (jmsProvider.equals("Server4"))
                            env.put("org.omg.CORBA.ORBInitialHost",COMPUTER4);
                    // Get an object of JNDI InitialContext
                    //from given JMS Provider
                    Context jndiContext = new InitialContext(env);
                    // Get JMS Administrator Objects
                    TopicConnectionFactory topicConnectionFactory =
                    (TopicConnectionFactory)
```

LISTING 12.2   continued

```
➡                      jndiContext.lookup("TopicConnectionFactory");
                Topic topic = (Topic) jndiContext.lookup(topicName);
                // Establish TopicConnection and TopicSession.
                topicConnection =
➡                      topicConnectionFactory.createTopicConnection();
                topicSession =
➡                          topicConnection.createTopicSession(false,
➡                          Session.AUTO_ACKNOWLEDGE);
                // Create the publisher for the topic of interest.
                topicPublisher = topicSession.createPublisher(topic);
                // Create Message Object and set the text.
                TextMessage message = topicSession.createTextMessage();
                message.setText(msg);
                // We are all set, Send message.
                topicPublisher.publish(message);
        } catch (JMSException e) {
                String err =
➡                      new String("Exception occurred: " + e.toString());
                return err;
        } catch (NamingException e) {
                String err =
➡                      new String ("Error in JNDI context= " + e.toString());
                return err;
        }

            finally {
                if (topicConnection != null) {
                    try {
                                topicPublisher.close();
                                topicSession.close();
                                topicConnection.close();
                    } catch (JMSException e) {
                                return "Connection Closing Exception: "
➡                                      + e.toString();
                    }
                }//if
        } // finally
                return "Message Sent Successfully";
    } //connectToProvider()
} // end MessageProducer Class
```

The MessageConsumer Class

As its name implies, the MessageConsumer class is responsible for tasks related to message consuming. This includes

- Creating a connection with the topic of interest registered with a JMS provider (topics are also referred to as *destinations*).

- Creating a session and registering interest in receiving messages related to a particular topic.

The MessageConsumer class has a public method connectToProvider that takes two strings as parameters. The first parameter is the name of the topic for which the MessageConsumer wants to register itself to receive messages. The second parameter is the provider address (the address of a JMS provider inside the other peer). We'll call it a *remote provider*.

The ConnectToServer method implements the following sequence:

1. Sets a system properties object to include parameters and creates the JNDI context.
2. Looks up the topic ConnectionFactory object in the JNDI context. (Recall that we created the topic connection factory while configuring the JML provider.)
3. Looks up the topic of interest in the topic ConnectionFactory. (Recall that we created topics while configuring the JML provider.)
4. Creates a topic connection and a session.
5. Creates a subscriber for the topic and sets a message listener. The message listener will be activated after receiving of a message.

Our MessageConsumer has an inner class called TextListener, which is an asynchronous event handler. The TextListener class implements the MessageListener interface, which requires implementing just one method named onMessage. onMessage receives control whenever a new message is detected. In the onMessage method, you define the actions to be taken when a message arrives. Our implementation of the onMessage method simply displays the incoming message in a text area.

The MessageProducer Class

Whereas the MessageConsumer class has the responsibility of receiving (or consuming) messages related to particular topics, the MessageProducer class is used to send messages to their corresponding topics (destinations), so that the messages can be consumed by interested MessageConsumer objects.

The MessageProducer class has a method named connectToProvider that works very much like the connectToServer method of the MessageConsumer class. The only difference occurs after the connection and session are both established. This time a publisher is created instead of a subscriber, and a message is published with the publisher. The message will reach the remote provider, which will route it to all interested peers.

GUI for the Messaging Application

We have implemented a simple JFC-based GUI for this messaging application. It puts the `MessageProducer` and `MessageConsumer` classes to work. The GUI is one of the downloads from this chapter at this book's Web site.

Limitations of our Messaging System

This messaging application presents a skeleton design and implementation of a messaging system. The purpose is to demonstrate JMS. You can build your own messaging logic on top of a similar architecture.

Java API for XML Parsing (JAXP)

As we have already said, Java provides two ways of processing XML: a Java API for XML processing (JAXP), and a Java API for XML binding (JAXB). Both of these APIs are complete in the sense that both fulfill all requirements for XML processing that might be required in any XML application. XML processing applications (such as P2P or Web services applications) will need to use one of them.

We will consider Simple Object Access Protocol (SOAP) as an example to elaborate XML processing requirements. Please refer to Chapter 4, "P2P As a Framework for Distributed Computing," where we introduced SOAP, and Chapter 11, "Web Services Explained," where we discussed the structure of SOAP messages and SOAP request/response mechanism.

We will use the SOAP request of Listing 12.3 and the response of Listing 12.4 to demonstrate the different capabilities of JAXP.

LISTING 12.3   `SoapRequest.xml`: A Simple SOAP Request to Demonstrate XML Authoring with DOM

```xml
<?xml version="1.0" encoding="UTF-8"?>
<SOAP-ENV:Envelope xmlns:SOAP-ENV="http://schemas.xmlsoap.org/soap/envelope/"
➥xmlns:xsi="http://www.w3.org/1999/XMLSchema-instance"
➥xmlns:xsd="http://www.w3.org/1999/XMLSchema">
  <SOAP-ENV:Body>
    <f:getFreight xmlns:f="www.freightservice.com/">
      <source xsi:type="xsd:string">Lahore</source>
      <destination xsi:type="xsd:string">Multan</destination>
      <packetWeight xsi:type="xsd:int">50</packetWeight>
    </f:getFreight>
  </SOAP-ENV:Body>
</SOAP-ENV:Envelope>
```

LISTING 12.4 SoapResponse.xml: Sample SOAP Response to Demonstrate SAX and XSL Transformations

```xml
<?xml version='1.0' encoding='UTF-8'?>
<SOAP-ENV:Envelope
        xmlns:SOAP-ENV="http://schemas.xmlsoap.org/soap/envelope/"
        xmlns:xsi="http://www.w3.org/1999/XMLSchema-instance"
        xmlns:xsd="http://www.w3.org/1999/XMLSchema">
        <SOAP-ENV:Body>
                <ns1:getFreightResponse xmlns:ns1="urn:FreightCalculationService"
                SOAP-ENV:encodingStyle=
                   "http://schemas.xmlsoap.org/soap/encoding/">
                        <return xsi:type="xsd:string">5000</return>
                </ns1:getFreightResponse>
        </SOAP-ENV:Body>
</SOAP-ENV:Envelope>
```

SOAP Request Authoring Through DOM Using JAXP

In this section, we will describe the XML authoring process by using the DOM-related features of JAXP. We will use Listing 12.3 as a sample SOAP message to demonstrate XML authoring.

DOM is a W3C specification. It specifies a way to process XML by representing it as a tree of nodes. Every element, attribute, content, comment, and processing instruction that appears inside an XML file becomes a node. You can traverse through, read, insert, edit, or delete nodes using the DOM specification.

We are discussing DOM-related features of JAXP, which is mostly used on the Web server side, or as part of standalone applications. The same DOM specification is also used on the client side (inside a Web browser) to author or process XML. Although we will not discuss DOM inside a Web browser, it is worth noting that Netscape and Microsoft have implemented their own versions of DOM in their browsers.

While authoring a SOAP request, we will start from scratch; that is, we do not have any XML file to begin with. We will first create a new empty XML document and then author XML nodes according to the SOAP structure one by one. At the end, we will get the completed XML string, ready to be sent via HTTP (or any other similar transport service).

Listing 12.5 is a Java class named SOAPRequest. Look at the constructor. The first three lines are a standard code to create a new empty XML document:

```
DocumentBuilderFactory
dbf = DocumentBuilderFactory.newInstance();
DocumentBuilder db = dbf.newDocumentBuilder();
ownerDoc = db.newDocument();
```

You create a new instance of `DocumentBuilderFactory`; then using the factory, you create a new `DocumentBuilder`, and finally using the `DocumentBuilder`, you create a new `Document`. This is a standard three-step procedure to create an empty XML document. This procedure gives you a reference for the newly created document. The private variable `ownerDoc` holds this reference for you.

LISTING 12.5 `SOAPRequest.java`: SOAP Request Author

```
import org.w3c.dom.*;
import javax.xml.parsers.*;
import org.apache.crimson.tree.XmlDocument;
import java.io.*;


public class SOAPRequest  {
        // Keeps reference of the complete XML document.
        private Document ownerDoc;

        // Keeps reference of the SOAP Envelope element.
        private Element soapEnvelope;

        // Keeps reference of the SOAP Body element.
        private Element soapBody;



        // We will author SOAPEnvelope
        // and an empty SOAP Body in the constructor.
        public SOAPRequest () {
                try {
                        // Create a Document Builder Factory,
                        // then create a Document Builder using the Factory,
                        // then create a Document using the Builder.
                        DocumentBuilderFactory dbf =
                                DocumentBuilderFactory.newInstance();
                        DocumentBuilder db = dbf.newDocumentBuilder();
                        ownerDoc = db.newDocument();
                }//try
                catch (ParserConfigurationException pce) {
                        System.out.println ("ParserConfigException:"+
                                pce.getMessage());
                }//catch
                try {
                        // Create the Envelope.
```

12

MESSAGING
AND JAVA APIS
FOR XML

LISTING 12.5   continued

```
                    soapEnvelope = ownerDoc.createElement("SOAP-ENV:Envelope");
                    // Set namespaces.
                    soapEnvelope.setAttributeNS(
➥                           "http://www.w3.org/2000/xmlns/",
➥                           "xmlns:SOAP-ENV",
➥                           "http://schemas.xmlsoap.org/soap/envelope/"
➥                                                  );
                    soapEnvelope.setAttributeNS(
➥                           "http://www.w3.org/2000/xmlns/",
➥                           "xmlns:xsi",
➥                           "http://www.w3.org/1999/XMLSchema-instance"
➥                                                  );
                    soapEnvelope.setAttributeNS(
➥                           "http://www.w3.org/2000/xmlns/",
➥                           "xmlns:xsd",
➥                           "http://www.w3.org/1999/XMLSchema"
➥                                                  );
                    // Create an empty SOAP Body and
                    // add it to the Envelope.
                    soapBody = ownerDoc.createElement ("SOAP-ENV:Body");
                    soapEnvelope.appendChild(soapBody);
                    ownerDoc.appendChild (soapEnvelope);

        }//try
        catch (DOMException de){
                System.out.println ("DOMException: "+de.getMessage());
        }//catch
}// Constructor

public void setBodyMethod (Node bodyMethod) {
        // bodyMethod belongs to some other owner document.
        // We will import the Node into our document
        // and append it to the soapBody.
        Node importedNode =
➥              ownerDoc.importNode(bodyMethod, true);
        soapBody.appendChild (importedNode);
        // Now save the SOAP request XML as SOAPRequest.xml.
        // This saving is only for demonstration.
        XmlDocument xmlDocument = (XmlDocument)ownerDoc;
        try{
                FileOutputStream fout =
➥                      new FileOutputStream(
➥                              new File(".\\SoapRequest.xml"));
                xmlDocument.write(fout);
                fout.close();
        }//try
        catch(Throwable th){th.printStackTrace();}
}//setBodyMethod()

// Main method only for demonstration.
```

LISTING 12.5   continued

```
        // Creates one node "method" with a few child elements.
        // Then it calls the setBodyMethod of SOAPRequest class
        // passing the "method" node as parameter.
        public static void main (String args[]){
                SOAPRequest soap = new SOAPRequest();
                Document doc = null;
                Element method;
                Element parameter1;
                Element parameter2;
                Element parameter3;
                try{
                        DocumentBuilderFactory dbf =
                        DocumentBuilderFactory.newInstance();
                        DocumentBuilder db =
                        dbf.newDocumentBuilder();
                        doc = db.newDocument();
                }//try
                catch (ParserConfigurationException pce) {
                        System.out.println(
                                "ParserConfigException: "+
                                pce.getMessage());
                }//catch
                try{
                        method = doc.createElement("f:getFreight");
                        method.setAttributeNS(
                                "http://www.w3.org/2000/xmlns/",
                                "xmlns:f","www.freightservice.com/");
                        parameter1 = doc.createElement("source");
                        parameter1.setAttribute ("xsi:type","xsd:string");
                        parameter1.appendChild(
                                doc.createTextNode("Lahore"));
                        method.appendChild(parameter1);
                        parameter2 = doc.createElement("destination");
                        parameter2.setAttribute ("xsi:type","xsd:string");
                        parameter2.appendChild(
                                doc.createTextNode("Multan"));
                        method.appendChild(parameter2);
                        parameter3 = doc.createElement("packetWeight");
                        parameter3.setAttribute ("xsi:type","xsd:int");
                        parameter3.appendChild(doc.createTextNode("50"));
                        method.appendChild(parameter3);
                        soap.setBodyMethod (method);
                }//try
                catch (DOMException de){
                        System.out.println(
                                "Method DOMException: "+de.getMessage());
                }//catch
        }//main
}//class
```

The next step is to start authoring the SOAP request. We will perform the common tasks of authoring an envelope and an empty body in the SOAPRequest constructor. This will allow you to later add user-defined structures to the body of your SOAP request.

Look at the following lines of code:

```
soapEnvelope = ownerDoc.createElement("SOAP-ENV:Envelope");
soapEnvelope.setAttributeNS ("http://www.w3.org/2000/xmlns/", "SOAP-ENV",
➥"http://schemas.xmlsoap.org/soap/envelope/");
soapEnvelope.setAttributeNS ("http://www.w3.org/2000/xmlns/", "xsi",
➥"http://www.w3.org/1999/XMLSchema-instance");
soapEnvelope.setAttributeNS ("http://www.w3.org/2000/xmlns/", "xsd",
➥"http://www.w3.org/1999/XMLSchema");
```

We have used the createElement method of the Document class to author the envelope (SOAP-ENV:Envelope) element. This envelope accompanies three namespace declarations.

The next step is to create an empty child element Body that belongs to SOAP-ENV namespace and add it to the envelope. The following three lines accomplish this:

```
soapBody = ownerDoc.createElement ("SOAP-ENV:Body");
soapEnvelope.appendChild(soapBody);
doc.appendChild (soapEnvelope);
```

This finishes the constructor in Listing 12.5. Listing 12.6 shows what we have authored in the constructor.

LISTING 12.6   SoapRequest.xml (partial)

```
<?xml version="1.0" encoding="UTF-8"?>
<SOAP-ENV:Envelope xmlns:SOAP-ENV="http://schemas.xmlsoap.org/soap/envelope/"
➥xmlns:xsi="http://www.w3.org/1999/XMLSchema-instance" xmlns:xsd=
➥"http://www.w3.org/1999/XMLSchema">
  <SOAP-ENV:Body />
</SOAP-ENV:Envelope>
```

Adding a User-Defined Body to the SOAP Request

The SOAP request constructor discussed previously creates an envelope and an empty body. The setBodyMethod() method will add the user-defined XML structure to the available empty body.

The setBodyMethod() method takes a parameter bodyMethod of type Node. Look at the following two lines of code:

```
Node importedNode =       document.importNode(header, true);
soapEnvelope.appendChild (importedNode);
```

The first line imports the incoming node (bodyMethod) into the document (ownerDoc). This is necessary because the bodyMethod node will be supplied by other Java classes that will use SOAPRequest. Therefore, it will always belong to some other owner Document. The second line simply appends the newly imported child to the soapBody node.

The rest of the lines in setBodyMethod() are only for demonstration. They are meant to save the authored XML structure as an XML file, so you can see what has been authored. The completed XML structure will look like Listing 12.3.

How to Use the SOAP Request Class

Our SOAPRequest class is supposed to be a reusable component. It can be used inside a JFC/Swing application, or as a server-side component. But in order to keep Listing 12.5 simple, we have included a main() method within the SOAPRequest class. The main() method demonstrates the use of the constructor and setBodyMethod() for SOAP request authoring. It instantiates the SOAPRequest class, authors a new node, and passes it to setBodyMethod().

SOAP Response Processing Through Simple APIs for XML (SAX) Using JAXP

SAX is a W3C specification. It was originally a Java-only API, the first widely accepted API for XML in Java. SAX represents an XML file (for example, a SOAP message) as a sequence of events. Every node in an XML document (start and end elements, text, and so on) is taken as an event, and the sequence of events represents an XML file.

We have already discussed the use of JAXP DOM in authoring SOAP requests. In response to the request, we will receive another SOAP message, called a SOAP response. We will now demonstrate the use of SAX to process a SOAP response. We will also describe how SAX represents an XML file as a sequence of events, and develop a small Java application.

SOAP Response Processing Inside a SOAP Client

Recall the SOAP request and response of Listings 12.3 and 12.4, respectively. Listing 12.4 contains a typical SOAP message that we would expect in response to our request in Listing 12.3.

The SOAP response in Listing 12.4 contains the following information:

- Name of the method that was invoked (`getFreight`) concatenated with a string `Response`. This forms the `<getFreightResponse>` tag inside the `<SOAP:ENV-Body>` tag.

- The return value string `5000` as contents of the `<return>` tag. The `<return>` tag has an attribute `type` that belongs to the `xsi` namespace. The type attribute value is `xsd:string`. This means the returned information is of type `string`.

We would like to extract information out of this SOAP response and present it to the user. HTML is one of the most popular formats for presentation, so we will generate the HTML format after extracting information from the SOAP response. You can use a similar technique to generate other formats, as well.

Listing 12.7 is a simple HTML file that we will generate from the SOAP response. This type of application, in which we take an XML file as input, read something from it and generate another format (for example, HTML), is referred to as *XML transformation*. This example helps to demonstrate what type of SOAP response processing is normally required.

LISTING 12.7   `SoapResponse.html`: Sample HTML File Generated by SAX and XSLT

```
<html>
     <body bgcolor="whitesmoke">
          <p align="center"><b> Method Name: getPriceResponse</b>
               <table>
                    <tr>
                          <td align="right"> Freight:</td>
                          <td>5000</td>
                    </tr>
               </table>
          </p>
     </body>
</html>
```

Compare the SOAP response of Listing 12.4 with the HTML file of Listing 12.7 to note the following important points:

- The name of the method in the SOAP response (`getFreightResponse`) appears within a `<b>` tag in HTML.

- The return value in the SOAP response (`5000`) appears within a `<td>` tag in HTML.

We will now see how we accomplish HTML generation from SOAP responses through SAX.

Simple API for XML (SAX)

The XML structure of Listing 12.4 can be represented by the following SAX events (the order of events is important):

1. Start of document event
2. Start element event `<SOAP-ENV:Envelope>`
3. Start element event `<SOAP-ENV:Body>`
4. Start element event `<ns:getFreightResponse>`
5. Start element event `<return>`
6. Character event (`5000`)
7. End element event `</return>`
8. End element event `</ns:getFreightResponse>`
9. End element event `</SOAP-ENV:Body >`
10. End element event `</SOAP-ENV:Envelope>`
11. End of document event

The preceding sequence of events suggests that you can have several types of SAX events in an XML file. The following is a list of the major types of SAX events (some of them don't occur in Listing 12.4):

- Start of document
- End of document
- Start of element
- End of element
- Character
- Processing instruction

Whenever you have a transformation requirement from XML to any format (for example, other XML DTDs, HTML, binary format, and so on), this event strategy will always help you. The simplest way of transforming XML through SAX events is to catch the events of your interest, read XML data in that event, and generate the output.

Our SOAP response to the HTML transformation requirements can be accomplished through the following strategy:

1. Look for the `getFreightResponse` start element and read the name of the element.
2. Look for the `character` event inside the return element and read the contents.
3. Insert the two bits of data read from XML into the HTML data stream.

Listing 12.8 is a Java class (SOAPResponse) that implements this parsing strategy using SAX implementation in JAXP. We will now have a detailed look at the working of SAX in the SOAPResponse class.

LISTING 12.8   SOAPResponse.java: Uses SAX Parser to Transform SOAP to HTML

```java
import javax.xml.parsers.*;
import org.xml.sax.helpers.*;
import org.xml.sax.*;
import java.io.*;

public class SOAPResponse extends DefaultHandler
{
        //Holds the HTML that we are authoring.
        private String html="<html>"+
                        "<body bgcolor=\"whitesmoke\">"+
                        "<p align=\"center\">";

        //These flags will be set when
        //corresponding events are found.
        private boolean body=false;
        private boolean method=false;
        private boolean value=false;


        // Constructor takes a File object (XML file).
        // It creates a SAXParserFactory.
        // Then creates a SAXParser on the Factory and
        // parses the input File object.
        public SOAPResponse(File file)
        {
                //Calling parser to parse the xml file.
                try
                {
                        SAXParserFactory parserfactory =
                                SAXParserFactory.newInstance();
                        SAXParser parser = parserfactory.newSAXParser();
                        parser.parse(file,this);
                }//try
                catch(Exception e)
                {
                        System.out.println(e.getMessage());
                }//catch
        }//Constructor


        public void startElement(String uri,
                        String localName,
                        String qName,
                        Attributes attributes)
        {
```

LISTING 12.8 continued

```
            if(localName.equals("Body"))
            {
                    //We've found SOAP Body.
                    body=true;
            }// if
            else if (body && !method && !value)
            {
                    //We've found SOAP Method.
                    html +="<b> Method Name: " + localName + "</b>";
                    method = true;
            }// else if
            else if (method && !value )
            {
                    //We can expect the value that we were looking for.
                    html +="<table>";
                    value = true;
                    //The character event will actually work
                    //after we've set the value equal to true.
            }// else if
    }//startElement

    public void characters(char[] ch, int start, int length)
    {
            String tstr = new String(ch,start,length);
            String str="";
            //Ignore everything except integers and alphabets.
            for (int i=0;i<tstr.length();i++)
            {
                    if ((tstr.charAt(i)>='0' && tstr.charAt(i)<='9') ||
                        (tstr.charAt(i)>='a' && tstr.charAt(i)<='z') ||
                        (tstr.charAt(i)>='A' && tstr.charAt(i)<='Z'))
                    {
                            str += tstr.charAt(i);
                    }//if
            }//for
            if (value && str.length()>0)
            {
                    // Value flag was set in startElement event handler.
                    // Now is the time to read contents of <return> tag.
                    html+= "<tr>"+
                            "<td align=\"right\"> Freight:</td>"+
                            "<td>"+ str+"</td>"+
                            "</tr>";
                    value=false;//don't read again.
            }//if
    }//characters

    public void printHTML(File file)
    {
```

LISTING 12.8 continued

```
        try
        {
                FileWriter fw = new FileWriter(file);
                fw.write(html,0,html.length());
                fw.close();
        }//try
        catch(Exception e)
        {
                System.out.println("File Write Error....");
        }//catch
        System.out.println(html);
    }//printHtml

    public void endDocument()
    {
            html+="</table>"+
                "</p>"+
                "</body>"+
                "</html>";
    }//endDocument

    public static void main(String arg[])
    {
            String fileName="SOAPResponse";
            SOAPResponse sr =
                    new SOAPResponse(new File(fileName+".xml"));
            sr.printHTML(new File(fileName+".html"));
    }//main
}//class
```

Using SAX to Read XML and Transform to Other Formats

The SOAPResponse constructor takes a File object (this File object represents an XML file). It creates an instance of a SAXParserFactory and then builds a SAXParser using the factory. Once the SAX parser is ready, we can call its parse() method. Have a look at the following lines of code that accomplish this:

```
SAXParserFactory parserfactory =
SAXParserFactory.newInstance();
SAXParser parser = parserfactory.newSAXParser();
parser.parse(file,this);
```

The parse() method takes two parameters. The first parameter is the File object that represents our XML file to be parsed.

The second parameter is a reference of an object that would receive control whenever a SAX event is detected. We have passed the address of SOAPResponse object (this) as the value of the second parameter. Therefore, SOAPResponse will receive control to handle all SAX events. JAXP requires that classes that will handle SAX events should be derived from the DefaultHandler class. That's why our SOAPResponse class is derived from the DefaultHandler class.

Now have a look at the startElement method. It is a SAX event handler, and receives control every time a start element is detected in the XML file being parsed. The parameters passed to this event handler specify the element name and attributes.

We have to do three things in this event handler. First, we have to look for the Body element. When Body is found, we'll read the name of its first (and only) child element. Body's first child is the name of a SOAP method response, and should be written in our output HTML.

The startElement method will then look for the return element, which is the only grandchild of Body element. When found, we will set the Value flag.

The Value flag is used by the characters event handler to decide when to read contents. The characters event handler receives control every time content is detected in an XML file, and the detected content is passed to the event handler. This event handler will only write the content to output HTML if the Value flag is set, which means the content inside Body's grandchild will be written to output HTML.

The main() and printHTML() methods in Listing 12.8 are only for demonstration, so you can run this class and save the resulting HTML.

Comparing SAX and DOM

SAX and DOM both represent the same information, but in different ways. SAX represents an XML document as a sequence of events, while DOM loads an XML file in memory and uses a hierarchical structure (a tree of nodes) to represent XML.

SAX does not load the XML data in memory. It keeps on firing events as they occur. Therefore, SAX is more suitable for applications where large XML documents need to be parsed.

Limitations of SAX

As we have seen while using JAXP's SAX parser, the order of SAX events corresponds to the XML file being parsed. All SAX events occur in an order that matches the arrangement of nodes in XML. This type of arrangement suits applications where you need to read specific bits of information from an XML file.

What if our requirement calls for reading a fragment identifier from an XML file and then jumping to that fragment? The destination fragment might be present prior to its reference. This means we need to jump to a SAX event that has already occurred in the past. This type of requirement is a bit tricky to handle in SAX. DOM-based parsing is more suitable for such applications.

XSLT in JAXP

Until now we have been writing Java code (either SAX- or DOM-based) to author, parse, process, or transform XML. But JAXP also allows the use of XSLT to process XML.

XSLT code is itself XML, and is much easier to write compared to Java code. In this section we will write an XSLT file that transforms the SOAP response of Listing 12.4 to the HTML of Listing 12.7 (the same task that we accomplished through SAX in the previous section). We will also demonstrate how to use a XSLT stylesheet from within Java code.

Most XML transformation tasks can be accomplished through XSLT. JAXP allows the use of XSLT code from within Java applications. Therefore, Java-based P2P applications can employ XSLT for P2P-related XML processing requirements.

XSLT at Work

XSLT is an XML-based grammar with which to specify transformation criteria directly in XML format, without needing to write the parsing logic that we wrote while discussing SAX-based transformations. JAXP includes an XSLT engine that can be used from within Java applications to make XSLT files perform XML transformations.

Listing 12.9 is an XSLT file that transforms the XML of Listing 12.4 to the HTML of Listing 12.7. This file basically contains three sections. The first section is the root element that contains namespace declarations, and the other two are templates.

The first section declares the four namespaces we will use. The first namespace is the XSLT namespace itself. The other three are SOAP namespaces that occur in the SOAP response that we are going to transform.

The use of namespaces is quite logical. As the XSLT file itself is XML, the transformation instructions in XSLT are also XML. Namespace declarations are used to identify which tags are part of XSLT code.

The second section starts with a template definition:

```
<xsl:template
➥match="SOAP-ENV:Envelope/SOAP-ENV:Body/node()[position()=2]">
```

The `match` attribute of this template element is an XPath query. XPath is another W3C specification that is normally used in conjunction with XSLT to specify particular sections within an XML document. The XPath query says: "Find the section in the input

XML file in which a SOAP `Envelope` element is the parent of a SOAP `Body` (`SOAP-ENV:Envelope/SOAP-ENV:Body/`). When you have found the SOAP `Body`, get its second node (`node()[position()=2]">`)." Body's second child node is the `<getFreightResponse>` element in the SOAP response (the first is the white space between two elements).

Once you have reached the `<getFreightResponse>` element, you want to output it to the HTML file being authored. The following XSLT code accomplishes this:

```
<xsl:value-of select="local-name(.)"/>
```

The next step is to find the contents of the `<return>` element. For this purpose, we have another XSLT template element. The following line jumps from one template to another template:

```
<xsl:apply-templates select="return"/>
```

The `apply-templates` element says "Now is the time to jump to the template whose `match` attribute matches my `select` attribute." Look at the second template element (the third section of Listing 12.9):

```
<xsl:template match="return">
```

This template will output the contents of the `<return>` element and finish our transformation job.

LISTING 12.9   XSLT That Transforms a SOAP Response to HTML

```
<?xml version="1.0"?>
<xsl:stylesheet version="1.0"
➡      xmlns:xsl="http://www.w3.org/1999/XSL/Transform"
➡      xmlns:SOAP-ENV="http://schemas.xmlsoap.org/soap/envelope/"
➡      xmlns:xsi="http://www.w3.org/1999/XMLSchema-instance"
➡      xmlns:xsd="http://www.w3.org/1999/XMLSchema">

    <xsl:output method="html"/>
    <xsl:template
➡        match="SOAP-ENV:Envelope/SOAP-ENV:Body/node()[position()=2]">
            <html>
                <body bgcolor="whitesmoke">
                    <p align="center">
                        <b>Method Name:
                        <xsl:value-of select="local-name(.)"/>
                        </b>
                        <table>
                        <xsl:apply-templates select="return"/>
                        </table>
                    </p>
                </body>
```

LISTING **12.9**   continued

```
            </html>
        </xsl:template>
        <xsl:template match="return">
            <tr>
                    <td align="right"> Freight:</td>
                    <td><xsl:value-of select="text()"/></td>
            </tr>
        </xsl:template>
</xsl:stylesheet>
```

How to Use XSLT from Within Java Code

The use of XSLT files from Java code is very simple in JAXB. The following lines of code accomplish this:

```
TransformerFactory tFactory = TransformerFactory.newInstance();
Transformer transformer =
➥        tFactory.newTransformer(new StreamSource(XSLTDocument));
transformer.transform( new StreamSource(XMLDocument),
new StreamResult(new FileOutputStream(ResultDocument)));
```

XSLTDocument, XMLDocument, and ResultDocument are three String type objects that specify the names of XSLT, XML, and the resulting output (for example, HTML) files, respectively.

First create an instance of TransformerFactory. Then pass the XSLT stream to the newTransformer() method of TransformerFactory. This returns a Transformer object. Then call the transform() method of the Transformer object and pass on the XML stream and a reference to an output stream. The transform() method will generate the output and write it to the output stream.

XML and the Java API for XML Binding (JAXB)

We have already discussed JAXP in detail and seen how JAXP supports SAX and DOM. JAXB is another way of processing XML through Java classes, and therefore provides all the features that SAX and DOM provide. JAXB features a newer approach, and an easier way of authoring and processing XML compared to SAX or DOM. You can generate Java classes directly from the XML DTD that you want to author or process. The following are the steps to accomplish this:

1. Take the DTD of the XML that you want to author or process through Java classes. DTDs are a way to describe the structure of XML documents. The latest way of

describing XML structures is to use XSD (XML Schema Definition) files. However, JAXB currently only supports DTDs. Support for XSDs can be expected in the future.

2. Write the JAXB binding schema. This schema allows you to customize Java classes that will be produced. For example, you can customize names of packages, classes, and methods. You can also decide the data type of return values from methods of Java classes. We'll give examples of doing this in the section "Writing the Binding Schema for JAXB." However, if you don't want to customize the creation of Java classes, you can leave it to the JAXB Schema Compiler to assume default behavior.

3. Provide the DTD from the first step and the binding schema from the second step to the JAXB Schema Compiler provided with Sun's implementation. The Compiler will generate the required Java class for you.

4. Java classes generated by the Schema Compiler use the packages provided by Sun in the reference implementation for JAXB. As a last step before you can use these newly generated Java classes, you will need to set the classpath to include all JAXB-related classes.

JAXB-generated classes are normally more efficient and require a smaller footprint in memory compared to using SAX and DOM. This is because Java classes generated by the JAXB Schema Compiler are custom-built for your specific DTD.

We will now give a step-by-step illustration of the previously mentioned steps using a sample XML structure.

Step 1: DTD

The following is a sample DTD that we'll take in our sample JAXB application. (We are not discussing P2P in this section, but JAXB is expected to have an important role in developing P2P applications. Therefore, the DTD that we have chosen for our sample application belongs to one of the JXTA specifications. JXTA uses this DTD to define the structure of search requests issued by peers.)

```
<?xml version="1.0" encoding="UTF-8"?>
<!ELEMENT request (query)>
<!ELEMENT query (author+, title)>
<!ELEMENT author (quote)>
<!ELEMENT title (#PCDATA)>
<!ELEMENT quote (#PCDATA)>
<!ATTLIST request
      id CDATA #REQUIRED
      query-space CDATA #REQUIRED
>
```

This sample DTD contains five elements: `request`, `query`, `author`, `quote`, and `title`. The `request` element contains a `query` element. The `query` element contains one or more (+ sign) `author` elements and exactly one `title` element. The `author` element contains one `quote` element, which in turn contains only `PCDATA` (*Parsed Character DATA*, which generally means content with escape character sequences such as < for <). The `title` element also contains only `PCDATA`. The `request` element contains the two attributes `id` and `query-space`.

For the sake of clarity, the following is a valid XML file that conforms to the preceding DTD:

```
<?xml version="1.0" ?>
<request id="1C8DAC3036A911D584BCC2C23"
➥query-space="http://bigbookseller.com/js">
<query>
<author>
<quote>Muhammad Imran</quote>
</author>
<author>
<quote>Bilal Siddiqui</quote>
</author>
<title>Java</title>
</query>
</request>
```

Step 2: Writing the Binding Schema

We will now demonstrate the authoring of binding schema, which enables you to specify exactly how you would like your Java classes to behave. Look at the following binding schema:

```
<xml-java-binding-schema version="1.0-ea">
<element name="request" type = "class" root="true" />
<element name="query" type="class" root="true" />
</xml-java-binding-schema>
```

This binding schema is itself an XML file. The first tag is `<xml-java-binding-schema>`, which specifies the version of JAXB specification that you're working with. Next is an empty `<element/>` tag with several attributes.

The `name` attribute refers to the root element of our DTD (the `request` element). This line of the binding schema simply says "The `request` element in your DTD should be handled by a separate Java class." When you compile the DTD and binding schema together in the next step to generate Java classes, you will see that there is a separate Java class named `Request` that handles the authoring and processing of the `request` element.

Similarly, the third line of the binding schema says that we also want a separate Java class to handle the query element.

Step 3: Compiling the DTD and Binding Schema Together into a Set of Java Classes

We are now ready to run the Schema Compiler and generate the required Java classes. Execute the Compiler with the following command:

```
Java com.sun.tools.xjc.Main Search.DTD search1.xjs
```

Notice that name of our DTD file is search.DTD, and name of the binding schema file is search1.xjc. You will need to save these files in your current working folder before you can compile them. Moreover, the JAXB compiler should be in your classpath (jaxb-xjc-1.0-ea.jar for the early-access release version 1.0).

This command will generate the following set of classes:

- Request.java
- Query.java
- Author.java

Have a look at Request.java. We have not included these Java files in this chapter, but you can either generate them yourself using the Schema Compiler as described previously, or download the files from this book's accompanying Web site. The following is a code extract from the Request.java class that specifies the private variable declarations for the class:

```
private String _Id;
private String _QuerySpace;
private Query _Query;
```

Here we have two strings _Id and _QuerySpace that will hold the attribute values of id and queryspace for our Request.Java class.

There is another private data member named _Query that's an object of the Query class. Query.java is another file generated by the Schema Compiler that corresponds to the query element in our DTD. Recall from the discussion in step 1 that the request element in our DTD can contain only one query. This is reflected in the Java file generated by the Schema Compiler.

We also have the public methods setQuery and getQuery. The setQuery method takes a Query object and places it in the private data member _Query. On the other hand, the getQuery() method returns the Query object from the internal data structure. The following is the simple code for the getQuery() method:

```
public Query getQuery() {
        return _Query;
    }
```

Similarly, the Query class will hold its own data members. But why do we have an Author class while we specified to have separate classes only for the request and query elements in the binding schema in Step 2? The reason for having a separate Author class is that there can be more than one author elements inside a query element (refer to the DTD of Step 1). Therefore, the Query class will have to maintain a list of author elements. JAXB accomplishes this by defining a separate Author class, so that Query can maintain a list of all Author objects (one Author object for each author element).

We will shortly describe how to use these Java classes, but first we have to set the classpath.

Step 4: Setting the Classpath for the Newly Generated Classes

In order to use the Java classes generated by the JAXB Schema Compiler, you need to set the classpath for the following two JAR files:

- jaxb-xjc-1.0-ea.jar
- jaxb-rt-1.0-ea.jar

The three Java classes that we generated in Step 3 use packages included in these JAR files. Therefore, you should have these JARs in your classpath. Once you have set the correct classpath, you can compile your Java classes as normal Java files.

Using JAXB Classes in a Java Application

We will now demonstrate how to use the newly generated Java classes in a Java application. Look at the following lines of code:

```
InputStream ins = new FileInputStream(
➥new File("SearchInput.xml"));
Request request = Request.unmarshal(ins);
OutputStream outs = new FileOutputStream(
➥new File ("SearchOutput.xml"));
request.marshal(outs);
```

These four lines of code demonstrate two important functions called *unmarshaling* and *marshaling*.

The first line creates an InputStream over an XML file named SearchInput.xml. You can use the XML file of Step 1 for this purpose. The second line calls the static method unmarshal() of the Request class and passes the InputStream to it. This unmarshal() method will internally parse the XML stream, load it into a Request object, and return the loaded Request object. We have stored the reference of the returned Request object in a variable. This process is called unmarshaling, in which an XML stream is loaded into Java objects.

The third and fourth lines of code demonstrate the reverse of unmarshaling, called marshaling. Here we take an OutputStream over a file named SearchOutput.xml and pass it to the marshal() method of the same Request object that we obtained through unmarshaling in the previous paragraph. The marshal() method will write the Java object as an XML stream to the OutputStream supplied to it. Therefore, marshaling is the process in which Java objects are converted into XML streams.

After the execution of these four lines of code, the two XML files SearchInput.xml and SearchOutput.xml should match with each other.

In some real-world applications, you will be required to unmarshal an XML stream and edit it before marshaling it back to an XML stream. For such applications, you will use the set and get methods of the Java classes that we explained in Step 3 to edit the XML data.

Message Profiling Using JAXM

Sun has released the Java API for XML Messaging (JAXM) to combine messaging and XML processing capabilities into one API. It enables both synchronous and asynchronous communication (refer to the discussion related to synchronous and asynchronous communications in the section "Messaging Versus Request-Response" earlier in this chapter).

JAXM follows the standard SOAP 1.1 and SOAP with Attachments specifications. It can generate SOAP-compatible messages and work in any of the following ways:

- JAXM as a simple SOAP client—JAXM can author a simple SOAP message with only a SOAP Body inside the SOAP Envelope. After authoring the SOAP message, JAXM will send it synchronously through HTTP communication. This is the simplest form of SOAP communication, in that JAXM acts like a simple SOAP-over-HTTP client.
- Using JAXM for SOAP Header authoring—JAXM can also add a SOAP Header in the SOAP message being sent. The SOAP Header is an extensibility mechanism used to build higher layers of protocols on top of the basic SOAP framework. This means that a protocol layer operating above SOAP will define its own XML syntax

to be included in the SOAP Header. The SOAP specification does not dictate anything about its header. So, you can build whatever mechanism you feel like using in the SOAP Header.

One of the most significant efforts in building SOAP-based protocols is in defining the Web services security mechanism for SOAP-based Web services. Another important use of SOAP Headers is to define the ebXML Messaging Service framework.

- Using JAXM providers and profiles—JAXM supports asynchronous communication for both the preceding points. This means that you can send SOAP messages with or without Headers asynchronously. You will use JAXM providers for asynchronous communication. A JAXM client will hand over the message to the JAXM provider. The JAXM provider is responsible to route the message to its destination asynchronously. The provider will also inform the client when a response is received from the other end.

JAXM also allows the use of preconfigured JAXM profiles. A JAXM profile represents a specific SOAP-based protocol. When you use the preconfigured profiles, you no longer need to author SOAP Headers yourself. The JAXM profile will create the correct Header according to the protocol that it supports. The JAXM 1.0 Reference Implementation comes with two profiles—one for the simple SOAP Remote Provider (SOAPRP), and one for the ebXML Messaging Service.

A JAXM provider implementation is required to support the basic features as specified by the SOAP 1.1 and SOAP with Attachments specifications. Anything beyond the basic SOAP features is optional. However, most JAXM provider implementations will implement at least something (probably one or more profiles supporting some SOAP-based protocols) on top of the basic SOAP functionality. Building profiles to support SOAP-based protocols is among the most important objectives of JAXM.

Note

Note that a JAXM provider may support multiple profiles, but an application can use only one at a time.

We will now see the details of how the three types of operations are accomplished using JAXM.

JAXM As a Simple SOAP Client

We will now discuss the first and simplest case, in which JAXM acts as a SOAP client. In this case, we will use JAXM to perform the following tasks:

1. Author a SOAP request consisting of a SOAP `Envelope` containing a SOAP `Body`. JAXM will also author the application-specific contents of the SOAP `Body`.

2. Create a connection with the remote server.

3. Send the SOAP request to the remote SOAP server synchronously and wait for the response.

4. Process and display the SOAP response received from the SOAP server.

Let's see how these tasks are accomplished using JAXM. The following lines of code author a complete SOAP request:

```
MessageFactory messageFactory = MessageFactory.newInstance();
SOAPMessage request = messageFactory.createMessage();
SOAPPart soapPartOfRequest = request.getSOAPPart();
SOAPEnvelope soapEnvelope = soapPartOfRequest.getEnvelope();
SOAPBody soapBody = soapEnvelope.getBody();
Name methodName = soapEnvelope.createName(
➡                   "invoke" ,
➡                   "jaxm",
➡                   "urn:P2PCarRental");
soapBody.addChildElement(methodName);
```

The first step is to instantiate a `MessageFactory` that will be used to author a SOAP request message using the `MessageFactory.createMessage` method. The `createMessage` method authors a default `SOAPMessage` object, which contains a SOAP `Envelope`. The SOAP `Envelope` in turn contains an empty SOAP `Header` and an empty SOAP `Body`.

The following is the XML representation of a default `SOAPMessage` object created by `createMessage` method:

```
<soap-env:Envelope
    xmlns:soap-env=http://schemas.xmlsoap.org/soap/envelope/">
    <soap-env:Header/>
    <soap-env:Body/>
</soap-env:Envelope>
```

SOAP messages can also optionally contain non-SOAP (or even non-XML) parts. They are treated as attachments with the SOAP part of the message.

Your interest lies with the SOAP part of the message, so you can add SOAP service invocation details to the SOAP `Body`. The `getSOAPPart` method of the `SOAPMessage` class will extract the SOAP part of the message (a `SOAPPart` object).

Next you will call the SOAPPart.getEnvelope method that returns the SOAPEnvelope object. The SOAPEnvelope class has a method named getSOAPBody. The getSOAPBody method will eventually bring you the SOAPBody object that you will manipulate.

You will now author the application-specific XML content of your SOAP request, and then add the content to the SOAPBody object. XML authoring with JAXM is generally a two-step procedure. You first create a new element, and then add the newly created element to the appropriate place.

A new element is created by using the createName method of the SOAPEnvelope class. This returns a Name object. A newly created element is empty, and therefore just carries an XML name (which might include an element name, a namespace prefix, and a namespace URI). That's probably the reason why JAXM calls a new element a Name object.

You will need to specify three parameters while creating a new element for the XML contents of SOAP Body: the name of the element, the namespace prefix, and the namespace URI. The name of the element in this case is invoke; the namespace prefix is jaxm; and the namespace URI is urn:P2PcarRental. The following is how this new element looks like in XML format:

```
<jaxm:invoke xmlns:jaxm="urn:P2PCarRental"/>
```

You have created the new element. Now just add the new element to the SOAP Body. The addChildElement method of the SOAPBody class does this job for you.

The following is the complete XML structure that you have just authored:

```
<soap-env:Envelope
    xmlns:soap-env=http://schemas.xmlsoap.org/soap/envelope/">
    <soap-env:Header/>
    <soap-env:Body>
        <jaxm:invoke xmlns:jaxm="urn:P2PCarRental"/>
    </soap-env:Body>
</soap-env:Envelope>
```

We have authored the SOAP request that we want to send to the remote SOAP server. It is time to connect to the SOAP server.

Connecting to a SOAP server using JAXM is a three-step procedure:

1. Create an end point by specifying the URL of the SOAP server. The following line of code accomplishes this by using the URLEndpoint constructor:

```
URLEndpoint soapServerAddress =
➡       new URLEndpoint(
➡       "http://localhost:8080/soap/servlet/rpcrouter");
```

> **Note**
>
> We tested all this code with an Apache SOAP server deployed on a Tomcat Web server. The SOAP server address used previously (`http://localhost:8080/soap/servlet/rpcrouter`) is the address of the local Apache SOAP server on our machine. You may want to specify some remote SOAP server over the Internet.

2. Create a new instance of `SOAPConnectionFactory`:

   ```
   SOAPConnectionFactory connectionFactory =
   SOAPConnectionFactory.newInstance();
   ```

3. Call the `createConnection` method of the newly instantiated `SOAPConnectionFactory`:

   ```
   SOAPConnection connection = connectionFactory.createConnection();
   ```

You are now ready to send the SOAP request over this connection. The following code sends your request synchronously to the remote server:

```
SOAPMessage soapResponse = connection.call(request, soapServerAddress);
```

Notice that it is a synchronous request, so `SOAPConnection.call` method will return only when the SOAP server responds.

The SOAP response is a `SOAPMessage` object. Recall that our request was also a `SOAPMessage` object. Therefore, to process this SOAP response, you can follow the same sequence of `getSOAPPart`, `getEnvelope`, and `getBody` methods that we explained earlier while authoring the SOAP request.

We have summed up all this code in Listing 12.10 as a simple Java program named `JAXMSOAPClient`, which is a simple JAXML-based SOAP client. To compile and execute this application , you will need the following JAR files in your classpath: `jaxm.jar`, `dom4j.jar`, `mail.jar`, and `client.jar`.

LISTING 12.10 JAXMSOAPClient

```
import java.io.*;
import javax.xml.soap.*;
import javax.xml.messaging.*;
import java.net.URL;
import javax.mail.internet.*;
import javax.xml.transform.*;
import javax.xml.transform.stream.*;
import org.dom4j.*;
```

LISTING 12.10   continued

```
public class JAXMSOAPClient{
        public static void main(String args[]) {
        try {
            //Author a SOAP request.
            MessageFactory messageFactory = MessageFactory.newInstance();
            SOAPMessage request = messageFactory.createMessage();
            SOAPPart soapPartOfRequest = request.getSOAPPart();
            SOAPEnvelope soapEnvelope = soapPartOfRequest.getEnvelope();
            SOAPBody soapBody = soapEnvelope.getBody();
            Name methodName = soapEnvelope.createName(
➥                "invoke" ,
➥                "jaxm",
➥                "urn:P2PCarRental");
            soapBody.addChildElement(methodName);

            //Add code for SOAP Header authoring here.

            //Establish the SOAP connection.
            URLEndpoint soapServerAddress =
➥                new URLEndpoint(
➥                    "http://localhost:8080/soap/servlet/rpcrouter");
            SOAPConnectionFactory connectionFactory =
➥                SOAPConnectionFactory.newInstance();
            SOAPConnection connection =
➥                connectionFactory.createConnection();

            //Display the request.
            System.out.println();
            System.out.println("Sending SOAP request:");
            request.writeTo(System.out);
            System.out.println();

            //Send the request and wait for the response.
            SOAPMessage soapResponse = connection.call(request,
➥                                            soapServerAddress);

            //We have received the response. Display it.
            System.out.println();
            System.out.println("Received reply from: "+soapServerAddress);
            soapResponse.writeTo(System.out);

            //Job done. Close the connection.
            connection.close();

        } catch(Throwable e) {
            e.printStackTrace();
        }//catch
    }//main
}//class
```

Using JAXM for SOAP Header Authoring

We'll now show how to author a SOAP Header and add it to a SOAP message. The following is how the completed SOAP message will look after authoring is complete:

```
<soap-env:Envelope
    xmlns:soap-env=http://schemas.xmlsoap.org/soap/envelope/">
    <soap-env:Header>
        <sh:sampleHeader xmlns:sh=http://sampleNamespace.com/>
    </soap-env:Header>
    <soap-env:Body>
        <jaxm:invoke xmlns:jaxm="urn:P2PCarRental"/>
    </soap-env:Body>
</soap-env:Envelope>
```

The following lines of JAXM code will author the preceding SOAP message:

```
SOAPHeader soapHeader = soapEnvelope.getHeader();
Name soapHeaderName = soapEnvelope.createName(
➥                         "sampleHeader",
➥                         "sh",
➥                         "http://sampleNamespace.com");
soapHeader.addHeaderElement(soapHeaderName);
```

You can add the lines of code shown here just after authoring the SOAP request message and before establishing the SOAP connection in Listing 12.10.

The first line in this code obtains a reference to the SOAP Header element. Recall that you used the getBody method of the SOAPEnvelope class to obtain a reference to the SOAP Body. Similarly, you will now use the getHeader method of the SOAPEnvelope class to obtain a reference to the SOAP Header.

The second line creates a new sampleHeader element with the fictitious namespace http://sampleHeaderName.com. The third line of code simply adds the sampleHeader element to the SOAP Header.

This is a generic procedure to author any Header. The actual element names and namespace declaration will depend on the protocol that you wish to support through the SOAP Header.

Using JAXM Providers and Profiles

This section describes the use of JAXM providers and profiles. The use of a JAXM provider enables asynchronous communication, which means you will hand your message over to the provider and will not wait for the response. The provider will take care of routing and delivery and will inform you upon receipt of the response.

The JAXM profile is used to author preconfigured SOAP Headers confirming to a specific SOAP-based protocol (such as the ebXML Message Service Specification).

The JAXM providers only work inside J2EE or servlet containers. They cannot work alone, so if you are designing a standalone client, you cannot use a JAXM provider.

Your application will use the following steps to make use of the JAXM providers and profiles:

1. Look for a provider connection factory in a JNDI-based naming service and create a connection with the provider using the ProviderConnectionFactory. createConnection method. The createConnection method returns an instance of the ProviderConnection class.

   An alternative way is to use the default provider connection (without the JNDI lookup) using the ProviderConnectionFactory.newInstance method. After calling the newInstance method, you will also call the ProviderConnectionFactory.createConnection to create the connection (a ProviderConnection instance) on the default ProviderConnectionFactory.

2. Check for supported profiles and create a message factory using the profile of your choice.

3. Include the routing and destination information in the message.

4. Author the message, and optionally the SOAP Header as well (if you want to include something in the Header not supported by your JAXM profile).

5. Hand the message over to the provider.

You might have noticed that these steps do not include any action about receiving messages. How will you implement the message receiving logic in your application? We'll make use of the OnewayListener interface to receive messages asynchronously. Let's see how all of this is accomplished.

We will use a sample application called soaprp to demonstrate these steps. The soaprp sample application comes bundled with the JAXM version 1.0 Reference Implementation. It's a WAR file that can be deployed directly on a J2EE or servlet container such as Tomcat.

You might want to see what this application does before going into the technical details. Deploying this application on Tomcat involves nothing more than copying the soaprp.war file in the webapps directory after you have successfully installed JAXM, for which you will find comprehensive instructions in the documentation accompanying the Reference Implementation.

If you deploy the `soaprp` application on your container and access it through a normal Web browser, you will see the following message on the browser window:

```
This is an example of a roundtrip JAXM message exchange via the
remote provider..
Click here to send the message
```

The message will contain a hyperlink. Click on the hyperlink and the message will be delivered to the provider, and in turn sent to its destination. You will also notice that the JAXM-based recipient of the message has some message-receiving logic that reported the receipt of the incoming message on the `System.out` console of your container.

How soaprp Uses JAXM

You can unzip the `soaprp.war` file using any unzipping tool. Look for the `src` folder that contains the source code for this application. You will find two JavaBeans inside: `SendingServlet.java` and `ReceivingServlet.java`.

`SendingServlet` is responsible for authoring messages and handing them over to the provider. `ReceivingServlet` demonstrates the use of the `OnewayListener` interface that's responsible for receiving messages. This is a simple and generic arrangement that you can use to build your own messaging logic.

Look at the `SendingServlet` JavaBean, which extends the `HttpServlet` class. The most interesting part is in the `doGet` method, where you will look for the profile of your interest and create the message factory with it. Look at the following code extract from the sample application (`mf` is a `MessageFactory` instance, and `pc` is a `ProviderConnection` instance in the following code):

```
if (mf == null) {
    ProviderMetaData metaData = pc.getMetaData();
    String[] supportedProfiles = metaData.getSupportedProfiles();
    String profile = null;
    for(int i=0; i < supportedProfiles.length; i++) {
        if(supportedProfiles[i].equals("soaprp")) {
            profile = supportedProfiles[i];
            break;
        }//if
    }//for
    mf = pc.createMessageFactory(profile);
}//if
// Create a message from the message factory.
SOAPRPMessageImpl soaprpMsg =
➡   (SOAPRPMessageImpl)mf.createMessage();
```

The `if (mf==null)` block is only meant to create the required message factory by selecting the correct profile. When you have the message factory, you can create the message the same way you created it in Listing 12.10. However, this time you will store the message in a SOAPRPMessageImpl object, which represents the profile-specific message format with the correct SOAP Header.

The rest is logically the same as in Listing 12.10, except that you will use the ProviderConnection.send method instead of the SOAPConnection.call method to send the message. The send and call methods differ from each other in the sense that send is asynchronous, or one-way (meaning it returns immediately without waiting for the response), whereas call is synchronous (meaning it waits and remains blocked until it gets a response).

Now look at the ReceivingServlet.java file. The ReceivingServlet class implements the OnewayListener interface, which consists of only one method, onMessage. This method assumes control upon receipt of an incoming message.

Summary

We started our discussion by stating the two basic requirements of any P2P architecture. This entire chapter is about how Java fulfills the two requirements.

We discussed messaging and XML-related Java APIs. We introduced the messaging framework of JMS API, and explained the concept of synchronous and asynchronous communications. We also demonstrated the use of JMS clients and providers.

We then moved on to Java-based XML authoring, and processing details. We introduced two Java APIs: JAXP and JAXB. JAXP provides the implementation of SAX, DOM, XSLT, and XPath, and we demonstrated the use of these technologies. JAXB is a newer approach to solve the same XML processing and authoring tasks. We generated Java classes through the use of the JAXB Schema Compiler, and used the classes in a small application.

We then looked at JAXM, which is a Java API that combines XML processing and messaging capabilities. We discussed a few sample applications that explore the SOAP authoring capabilities of JAXM. We also discussed asynchronous communication using JAXM, and the use of messaging profiles in JAXM.

Working with Registries

by Bilal Siddiqui

IN THIS CHAPTER

This chapter is dedicated to XML registries, such as the discovery stack of Web services, which was introduced in Chapter 11, "Web Services Explained." In this chapter, we will first discuss the use of XML registries in P2P applications. We will then extend the UDDI discussion of Chapter 11 and the details of using UDDI's XML structures to publish and find Web services. The UDDI API discussion will be followed by a Java code example that shows UDDI request authoring in Java.

We will also introduce ebXML, which is a set of XML-based grammars to describe, register, store, and discover business processes. Another related topic that we will discuss in this chapter is Java API for XML Registries (JAXR), an API that provides a layer of abstraction over all XML registries, including the UDDI registry. We will conclude this chapter with a brief note about the Web service usage models, especially with reference to P2P networks.

XML Registries for P2P

In Chapter 11 we discussed the three Web services stacks: the wire stack, the description stack, and the discovery stack. As this chapter is dedicated to XML registries, we will therefore be covering the discovery stack here. Let's first establish a case for using XML registries in P2P applications.

Recall that Web services do not essentially reside over the Internet. They may reside on a network, on an intranet, or even on a P2P network. XML registries will act as the discovery stack, irrespective of the type of network that hosts the Web services being discovered.

Therefore, if we try to define the role of XML registries over P2P networks, we can say that XML registries play the same role over P2P networks that they play over the client-server model of the conventional Internet. Web services residing over P2P networks can be published on XML registries, and users looking for those services will find them in the same way.

To understand exactly how to publish P2P-based Web services on a UDDI registry, recall the WSDL and UDDI sections of Chapter 11. The WSDL section describes the roles of `portType`, `binding`, and `port` elements in WSDL authoring. These three elements of a WSDL file together achieve decoupling between abstract Web service definitions and their concrete correspondence to actual protocols. This decoupling framework assures that a Web service is independent of the wire-level protocol (such as SOAP over HTTP, an example in Chapter 11) and the address used for hosting. As a practical example, Chapter 20, "Using SOAP with P2P," demonstrates how to use SOAP over P2P instead of SOAP over HTTP as the Web services interoperability wire stack.

The `tModel`-related discussion of the UDDI section in Chapter 11 builds on this idea of decoupling. A UDDI `tModel` provides the abstract definitions of a Web service interface, which can be referred to by any implementation or instance of that particular service. For instance, a P2P Web service publisher will refer to the corresponding `tModel` for the abstractions, and provide the remaining concrete part of the definitions.

The last section of this chapter, "Accessing Web Services," explains why, when, and how to use the different Web service-related technologies (XML, SOAP, WSDL, UDDI, and so on) in P2P applications.

UDDI

Chapter 11 concluded with the introduction of Universal Description, Discovery, and Integration (UDDI) APIs. We will now look at what UDDI APIs are available, what they can do for us, and how they work.

UDDI Publishing API

The UDDI Publishing API is designed to publish all the data structures shown in Figures 11.7 to 11.11. It offers one publishing method for each data structure. The following is a list of all available methods:

```
save_business and delete_business
save_service and delete_service
save_binding and delete_binding
save tModel and delete_tModel
set_publisherAssertions, add_publisherAssertions and delete_publisherAssertions
```

All the save, set, and add methods are meant to publish new or edit existing information on the UDDI registry. The delete methods will hide the previously published information from the registry users. We'll first cover all the save methods, and then see the delete methods.

The `save_business` Method

This method publishes the `businessEntity` structures conforming to Figure 11.7 (repeated here in Figure 13.1). An example of the XML structure for a `save_business` method call will look like the following:

```
<save_business generic="2.0" xmlns="urn:uddi-org:api_v2">
    <authInfo>An authorization token string.</authInfo>
    <businessEntity businessKey = "">
        <discoveryURLs>
            <discoveryURL useType = "businessEntity">
                An HTTP URL pointing at an alternate discovery mechanism.
            <discoveryURL>
```

```
<discoveryURLs>
<name>Name of a contact person</name>
<description>A short business description</description>
<contacts>
    <contact useType = "Technical Support">
        <description>How this contact can be useful</description>
        <personName>Name of the contact</personName>
        <phone>Phone number</phonse>
    </contact>
</contacts>
<identifierBag>
    <keyedReference tModelKey = "dnb-com:D-U-N-S" keyName = "D-U-N-S"
        keyValue = "DUNS identification number"/>
    <!—Other keyed references. —>
</identifierBag>
<categoryBag>
    <keyedReference tModelKey = "unspsc-org:unspsc:3-1"
    keyName = "UNSPSC"
        keyValue = "UNSPSC code"/>
    <!—Other keyed references. —>
</categoryBag>
<!—Other businessEntity structures. —>
    </businessEntity>
</save_business>
```

The save_business method call shown here has two child elements: an authInfo element and a businessEntity element.

The authInfo Element

The authInfo element is used in all methods of the Publishing API. It is used to authenticate the publishing request and contains an authorization token. Therefore, you will need an authorization token before you can publish anything on a UDDI registry.

You can use a get_authToken method call to get an authorization token. This method call looks like the following structure:

```
<get_authToken generic="2.0" xmlns="urn:uddi-org:api_v2">
    userID = "login name"
    cred = "password"/>
```

The get_authToken method call takes two parameters, a login name and a password. The UDDI specification does not define the process through which an operator issues user login names and passwords. Therefore, each UDDI operator will design its own mechanism to issue login names and passwords.

FIGURE 13.1

The
`businessEntity`
structure.

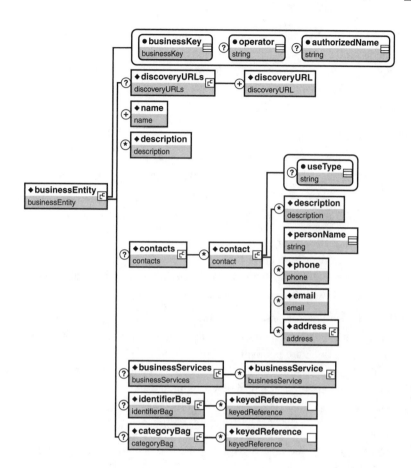

Return value from the `get_authToken` is another XML structure that contains the required authorization token:

```
<authToken generic="2.0" operator = "some UDDI operator"
    xmlns="urn:uddi-org:api_v2">
    <authInfo>An authorization token string.</authInfo>
</authToken>
```

UDDI users can discard authorization tokens by using the discard_authToken method:
```
<discard_authToken generic="2.0" xmlns="urn:uddi-org:api_v2">
    <authInfo>An authorization token string.</authInfo>
</discard_authToken>
```

The discard_authToken method will effectively end the secure session; that is, any subsequent method calls that use a discarded authorization token will be rejected.

UDDI also enables operators to implement their own mechanism of communicating authorization tokens to the publishers. For instance, an alternative technique is to exchange certificates instead of a login/password mechanism. In this case, it is optional for the UDDI operator to implement the get_authToken and discard_authToken methods.

The businessEntity Structure

A single save_business method call can contain any number of the businessEntity elements to be published, each conforming to the structure of Figure 13.1.

All the businessEntity substructures have been well explained in the discussion associated with Figure 11.7. The intent here is just to explain a few points.

The businessKey attribute of the businessEntity element in the save_business call shown previously is an empty string. The empty string means that we are publishing a new businessEntity structure. If we want to edit or update an existing businessEntity structure, we will pass its businessKey value along with the save_business call.

Also look at the discoveryURLs child element inside the businessEntity structure, which is a collection of URLs that can be used to point to the same businessEntity structure that you are publishing. This is useful if you have also published your business at other (probably non-UDDI) data repositories and discovery mechanisms, and you want your UDDI version of the business to point to other places where the same information can be found.

Another point to be noticed is that Figure 13.1 includes a collection of businessService elements that we have not shown in our save_business call. You may include businessService elements within the same call, or you may use separate save_service calls (explained in the next section) to publish businessService structures. If you include businessService elements within a businessEntity structure, you can publish both in the same save_business call. Moreover, as depicted in Figure 11.8 (repeated here as Figure 13.2), a businessService structure can in turn contain one or more bindingTemplate structures. Therefore, the same save_business call can publish all structures in one go. This shows that save_business has the broadest publishing scope.

The save_business method returns a businessDetail message as shown here:

```
<businessDetail generic="2.0" operator = "some uddi operator"
    xmlns="urn:uddi-org:api_v2">
    <businessEntity businessKey="F5E65…">
        <!—Content of the businessEntity structure. —>
    </bindingTemplate>
    <!—Other businessEntity elements. —>
</bindingDetail>
```

FIGURE **13.2**

The businessService *structure.*

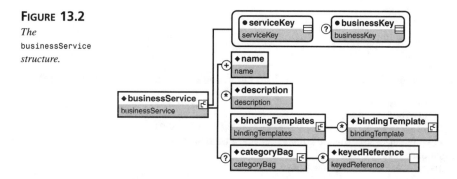

The businessDetail structure contains a number of businessEntity elements that reflect the information you have just published.

Notice that we passed an empty string as the value of the businessKey attribute with the save_business call. The UDDI registry generated the businessKey and returned the same to us. The businessKey attribute is not an empty string in the businessDetail message shown here.

The save_service Method

This method call publishes the businessService structures of Figure 13.2. The following is a typical method call:

```
<save_service generic="2.0" xmlns="urn:uddi-org:api_v2" >
    <authInfo>An authorization token string.</authInfo>
    <businessService serviceKey =""
            businessKey="F5E65...">
        <name>The name of the service.</name>
        <description>
            Textual description of the Binding Template.
        </description>
        <categoryBag>
            <keyedReference tModelKey = "unspsc-org:unspsc:3-1"
                    keyName = "UNSPSC"
                    keyValue = "UNSPSC code"/>
            <!—Other keyed references. —>
        </categoryBag>
    </businessService>
    <!—Other businessService elements.—>
</save_service>
```

The save_service method has the same logical structure as that of the save_business call. There is an authInfo element for authorization, followed by a number of businessService elements that need to be published.

The businessService element contains a businessKey as well as a serviceKey. The businessKey attribute refers to the parent businessEntity that contains this businessService structure.

The save_service element method returns a serviceDetail message, as shown here:

```
<serviceDetail generic="2.0" operator = "some uddi operator"
    xmlns="urn:uddi-org:api_v2">
    <businessService businessKey="F5E65…" serviceKey="3D21…">
        <!—Contents of the businessService structure.—>
    </businessService>
    <!—Other businessService elements.—>
</serviceDetail>
```

The save_binding Method

This method publishes the bindingTemplate structure of Figure 11.9 (repeated here as Figure 13.3). The following is a typical save_binding method call:

```
<save_binding generic="2.0" xmlns="urn:uddi-org:api_v2" >
    <authInfo>An authorization token string.</authInfo>
    <bindingTemplate bindingKey = ""
        serviceKey = "key of the parent businessService">
        <description>
            Textual description of the Binding Template.
        </description>
        <accessPoint URLType = "http">
            www.mySOAPServices.com/SOAPServer
        </accessPoint>
        <tModelInstanceDetails>
            <tModelInstanceInfo tModelKey = "The tModel Key">
                <description>
                    Textual description of this tModel instance.
                </description>
                <instanceDetails>
                    <description>
                        Textual description of the instance details.
                    </description>
                    <overviewDoc>
                        <description>
                            Textual description of this overviewDoc.
                        </description>
                        <overviewURL>
                            URL of our WSDL file that describes
                            the interface that our SOAP server is expecting.
                        </overviewURL>
                    </overviewDoc>
                    <instanceDetails>
                </tModelInstanceInfo>
            </tModelInstanceDetails>
    </bindingTemplate>
    <!—Other binding templates. —>
</save_binding>
```

FIGURE 13.3

The `bindingTemplate` *structure.*

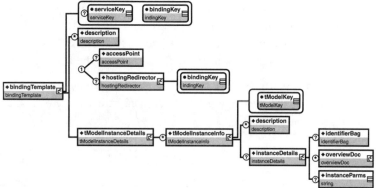

The `save_binding` method call shown here has two child elements. The first is the `authInfo` element that we have already discussed in the `save_business` method call.

The second is a complete instance of `bindingTemplate` structure shown in Figure 13.3 that we want to save (publish) using the `save_binding` method call. A single `save_binding` call can have one or more `bindingTemplate` structures (we have shown just one).

The `bindingTemplate` structure shown previously has two attributes and three child elements. The two attributes are actually two keys. The first is a `bindingKey`, which identifies the `bindingTemplate` that you are publishing. If you want to update an existing `bindingTemplate`, you will provide its key. If you are publishing a new `bindingTemplate`, you will pass an empty string as the value of the `bindingKey` attribute.

The `serviceKey` identifies the registered `businessService` object that is the parent of the `bindingTemplate` being published.

The three child elements are `description`, `accessPoint`, and `tModelInstanceDetails`. The `description` element is simply a textual description of the binding template.

The `accessPoint` element provides a URL that is the address of a location where an actual service is deployed. The service might be in any form: it might be a SOAP-based Web Service (the URL points to a SOAP server), a Web page, a customer service phone, fax number, or an email address. The `URLType` attribute tells the type of the service. Its possible values are `mailto`, `http`, `https` (secure HTTP channel), `ftp`, `fax`, `phone`, or `other` (any other type). The `bindingTemplate` structure shown previously assumes a SOAP-over-HTTP Web service, so we have specified `http` as the `URLType` and included a SOAP server address as the content of `accessPoint` element.

The `tModelInstanceDetails` structure acts as a technical fingerprint of the binding template, and explains what you can expect to be waiting for you when you visit the URL specified by the `accessPoint`. To explain the technical details of the binding template, the `tModelInstanceDetails` contains one or more `tModelInstanceInfo` structures (again, we have shown just one). All the `tModelInstanceInfo` structures together inside a `tModelInstanceDetails` structure define a single technical fingerprint.

Each `tModelInstanceInfo` structure contains a `tModelKey` attribute that refers to a `tModel` structure (refer to Figure 11.10, repeated here as Figure 13.4, and the accompanying discussion in Chapter 11).

Figure 13.4

The `tModel` *structure.*

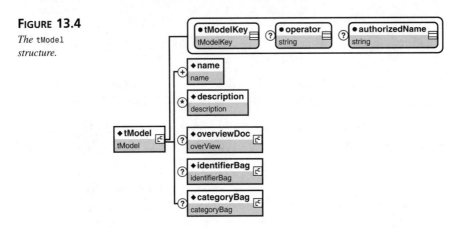

The `tModelInstanceInfo` structure might also optionally contain an `instanceDetails` substructure. Although a `tModel` provides an abstract service description, an `instanceDetails` element will provide implementation-specific details (if any) relative to the `tModel`. The `overviewDoc` child element holds the `overviewURL`, which points to a resource that describes the implementation-specific details of the `tModel` instance. In the case of WSDL and SOAP-based Web services, the `overviewURL` will point to a WSDL file.

The `save_binding` method call returns a `bindingDetail` structure that contains the `bindingTemplate` that is published as a result of the `save_binding` method call:

```
<bindingDetail generic="2.0" operator = "some uddi operator"
    xmlns="urn:uddi-org:api_v2">
    <bindingTemplate bindingKey="F5E65…" serviceKey="E4D6…" >
        <!—Content of the binding template. —>
    </bindingTemplate>
    <!—Other binding templates. —>
 </bindingDetail>
```

The `save_tModel` Method

This method publishes a `tModel` structure. Recall the `tModel` structure of Figure 13.4 and the associated discussion in Chapter 11.

The following is how a `save_tModel` method call looks:

```
<save_tModel generic="2.0" xmlns="urn:uddi-org:api_v2" >
    <authInfo>An authorization token string.</authInfo>
    <tModel tModelKey = "">
        <name>A logical and meaningful name of the tModel</name>
        <description> Textual description of the tModel. </description>
        <overviewDoc>
            <description>
                Textual description of this overviewDoc.
            </description>
            <overviewURL>
                URL to a file that describes
                details of how this tModel fits in
                the Web Service description.
                It may refer to a WSDL file.
            </overviewURL>
        </overviewDoc>
        <identifierBag>
            <keyedReference tModelKey = "dnb-com:D-U-N-S" keyName = "D-U-N-S"
                keyValue = "DUNS identification number"/>
            <!—Other keyed references. —>
        </identifierBag>
        <categoryBag>
            <keyedReference tModelKey = "unspsc-org:unspsc:3-1"
                keyName = "UNSPSC"
                keyValue = "UNSPSC code"/>
            <!—Other keyed references. —>
        </categoryBag>
    </tModel>
    <!—Other tModels. —>
```

A single `save_tModel` method call can include any number of `tModel` structures. The XML code block given here shows only one.

In addition to the name and `description` child elements already discussed, a `tModel` structure also contains an `overviewDoc` substructure. It is the same substructure that you saw in the `save_binding` discussion (inside the `instanceDetails` structure). Note that when an `overviewDoc` substructure appears inside an `instanceDetails` structure, it provides information about a particular instance of a `tModel`. On the other hand, when it appears inside a `tModel` structure, it contains information about the abstract `tModel` definition.

The save_tModel method returns a tModelDetail structure, which is a simple structure that contains the tModel structures published by the save_tModel method:

```
<tModelDetail generic="2.0" operator = "some uddi operator"
    xmlns="urn:uddi-org:api_v2">
    <!—List of tModels. —>
</tModelDetail>
```

The set_publisherAssertions and add_publisherAssertions Methods

The set_publisherAssertions method call publishes one or more publisherAssertion structures, which represent relationships between two different businessEntities. A single call to set_publisherAssertions manages all the tracked relationship assertions associated with an individual publisher account. The set_publisherAssertions method call uses the following XML structure:

```
<set_publisherAssertions generic="2.0" xmlns="urn:uddi-org:api_v2" >
    <authInfo>An authorization token string.</authInfo>
    <publisherAssertion>
        <fromKey>F5E65…</fromKey>
        <toKey>A237B…</toKey>
        <keyedReference tModelKey="uuid:34D5…" keyName = "Holding Company"
            keyValue = "parent-child" </keyedReference>
    </publisherAssertion>
    <!—Other publisherAssertion elements. —>
</set_publisherAssertions>
```

The fromKey and toKey elements are the unique keys of the first and second businessEntities, respectively, which are being asserted to become related to each other. The keyedReference element defines the actual relationship.

You can also use the add_publisherAssertions method instead of the set_publisherAssertions method shown earlier (the structure is exactly the same; you just need to replace the method name). The add_publisherAssertions method adds one or more assertions to the existing collection of assertions.

Note that to make the relationship visible on the UDDI registry, both businessEntities have to publish exactly the same asserting information.

How To Delete Data From a UDDI Registry

You have seen the five save_XX method calls. There are also five corresponding delete_XX method calls available, each meant to delete a data structure from the UDDI registry. The five delete methods are

```
delete_binding
delete_business
```

```
delete_publisherAssertions
delete_service
delete_tModel
```

All the delete_XX methods are similar to each other. They just need all the authentication tokens and keys that can uniquely identify the object that needs to be deleted. For example, the delete_business method looks like

```
<delete_business generic="2.0" xmlns="urn:uddi-org:api_v2" >
    <authInfo>An authorization token string.</authInfo>
    <businessKey>KB2</businessKey>
    <!—Other businessKey elements —>
</delete_business>
```

Only the delete_publisherAssertions is different from the rest. It takes the all the assertion structures that are to be deleted:

```
<delete_publisherAssertions generic="2.0" xmlns="urn:uddi-org:api_v2" >
    <authInfo>An authorization token string.</authInfo>
    <publisherAssertion>
        <fromKey>F5E65…</fromKey>
        <toKey>A237B…</toKey>
        <keyedReference tModelKey="uuid:34D5…" keyName = "Holding Company"
            keyValue = "parent-child" </keyedReference>
    </publisherAssertion>
    <!—Other publisherAssertion elements that need to be deleted. —>
</set_publisherAssertions>
```

UDDI Request Authoring in Java

Having seen the UDDI's XML structures for publishing, let's consider a Java code sample to author a UDDI request. Refer to Listing 13.1, which authors the save_service method call that we presented earlier.

LISTING 13.1 SOAPRequest.java: A UDDI Request Authoring Example

```
import org.w3c.dom.*;
import javax.xml.parsers.*;
import org.apache.crimson.tree.XmlDocument;
import java.io.*;

public class SOAPRequest {
        // Keeps reference of the complete XML document.
        private Document ownerDoc;

        // Keeps reference of the SOAP Envelope element.
        private Element soapEnvelope;
```

LISTING 13.1   continued

```
        // Keeps reference of the SOAP Body element.
        private Element soapBody;

        // We will author SOAPEnvelope
        // and an empty SOAP Body in the constructor.
        public SOAPRequest () {
                try {
                        // Create a Document Builder Factory,
                        // then create a Document Builder using the Factory,
                        // then create a Document using the Builder.
                        DocumentBuilderFactory dbf =
➡                               DocumentBuilderFactory.newInstance();
                        DocumentBuilder db = dbf.newDocumentBuilder();
                        ownerDoc = db.newDocument();
                }//try
                catch (ParserConfigurationException pce) {
                        System.out.println ("ParserConfigException:"+
➡                               pce.getMessage());
                }//catch
                try {
                        // Create the Envelope.
                        soapEnvelope =
➡                           ownerDoc.createElement("SOAP-ENV:Envelope");
                        // Set namespaces.
                        soapEnvelope.setAttributeNS(
➡                               "http://www.w3.org/2000/xmlns/",
➡                               "xmlns:SOAP-ENV",
➡                               "http://schemas.xmlsoap.org/soap/envelope/"
➡                                               );
                        soapEnvelope.setAttributeNS(
➡                               "http://www.w3.org/2000/xmlns/",
➡                               "xmlns:xsi",
➡                               "http://www.w3.org/1999/XMLSchema-instance"
➡                                               );
                        soapEnvelope.setAttributeNS(
➡                               "http://www.w3.org/2000/xmlns/",
➡                               "xmlns:xsd",
➡                               "http://www.w3.org/1999/XMLSchema"
➡                                               );
                        // Create an empty SOAP Body and
                        // add it to the Envelope.
                        soapBody = ownerDoc.createElement ("SOAP-ENV:Body");
                        soapEnvelope.appendChild(soapBody);
                        ownerDoc.appendChild (soapEnvelope);

                }//try
                catch (DOMException de){
                        System.out.println (
➡                               "DOMException: "+de.getMessage());
```

LISTING **13.1**   continued

```
        }//catch
}// Constructor

public void setBodyMethod (Node bodyMethod) {
        // bodyMethod belongs to some other owner document.
        // We will import the Node into our document
        // and append it to the soapBody.
        Node importedNode =
                ownerDoc.importNode(bodyMethod, true);
        soapBody.appendChild (importedNode);
        // Now save the SOAP request XML as SOAPRequest.xml.
        // This saving is only for demonstration.
        XmlDocument xmlDocument = (XmlDocument)ownerDoc;
        try{
                FileOutputStream fout =
                        new FileOutputStream(
                                new File(".\\SoapRequest.xml"));
                xmlDocument.write(fout);
                fout.close();
        }//try
        catch(Throwable th){th.printStackTrace();}
}//setBodyMethod()

// UDDI request authoring.
public static void main (String args[]){
        SOAPRequest soap = new SOAPRequest();
        Document doc = null;
        Element method;
        Element businessService;
        Element authInfo;
        Element name;
        Element description;
        Element categoryBag;
        Element keyedReference;

        try{
        // We will author the UDDI part
        // independently of the SOAP part of the request.
        // Therefore, we have to create a new XML document.
        // The steps of creating a new XML document are:
        // Create a Document Builder Factory,
        // then create a Document Builder using the Factory,
        // then create a Document using the Builder.
        DocumentBuilderFactory dbf =
                DocumentBuilderFactory.newInstance();
        DocumentBuilder db =
                dbf.newDocumentBuilder();
        doc = db.newDocument();
        }//try
```

LISTING 13.1 continued

```
                catch (ParserConfigurationException pce) {
                        System.out.println(
➡                               "ParserConfigException: "+
➡                               pce.getMessage());
                }//catch
                try{
                        // The newly created empty XML document
                        // is stored in the object named doc.
                        // We can start authoring the UDDI structure.

                        // The first step is to author the root element.
                        method = doc.createElement("save_service");
                        method.setAttributeNS(
➡                               "http://www.w3.org/2000/xmlns/",
➡                               "xmlns","urn:uddi-org:api_v2");
                        method.setAttribute("generic", "2.0");

                        // We'll now author root element's child elements.
                        // We will perform the following steps for each
                        // child of the save_service element:
                        // First create the new element
                        // using the createElement method,
                        // then set the attributes (if any),
                        // then append the element to its immediate parent
                        // using the appendChild method.
                        // Text nodes are created using the createTextNode method.

                        authInfo = doc.createElement("authInfo");
                        authInfo.appendChild(
➡                               doc.createTextNode(
➡                                   "An authorization token string."));
                        method.appendChild(authInfo);

                        businessService = doc.createElement("businessService");
                        businessService.setAttribute ("serviceKey","");
                        businessService.setAttribute ("businessKey","F5E65...");
                        method.appendChild(businessService);

                        name = doc.createElement("name");
                        name.appendChild(
➡                               doc.createTextNode(
➡                                       "The name of the service."));
                        businessService.appendChild(name);

                        description = doc.createElement("description");
                        description.appendChild(
                                doc.createTextNode(
                            "Textual description of the Binding Template."
➡                                       ));
                        businessService.appendChild(description);
```

LISTING 13.1   continued

```
                    categoryBag = doc.createElement("categoryBag");
                    businessService.appendChild(categoryBag);

                    keyedReference = doc.createElement("keyedReference");
                    keyedReference.setAttribute("keyName","UNSPSC");
                    keyedReference.setAttribute("keyValue","UNSPSC code");
                    categoryBag.appendChild(keyedReference);

                    doc.appendChild (method);

                    // Now save the UDDI request as UDDIRequest.xml.
                    XmlDocument xmlDocument = (XmlDocument)doc;
                    try{
                    FileOutputStream fout =
                            new FileOutputStream(
                                    new File(".\\UDDIRequest.xml"));
                    xmlDocument.write(fout);
                    fout.close();
                    }//try
                    catch(Throwable th){th.printStackTrace();}

                    // Finally call setBodyMethod,
                    // which will copy the UDDI part inside the
                    // SOAP part.
                    soap.setBodyMethod (method);
              }//try
              catch (DOMException de){
                    System.out.println(
                            "Method DOMException: "+de.getMessage());
              }//catch
        }//main
}//class
```

The code in Listing 13.1 builds on the class SOAPRequest that we developed in Chapter 12, "Messaging and Java APIs for XML" (refer to Listing 12.5). There is no change in the SOAPRequest constructor. The main() function has been rewritten to demonstrate that UDDI requests are actually SOAP requests. The UDDI part of the request appears inside the SOAP Body element.

The UDDI Inquiry API

The UDDI API offers ten methods for inquiry, or searching through the registry. The ten methods jointly form the UDDI Inquiry API. Five of the ten methods are used for general search and are named find_XX methods. The other five are used for specific (drill-down) search and are called get_XX methods.

13

WORKING WITH
REGISTRIES

The find_XX methods will take the search criteria as search parameters from the user and return a list of required objects. On the other hand, the drill-down (or get) methods simply take the key of an object and return the complete structure representing that object. The 10 methods are find_binding, find_business, find_relatedBusinesses, find_service, find_tModel, get_bindingDetail, get_businessDetail, get_businessDetailExt, get_serviceDetail, and get_tModelDetail. All the method names are self-explanatory, except find_relatedBusinesses and get_businessDetailExt. The find_relatedBusinesses method will find all businessEntities, which are related to a particular businessEntity through publisher assertions. The get_businessDetailExt method returns information about business entities with some additional attributes. These additional attributes are not defined by the UDDI specification, and a UDDI-compatible registry is allowed to choose what extra information it would like to provide. Refer to the UDDI API documentation for complete details.

ebXML

The current challenge in e-business development is to cross the boundaries of traditional enterprise and seamlessly integrate businesses into an interoperable set of loosely coupled components. This is the basic concept of collaborative commerce, in which across-the-enterprise communication through open standards plays a key role. In other words, this is the era of interoperability, which is fast becoming as important as the more traditional and well recognized requirements of portability and scalability in e-business solutions.

ebXML ("electronic business XML") is a set of specifications to define a modular yet complete framework for collaborative commerce. The ebXML set of specifications is a combined effort of two organizations—OASIS (Organization for the Advancement of Structured Information Standards; see http://www.oasis-open.org/) and UN/CEFACT (United Nations Centre for Trade Facilitation and Electronic Business; see http://www.unece.org/cefact/).

ebXML defines XML-based grammars to facilitate interoperability. The following are the main features that the ebXML specification suite offers:

1. The first step toward interoperability is to analyze and document a particular B2B process. The ebXML set of specifications include Business Process Specification Schema (BPSS), which is a grammar to define business processes. For instance, the tourism industry is a suitable candidate to be documented as a B2B process.

2. The companies that want to take part in the B2B process that we have documented in Step 1 will use another ebXML specification called Collaboration Protocol

Profile (CPP). CPP enables companies to document their roles in a particular B2B scenario. For example, tour operators, hotels, car rental companies, and so on all have different roles to play in a tourism B2B process.

3. We'll want to publish the metadata of our business process and capabilities at a public data repository so the interested trading partners and prospective customers can access and use the information. The ebXML Registry Services (ebRS) expose interfaces to publish and manage information and search for it.

4. The Collaboration Protocol Agreement (CPA) is an agreement between companies that have published CPPs. The CPA documents represent the agreed-on intersection of two or more CPPs.

5. ebXML also defines the communication architectures for transport, packaging, routing, and security.

A complete discussion of the entire ebXML architecture is beyond the scope of this section. We will keep our focus on the third point (the ebXML registry services).

The ebXML Registry Services

The ebXML registry services are meant to manage publishing, indexing, and the categorization of information. It serves as a storage facility for business information and associated metamodels. The main aim of this effort is the same as that of all search engines such as Yahoo!—the information should be available to those searching for it. For this purpose, the ebXML registry services include a set of data structures that collectively form the *ebXML Registry Information Model (ebRIM)*.

We will first discuss the information model of the ebXML registry services, and then move on to the programmatic interface necessary to access the services.

The ebXML Registry Information Model

This section describes the information model for the ebXML registry services. The information model explains the data structures and data types of objects contained in an ebXML registry. The official documentation for ebRIM defines interfaces instead of classes to describe the information model. The use of interfaces reminds us that the ebRIM documentation is an abstract definition, and does not imply any specific implementation.

Therefore, the interfaces included in ebRIM are *not* the actual interfaces that will be used to interact with the objects in an ebXML data repository. We will discuss the XML-based interfaces that expose the functionality of the ebXML registry services separately in a later section.

Another important thing to remember is that the interfaces in ebRIM only govern the metadata structures describing the content residing in an ebXML data repository. The ebRIM interfaces do not say anything about the actual content submitted to the data repository. The actual content is normally in the form of XML files, DTDs, schema documents, and so on. The ebXML registry service users might control the structure of the actual content, instead of the registry service itself.

A content item (an XML file, for example) that a registry service user submits to the registry service is called a *repository item*. A metadata structure that describes a repository item is referred to as a *registry entry*. Therefore, repository items and registry entries are related to each other, but are not the same. The ebXML registry information model is all about defining structures for the registry entry objects.

> **Note**
>
> Note that this section only aims to present the basic concepts of the ebXML information model to support the next section, in which we describe the programmatic interfaces for accessing the ebXML registry services. It is not possible to cover the entire information model in this section, so the interfaces and data structures presented here are not exhaustive.

The `RegistryObject` Interface

The `RegistryObject` interface forms the base interface in the information model. Most of the registry entries extend the `RegistryObject` interface. It contains set and get methods for four important parameters: `name`, `id`, `description`, and `accessControlPolicy`. The first three parameters are related to the identity of the object instantiating this interface. All three parameters map to XML attributes with the same names while accessing a registry service.

The fourth parameter defines a security model in terms of access control (who is allowed to do what with this object).

All registry entry interfaces that require an identity (ID, name, and description) and security model (access control policy) will extend from the `RegistryObject` interface.

The most important interface that extends the `RegistryObject` interface is the `RegistryEntry` interface.

The `RegistryEntry` Interface and Its Sub-Interfaces

`RegistryEntry` is the base interface for all the metadata interfaces that describe the content submitted to the ebXML registry.

One of the important attributes in this interface is the status attribute. The getStatus method in the RegistryEntry interface tells the status of any RegistryEntry object. The status attribute depicts the lifecycle of a repository item. A repository item can have one of the four predefined status values: Submitted, Approved, Deprecated, and Withdrawn. When a repository item is first submitted by a submitting organization, the value of its status attribute is Submitted. The submitting organization can approve a previously submitted RegistryEntry instance, so that its status will change to Approved. Similarly, RegistryEntry instances can be Deprecated and Withdrawn by the submitting organizations.

Another important attribute in the RegistryEntry interface is the stability attribute. A submitting organization needs to indicate the stability of content being submitted. The stability attribute can have one of three possible predefined values: Dynamic (meaning it's not stable and can change arbitrarily), DynamicCompatible (meaning it's not stable, but will change in a backward-compatible manner) and static (meaning it's stable).

The RegistryEntry interface is directly extended by two interfaces—the ExtrinsicObject interface and the IntrinsicObject interface.

The ExtrinsicObject interface describes the repository items whose type is not intrinsically known to the ebXML registry service. The exact type of an ExtrinsicObject is normally determined through additional means, such as MIME types and so on. The ExtrinsicObject interface is not extended further to produce other interfaces, and therefore different ExtrinsicObject instances only differ from each other in their data types. The following is how an ExtrinsicObject will look like in XML format:

```
<ExtrinsicObject id = "CarRentalProfile"
            contentURI = "A resolvable URI to a Car Rental Profile."
            objectType = "CPP"
            name = "CarRentalCPP"
            description = "Profile to rent a car on-line." />
```

The name, id, and description attributes are inherited from the RegistryObject interface. The objectType attribute is inherited from the RegistryEntry interface (we'll explain what this means shortly). The contentURI attribute contains a URI that points to the actual content catalogues by this ExtrinsicObject.

The IntrinsicObject interface describes the content submitted to the ebXML data repository whose type is intrinsically known to the registry service. This interface is further extended by these interfaces: Package, ExternalIdentifier, ExternalLink, Organization, Association, ClassificationNode, and Classification.

Therefore, the RegistryEntry interface is directly and indirectly extended to produce many other interfaces. To identify the interface or data type of a particular

RegistryEntry instance, the RegistryEntry interface has an attribute named
objectType. The objectType attribute tells the type of interface of a particular
RegistryEntry instance.

The objectType attribute can have one of several predefined values. Each value corresponds to a data type (in the case of an ExtrinsicObject instance) or an interface (in the
case of an IntrinsicObject instance). The predefined values for ExtrinsicObject data
types are as follows:

- Unknown—Indicates that the ebXML registry does not know the type of the object.

- CPA—Provides metadata about Collaboration Protocol Agreement (CPA). Recall
  that CPA is an XML document that describes an agreement between two parties
  regarding how they want to communicate with each other using a specific protocol.

- CPP—Provides metadata about Collaboration Protocol Profile (CPP). Recall that
  CPP is an XML document that describes the role of a party that wants to take part
  in a business process (a B2B scenario).

- Process—Provides metadata about a business process.

- Role—Describes a CPP role.

- ServiceInterface—Provides metadata about an XML description of a service
  interface (for example, a Web service interface, such as a WSDL file).

- SoftwareComponent—Provides metadata about software components (for example,
  JavaBeans and COM components, and so on).

- Transport—Provides metadata about a transport configuration. For example,
  SOAP is fast becoming the de facto framework to define other higher layers of
  XML-based transport protocols. We will discuss SOAP-based protocols in the section "Message Profiling Using JAXM." This type of ExtrinsicObject may be
  used to describe a particular SOAP-based transport configuration.

- UMLModel—Provides metadata about UML documentation.

- XMLSchema—Provides metadata about documents describing the structure of XML
  documents (for example, DTDs and XSDs).

The predefined values for IntrinsicObject interfaces are as follows:

- Package—Groups together the logically similar registry entries. There may be several reasons for grouping together different registry entries. For example, registry
  entries in a package can be processed together (they can be deleted in one go).
  Packages can also be searched for directly. If you have grouped your registry
  entries into appropriate packages, your registry entries will be more readily available to search operations. The following is the XML form of a Package instance:

```
<Package id = "TourismPackage" name = "Package #1"
         description = "Everything related to tours."/>
```

- **ExternalLink**—Refers to some content external to the registry by using Uniform Resource Indicators (URIs). The ebXML registry does not care about the type of the content being linked. It can be a Web site or any other type of resource over the Internet.

- **ExternalIdentifier**—Identifies registry entries with some identification scheme that exists independently of the ebXML registry services. For example, you might want to have your company identified through Social Security numbers, National Tax numbers, or DUNS numbers. In this case, you will use `ExternalIdentifier` instances.

  An `ExternalIdentifier` works in addition to the ebXML identification scheme that uses the `id` attribute (inherited from the `RegistryObject` interface). You can compare ebXML `ExternalIdentifiers` with the `identifierBag` in UDDI.

  An `ExternalIdentifier` works with two attributes: a name and a value. The `name` attribute is inherited from the `RegistryObject` interface and specifies the name of the identification scheme (for example, a Social Security number). The `value` attribute is included in the `ExternalIdentifier` interface and specifies the actual value of the identification (the actual Social Security number).

  You can *associate* any number of `ExternalIdentifier` instances with a single registry entry.

- **Association**—Associates a `RegistryEntry` instance with some `RegistryObject` instance such as an `ExternalIdentifier`, an `ExternalLink`, or an `ExtrinsicObject` instance and so on. `Association` has a source object and a target object. Both source and target objects are `RegistryEntry` instances. An `Association` instance simply associates the source with the target object. You can associate a `RegistryEntry` instance with any number of `RegistryObject` instances. One possible use of `Association` instances is to associate different versions of the same document (such as a CPP document) with each other. Look at the following example, where we have shown the source and target objects, as well as the type of association:

```
<Association id = "TourismPackage - CarRentalProfile"
    associationType = "RelatedTo"
    sourceObject = "TourismPackage"
    targetObject = "CarRentalProfile" />
```

- **ClassificationNode**—Defines classification schemes, which are tree-like structures used to classify repository items. Some of the most common classification trees are industrial, product, and geographical classification trees.

For example, an industrial classification scheme starts with a broad definition, such as automotive industry or computer industry. Each category will be further divided into subcategories, (such as motor vehicle assembly and engine parts manufacturing). Subcategories will be divided into more specific sub-subcategories.

This XML-like hierarchical arrangement has nodes, parents, and children. Every category or subcategory is a classification node. All classification nodes have children (except the leaf nodes that don't have any further division into subcategories).

Similarly, all classification nodes have parents (except the root classification nodes, which are the points where a classification tree starts).

Every node in a classification scheme is represented by a `ClassificationNode` interface that is an intrinsic object. Look at the following example that shows a parent-child pair of classification nodes:

```
<ClassificationNode id = "Industry"
    name = "Industrial Classification Scheme"
    description = "The Industrial Classification example."/>
<ClassificationNode id = "AutomotiveIndustryNode"
    name = "Automotive industry"
    description = "Automotive industry node under the industrial
➥    classification."
    parent = "Industry"/>
<ClassificationNode id = "MotorVehicleAssemblyNode"
    name = "Motor Vehicle Assembly"
    description = "The Motor Vehicle Assembly node under the
➥    AutomotiveIndustryNode"
    parent = "AutomotiveIndustryNode"/>
```

- Classification—Associates a `RegistryEntry` instance with a `ClassificationNode`. Repository items are classified by associating their `RegistryEntry` instances with `ClassificationNodes`.

The `Classification` interface contains two attributes that are used to associate `RegistryEntry` instances with `ClassificationNodes`: `classifiedObject` and `classificationNode`. Look at the following example:

```
<Classification id = "sampleClassification"
    description = "Classifies the CarRentalProfile extrinsic object
➥    by Industry/AutomotiveIndustryNode/MotorVehicleAssemblyNode"
    classifiedObject = "CarRentalProfile"
    classificationNode = "MotorVehicleAssemblyNode" />
```

The `classificationNode` attribute refers to the classification node being used to classify a registry entry that the `classifiedObject` attribute refers to. In this example, the classification node is referring to the `MotorVehicleAssemblyNode`, and `CarRentalProfile` is the ID of the object being classified.

- Organization—Represents organizations such as those submitting information to an ebXML data repository. The Organization interface has attributes such as primary contact, address, phone numbers, and so on.

Programmatic Interfaces for the ebXML Registry Services

We'll first see how to submit (or publish) information on an ebXML registry service. The discussion on searching or browsing through the registry will be next.

Publishing to an ebXML Registry

The ebXML registry services manage information as objects through an interface named ObjectManager. Whenever an ebXML client wants to submit some information to ebRS, it will invoke the submitObjects methods of the ObjectManager interface.

The submitObjects method takes a parameter named SubmitObjectsRequest, which specifies all objects that need to be published. For example, look at the following XML structure:

```
<SubmitObjectsRequest>
    <RegistryEntryList>
        <Package id = "TourismPackage" name = "Package #1"
            description = "Everything related to tours."/>
        <ExtrinsicObject id = "CarRentalProfile"
            contentURI = "A resolvable URI to a Car Rental Profile."
            objectType = "CPP"
            name = "CarRentalCPP"
            description = "Profile to rent a car on-line." />
        <Association id = "TourismPackage - CarRentalProfile"
            associationType = "Packages"
            sourceObject = "TourismPackage"
            targetObject = "CarRentalProfile" />
        <ObjectRef id = "urn:uuid:a2345678-1234-1234"/>
        <Association id = "TourismPackage - HotelBookingProfile"
            associationType = "Packages"
            sourceObject = "TourismPackage"
            targetObject = "urn:uuid:a2345678-1234-1234"/>
    </RegistryEntryList>
</SubmitObjectsRequest>
```

We'll now look into the details of SubmitObjectsRequest.

The SubmitObjectsRequest shown here has only one child element: RegistryEntryList, which is a list of entries that we want to publish on the ebXML registry services.

Our entries are very simple. There is a `Package` element, an `ExtrinsicObject` instance, two `Association` instances, and another object referred to by an `ObjectRef` element. An `ObjectRef` element simply refers to another registry entry through its `id` attribute. The registry entry being referred to should be available at the ebXML registry.

First, look at the two `Association` elements. Each `Association` element has a `sourceObject` attribute. Both `sourceObject` attributes have the same value (`TourismPackage`). This means that the source object of the two associations is the same. Compare this source object with the `id` attribute of the `Package` element. They are the same. Therefore, the source object of the two associations is the `Package` element in the `SubmitObjectsRequest`.

Now look at the `targetObject` attributes of the two `Association` elements. The two target objects are different from each other. One of the two matches with the `id` attribute of the `ExtrinsicObject` instance, whereas the other matches with the `id` attribute of the `ObjectRef` element. Therefore, the target objects of the associations are the `ExtrinsicObject` and the `ObjectRef` elements.

This is how we can package or group different objects. The `sourceObject` attribute of an `Association` element refers to a `Package` element, and the `targetObject` attribute of the association refers to the object that needs to be packaged.

You can include any number of objects in the same package. Moreover, you can create any number of packages in the same `SubmitObjectsRequest`.

Removing Objects from an ebXML Registry

We will now explain how to delete metadata objects from an ebXML registry service. The following XML message accomplishes this:

```
<RemoveObjectsRequest deletionScope = "Delete All"
    <ObjectRefList>
        <ObjectRef id = "urn:uuid:b2345678-1234-1234"/>
    </ObjectRefList>
</RemoveObjectsRequest>
```

The `RemoveObjectsRequest` contains an `ObjectRefList` that is actually a list of `ObjectRef` elements (we have shown only one). This request will remove all objects referred to by the `ObjectRef` elements in the `ObjectRefList`.

Note that you will need to remove all references to a `RegistryEntry` before removing the entry itself. For example, if you want to remove the `CarRentalProfile` `ExtrinsicObject` that we previously published while explaining the `SubmitObjectsRequest` method, you will first have to remove all association instances whose `targetObject` is referring to the `CarRentalProfile` `ExtrinsicObject`.

The deletionScope attribute of RemoveObjectsRequest shown in the preceding code controls the scope of deletion. The deleteAll value of this attribute will delete both the repository item and the registry entry associated with it. If you want to delete only the registry entry and not the repository item, you will specify DeleteRepositoryItemOnly as the value of the deletionScope attribute.

Publishing Classifications

The following SubmitObjectsRequest call will publish the classificationNode and Classification elements that we presented during the discussion on ClassificationNode and Classification elements (refer to the section "The ebXML Registry Information Model"):

```
<SubmitObjectsRequest>
    <RegistryEntryList>
        <ExtrinsicObject id = "CarRentalProfile"
            contentURI = "A resolvable URI to a Car Rental Profile."
            objectType = "CPP"
            name = "CarRentalCPP"
            description = "Profile to rent a car on-line." />
        <ClassificationNode id = "Industry"
            name = "Industrial Classification Scheme"
            description = "The Industrial Classification example."/>
        <ClassificationNode id = "AutomotiveIndustryNode"
            name = "Automotive industry"
            description = "Automotive industry node under the industrial
              classification."
            parent = "Industry"/>
        <ClassificationNode id = "MotorVehicleAssemblyNode"
            name = "Motor Vehicle Assembly"
            description = "The Motor Vehicle Assembly node under the
              AutomotiveIndustryNode"
            parent = "AutomotiveIndustryNode"/>
        <Classification id = "sampleClassification"
            description = "Classifies the CarRentalProfile extrinsic object
          by Industry/AutomotiveIndustryNode/MotorVehicleAssemblyNode"
            classifiedObject = "CarRentalProfile"
            classificationNode = "MotorVehicleAssemblyNode" />
    </RegistryEntryList>
</SubmitObjectsRequest>
```

Searching and Browsing Through the ebXML Registry

ebXML offers an Object Query Management service that exposes an ObjectQueryManager interface. The ObjectQueryManager interface is responsible for performing all browsing and search operations. An ebXML registry user who wants to browse through or search for information on an ebXML data repository will use the ObjectQueryManager interface. Such users are called ObjectQueryManagerClients.

You have already seen that there are several types of registry entries: Classification and association instances, intrinsic and extrinsic objects, and business organizations are all registry entries. The XML syntax of ebXML search queries aims at testing the relationships between different types of registry entries to find the required information. Let's consider a few search requirements to elaborate upon this point.

We will start with the most primitive and slowly move to the advanced searches.

Search Scenario 1: We want to search for companies offering specific products and services on an ebXML registry, but we don't know the keywords to search for. So, we'll want to browse through the classification tree in the ebXML registry. If there is more than one classification of trees available, we'll want to learn about all of them.

This basic search requirement is fulfilled in two steps using the `ObjectQueryManager` interface: Discovering all available classification trees and browsing through the classification trees.

`GetRootClassificationNodesRequest` will return the root nodes of all classification trees. A root node in the classification tree is like the root element of an XML file—it has no parent, so that's the point where the classification tree starts. All other classification nodes are descendants of the root classification nodes. There can be any number of root classification nodes in an ebXML registry. For example, there will be separate classification root nodes (and therefore separate classification trees) for industrial and geographical classifications.

`GetRootClassificationNodesRequest` has the following XML syntax:

```
<GetRootClassificationNodesRequest namePattern = "*"/>
```

The `namePattern` attribute uses a wildcard pattern specified by SQL. We have specified the asterisk mark as the name pattern, which means we are interested in all root classification nodes. The following is a typical registry response of `GetRootClassificationNodesRequest`:

```
<RegistryResponse status = "success">
    <GetRootClassificationNodesResponse>
        <ClassificationNode id="urn:uuid:a2345678-1234-1234-123456789012"
          name = "Name of this classification node."
          description = "Some descriptive text for this classification node"/>
        <ClassificationNode id="urn:uuid:b2345678-1234-1234-123456789012"
          name = "Name of this classification node."
          description = "Some descriptive text for this classification node"/>
        <ClassificationNode id="urn:uuid:c2345678-1234-1234-123456789012"
          name = "Name of this classification node."
          description = "Some descriptive text for this classification node"/>
    </GetRootClassificationNodesResponse>
</RegistryResponse>
```

Notice that the `RegistryResponse` element has a `status` attribute that says `"success"`. If there was an error during request processing, this attribute would have said `"failure"`.

The registry response will contain one `ClassificationNode` element for each classification tree present in the registry. We have shown three nodes in the registry response, each of which has an `id` attribute. The `id` attribute uniquely identifies a `ClassificationNode`. Each `ClassificationNode` also contains a `description` attribute. Upon receipt, the `ObjectQueryManagerClient` will parse the registry response and decide which `ClassificationNodes` are of interest. When it has chosen the `ClassificationNodes` that it wants to peruse further, it can go ahead with the next step and browse the classification trees.

The browsing consists of opening a classification tree to the required number of levels. This is like browsing through a list of folders using Windows Explorer. You can click on a folder to view another level of child folders. In this way, you can open the tree of folders to the deepest level. Let's see how we can follow the same technique to browse through and open a classification tree to our desired level.

The following code shows a `GetClassificationTreeRequest`, which takes two parameters, `parent` and `depth`:

```
<GetClassificationTreeRequest
    parent = "parent that needs to be drilled down" depth = "1"/>
```

The `parent` parameter identifies the `ClassificationNode` that needs to be drilled down. The `depth` attribute specifies the number of levels that we want to drill down. A depth value of 1 will return only the immediate children of the classification node specified by the parent attribute. A zero or negative depth value will return the entire subtree of the parent classification node.

The following is a typical response of `GetClassificationTreeRequest`:

```
<RegistryResponse status = "success">
    <GetClassificationTreeResponse>
        <ClassificationNode id="urn:uuid:a2345678-1234-1234-123456789012"
          name = "Name of this classification node."
          description = "Some descriptive text for this classification node"
          parent = "parent of this classification node"/>
        <ClassificationNode id="urn:uuid:b2345678-1234-1234-123456789012"
          name = "Name of this classification node."
          description = "Some descriptive text for this classification node"
          parent = "parent of this classification node"/>
        <!—Other classification nodes. —>
    </GetClassificationTreeResponse>
</RegistryResponse>
```

An `ObjectQueryManagerClient` might use a number of `GetClassificationTreeRequest` calls to arrive at the required classification node(s).

Search Scenario 2: Search for all companies that offer a certain product and are located in a certain region.

We will now see a search scenario in which an ebXML registry service client will use the classification nodes previously obtained to search for other types of registry entries. This scenario requires finding organizations that have been classified with certain geographical and product classifications.

The `GetClassifiedObjectsRequest` element can specify this query in XML syntax. Look at the following XML code:

```
<GetClassifiedObjectsRequest>
    <ObjectRefList>
        <ObjectRef id="urn:uuid:a2345678-1234-1234-123456789012"/>
        <ObjectRef id="urn:uuid:b2345678-1234-1234-123456789012"/>
    <ObjectRefList>
</GetClassifiedObjectsRequest>
```

The `GetClassifiedObjectsRequest` element contains a single `ObjectRefList` element. The `ObjectRefList` element contains a list of references to classification nodes. Each classification node is referenced through an `ObjectRef` element. The `GetClassifiedObjectsRequest` will bring all registry entries that have been classified by *all* the classification nodes being referenced by the `ObjectRef` elements.

The first `ObjectRef` element might point to the product classification, and the other might refer to the geographical classification of our interest.

How do we know the values of `id` attributes of classification nodes? The previously discussed `GetRootClassificationNodesRequest` and `GetClassificationTreeRequest` methods used one after the other will fetch the `id` attributes of classification nodes to be passed to the `GetClassifiedObjectsRequest`.

A response to `GetClassifiedObjectsRequest` is supposed to contain registry entries that have been classified with *all* the classification nodes specified in the request. This means that there is a logical AND between individual classification nodes included in the `ObjectRefList` element.

It's possible that some of the classification nodes we specify in the `ObjectRefList` structure have further child nodes. As an example, consider the `Product` classification tree shown in Figure 13.5.

Figure 13.5 shows a root classification node `Product` that has a child classification node `Engineering Services`. The `Engineering Services` node has three child nodes: `Mechanical Engineering`, `Electrical Engineering`, and `Software Engineering`. The `Mechanical Engineering` node has further children: `Process Plant Fabrication` and `Power Generation Set Repairs`.

FIGURE 13.5

A sample product classification tree.

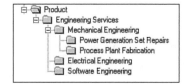

Let's suppose, we included a reference to the Mechanical Engineering classification node in the ObjectRefList. This means that the response to our GetClassifiedObjectsRequest will contain any registry entry that has been classified with the Mechanical Engineering node or with the Process Plant Fabrication node, or with the Power Generation Set Repairs node. So, there is a logical OR between the entries of a subtree of a classification node included in the ObjectRefList.

Combining the logical AND with the logical OR rules is simple. Suppose there were two classification nodes in the GetClassifiedObjectsRequest: Asia under the geographical classification parent and Mechanical Engineering under the product classification parent node. In this case, the registry entries fulfilling *both* of the following conditions will be returned:

1. Geographically classified under the node Asia, or any Asian country or region.
2. Classified with Mechanical Engineering, or Process Plant Fabrication, or the Power Generation Set Repairs node under the Product classification.

The GetClassifiedObjectsRequest given previously will return the following XML structure:

```
<RegistryResponse status = "success">
    <GetClassifiedObjectsResponse>
        <RegistryEntryList>
            <Organization
                primaryContact = "id of a User object
                    that acts as a primary contact for the
                    organization.">
                <PostalAddress street = "Street" city = "City"
                    country = "Country" postalCode = ""postal code"/>
                <TelephoneNumber number = "5834567"
                    areaCode = "42" contryCode = "92"/>
                <FaxNumber number = "5834568"
                    areaCode = "42" contryCode = "92"/>
            </Organization>
            <ExtrinsicObject id = "some CPP document"
                contentURI = "CPP1" objectType = "CPP"
                name = "Name of this profile"
                description = "Textual description of this profile."/>
            <!—Other registry entries. —>
        </RegistryEntryList>
```

13

WORKING WITH
REGISTRIES

```
        </GetClassifiedObjectsResponse>
    </RegistryResponse>
```

The `GetClassifiedObjectsResponse` structure shown here contains two registry entries: an `Organization` structure and an `ExtrinsicObject` instance.

Search Scenario 3: We want to search for all hotels that have classified themselves under tourism-related services and are located in Lahore. We know the UNSPSC code of tourism-related services, and will look for all organizations that have the keyword *hotel* in their name, and have classified them under *both* the following conditions:

- The UNSPSC product classification code for tourism-related services.
- The geographical classification code for Lahore.

We have so far considered how to browse and drill down the classification trees in an ebXML registry service. We have also considered the case in which classification nodes are used to search all registry entries classified against specific classification nodes.

We will now consider another search scenario, in which none of the previously discussed search techniques are useful. This search scenario requires finding the registry entries that fulfil the following criteria:

- Classified under the specified product and geographical classifications.
- Are of type `Organization`.
- Contain the keyword *hotel* in its name.

The `GetClassifiedObjectsRequest` that we discussed previously can take care of only the first criterion (classified under the specified product and geographical classifications). The latter two search criteria need the support of filtering the results.

The ebXML registry service provides a comprehensive mechanism of filter queries to search according to filtering requirements. Probably the most frequently used filter query is `RegistryEntryQuery`. Have a look at the following code that demonstrates the use of `RegistryEntryQuery`:

```
<RegistryEntryQuery>
    <RegistryEntryFilter>
        <Clause>
            <CompoundClause connectivityPredicate = "And">
                <Clause>
                    <SimpleClause leftArgument = "objectType">
                        <StringClause stringcomparepredicate = "equal">
                            Organization
                        </StringClause>
                    </SimpleClause>
                </Clause>
                <Clause>
```

```
                <SimpleClause leftArgument = "status">
                    <StringClause stringcomparepredicate = "equal">
                    Approved
                    </StringClause>
                </SimpleClause>
            </Clause>
        </CompoundClause>
    </Clause>
</RegistryEntryFilter>
<HasClassificationBranch>
    <ClassificationNodeFilter>
        <Clause>
            <SimpleClause leftArgument = "id">
                <StringClause stringcomparepredicate = "startswith">
                urn:un:spsc:XXXX
                </StringClause>
            </SimpleClause>
        </Clause>
    </ClassificationNodeFilter>
    <ClassificationNodeFilter>
        <Clause>
            <SimpleClause leftArgument = "id">
                <StringClause stringcomparepredicate = "startswith">
                urn:un:spsc:YYYY
                </StringClause>
            </SimpleClause>
        </Clause>
    </ClassificationNodeFilter>
</HasClassificationBranch>
<SubmittingOrganizationBranch>
    <OrganizationFilter>
        <Clause>
            <SimpleClause leftArgument = "name">
                <StringClause stringcomparepredicate = "contains">
                hotel
                </StringClause>
            </SimpleClause>
        </Clause>

    </OrganizationFilter>
    </SubmittingOrganizationBranch>
</RegistryEntryQuery>
```

This `RegistryEntryQuery` structure contains three child elements: `RegistryEntryFilter`, `HasClassificationBranch`, and `SubmittingOrganizationBranch`. These three elements represent three filters that will be applied one by one to the search results.

The search filter query process starts with all the registry entry objects in the ebXML registry. The first filter to be applied is the `RegistryEntryFilter`, which has two requirements:

- The first requirement is that we are only interested in `Organization`-type registry entry objects.
- The second requirement says give us only the approved objects and filter out the objects that do not have the `Approved` status (the other three predefined possible status values for the registry entry objects are `Submitted`, `Deprecated`, and `Withdrawn`).

There is a logical `AND` operation between the two requirements; therefore the search results will contain only the registry entries that fulfill *both* requirements.

The two filtering requirements of the `RegistryEntryFilter` are accomplished through the `Clause` child element. ebXML has defined an XML-based grammar to specify filtering queries. The `Clause` element belongs to this grammar.

For clarity, look at the `Clause` structure separately, which we have extracted from the main structure:

```
<Clause>
    <CompoundClause connectivityPredicate = "And">
        <Clause>
            <SimpleClause leftArgument = "objectType">
                <StringClause stringcomparepredicate = "equal">
                    Organization
                </StringClause>
            </SimpleClause>
        </Clause>
        <Clause>
            <SimpleClause leftArgument = "status">
                <StringClause stringcomparepredicate = "equal">
                    Approved
                </StringClause>
            </SimpleClause>
        </Clause>
    </CompoundClause>
</Clause>
```

The main `Clause` structure shown here has a child element named `CompoundClause`. You will need a `CompoundClause` only when you have more than one logical condition to specify (recall that we have two conditions to specify). The `CompoundClause` element has an attribute named `connectivityPredicate` that specifies the logical operator between the logical conditions inside the `CompoundClause` (we have specified `AND`).

There are two `Clause` elements inside the `CompoundClause` element. Each `Clause` element will specify one logical condition. The first `Clause` element specifies the first condition: "`objectType` of the registry entry should be `Organization` (`objectType` EQUALS `"Organization"`)." This is a string comparison operation that requires a combination of

`SimpleClause` and `StringClause` elements. There are other types of comparison operations also available, such as Boolean comparison (using `BooleanClause`), integer comparison (using `IntClause`), and so on, but for this example, we need only the string comparison function.

Every string comparison operation requires specifying three things:

- The `leftArgument` attribute of the `SimpleClause` element specifies the left-hand argument (`objectType`) of the logical condition.

- The `stringcomparepredicate` attribute of the `StringClause` element specifies the string operation (`EQUALS`)

- The contents of the `StringClause` element (`"Organization"`) specify the right hand argument.

You can follow the other clause in a similar way. The second filter (`HasClassificationBranch`) operates on the set of registry entries that have passed the first filter (`RegistryEntryFilter`). The `HasClassificationBranch` element will filter out all those entries that do not have any classification. The remaining set of entries will be passed on to the two `ClassificationNodeFilter` elements one by one. The first `ClassificationNodeFilter` element is for the UNSPSC product classification for tourism, and the second is for the geographical classification node.

Similarly, the third filter (`SubmittingOrganizationBranch`) will act on the set of remaining nodes that have passed all the filters encountered thus far. This last filter will block all registry entries that do not have keyword *hotel* in their name.

We have presented only a few search scenarios in this section to convey the basic concept. It is not feasible to cover all logical cases in this section. Many other search and query features are comprehensively covered in the ebRS document that is part of the official ebXML documentation.

Java API for XML Registries

We have discussed XML registries and seen the UDDI and ebXML registry service specifications in detail. Now let's put these concepts to service by using the Java API for XML Registries (JAXR).

What Is JAXR?

JAXR specifies a standard interface to invoke all types of XML registries. This allows Java developers to use simple Java method calls to JAXR objects, called *JAXR providers*, without worrying about how to author XML according to the registry specification. The JAXR provider will author the correct XML structures itself. We'll look at the JAXR specification and architecture in detail here.

JAXR Architecture

Figure 13.6 is a simple illustration of the JAXR architecture.

FIGURE 13.6

The JAXR architecture.

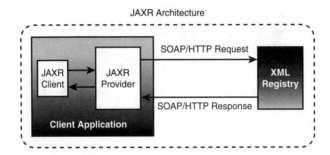

The following entities are identified in Figure 13.6:

- A client application consisting of two modules: a JAXR client and a JAXR provider.
- An XML registry—this might be a UDDI registry or an ebXML registry.

The client application could be a JFC/Swing application that needs to invoke an XML registry. Alternately, it could be a server-side component.

The JAXR client talks to the JAXR provider to invoke the XML registry. The JAXR client does not know anything about the XML syntax or format required by the XML registry. It will issue simple Java method calls to the JAXR provider, which will in turn author the required XML, invoke the XML registry, and bring back the results. Naturally, JAXR providers will have to implement (and expose) several interfaces so that JAXR clients can use them. We'll shortly see the details of these interfaces.

Arrangement of Registry Objects in JAXR

The following are the major classes that JAXR has defined. They map to different data structures of XML registries:

- Organization is the parent structure of all other smaller structures. It represents an organization (perhaps a business organization) that might need several attributes associated with it, such as its description, the name of its contact person, phone number, email address, a list of services that it provides, and so on. All these attributes are also defined as classes.

- InternationalString defines the description about an organization.

- ExternalLink is used whenever we need to refer to some URI that is external to the XML registry.

- PersonName specifies the name of a person (maybe the contact person of an organization). Similarly, EmailAddress specifies an email address, PhoneNumber specifies a phone number, and PostalAddress specifies an address. All these classes (PersonName, EmailAddress, PhoneNumber, and PostalAddress) form structures that combine in a User class. The User object eventually becomes part of the Organization.

- Service represents a service that an Organization offers. Therefore, an Organization may have more than one Service object.

The preceding list is not exhaustive. It only gives you an idea about how JAXR has modeled objects within objects (a tree of objects) to handle XML registry structures. In fact, UDDI also defines a similar tree. You'll see more about UDDI in upcoming chapters.

Putting JAXR to Work

All JAXR classes are packaged in two packages:

- javax.xml.registry—Contains API interfaces and classes that define the mechanism for accessing the registry.

- javax.xml.registry.infomodel—Contains interfaces and classes that define the types of objects that reside in a registry.

We'll now describe the steps for using JAXR to invoke an XML registry.

Connecting to a Registry

No matter what you want to do with a registry, first you should connect to it. For this purpose, you'll start from the Connection interface (included in the javax.xml.registry package). Connection represents a client session with a JAXR provider. A client must establish a connection with a JAXR provider to use it. The javax.xml.registry package contains a class named ConnectionFactory, which has a static method newInstance. The newInstance method creates a new connection.

You also need to specify the properties of the target XML registry (for example, whether it is a UDDI registry).

Once you have established a connection, you will use the getRegistryService method of the Connection interface to get a RegistryService object. RegistryService is another interface included in the `javax.xml.registry` package. It enables the client to obtain other interfaces it uses to access the registry.

The following lines of code accomplish this by first creating a `Connection` and then getting a `RegistryService` object:

```
Properties properties = new Properties();
properties.setProperty("javax.xml.registry.queryManagerURL", file);
properties.setProperty("javax.xml.registry.lifeCycleManagerURL",filep);
properties.setProperty("javax.xml.registry.factoryClass",
➥          "com.sun.xml.registry.uddi.ConnectionFactoryImpl");
ConnectionFactory connectionFactory = ConnectionFactory.newInstance();
connectionFactory.setProperties(properties);
Connection connection = connectionFactory.createConnection();
RegistryService regService = connection.getRegistryService();
```

After you have the registry service object, the next step depends upon what you want to do with the registry. Logically, you can either read from (search) the registry, or write to it (publish).

Reading from an XML Registry Through the JAXR Provider

JAXR has provided a `BusinessQueryManager` interface (also included in the `javax.xml.registry` package) that handles all types of read operations (search queries) that you might want to execute. The `RegistryService` object that you already have will give you the `BusinessQueryManager` object. The following line of code will bring you the `BusinessQueryManager` object:

```
BusinessQueryManager bqm = regService.getBusinessQueryManager();
```

`BusinessQueryManager` has a number of `find` methods. For example, `findOrganizations()` will find a number of `Organizations` matching the search criteria, and `findServices()` will find all the `Service` objects matching the search criteria.

We will now look at `findOrganizations` and `findServices` in detail. The following lines of code will bring a bulk response containing a list of organizations:

```
Collection listOfBusinessNames = new ArrayList();
listOfBusinessNames.add("WaxSys");
listOfBusinessNames.add("Crystal");
listOfBusinessNames.add("Chimera");
BulkResponse response =
➥bqm.findOrganizations(null, listOfBusinessNames,
➥null, null, null, null);
```

Notice that we have passed a collection of strings (`listOfBusinessNames`) to the `findOrganizations()` method. This will bring all `Organizations` with names matching any of the strings that we have included in the `listOfBusinessNames` collection (WaxSys, Crystal, Chimera).

The findOrganizations() method has several other parameters as well that help in specifying search criteria, but we have used only the listOfBusinessNames as the search criteria.

The BulkResponse returned by the findOrganizations() method might contain a number of organizations. Each organization is represented by an Organization object. The Organization interface is included in the javax.xml.registry.infomodel package. The javax.xml.registry.infomodel package represents the information model of JAXR. All data structures (such as Organization, Service, ServiceBinding, User, and so on) representing information contained in an XML registry are included as interfaces in this package.

The following lines of code will read the first Organization object from the BulkResponse:

```
Collection organizations = br.getCollection();
Iterator orgIter = organizations.iterator();
while (orgIter.hasNext())
{
  Organization org =(Organization) orgIter.next();
  System.out.println("Organization name: " + org.getName());
  System.out.println("Organization description: " + org.getDescription());
  System.out.println("Organization Key ID: " + org.getKey().getId();
}
```

Every organization in BulkResponse is identified by a unique identification. We can use this identification to get more details about the organization, such as the services it offers. The following line of code shows how to get the key:

```
String myBusinessKey = org.getKey().getId()
```

We will pass this key to the findServices() method to get a list of all the services that this organization offers:

```
BulkResponse response =
➥bqm.findServices (myBusinessKey, null, null, null, null);
```

The findServices() method also returns a BulkResponse. You can iterate through the BulkResponse to learn more details about the service. For this, you will call the getCollection() method of BulkResponse to get a collection of Service objects. You will then call the Iterator() method of the Collection object and iterate on the returned Iterator object.

We have discussed the use of BusinessQueryManager for reading business services data from an XML registry. There are a number of possible read operations (queries) that can be performed on an XML registry. You will follow the preceding approach for any query requirement.

13

WORKING WITH REGISTRIES

Writing Data to an XML Registry Through a JAXR Provider

JAXR has provided a `BusinessLifeCycleManager` interface in the `javax.xml.registry` package that handles all write operations (create, save, update, delete, and so on) that you might want to perform on an XML registry.

The first step for writing to an XML registry is the same as the read operation: get the `RegistryService` object. After you have the `RegistryService` object, you will call its `getBusinessLifeCycleManager()` method to get the `BusinessLifeCycleManager` object:

```
BusinessLifeCycleManager blcm = regService.getBusinessLifeCycleManager();
```

Writing data to an XML registry requires authentication. Before you can use the `BusinessLifeCycleManager` to write data to an XML registry, you should get authentication from the registry by providing a username and password. The question of how to obtain a username and password are not addressed by JAXR. Obtaining a username and password is a registry-specific task, so you will have to obtain them from some other process.

When you have the username and password, you will pass them on to the `PasswordAuthentication` constructor. The next step is to add this to your credentials. The following code shows how to do this:

```
String username = "bsiddiqui";
String password = "121lhr";
PasswordAuthentication passwdAuth =
➥new PasswordAuthentication (username, password.toCharArray());
Set creds = new HashSet();
creds.add(passwdAuth);
connection.setCredentials(creds);
```

Now you are all set to start writing to the registry. `BusinessLifeCycleManager` has a number of methods to write an organization record in an XML registry; for example, organization, classification, service and service binding, and so on. We will demonstrate how to create a new organization and add a service to it.

The first step is to create a new organization:

```
Organization organization = blcm.createOrganization("MyBusinessOrganization");
```

The `CreateOrganization()` method returns a newly created `organization` object. We will add the following structures one by one to this organization object:

- Description (an `InternationalString` object containing a brief description about the organization)

- Contacts (whom to contact in this organization, specified by a `User` object)
- Services (services offered by this organization)

The following line of code shows how to add a description to the organization. You first create a description on the `BusinessLifeCycleManager` and then call the `setDescription()` method of the organization object:

```
InternationalString description =
➥blcm.createInternationalString("J2EE and XML get married");
organization.setDescription(description);
```

To add a contact, you will use several JAXR classes, namely `PersonName`, `TelephoneNumber`,and `EmailAddress`. You will create objects of these classes and then add them to the `User` class one by one:

```
User primaryContact = blcm.createUser();
PersonName pName = blcm.createPersonName("BiBi");
primaryContact.setPersonName(pName);
TelephoneNumber tNum = blcm.createTelephoneNumber();
tNum.setNumber("(92) 300-8484756");
Collection phoneNums = new ArrayList();
phoneNums.add(tNum);
primaryContact.setTelephoneNumbers(phoneNums);
EmailAddress emailAddress =
➥blcm.createEmailAddress("bsiddiqui@waxsys.com ");
Collection emailAddresses = new ArrayList();
emailAddresses.add(emailAddress);
primaryContact.setEmailAddresses(emailAddresses);
```

After the user is ready, you will set this user as the primary contact in the organization:

```
organization.setPrimaryContact(primaryContact);
```

To add services to an organization, you will create services individually, set their descriptions, add these services to a collection, and then add this collection to the `organization` object:

```
Collection services = new ArrayList();
Service service = blcm.createService("Service Name");
InternationalString serviceDesc =
➥blcm.createInternationalString("My Service Desc");
service.setDescription(serviceDesc);
services.add(service);
organization.addServices(services);
```

In the preceding code, you can see that we have a hierarchy of data structures (objects). Smaller data objects become a part of larger data objects and so on, until everything finally gets placed in an `organization` object.

Accessing Web Services

How do you apply the XML, SOAP, UDDI, WSDL, ebXML, and messaging concepts to P2P applications?

Can you develop applications that expose Web service interfaces over the P2P infrastructure and use SOAP to expose your P2P Web service interfaces? There is no conceptual problem in doing this. Chapter 20, "Using SOAP with P2P," demonstrates how to use SOAP over P2P networks.

You can also go one step further. Recall that WSDL is the grammar used to describe Web service interfaces, and UDDI tModels represent technical fingerprints. You can describe the interfaces of your applications using WSDL, and you can also publish your P2P Web service applications as technical fingerprints using the UDDI tModel structures.

This means that you can publish your P2P Web services on an XML registry like UDDI, search for P2P Web services published by other peers, describe your P2P Web services using a grammar such as WSDL, and bind your P2P Web services with concrete implementations using a binding mechanism, like SOAP.

For example, let's consider an application scenario in which a company has already written its WSDL interfaces, hosted its Web services on a SOAP server, and published all the relevant information and documents on a UDDI registry (or probably an ebXML registry). Now the company has come across a prospective customer base in a community of peers sharing a P2P infrastructure. The company would like to expose its existing Web services to the community of P2P users. For this purpose, the company will be required to do the following:

1. Publish new binding information for its existing Web services on the UDDI (or ebXML) registry. This new information will be in addition to the information already published, so the existing Web services will continue to serve as such. The new information will establish new service end points. For example, the old service end points were SOAP-based (they were pointing to the company's SOAP server); the new end points will point to some P2P resources (for example, in a JXTA network, pipe end points can be used as service end points. Refer to Chapter 16 for details on JXTA).

2. Create appropriate listeners for the P2P infrastructure, which will receive service invocation requests from peers, translate the requests to appropriate SOAP format, send the SOAP requests to the existing SOAP server, receive responses from the SOAP server, translate the SOAP responses back in a format acceptable to P2P users, and send the responses back to the requesting peers. This way you can get

the benefits of P2P architecture over the conventional client-server model, as well as simultaneously integrate your loosely coupled Web service components into a global P2P-based Web services model.

Summary

In this chapter, we discussed the UDDI Publishing API in detail. You learned how to publish new information and update existing information on a UDDI registry using XML-based programmatic interfaces.

We also briefly discussed how the ebXML set of specifications provide a modular yet complete framework to ensure interoperability in an e-business application. We then discussed in detail the registry services that are part of the ebXML set of specifications.

We then discussed the concept of XML registries, and explained how JAXR allows its clients to access XML registries for read/write operations. Finally, we proposed a P2P-based Web services model.

Jini and JavaSpaces

by Robert Flenner

IN THIS CHAPTER

Jini is about federating and organizing services on a network and enabling clients to discover and use services. Jini's network capabilities and JavaSpaces' support for persistent communication make them strong candidates for P2P systems.

Obtaining Jini

You can download the Jini binaries and source from the Java Developer Connection at `http://developer.java.sun.com/developer/products/jini`.

You must register to be a member of the Java Developer Connection. These downloads are available after accepting the Sun Community Source License Agreement.

In addition, there is a Jini TCK (Technology Core Platform Compatibility Kit v 1.1B) available. The TCK consists of a set of tests to ensure that Jini technology-enabled services and clients are compatible with the Jini specification.

The installation instructions are available at `http://developer.java.sun.com/developer/products/jini/installation.index.html`.

You can download the Jini specifications from `http://java.sun.com/products/jini/specs/`.

Standardizing Interfaces

Jini services are manifested as Java objects that expose interfaces conforming to the Jini specification. The type of the service determines the interfaces that comprise the service. Jini relies on the richness of Java type semantics. These type definitions and the ease with which they support subtyping (inheritance) resembles the way we build systems. Systems can evolve as the technology evolves. Many of the other approaches rely on XML definitions or APIs that might limit the systems' adaptability to change: For instance, versioning has always been problematic with XML.

Jini services advertise their operations by registering an object with a Jini-compliant lookup service. Service registration is at the core of building the Jini network community. Jini does define special roles for service discovery, but does not limit the number of lookup services that a network can support.

There are three infrastructure services that are required somewhere on your Jini network:

- An HTTP server that supports the dynamic downloading of code
- The Remote Method Invocation daemon (`rmid`) that provides the distributed remote object lookup and activation mechanism

- The Jini Lookup Service (LUS) that provides the service registry and the service lookup capabilities on the Jini network

The HTTP Server and Protocol

Jini requires that an HTTP server be available on the network, because Jini uses the HTTP protocol to transport files (code) from machine to machine.

Any HTTP server should be able to satisfy the requirements of Jini. The GET method of the HTTP protocol is used to request a specific file (URL) for download. The files requested are JAR or class files necessary to instantiate objects to process distributed requests.

The class com.sun.jini.tool.ClassServer that's supplied with the Jini distribution implements a simple HTTP server for transporting JAR and class files.

Remote Method Invocation

The Sun-supplied Jini services rely heavily on the Remote Method Invocation (RMI) framework. Understanding RMI is critical to understanding Jini.

RMI is another Java-based technology enabling distributed processing. RMI enables Java applications running on different Java Virtual Machines (JVMs) to communicate. Whether these JVMs exist on the same host machine or on different machines does not matter. Just like RPCs (Remote Procedure Calls), the processes need not exist in the same address space, or even on the same machine. However, RMI is able to offer a number of advantages over other distributed models because it assumes the environment is Java-enabled.

The Java platform's RMI system has been specifically designed to operate in the Java application environment. Client applications invoke local calls through a stub interface that communicates with the actual remote object, as seen in Figure 14.1. The RMI runtime performs all the necessary communication housekeeping to ensure that two processes running on separate JVMs can exchange invocation requests and results through an exposed common interface definition.

In the Java platform's distributed object model, a remote object is described by one or more remote interfaces, which are written in the Java programming language. A remote interface is a Java interface that extends java.rmi.Remote and defines the methods, which are made available to remote clients. All methods declared in the interface that can be invoked remotely must declare that they throw a java.rmi.RemoteException. For example, the following simple Agent interface extends Remote, and the talk method

14

JINI AND JAVASPACES

FIGURE **14.1**

Client invocation using RMI.

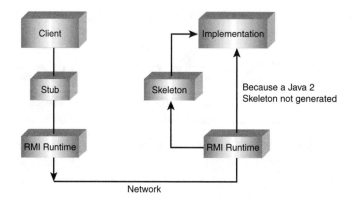

throws `RemoteException`. The object that implements this interface is exposing its `talk` method to clients in other JVMs:

```
import java.rmi.Remote;
import java.rmi.RemoteException;

public interface Agent extends Remote {
    public String talk() throws RemoteException;
}
```

A client with a reference to the `Agent` can invoke the `talk` method regardless of where the `Agent` implementation physically resides. Of course, there are network and security considerations that affect this capability. Like P2P systems, firewalls are one of the most frequently encountered inhibitors to RMI communication. To address this issue, RMI uses direct and indirect forwarding. RMI creates HTTP tunnels that encapsulate remote requests, and the Java Remote Method Invocation Protocol (JRMP).

Figure 14.2 demonstrates indirect forwarding, which requires a CGI script running on the remote server to forward requests to the RMI server. Because this is still a hit-and-miss proposition, it has limitations.

FIGURE **14.2**

The HTTP tunnel for RMI.

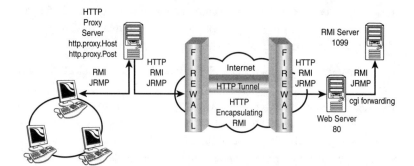

The RMI Registry

Let's look at how remote objects in RMI are discovered.

The RMI registry is used to associate a remote object with a user-defined name. This name is simply a Java String. The `java.rmi.Naming` class provides the methods to `bind` and `unbind` an object to a name using the RMI registry. The name takes the form of

`[rmi:][//][host][:port][/name]`

where:

- `rmi` names the protocol and may be omitted
- *host* is the host (remote or local) where the registry is located
- *port* is the port number on which the registry accepts calls
- *name* is a string that represents the remote object

Both *host* and *port* are optional. If *host* is omitted, the host defaults to the local host. If *port* is omitted, then the port defaults to 1099.

Binding a name to a remote object associates the name with the remote object. If you have used other distributed object systems such as CORBA, this process should not be new. A remote object can be associated with a name using the `Naming` class's `bind` or `rebind` methods. For security reasons, the `Naming.bind`, `Naming.rebind`, and `Naming.unbind` methods can only be executed on the same host as the RMI registry.

After a remote object is registered (bound) with the RMI registry on the local host, callers on a remote (or local) host can look up the remote object by name, obtain its reference, and then invoke remote methods on the object.

Unicast and Activatable Services

RMI provides two convenience classes that remote object implementations can extend to facilitate remote object creation, both shown in Figure 14.3:

- `java.rmi.server.UnicastRemoteObject`
- `java.rmi.activation.Activatable`

A remote object implementation must be exported to RMI. Exporting a remote object makes that object available to accept incoming calls from clients. For a remote object implementation that is exported as a `UnicastRemoteObject`, the exporting involves listening on a TCP port for incoming calls. More than one remote object can accept incoming calls on the same port. A remote object implementation can extend the class `UnicastRemoteObject` to make use of its constructors that export the object, or it can export the object via `UnicastRemoteObject`'s static `exportObject` methods.

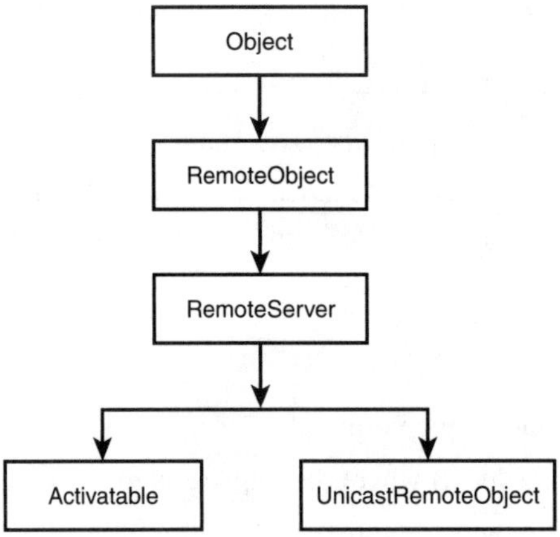

FIGURE 14.3

Class hierarchy for remote objects.

The `UnicastRemoteObject` class is as follows:

```
public class UnicastRemoteObject extends RemoteServer{
    protected UnicastRemoteObject()
    protected UnicastRemoteObject(int port)
    protected UnicastRemoteObject(int port, RMIClientSocketFactory csf,
➥RMIServerSocketFactory ssf)
    public Object clone()
    public static RemoteStub exportObject(Remote obj)
    public static Remote exportObject(Remote obj, int port)
    public static Remote exportObject(Remote obj, int port,
    RMIClientSocketFactory csf, RMIServerSocketFactory ssf)
    public static boolean unexportObject(Remote obj, boolean force)
}
```

The no-argument constructor of `UnicastRemoteObject` creates and exports a remote object on an anonymous port chosen at runtime. The second form of the constructor takes a single argument, `port`, that specifies the port number on which the remote object accepts incoming calls. The third constructor creates and exports a remote object that accepts incoming calls on the specified `port` via a `ServerSocket` created from the `RMIServerSocketFactory`. Clients make connections to the remote object via sockets supplied from the `RMIClientSocketFactory`. You make use of socket factories to change the underlying socket behavior to support additional connection features, such as security and encryption.

Implementing Unicast Services

Let's start with a simple `AgentService` that implements the `Agent` interface and extends `UnicastRemoteObject`:

```
public class AgentService extends UnicastRemoteObject
        implements Agent
```

```
{
    public AgentService() throws RemoteException {
        super();
    }
```

The `UnicastRemoteObject` class defines a remote object whose references are valid only while the server process is running. The `UnicastRemoteObject` class provides support for point-to-point active object references using TCP streams.

Because you are extending `UnicastRemoteObject`, the object is automatically exported to the RMI runtime during construction. Inheriting from `UnicastRemoteObject` eliminates the need to call `exportObject`.

Let's look at the `main` method for `AgentService`:

```
public static void main(String[] args) {
    // must set a security manager to load classes
    if(args.length < 1) {
        System.out.println("usage [hostname]");
        System.exit(1);
    }
    // set the hostname from the first argument
    String hostname = args[0];
    if (System.getSecurityManager() == null) {
        System.setSecurityManager(new RMISecurityManager());
    }
    try {
        Agent agent = new AgentService();
        // prepare to bind the server with a name
        String name = "//" + hostname + "/Agent";
        Naming.rebind(name, agent);
            System.out.println("AgentService bound");
    } catch (Exception e) {
        System.err.println("AgentService exception: " +
        e.getMessage());
    }
}

    // implementation of the Agent interface
    public String talk() {
        return "P2P is very cool";
    }
}
```

The first thing you must do is install and set an appropriate security manager that protects access to system resources from untrustworthy downloaded code. Forgetting to do this will result in a runtime error, which will throw a `java.lang.SecurityException`. The security manager determines whether downloaded code has access to the local filesystem or can perform any other privileged operations.

All programs using RMI must install a security manager, or RMI will not download classes other than from the local classpath in remote method calls. This restriction ensures that the operations performed by downloaded code go through a set of security checks. In addition to installing a security manager, you also define an associated security policy:

```
grant {
    permission java.security.AllPermission "", "";
};
```

This is a simple text file that you pass the location to as a property of the Java virtual machine when you invoke the program.

After you have installed a security manager and exported the remote object to RMI, you need to associate a name to the object so clients can find the service. As mentioned before, you use the java.rmi.Naming class to do this. The Naming class takes a name that is a URL-formatted java.lang.String.

A sample fragment would look like the following:

```
String name = "//hostname/AgentService";
Naming.rebind(name, agent);
```

This code fragment associates the name AgentService with the remote object running on the designated host machine. The port is optional and defaults to 1099, which is the default port for the RMI registry.

The only thing left to complete our service is to implement the Agent interface:

```
public String talk() {
    return "P2P is very cool";
}
```

The implementation of the interface can be as simple or as complex as required. Standardizing the interface would enable P2P agents from different systems to engage in conversations resembling human communication.

Implementing Activatable Services

A unicast service must be started manually. An activatable service is one that RMI can start automatically. RMI has the capability to restart services when it is activated, or to start services when they receive their first incoming call. This automatic activation is instrumental to enabling a more robust distributed environment. An activation daemon takes care of restarting, deactivating, and reactivating services.

There are a number of key components to the activation model that should be highlighted. Because many of the Jini services are activatable services, this background will be beneficial.

The `java.rmi.activation.Activator` interface provides the basic functionality of activation. The Sun implementation of this interface is provided through `sun.rmi.server.ActivationGroupImpl`, and is invoked by starting the RMI daemon process.

`rmid` (the RMI daemon) is a daemon process that is started when you boot or reboot your system. The typical command to start the process is

```
rmid -J-Dsun.rmi.activation.execPolicy=policy.file
```

In addition to the `Activator`, other key elements of the activation model include the following:

- `java.rmi.activation.ActivationGroup`, which is a group of services that have been identified to share a common JVM.

- `java.rmi.activation.ActivationMonitor`, which tracks and monitors the state of an object in an activation group, and the state of the activation group as a whole.

- `java.rmi.activation.ActivationSystem`, which provides the interface to register activatable objects and groups.

The activation system will call the constructor with a unique activation ID and a marshalled object that contains any information that you want to pass to the activated object. This information is passed when you register the service, as illustrated in the following fragment:

```
public class AgentService extends Activatable
        implements Agent
{
    public AgentService(ActivationID id, MarshalledObject data)
        throws RemoteException
    {
        // register object using anonymous port
        super(id, 0);
    }
}
```

An activation group descriptor contains the information necessary to create and re-create an activation group in which to activate objects. The description contains

- The group's class name

- The group's code location (the location of the group's class)

- A marshalled object that can contain group-specific initialization data

The group's class must be a concrete subclass of `ActivationGroup`. A subclass of `ActivationGroup` is created/re-created via the `ActivationGroup.createGroup` static method, which invokes a special constructor that takes two arguments: the group's `ActivationGroupID`, and the group's initialization data (in a `java.rmi.MarshalledObject`).

14

You can construct an activation group descriptor that uses the system defaults for group implementation and code location. Properties specify Java environment overrides, which will override system properties in your group implementation's JVM. The command environment can control the exact command/options used in starting the child JVM, or can be `null` to accept `rmid`'s default. The following example creates a group description:

```
// Set the policy and codebase properties to start the group
Properties props = new Properties();
props.put("java.security.policy", policy);
props.put("java.rmi.server.codebase", codebase);

// use the rmid default command environment
ActivationGroupDesc agd = new ActivationGroupDesc(props, null);

// get the activation group id
ActivationGroupID agi =
    ActivationGroup.getSystem().registerGroup(agd);

// create the group
ActivationGroup.createGroup(agi, agd, 0);
```

Now you need to create a specific object description. An object activation descriptor contains the information necessary to activate an object, which includes the following:

- The object's group identifier
- The object's fully qualified class name
- The object's code location (the location of the class) and a codebase URL path
- The object's restart mode
- A marshalled object that can contain object-specific initialization data

A descriptor registered with the activation system can be used to re-create/activate the object specified by the descriptor. The `MarshalledObject` in the object's descriptor is passed as the second argument to the remote object's constructor for objects to use during re-initialization/activation:

```
ActivationDesc ad =
    new ActivationDesc("AgentService", // class name
                       codebase,        // codebase
                       null,            // no marshalled data passed
                       true);           // restart
```

Register the object with `rmid` and then bind the name to the registry:

```
Agent agent = (Agent) Activatable.register(ad);
String name = "//" + hostname + "/AgentService";
Naming.rebind(name, agent);
```

That is all that is required to create an activatable object. You now have an object implementation that can be created on demand, and if a failure occurs, it will be automatically started when the rmid process is restarted.

RMI's Role in P2P

RMI provides P2P systems with the capability to exchange objects—not just messages or XML. These objects are capable of running in the JVM they are downloaded into. This is a powerful concept in distributed computing that has yet to gain widespread adoption. One reason for this is because of the security considerations that must be addressed. Code from untrustworthy sources can do considerable damage if left unchecked. Security must be standardized through security managers like the RMI security manager. This level of homogenous platform architecture across the Internet has not been achieved. Therefore, RMI and Jini can play a role in P2P systems, but most likely that will be limited to Java-based implementations.

Lookup and Discovery

Jini services are found and resolved by a *lookup service (LUS)*. Every Jini community must have at least one lookup service available. The lookup service is the central bootstrapping mechanism for the system, and provides the major point of contact between the system and users of the system. A lookup service maps Java language-defined interfaces that indicate they possess the functionality provided by a service to sets of objects implementing the service.

In contrast to the RMI registry, which uses name-to-object mapping, the Jini lookup service uses interface-to-object mapping, as illustrated in Figure 14.4. This is a powerful concept, because interfaces are inherently extensible.

FIGURE 14.4

Jini uses interface-to-object lookup as opposed to the name-to-object method provided through RMI.

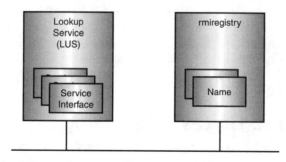

Jini lookup services are organized into groups. You can create groups with any name that you desire. There is also a default group called the *public group*. When you start a lookup service, you specify the groups that the lookup service will support. In addition, when you search for a lookup service, you specify the groups you require the lookup service to support.

Groups can be organized along departmental boundaries, such as marketing or advertising departments, or along other dimensions, such as sports services, vacation services, and so on. The organization of lookup services is really system- and application-dependent. However, security considerations often influence—if not dictate—the configuration.

A service is added to a lookup service, and therefore to a group, by a pair of protocols called discovery and join.

Understanding Discovery Management

The *discovery* and *join protocols* enable services to discover, become part of, and advertise supplied services to other members of the Jini community.

The discovery protocol is used to:

- Announce the presence of a lookup service on a local area network (LAN multicast)
- Discover one or more lookup services on a local area network (LAN multicast)
- Establish communication with a specific lookup service over a wide area network (WAN unicast)

The discovery protocol requires support for multicast or restricted-scope broadcast (such as UDP), along with support for reliable unicast delivery in the transport layer (such as TCP). The discovery protocol makes use of the Java platform's object serialization capabilities to exchange information in a platform-independent manner.

The join protocol makes use of the discovery protocol to provide a standard sequence of steps that services should perform when they are starting up and registering themselves with a LUS. The join protocol is used to register a service and advertise its functionality in all lookup services of interest.

The discovery protocol supports multicast and unicast messaging.

Multicast and Unicast Messaging

Jini uses both multicast and unicast messaging to support the discovery protocols. Unicast messaging is used when the location of the lookup service is known. For instance, the TCP/IP address of the lookup service is known to the querying entity.

Multicast messaging is used when the lookup service must be found or discovered. It is more dynamic and typical of P2P discovery.

Multicast Discovery Protocol

Multicast addresses are in the 224–239 range. Jini has reserved the following two multicast addresses for its use:

- 224.0.1.84—jini-announcement
- 224.0.1.85—jini-request

How do lookup services bootstrap to the community and use these multicast addresses?

Jini uses the jini-announcement address (224.0.1.84) and the *multicast announcement protocol* for lookup services to advertise their existence. When a new lookup service is started, it announces its availability to potential clients. Also, if a network failure occurs, this protocol can be used by the lookup service to make clients aware that it is available after the network has been restored.

The multicast announcement protocol follows these steps:

1. Interested entities on the network listen for multicast announcements from lookup services. If an announcement of interest arrives at such an entity, the entity uses the unicast discovery protocol to contact the specific lookup service.

2. Lookup services take part in the unicast discovery protocol (see Figure 14.5) by sending multicast announcements of their existence at regular intervals.

So, the lookup service can broadcast its existence like a "heartbeat" on the network, and interested clients listen for heartbeats.

FIGURE 14.5

The multicast announcement protocol provides a heartbeat broadcast for lookup services to advertise their presence.

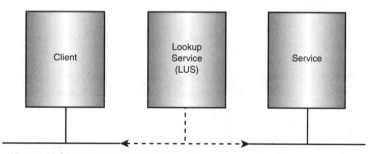

When an LUS becomes active it multicasts an announcement to notify nearby members

It is assumed that lookup services are relatively stable in the community. In other words, lookup services should not be entering and leaving the community as frequently as other services or clients.

Let's consider how other services that become active by broadcasting their existence.

Multicast request datagrams are encoded as a sequence of bytes, using the data and object serialization facilities of the Java programming language. A multicast discovery request packet must be 512 bytes in size or less to fit into a single UDP datagram.

Table 14.1 illustrates the contents of a multicast request packet body.

TABLE 14.1 Multicast Request Datagrams

Multicast Request Packet Description	*Count (Occurrences)*	*Serialized Type*
Protocol version	1	Int
The port to respond to	1	Int
The count of lookups	1	Int
An array of lookups that have already responded	Variable	ServiceID
The count of groups	1	Int
An array of groups of interest	Variable	String

In Figure 14.6, a service becomes active and broadcasts a request to find nearby LUSs of interest: for example, groups that it wants to join. Each LUS discovered will return a MarshalledObject that implements the net.jini.core.lookup.ServiceRegistrar interface. This will enable the service to register with the LUS, and in effect, join and advertise its functionality to the Jini community.

FIGURE 14.6

When a service becomes active, it multicasts a request to find nearby LUSs.

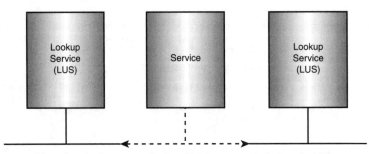

When a service becomes active it multicasts a request to find nearby LUSs

The multicast protocol is a key to enabling the dynamics of a Jini community. It permits the community to grow and form dynamically based on network "closeness," versus traditional programming lookups or network IP configurations. The using entity does not have prior knowledge of the request recipient.

Unicast Discovery Protocol

Unlike the multicast protocol, the *unicast discovery protocol* is used to communicate with a specific service or LUS. This is useful for dealing with nonlocal communities, and for using services in specific communities over a long period of time. This protocol is able to bypass the constraints of the multicast radius.

The unicast discovery protocol works as follows:

1. The LUS listens for incoming connections, and when a client makes a connection, responds with a `MarshalledObject` that implements the `net.jini.core.lookup.ServiceRegistrar` interface. This is also what occurred as a result of the preceding multicast request.

2. An entity that wants to contact a particular LUS uses known host and port information to establish a connection. The client-entity sends a unicast discovery request and listens for a `MarshalledObject` in response.

The LUS is crucial to the establishment of a Jini community. The discovery protocol provides both a dynamic multicast and a directed unicast approach to finding LUSs.

Many of the requirements of P2P discovery can be satisfied by Jini discovery and join protocols. Of course, the major constraint is that the systems have to publish a Java interface. Systems that are dependent on language-neutral protocols such as XML will probably bridge to Jini services through a Jini gateway.

The Jini Lookup Service

The Jini reference implementation provides a LUS named *reggie*. `reggie` is an activatable RMI service. When `reggie` is started, it will register with `rmid` and multicast its announcement packets on the network.

Be sure that `rmid` is running when you start `reggie`, or an exception will be thrown.

The following script starts `reggie` on Windows:

```
@echo off
set HTTP_ADDRESS=172.16.1.3:8080
set JINI_HOME=c:\files\jini1_2
set HTTP_HOME=c:\services\logs
set GROUPS=public

echo P2P Unleashed
echo — — — — — — — — — — — — — — — — — — — — —.
echo Jini install directory          %JINI_HOME%
echo Web server                      %HTTP_ADDRESS%
echo Default group                   %GROUPS%
echo — — — — — — — — — — — — — — — — — — — — —.
```

```
java -jar -Djava.security.policy=%JINI_HOME%\policy\policy.all %JINI_HOME%\
➥lib\reggie.jar http://%HTTP_ADDRESS%/reggie-dl.jar %JINI_HOME%\policy\
➥policy.all %HTTP_HOME%\services\logs\reggie_log %GROUPS%
```

The following properties are set:

- JINI_HOME\lib—Executable JAR file path to the Jini reggie.jar
- JINI_HOME\policy—Security policy file path to the policy.all file
- HTTP_ADDRESS—Codebase path to the downloadable reggie-dl JAR file
- HTTP_HOME\services\logs—Log directory path to reggie persistent state
- Groups—Groups this LUS will support

reggie will create a log file under the directory specified by the log directory property. You might want to verify the existence of that file after you have started the service.

After you have started reggie, you should be able to start the lookup browser, which permits you to browse the services that are currently running in your Jini community. At this point, the only service running will be the LUS itself.

The following script can be used to start the service lookup browser on Windows:

```
@echo off
set HTTP_ADDRESS=172.16.1.3:8080
set JINI_HOME=c:\files\jini1_2
set HTTP_HOME=c:\services\logs
set GROUPS=public
echo P2P Unleashed
echo — — — — — — — — — — — — — — — — — — — ·
echo Jini install directory     %JINI_HOME%
echo Web server                 %HTTP_ADDRESS%
echo Default group              %GROUPS%
echo — — — — — — — — — — — — — — — — — — — ·
echo Starting the Service Browser
java -cp %JINI_HOME%\lib\jini-examples.jar
➥-Djava.security.policy=%JINI_HOME%\example\browser\policy
➥-Djava.rmi.server.codebase=http://%HTTP_ADDRESS%/jini-examples-dl.jar
➥ com.sun.jini.example.browser.Browser –admin
```

The lookup browser can be used to view your LUS environment. You can display the services that are currently registered at each LUS that is active. You can use the browser as an aid in determining what services are active, how many LUSs are running, attributes of a service, and so on.

The administration of services is possible by highlighting the service and right-clicking on the service item. Selecting Service Admin displays the administration. You can change groups, locators, and remove the service from the LUS and rmid.

At this point, `reggie` should be sending announcement packets out on the network. By default, `reggie` sends an announcement packet every two minutes.

Jini Finding and Binding

Now that you have the LUS in place and have been able to verify the heartbeat of `reggie`, let's discuss the join and lookup process. These are the processes that implement the find and bind semantics of service-oriented architectures. These processes enable you to provide and access services in the Jini community.

As mentioned, the join protocol makes use of the discovery protocols to provide a standard sequence of steps that services should perform when they are starting up and registering themselves with a LUS.

The discovery protocol is used to discover LUSs, and for LUSs to return a proxy object that implements the ServiceRegistrar interface, shown in Listing 14.2.

LISTING 14.2   ServiceRegistrar Interface

```
public interface ServiceRegistrar {
   ServiceRegistration register(ServiceItem item, long leaseDuration)
       throws RemoteException;
   ServiceMatches lookup(ServiceTemplate tmpl, int maxMatches)
       throws RemoteException;
   int TRANSITION_MATCH_NOMATCH = 1 << 0;
   int TRANSITION_NOMATCH_MATCH = 1 << 1;
   int TRANSITION_MATCH_MATCH = 1 << 2;

   EventRegistration notify(ServiceTemplate tmpl, int transitions,
                            RemoteEventListener listener,
                            MarshalledObject handback,
                            long leaseDuration) throws RemoteException;

   Class[] getEntryClasses(ServiceTemplate tmpl) throws RemoteException;

   Object[] getFieldValues(ServiceTemplate tmpl, int setIndex, String field)
       throws NoSuchFieldException, RemoteException;

   Class[] getServiceTypes(ServiceTemplate tmpl, String prefix)
       throws RemoteException;

   ServiceID getServiceID();
   LookupLocator getLocator() throws RemoteException;
   String[] getGroups() throws RemoteException;
}
```

Service Registration

After the LUS has been discovered and returns the ServiceRegistrar proxy, you invoke the register method to register your service. You will do this with all LUSs that are of interest to you (that is, LUSs that support specific groups):

```
ServiceRegistration register(ServiceItem item, long leaseDuration)
    throws RemoteException;
```

The register method takes two parameters:

- A ServiceItem
- A lease duration

The ServiceItem includes a service ID that must be globally unique and is initially generated by the LUS. In addition, a ServiceItem contains a set of attributes that are used to augment the service definition, and a proxy object that's used to communicate with the service.

The lease parameter is used to indicate a time-based duration to keep the service active. We will discuss leasing in general later in this chapter. For now, just realize that every service has a lease associated with it that controls how long the service will remain active in the LUS. The lease duration is expressed in milliseconds.

The register method of the ServiceRegistrar interface returns an object that implements the ServiceRegistration interface (see Listing 14.3). This interface enables the service to retrieve its service ID and lookup registration and to manage its service attributes. You will need the service ID to register with other LUSs to ensure that your identification is consistent and unique across the network.

Each implementation of the LUS exports proxy objects that implement the ServiceRegistration interface.

LISTING 14.3 ServiceRegistration Interface

```
public interface ServiceRegistration {
   ServiceID getServiceID();
   Lease getLease();
   void addAttributes(Entry[] attrSets)
       throws UnknownLeaseException, RemoteException;
   void modifyAttributes(Entry[] attrSetTemplates, Entry[] attrSets)
       throws UnknownLeaseException, RemoteException;
   void setAttributes(Entry[] attrSets)
       throws UnknownLeaseException, RemoteException;
}
```

After a service has registered with the LUS, it has joined the community. Clients can now find the service by performing a lookup on any LUS with which the service has registered.

The `JoinManager` Class

Services will often use the `net.jini.lookup.JoinManager` class to discover and join a Jini community. This helper class implements the discovery and join protocols, making it easier for services to manage the "good Jini citizen" process requirements.

There are five parameters required to construct a `JoinManager`:

- `java.lang.Object` is the object/service to be registered. This is the proxy object that implements the service interface. For example, the Jini LUS registers an object that implements the `ServiceRegistrar` interface.

- `net.jini.core.entry.Entry[]` is an array of attributes associated with the service. `Entry` objects are used to augment the service definition, so users can perform specific searches for services. For example, an `Entry` might be used to specify a location of a service, or a specific vendor's implementation. In that case, only services matching that criteria would be returned from lookup requests.

- `net.jini.lookup.ServiceIDListener` or `net.jini.core.lookup.ServiceID` is the unique service identifier assigned to the service. If the service has already received the identifier from the LUS, it uses the ID as a parameter; otherwise it supplies an ID listener to receive the ID. The ID listener stores the ID for subsequent registration(s). Where and how the ID is stored depends on the service. Typically, the service will log this information to safe-storage upon receipt, and retrieve the ID during subsequent starts from a known location.

- `net.jini.discovery.DiscoveryManagement` is an interface that defines the discovery operations as outlined in the previous section. The `LookupDiscovery` class implements this interface. In addition, the `LookupLocatorDiscovery` class implements this interface using the unicast, rather than the multicast, discovery protocol.

- `net.jini.lease.LeaseRenewalManager` is the lease renewal manager responsible for renewing your lease with the LUS. This is how resources are managed across the Jini network, based on time-allocation management. Leasing is often referred to as providing the "self-healing" properties of a Jini network.

The `AgentService` Example

Let's convert the RMI `AgentService` into a Jini service to demonstrate the changes required (see Listing 14.4). This will serve to reinforce our discussion and highlight the extensions Jini provides on top of RMI.

14

JINI AND
JAVASPACES

LISTING 14.4 `JiniAgentService` Class

```
// These classes form the basis of the RMI support
import java.rmi.RemoteException;
import java.rmi.RMISecurityManager;
import java.rmi.server.UnicastRemoteObject;
import java.io.IOException;

// We will require a number of Jini classes to support our Jini service
import net.jini.core.discovery.LookupLocator;
import net.jini.core.lookup.ServiceID;
import net.jini.discovery.DiscoveryGroupManagement;
import net.jini.discovery.LookupDiscoveryManager;
import net.jini.lookup.JoinManager;
import net.jini.lookup.ServiceIDListener;

//
// Extend the UnicastRemoteObject to create a non-activatable Jini service.
//
public class JiniAgentService extends UnicastRemoteObject
    implements Agent
{

    // The LookupDiscoveryManager you are using to find (request) LUSs
    private LookupDiscoveryManager lookupDiscMgr;

    // The lookup locator array that contains specific LUSs
    private LookupLocator locators[];

    // The groups array that contains specific groups, no groups, or all groups
    private String groups[] = DiscoveryGroupManagement.ALL_GROUPS;

    // The manager for joining LUSs
    private JoinManager joiner = null;

    // ServiceID returned from the lookup registration process
    private ServiceID serviceID = null;
//
// Add an init method to your constructor to do initialization
➥specific to Jini.
//
    public JiniAgentService() throws IOException {

    // call the UnicastRemoteObject to export the object
        super();

    // Initialize the Jini service
        init();
    }
//
//
```

LISTING 14.4 continued

```
// Create a discovery manager by passing parameters
// to discover all LUSs within the multicast radius.
// Do this by specifying ALL_GROUPS and null parameters.
//
//
    private void init() throws IOException {

        try {
          lookupDiscMgr = new LookupDiscoveryManager(groups, locators, null);
        } catch (IOException e) {
          System.err.println("Problem starting discovery");
          e.printStackTrace();
              throw new IOException("Problem starting discovery:" +
                  e.getLocalizedMessage());
        }
        /* Register this service with any configured LUSs */
        if (serviceID == null) {
        // First instance ... need service id
          joiner = new JoinManager(
          this,                     // service object
          null,                     // service attributes - none at this time
          new SrvcIDListener(),     // ServiceIDListener  - internal helper class
          lookupDiscMgr,            // DiscoveryManagement - default
          null);                    // LeaseRenewalManager - default

        } else {                    // Rejoin with (recovered) state information
          joiner = new JoinManager(
          this,                     // service object
          null,                     // service attributes - none at this time
          serviceID,                // Service ID - already have an ID
          lookupDiscMgr,            // DiscoveryManagement - default
          null);                    // LeaseRenewalManager - default
        }
    }

    // implementation of the Agent interface
    public String talk() {
        return "P2P is very cool";
    }
//
//
// The main method does not differ significantly from prior examples
// however, you no longer need to bind to the RMIregistry because you
// now will use the LUS (ServiceRegistrar) to return a reference to the
// remote object.
//
//
    public static void main(String[] args) {
    // set the security manager
```

LISTING 14.4 continued

```
        if (System.getSecurityManager() == null) {
            System.setSecurityManager(new RMISecurityManager());
        }
        try {
            Agent agent = new JiniAgentService();
            System.out.println("JiniAgentService bound");
            Thread.currentThread().join();
        } catch (Exception e) {
            System.err.println("JiniAgentService exception:
➥" +  e.getMessage());
            e.printStackTrace();
        }
    }
    // Utility method for setting the service's ID obtained from
    // the lookup registration process.
    private void setServiceID(ServiceID id) {
        serviceID = id;
    }
//
//
// The SrvcIDListener inner class handles the callback of the service ID
// assignment from the JoinManager.
//
private class SrvcIDListener implements ServiceIDListener
    {

        public SrvcIDListener() {
            super();
        }
        /**
        * The JoinManager will invoke this method when it receives a
        * valid ServiceID from a LUS.
        */
          public void serviceIDNotify(ServiceID id) {
            // Set the ID
            setServiceID(id);
            System.out.println("Received service id");
        }
    }
}
```

There are a number of important aspects of being a Jini service that have been omitted. The preceding service only demonstrates the core requirements to registration. For example, we did not persist the service ID, so restarts of the service would pass a listener, and thus the LUS would generate a new unique ID instead of reusing the existing ID. Any client who had saved the original ID would not be able to find the service again.

A Simple Jini-P2P Client

Let's now build a simple client to test the service, shown in Listing 14.5.

LISTING 14.5 JiniUserAgent Class

```java
import java.rmi.*;

import java.io.IOException;
import java.util.Vector;

// Jini classes used to find and bind to a Jini service
import net.jini.core.lookup.ServiceItem;
import net.jini.core.lookup.ServiceTemplate;
import net.jini.discovery.DiscoveryEvent;
import net.jini.discovery.DiscoveryListener;
import net.jini.discovery.DiscoveryManagement;
import net.jini.discovery.LookupDiscovery;
import net.jini.core.lookup.ServiceMatches;
import net.jini.core.lookup.ServiceRegistrar;

public class JiniUserAgent  {

    public JiniUserAgent() {}

    public static void main(String args[]) {
        // set security manager if not set
        if (System.getSecurityManager() == null) {
            System.setSecurityManager(new RMISecurityManager());
        }
        try {
            JiniUserAgent userAgent = new JiniUserAgent();

            // create a service template to represent the required service
            ServiceTemplate template;

            // We pass a class that identifies an interface rather than a name
            Class[] types = {  Class.forName("Agent")  };

            // We do not constrain our service search other than interface type
            // null indicates match anything on service ID and attributes
            template = new ServiceTemplate(null, types, null);

            // call the lookup passing our template
            Agent agent = (Agent)userAgent.lookup(template);

            // Now call the JiniAgentService
            System.out.println(agent.talk());

        } catch (Exception e) {
```

LISTING 14.5   continued

```java
                System.err.println("Agent exception: " +
                    e.getMessage());
                    e.printStackTrace();
        }
    }
    // method to find a service given a service template
    private Object lookup(ServiceTemplate template) throws IOException
    {
        // Your internal class ServiceListener does the actual work
        ServiceListener serviceListener = new ServiceListener(template);
        return serviceListener.lookup();
    }
}

private class ServiceListener implements DiscoveryListener {

    // Our discovery management support
    private DiscoveryManagement mgt;

    // A vector to hold all services discovered
    private Vector services = new Vector();

    // A template used to indicate the service requested by the client
    private ServiceTemplate template;

    public ServiceListener(ServiceTemplate template) throws IOException  {
        super();
        this.template = template;

        // sequence to ensure all lookups are heard
        mgt = new LookupDiscovery(LookupDiscovery.NO_GROUPS);

        // we implement the listener interface
        mgt.addDiscoveryListener(this);

        // now set all groups
        ((LookupDiscovery)mgt).setGroups(LookupDiscovery.ALL_GROUPS);
    }

    // client will wait until matching service is discovered
    public synchronized Object lookup() {
        while(services.size() == 0) {
            try {
                wait();
            } catch (InterruptedException ex) {}
        }
         // just return the first match found
          return ((ServiceItem)services.elementAt(0)).service;
    }
```

LISTING 14.5 continued

```
    public synchronized void discovered(DiscoveryEvent de) {
        System.out.println("Discovered LUS: ");
        ServiceRegistrar[] registrars = de.getRegistrars();
        for(int i=0; i < registrars.length; i++) {
            try {
                System.out.println("URL:     " + registrars[i].getLocator().
➥toString());
                System.out.println("ID:      " + registrars[i].getServiceID());
                String groups[] = registrars[i].getGroups();
                // simply display the first group returned
                System.out.println("GROUPS: " + groups[0]);
                ServiceMatches sm = registrars[i].lookup(template,
➥Integer.MAX_VALUE);
                System.out.println("Matching services found ———: " +
➥sm.totalMatches);
                System.out.println("");
                for(int j=0; j < sm.items.length; j++) {
                    // Process each ServiceItem
                    if(sm.items[j].service != null) {
                        services.addElement(sm.items[j]);
                    } else {
                        System.out.println("Service item null" +
➥sm.items[j].service);
                    }
                }
                // notify the client a matching service has been found
                System.out.println("Notifying...");
                notifyAll();
            } catch(Exception e) { e.printStackTrace(); }
        }
    }

    // we ignore discarded LUS objects in this example
    public void discarded(DiscoveryEvent de) {}

}
```

You create a ServiceTemplate to indicate the service you want the discovery process to find (Agent). A ServiceTemplate is used to match service items that are registered in the LUS. The template contains the service ID (if known), an array of java.lang.Class objects of supported interfaces, and the attributes to limit the returned services. Null values are supplied for the service ID and attribute parameters, which instructs the LUS to match anything. You ask for any object that implements the Agent interface by setting the java.lang.Class array parameter to the Agent class name.

The `ServiceListener` implements the `DiscoveryListener` interface. The internal class `ServiceListener` is a helper class for the client, and it is passed the template that the client wants to find.

The `DiscoveryListener` interface defines two methods, `discovered` and `discarded`:

```
public interface DiscoveryListener extends java.util.EventListener
    // Called when one or more LUS registrars has been discarded.
    void discarded(DiscoveryEvent e);
    // Called when one or more LUS registrars has been
    // discovered.
    void discovered(DiscoveryEvent e);
}
```

The `discovered` method receives a `DiscoveryEvent`, which is passed by the `LookupDiscovery` object when it discovers one or more LUSs. The `getRegistrars` method of the `DiscoveryEvent` returns an array containing the `ServiceRegistrar` for each newly discovered LUS.

The `lookup` method of the `ServiceRegistrar` is used to return an array of `ServiceMatches` objects. The service template containing the service `Agent` interface is used as a parameter to request only services implementing the `Agent` interface be returned.

The `ServiceMatches` object returned by the LUS will contain an array of `ServiceItem` objects and a count of the number returned. The `ServiceItem` is added to the `Vector` of services, which in this simple example is used to trigger the notification to the suspended client that an object implementing the `Agent` interface has been found.

Jini Services

To help simplify the process of developing clients and services for the Jini environment, several helper services have been defined. The Jini specifications define two categories of helper entities: helper utilities and helper services. These utilities and services provide a basis for building applications that demonstrate desirable behavior in a Jini community.

Helper utilities are programming components that aid in the construction of Jini services and clients. They help to reduce the coding effort required. They are not services that register with a lookup service, but rather aid in the process of being a good Jini citizen. Helper utilities include the following:

- `LookupDiscovery`
- `LeaseRenewalManager`

- JoinManager
- ServiceDiscoveryManager

A helper service, on the other hand, is a Jini service. Helper services register with lookup services and can be invoked on remote hosts. A helper service consists of an interface or set of interfaces and an associated implementation encapsulating behavior that is either required or highly desirable in services that adhere to the Jini technology programming model. Helper services include the following:

- Lookup Discovery Service
- Lease Renewal Service
- Event Mailbox Service

Lookup Discovery Service

The Lookup Discovery Service (LDS) is a helper service that uses the Jini discovery protocols to find LUSs in which an entity (a client or service) has expressed interest, and to notify the entity when a previously unavailable LUS becomes available. An activatable service that deactivates might want to use the LDS to perform discovery duties on its behalf.

Lease Renewal Service

The Jini framework supports the notion of leasing. In a Jini environment, resources like service references are not simply created and deleted. They must be managed and maintained. You must periodically inform the service that has granted you access to a resource that you are still using that resource and want to continue using that resource. If you fail to renew the lease on a leased resource, the Jini framework or specific service instance will release the resource from your control. The Lease Renewal Service (LRS) is a helper service that can be employed by both Jini clients and services to perform all lease renewal duties on their behalf.

Event Mailbox Service

The Event Mailbox Service (EMS) is a helper service that can be used by entities to store event notifications on their behalf. This permits a service to deactivate and not miss events of interest while deactivated. The service in effect has more control over when and where events are delivered. Services register with the event mailbox service using the `MailboxRegistration` interface. The using entity retrieves a `RemoteEventListener` object from the EMS and uses this reference in any method call that requires a remote listener. The using entity can then disconnect from the network and not worry about losing events. The events will be directed and stored by the mailbox listener. The using entity can then activate at some point and request delivery of the stored events. You might think of this as implementing store-and-forward semantics for distributed event processing.

The general theme in the usage patterns mentioned previously is support for disconnected entities, and entities or environments where computational conservation is of paramount importance.

Enabling P2P Transactions

As P2P gains popularity in commercial applications, support for transactions will become critical. Jini defines a two-phase, commit-based interface to support the notion of distributed transactions.

The Transaction Service

Jini uses the traditional two-phase commit transaction protocol. Transaction monitors specialize in managing transactions from clients across one or more servers. When a transaction ends, the TP monitor ensures that all systems involved in the transaction are left in a consistent state. The classic example of the bank credit transaction followed by the bank debit transaction is often cited to demonstrate the need for transactional integrity.

Transaction monitors are able to cross system boundaries to manage the transaction process. This includes starting server processes, routing and monitoring their execution, and balancing their workloads. In addition, TP monitors are used to guarantee the *ACID properties* to all programs that run under its control:

- Atomicity—All the operations grouped under a transaction occur or none of them do.
- Consistency—The completion of a transaction must leave the system in a consistent state. If the transaction cannot achieve stable end-state, it must return the system to its initial state.
- Isolation—Transactions should not be affected by other transactions that execute concurrently. Participants in a transaction should see only intermediate states resulting from the operations of their own transaction, not the intermediate states of other transactions.
- Durability—The results of a transaction should be as persistent as the entity on which the transaction commits.

TP monitors often use thread pools to assign work to available threads that act as a mechanism to balance and control the load on any one-server process. The TP monitor is able to funnel work to shared server processes and act as a gatekeeper for the OS. This load-balancing function is a primary benefit to systems that must scale to support high transaction volumes. TP monitors are able to establish priorities for tasks, and thus prioritize transactions within the system.

Fundamentally, the TP monitor assures the ACID properties while enabling high throughput. This alleviates much of the work application programmers would normally have to be concerned with, such as network failures, concurrency, load balancing, and the synchronization of resources across multiple nodes.

Implementers of the Jini transaction service are free to develop various levels of transactional assurance. In other words, the degree to which a Jini transaction service ensures the ACID properties of transactions is implementation-dependent. Some implementations might go to great lengths to ensure recovery from failures, whereas others might simply rollback transactions in light of any failure, and attempt to optimize other aspects of distribution such as performance, or minimize the resources required to support distributed transactions. Jini provides a lightweight reference implementation of the transaction service named `mahalo`.

Enabling P2P Communication (JavaSpaces)

One of the most important services for Jini-P2P is the JavaSpaces service.

JavaSpaces is a Jini service that supports distributed persistence and the design of distributed algorithms. JavaSpaces is closely tied to the Jini architecture. JavaSpaces was heavily influenced by the concept of the tuple space, first described in 1982 in a programming language called Linda that was developed at Yale University. Linda was designed as a coordination language for ensemble (distributed and parallel) computing. Like Linda, JavaSpaces is designed to significantly ease the development of distributed and parallel processing systems.

JavaSpaces, however, extends this model of communication by defining the data as objects. So, rather than simply passing data between processes, you are able to pass objects, and thus behavior. JavaSpaces uses RMI and object serialization from the Java programming language to provide these features. In addition, JavaSpaces leverages the Jini infrastructure that includes distributed events, leasing, and lightweight transactions.

A JavaSpaces server is used to mediate the communications between networked systems. It provides much of the common functionality required for distributed systems, which simplifies the development task, particularly when you can model your task as a flow of objects between systems distributed over a network.

With JavaSpaces, distributed processes communicate by reading and writing entries into space. A space is defined by JavaSpaces as a shared, network-accessible repository for objects. This shared repository can save objects written to a space beyond the lifetime of the process that created them. Spaces provide reliable storage for objects and support leases. The JavaSpace API provides an event notification mechanism, which enables processes to register for notification when a specific object is written to space.

Objects in a space are located via *associative lookup,* as opposed to more traditional keys or identifiers. More is said about associative lookup when entries are discussed in the next chapter. When you read or take an object from a space, a local copy of the object is created. As with any other local object, you can modify its public fields and invoke its methods. In addition, JavaSpaces supports transactions for single operations, such as writing an object to a single space, as well as multiple operations over one or more spaces.

So, how does JavaSpaces differ from traditional message-oriented middleware or traditional database technology?

Message Oriented Middleware (MOM)

MOM permits general message exchange using message queues. MOM has become a popular approach to integrating inter- and intra-enterprise applications. The message queuing facility enables clients and servers to communicate indirectly, which provides several advantages:

- Applications are provided a higher level of abstraction when dealing with network communication. Destinations, or queues, can have logical names and be built up hierarchically.

- Clients and servers do not have to be running at the same time to carry on a conversation. Messaging products can therefore help support the disconnected client.

- Traffic can be distributed or the load balanced across multiple queues and multiple systems. This provides a scalable solution to high-throughput requirements.

- Messaging queues are versatile. They enable you to define communication models that support one-to-one or one-to-many patterns of message transfer.

- MOM products offer various levels of message assurance, from best effort to guaranteed delivery. This is provided through persistent queues that are capable of storing messages until acknowledged.

Messaging products should continue to gain in popularity because of their broad range of capabilities in application communication. However, these products are more prevalent within an enterprise rather than between enterprises because of the proprietary protocols that often need to be supported. Popular commercial products include IBM's MQSeries, Microsoft's MSMQ, and BEA's MessageQ.

JavaSpaces Versus MOM

Although JavaSpaces also provides loose coupling for distributed processes and MOM models of communication, there are a number of important differences:

- MOM supports messages; JavaSpaces supports objects. Most messaging products support the exchange of data. JavaSpaces supports the exchange of objects, and therefore active processes or behavior.

- MOM products often involve extensive administrative overhead. JavaSpaces are simple to set up and administer.

- Messaging products have proprietary interfaces, which means that two different messaging products might not be able to communicate without some gateway or bridging technology.

- JavaSpaces supports persistent messaging. A JavaSpaces message is an object in its own right, and can persist and manage its lifecycle independent of the originating process.

- JavaSpaces supports transactions and leases inherently. The concept of leases has no counterpart in MOM products.

SQL Middleware

Unfortunately, while SQL has been standardized for years, vendor extensions and variations still make access across products a challenge. Many middleware products exist to provide access to multiple databases and transform SQL calls to a native database server's access language.

Typically, SQL middleware must deal with vendor-proprietary APIs across Windows, Linux, Macintosh, and Unix clients. In conjunction with the API is a unique driver that handles runtime calls and formats SQL messages. The driver typically provides a proprietary transport exchange format with the server. Therefore, the format and protocols defined to access the database are vendor-defined.

Most vendors support multiple protocol stacks that might include a common transport interface, such as sockets or named pipes. Even providing a common SQL interface still requires management of multiple vendor drivers. In addition, although a common API exists, multiple formats and protocols are still supported under the covers. A number of solutions, such as ODBC and JDBC, have emerged, but often run into performance and scalability issues in high-access scenarios. Gateway protocol converters are often used, such as Remote Data Access (RDA), and IBM's Distributed Relational Data Access (DRDA).

14

JINI AND
JAVASPACES

JavaSpaces Versus Traditional Database Technology

JavaSpaces is not a database, although it does have database characteristics. For instance, the capability to persist objects would lead to comparing it to object database technology. However, you will find that the API to JavaSpaces is so simple that it could not possibly cover all the functions and features normally associated with databases.

The differences include the following:

- Objects are retrieved with templates, not a specifically designed query language such as SQL or OQL.
- No transparent access provided to objects: Rather than blurring the distinction between in-memory and storage access of objects, JavaSpaces works on serialized copies of entries.
- A general lack of database tools and utilities: JavaSpaces provides a simple API and defines a minimal and lightweight persistence engine.

JavaSpaces' strength lies in its capability to simplify the programming required to coordinate distributed communication and parallel processing.

Although comparisons to database technology and message-oriented middleware are valid, JavaSpaces still provides significant differences. These differences point to a new environment supporting networked-applications as the norm, rather than the exception.

Summary

Jini services are manifested as Java objects that expose an interface conforming to the Jini specification. This is in contrast to JXTA and other P2P protocols that maintain programming language-neutrality.

Jini services advertise their operations by registering an object with a Jini-compliant lookup service. Service registration is at the core of building the Jini network community.

There are three infrastructure services that are required somewhere on your Jini network. They are as follows:

- An HTTP server that supports dynamic downloading of code
- The Remote Method Invocation daemon (`rmid`) that provides the distributed remote object lookup and activation mechanism
- The Jini Lookup Service that provides the service registry and the service lookup capabilities on the Jini network

The Sun-supplied Jini services rely heavily on the Remote Method Invocation (RMI) framework. Understanding RMI is critical to understanding Jini. RMI provides P2P systems with the capability to exchange objects, not just messages or XML.

The discovery and join protocols are protocols that enable services to discover, become part of, and advertise supplied services to other members of the Jini community.

The discovery protocol requires support for multicast or restricted-scope broadcast (such as UDP), along with support for reliable unicast delivery in the transport layer (such as TCP). The discovery protocol makes use of the Java platform's object serialization capabilities to exchange information in a platform-independent manner.

The join protocol makes use of the discovery protocol to provide a standard sequence of steps that services should perform when they are starting up and registering themselves with a LUS. The join protocol is used to register a service and advertise its functionality in all lookup services of interest.

To help simplify the process of developing clients and services for the Jini environment, several helper services have been defined. The Jini specifications define two categories of helper entities: helper utilities and helper services. These utilities and services provide a basis for building applications that demonstrate desirable behavior in a Jini community.

One of the most important services for Jini-P2P is the JavaSpaces service. JavaSpaces is a Jini service that supports distributed persistence and the design of distributed algorithms. We will look at this service in more detail in the next chapter.

14

**JINI AND
JAVASPACES**

P2P Jini and JavaSpaces

Jini and JavaSpaces can provide support for a number of services that are critical to building robust P2P systems. They include the following:

- Service discovery
- Distributed communication
- Transactions
- Self-healing networks
- P2P software agents

As mentioned in Chapter 14, "Jini and JavaSpaces," service discovery and service federation is fundamental to a Jini community. In addition, JavaSpaces supports distributed persistence and the design of distributed algorithms. JavaSpaces can provide a platform for rendezvous points in a P2P network. It can provide a point in the network where cooperating processes can exchange information in the form of objects.

Edge Services

Peer-to-peer networks make use of resources at the edge of the Internet. Peering organizes a variable-sized pool of distributed resources. P2P systems are forcing processing, storage, and intelligence responsibilities to edge devices. Devices on the edge of the network require new levels of management.

The new network reality is that devices, computers, automobiles, and even appliances are forming a new "infosphere" that will interconnect us all, as seen in Figure 15.1. Traditional network management and administration will not keep pace with this change. Complementary technologies such as Jini can build more intelligent services, reduce administration, manage connectivity complexity, and provide a unifying framework for service delivery.

Interconnected devices have already changed our communication and information exchange capabilities. The market for network-connected devices continues to grow. In fewer than five years we have witnessed the Internet connecting the world, cell phones connecting individuals, and devices connecting everything in between. P2P devices and services should continue to proliferate.

Distributed Communication

JavaSpaces provides a compelling model for distributed P2P communication between peers. The model can be implemented by traditional applications, or by new service-oriented architectures. P2P edge services (services implemented on edge devices) can use JavaSpaces as a platform for distributed communication, coordination, and rendezvous.

FIGURE 15.1

The new network reality is an "infosphere" of pervasive computing.

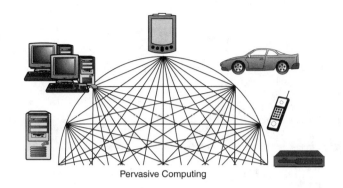

Pervasive Computing

In Chapter 14 we introduced entries to build templates to define and find services in a Jini network. Recall that when you register a service, you can associate attributes with the service, such as address or service-specific information. These attributes were defined by the net.jini.core.entry.Entry interface:

```
package net.jini.core.entry;
public interface Entry extends java.io.Serializable {}
```

The net.jini.core.entry.Entry interface is also implemented by objects that are used in JavaSpaces. You can implement this interface directly, or use the AbstractEntry class that implements this interface and provides some additional JavaSpaces-related methods.

There are a number of rules associated with the use of Entry objects:

- They must have a default no-argument constructor, which assists in object serialization.

- They should contain only public instance variables, which are required for associative lookups.

- All instance variables must be serializable; no primitive types are written or read from space.

In addition, each public field is serialized separately. So, two fields referencing the same object prior to serialization will reference two separate but equal objects after being written to space.

AbstractEntry is a basic implementation of the Entry interface. This class is often used as the base class for defining entries because it adheres to the Entry specification. For instance, it implements the proper semantics for equality and comparisons.

Listing 15.1 demonstrates the use of the AbstractEntry class as a base class for a message used in a simple P2P chat application.

LISTING 15.1   Message Class

```java
import net.jini.entry.AbstractEntry;

public class Message extends AbstractEntry {

    public String to;
    public String from;
    public String text;

    public Message()
    {
        this(null,null,null);
    }

    public Message(String to, String from, String text) {
        super();
        this.to = to;
        this.from = from;
        this.text = text;
    }
}
```

The Message class extends AbstractEntry and has a no-argument constructor. The text of the message and the From/To addresses are contained in public fields that are serializable, so all the requirements of the Entry specification have been met.

Retrieving entries from JavaSpaces requires a template of the type or subtype of the entry to be retrieved. Entries are compared, public field by public field, based on the template. If two fields have the same value, they are considered equal. When you want to retrieve an Entry from JavaSpaces, you need to create a template for the system to compare for equality. For example:

```java
Message template = new Message("tjones", "rflenner", null);
```

The preceding fragment constructs a Message template that can be used to match and return any Message that has been addressed to "tjones" from "rflenner".

The following template can be used to match and return any message addressed to "tjones":

```java
Message template = new Message("tjones", null. null);
```

Finally, a template with all null values will match any entry of the same type:

```java
Message template = new Message();
```

The null value acts as a wildcard in matching fields in an Entry. The null value will therefore match any and all values. There are a couple of implications as a result of this idiom.

First, you cannot use `null` to match on an uninitialized value. You need to introduce another field, such as a `Boolean`, to perform such a comparison for each field in your `Entry` definition. This is because, as mentioned, `null` matches on anything. In addition, matching on `null` (or for that matter, any field) makes no guarantee on which object will be returned as a result of the match.

Suppose you have 10 messages that have been addressed to `"tjones"` in JavaSpaces. If you fetch the message 10 different times using just the `"tjones"` argument, you might get

- The same message object returned 10 times
- A different message object returned each time
- Some combination of repetitive and unique message objects

JavaSpaces makes no guarantee on which object will be returned. This has enormous implications on the design of your entries and the applicability of JavaSpaces as a solution.

If you normally deal with traditional database technologies, this requirement might catch you off guard the first time you find yourself looking for a collection or set of objects with a specific value. In the relational world, this type of programming is done all the time. For example, you might have the statement "Bring me back all rows where column x equals y." The set returned permits you to iterate through each record. Converting this table/data structure to an `Entry` will almost always fail.

Entries are used when exact-match lookup semantics are useful. In other words, you supply the value you are looking for in the template to the lookup function. However, this should not be construed to imply the statement "I need to know the entire value of the entry in order to find the one that matches." The wildcard value (`null`) provides the "I don't care" or "any will do" semantics for a specific field.

JavaSpaces also provides us with the powerful capability to match on subtypes. All fields added by a subtype are considered to be wildcards. This enables a template to match the entries of any of its subtypes. This capability, combined with dynamic downloading of code with RMI, provides a natural solution to the evolution of service functionality. New class structures can be defined without affecting current applications using old interface semantics, or new functionality can be dynamically invoked by downloading new class definitions on demand.

The Simple JavaSpaces API

JavaSpaces exposes a powerful but simple API supporting distributed communication. You can easily create a message to be used in an instant messaging-style application that uses JavaSpaces as a platform for persistent communication:

```
// Gain access to an instance of JavaSpace
JavaSpace space = getSpace();

// Create an entry
Message entry = new Message();

// initialize the public fields

entry.to = "tjones";
entry.from = "rflenner";
entry.text = "P2P messaging is now available using JavaSpaces";

// write the entry to space and allow it to exist for 1 hour
space.write(entry, null, 60 * 60* 1000);
```

The net.jini.space package provides the service interface and related classes for the Sun/Jini outrigger implementation.

The JavaSpace interface is defined as shown in Listing 15.2.

LISTING 15.2 JavaSpace Interface

```
package net.jini.space;

import java.rmi.*;
import net.jini.core.event.*;
import net.jini.core.transaction.*;
import net.jini.core.lease.*;

public interface JavaSpace {

    public final long NO_WAIT = 0; // don't wait at all

    Lease write(Entry e, Transaction txn, long lease)
        throws RemoteException, TransactionException;

    Entry read(Entry tmpl, Transaction txn, long timeout)
        throws TransactionException, UnusableEntryException,
            RemoteException, InterruptedException;

    Entry readIfExists(Entry tmpl, Transaction txn,
                        long timeout)
        throws TransactionException, UnusableEntryException,
            RemoteException, InterruptedException;

    Entry take(Entry tmpl, Transaction txn, long timeout)
        throws TransactionException, UnusableEntryException,
            RemoteException, InterruptedException;
```

LISTING 15.2 continued

```
    Entry takeIfExists(Entry tmpl, Transaction txn,
                        long timeout)
        throws TransactionException, UnusableEntryException,
            RemoteException, InterruptedException;

    EventRegistration notify(Entry tmpl, Transaction txn,
            RemoteEventListener listener, long lease,
            MarshalledObject handback)
        throws RemoteException, TransactionException;

    Entry snapshot(Entry e) throws RemoteException;
}
```

JavaSpaces supports distributed transactions. The `Transaction` and `TransactionException` types are imported from `net.jini.core.transaction`. You can exclude transaction support from a method invocation by setting the `Transaction` parameter to `null`. This implies that there is no transaction object managing the operation.

JavaSpaces also supports the concept of leases. The `Lease` type is imported from the `net.jini.core.lease package`. The `Lease` parameter assists with the effective resource management of JavaSpaces entries. JavaSpaces implementations will typically export a proxy object that communicates with the remote `JavaSpace` interface. The details of each `JavaSpace` method are given in the sections that follow.

write

A `write` statement copies an `Entry` object to a JavaSpaces service. It uses a lease parameter to indicate to JavaSpaces the length of time desired to store the entry:

```
long lease_requested = 60 * 60 * 1000;
Lease lease = space.write(template, null, lease_requested);
```

Even if you use the same object in each `write` request, JavaSpaces will still store a new entry. An update to an existing entry is accomplished through a combination of `take` (explained a little later in this chapter) and `write` operations.

Each `write` invocation returns a `Lease` object. The long parameter on the `write` operation indicates your desired lease time on the entry being placed in the space. The `Lease` object returned contains what the space was willing to grant—they might not be the same value. The space might be unable to commit to the duration you requested. Perhaps resources are not available to satisfy the length of the request. When the lease expires, the entry is removed from the space. The following code fragment demonstrates how to determine whether the lease granted is different from the lease requested:

15

```
long expires = lease.getExpiration();
if(expires < lease_requested) {
    // code to handle case where lease is less than requested
}
```

If a RemoteException is thrown, the write request might or might not have been successful. If any other exception is thrown, the entry was not written into the space.

Writing an entry into a space can also generate notifications to registered objects (notify will be discussed a little later).

read and readIfExists

The two forms of the read request, read and readIfExists, will search the JavaSpaces service for an entry that matches the template provided as an Entry:

```
static long TIMEOUT_VALUE = 10000L;
Message template = new Message();
template.to = "tjones";
Message msgEntry = (Message)space.read(template, null, TIMEOUT_VALUE);

Message template = new Message();
template.from = "rflenner";
Message msgEntry = (Message)space.readIfExists(template, null, TIMEOUT_VALUE);
```

If the template matches an entry involved in a transaction, the timeout value is used to indicate how long the invoking process will wait for the transaction to commit. If the transaction has not committed prior to the timeout value, the space will return a null value. As described in the Jini specification (http://wwws.sun.com/software/jini/specs/jini1.1html/js-spec.html):

> A read request acts like a readIfExists, except that it will wait until a matching entry is found or until transactions commit, whichever is longer, up to the timeout period.
>
> In both read methods, a timeout of NO_WAIT means to return immediately, with no waiting, which is equivalent to using a zero timeout.

take and takeIfExists

The take and the takeIfExists requests perform exactly like the corresponding read and readIfExists requests, except that the matching entry is removed from the space. If a take or takeIfExists request returns a non-null value, the entry has been removed from the space.

notify

A notify request registers for notification when a matching entry is written to a JavaSpace. Matching is done as it is for the read operation.

When you invoke `notify`, you provide a `RemoteEventListener`, which is notified when a matching entry is written. You also supply a desired lease time for the space to keep the registration active. The following sample `Subscriber` class extends `RemoteEventListener`, and uses the `UnicastRemoteObject.exportObject` function to export itself to the RMI runtime. This class receives notification any time an object is written to JavaSpaces that matches the template used for registration:

```
import java.io.*;
import java.rmi.*;
import java.rmi.server.*;
import net.jini.core.event.*;

public class Subscriber implements net.jini.core.event.RemoteEventListener {

    public Subscriber() throws RemoteException {
       UnicastRemoteObject.exportObject(this);
    }

    public synchronized void notify(RemoteEvent event)
    {
      try {

          System.out.println("Notification of matching entry");
          MarshalledObject marshalledObject = event.getRegistrationObject();
          Object object = marshalledObject.get();

          // application specific code inserted here

    } catch (Exception e) { e.printStackTrace(); }
}
```

When an object is written that matches the template supplied, the listener's `notify` method is invoked with a `RemoteEvent` object. A `MarshalledObject` can be included in the registration, and is returned by JavaSpaces with the `RemoteEvent`. This enables you to pass application-specific context to JavaSpaces, which will return it intact. An `EventRegistration` is returned from the `notify` method. It is the caller's responsibility to ensure that the registration's lease is managed.

snapshot

The `snapshot` method optimizes the serialization process required when you repeatedly use the same template to `read` or `take` an entry from space. The JavaSpaces implementor can reduce the impact of repeated serialization by providing the `snapshot` method. Invoking `snapshot` with an `Entry` will return another `Entry` object that contains a snapshot of the original entry. Using the returned snapshot entry is equivalent to using the unmodified original entry in all operations on the same JavaSpaces service.

read, write, take, notify, and snapshot comprise the entire JavaSpace API—simple, but extremely powerful in developing distributed applications.

Distributed Data Structures

JavaSpaces is built using distributed data structures. Distributed data structures enable multiple processes to access and manipulate the content of a structure in parallel.

Distributed data structures require a different approach to data access and control. In a typical database system, processes are defined to act as barriers or locks at a level in the structure that inhibits concurrent access. This is done to ensure that the database remains in a consistent state, often referred to as supporting the ACID properties of atomicity, concurrency, isolation, and durability. Other programming techniques include defining manager objects that provide a barrier around data, and files that ensure data is accessed serially.

Distributed data structures offer a number of advantages to traditional database processing by enabling multiple processes to access and change information concurrently. Distributed data structures

- Scale to large, rapidly growing user populations
- Provide high availability over an unreliable network, even during partial failure
- Maintain user data consistency across a large user base
- Improve or ease operational management of large data structures

In the book *JavaSpaces Principles, Patterns, and Practice* (Addison Wesley), a significant amount of detail is provided on building and using distributed data structures in JavaSpaces. The book classifies distributed data structures according to common usage patterns, such as shared variables, ordered structures, and distributed arrays.

Shared Variables

A shared variable enables multiple processes to change the shared value in an atomic manner. JavaSpaces provides an easy approach to support such changes. For instance, the following entry definition represents an index into a data structure:

```java
public class Index implements AbstractEntry {
    public Integer value;
    public String name;
    public Index() {}

    public increment() {
        value = new Integer(value.intValue()+1);
    }
}
```

```
    public decrement() {
        value = new Integer(value.intValue()-1);
    }

}
```

The following code fragment takes the index entry and increments it by using the `take` and `write` methods of the JavaSpace API:

```
Index template = new Index();
Index index = (Index)space.take(template, null, Long.MAX_VALUE);
index.increment();
space.write(index, null, Lease.FOREVER);
```

The `take` method removes the entry from space. Any process trying to read the entry will be blocked until the entry is returned with the `write` method. Therefore, serialization of updates across distributed processes is guaranteed. You can use the index entry to iterate through ordered structures, such as distributed arrays (discussed in the following section). By following the `take` method, and then the `write` protocol for updating the structure, the ACID properties for data reliability are assured. This is all under the control of JavaSpaces, and simplifies the development task for the programmer.

Ordered Structures

Ordered structures are collections that have an index or position field defined in each entry. If you are defining a process that might need to iterate through the entries of a space or requires sequencing, ordered structures provide one solution.

Distributed Arrays

Distributed arrays are the most popular example of an ordered structure. They are built from space entries that include an index and name reference.

The distributed array enables you to access individual elements within the array by going directly to an element via the position index. No locking is required at a start or root element. This permits and promotes concurrent access, and thus reduces wait and blocking issues, as illustrated in Figure 15.2.

In addition to the position field, you need to define a name field. The name field provides a mechanism to reuse the index entry across multiple data structures, as opposed to subtyping the index entry for each structure. However, either approach is valid. The naming approach reduces the amount of object types that result in the space.

FIGURE 15.2

Traditional data-bases use barriers to restrict concurrent access. Distributed data structures promote concurrent access.

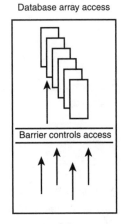

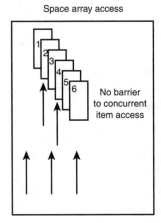

Unordered Structures

Unordered structures, illustrated in Figure 15.3, are used when sequence or order is not important. For instance, workflow applications are often based on a `Task` entry that is written to space. Worker processes do not care which `Task` they take from space, as they can operate or use any task that they retrieve. The idea is that as the number of tasks grows, so can the number of worker processes that take and process task objects. The system can expand and contract based on demand. Workers will often write a `Result` object to space on completion, which is read or taken by a `Boss` or `TaskManager` object. The manager is responsible for controlling or aggregating the results from many tasks.

FIGURE 15.3

An unordered structure is used when sequence is not important. In effect, the structure implements "any object will do" semantics.

Unordered Structure

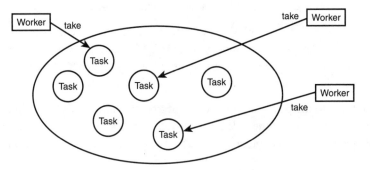

Bags

Unordered structures are referred to as *bags* because you can throw any type of object into them without concern for the sequencing of the structure.

Bags are created by defining an entry class and writing as many instances of that entry into the space as you want.

Persistent Communication Channels

JavaSpaces' strength lies in its capability to simplify the programming required to coordinate distributed communication and parallel processing.

Developing applications with JavaSpaces requires the following:

- Experience with synchronization techniques in distributed processing
- Experience defining data structures supporting loosely coupled communication

Fortunately, JavaSpaces minimizes the learning curve required.

Synchronization Techniques

The complexity of synchronization is radically reduced using the JavaSpace API. As mentioned, `read`, `write`, and `take` operations can be performed in parallel. However, there is no explicit update operation. Processes must `take`, (remove an entry from space) and then modify and `write` the entry back to space. This technique enforces coordinated access to entries. In addition, transaction support provides additional assurances that distributed updates are performed in a consistent and atomic manner. The JavaSpace API gives you everything you need to build complex synchronization and object coordination patterns.

Loosely Coupled Communication

JavaSpaces provides a simple foundation for the exchange of information between loosely coupled processes. For example, by writing a message to a space, any process can read or take the message from that space.

Combined with the Jini discovery process, it is easy to recognize the power and flexibility of dynamically discovering a space and interfacing with it. Coupled with RMI, the options for exchanging data and objects become almost limitless.

Sun provides a reference implementation of the JavaSpace Service called `outrigger`. You can run `outrigger` as an activatable service or as a transient service—which version you use will depend on your requirements for persistence. In other words, will you require the service to survive restarts or system crashes? The transient space does not provide persistence across system restarts. If the system crashes or you need to restart the service, the information stored in the transient space will not be available.

The following script starts the `outrigger` persistent service (Note that you must change the set arguments to match your installation):

```
@echo off
set HTTP_ADDRESS=172.16.1.3:8080
set JINI_HOME=c:\files\jini1_2
set HTTP_HOME=c:\services\logs
set GROUPS=public
set SPACENAME=JavaSpaces

echo P2P Unleashed
echo — — — — — — — — — — — — — — — — — — —·
echo Jini install directory          %JINI_HOME%
echo Web server                      %HTTP_ADDRESS%
echo Default group                   %GROUPS%
echo Default SpaceName property      %SPACENAME%
echo — — — — — — — — — — — — — — — — — — —·
echo Starting the outrigger JavaSpaces service...

java -jar -Djava.security.policy=%JINI_HOME%\policy\policy.all
➥-Dcom.sun.jini.outrigger.spaceName=%SPACENAME% %JINI_HOME%\lib\
➥outrigger.jar http://%HTTP_ADDRESS%/outrigger-dl.jar %JINI_HOME%\
➥policy\policy.all%JWORK_HOME%\services\logs\js_log GROUPS
```

Notice the `-Dcom.sun.jini.outrigger.spaceName` property, which is used to name this instance of `outrigger`.

In order to start `outrigger`, your Jini environment will need the following:

- An HTTP server running with a public directory available for downloading files
- An RMI daemon (`rmid`) running to activate services
- An LUS (`reggie`) running to register and look up services
- The transaction service (`mahalo`) required for JavaSpace transaction support

The following script can be used to start the transaction service. Note that you will need the `mahalo-dl.jar`, `reggie-dl.jar`, and `outrigger-dl.jar` files available on your HTTP server path:

```
@echo off
set HTTP_ADDRESS=172.16.1.3:8080
set JINI_HOME=c:\files\jini1_2
set HTTP_HOME=c:\services\logs
set GROUPS=public

echo P2P Unleashed
echo — — — — — — — — — — — — — — — — — — —·
echo Jini install directory          %JINI_HOME%
echo Web server                      %HTTP_ADDRESS%
echo Default group                   %GROUPS%
echo — — — — — — — — — — — — — — — — — — —·
echo Starting the mahalo transaction service...
```

```
java -jar -Djava.security.policy=%JINI_HOME%\example\lookup\policy.all
➥-Dcom.sun.jini.mahalo.managerName=TransactionManager %JINI_HOME%\
➥lib\mahalo.jar http://%HTTP_ADDRESS%/mahalo-dl.jar %JINI_HOME%\
➥example\txn\policy.all %JWORK_HOME%\services\logs\txn_log %GROUPS%
```

After your environment is in place, subsequent startups only require you to start the
HTTP server for downloading code, and the RMI daemon for activating services.
`reggie`, `mahalo`, and `outrigger` are started as activatable services, and they will be
restarted by RMI automatically when `rmid` starts.

The process to access the JavaSpaces service is like accessing any other Jini service; you
perform the lookup process with an LUS that has the JavaSpace service registered. The
`SpaceAccessor` class, shown in Listing 15.3, can be used to access an instance of
JavaSpaces on your network.

LISTING 15.3   The SpaceAccessor Class

```java
import java.rmi.*;
import java.util.*;
import net.jini.space.JavaSpace;
import net.jini.core.entry.*;
import net.jini.core.lookup.*;
import net.jini.lookup.entry.*;
import net.jini.core.discovery.*;

/*
 *  The SpaceAccessor class is a utility class used to resolve the reference
 *  to the outrigger JavaSpace service
 */

public class SpaceAccessor {
    // host name running LUS and name of JavaSpace instance
    public synchronized static JavaSpace getSpace(String hostname, String name) {

        try {
            if (System.getSecurityManager() == null) {
                System.setSecurityManager(
                    new RMISecurityManager());
            }

            // unicast discovery
            LookupLocator lookup = new LookupLocator("jini://" + hostname);
            System.out.println("SpaceAccessor using locator: " + lookup);
            ServiceRegistrar registrar = lookup.getRegistrar();

            // create Name entry to match on
            Entry entries[] = { new Name(name) };

            // lookup the service in the LUS
```

LISTING 15.3   continued

```
        JavaSpace space = (JavaSpace)registrar.lookup(new
                                ServiceTemplate(null,null,entries));

        // return the proxy
        return space;
    } catch (Exception e) {
        System.err.println(e);
    }
      return null;
    }
}
```

To use this utility, you must know the location of the LUS that has the JavaSpaces instance running as referenced by the hostname parameter. The name argument refers to the `-Dcom.sun.jini.outrigger.spaceName=JavaSpaces` property that was used to launch JavaSpaces. In Chapter 19, "The P2P Dashboard," we will present a more dynamic approach to service discovery.

JavaSpaces Instant Messaging Example

In this example, you will build on the concept of a channel. A *channel* is an implementation of a distributed data structure that has an index or position field defined in each entry of the collection. This enables you to sequence the messages in the collection, and to iterate through the entries.

The `ChatMessage` class, shown in Listing 15.4, extends `Message` by providing two new fields: a channel name and a position. The name is used to uniquely identify the channel to a specific instance of JavaSpace. The position is used to indicate where in the channel sequence the message resides. The text field contains the actual message data.

LISTING 15.4   ChatMessage Class

```
import net.jini.entry.AbstractEntry;

/*
 * The Message class is used to create messages for a chat channel.
 */

public class ChatMessage extends Message {

    public String channel;
    public Integer position;

    public ChatMessage()    {}
```

LISTING 15.4 continued

```
    public ChatMessage(String channel, Integer position, String to,
➥String from, String text) {
        this.channel = channel;
        this.position = position;
        this.to = to;
        this.from = from;
        this.text = text;
    }
}
```

The combination of the channel name and the position uniquely identifies a chat message in space. In addition, because you sequentially increment the position for each message written to a channel, you can determine the number of messages in a channel by starting at the first message and incrementing the position with each read until a null is returned.

You also create a Tail entry, shown in Listing 15.5, to indicate the last entry in the channel. If you have worked with queues before, then the heads and tails technique to indicate the start and end of a queue structure should not be new. However, what might be new is having a named tail that equals the named queue (channel).

LISTING 15.5 Tail Class

```
import net.jini.entry.AbstractEntry;

public class Tail extends AbstractEntry {

    public String name;
    public Integer position;

    public Tail() {
        super();
        this.name = null;
        this.position = null;
    }

    public int increment() {
        position = new Integer(position.intValue() + 1);
        return position.intValue();
    }

    public int decrement() {
        position = new Integer(position.intValue() - 1);
        return position.intValue();
    }
}
```

The `ChatController` class, shown in Listing 15.6, uses `ChatMessage` and `Tail` entries to enable space chat. If a `Tail` entry for the designated channel does not exist, create a new channel.

LISTING 15.6 ChatController Class

```java
import java.awt.*;
import java.awt.event.*;
import java.util.*;
import javax.swing.*;
import net.jini.space.JavaSpace;
import net.jini.core.lease.*;
import org.jworkplace.*;

/**
 *  The ChatController class is used to create the ChatView and control the
 *  reading and writing of messages to the chat channel
 */

public class ChatController implements ActionListener {

    // The name of the channel
    private String channel = null;

    // name of user in chat session
    private String userName = null;

    // Simple Swing JPanel
    private ChatViewer viewer = null;

    // Thread to read new messages
    private ChannelListener cl = null;
    private volatile Thread listener;

    // Messages exist for 1 hour
    public long CHAT_TIME = 60 * 60 * 1000; // 1 hour

    private JavaSpace space;
    private JFrame frame;

    public ChatController(JFrame frame, JavaSpace space, String channel,
    ➥String user) {

            this.frame = frame;
            this.space = space;
            this.userName = user;
            this.channel = channel;
            viewer = new ChatViewer(this,channel);
```

LISTING 15.6   continued

```
        // start the channel listener thread
        cl = new ChannelListener();
        cl.start();

        // determine if there is already a session open
        if(!activeChannel())
          createChannel();
    }

// Does Tail entry exists for this channel?
synchronized boolean activeChannel() {
    Tail template = new Tail();
    template.name = channel;
    try {
        Tail tail = (Tail)space.readIfExists(template, null,
                            JavaSpace.NO_WAIT);
        if(tail == null) return false;
    } catch (Exception e) {}
    return true;
}
// if no active channel create and initialize new Tail
private void createChannel() {
        Tail tail = new Tail();
        tail.name = channel;
        showStatus("Creating channel "+ channel);
        tail.position = new Integer(0);
        try {
            Lease lease = space.write(tail, null, CHAT_TIME);
        } catch (Exception e) {
            e.printStackTrace();
            return;
        }
    }
}
```

When you press the Send button, an `ActionEvent` is triggered and delivered to the
`actionPerformed` method. The message is displayed in a `JTextArea` and appended to the
channel, meaning it is written to space:

```
// Action to display message and append to channel
public void actionPerformed(ActionEvent event) {
    Object object = event.getSource();
    if (object == viewer.chatControl) {
        String message = userName+ "> "+viewer.getMessage();
        String to = viewer.getToAddress();
        String from = viewer.getFromAddress();
        if (message.equals("")) {
            JOptionPane.showMessageDialog(frame, "Enter message");
            return;
```

```
      }
      viewer.setMessage("");
      append(channel, to, from, message);
    }
  }

    // append message to channel
    private void append(String channel, String to, String from, String msg) {
        // get the next available position
        Integer messageNum = getMessageNumber();
        // create a new message using the new position
        ChatMessage message = new ChatMessage(channel,
➥messageNum, to, from, msg);
        try {
            // write to space
            Lease lease = space.write(message, null, CHAT_TIME);
        } catch (Exception e) { e.printStackTrace();  return; }
    }
```

The getMessageNumber method determines whether a Tail entry exists. If a Tail entry exists, you take the Tail from space, increment the position, and write it back. While you have taken the Tail entry, no other process will be able to read the Tail. Here again, JavaSpaces provides an easy technique for serializing distributed processes.

If the Tail does not exist, create a new channel:

```
    // get the current tail and increment
    private Integer getMessageNumber() {
      try {
        Tail template = new Tail();
        template.name = channel;
        Tail tail = (Tail)space.take(template, null, 10 * 1000);
        // If no tail exists create a new channel
        if (tail == null) {
            createChannel();
            tail = (Tail) space.take(template, null, Long.MAX_VALUE);
        }
        // increment the tail position
        tail.increment();
        // write the tail to space
        Lease lease = space.write(tail, null, CHAT_TIME);
        // return the next position
        return tail.position;
      } catch (Exception e) {
          e.printStackTrace();
          return null;
        }
    }

    public JPanel getChatView() { return viewer; }
```

On a `WindowClosingEvent`, you interrupt and kill the channel listener thread:

```
// set the listener to null and interrupt the thread
public void windowClosing() {
    listener = null;
    cl.interrupt();
}
```

The ChannelListener thread is an inner class. It reads messages on startup that already exist in the channel if you are joining an active session:

```
// The channel listener
public class ChannelListener extends Thread  {
    int position = 1;
    String newline;

    public ChannelListener() {
        newline = System.getProperty("line.separator");
        // If joining an existing chat display chat history
        if(activeChannel()) {
            try {
                ChatMessage template = new ChatMessage();
                template.channel = channel;
                ChatMessage msg = template;
                // loop through all messages starting at 2
                while(msg != null) {
                    template.position = new Integer(position++);
                    msg = (ChatMessage)space.readIfExists(template, null,
                                            JavaSpace.NO_WAIT);
                    if(msg != null) {
                        viewer.append(msg.text + newline);
                    } else {
                        position—;
                    }
                }
            } catch (Exception e) { e.printStackTrace(); }
        }
    }
```

The `run` method simply blocks on `read` requests, incrementing the position after each read, then waits for the next message to arrive, or until it's interrupted:

```
// run until interrupted
public void run() {
    listener = Thread.currentThread();
    while(listener != null) {
        ChatMessage template = new ChatMessage();
        template.channel = channel;
        ChatMessage msg = null;
        // increment the current position
        template.position = new Integer(position++);
        try {
```

```
        // wait till message arrives
        msg = (ChatMessage)space.read(template, null, Long.MAX_VALUE);
        // display new message
        viewer.append(msg.text + newline);
      } catch (Exception e) { }
    }
  }
}
```

The ChatFrame class, shown in Listing 15.7, contains the main method that accepts the command-line arguments, resolves the JavaSpace reference using the SpaceAccessor utility, and creates the view.

LISTING 15.7 ChatFrame Class

```
import java.awt.*;
import java.awt.event.*;
import java.io.*;
import java.rmi.*;
import java.util.*;
import javax.swing.*;
import javax.swing.event.*;
import net.jini.space.JavaSpace;
import org.jworkplace.*;
import org.jworkplace.util.SpaceAccessor;

public class ChatFrame extends JFrame {

    public static void main(String[] args) {
        if(args.length < 4) {
            System.out.println("Usage [hostname] [spacename] [channel] [user]");
            System.exit(1);
        }
        ChatFrame frame = new ChatFrame(args[0], args[1], args[2], args[3]);
    }


    public ChatFrame(String hostname, String spacename, String channel,
                        String user)
    {
        super("JWorkPlace");
        JavaSpace space =  SpaceAccessor.getSpace(hostname, spacename);
        addWindowListener(new WindowEventHandler());
        getContentPane().setBackground(Color.black);
        getContentPane().add(new ChatController(this, space,
                                        channel,user).getChatView());
        setSize(480,640);
        setVisible(true);
    }
```

LISTING 15.7   continued

```
class WindowEventHandler extends WindowAdapter {
        public void windowClosing(WindowEvent evt) {
            System.exit(0);
        }
    }
}
```

Figure 15.4 depicts a chat channel with four active messages. The chat controller would append the next message using Position 5. Each participant (`ChannelListener`) in the chat is blocking on a read request using a template with Position 5. When the entry is written, each participant will read the entry and increment the template position number to block on Position 6. This approach to retrieving messages using blocking threads is called *fetching*. You could also use an approach that relies on notification, such as the `Subscriber` class that was introduced earlier in this chapter.

FIGURE 15.4

A distributed array structure can be used to implement a message channel. The channel is used to sequence messages and control access to message content.

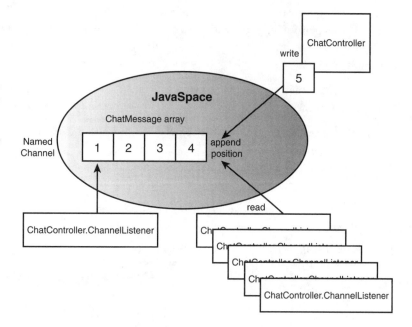

Rendezvous Points

JavaSpaces provides a shared memory that can be used to build rendezvous peers. A *rendezvous peer* is a special-purpose peer capable of supporting key services in P2P networks. These services might include routing information, identity information, or presence services. JavaSpace clusters can also be used to scale systems and provide fault resiliency.

Self-Healing Networks

As demonstrated, one of the concepts introduced in Jini is the concept of resource leasing, or time-based resource allocation. Leasing of resources has direct implications on the programming model used, and the services that must be implemented to support a Jini network.

When a service registers with the LUS, it receives a lease from the LUS. More specifically, the `ServiceRegistrar` interface returns a `ServiceRegistration` object when the `register` method is invoked. The `ServiceRegistration` contains a `getLease` method that returns a `Lease` object.

Proper lease management requires that a service maintain and manage its lease in all service registrars it has registered with and has active residency.

If the service fails to renew the lease when it expires, the LUS will remove the service from its list of available services. The LUS assumes the service is having a problem that keeps it from performing satisfactorily. This is why the Jini network is often referred to as "self-healing." It proactively grooms the service environment without the need for human intervention.

The `net.jini.lease` package introduced with Jini 1.1 contains the classes related to lease management.

The `LeaseRenewalManager` is a utility class that can be used to ease the development required to manage leases. The class creates a thread that sleeps until it is time to renew the leases under its management. The `LeaseRenewalManager` is active as long as the virtual machine that activated the manager is active.

Recall that we have already used a `LeaseRenewalManager` (LRM), although we did not explicitly provide one when you instantiated a `JoinManager` in Chapter 14:

```
JoinManager   joiner = new JoinManager(
  this,                    // service object
  entries,                 // service attributes
  new SrvcIDListener(),    // ServiceIDListener  - internal helper class
  lookupDiscMgr,           // DiscoveryManagement - default
  null);                   // LeaseRenewalManager - default
```

The last parameter to the `JoinManager` takes a renewal manager. If one is not supplied, the `JoinManager` instantiates one on your behalf. You can gain access to the LRM (see Listing 15.9) through the `JoinManager`'s `getLeaseRenewalManager` method:

```
public LeaseRenewalManager getLeaseRenewalManager()
```

Using entities of the LRM delegates lease renewal management to the LRM. The LRM will renew leases as necessary. This can help minimize the development requirements of services and clients joining a Jini community. Errors encountered during the lease renewal process can optionally be directed to a lease listener supplied by the using entity.

LISTING 15.9   The `LeaseRenewalManager` Class as Defined by Sun Microsystems

```
public class LeaseRenewalManager
   LeaseRenewalManager()
   LeaseRenewalManager(Lease lease, long desiredExpiration,
       LeaseListener listener)
   public void cancel(Lease lease)
   public void clear()
   public long getExpiration(Lease lease)
   public void remove(Lease lease)
   public void renewFor(Lease lease, long desiredDuration,
       LeaseListener listener)
   public void renewFor(Lease lease, long desiredDuration, long renewDuration,
       LeaseListener listener)
   public void renewUntil(Lease lease, long desiredExpiration,
       LeaseListener listener)
   public void renewUntil(Lease lease, long desiredExpiration,
       long renewDuration, LeaseListener listener)
   public void setExpiration(Lease lease, long expiration)
}
```

Intelligent Agents

The popularity of the Internet has ushered in a new era of communication and collaboration. Software agents are being developed to provide a framework for organizing and interpreting the vast amount of information available on the Internet. Agent development has also increased in popularity because the Web has become the prominent channel for user and business communication. This popularity has also blurred the distinction between traditional software and agent-based modules.

Agent technology has also been affected by the growth of e-commerce. A new breed of software agent is attempting to increase the efficiency of transactions across electronic markets and exchanges. Often we think of business-to-business (B2B) and business-to-consumer (B2C) as two separate models of participation and communication. However, B2B and B2C are not discrete models, but rather exist on a continuum. Agents can be used to acquire knowledge about customers, partners, and product preferences. As a result, the capability to leverage software agents at key points, such as in distribution, manufacturing, sales, and customer relationship management, is compelling.

Imagine a business engaged in distributing products and services over the Web. A tremendous amount of marketing research is involved in determining the effectiveness of distribution channels. Many companies are looking for more effective data capture and analysis techniques. Software agents provide one solution.

Software agents are also envisioned to play a significant role in P2P systems. Jini and JavaSpaces can provide a foundation for building P2P agent frameworks. The benefits include the following:

- Software mobility "out of the box"
- Distributed storage using JavaSpaces
- Support for communicating agents using distributed events
- A framework to find information, services, and agents
- A framework supporting transactions using the two-phase commit protocol
- The capability to use cryptographic channels to communicate

Simple Agent Frameworks

The distinction and refinement of what is and what is not an agent has generated a lot of press and discussion. A considerable amount of effort has been focused on classifying types of software agents. Researchers often use role-based classification in an attempt to elucidate agent definition. Accordingly, we have search agents, navigation agents, management agents, domain-specific agents, as well as development and help agents.

Although the line between agent and software program can be hard to determine, other characteristics of agents help to delineate the distinction:

- Learning—The capability for a software program to acquire knowledge without reprogramming
- Goal-oriented direction—The capability of a software program to be instructed as to a desired result, and then to determine the accuracy of the attained result
- Community—The capability for software to communicate with other software to emulate knowledge acquisition and goal-oriented behavior

In the paper "Software Agents: An Overview,"(`http://agents.umbc.edu/ introduction/ao/4.shtml`) Hyacinth Nwana provides a typology for classifying agents. The three attributes or characteristics of agents are identified as autonomy, learning, and cooperation.

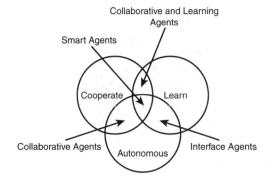

FIGURE 15.5
A model for classifying software agents.

Mobile Agents

Autonomous agents are often defined as systems that can act on behalf of the user and exhibit capabilities to learn and cooperate with their environment. Typically, an agenda or goal drives an agent's behavior. A mobile agent can move across machines and networks to carry out this mission. There is a significant amount of work being done to provide mobile agents for network management. It is easy to envision the benefits gained by network managers using mobile agents to relay conditions and instructions to network elements.

Jini provides a foundation for many of the requirements for mobile agents. As discussed previously in Chapter 4, "P2P As a Framework for Distributed Computing," the capability to move code from machine to machine through downloadable proxies is a key enabler of the Jini framework.

You can quickly define an interface for a remote agent and a mobile agent by exploiting RMI interface semantics. For instance, extending Remote provides an interface that is accessed remotely through a stub reference by the caller:

```
public interface RemoteAgent extends java.rmi.Remote {
    public void tell(Sender sender, Receiver receiver, String speechAct)
        throws RemoteException;
}
```

On the other hand, extending Serializable provides a mechanism to move the object to the caller:

```
public interface MobileAgent extends java.io.Serializable {
    public void tell(Sender sender, Receiver receiver, String speechAct)
        throws RemoteException;
}
```

You can even pass references from caller to receiver and implement powerful callback mechanisms.

Summary

JavaSpaces provides a compelling model for distributed P2P communication. The JavaSpaces API is very simple. All operations are invoked on an object that implements the `JavaSpace` interface. `read`, `write`, `take`, `notify`, and `snapshot` comprise the entire JavaSpace API. This simple yet extremely powerful API helps in developing distributed applications because much of the complexity is implemented by the service.

JavaSpaces is built using distributed data structures, which enable multiple processes to access and manipulate the content of a structure in parallel. Distributed data structures offer a number of advantages to traditional database processing by enabling multiple processes to access and change information concurrently.

One of the concepts introduced in Jini is the concept of resource leasing, which has direct implications on the programming model used and the services that must be implemented to support and manage a Jini network. The Jini network is often referred to as "self-healing," as it grooms the service environment without the need for human intervention.

JavaSpaces provides a distributed shared-memory that can be used to build rendezvous peers to assist in community formation and management.

JXTA and XML

by Frank Sommers

IN THIS CHAPTER

CHAPTER

16

Although all peer-to-peer systems are distributed systems, not all distributed systems aim to facilitate peer-to-peer-style computing. Growing experience with real-life P2P computing indicates that peer-to-peer systems share a common set of needs above and beyond what a general purpose distributed computing framework needs to provide. JXTA is an attempt to factor out the needs common to peer-to-peer systems, and offer a set of APIs around those functionalities.

In essence, JXTA is a peer-to-peer developer's library. It enables a developer to delegate to it the grunt work involved in the P2P-specific aspects of an application, and to focus instead on what makes his application unique. The purpose of this chapter is to show you what P2P-specific functionalities JXTA abstracts out, and how you might incorporate the JXTA libraries into your application.

We will start out by outlining the central problems of P2P systems that JXTA uniquely addresses. This discussion will introduce the key JXTA concepts, and will show how JXTA differs from other distributed computing frameworks, such as Jini. The subsequent sections will map those concepts to JXTA API programming constructs, and provide examples of using the most important JXTA capabilities. By the end of these sections, you will be able to design and implement simple P2P applications with JXTA.

The book's next chapter illustrates a full-fledged JXTA application—the JXTA Shell— which is an excellent tool to get acquainted with JXTA's key concepts without having to write a single line of code.

The Virtualization of Networks

By way of introduction, consider the familiar scenario depicted in Figure 16.1. It depicts a run-of-the-mill campus network or corporate intranet. The network itself is made up of different sorts of nodes: servers, desktop PCs, notebook computers, personal digital assistants, and cellular phones. The lines interconnecting the nodes outline the network's topology. Communication on this network takes place by sending messages from one node to another, typically along client-server communication channels.

Each node on this network assumes a unique identity, denoted by an IP address. Some nodes have statically assigned IP addresses, while others might dynamically obtain one each time they connect to the network. A node's IP address determines message routing to that node: When a message is destined to a node, the sender must first obtain the target's IP address and attach that address to every message packet it sends. This is how communication takes place on much of the Internet or on an organization's intranet.

FIGURE 16.1

Computing on the edge. A traditional client-server environment is juxtaposed with devices directly communicating along the network's edges.

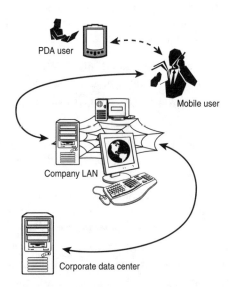

PDA user

Mobile user

Company LAN

Corporate data center

As networks grow in size, and users demand anywhere/anytime access to networked resources, the assumptions underpinning that mode of operation become increasingly harder to ensure. As an example, consider what happens when a user of the cell phone depicted in Figure 16.1 sends a message to the user of the PDA. Both the cell phone and the PDA use dynamically assigned IP addresses. Thus, they might receive different network identities each time they connect to the network. Yet, the cell phone user might want to send messages to the PDA even after the PDA detaches and then re-attaches to the network; that is, even after it obtains a new IP address. As well, servers behind firewalls and NAT points hide their identities from entities outside the firewall. In such dynamic network environments, the assumption that an IP address uniquely identifies a network entity starts to fall apart.

One solution to these problems centers around constructing a virtual network independent of physical topology. To illustrate this concept, consider a city map. On this map, imagine a point that indicates a company's offices; let's call it JXTA Systems, Inc. When you decide to meet a customer at that office, you might arrange the meeting by referring to the meeting place as "the JXTA Systems offices." This follows the assumption that your meeting partner knows where that office is, and is able to resolve its human-friendly name to a street address (such as 85th Floor, 350 Fifth Avenue, New York). Resolving the address might mean looking it up in a personal address book, on a business card, or, if your office is well-known, by asking a cab driver to simply take him there.

Networking terminology similarly considers an entity's physical address (IP address or Ethernet MAC address) and its human-friendly name (such as `server.juxtacorp.com`).

In a traditional TCP/IP networking environment, domain name servers (DNS) are used to resolve a human-friendly name to a machine name.

P2P systems strive along a network's edges. As a result, they cannot make the same assumptions about network infrastructure as traditional, client-server style systems can. In particular, they cannot assume the presence of a centralized naming and directory service.

Network identities are also typically shorter in P2P systems than in the traditional client-server world, because devices might frequently disconnect, causing them to obtain new IP addresses with each reconnection. A peer's networked identity might change too frequently for a centralized naming service to catch up. This is similar to JXTA Systems, Inc., moving to a new office every month. It would be very hard, if not impossible, for its customers and clients (and even its employees) to track the office's current location. In essence, you would need a dynamic address book that updates the office's current location just in time as you are about to go there. In other words, your address book would have the capability to find out the mapping of the office's name to its address on demand, instead of storing away that information.

On a network, the capability to delay binding a virtual identifier to an IP address as late as possible in the communication process is referred to as *late binding*. Late binding is a crucial requirement for both mobile and peer-to-peer systems. JXTA's most remarkable capability is to facilitate the late binding of network resources.

JXTA offers late binding for peer-to-peer networks in two ways:

- By assigning identifiers to a networked resource, and
- By providing a resolver capability to map between virtual and physical network identities at the time access to a resource is requested.

In other words, a network node is identified independently of its IP address, and a mechanism exists to bind a node's (virtual) JXTA identifier to its current IP address whenever a message aims for that node. JXTA's resolver mechanism is independent of centralized naming and directory services such as DNS. A JXTA network based on virtual identifiers is illustrated in Figure 16.2. As you see from the figure, the virtual and IP-based network identities can change independently: The red dots represent "virtual" network identifiers, and the IP addresses assigned to the nodes identify those nodes on the TCP/IP network. The two types of identities can change independently.

FIGURE **16.2**
Virtual and IP-based network topologies super-imposed. Virtual and IP-based identities can change indepen-dently of one another.

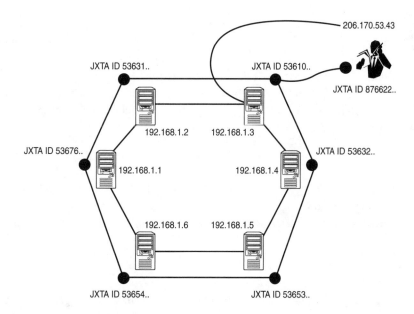

JXTA IDs, Credentials, and Advertisements

JXTA tags identifiers not only to nodes or peers, but also to any networked resource of importance on the peer-to-peer network. That includes chunks of data, pieces of code, groups of peers, or virtual communication channels between peers. Services—pieces of software functionality accessible by peers—also have their identifiers. JXTA IDs are expressed as text URNs (universal resource names).

A resource's identity on the JXTA network is also determined by that resource's creden-tials. A *credential* is a piece of information verifying a resource's identity in human terms. Although IDs are given to resources by the JXTA system, humans assign a resource's credentials. Thus, a peer might have a credential identifying it as belonging to a company. Before trusting that peer, others would request and verify its credential. Credentials don't play a role in building a virtual network; instead, they play a role in making that network trustworthy: Without them, confidence would not be possible in an ever-changing network environment.

What JXTA IDs *identify*, JXTA advertisements *describe*. A JXTA advertisement is a structured XML document, which typically includes a resource's unique JXTA identifier, in addition to other pieces of information that describe the resource, such as its creden-tials. An advertisement might also have an expiration date—an absolute time value beyond which the advertisement loses its validity on the JXTA network.

The JXTA network locates resources through advertisements. A peer that decides to advertise itself creates an advertisement, and announces that advertisement on the JXTA network. JXTA's *discovery* capability facilitates the searching of the network for advertisements that describe a desired resource (for example, another peer's ID). *Queries* for resources propagate through the JXTA network until a query matches a suitable advertisement. Indeed, much of JXTA's infrastructure facilitates the propagation of advertisements and queries on the network.

When a peer sends out a query message, that query message automatically reaches all peers that are within the sender's multicast radius. (Multicast radius typically implies that the peers reside on the same network subnet; that is, a router is not needed to communicate between them.) Because a query might not match a desired advertisement within the narrow confines of a subnet, JXTA provides a mechanism to propagate queries to a larger network.

Relays

Intuitively, you can imagine JXTA's query mechanism as though you want to find an answer to a question by asking that question from everyone you know. For instance, you might want to find out who played the role of Gelsomina in Fellini's movie *La Strada*. You would start out by asking that question of everyone in your office and your immediate family. If no one knew the answer, some of your colleagues and relatives would *relay* that question, along with your phone number or email address, to their friends, who in turn could ask their friends, and so forth. Those with the answer would reply to you, hopefully with the right response (Giulietta Masina).

Message relay offers several advantages. The obvious advantage is that it enlarges the set of peers that can answer a query. In JXTA terminology, relay peers that facilitate query transmission beyond a peer's multicast radius are *rendezvous peers*. Rendezvous peers are special in that they know about other rendezvous peers, forming a rendezvous network. A peer registers with a rendezvous peer in order to benefit from the rendezvous network's query propagation (see Figure 16.3).

It might also be that you or your friends know of someone particularly knowledgeable about Italian movies. Thus you'd like to send the query to that particular friend, but you only know her name, not how to deliver a message to her. In that case, you would employ a *router*, a peer that has the capability to construct and maintain routes to other peers. A route consists of a series of hops that terminate with the desired destination. In JXTA, each hop in a route is denoted by that peer's virtual identifier (see Figure 16.4). Thus routes in JXTA are not related to routes constructed by IP routers on the Internet.

FIGURE 16.3

Query propagation on the JXTA rendezvous network. Rendezvous peers pass a query message to other rendezvous peers. As matching advertisements are found, they are returned to the query's originator, and are also cached by peers along the query's route.

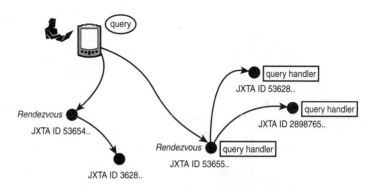

FIGURE 16.4

JXTA routers are peers with the capability to construct routes to a peer. A route is a list of hops a message has traveled through to reach a destination.

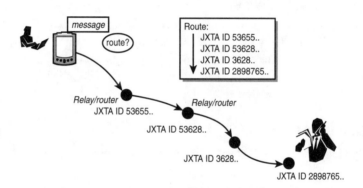

Finally, imagine that your knowledgeable friend speaks only Italian, a language you don't understand. In that case, you could ask a mutual friend who speaks your native language as well as Italian to act as a gateway between you and your Italian friend. On the JXTA network, gateway peers facilitate message relay in environments with heterogeneous network protocols. For instance, a peer might support the HTTP protocol, but another peer might only offer TCP. Sending a message in this network requires a third party capable of acting as a gateway between the two network partitions. Gateways are also useful when communicating with peers partitioned off by firewalls or NAT proxies (see Figure 16.5).

Any peer may assume relay responsibilities, and the more peers do so, the more reliable and robust the JXTA network becomes. A relay peer might be implemented such that it caches advertisements and saves them in persistent store. For instance, a rendezvous peer might cache answers to a query. The next time it receives that query, it uses the answer it already has instead of propagating the query further down the rendezvous network. Similarly, a router might already have route information to a peer; it then no longer needs to forward route requests to other routers. Finally, a gateway might also offer a message caching mechanism, allowing a peer across a network partition to pick up messages intended for it from peers on the outside.

FIGURE 16.5

Gateways help messages bridge network partitions.

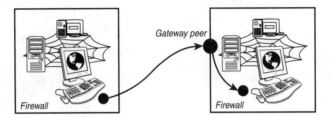

Indeed, one assumption JXTA makes of a network is that there are relays with advertisements matching a query. Without them, query and message propagation would continue ad infinitum. In smaller networks, JXTA operates well with only a handful of peers offering relay capabilities. The JXTA reference implementation in Java provides a configuration option to indicate whether a peer wants to act as a relay, and the kinds of relay functionality it wants to offer.

Endpoints

When you ask for a person's business card, that card typically lists several methods of contacting that person: by telephone, postal mail, email, fax, pager, or mobile phone. In a JXTA network, a peer might similarly be reachable via a number of virtual addresses, or *endpoints*. An endpoint's advertisement informs other peers about the particular protocol that that endpoint understands (such as HTTP or TCP), and a peer's advertisement might include the endpoints through which to reach that peer (see Figure 16.6).

FIGURE 16.6

Endpoints abstract out access to a peer. A peer can have several endpoints, each possibly using a different communication protocol.

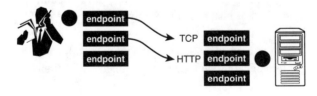

By abstracting out a peer into a set of endpoints, the JXTA network gains resiliency in the face of changes occurring in a peer's state. For instance, a given endpoint might not always be available on a peer, or a peer might decide to communicate only via certain protocols, depending on the environment a peer operates in (for instance, to conserve bandwidth or to conform to security requirements).

The Significance of Pipes

In JXTA, a communication channel between peers can assume a (virtual) identity. That channel's endpoints are identified, not by the peers' IP addresses, but by their endpoints. Thus, the peers can refer to that channel independently of IP addresses. Should any of the peers' IP address change, the JXTA network simply adjusts message routing to reflect that change—the communication via the channel is not interrupted. Because endpoints abstract out access to a peer, the two endpoints of a channel might understand different communication protocols.

In JXTA terminology, virtual communication channels are *pipes*. Although two peers can exchange messages via JXTA's simple message and query propagation mechanisms, pipes are the main abstraction for direct peer-to-peer communication. Each pipe receives its own JXTA identifier, and the system resolves a pipe's endpoints to physical IP addresses following the principle of late binding. In the subsequent programming example, you will learn how to create pipes and send messages through them.

JXTA pipes assume that only one-way message exchange is possible between two peers. Bidirectional communication between two peers is possible by constructing two pipes, one going each way.

A pipe is not restricted to placement between two peers. *Propagate pipes* allow the transfer of a message from a node to multiple destinations. How such a delivery takes place is not specified by JXTA. When all peers share a network partition and are within the multicast radius of the sender, IP multicast may be used; otherwise propagate pipes can take advantage of JXTA's relay capability described earlier.

Because JXTA must account for the peculiar conditions on a network's edge, pipes are not assumed to be reliable. Reliable pipes can be constructed by adding a layer of software to the communication channel, ensuring message integrity. In addition to reliable pipes, a JXTA pipe can also be secure, encrypting messages as they travel through it. Figure 16.7 illustrates different types of JXTA pipes.

FIGURE 16.7

JXTA pipes: (a) The unicast pipe is JXTA's main abstraction mechanism for peer-to-peer communication. It accounts for the asymmetric nature of communication along a network's edge. (b) Secure unicast pipes add message encryption to the basic pipe variety. (c) Propagate pipes facilitate one-to-many communication. (d) Roundtrip communication between two peers is possible by constructing two unicast pipes.

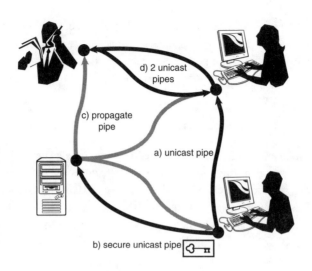

The JXTA Protocols

JXTA's designers chose to define the operations of the JXTA virtual network in terms of a set of *protocols*. A protocol, in essence, is a form of agreement in support of an activity. As long as all parties to an activity understand and follow the required protocols, the activity can take place. A corollary to that statement is that those protocols are the only thing each party has to understand to participate in the desired action.

In programming terminology, this means that if two peers want to participate on the JXTA network, the only thing they must have in common is an understanding of the protocols required for that participation. As far as JXTA is concerned, the peers might be implemented in different programming languages, run on different types of machines, or transmit messages through different network transport layer protocols (for example, TCP, HTTP, or Bluetooth). As long as the peers understand the JXTA protocols, they can become part of the JXTA virtual network and communicate with each other.

The JXTA protocols are expressed in terms of message exchanges. Regardless of what programming language a peer uses, at some point in the communication process, it must translate—or bind—JXTA messages to constructs in that programming language. Currently, several JXTA programming *language bindings*—or JXTA bindings, for short—exist or are being developed for Java, C, Objective C, Perl, Python, and Smalltalk, just to mention a few. The JXTA community actively develops new language bindings, so this list is growing.

From a programmer's viewpoint, a peer interacts with the JXTA system via an API provided by the JXTA bindings to the peer's programming language. An implementation of that API exposes the core functionality defined by the JXTA protocols as *services* a client can use to participate in P2P interactions. Because this book is about peer-to-peer programming in Java, we will only discuss the Java API to JXTA; other books and online resources provide descriptions of programming JXTA in other programming languages. Although the APIs to the JXTA protocols are different from programming language to programming language—and it is indeed possible to design different APIs for a single language—the JXTA protocols are defined via their message formats alone, and without reference to any specific programming language API.

The protocol specifications define JXTA messages in terms of XML data structures, as XML is a de facto standard for cross-platform representation of structured data. However, JXTA does not require that a peer have full XML-processing capability. Peers with limited resources, for example, might choose to precompile JXTA protocol exchanges into a binary representation. As long as those messages conform to the protocol specifications, that peer is able to participate on the JXTA network without having to process XML.

Although the JXTA specifications currently define seven protocols, a peer is not required to understand all seven to become part of the JXTA virtual network. Rather, the protocols define how a peer should act *if* it decides to implement the behavior defined by a protocol. Of course, the more protocols a peer supports, the fuller its participation in the JXTA network. In addition, a peer can also extend any of the existing protocols with new behavior.

Peer Resolver Protocol

The JXTA protocol messages form sets of query-response pairs: A peer sends a query, and some other peer sends a response to that query (see Figure 16.8). The format of the query and response messages are what the protocol specification defines. Responses to a query occur asynchronously in JXTA. The Peer Resolver Protocol (PRP) is the most fundamental JXTA protocol that specifies how a query is paired up with one or more responses.

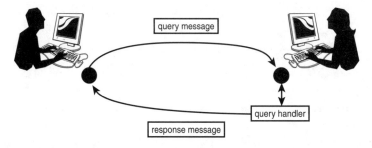

FIGURE 16.8

The Peer Resolver Protocol: A query message is directed to a query handler. A peer that implements that handler might choose to process the query and respond. Processing a query can include any computation on the peer offering the query handler, and that computation might consume an arbitrary query string or document. Similarly, the processing of the query may result in an arbitrary string. Responses are matched up with queries by a service providing the PRP.

All other protocols needing a generic query-response mechanism rely on PRP. PRP helps standardize the formats of queries and query resolution. An implementation of PRP offers a generic query service to the JXTA network. With PRP, a query message is addressed not to a specific peer, but to a named *query handler*. A peer registers a query handler, and it can then answer queries addressed to that handler. Note, however, that a peer is not obligated to answer a query; also, answers as well as queries might be lost on the network because of network or peer failure.

The following XML schema defines the resolver query message:

```
<xs:element name="ResolverQuery" type="jxta:ResolverQuery"/>
<xs:complexType name="ResolverQuery">
    <xs:element name="Credential" type="xs:anyType" minOccurs="0"/>
    <xs:element name="SrcPeerID" type="JXTAID"/>
    <xs:element name="HandlerName" type="xs:string"/>
    <xs:element name="QueryID" type="xs:string" minOccurs="0"/>
    <xs:element name="Query" type="xs:anyType"/>
</xs:complexType>
```

As the schema definition shows, a query includes the sending peer's credential and peer ID, the name of the handler for the query, a unique query ID, as well as a chunk of free text that forms the body of the query. A peer that registers as a handler for the query can use the query text to perform some processing in order to determine a response.

The response message format is as follows:

```
<xs:element name="ResolverResponse" type="ResolverResponse"/>
<xs:complexType name="ResolverResponse">
    <xs:element name="Credential" type="xs:anyType" minOccurs="0"/>
    <xs:element name="HandlerName" type="xs:string"/>
```

```
    <xs:element name="QueryID" type="xs:string" minOccurs="0"/>
    <xs:element name="Response" type="xs:anyType"/>
</xs:complexType>
```

The response contains the credential of the responding peer, as well as a text element `Response`. We will shortly explore the API offered by the Java bindings to take advantage of the PRP.

The Query-Response Paradigm

JXTA requires two-way communication between peers—a query is of little importance if the sender is not able to receive a reply because of network limitations. Although this requirement appears easy to satisfy, some networks, such as pager networks, support only one-way communication. Those networks are not able to participate in the PRP.

Because the PRP is a fundamental JXTA protocol in the sense that other protocols depend on it for query/response resolution, such limited peers are not able to participate in the JXTA virtual network. However, the requirement to support two-way communication does not exclude networks with highly asymmetric characteristics. For example, it might not be possible to directly contact a peer inside a firewall, but a network might provide a mechanism to contact that peer in some indirect way, such as through a gateway. As long as that is possible, the peer inside the firewall can participate in the JXTA protocols with peers outside of it.

Endpoint Routing Protocol

The Endpoint Routing Protocol (ERP) specifies message routing in JXTA. We earlier described how routing consists of constructing an ordered list of hops through which a message travels from a peer to its desired destination. Relay peers that offer routing capability perform this task. If a router receives a route query and knows the route to the requested destination, it answers that route request with a list of hops that constitute the route. The sender of that message will use the first address in that list and dispatch the message to it. Network changes can cause a route to become obsolete at any time during the message's transmission, necessitating the discovery of a new route. The following XML schema defines the structure of a route:

```
<?xml version="1.0" encoding="UTF-8"?>
<jxta:EndpointRouter>
        <Src> peer id of the source </Src>
        <Dest> peer id of the destination </Dest>
        <TTL> time to live </TTL>
        <Gateway> ordered sequence of gateway </Gateway>
        <.................>
        <Gateway> ordered sequence of gateway </Gateway>
</jxta:EndpointRouter>
```

As the message winds its way through the network toward its destination, each peer it goes through leaves a trace on that message. Those traces enable routers to remember new routes to destinations. As more peers cache correct route information to a destination, the faster route discovery becomes. The trace information left by peers on a message is also useful to detect loops, or to detect duplicate messages by routers.

The following XML schema defines the route query message, and shows how route caching is controlled:

```
<?xml version="1.0" encoding="UTF-8"?>
<jxta:EndpointRouterQuery>
    <Credential> credential </Credential>
    <Dest> peer id of the destination </Dest>
    <Cached>
       true: if the reply can be a cached reply
       false: if the reply must not come from a cache
    </Cached>
</jxta:EndpointRouterQuery>
```

In response to this message, a peer router that has the requested route information returns an answer conforming to the following format:

```
<?xml version="1.0" encoding="UTF-8"?>
<jxta:EndpointRouterAnswer>
       <Credential> credential </Credential>
       <Dest> peer id of the destination </Dest>
       <RoutingPeer>
             Peer ID of the router that knows a route to DestPeer
       </RoutingPeer>
       <RoutingPeerAdv>
             Advertisement of the routing peer
       </RoutingPeerAdv>
       <Gateway> ordered sequence of gateway </Gateway>
       < ..................>
       <Gateway> ordered sequence of gateway </Gateway>
</EndpointRouterAnswer>
```

By defining this somewhat cumbersome protocol, ERP's objective was to ensure a high degree of success in guiding a message to its destination, not to ensure efficiency in message transmission. Thus, more intelligent peers might implement specialized routing algorithms to optimize route discovery. Figure 16.9 illustrates ERP in action.

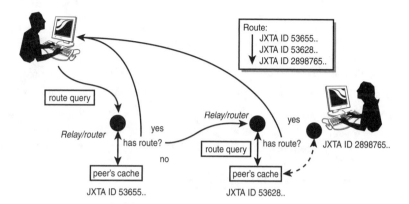

FIGURE 16.9
ERP discovers routes and aids in message delivery.

Peer Discovery Protocol

You might recall from earlier in this chapter that advertisements provide the mechanism to describe resources on the JXTA virtual network. The discovery of resources based on their advertisements is what the Peer Discovery Protocol (PDP) specifies. The query message for PDP offers three pieces of information:

- Advertisement type
- An XML key or tag name
- A value that must correspond to the XML key

The message format is specified as follows:

```
<xs:element name="DiscoveryQuery" type="jxta:DiscoveryQuery"/>
<xs:complexType name="DiscoveryQuery">
        <xs:element name="Type" type="xs:string"/>
        <xs:element name="Threshold" type="xs:unsignedInt" minOccurs="0"/>
        <xs:element name="PeerAdv" type="xs:string" minOccurs="0"/>
        <xs:element name="Attr" type="xs:string" minOccurs="0"/>
        <xs:element name="Value" type="xs:string" minOccurs="0"/>
</xs:complexType>
```

The threshold attribute in the query message defines how many responses per peer we are expecting. The response message is as follows:

```
<xs:element name="DiscoveryResponse" type="jxta:DiscoveryResponse"/>
<xs:complexType name="DiscoveryResponse">
        <xs:element name="Type" type="xs:string"/>
        <xs:element name="Count" type="xs:unsignedInt" minOccurs="0"/>
        <xs:element name="PeerAdv" type="xs:anyType" minOccurs="0">
                <xs:attribute name="Expiration" type="xs:unsignedLong"/>
        </xs:element>
        <xs:element name="Attr" type="xs:string" minOccurs="0"/>
```

```
    <xs:element name="Value" type="xs:string" minOccurs="0"/>
    <xs:element name="Response" type="xs:anyType" maxOccurs="unbounded">
        <xs:attribute name="Expiration" type="xs:unsignedLong"/>
    </xs:element>
</xs:complexType>
```

The response element in this message includes the advertisement that the JXTA peer located in response to the query, in addition to the responding peer's own advertisement. The message exchange defined by PDP represents the lowest-level discovery mechanism in JXTA. Applications can build higher-level discovery protocols based on PDP.

Rendezvous Protocol

By default, query messages only reach peers that share a physical network with the inquiring peer. The Rendezvous Protocol (RP) defines how queries propagate through rendezvous peers. The propagation scope for messages via the RP is limited to a set of peers that form a logical group, or peer group. (We will discuss peer groups shortly.) This scope is reflected in the advertisement message of a peer that announces itself as a rendezvous peer, as the following XML message from the JXTA specifications shows:

```
<?xml version="1.0" encoding="UTF-8"?>
<jxta:RdvAdvertisement>
        <Name> name of the rendezvous peer</Name>
        <RdvGroupId> PeerGroup UUID </RdvGroupId>
        <RdvPeerId>Peer ID of the rendezvous peer</RdvPeerId>
</jxta:RdvAdvertisement>
```

A peer discovers a rendezvous peer via this advertisement type and then connects to it. When a peer requests that connection, the rendezvous peer assigns a lease to the connection; the request for the connection includes the desired lease time. A rendezvous peer receives a message and propagates that message to other rendezvous peers it knows. The message format that controls that propagation assumes the following format:

```
<xs:element name="RendezVousPropagateMessage"    type="jxta:
➥RendezVousPropagateMessage"/>

<xs:complexType name="RendezVousPropagateMessage">
        <xs:element name="MessageId" type="xs:string"/>
        <xs:element name="DestSName" type="xs:string"/>
        <xs:element name="DestSParam" type="xs:string"/>
        <xs:element name="TTL" type="xs:unsignedInt"/>
        <xs:element name="Path" type="xs:anyURI" maxOccurs="unbounded"/>
</xs:complexType>
```

Pipe Binding Protocol

A pipe defines a communication channel between two peers. Each pipe has two ends: an input pipe and an output pipe, for receiving and sending messages through the pipe, respectively. The Pipe Binding Protocol (PBP) defines how a pipe's input and output ends bind to a peer's endpoint. JXTA defines different types of pipes, and a pipe's advertisement includes an indication of the pipe's type, in addition to its name and ID:

```
<?xml version="1.0" encoding="UTF-8"?>
<jxta:PipeAdvertisement>
        <Name> name of the pipe</Name>
        <Id> Pipe Id </Id>
        <Type> Pipe Type </Type>
</jxta:PipeAdvertisement>
```

The following message format defines a pipe binding request message:

```
<xs:element name="PipeResolver" type="jxta:PipeResolver"/>
<xs:complexType name="PipeResolver">
        <xs:element name="MsgType" type="xs:string"/>
        <xs:element name="PipeId" type="JXTAID"/>
        <xs:element name="Type" type="xs:string" minOccurs="0"/>
        <xs:element name="Cached" type="xs:boolean" default="false"
➥minOccurs="0"/>
        <xs:element name="Peer" type="JXTAID" minOccurs="0"/>
        <xs:element name="Found" type="xs:boolean" minOccurs="0"/>
        <xs:element name="PeerAdv" type="xs:string" minOccurs="0"/>
</xs:complexType>
```

The Found and PeerAdv elements in this message are sent by the peer that was able to resolve the pipe's endpoint. We will see shortly how pipe endpoint resolution occurs via the Java API.

Peer Information Protocol

The Peer Information Protocol (PIP) fills a bit of a different role in the JXTA universe than the other protocols. Its purpose is to allow peers to exchange runtime information, such as a peer's uptime, or the number of messages a peer processed in a given period of time. That PIP exists in the JXTA specifications reveals the importance of such metadata about peers for the proper functioning of a P2P network. Tool vendors can use this protocol to hook network-monitoring software into peers and allow system administrators to track the performance of the JXTA network.

As it exists in the JXTA specifications, PIP is rather limited in the kinds of information it defines about a peer. In addition, some peers that claim to support PIP might only provide a partial set of that information. The idea behind PIP, though, is that implementers of this protocol can extend it with other sorts of information; because this protocol, as every other JXTA protocol, uses XML to define its message formats, extending PIP with new information is as easy as adding elements to an XML document. As it stands now, PIP's message format is as follows:

```
<xs:element name="PeerInfoResponse" type="jxta:PeerInfoResponse"/>
<xs:complexType name="PeerInfoResponse">
        <xs:element name="sourcePid" type="xs:anyURI"/>
        <xs:element name="targetPid" type="xs:anyURI"/>
        <xs:element name="uptime" type="xs:unsignedLong" minOccurs="0"/>
        <xs:element name="timestamp" type="xs:unsignedLong" minOccurs="0"/>
        <xs:element name="response" type="xs:anyType" minOccurs="0"/>
        <xs:element name="traffic" type="jxta:piptraffic" minOccurs="0"/>
</xs:complexType>
<xs:complexType name="piptraffic">
        <xs:element name="lastIncomingMessageAt" type="xs:unsignedLong"
➥minOccurs="0"/>
        <xs:element name="lastOutgoingMessageAt" type="xs:unsignedLong"
➥minOccurs="0"/>
        <xs:element name="in" type="jxta:piptrafficinfo" minOccurs="0"/>
        <xs:element name="out" type="jxta:piptrafficinfo" minOccurs="0"/>
</xs:complexType>

<xs:complexType name="piptrafficinfo">
        <xs:element name="transport" type="xs:unsignedLong"
➥maxOccurs="unbounded">
                <xs:attribute name="endptaddr" type="xs:anyURI"/>
        </xs:element>
</xs:complexType>
```

Peer Groups and the Peer Membership Protocol

One of the most powerful aspects of JXTA is its capability to overcome the physical partitioning of a network. Peers can communicate on the JXTA network, even though they might reside on different sides of firewalls and NAT points, or use different network communication protocols. However, network partitioning in the physical world is useful for various reasons. For example, by using a set of private IP addresses behind a secure NAT point, a company's computers form a group inaccessible from the outside. The company can provide services on that private network, such as databases or application software, without having to be concerned about unauthorized access from the outside. JXTA offers the equivalent of network partitions in the form of *peer groups*.

Any sort of peer group can be created, each with a unique ID and a name. As other JXTA entities with IDs, each peer group has an advertisement. Peers that share a common interest join a peer group, and a peer may be a member of one or more groups. There are several reasons why a peer might want to become member of a group.

First, groups form a scoping environment for JXTA queries: When a peer propagates a query for an advertisement, that query will by default propagate only through peers that are members of the peer group in which message propagation commenced. Because of query propagation scoping, resources available to one peer in a group are accessible to other group members as well, facilitating resource sharing. Such resources include anything with an advertisement, such as pipes or other peers. Because pipes and message propagation are the mechanisms through which peers communicate, peers must belong to the same peer group to send messages to one another.

Second, peer groups outline security boundaries on the JXTA network. When a peer wants to join a peer group, it must apply for membership in that group. The Peer Membership Protocol (PMP) defines how a peer obtains group membership.

In essence, the application is similar to someone applying for membership in a professional organization. An applicant initiates the process by filling out an application form with some basic information, such as job history and educational background. Because many professional organizations require a minimal education level or job history from candidates, the organization's membership committee then evaluates the application, possibly confirming the information the applicant provided. After that information has been verified, the applicant is qualified to join. At that point, the applicant joins by paying the initial membership dues and signing a membership form. Thereafter, the new member receives a membership card, verifying his standing as the organization's member.

The JXTA PMP outlines a similar protocol, consisting of an application phase and a joining phase. Figure 16.10 illustrates the process of joining a JXTA peer group. Each peer group operates a service implementing PMP. When a peer applies for group membership, it specifies its credentials, in addition to a reference to the authenticator capable of verifying those credentials. The group's membership service then uses that information to verify the peer's identity via the specified authenticator. That verification might take any form, including contacting third-party components, such as a centralized database, or asking a peer to answer an arbitrary set of questions. After the peer prequalifies for group membership in this manner, it can request to join the group. Joining results in a credential issued by the membership service. That credential will thereafter be used in all peer operations requiring group membership, such as accessing services and other resources specific to a group.

Finally, JXTA groups provide mechanisms for peers to monitor other peers sharing a peer group. In that way, JXTA peer groups define a monitoring environment as well.

Figure 16.11 gives an overview of the manner in which peer groups impose a virtual partitioning on a network. The driver in the automobile accesses a network via a handheld device. The network provider offers various services, and those services are usable by anyone belonging to the provider's peer group (gas station locator, weather service). In addition, the mobile user created his own secure peer group to share notes from a business meeting with the company's sales representatives on the road, and with a partner company's employees. Finally, the user is also a member of his corporation's secure internal peer group, enabling him to use services offered by the company (employee directory, factory floor status reporting, and a printer).

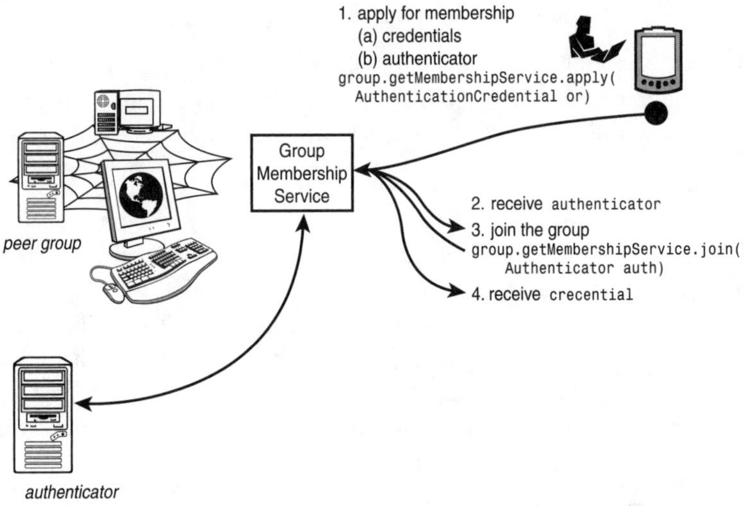

FIGURE 16.10

Joining a JXTA peer group.

1. apply for membership
   (a) credentials
   (b) authenticator
   `group.getMembershipService.apply(`
   `   AuthenticationCredential or)`

Group Membership Service

peer group

2. receive authenticator
3. join the group
   `group.getMembershipService.join(`
   `   Authenticator auth)`
4. receive crecential

authenticator

FIGURE 16.11

Virtual network partitioning via peer groups.

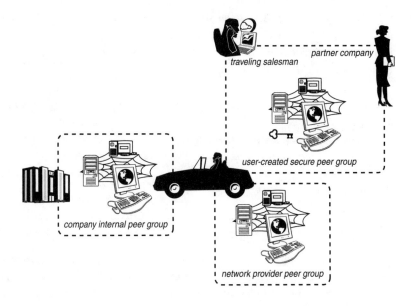

traveling salesman

partner company

user-created secure peer group

company internal peer group

network provider peer group

The JXTA specifications define two kinds of peer groups: a Platform Peer Group and a Standard Peer Group. By default, every peer is a member of the Platform, or World Peer Group, and joins that group when the peer boots up. The World Peer Group defines implementations of the basic JXTA protocols, such as the membership, discovery, and resolver protocols. Peer groups form a parent-child hierarchy. All the services available in a parent group are also available in child groups.

By virtue of membership in the World Peer Group, every peer on the global JXTA network can potentially communicate with every other peer. The Standard Peer Group, in turn, can be used to implement user-defined peer groups (to provide a scoping, security, or monitoring environment).

JXTA Services

The JXTA protocols are definitions of abstract behavior, by means of the message formats that pass between peers. In order for the peers to participate in the JXTA virtual network, they must have implementations of those protocols available, and exposed via an application programmer's interface (API). JXTA protocol implementations are *services*. Services also include software components that support activities other than the core JXTA protocols, and which are available for other peers to use. Those services rely on the core JXTA service implementations. Higher-level JXTA-based applications depend on an increasingly higher-level service layer. Figure 16.12 illustrates that structure.

FIGURE 16.12

Three layers of JXTA services. The core layers implement the fundamental JXTA protocols. Those services in turn are employed by a higher-level service layer. Finally, applications take advantage of those services to interoperate on the JXTA network.

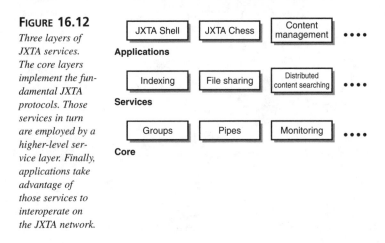

As any other JXTA resource, services assume unique identifiers, and announce their presence via JXTA advertisements. If a service is capable of communicating with other peers via JXTA pipes, its advertisement might include the communication pipes' advertisements as well.

Because services have IDs and corresponding advertisements, service discovery is similar to peer discovery: A peer issues a query for a specific service. That query, in turn, propagates through the peer group via the rendezvous network until rendezvous peers locate an advertisement for the specified service. At that point, the service's advertisement is returned to the requestor, causing that advertisement to be cached by rendezvous peers along its way. The service advertisement could contain the advertisement of a pipe described in the service's advertisement. The requestor peer can invoke the service through that pipe.

Although pipes are the JXTA-specified means of peer-to-peer message passing, JXTA does not prescribe how a service should be invoked: Any service invocation is possible, including opening direct socket connections to the service, performing remote method invocations (RMI) on a remote service object, or simply sending messages to the target peer formatted in accord with the Simple Object Access Protocol (SOAP) document model.

To support flexible service invocation, some services might specify a proxy object: An object that represents the service on the JXTA network, and has the capability to communicate to other network resources, some of which might not be accessible via JXTA communication mechanism. This proxy-based service invocation is similar to Jini's service proxies, which are free to choose any communication mechanism to connect to other network resources. Figure 16.13 illustrates some of the ways a peer can invoke a service.

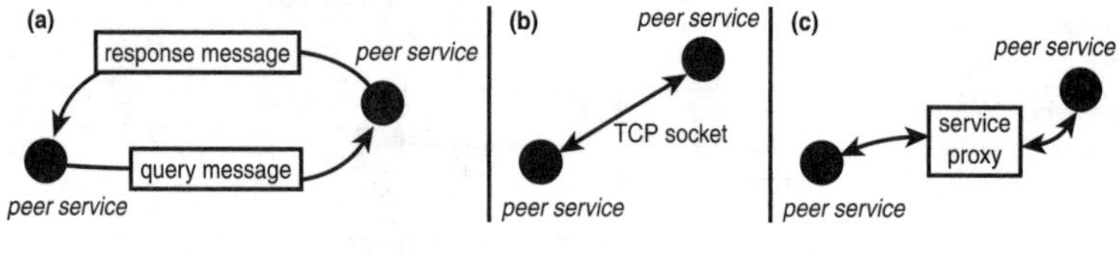

FIGURE 16.13
A sampling of service invocation methods:
(a) Query/
response message,
(b) TCP sockets,
(c) service
proxies.

Peer Group Services

JXTA provides for high service availability by having certain services belong, not to a single peer, but to the whole peer group. In essence, several peers implement the service, and those implementations are deemed equivalent by the JXTA system; that is, they have the same IDs and advertisements. A peer requesting a peer group service can use any of those service instances. The services implementing the core JXTA protocols are peer group services.

Note that JXTA does not provide for load balancing or service fail-over. If a peer providing a peer group service fails, the client of a service on the failed peer must discover a new instance of the service. If the failed peer contains data that was modified in the course of using that service, that data will not be available on other peers running instances of the service, unless an application developer built data replication into his JXTA service implementation. The concept of a peer group service is illustrated in Figure 16.14.

Figure 16.14

Peer group services.

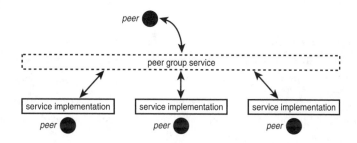

JXTA Modules

In locating and interacting with other services, JXTA aims to facilitate peer-to-peer computing across a diversity of language and execution environments. A *module* denotes a chunk of functionality (code) available to JXTA peers in a peer group. JXTA uses the concept of module IDs and advertisements to define services and service types.

In JXTA, you can locate a service based on its abstract behavior, a particular specification or wire protocol for that service, or an implementation of a specification. An underlying assumption is that you have some prior knowledge to construct a query for any of those advertisements. That prior knowledge typically means knowing the IDs for a module's class, spec, or implementation, respectively.

An identifier for an API, or some *local behavior*, is the module's class ID, which also includes a base class ID, declaring what class this module specializes (extends). Services available in a group are defined by a set of module class IDs. Different groups might use specifications of common classes which are not network-compatible, but the local APIs for those classes will be similar, if their module class IDs are identical. Combining the peer group's ID with the module's class ID uniquely identifies a service.

When constructing a JXTA service, you would normally describe what other JXTA services your service depends on based on those services' module class IDs. To draw a comparison to Java classes, a module class is somewhat analogous to a Java interface—a Java interface also defines some local behavior, but how that behavior might be accessed over the network is specific to an implementation of that interface. (Keep in mind that JXTA module classes are not specified in the Java programming language, but by abstract IDs and advertisements.)

Module class IDs are advertised by module class advertisements. A module class advertisement provides a description of what a module class ID *means*. These advertisements are meant for programmers who want to create modules offering the abstract behavior designated by the module's class ID. It does not specify how to invoke the service.

There can be many embodiments of a module class, each of which is termed a module specification, or *module spec*. A module specification represents *network behavior*, or wire protocols, that a module might embed. Module specs with identical Module Spec IDs are network-compatible.

A *module spec advertisement* provides the description of the protocol defined by the module spec. Although a module class defines a service's dependency on some abstract behavior, a module spec designates dependency on a given *specification* for that behavior. As such, module spec advertisements might also describe how to access a module. Similar to module class advertisement, module spec advertisements are also chiefly aimed at a programmer implementing a specification.

Using a module's spec ID, an implementation of that module can be located in the peer group. These implementations themselves are defined by *module implementation IDs*. Module implementation IDs are advertised via module implementation advertisements. This type of advertisement might provide a complete URI to the code and JAR files needed to execute the implementation, in addition to other descriptive elements; a peer could use those URIs to download the needed code. The module spec ID on which an implementation is based is also included.

The relationship between the different module IDs and advertisements is depicted in Figure 16.15. Note that JXTA does not mandate that a module's implementation be available locally to a peer. Rather, using information in the module implementation advertisement, a peer can download pieces of code (JAR files) needed to instantiate and invoke a service. How a peer might download that code is not specified by JXTA—the peer could use HTTP, FTP, or any other network protocol. A peer might even use the Java mobile object paradigm specified in RMI.

FIGURE 16.15
Modules define some behavior in JXTA. Module class IDs denote local behavior (an API), module spec IDs designate network behavior, and module implementation IDs describe the implementation of a specification.

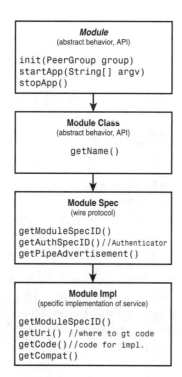

```
              Module
       (abstract behavior, API)

init(PeerGroup group)
startApp(String[] argv)
stopApp()
```

```
            Module Class
       (abstract behavior, API)

             getName()
```

```
            Module Spec
            (wire protocol)

getModuleSpecID()
getAuthSpecID()//Authenticator
getPipeAdvertisement()
```

```
            Module Impl
    (specific implementation of service)

getModuleSpecID()
getUri() //where to gt code
getCode()//code for impl.
getCompat()
```

In summary, to find a module, you'd need to know the module's class ID, spec ID, or implementation ID, depending on whether you're looking for some abstract behavior, a specific wire protocol to access that behavior, or an implementation. In the next section, you will see an example of defining a service's module class and spec, and specifying an input pipe in the module spec advertisement through which other peers can send messages.

The JXTA J2SE API

The main purpose of the J2SE API to JXTA is to allow Java programs to take advantage of the unique capabilities offered by this P2P platform. A secondary purpose of the J2SE implementation is to offer a test bed for the JXTA protocols, and to enable programmers to see how well those protocols serve real-life applications. Because APIs are for programmers, the J2SE API aims to simplify interaction with the JXTA protocols and core services from a Java programmer's viewpoint.

From now on throughout this chapter, we'll refer to the APIs of the J2SE reference implementation as simply the JXTA API. During this discussion, bear in mind that this

API is just one of many possible APIs in Java—If you don't like certain aspects of it, you can propose different mechanisms to access what JXTA has to offer. Rapid progress in the development of this API also means that things will change with time. We've tried to use relatively stable aspects of the API here; however, if you find that some things don't work, please visit the book's Web site for an update regarding errata.

A First JXTA Program

You can download the current version of the J2SE implementation from http://www.jxta.org; follow the download instructions for the appropriate packages. My recommendation is that you choose the full download option, which includes all the JXTA libraries, as well as the JXTA Shell and other sample applications. The only requirements for the JXTA J2SE binding is the presence of a J2SE implementation. Other Java-based JXTA implementations might require various configurations of J2ME.

Although the JXTA download comes with several sample applications that enable you to experiment with the platform, we will write here a very simple JXTA program that initializes the platform and displays some information about peers and peer groups. Successful termination of this program indicates that you have correctly installed the JXTA libraries. Listing 16.1 shows the complete source code for this simple program that starts up the JXTA runtime environment and then prints out the peer and peer group names and IDs, respectively.

LISTING 16.1 PlatformTest

```
import net.jxta.peergroup.PeerGroup;
import net.jxta.peergroup.PeerGroupFactory;
import net.jxta.exception.PeerGroupException;
/**
 * Platform test. This program simply initializes the JXTA platform,
 * obtains a reference to the NetPeerGroup, and displays the names and IDs
 * of the peer and the group, respectively.
 */
public class PlatformTest {
        public static void main(String[] argv) {
                PeerGroup netPeerGroup = null;
                try {
                        netPeerGroup = PeerGroupFactory.newNetPeerGroup();
                        System.out.println("Group name: " +
                                netPeerGroup.getPeerGroupName());
                        System.out.println("Group ID: " +
                                netPeerGroup.getPeerGroupID());
                        System.out.println("Peer name: " +
                                netPeerGroup.getPeerName());
```

LISTING 16.1   continued

```
                System.out.println("Peer ID: " +
                        netPeerGroup.getPeerID());
        } catch (PeerGroupException e) {
                System.out.println("Can't initialize net peer group: " +
                        e.getMessage());
        }
        System.exit(0);
    }
}
```

When you compile and run this program for the first time, the JXTA runtime brings up a window requesting that you configure your peer. This window represents the JXTA Configurator, shown in Figure 16.16. It asks you to give your peer a name, and to indicate whether your peer will offer any relay services, such becoming a rendezvous, a router, or a gateway. You also need to specify whether to use any outside relays to aid the discovery of advertisements outside of your local network. You have the option of asking the system to download a list of well-known rendezvous and relays. Once you opt to download that list, your peer will use those in message propagation and discovery. Finally, you also need to specify a secure username and password for your peer. This information will be used when your peer applies for group membership, and in other situations when it needs to be authenticated.

FIGURE 16.16

The JXTA Configurator window.

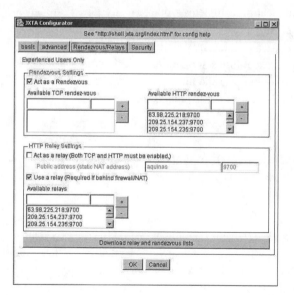

As we mentioned earlier, at startup a peer initializes the World Peer Group and the Net Peer Group. This application simply obtains a reference to the latter, and prints out that peer group's name, group ID, as well as the peer's own name and ID:

```
aquinas% java PlatformTest
 Group name: NetPeerGroup
 Group ID: urn:jxta:jxta-NetGroup
 Peer name: aquinas
 Peer ID: urn:jxta:uuid59616261646162614A7874
➡6150325033D5A4650661A84DF1867897A0FC52E4FF03
```

If you examine the files in the directory you started the application from, you will see that the JXTA runtime created several files and subdirectories. The peer's configuration itself is stored in the file `PlatformConfig`; this is an XML file, and you can examine its contents with a text editor. If you ever need to reconfigure the peer, removing this file will cause the JXTA Configurator to display the set of configuration screens again. The `cm` directory stands for the cache manager, and contains cached advertisements. The files in that directory are also XML files; examining them is a good way to learn about the structure of JXTA advertisements. Finally, the `pse` directory contains credential information.

JXTA Prime Cruncher

After this simple application completes, you are ready for a more advanced tour of the JXTA API. In this example, we will design and write a distributed JXTA application that solves parallel computing problems. We will construct this application in an iterative fashion, expanding its capabilities and the set of APIs it uses with each step. The source code in this book can only cover the most important parts of the application; please check the book's Web site for the full source code.

A large subset of computational problems lend themselves to a parallel solution. Parallel execution of a task means that you break a problem into many smaller sub-problems, and cause those sub-problems to execute simultaneously. After a subtask completes, it returns its result to a master process, which then assembles the answer to the larger problem from those small results.

As an example, consider the task of creating a list of prime numbers between any two integers. Prime numbers are natural numbers that divide only by themselves and one. Natural numbers that divide by one and any other integer less than themselves are composite numbers. Thus, the simplest way to produce a list of prime numbers is to eliminate from a list of natural numbers all composites; the elements remaining in the list will all be primes.

That method is the essence of a very old—albeit not very efficient—algorithm: the Sieve of Eratosthenes. It is named after Eratosthenes of Cyrene (ca. 275–195 B.C.), a mathematician chiefly known for being the first to accurately estimate the diameter of the Earth; he also served as director of the famous Alexandria library.

The Sieve of Eratosthenes identifies prime numbers by iterating through a list of natural numbers and attempting to eliminate from that list all composites. It does that by dividing every number in the list by each natural number between two and the square root of the ultimate number in the list. If any number in the list divides by a number other than itself without leaving a remainder, then that number is a composite and is marked as such. After the iterations complete, eliminating all marked numbers leaves only primes in the list. The following example illustrates how the Sieve works.

Consider the list of natural numbers between 10 and 20. To find all primes between these two numbers, we will divide every element in the list by 2, 3, and 4 (4.47 being the approximate square root of 20). The original list is as follows: 10, 11, 12, 13, 14, 15, 16, 17, 18, 19, and 20. Eliminating the numbers that divide by 2 without a remainder leaves 11, 13, 15, 17, and 19. Next, removing all numbers that divide by 3 leaves 11, 13, 17, and 19. Doing the divisions by 4 does not change the list. Therefore, we have obtained the complete list of primes between 10 and 20.

With a very long list of natural numbers—for instance, with numbers several million digits long—we can divide that list into multiple smaller lists, and perform the Sieve on each list simultaneously. Each of those computations might be handed out to different machines on the network, taking advantage of distributed computing resources. Prime number searching is but one of a large set of problems that can be parallelized. Among the popular uses of P2P-style software are applications such as the SETI@HOME project, which aims to decode signals from outer space in search of intelligent life on other planets, or similar projects enabling users to contribute their idle CPU resources to tasks such as simulating protein folding or decoding strands of DNA.

In this application, a master process will request two numbers from the user and produce a list of all primes between those two numbers. The master process will attempt to discover other peers on the JXTA network offering the prime number search service, and try to parcel out list segments to them for processing. After a peer completes its part of the work, it will send back an array of primes for its segment of the list. For that distribution to work, we will enable a JXTA peer to advertise its prime searching capability on the network so that others can find and connect to it. Figure 16.17 outlines this generic JXTA prime cruncher.

FIGURE 16.17

A server architecture suitable for finding large prime numbers in a distributed manner.

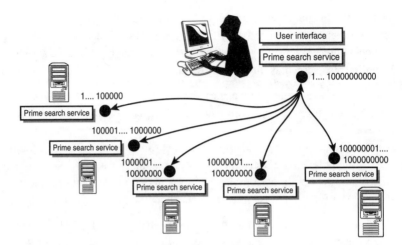

JXTA Application Design

Perhaps the most unusual aspect of this application is that every peer acts both as a master process and a slave, helping compute a sublist handed to it by a master. It is also conceivable that a slave might decide to further break down the problem into small subtasks, and act as a master process itself. This server-mode/client-mode operation is an essential P2P application design pattern. We will refer to that pattern as a *SM/CM operation*. It's worth noting that we will exploit SM/CM to reuse code: The master process itself will act as a slave to an adapter standing between it and the user interface: When a user specifies the two extremes of the natural number list, that adapter constructs the list and passes it to the prime cruncher component. Figure 16.18 illustrates this design.

Message Definition

When designing a JXTA application, we must bear in mind that JXTA is a message-based system: The primary contract between peers is defined by a set of messages. Thus, the first design task is to define that message exchange. In the prime cruncher application, a peer passes a message to another peer containing the two boundaries of the list. The receiving peer then computes a list of all primes between those two extremes, and returns that sublist to the original peer. The net.jxta.endpoint.Message class abstracts out the concept of a message. It allows one to associate an arbitrary set of message elements with a key. We will use instances of that class with the following key-value structures seen in Tables 16.1 and 16.2.

FIGURE 16.18

A peer offers both server-mode and client-mode operations (SM/CM).

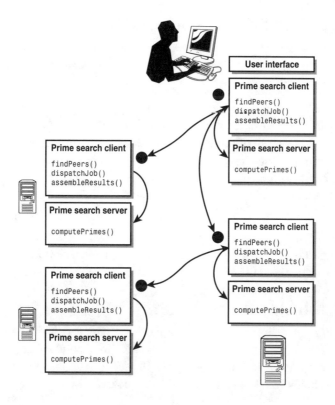

TABLE 16.1   Request Message

Key	Value
ServiceConstants.LOW_INT	Lower boundary of the (sub)list
ServiceConstants.HIGH_INT	Upper boundary of the (sub)list

TABLE 16.2   Response Message

Key	Value
ServiceConstants.LOW_INT	Lower boundary of the (sub)list
ServiceConstants.HIGH_INT	Upper boundary of the (sub)list
ServiceConstants.PRIMELIST	A string containing all primes between the bounds of the list. The primes are separated by ; characters.

Service Definition and Discovery

Next we must define a way for a master to find slaves on the network. In other words, we must specify the prior knowledge a peer must have in order to discover other peers offering the prime crunching service.

As mentioned earlier, a JXTA service is defined by its module class and specification. Thus, we will define advertisements for the number-crunching module's class and specification, and cause a peer offering that service to propagate those advertisements on the JXTA network. The prime-crunching module class will assume the name JXTACLASS: com.sams.p2p.primecruncher, and the module's spec will have the name JXTASPEC: com.sams.p2p.primecruncher.

Masters will discover peers that advertise module specifications with that name. Thus, in addition to the message definition, the service name string is another piece of information peers must posses at design time. All other information pertinent to peer interaction will be discovered at runtime.

Service Implementation

When a prime-crunching peer starts up, it must first initialize the JXTA platform to gain access to the World and Net Peer Groups. The code for that initialization is similar to our earlier example. After the platform initiated, the peer creates and publishes its advertisements, including its module class and module spec advertisements.

The module spec advertisement will include the advertisement of a pipe. Clients discovering a module spec advertisement for the service must obtain the pipe advertisement, and connect to the service via that pipe.

After it has published its advertisements, our service opens an input pipe and listens for incoming messages. When a message arrives, the service attempts to obtain the high and low boundary numbers from it, and pass those onto a component responsible for generating the primes-only sublist. When that component returns its results (an array containing the primes), the prime cruncher service attempts to create a message with a result and then send that message back to the client. In the first iteration, the service will simply print out the message it receives. In subsequent refinements, it will open a pipe back to the client and send the results back to it. The client will then assemble the results from all the peers it heard back from and save the resulting master list into the file.

The outline of this server component is shown in Listing 16.2.

LISTING 16.2 Outline of `PrimePeer` and Initialization of a JXTA Peer

```java
package primecruncher;
import net.jxta.peergroup.PeerGroup;
import net.jxta.peergroup.PeerGroupFactory;
import net.jxta.peergroup.PeerGroupID;
import net.jxta.discovery.DiscoveryService;
import net.jxta.pipe.PipeService;
import net.jxta.pipe.InputPipe;
import net.jxta.pipe.PipeID;
import net.jxta.exception.PeerGroupException;
import net.jxta.protocol.ModuleClassAdvertisement;
import net.jxta.protocol.ModuleSpecAdvertisement;
import net.jxta.protocol.PipeAdvertisement;
import net.jxta.document.*;
import net.jxta.platform.ModuleClassID;
import net.jxta.platform.ModuleSpecID;
import net.jxta.id.IDFactory;
import net.jxta.endpoint.Message;
import java.io.FileInputStream;
import java.io.IOException;
import java.io.FileOutputStream;
import java.io.StringWriter;
public class PrimePeer {
        private static PeerGroup group;
        private static DiscoveryService discoSvc;
        private static PipeService pipeSvc;
        private InputPipe inputPipe;
        private static final String PIPE_ADV_FILE = "primeserver_pipe.adv";
        public static void main(String[] argv) {
                PrimePeer pp = new PrimePeer();
                pp.startJxta();
                pp.doAdvertise();
                pp.startService();
        }
        public PrimePeer() {
        }
        private void startJxta() {
                try {
                        group = PeerGroupFactory.newNetPeerGroup();
                        discoSvc = group.getDiscoveryService();
                        pipeSvc = group.getPipeService();
                } catch (PeerGroupException e) {
                        System.out.println("Cannot create Net Peer Group:
➥" + e.getMessage());
                        System.exit(-1);
                }
        }

    /**
     * Create and propagate advertisements
     */
```

LISTING 16.2 continued

```
        private void doAdvertise() {
            …
        }
        /*
         * Start up the service, listen for incoming messages on the service's
➥input pipe.
         */
        private void startService() {
            …
        }
    /**
         * Compute the requested list of prime numbers.
         */
        private void processInput(String high, String low) {
            …
        }
}
```

In the `startJxta()` service initialization method, we first obtain a reference to the World Peer Group; this is done via a static `PeerGroupFactory` method. Calling that method will cause the JXTA runtime to bootstrap. Next, we obtain references to two peer group services that the Net Peer Group provides: the `DiscoveryService` and the `PipeService`. We will use both when creating the service's advertisements.

Creating and Publishing Advertisements

As we mentioned earlier, the JXTA virtual network relies on JXTA IDs to identify network resources. The discovery of those resources occurs via advertisements. The `net.jxta.id` package contains the `ID` class, as well as a factory for creating various kinds of IDs—`IDFactory`. Listing 16.3 uses `IDFactory` to create a `ModuleClassID` for our new module.

In JXTA, a `net.jxta.document.Document` serves as a general container for data. A `Document` in JXTA is defined by the MIME media type of its content, and it has the capability of producing an `InputStream` with the content itself. In that sense, `Document` is somewhat analogous to an HTTP stream. JXTA makes no attempt to interpret the content of a `Document`; that content is part of an application-level protocol.

A `Document` that holds the advertisement of a JXTA network resource is a `net.jxta.document.Advertisement`. An `Advertisement` is a `StructuredDocument`, composed of a hierarchy of elements similar to XML. Structured documents can be nested, which enables a document to be manipulated without regard to the physical representation of its data.

As with any `StructuredDocument`, an `Advertisement` can be represented in XML or plain text formats. An `Advertisement` contains the ID of the resource it advertises, the type of the `Advertisement`, as well as an expiration time specified as an absolute time value. The JXTA API provides a convenient factory, `AdvertisementFactory`, to create different types of advertisements. Listing 16.3 shows the creation of a new `ModuleClassAdvertisement` via that factory class. Note the manner in which the `ModuleClassID` is added to the advertisement.

LISTING 16.3 Creating and Advertising a Module Class

```
private void doAdvertise() {
        ModuleClassAdvertisement classAd =
                (ModuleClassAdvertisement)AdvertisementFactory.newAdvertisement(
                        ModuleClassAdvertisement.getAdvertisementType());
        ModuleClassID classID = IDFactory.newModuleClassID();
        classAd.setModuleClassID(classID);
        classAd.setName(ServiceConstants.CLASS_NAME);
        classAd.setDescription("A prime number crunching service.");
        try {
                discoSvc.publish(classAd, DiscoveryService.ADV);
                discoSvc.remotePublish(classAd, DiscoveryService.ADV);
                System.out.println("Published module class adv.");
        } catch (IOException e) {
                System.out.println("Trouble publishing module class adv: " +
                        e.getMessage());
        }
}
```

The JXTA `net.jxta.discovery.DiscoveryService` is a group service provided by the Net Peer Group, and its main purpose is to facilitate the publishing and discovery of advertisements. It provides two modes of both publishing and discovery: local and remote. The local mode has to do with the peer's local cache—local discovery means looking for advertisements in that cache, and local publishing means entering an advertisement into the local cache. Remote, as its name says, means performing discovery and publishing in the context of the entire peer group. Thus, query messages propagate throughout the JXTA virtual network in accord with the protocols we described previously, and responses are resolved to those queries as they arrive from the network. Thus, remote discovery is asynchronous—it might take quite a while for a desired advertisement type to be found on the JXTA network. Listing 16.3 shows both the remote and local publishing of the `ModuleClassAdvertisement`.

Similar to the preceding process, we create a `ModuleSpec` ID via the `IDFactory` class, and its corresponding advertising is obtained from the `AdvertisementFactory` (see Listing 16.4).

LISTING 16.4   Creating a New `ModuleSpecAdvertisement`

```
ModuleSpecAdvertisement specAd =
        (ModuleSpecAdvertisement)AdvertisementFactory.newAdvertisement(
                ModuleSpecAdvertisement.getAdvertisementType());
ModuleSpecID specID = IDFactory.newModuleSpecID(classID);
specAd.setModuleSpecID(specID);
specAd.setName(ServiceConstants.SPEC_NAME);
specAd.setDescription("Specification for a prime number
➥crunching service");
specAd.setCreator("Sams Publishing");
specAd.setSpecURI("http://www.samspulishing.com/p2p/primecruncher");
specAd.setVersion("Version 1.0");
```

Recall that a `ModuleSpecAdvertisement` defines a wire protocol, or a network behavior,
to access a service. Thus, we need to provide a `PipeAdvertisement` as a parameter to the
`ModuleSpecAdvertisement`. Because the module's advertisements will be cached by
peers on the network, it is important to ensure that each `ModuleSpecAdvertisement`
refers to the same pipe. Thus, we must save the pipe's advertisement to persistent storage
and read that data from storage whenever creating a new pipe advertisement, as shown in
Listing 16.5. (If the advertisement has not been saved to disk yet, create and save a new
one.)

LISTING 16.5   Creating a Pipe Advertisement

```
PipeAdvertisement pipeAd = null;
try {
        FileInputStream is = new FileInputStream(PIPE_ADV_FILE);
        pipeAd = (PipeAdvertisement)AdvertisementFactory.
➥newAdvertisement(
                new MimeMediaType("text/xml"), is);
        is.close();
} catch (IOException e) {
        pipeAd = (PipeAdvertisement)AdvertisementFactory.
➥newAdvertisement(
                PipeAdvertisement.getAdvertisementType());
        PipeID pid = IDFactory.newPipeID(group.getPeerGroupID());
        pipeAd.setPipeID(pid);
        //save pipeAd in file
        Document pipeAdDoc = pipeAd.getDocument(new MimeMediaType
➥("text/xml"));
        try {
                FileOutputStream os = new FileOutputStream(PIPE_ADV_FILE);
                pipeAdDoc.sendToStream(os);
                os.flush();
                os.close();
                System.out.println("Wrote pipe advertisement to disk.");
        } catch (IOException ex) {
```

LISTING **16.5**   continued

```
                    System.out.println("Can't save pipe advertisement
➥to file " +
                        PIPE_ADV_FILE);
                    System.exit(-1);
            }
        }
```

The following code segment saves a pipe advertisement to disk in XML format. For instance, one running of this code produced the following XML document:

```
<?xml version="1.0"?>
<!DOCTYPE jxta:PipeAdvertisement>
<jxta:PipeAdvertisement xmlns:jxta="http://jxta.org">
        <Id>
urn:jxta:uuid-59616261646162614E5047205032503382CCB236202640F5A242ACE15A8F9D7C04
        </Id>
        <Type>
                JxtaUnicast
        </Type>
</jxta:PipeAdvertisement>
```

We subsequently pass this new `PipeAdvertisement` as a parameter to the `ModuleSpecAdvertisement`, as shown in Listing 16.6.

LISTING **16.6**   Adding the `PipeAdvertisement` as a Parameter to the `ModuleSpecAdvertisement`

```
specAd.setPipeAdvertisement(pipeAdv);
```

At this point, we are ready to publish the `ModuleSpecAdvertisement` both locally and remotely, as illustrated in Listing 16.7.

LISTING **16.7**   Local and Remote Publishing of a `ModuleSpecAdvertisement`

```
        try {
                discoSvc.publish(specAd, DiscoveryService.ADV);
                discoSvc.remotePublish(specAd, DiscoveryService.ADV);
                System.out.println("Published module spec adv");
        } catch (IOException e) {
                System.out.println("Trouble publishing module spec adv: " +
                        e.getMessage());
}
```

Finally, we create an `InputPipe` based on the pipe advertisement in Listing 16.8.

LISTING 16.8 `InputPipe` Creation from a `PipeAdvertisement`

```
//create an input pipe based on the advertisement
try {
        inputPipe = pipeSvc.createInputPipe(pipeAd);
        System.out.println("Created input pipe");
} catch (IOException e) {
        System.out.println("Can't create input pipe. " + e.getMessage());
}
}
```

These are all the steps needed to publish a new JXTA service. Recall that a module's class advertisement advertises the fact that the module functionality exists in a peer group; it is a fairly abstract concept, somewhat analogous to a Java interface that defines an API, but does not provide an implementation. A module's spec advertisement, on the other hand, specifies a wire protocol to access the service. In this case, that wire protocol consists of an `InputPipe` to which other peers can send messages. It is to that `InputPipe` that the messages specifying the two boundary numbers will arrive.

Processing Messages from an `InputPipe`

The next step in implementing the prime cruncher peer is to process the received messages. We will break this task down into handling incoming messages, calculating the desired list of prime numbers, and sending back a response. Listing 16.9 shows the first part of the activity.

LISTING 16.9 Processing Messages on an `InputPipe`

```
private void startService() {
        while (true) {
                Message msg = null;
                try {
                        msg = inputPipe.waitForMessage();
                } catch (InterruptedException ex) {
                        inputPipe.close();
                        return;
                }
                String highInt = msg.getString(ServiceConstants.HIGH_INT);
                String lowInt = msg.getString(ServiceConstants.LOW_INT);
                if (highInt != null || lowInt != null) {
                        processInput(highInt, lowInt);
                }
        }
}
```

As mentioned before, the `net.jxta.endpoint.Message` object is sent between two peers by `EndpointService` (an implementation of the Endpoint Protocol discussed earlier). A `Message` consists of a set of `MessageElements`, and features a destination `EndpointAddress` to facilitate its routing through the JXTA network. A message element can be any array of bytes, and `Message` has the capability to retrieve an element as a `String`. When a new message element is specified, it can be associated with a MIME type, as well as a `String` that serves as the element's key. In this method implementation, we retrieve the message elements referenced by the keys `ServiceConstants.HIGH_INT` and `ServiceConstants.LOW_INT`. If both elements are valid `Strings`, we pass them onto a private method, `processInput()`.

`processInput()` is responsible for executing the Sieve of Eratosthenes algorithm (or any other algorithm) to produce a list of all prime numbers between `LOW_INT` and `HIGH_INT`. To save space, we will not show that part of the code here; instead, the full source code is available for download from `samspublishing.com`. In addition, the full source code also contains a version of `startService()` that retrieves a `PipeAdvertisement` from the `Message` (as another message element), opens a pipe back to the client, and sends the list of prime numbers back to the client.

The Prime Cruncher Client

The purpose of the client in this application is to distribute the computation load to as many peers advertising the number-crunching service as possible. Consider a user wanting to obtain all prime numbers between 1 and 10,000. When a peer receives that user request, it needs to determine how many other peers it can share the task with. Thus, it must continuously discover peers advertising the prime number service and maintain a cache of those peers' advertisements. If a peer has, for example, 10 other peers it can share the work with, then it might then create a message with `LOW_INT` set to 1 and `HIGH_INT` set to 1000, then another message with the numbers set to 1001 and 2000, respectively, and so forth. Finally, the client would open a pipe to each of the 10 peers, and transmit one message to each. Figure 16.19 describes that peer-to-peer message exchange.

The client's skeleton looks similar to the server's (see Listing 16.10). It also initializes the Net Peer Group, and obtains from it the group's discovery and pipe services.

FIGURE 16.19

The peer-to-peer message exchange.

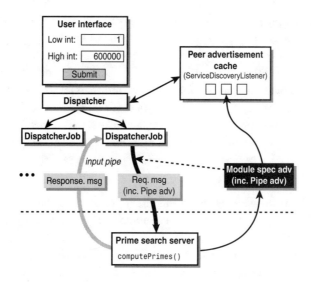

LISTING 16.10   PrimeClient

```
package primecruncher;
import net.jxta.peergroup.PeerGroup;
import net.jxta.peergroup.PeerGroupFactory;
import net.jxta.discovery.DiscoveryService;
import net.jxta.discovery.DiscoveryListener;
import net.jxta.discovery.DiscoveryEvent;
import net.jxta.pipe.PipeService;
import net.jxta.pipe.OutputPipe;
import net.jxta.pipe.PipeID;
import net.jxta.exception.PeerGroupException;
import net.jxta.protocol.DiscoveryResponseMsg;
import net.jxta.protocol.ModuleSpecAdvertisement;
import net.jxta.protocol.PipeAdvertisement;
import net.jxta.document.StructuredTextDocument;
import net.jxta.document.MimeMediaType;
import net.jxta.document.TextElement;
import net.jxta.document.AdvertisementFactory;
import net.jxta.id.IDFactory;
import net.jxta.endpoint.Message;
import java.util.Enumeration;
import java.io.StringWriter;
import java.io.IOException;
import java.net.URL;
import java.net.MalformedURLException;
import java.net.UnknownServiceException;
import java.util.HashSet;
import java.util.Set;
public class PrimeClient implements DiscoveryListener {
        private static PeerGroup group;
```

LISTING **16.10**   continued

```
        private static DiscoveryService discoSvc;
        private static PipeService pipeSvc;
        private OutputPipe outputPipe;
        private Set adverts = new HashSet();
        public PrimeClient() {
        }
        public static void main(String[] argv) {
                Client cl = new Client();
                cl.startJxta();
                cl.doDiscovery();
        }
        public int[] processPrimes(int low, int high) {
        }
        private void startJxta() {
                try {
                        group = PeerGroupFactory.newNetPeerGroup();
                        discoSvc = group.getDiscoveryService();
                        pipeSvc = group.getPipeService();
                } catch (PeerGroupException e) {
                        System.out.println("Can't create net peer group: " +
                                e.getMessage());
                        System.exit(-1);
                }
        }
        private void doDiscovery() {

        }
}
```

Although `PrimePeer`'s key responsibility is to advertise its service and process incoming messages, `PrimeClient` must participate in the service discovery process. The `doDiscovery()` method initiates service discovery. First, the peer looks into its local cache for advertisements that match a `Name` attribute in the prime computing module's specification. It then processes each advertisement it finds there (see Listing 16.11).

LISTING **16.11**   Performing Local Discovery

```
        System.out.println("Starting service discovery...");
        System.out.println("Searching local cache for " +
                ServiceConstants.SPEC_NAME + " advertisements");
        Enumeration res = null;
        try {
                res = discoSvc.getLocalAdvertisements(DiscoveryService.ADV,
                        "Name", ServiceConstants.SPEC_NAME);
        } catch (IOException e) {
                System.out.println("IO Exception.");
        }
```

LISTING 16.11   continued

```
if (res != null) {
        while (res.hasMoreElements()) {
                processAdv((ModuleSpecAdvertisement)res.nextElement());
        }
}
```

Next, the peer initiates remote advertisement discovery. *Remote discovery* means that discovery queries propagate through the JXTA network, and responses arrive as suitable advertisements are found. Thus, remote discovery is an asynchronous process. We pass a `DiscoveryListener` as an argument to `DiscoveryService`'s `getRemoteAdvertisements()` method. In addition, we must also specify a threshold of the number of advertisements we desire to receive from each peer (see Listing 16.12).

Once remote discovery is initiated, discovered advertisements are cached in the local advertisement cache. So, the next time the peer starts up, it will likely discover advertisements from that cache.

LISTING 16.12   Initiating Remote Service Discovery

```
System.out.println("Starting remote discovery...");
discoSvc.getRemoteAdvertisements(null, DiscoveryService.ADV,
        "Name", ServiceConstants.SPEC_NAME, 1, this);
}
```

`DiscoveryListener` specifies the `discoveryEvent()` method that gets called each time an advertisement matching our criteria is found. A `DiscoveryEvent` contains a `DiscoveryReponseMsg`, containing the actual advertisements found through remote discovery. We obtain an enumeration of those advertisements and process each, as seen in Listing 16.13.

LISTING 16.13   Implementing a DiscoveryListener

```
public void discoveryEvent(DiscoveryEvent event) {
        System.out.println("DiscoveryEvent called");
        DiscoveryResponseMsg  mes = event.getResponse();
        //these contain the responses found
        Enumeration res = mes.getResponses();
        if (res != null) {
                while (res.hasMoreElements()) {
                        processAdv((ModuleSpecAdvertisement)
➥res.nextElement());
                }
        }
}
```

Our processAdv() method is very simple: It inserts each ModuleSpecAdvertisement into a set. A *set* ensures that no duplicate advertisements are stored. This set acts as a cache for module spec advertisements:

```
private void processAdv(ModuleSpecAdvertisement ad) {
        adverts.add(ad);
}
```

Advertisement Processing

After we've set up a discovery listener, it will keep adding newly discovered module spec advertisements to our simple local cache. Each time the processPrimes() method gets called, the client peer will attempt to contact the peers represented by these module spec advertisements, connect to their input pipes, and pass a message that initiates the prime number search on each of those peers.

The first item in this method is to determine the set of peers we can delegate work to. Recall that an advertisement has an expiration date associated with it. Thus, we must eliminate advertisements that are no longer valid:

```
Public int[] processPrimes(int low, int high) {
        Set setCopy = null;
        synchronized(adverts) {
                Set setCopy = (Set) adverts.clone();
        }
        ArrayList workingList = new ArrayList();
        ArrayList expired = new ArrayList();
        long currentTime = System.getCurrentTimeMillis();
        Iterator it = workingSet.iterator();
        while (it.hasNext()) {
                ModuleSpecAdvertisement ad = (ModuleSpecAdvertisement)it.next();
                if (ad.getLocalExpirationTime() > currentTime + (2 * 60 *1000)) {
                        workingList.addElement(ad);
                } else {
                        expired.addElement(ad);
                }
        }
removeExpired(expired);
```

The preceding code segment performs a simple cache management of discovered advertisements, delegating the removal of all advertisements that have either expired or about to expire shortly to the removeExpired() method (not shown here, but is included in the full source code).

After we have a set of valid advertisements, we can start processing them in order to obtain from them the pipe advertisement that we must use to send the messages. Because we assume (at least in this example) that all those advertisements refer to peers that we will actually use in our prime searching task, we first break down the job into smaller tasks corresponding to each peer.

Note that this job distribution is rather contrived: Some peers might be more capable than others, and some might have better network connections than others. Those differences should be taken into account when assigning tasks to a peer. Also, in practice it might not make sense to divide the job into too many small segments, because the network communication time could easily dominate the time spent on the actual processing of the prime numbers list. However, this example aims to illustrate how to obtain a pipe advertisement from a `ModuleSpecAdvertisement`, how to create a new message, and then how to send that message down the pipe.

Listing 16.14 shows how the natural number list is broken into sublists, each sublist corresponding to a message that will be sent to a peer participating in the computation. Messages are then inserted into a hash map, and the key of the map indicates a message's status: Was it sent out already? Have we received a result for that computation yet?

LISTING 16.14   Creating New Messages

```
Map messageMap = new HashMap();
int size = workingList.size()
int mod = high % size;
high -= mod;
int perPiece = high / size;
for (int i=0; i < size; i++) {
        //create a new message
        Message msg = pipeSvc.createMessage();
        msg.setString(ServiceConstants.LOW_INT, low);
        //last message will get to compute a bit more
        if (i == size-1) {
                high = low + perPiece - 1 + mod;
        } else {
                high = low + perPiece -1;
        }
        msg.setString(ServiceConstants.HIGH_INT, high);
        low += perPiece;

        //we neither sent the message, nor did we get a response
        StatusMap statusMap = new StatusMap(false, false);
        StatusMap statusMap = new StatusMap(false, false);
        messageMap.put(statusMap, msg);
}
```

`StatusMap` is simply a pairing of two Boolean values; it is not listed here.

Our final step is to extract the pipe advertisements from each `ModuleSpecAdvertisement`, open each pipe, and send a message to that pipe. Finally, we will mark the message as sent.

Recall that an advertisement is just a structured document, similar to an XML document. It can easily be converted to a text document and printed out. It's useful to inspect the contents of the advertisement during development and at debug-time (see Listing 16.15).

LISTING 16.15   Printing an Advertisement

```
Collection ads = messageMap.values();
Iterator it = ads.iterator();
while (it.hasNext()) {
        ModuleSpecAdvertisement ad = (ModuleSpecAdvertisement)it.next();
        //First, print out ModuleSpec advertisement on standard output
        StructuredTextDocument doc =
                (StructuredTextDocument)ad.getDocument(new MimeMediaType
➥("text/plain"));
        try {
                StringWriter out = new StringWriter();
                doc.sendToWriter(out);
                System.out.println(out);
                out.close();
        } catch (IOException e) {
        }
...
```

As we discussed earlier, a `StructuredTextDocument` consists of elements, and one such element is a parameter. When we constructed the `ModuleSpecAdvertisement` for our service, we entered the service's pipe advertisement as a parameter. The parameter is just another `StructuredDocument` element that we can manipulate in the same way we would an XML document.

In parsing the advertisement's parameter element, we first obtain the pipe's ID and type. The pipe's ID conforms to a URN specification, outlined in the JXTA specifications, which encodes the 128-bit special identifier for the pipe. The following is an example of such a URN:

```
urn:jxta:uuid-59616261646162614E5047205032503382CCB236202640F5A242ACE15A8F9D7C04
```

The `IDFactory` class is capable of constructing the `PipeID` object from such a URN. That is the mechanism we use to assign the pipe ID to the pipe advertisement (see Listing 16.16).

LISTING 16.16 Working with Advertisement Parameters

```java
StructuredTextDocument param = (StructuredTextDocument)ad.getParam();
String pipeID = null;
String pipeType = null;
Enumeration en = null;
 if (param != null) {
        en = param.getChildren("jxta:PipeAdvertisement");
}
Enumeration child = null;
 if (en != null) {
        child = ((TextElement)en.nextElement()).getChildren();
}
 if (child != null) {
        while (child.hasMoreElements()) {
                TextElement el = (TextElement)child.nextElement();
                String elementName = el.getName();
                if (elementName.equals("Id")) {
                        pipeID = el.getTextValue();
                }
                if (elementName.equals("Type")) {
                        pipeType = el.getTextValue();
                }
        }
}
if (pipeID != null || pipeType != null) {
        PipeAdvertisement pipeAdvert = (PipeAdvertisement)
                AdvertisementFactory.newAdvertisement(
                        PipeAdvertisement.getAdvertisementType());
        try {
                URL pidURL = new URL(pipeID);
                PipeID pid = (PipeID)IDFactory.fromURL(pidURL);
                pipeAdvert.setPipeID(pid);
        } catch (MalformedURLException e) {
                System.out.println("Wrong URL: " + e.getMessage());
                return;
        } catch (UnknownServiceException e) {
                System.out.println("Unknown Service: " + e.getMessage());
                return;
        }
}
```

Based on this `PipeAdvertisement`, we are now able to construct an output pipe that connects to the remote peer's input pipe, as shown in Listing 16.17. Recall that a pipe is unidirectional communication channel. Thus, we do not expect to hear back from the remote peer via this pipe. The remote peer performs an essentially similar task, opening a pipe back to the client and sending it a message with the results of the computation. (We do not show that part of the code here; please see the Web site for the full sample source code.)

LISTING 16.17   Creating an Output Pipe

```
try {
        outputPipe = pipeSvc.createOutputPipe(pipeAdvert, 30000);
        outputPipe.send(msg);
        System.out.println("Sent message on output pipe");
} catch (IOException e) {
        System.out.println("Can't send message through pipe:
➥" + e.getMessage());
    }
}
```

An interesting thing about this pipe-creation mechanism is that a peer might have changed network identities between sending out the ModuleSpecAdvertisement and a client contacting it for useful work. However, the peer's virtual identity on the JXTA network remains the same, and the runtime services ensure that the pipe advertised by the ModuleSpecAdvertisement connects.

After you have downloaded the full source code from the Web site and made the decision to run both peers on the same machine, you'll need to start them from separate directories and specify a different network communication port for each in the JXTA Configurator.

To start the server application, ensure that all the JXTA classes are in your classpath (this process is detailed in the JXTA installation document), and then type the following command:

```
java primecruncher.PrimePeer
```

You might also run the command with the following optional parameters. These parameters allow you to bypass the JXTA login screen:

```
java -Dnet.jxta.tls.principal=USERNAME
    -Dnet.jxta.tls.password=PASSWORD primecruncher.PrimePeer
```

By substituting your JXTA username and password you can run the client similarly:

```
java -Dnet.jxta.tls.princincipal=USERNAME
    -Dnet.jxta.tls.password=PASSWORD primecruncher.PrimeClient
```

The prime-finder application of this chapter operates as a full-fledged Java application, with its own user interface and main() method. In the next chapter, we will learn how to interactively invoke this application from the JXTA Shell.

Summary

This chapter demonstrated JXTA's ability to construct a virtual network across existing network topologies and protocols. The sample application presented in this chapter can run on any operating system, utilizing any implementation of JXTA; it does not require a peer to have any Java language processing capability. The only requirement is for each peer to implement the JXTA protocols used in this application, and to understand an application-level protocol defined in the message exchanges.

The JXTA Shell

by Frank Sommers

IN THIS CHAPTER

At the 2001 O'Reilly Peer-to-Peer Conference, Bill Joy, Sun Microsystems' co-founder and chief technologist, introduced JXTA with a comparison to the Unix operating system. In the early days of Unix, when Joy was a student at the University of California at Berkeley, many versions of that operating system were in use. In addition, crucial parts of Unix, such as the filesystem, had a variety of implementations. Although that diversity fueled Unix innovation, it resulted in many incompatible software packages all trying to solve similar problems.

The peer-to-peer space, Joy argued, exhibits a similar situation: File sharing, peer-to-peer communication, security, and peer groups are issues all P2P systems must deal with. Chapter 16, "JXTA and XML," gives you a glimpse of how JXTA abstracts out those common functionalities into a set of reusable APIs, much like the Berkeley version of Unix (BSD) aimed to provide a common platform for all to build on. Unix's design inspired JXTA in other ways, too. This chapter will show you a JXTA application, the JXTA Shell, that takes many useful concepts from the Unix shells and extends those capabilities to P2P networks.

Why a Shell?

Just as a shell protects its inhabitant from the vicissitudes of the ocean, an operating system shell enables a human user to interact with an otherwise uninviting machine environment. And, just like a sea shell, an operating system shell defines an environment that governs the behavior of things executing inside. With an operating system shell, environment variables permit programs executing from a shell to share common information. A user interacts with the operating system and application software running on it via shell commands. Figure 17.1 illustrates a shell's shared environment and commands.

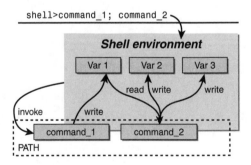

FIGURE 17.1

A shell provides a common environment for executing commands and applications.

A shell presents a minimalist user interface: only a command line. All interaction with the shell occurs via commands. When a user submits a command, the shell evaluates the entire line, starting from left to right. Some elements of that command line might refer to a shell's built-in commands, in which case the shell interprets them directly. Or, a command might be the name of an external program, in which case the shell searches for that program and requests the operating system to invoke it. The PATH shell environment variable specifies the location of that search.

Whether built-in or external, shell commands often have well-defined input and output streams. Whereas a Java object, for example, might offer various data input and output mechanisms—such as method invocations, sockets, or message interfaces—a shell command also has in addition *standard input* and *standard output* streams. These are standard in the sense that a shell considers them the primary mechanisms to get data in and out of a shell command. System.out and System.in are similar concepts for Java programs, in that the Java VM defines these as "standard" input and output streams to and from an object. Figure 17.2 illustrates an object executing as a shell command with standard input and standard output streams.

FIGURE 17.2
Shell command with standard input and output streams.

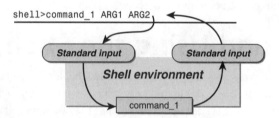

Because the shell tracks each command's standard input and output streams, it can arrange the input stream of one command to be connected to the output stream of another command. The abstraction for that connection is a pipe. A user requests that a pipe be created with the built-in shell operator |. As an example, consider a pipe between the Unix cat and grep commands. Cat concatenates a list of files and sends that output to its standard output stream. grep is a searching utility—it lets you specify a pattern and search for it in a set of files you list. Suppose that you wanted to find the pattern JXTA in the file P2P_article.txt. You would pipe the output of cat to the input of grep:

```
cat P2P_article.txt | grep JXTA
```

Pipes can assume any length, provided that one program's input stream can process another's output stream. Pipes therefore offer a powerful way to arrange sophisticated interaction between simple programs. At the end of that chain is the shell's standard output stream. By default, that output stream is the command line.

Shells not only let you pipe one command's output into another's input, they also enable you to redirect a command's output and input in any fashion. The operators for that arbitrary input and output redirection are < and >, respectively. For instance, the > operator enables you to redirect the output from the previous command line to a file:

```
cat P2P_article.txt | grep JXTA > resultfile.txt
```

In his presentation at the O'Reilly conference, Bill Joy suggested that a shell's capability to combine simple commands into complex interactions would be helpful in the P2P world as well: That capability would let P2P applications remain small and simple, and users would be able to compose sophisticated P2P functionality out of those simple components. If each component does one thing, but does it well, that component can be reused as often as necessary, enabling developers to build on each others' work. Chapter 16 gives you an overview of how JXTA abstracts out components common to P2P systems, and offers reusable, programming language-neutral abstractions for those components. The JXTA Shell in this chapter is an application built on the core JXTA components, and it enables you to interact with the JXTA network in the same way a Unix shell enables you to interact with the operating system.

Starting and Using the Shell

If you opted for a full download of the JXTA libraries in Chapter 16, you already have the code to run the JXTA Shell. If you did not use a graphical installer, go to the directory where you installed the JXTA libraries and find the `shell` subdirectory. If you don't have that directory, you will need to download the JXTA Shell from `http://www.jxta.org`.

Inside that directory, find `jxta.exe` (or on Unix, the `run.bat` file) and execute it. This batch file will cause the JXTA Shell to start up. As with all JXTA applications based on the J2SE JXTA binding, you will need to ensure that the JXTA environment has been properly set up. Please refer to Chapter 16 for an overview of the JXTA Configurator. After the JXTA Shell starts up, you will see a window similar to Figure 17.3.

Using the man Command

The best way to get acquainted with the JXTA Shell is to type in the `man` command, which stands for manual pages. The output of that command will be a list of all the commands the shell recognizes, along with a one-line description for each command. If you are familiar with some of the Unix shells, you will recognize many of the commands.

We've already seen the `cat` and `grep` commands, but the JXTA shell has the equivalent of `clear`, `env`, `more`, `talk`, `wc` (word count), `who`, `whoami`, and `help`, to mention just a few. If you type **man** followed by any of the JXTA shell commands, a detailed manual page for that command will be displayed.

FIGURE 17.3

The JXTA Shell.

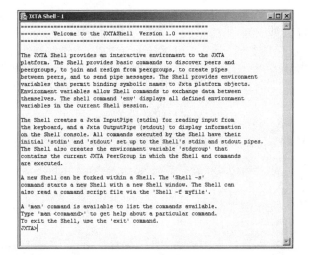

Differences Between the JXTA Shell and Unix

The main difference between the JXTA Shell and its typical Unix relative is that the JXTA Shell's primary function is to let you interact with the JXTA virtual network, whereas the Unix shell enables you to interface with the operating system. As a result, the JXTA Shell supports only minimal interaction with the operating system; it is not able to run arbitrary OS commands, for instance. As well, each shell command interacts with objects relevant to the JXTA P2P network, not with objects defined by an operating system.

To appreciate that difference, consider the cat command in the context of the JXTA Shell. In the Unix version of that command, it concatenates a set of files, producing its output in the shell's standard output. JXTA does not directly interact with the filesystem; the JXTA equivalent of a "file" would be Document. The shell has to be able to identify a Document, and the cat command then takes as its parameter that document identifier and displays the document's content.

Environment Variables

The JXTA Shell takes advantage of the shell environment to associate JXTA-specific objects with variables. If you type the env command, it displays all the variables the current JXTA Shell instance knows of. Variable assignment occurs either explicitly, via the set or setenv commands, or implicitly as a result of executing certain commands.

Among the commands that implicitly assign environment variables are those that manipulate peers, peer groups, pipes, advertisement, and documents. The `peers` command, for example, prints a list of all peers the shell is aware of. Recall that peers are represented by peer advertisements; the `peers` shell command displays the peer advertisements it has discovered in its local cache, a behavior that corresponds to `DiscoveryService`'s `getLocalAdvertisements()` method. For the advertisement search to propagate throughout the JXTA network, use the `-r` flag: `peers -r` (`-r` meaning `remote`). The command itself exits, but the discovery messages will propagate via relay peers, causing newly discovered peer advertisements to add to the local cache. Thus, issuing `peers` again after a while will likely produce a list including those newly discovered peers:

```
JXTA>peers
peer0: name = aristotle
peer1: name = aquinas
```

As this example shows, the `peers` command assigns environment variables, which are listed on the left side. For instance, `peer1` corresponds to a peer by the name `aquinas`. You can use the `cat` command to display the contents of that environment variable (see Listing 17.1).

LISTING 17.1   Displaying a Peer Advertisement's Content

```
JXTA>cat peer1
<?xml version="1.0"?>
<!DOCTYPE jxta:PA>
<jxta:PA xmlns:jxta="http://jxta.org">
    <PID>
     urn:jxta:uuid-59616261646162614A78746
        150325033F09E3FC87DD34E52864FB8CDEB0398B803
    </PID>
     <GID>
        urn:jxta:jxta-NetGroup
     </GID>
     <Name>
        aquinas
     </Name>
     <Svc>
     <MCID>
        urn:jxta:uuid-DEADBEEFDEAFBABAFEEDBABE0000000605
     </MCID>
      <Parm>
        <Rdv>
          true
        </Rdv>
      </Parm>
     </Svc>
     <Svc>
```

LISTING 17.1 continued

```
    <MCID>
        urn:jxta:uuid-DEADBEEFDEAFBABAFEEDBABE0000000805
    </MCID>
    <Parm>
      <Addr>
          tcp://192.168.1.10:9701/
      </Addr>
      <Addr>
          jxtatls://uuid-
59616261646162614A78746150325033F09E3FC87DD
34E52864FB8CDEB0398B803/TlsTransport/jxta-WorldGroup
      </Addr>
      <Addr>
          jxta://uuid-59616261646162614A78746
150325033F09E3FC87DD34E52864FB8CDEB0398B803/
      </Addr>
      <Addr>
          http://JxtaHttpClientuuid-
59616261646162614A78746150325033F09E3FC87DD34E52864FB8CDEB0398B803/
      </Addr>
    </Parm>
    </Svc>
    <Svc>
    <MCID>
        urn:jxta:uuid-DEADBEEFDEAFBABAFEEDBABE0000000105
    </MCID>
    <Parm>
      <RootCert>
```

MIICPDCCAaWgAwIBAgIBATANBgkqhki
G9w0BAQUFADBmMRUwEwYDVQQKEwx3d3
cu anh0YS5vcmcxCzAJBgNVBAcTAlNGMQswCQ
YDVQQGEwJVUzEUMBIGA1UEAxMLZnNv
bW1lcnMtMtQ0ExHTAbBgNVBAsTFDA2M0E
xNEZGODREOUQwMEI2NDUyMB4XDTAyMDQw
 ODA1MDYyOVoXDTEyMDQwODA1MDYyOVo
wZjEVMBMGA1UEChMMd3d3Lmp4dGEub3Jn
MQswCQYDVQQHEwJTRjELMAkGA1UEBhMCVVM
xFDASBgNVBAMTC2Zzb21tZXJzLUNB
MR0wGwYDVQQLExQwNjNBMTRGRjg0
RDlEMDBCNjQ1MjCBmzALBgkqhkiG9w0BAQED
 gYsAMIGHAoGBALwcEz8GNFp/7RybRFK
3Nw/Qz2bHjeLGA2XZqZi0Xlh6TUHumbE5
 0VFPUuZBzRbIbp/vikRmy16NeG4MLM8
/iTT3HfKjxXNByDKtOtrCQPfLnQXiGLkM
vXY2ksI4FHfmI6QbIEW2S/ND6jcVZ
gtRddhr3XJUX3z5CjCAx8E8YRr/AgERMA0G
CSqGSIb3DQEBBQUAA4GBAC7Uh+Q0WzRkMM
0TYmMDyLNiph5a7vxUO7RM/kI/qS7i
i59e3rJDRtV2hFrK2J6q003Vj9o9TOX

LISTING 17.1 continued

```
cAxzzv31JDTGutSC9IaoHnKWFj973tk+j
wjghmbtPFTDppZsqjvDJVf/rBxP1tVBVP
gqc+vZfEox4ZETbrT9XQqvQI4JnKbok
        </RootCert>
      </Parm>
    </Svc>
</jxta:PA>
```

As you can see, the content of the peer1 environment variable corresponds to a peer advertisement. If you call cat with the -p argument, it will display the content a variable refers to in a "pretty" format (without the XML tags). The groups command similarly displays peer groups (peer group advertisements). If presented with the -r argument, it likewise initiates remote peer group discovery.

The JXTA shell enables you to search for any sort of advertisement on the JXTA network. The following command searches for module spec advertisements with a Name attribute JXTASPEC:com.sams.p2p.primecruncher:

```
JXTA>search -a Name -v JXTASPEC:com.sams.p2p.primecruncher -r
```

The -a and -v parameters signify an attribute and value pair, whereas the -r parameter indicates that we'd like to propagate the discovery request on the JXTA network to remote peers. If you run the JXTA service application from Chapter 16 and type the search command again, in a few seconds you should have at least one advertisement matching that search criteria. You can then look at the contents of that advertisement with the cat command. Listing 17.2 locates the advertisement for the prime number-searching service. The module spec includes a pipe specification through which a client can contact the service.

LISTING 17.2 Locating the Advertisement for the Prime Number-Searching Service

```
JXTA>cat adv0
<?xml version="1.0"?>
<!DOCTYPE jxta:MSA>
<jxta:MSA xmlns:jxta="http://jxta.org">
    <MSID>
        urn:jxta:uuid-C4919B07BDBD4BDD923189BB
623CCF96D14DC34ECEE04C9688688FAEFE56DEBB06
    </MSID>
    <Name>
        JXTASPEC:com.sams.p2p.primecruncher
    </Name>
    <Crtr>
        Sams Publishing
    </Crtr>
```

Listing 17.2   continued

```
        <SURI>
            http://www.samspublishing.com/p2p/primecruncher
        </SURI>
        <Vers>
            Version 1.0
        </Vers>
        <Desc>
            Specification for a prime number crunching service
        </Desc>
        <jxta:PipeAdvertisement xmlns:jxta="http://jxta.org">
            <Id>
                urn:jxta:uuid-59616261646162614E50472050050325
0333BA0BA91BA4A48F48E98AB94400A8EF704
            </Id>
            <Type>
                JxtaUnicast
            </Type>
            <Name>
                JXTAPIPE:com.sams.p2p.primecruncher
            </Name>
        </jxta:PipeAdvertisement>
</jxta:MSA>
```

You can also assign the contents of a file to an environment variable with the importfile command. As an example, consider the pipe advertisement created by the prime number compute server in Chapter 16. To persist the pipe information, that JXTA service wrote its pipe advertisement to a file. Using the importfile command, we can assign the contents of that file to a shell environment variable:

```
JXTA>importfile -f /export/home/myfiles/primeserver_pipe.adv primepipe
```

If you subsequently run the env command, you will notice the new environment variable primepipe. Running cat on the primepipe variable displays the contents of the advertisement file. As you can see, the advertisement read from the file is identical to the pipe advertisement section of the module spec advertisement we discovered via the search command:

```
JXTA>cat primepipe
<?xml version="1.0"?>
<!DOCTYPE jxta:PipeAdvertisement>
<jxta:PipeAdvertisement xmlns:jxta="http://jxta.org">
    <Id>
<urn:jxta:uuid-59616261646162614E5047
2050050325033AD6840F7B55347E4AE79AD0A65D5C42004
    </Id>
    <Type>
        JxtaUnicast
```

```
    </Type>
    <Name>
        JXTAPIPE:com.sams.p2p.primecruncher
    </Name>
</jxta:PipeAdvertisement>
```

After you have that file content assigned to an environment variable, you can create an actual pipe advertisement from it with the `mkadv` command:

```
JXTA>primepipeadv = mkadv -p -d primepipe
```

The `-p` argument signifies that you want to create a pipe advertisement (`mkadv` can also create group advertisements with the `-g` argument), whereas the `-d` argument requests that the advertisement be created from the specified document. (We assigned the document name `primepipe` earlier.)

With a pipe advertisement in hand, you can create the actual pipe that connects to the prime search service. Because that service referred to its input pipe via the published pipe advertisement, you will need to create an *output* pipe to connect to that input pipe:

```
JXTA>primeservice = mkpipe -o primepipeadv
```

The `mkpipe` command creates output pipes with the `-o` parameter, and can create input pipes if you specify the `-i` parameter. When creating an output pipe, `mkpipe` returns only when that pipe is actually resolved. (Recall from Chapter 16 that an output pipe must first resolve the pipe's endpoint, which can take time.) When `mkpipe` returns, the `prime-service` shell variable contains a reference to an actual input pipe to the service.

Interacting with a Remote Peer via a Shell

After we've created a pipe to the peer offering the prime-finding service, we can use that pipe to interact with the peer. Recall from Chapter 16 that the interaction between the prime-finding service and a peer wanting to use that service is via a message exchange: A client peer would need to format a message and send it to the prime-finder service's output pipe. The message must contain the advertisement for an input pipe through which the prime finder service can send back its response. Figure 17.4 shows that interaction.

Therefore, we first must create a message from the JXTA Shell, which is accomplished via the `mkmsg` command:

```
JXTA>querymessage = mkmsg
```

Figure 17.4

Message interfaces between the prime-finder service and other peers.

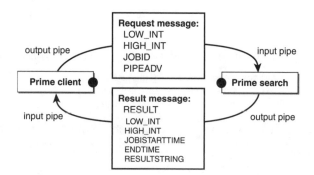

A message initially contains no message elements. We will need to add message elements corresponding to the high and low numbers, indicating the range of prime numbers we want to search for, a job ID, as well as an input pipe advertisement. We will then use the put command to add each of those elements to the message.

The put command takes three arguments: a reference to a message, a unique identifier tag, and a document. The unique tag can be any string. put assigns the document's content to the unique tag inside the message. The document argument must refer to a structured document assigned to a shell variable.

At the time of this writing, the JXTA Shell does not have a built-in command to construct structured documents from the command line. As we've seen earlier, the shell does have the capability, however, to import the contents of an arbitrary file and assign that content to a document. Therefore, we will create three files, corresponding to the high, low, and jobID message elements, respectively. These documents are very simplistic XML files.

The high.xml file is as follows:

```
<?xml version="1.0"?>
<high>
100
</high>
```

Here's low.xml:

```
<?xml version="1.0"?>
<low>
10
</low>
```

And this is id.xml:

```
<?xml version="1.0"?>
<id>
```

17

THE JXTA SHELL

```
12345
</id>
```

We can now import each of these files and assign their contents to shell variables:

```
JXTA>importfile -f /export/home/myfiles/high.xml highdoc
JXTA>importfile -f /export/home/myfiles/low.xml lowdoc
JXTA>importfile -f /export/home/myfiles/id.xml iddoc
```

You can verify the contents of any of the these variables with the `cat` command:

```
JXTA> cat highdoc
<?xml version="1.0"?>
<high>
100
</high>
```

We are ready to use the `put` command to assign these documents to the message. Note that the service's wire protocol specifies that each message element be tagged with a well-known name. Those names are contained in the `ServiceConstants` interface (see Chapter 16). We will use the appropriate names from that interface when assigning each message element to the message:

```
JXTA>put querymessage HIGH_INT highdoc
JXTA>put querymessage LOW_INT lowdoc
JXTA>put querymessage JOBID iddoc
```

Finally, we must specify an input pipe so that we can receive a response from the prime-finder service. Creating an input pipe from the JXTA shell is similar to creating an output pipe: You first create a pipe advertisement with the `mkadv` command, and then create the pipe itself from that advertisement.

```
JXTA>inpipeadv = mkadv -p
JXTA>inputpipe = mkpipe -i inpipeadv
```

The `-i` parameter to `mkpipe` specifies that we are interested in creating an input pipe, not an output pipe.

The final step in preparing the message to be sent is to add the input pipe's advertisement as an element to the message. Because the `put` command accepts only document arguments, and because a pipe advertisement is not a JXTA-structured document type, we need to again overcome this limitation by exporting the advertisement to the filesystem and reading it back from that file into a document. The resulting document can then be assigned as a message element:

```
JXTA>exportfile -f /export/home/mydocuments/inpipeadv.adv inpipeadv
JXTA>importfile -f /export/home/mydocuments/inpipeadv.adv pipeadvdoc
JXTA>put querymessage PIPEADV pipeadvdoc
```

Finally, we are ready to transmit the message via the prime-finder service's output pipe. The send command accomplishes that:

```
JXTA>send primeservice querymessage
```

The prime-finder service has no knowledge that it is interacting with a user via the JXTA Shell rather than the client application we constructed in Chapter 16 because both use identical wire protocols. The service's response is also identical: Upon computing the list of prime numbers between the HIGH and LOW values, the service constructs a response message, opens a pipe back to the client, and sends that response message back via the newly opened pipe. Because we specified the advertisement of the input pipe we created earlier, the service will use that pipe to send its response. We instruct the input pipe to receive a message using the recv command:

```
JXTA>response = recv inputpipe
recv has received a message
```

At this point, the reply message the service sent is assigned to the response environment variable. The reply message protocol specifies (see Chapter 16) that a RESULT tag mark the message element containing the service's response. We can obtain that message element via the get command, which is the counterpart of put:

```
JXTA>result = get response RESULT
```

Finally, we can display the contents of the response with the cat command:

```
JXTA>cat result
<?xml version="1.0"?>
<!DOCTYPE RESULT>
<RESULT>
      <JOBID>
            12345
      </JOBID>
      <LOW_INT>
            10
      </LOW_INT>
      <HIGH_INT>
            100
      </HIGH_INT>
      <STARTTIME>
            1021004688485
      </STARTTIME>
      <ENDTIME>
            1021004688485
      </ENDTIME>
      <RESULTSTRING>
            11,13,17,19,23,29,31,37,41,43,47,53,59,61,67,71,73,79,83,89,97
      </RESULTSTRING>
</RESULT>
```

Thus, we were able to interact with the remote peer's service entirely via the JXTA Shell, without having to write a single line of code. Granted, this prime-finding method communicates with only one remote peer, but the example demonstrates some of the simple yet powerful JXTA Shell capabilities.

Extending the Shell

However useful the JXTA Shell is, you'll often find it lacking certain necessary capabilities. For instance, we've already encountered the shell's lack of document-creation capability: We had to export and then import an advertisement to convert it to a document suitable for adding to a message. The JXTA Shell addresses these limitations with an extensibility framework, enabling any user to add custom shell commands. In this section, we will create a new shell command that computes prime numbers using a set of remote prime-searching peers. Thus, this shell command performs the equivalent of the JXTA client we constructed in Chapter 16, except that it serves up that functionality as a JXTA command.

The new command's name will be primefind, and it will take as arguments the integers delimiting the list of prime numbers to produce. After the command is invoked, it will discover peers offering the prime-finding service, distribute the list of primes between them, and wait to receive the results. After the results arrive, the command produces an output consisting of the list of all primes between the argument integers. An sample invocation is as follows:.

```
JXTA>primefind 10 100
11,13,17,19,23,29,31,37,41,43,47,53,59,61,67,71,73,79,83,89,97
```

A JXTA *shell extension* is a Java program with a few special requirements. The program must occupy a subpackage in the net.jxta.impl.shell.bin hierarchy, and that subpackage's name must correspond to the command's name. In addition, the Java class implementing the command must also assume a name identical to the command's name. Thus, the fully qualified class name for the primefind command will be net.jxta. impl.shell.bin.primefind.primefind. The JXTA Shell uses Java's reflection capability to invoke the command based on a user's command-line input.

In addition, the program must be an extension of net.jxta.impl.shell.ShellApp. ShellApp in turn implements the net.jxta.platform.Application interface, which is a type of net.jxta.platform.Module. Module defines three methods corresponding to the life cycle of a JXTA shell extension.

A shell extension is loaded at the time a user invokes its corresponding command. Two methods in Module address a module's—and a ShellApp's—initialization, and one method enables a module's execution to be halted. The following method initializes the module as it is loaded:

```
init(PeerGroup group, ID assignedID, Advertisement implAdv)
```

Following that, the `int startApp(java.lang.String[] args)` method is called. The arguments array for `startApp()` corresponds to the command-line arguments specified by the user. For the `primefind` command, there must be two elements: the low and high limits of the primes list. `StartApp()` returns a status indicator integer; if all goes well, that integer is the constant `ShellApp.appNoError`. Finally, the module can be stopped with a call to `stopApp()`. Our implementation of the `primefind` command will override only the `startApp()` method.

Another requirement for a shell command is that it must implement `ShellApp`'s `getDescription()` and `help()` methods. The former should return a line of text, offering a brief description of the command. When a user types the `man` command on the JXTA Shell's command line, that line of text will display next to the command's name. If a user wants to obtain a more detailed command description and types `man primefind`, the text displayed as the `man page` is obtained from the command's `help()` method.

Finally, a shell command must be able to access the shell's standard output and input streams. That last requirement is attained via a number of instance variables a shell extension inherits from `ShellApp`.

Writing a New Shell Command

With these requirements in mind, we are ready to start coding the new shell command. We will reuse most of the code developed in Chapter 16, except for the graphical user interface elements. We start out by implementing the two information-providing methods (see Listing 17.3).

LISTING 17.3   The Information-Providing Methods `help()` and `getDescription()`

```
package net.jxta.impl.shell.bin.primefind;
....
public class primefind extends ShellApp {
    public void help() {
        println("NAME");
        println("    primefind — find prime numbers between two integers");
        println(" ");
        println("SYNOPSYS");
        println(" ");
        println("    primefind X Y");
        println(" ");
```

LISTING 17.3   continued

```
            println("DESCRIPTION");
            println("'primefind' utilizes peers offering a prime number finding ");
            println("service to search prime numbers in a distributed manner.");
            println("When invoked, 'primefind' discovers peers offering that ");
            println("service, distributes the list of numbers between the two");
            println("parameters among those peers, and waits for the peers to");
            println("respond with their results. Once all results are obtained,");
            println("'primefind' produces a comma-separated list of prime numbers");
            println("on its standard output. Note that this command relies on ");
            println("other peers to search prime numbers; If no peer offering");
            println("that service is available, 'primefind' will block until ");
              println("at least one such peer is discovered.");
            println(" ");
            println("EXAMPLE");
            println(" ");
            println("    JXTA>primefind 10 100");
            println(" ");
            println("This command produces a list of all prime numbers between");
            println("10 and 100 on its standard ouput.");
            println(" ");
        }
        public String getDescription() {
            return "Search for prime numbers";
        }
        public int startApp(String[] argv) {
            ....
            return ShellApp.appNoError;
        }
    }
}
```

The import statements are available from the full source code, which you can download from this book's Web site. In this code, we simply print the needed information to the shell's standard output via the `println` method, inherited from `ShellApp`. After you compile the code, you must generate a JAR file for the binaries; that file serves as the classpath the shell attempts to load the extension's classes from. Thus, you need to ensure that that JAR file contains all the classes used by the shell extension.

With the `primefind` command's JAR file ready, we can install the new extension to the JXTA Shell. The Shell's `instjar` command facilitates the loading of new extensions:

```
JXTA>instjar /export/home/myfiles/primefind.jar
```

Having installed `primefind`, a call to man shows the new extension (see Figure 17.5).

FIGURE 17.5

Output from the man *command with the* primefind *custom shell command.*

You can also type **man primefind** to receive the complete manual page for the command (see Figure 17.6).

FIGURE 17.6

Manual page for the primefind *command.*

The one remaining task is to make the command do what it advertises. We'll do that by implementing the startApp() method. Our implementation of startApp() consists of three logical parts:

1. Obtain and process command arguments.

2. Start up the prime-finding service, and wait for it to compute the results.

3. Present the results on the shell's standard output.

We will reuse the Dispatcher class developed in Chapter 16 to distribute the computation among different peers. Recall that an instance of the Dispatcher class registers a ResultListener to report the computation's results. We will register primefind as a ResultListener: primefind blocks until Dispatcher notifies it of the results. Listing 17.4 shows the entire code for startApp() as well as resultEvent() (specified in ResultListener).

Listing 17.4 Implementing startApp() and ResultListener

```
public class primefind extends ShellApp implements ResultListener {
.....
//a few variables
private ShellEnv enviroment = null;
private Dispatcher dispatcher = null;
String result = null;
public int startApp(String[] argv) {
    //assign the shell's enviroment
    environment = getEnv();
    //1. Obtain and process the command line arguments
    if (argv.length != 2) {
        return ShellApp.appParamError;
    }
    int low;
    int high;
    try {
        low = Integer.parseInt(argv[0]);
        high = Integer.parseInt(argv[1]);
    } catch (NumberFormatException e) {
        return ShellApp.appParamError;
    }

    //2. Create a new dispatcher, and submit a job to it
    //   Block until resultEvent is called by Dispatcher
    dispatcher = new Dispatcher(getGroup());
    dispatcher.processPrimes(low, high, this);
        synchronized(this) {
          try {
                wait();
            } catch (InterruptedException me) {
```

Listing 17.4   continued

```
        }
      }
//3. Process the result
//3(a) send a message with the result to the shell's standard output
   Message mes = getGroup().getPipeService().createMessage();
   MessageElement el = mes.newMessageElement("results", new
     MimeMediaType("text/plain"), result.getBytes());
   mes.addElement(el);
   try {
     outputPipe.send(mes);
       //3(b) Create a document with the results, and assign that document
       //      to an environment variable
       StructuredTextDocument doc = (StructuredTextDocument)
       StructuredDocumentFactory.newStructuredDocument(
          new MimeMediaType("text/xml"), "result", result);
       ShellObject so = new ShellObject("results", doc);
       environment.add("results", so);
   } catch (IOException e) {
       e.printStackTrace();
   }
   return ShellApp.appNoError;
}//end of startApp()

//this implementation of ResultListener assigns the list of prime
//numbers to the results variable, and notifies the blocking
//thread of the available result
public void resultEvent (Map resultMap) {
   synchronized(this) {
     result = (String)resultMap.get(ServiceConstants.RESULTSTRING);
     notifyAll();
   }
} //end of resultEvent
}//END OF primefind
```

The most interesting aspect of this code is startApp()'s third part. The outputPipe variable, inherited from ShellApp, references the shell's standard output. That's just a regular JXTA OutputPipe, and we need to create a message to send through that pipe. Recall that, by default, the shell's output pipe connects to the console (command line). Thus, the message's content is displayed on the command line—in this case, consisting of the comma-separated list of prime numbers.

In addition to displaying the results, the code also creates a StructuredDocument with the results, and assigns that document to a shell environment variable. You can call cat on the environment variable result to display the content of the document. You can also use exportfile to write the result document to a file.

Connecting Shell Commands

The final iteration of this application shows how to redirect primefind's standard output. It requires no changes to primefind's code. Instead, we define another shell extension, compress, that compresses its standard input and writes that compressed data to a specified file. The two commands can be combined as follows:

```
JXTA>primefind 1 100 | compress /export/home/myfiles/primesfile
```

The parameter to compress takes the name of the file to which the compressed output is written. Listing 17.5 shows compress' startApp() method.

LISTING 17.5 A Message Compression Shell Command

```java
package net.jxta.impl.shell.bin.compress;
...
public class compress extends ShellApp {
    /**
            This method uses Java's ZIP compression utility to compress its
    standard output.
            /
    public int startApp(String[] argv) {
        if (argv.length == 1) {
            try {
                Message mes = inputPipe.waitForMessage();
                FileOutputStream os = new FileOutputStream(argv[0] + ".zip");
                ZipOutputStream zipStream = new ZipOutputStream(os);
                MessageElementEnumeration en = mes.getElements();
                while (en.hasMoreElements()) {
                    MessageElement element = (MessageElement) en.nextElement();
                    ZipEntry entry = new ZipEntry(element.getName());
                    zipStream.putNextEntry(entry);
                    byte[] content = element.getBytesOffset();
                    zipStream.write(content, 0, content.length);
                    zipStream.closeEntry();
                }
                zipStream.close();
                os.close();
            } catch (InterruptedException e) {
            } catch (IOException e) {
                e.printStackTrace();
                return ShellApp.appMiscError;
            }
        } else {
            return ShellApp.appParamError;
        }
        return ShellApp.appNoError;
    }
    ...
}
```

This shell command uses the `java.util.zip` package's zip compression classes. Having obtained the command's argument from the command line—the filename to write the compressed output to—the program waits for a message on its standard input. As with the standard output, the standard input is referenced by a variable inherited from `ShellApp`—`inputPipe`.

The | sign on the command line tells the shell to connect the standard output of `primefind` into the standard input of `compress`. Thus, instead of sending the output message to the console, `primefind`'s output message flows into `compress`'s input stream. `waitForMessage()` then retrieves that message, and each element of that message is subsequently written to a compressed file.

Compressing `primefind`'s output might be useful when searching for very long lists for prime numbers: Instead of overwhelming the console screen, the piped output simply writes a compressed list to the file system. You can then use your favorite unzipping utility to decompress that file; the message element `result` will contain the comma-separated list of primes.

Summary

After reading through the sample applications in this and the previous chapter, you might wonder why you should go to the trouble of programming with the JXTA APIs, when you could just send messages between peers via simple Java sockets, or pass information as parameters in remote method invocations. To see the benefit JXTA brings to an application, you might want to set up a small experiment.

If you are able to use two or more computers, start up several peers with the prime-finding service. Then, start at least one peer with the client application, or the JXTA Shell with the `primefind` command installed. After issuing a few requests from your client peer, disconnect one of the peers offering the service and change that host's IP address. Or, if you can, put that host on a different network partition altogether. Next, start up that peer again, and issue the prime search commands from the client.

This experiment should show that, although a peer changed its network, or physical identity, its virtual identity on the JXTA network remained the same. When the client tries to connect to that peer's input pipe, the underlying JXTA implementation will realize that one of the pipe endpoints moved. The implementation will then try to discover the new endpoint location and reconnect the pipe. That searching and reconnecting is hidden from a client application of the JXTA implementation. In addition, note that at no time does the prime-finding service use centralized naming and directory services—all endpoint resolutions and message deliveries take place via JXTA's capability to manage virtual network identities.

Another important item to note about these sample applications is that peers can be programmed in any programming language. On the application level, the only agreement between peers is the wire protocol specified by the prime-finding service. That wire protocol defines what messages are exchanged, and what format those messages must follow. A developer has to know only that wire protocol to provide new clients for the prime number search service. On a lower level, peers need only implement the JXTA protocols. At no point does any peer depend on the Java language, or the presence of a Java virtual machine—some peers might use JXTA's C binding, others might be implemented in C# or Python. As long as each peer provides a correct JXTA binding, and as long as each of those bindings implements the needed JXTA protocols, peer interaction can take place.

Sample P2P Applications

PART
IV

IN THIS PART

Building a
Personal Portal

by Robert Flenner

IN THIS CHAPTER

The sample application presented in this chapter demonstrates distributed content management, file sharing, and publishing content over the Web using P2P shared spaces and XML metadata definitions.

Portals became popular in the late 90s. The idea was to become the "hot spot" on the Internet for your industry. Initially, generic portals emerged. These were focused on information across all industry segments, with a special focus on finding information on the Web. Leaders like Yahoo!, Netscape, and Lycos quickly emerged as portals for searching and advertising products. They became the first logical search engines and directories for the new Internet economy. They actually provided the first ontologies for Web content. To this day, most sites still mimic the definitions and organization that these sites established. In effect, they defined the concepts still prevalent on Web sites today. Businesses often offer categories such as "Products and Services," "About Us," "Search," "Chat," and so on.

Quickly industry-specific portals began to emerge. Their services were not as generic as the first informational offerings. They focused on industry-specific topics, which complemented their products and services. eBay in effect became the portal for personal auctions, E*Trade the portal for stock trading, and Amazon.com the portal for retail books.

Today, there are e-markets and trading hubs that dot the Internet landscape. They have taken the portal concept and the "hot spot" idea to new levels of business-to-business electronic commerce.

What Is a Personal Portal?

A personal portal is designed for the individual. It is your address on the Internet. It provides you with the opportunity to promote yourself, your family, or manage your relationships on both a personal and business level electronically.

Today's personal portals are based on individual interests. These sites are primarily informational, and relatively simple in their composition and content. Many Internet service providers offer personal portals, which typically are just personalized Web pages filled with text and images.

The personal portals of tomorrow will be much more. They will be the home servers that interface with friends, business colleagues, and the emerging home automation market. They will complement the software engines that keep the home running in an automated and connected world. Peer-to-peer technologies offer the most promising approach to realizing this vision.

Imagine scheduling appointments with doctors, business associates, and friends with the help of a home server that is constantly updating your calendar and contact information—

and that information is available to you anywhere. Or imagine automating bill payment and banking to a new level of completeness and efficiency almost effortlessly with bank statements fed into investment software, and software agents that assist in financial planning. It is possible today!

In this chapter, you will look at the details of a personal portal in the light of P2P technologies, specifically content management and the sharing of information from a personal perspective. Think of this as starting construction on your software `HomePlace` that will begin to automate your connections to the outside world.

Let's begin with content management in a connected and distributed world.

Content Management

You usually don't think in terms of content management from a personal perspective. In fact, neither do most businesses offering content products in the world today. Most content management products are directed at corporations that must maintain and manage informational assets on a large scale.

However, personal information such as photos, music, investments, payments, and so on, comprises some of the most important content in your life. To date, this type of personal information is rarely organized to the level that you organize your business assets.

As new devices emerge that provide informational mobility, new opportunities will exist to capture information and store it in a personal repository.

How many devices must you "sync" before the benefits of mobile information capturing are outweighed by the manual maintenance effort?

Thinking in terms of a personal portal like the one illustrated in Figure 18.1 will help you envision the home server in which automation truly offers a great computing opportunity.

Figure 18.1

The Personal Portal will evolve into a central nervous system for your personal content. Event notification will become increasingly important as personal devices integrate with home automation.

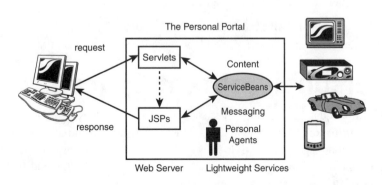

Personal Portal Requirements

Your personal portal will go far beyond showing images of your last vacation or the birth of your new child. This is not to say these are not important events, but merely to highlight that it is only the beginning!

The requirements for home portals of the future include the following:

- A gateway to the Internet—This is a bidirectional gateway that allows communication with home portal systems.

- Event notification—The system must act as an alarm for personal events.

- Support for many different data formats—Data will be received and transmitted in the form that makes sense for the medium; for example, text, image, sound, video.

- Support for many different application types—It must interface to applications that reside on traditional workgroup hardware, in addition to devices and mobile appliances.

- Support many different sources of information—Sources of information will be as varied as the content received.

- Support many different device types—Appliances both internal and external to the home will have access through wired and wireless technology.

- Provide information-sharing capabilities—Controlled sharing of information and group collaboration will be required.

- Provide remote access to information—Services and content must be accessed from any location.

- Minimize support and maintenance requirements—The home portal must minimize maintenance requirements to become an effective and omnipresent application entity.

- Provide flexibility in information organization—The system must be highly configurable and adaptable to change.

This is just a start to the requirements for the personal portal of the future. As we realize the potential in the connected world, new requirements will continue to surface.

Personal Content Space

Traditional database technologies, such as relational databases, provide a robust environment for building corporate systems. However, what is required in the personal portal is a much more agile and flexible information repository. Jini and JavaSpaces, as discussed in Chapter 14, "Jini and JavaSpaces," and Chapter 15, "P2P Jini and JavaSpaces," provide an alternative to meet the requirements of your personal content space.

With JavaSpaces, distributed processes communicate by reading and writing entries into a space. A *space* is defined by JavaSpaces as a shared network-accessible repository for objects. This shared repository can persist objects written to a space beyond the lifetime of the process that created them. Spaces provide reliable storage for objects, and support the concept of leasing. The JavaSpace API provides an event notification mechanism, which enables processes to register for notification when a specific object is written to space. This can be a powerful mechanism to activate and automate content-related tasks.

Objects in a space are located via *associative lookup,* as opposed to more traditional keys or identifiers. When you read or take an object from a space, a local copy of the object is created. As with any other local object, you can modify its public fields and invoke its methods.

Recall the JavaSpace API from Chapter 15 (shown again in Listing 18.1).

LISTING 18.1   JavaSpace API Interface

```
package net.jini.space;

import java.rmi.*;
import net.jini.core.event.*;
import net.jini.core.transaction.*;
import net.jini.core.lease.*;

public interface JavaSpace {

    public final long NO_WAIT = 0; // don't wait at all

    Lease write(Entry e, Transaction txn, long lease)
        throws RemoteException, TransactionException;

    Entry read(Entry tmpl, Transaction txn, long timeout)
        throws TransactionException, UnusableEntryException,
            RemoteException, InterruptedException;

    Entry readIfExists(Entry tmpl, Transaction txn,
                    long timeout)
        throws TransactionException, UnusableEntryException,
            RemoteException, InterruptedException;

    Entry take(Entry tmpl, Transaction txn, long timeout)
        throws TransactionException, UnusableEntryException,
            RemoteException, InterruptedException;

    Entry takeIfExists(Entry tmpl, Transaction txn,
                    long timeout)
        throws TransactionException, UnusableEntryException,
            RemoteException, InterruptedException;
```

LISTING **18.1**   continued

```
EventRegistration notify(Entry tmpl, Transaction txn,
        RemoteEventListener listener, long lease,
        MarshalledObject handback)
    throws RemoteException, TransactionException;

Entry snapshot(Entry e) throws RemoteException;
}
```

The space interface consists of only seven methods. JavaSpaces simplifies the process of building and managing distributed applications. This will be an important property for building future personal applications that extend your portals capabilities. Because it is based on Jini, it has some immediate network benefits. JavaSpaces can provide a notification platform capable of informing services and individuals of changes in information content. In effect, it can become the central nervous system of your content environment. Management of the service is minimized, and the self-healing properties of a Jini network can be leveraged to provide constant communication over less-than-reliable communication networks.

Peer-to-peer systems have already demonstrated the need for a distributed network of loosely coupled collaborating processes. These processes require identity, task management, and coordination. JavaSpaces provides a lightweight implementation of persistence that can aid in implementing a collective memory—a collective memory that is actually applicable not only in a business environment, but in the home of the future.

JavaSpaces is built on object database technology. Object databases are known for being extremely flexible in content storage capabilities and in the level of granularity that they support. Object technology is at the heart of Java, so it makes sense that an object database or a personal object repository should be implemented using object-based technology.

The personal portal envisioned is not a static entity only capable of serving Web pages. Rather, it is an active member of the global P2P network space. It is able to discover services, such as banking, investment, and entertainment, and integrate those services into its knowledge of the outside world.

Sharing Information

Networks today are very interconnected. The Web and the Internet leveraged the connectivity of networks to elevate information sharing to a new level. The global use of the HTTP protocol coupled with URL identity simplified content access, and in the process, distributed content sharing.

Your personal portal must permit content sharing. However, the approach of using a content space will be different than just a central repository. It will be akin to a content-addressable network. Content will be indexed in the space, and not necessarily require migration or transfer to a central personal repository. Using JavaSpaces, HTTP, and Web server technology makes this a simple and viable alternative.

Publishing

Publishing in your personal portal or personal content space will require updating the repository with the metadata associated with the content. For instance, your content will be defined using the metadefinitions developed by the Dublin Core Metadata Initiative (DMCI), which states that "The DCMI is an organization promoting the widespread adoption of interoperable metadata standards and developing specialized metadata vocabularies for describing resources that enable more intelligent information discovery systems"; see `http://www.dublincore.org` for additional information.

The Dublin Core Metadata Element Set is a set of 15 descriptive semantic definitions. It represents a core set of elements likely to be useful across a broad range of vertical industries and disciplines of study. The Dublin Core Metadata Element Set was created to provide a core set of elements that could be shared across disciplines, or within any type of organization needing to organize and classify information. It includes common cataloging information, such as the following:

- Description—Contains a textual description of the content.
- Subject—The subject of the document.
- Creator—Identifies the creator of a document, such as the author.
- Publisher—Identifies the publisher of the document.
- Date—The date the content was created.
- Type—The type of content, such as an article or a book.
- Language—The language the document was written in.
- Format—The media format of the content: text, video, and so on.

By using an extensive array of metadata elements to describe your content, searching and organizing can be drastically improved. But more importantly, information can be accessible not only to other users, but also to programs and software agents.

Design

Let's look at the major components of a personal portal.

You will need the following:

- A Web server—You will need a lightweight Web server capable of supporting Java Servlets and JavaServer Pages.

- Jini Services—Implementing a shared content space will require a number of Jini services, including `reggie`, `mahalo`, and JavaSpaces.

- Of course, a connection to the Internet will be required to put your portal on the Web.

We will use Tomcat from the Apache software group to support our content portal. Tomcat is the servlet container that is used in the official reference implementation for the Java Servlet and JavaServer Pages technologies (see Figure 18.2). The Java Servlet and JavaServer Pages specifications were developed by Sun under the Java Community Process.

Tomcat 4.0 supports the Servlet 2.2 and JSP 1.1 specifications (see www.apache.org for additional information and to download the software).

FIGURE 18.2

The personal portal uses standard Java-based technologies, all of which are freely available for personal use!

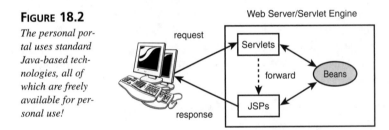

Tomcat can be easily installed and is written in Java. It can provide your personal portal with the required HTTP support for serving HTML pages over the Web. It also supports an environment for dynamically creating and fetching Web pages through the use of servlets and JSPs. More information on servlets can be found at www.sun.com/products/servlets and information on JavaServer Pages is available at www.sun.com/products/jsp.

You will extend the servlet architecture through the use of beans. A `SpaceBean` will provide access to an instance of JavaSpaces. A `MetaDataEntryBean` and a `MetaBean` will encapsulate the Dublin Core metadata Set elements and provide a wrapper to the JavaSpace API. A `MetaDataEntry` will be written and read to JavaSpaces, which includes metadata elements and a location URL for the document being catalogued in your content space. Documents in your personal repository can be local content, or may be distributed across a number of cooperating and collaborating nodes (see Figure 18.3).

FIGURE 18.3

The personal portal extends centralized content management to include a web of connections to information important to your portal presence.

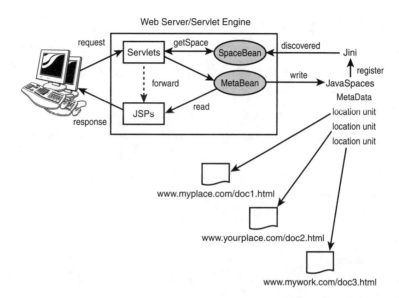

Use Cases

Our portal will initially support three primary functions:

- Cataloging—Cataloging a document involves adding the metadata elements and the location URL that points to the document.

- Search—Searching allows you to specify one or more metadata elements to find matching content that has been catalogued. Once found, the content can be accessed by following the link to the document using normal browser navigation.

- View—Viewing presents a list of the content currently accessible through your portal.

Typically, you would log in to a content space to authenticate and authorize login credentials. In a personal space, this might be simply a user identifier and password.

You can grant access rights to other users by establishing an account and allowing remote users to access your content repository. You could even allow other group members to update your repository with files located on their Web site or PC.

Once you have been authenticated, you can catalogue documents or search and view content. Authentication is outside the scope of this chapter, but numerous examples exist on the Web that demonstrate the use of session objects to maintain and manage user credentials.

18

BUILDING A
PERSONAL PORTAL

Class Design

The classes used in the personal portal (see Figure 18.4) are as follows:

- `HomePlace`—Extends `HttpServlet` and becomes the initial point of request intervention and routing.
- `SpaceBean`—Implements `DiscoveryListener` and resolves references to JavaSpaces.
- `MetaBean`—Provides access to `MetaData` defined for portal content.
- `MetaDataEntry`—Encapsulates Dublin Core Metadata in class entry definitions maintained in JavaSpaces.
- `MetaDataEntryBean`—Provides a link to the `MetaDataEntry`.

It also uses the following JSPs:

- `view.jsp`—The presentation JSP used to display a table of catalogued content entries.
- `document.jsp`—The presentation JSP used to acknowledge portal space updates.
- `find.jsp`—The presentation JSP used to search for specific content.

FIGURE 18.4

The beginning of the class design supporting the personal portal.

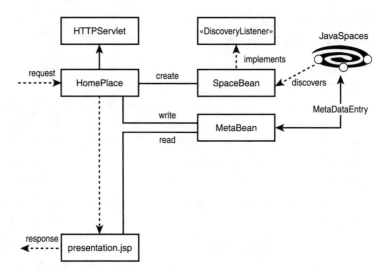

Code Details

The `MetaDataEntry` class (Listing 18.2) is the equivalent to an XML-defined Dublin Core Metadata element set. JavaSpaces requires classes to extend the `Entry` interface or the `AbstractEntry` class to be capable of storage in a tuple space.

LISTING 18.2   The MetaDataEntry Class

```
package org.jworkplace.content;
import net.jini.entry.AbstractEntry;

public class MetaDataEntry extends Index {

    public String description;
    public String subject;
    public String creator;
    public String publisher;
    public String date;
    public String type;
    public String language;
    public String format;
    public String location;

    public MetaDataEntry() {
        this(null,null,null,null,null,null,null,null,null);
    }

    public MetaDataEntry(String subject,
                         String creator,
                         String publisher,
                         String date,
                         String type,
                         String language,
                         String format,
                         String location,
                         String description)
    {
        super();
        this.name = "MyCatalog";
        this.subject = subject;
        this.creator = creator;
        this.publisher = publisher;
        this.date = date;
        this.type = type;
        this.language = language;
        this.format = format;
        this.location = location;
        this.description = description;
    }

    public void setName(String name) {
        this.name = name;
    }
}
```

Take special note of the no-argument constructor, which is required of JavaSpaces entries, and that the fields in the class must be serializable. Also, we have added the location element that will be used to capture a URL representing the location of the content being described.

The `MetaDataEntry` class also extends the `Index` class (Listing 18.3), which is used to create indexing capabilities for JavaSpaces entries. There are many approaches to accomplishing this same task in a space. This technique uses a unique collection name and position element. For instance, in this example we use `MyCatalog` to define a collection name. Every time an entry is written to a space, you increment the position element. So in effect, specifying the name of the set and position of the element can retrieve a specific element. This is useful when you need to loop through all entries within a specific entry set.

You could have created a separate index that was synchronized with the entries being written to or taken from JavaSpaces. You then could loop through the index to retrieve the associated entries. Alternatively, you could create an entry that contains a collection container; perhaps a `Map` set, which maintains a collection of metadata elements that do not extend `AbstractEntry`. However, once you begin to "hide" entries in collections, you lose some of the inherent capabilities of a space. A space has the capability to notify you when an entry that matches a template is written, which you provide. In this way, you can request notification when specific content is defined in your portal. Better yet, you can associate software agent activation with matching specific entries. The notification platform becomes more powerful when content begins to trigger automated activities.

LISTING 18.3   The Index Class

```
package org.jworkplace.content;
import net.jini.entry.AbstractEntry;

abstract public class Index extends AbstractEntry {
    public String name;
    public Integer position;

    public int increment() {
        position = new Integer(position.intValue() + 1);
        return position.intValue();
    }

    public int decrement() {
        position = new Integer(position.intValue() - 1);
        return position.intValue();
    }
}
```

To use the Index class, simply increment the counter each time you write an entry to the named collection.

Resource Leasing

One of the concepts introduced in Jini is the concept of *resource leasing*, or time-based resource allocation. Leasing resources has direct implications on the programming model used, and the services that must be implemented to support a Jini network. Leasing implies that nothing is permanent in the Jini system. You must renew leases and renew interest in resources for them to remain active and available. Otherwise, they will be purged from the network by their removal from the lookup service.

There is a lease renewal service defined as a helper service in the Jini framework that renews interest in resources for you. This service enables disconnected clients, and minimizes the amount of development work required by developers that use the Jini model.

The MetaBean class (Listing 18.4) is used to process catalog requests. It first processes the Request object and creates a MetaDataEntry and an associated MetaDataEntryBean (Listing 18.5). It supports the catalog method, which writes a MetaDataEntry to JavaSpaces. In addition, it supports the proper handling of the collection capabilities of an index and retrieval of MetaDataEntry information by presentation pages.

LISTING 18.4   The MetaBean Class

```
package org.jworkplace.content;

import java.beans.*;
import java.util.ArrayList;
import javax.servlet.http.*;
import javax.servlet.*;
import net.jini.core.entry.Entry;
import net.jini.core.lease.Lease;
import net.jini.space.JavaSpace;

public class MetaBean {

    private JavaSpace space;
    private LeaseManager leaseMgr;
    private int nextPosition = 0;
    private boolean processError = false;

    // use a lease manager to renew leases.
    // Note the lease manager is only active as long as
    // this process is active. A better alternative might be
    // to use a separate process for lease renewal, such as
    // the LeaseRenewal Service
```

LISTING 18.4   continued

```
  //
  public MetaBean() {
   leaseMgr = new LeaseManager();
}

  / set by HomePlace once JavaSpaces has been discovered
  public void setSpace (JavaSpace space) {
    this.space = space;
  }

  public JavaSpace getSpace() {
    return this.space;
  }


    // called to process a request
public synchronized MetaDataEntryBean processRequest (HttpServletRequest
➥ request) {

    this.processError = false;
    MetaDataEntry entry = new MetaDataEntry(request.getParameter ("subject"),
                                    request.getParameter ("creator"),
                                    request.getParameter ("publisher"),
                                    request.getParameter ("date"),
                                    request.getParameter ("type"),
                                    request.getParameter ("language"),
                                    request.getParameter ("format"),
                                    request.getParameter ("location"),
                                    request.getParameter
➥("description"));

    MetaDataEntryBean bean = new MetaDataEntryBean();
    bean.makeLink(entry);
    return bean;
  }

    // returns an array of MetaDataEntry elements
    public MetaDataEntry[] getEntries() {
      Entry entry = null;
      ArrayList list = new ArrayList();
      int position = 0;
      for(;;){
        entry = read(position++);
        if(entry == null) break;
        list.add(entry);
      }

      nextPosition = list.size();
```

LISTING **18.4** continued

```java
        return (MetaDataEntry[])list.toArray(new MetaDataEntry[0]);
    }

    // called to catalog content
    public void catalog(MetaDataEntryBean bean) {
        write((MetaDataEntry)bean.followLink());
    }

    //
    // Find a matching catalog entry given a request object
    //
    public MetaDataEntry find(HttpServletRequest request) {

        MetaDataEntry template = new MetaDataEntry();

        String element = request.getParameter("subject");
        template.subject = ( (element.equals("") || element == null) ? null :
➥element);
        element = request.getParameter("creator");
        template.creator = ( (element.equals("") || element == null) ? null :
➥element);
        element = request.getParameter("publisher");
        template.publisher = ( (element.equals("") || element == null) ? null :
➥element);
        element = request.getParameter("date");
        template.date = ( (element.equals("") || element == null) ? null :
➥element);
        element = request.getParameter("type");
        template.type = ( (element.equals("") || element == null) ? null :
➥element);
        element = request.getParameter("language");
        template.language = ( (element.equals("") || element == null) ? null :
➥element);
        element = request.getParameter("format");
        template.format = ( (element.equals("") || element == null) ? null :
➥element);
        element = request.getParameter("location");
        template.location = ( (element.equals("") || element == null) ? null :
➥element);
        element = request.getParameter("description");
        template.description = ( (element.equals("") || element == null) ? null :
➥element);

        return (MetaDataEntry)read(template);
    }

    // Write a MetaDataEntry to JavaSpaces
    // Uses the correct idiom to support an indexed collection
    // Changing the lease time would require changes to keep the index
```

18

BUILDING A
PERSONAL PORTAL

LISTING 18.4 continued

```
// in sync with entries as they expire or are removed from the space.

private synchronized void write(MetaDataEntry entry)
{
   entry.position = new Integer(nextPosition);
   try {
     Lease lease = space.write(entry, null, Lease.FOREVER);
     nextPosition++;
     leaseMgr.renewFor(lease, leaseTime, this);
   } catch (Exception e) { e.printStackTrace();
                           this.processError = true;
                           nextPosition-; }


}

// Given a position will attempt to retrieve matching entry
// Non-Blocking read uses readIfExists

private Entry read(int position)
{
   Entry entry = null;
   MetaDataEntry template = new MetaDataEntry();
   template.position = new Integer(position);
   try {
       // Will return immediately if no matching entry is found
       entry = space.readIfExists(template, null, 10*1000);
   } catch (Exception e) { e.printStackTrace();
                           this.processError = true; }
   return entry;
}

// Given a MetaDataEntry template attempts to read
// a matching space entry
// Blocking Read - increase wait time e.g. 10*1000 to
// wait longer for matching entry

private Entry read(MetaDataEntry template)
{
   Entry entry = null;
   try {
       // Set to wait for 10 seconds
       entry = space.read(template, null, 10*1000);
   } catch (Exception e) { e.printStackTrace();
                           this.processError = true; }
   return entry;

}

// used to determine if an error occurred
```

LISTING **18.4**   continued

```
// during space access
public boolean getProcessError () {
   return this.processError;
}



}
```

LISTING **18.5**   The MetaDataEntryBean Class

```
package org.jworkplace.content;

import java.io.Serializable;
import net.jini.core.entry.Entry;
import net.jini.lookup.entry.EntryBean;

public class MetaDataEntryBean implements EntryBean, Serializable {

    protected MetaDataEntry assoc;

    public MetaDataEntryBean() {
        assoc = new MetaDataEntry();
    }

    public void makeLink(Entry e) {
        assoc = (MetaDataEntry) e;
    }

    public Entry followLink() {
        return assoc;
    }

  public void setDescription (String description) {
    assoc.description  = description;
  }

  public String getDescription () {
    return assoc.description;
  }

  public void setSubject (String subject) {
    assoc.subject = subject;
  }

  public String getSubject() {
    return assoc.subject;
  }
```

LISTING 18.5 continued

```java
public void setCreator(String creator) {
  assoc.creator = creator;
}

public String getCreator() {
  return assoc.creator;
}

public void setPublisher (String publisher) {
  assoc.publisher = publisher;
}

public String getPublisher() {
  return assoc.publisher;
}

public void setDate (String date) {
  assoc.date = date;
}

public String getDate() {
  return assoc.date;
}

public void setType (String type) {
  assoc.type = type;
}

public String getType() {
  return assoc.type;
}

public void setLanguage (String language) {
  assoc.language = language;
}

public String getLanguage() {
  return assoc.language;
}

public void setFormat(String format) {
  assoc.format = format;
}

public String getFormat() {
  return assoc.format;
}
```

LISTING 18.5   continued

```
public void setLocation(String location) {
  assoc.location = location;
}

public String getLocation() {
  return assoc.location;
}


}
```

The HomePlace class (Listing 18.6) extends the HttpServlet class. It is used to route user requests and resolves a reference to the JavaSpaces services. The init method sets the security manager required by RMI and Jini. In addition, it performs the lookup of the service registrar (reggie) and the JavaSpaces service. This is done once when the servlet is initialized. The first call to the process will be slow, but subsequent calls are substantially faster. It is in this method that the MetaBean used by the application is created and initialized.

As an alternative to using a static reference to the MetaBean, you could place the reference to the bean in a named attribute. Other pages could reference the bean by using a getAttribute("metabean").

LISTING 18.6   The HomePlace Class

```
package org.jworkplace.homeplace;

import java.io.*;
import java.rmi.*;
import java.text.*;
import java.util.*;
import javax.servlet.*;
import javax.servlet.http.*;
import net.jini.space.JavaSpace;

import org.jworkplace.util.*;
import org.jworkplace.content.*;

public class HomePlace extends HttpServlet {

   private SpaceBean spaceBean;
   private static MetaBean metaBean;
   private JavaSpace space;

   private String updatePage = "/document.jsp";
   private String searchPage = "/find.jsp";
```

LISTING 18.6 continued

```java
private String listPage = "/view.jsp";
private String errorPage = "/error.jsp";

public void init() {

    System.setSecurityManager(new RMISecurityManager());

    try {
        spaceBean = new SpaceBean();
    } catch(Exception e) { e.printStackTrace();
                          System.exit(1); }
    try {

        space = getHomeSpace();

        metaBean = new MetaBean();
        metaBean.setSpace(space);

    } catch (InterruptedException e) {}

}

public void doPost(HttpServletRequest request,
                   HttpServletResponse response)
                   throws IOException, ServletException
{
    response.setContentType("text/html");

// default page
String nextPage = listPage;
String action = request.getParameter("action");

if(action != null) {
    if(action.equals("Update"))
    {
        MetaDataEntryBean entryBean = metaBean.processRequest(request);
        metaBean.catalog(entryBean);
        nextPage = updatePage;

    } else if( action.equals("Search")) {
        nextPage = searchPage;
    }
}

    ServletContext ctx = getServletContext();
    RequestDispatcher dispatcher = ctx.getRequestDispatcher(nextPage);
    dispatcher.forward(request, response);

}
```

LISTING 18.6 continued

```java
public void doGet(HttpServletRequest request,
                  HttpServletResponse response)
                  throws IOException, ServletException
{
    doPost(request,response);
}


public void destroy() {}

public JavaSpace getHomeSpace() throws InterruptedException
{
    return spaceBean.getSpace();
}

public static MetaBean getMetaBean() {
    return metaBean;
}

}
```

Service Discovery

The SpaceBean (Listing 18.7) implements the DiscoveryListener interface. When the SpaceBean is instantiated, it creates a LookupDiscovery manager. The LookupDiscovery manager is used to discover lookup services such as reggie.

When a lookup service is found, it invokes the discovered method of the DiscoveryListener interface. The DiscoveredEvent returns a list of lookup services discovered. Using these lookups, you can build service-specific templates to query the lookup service for matching services. In our example, we simply want to find an instance of JavaSpaces.

The lookup service enables service-using entities to register and find services that meet specific criteria. In this respect, the lookup service provides functions similar to a yellow page service. The lookup service is what in effect bootstraps the Jini network. Services register with the lookup service, and applications find services of interest using the lookup service. After a service is found, an application can invoke the methods that the service exposes through its public interface.

LISTING 18.7 The SpaceBean Class

```java
package org.jworkplace.util;
import java.rmi.*;
import java.io.IOException;
```

18

BUILDING A
PERSONAL PORTAL

LISTING 18.7 continued

```
import net.jini.core.entry.*;
import net.jini.core.lookup.ServiceRegistrar;
import net.jini.discovery.DiscoveryListener;
import net.jini.discovery.DiscoveryEvent;
import net.jini.discovery.LookupDiscovery;
import net.jini.space.JavaSpace;

public class SpaceBean implements DiscoveryListener {

    private JavaSpace space;
    private ServiceRegistrar[] registrars;

    public SpaceBean() throws IOException  {

        // start finding registrars (lookup services)
        LookupDiscovery mgt = new LookupDiscovery(LookupDiscovery.NO_GROUPS);
        mgt.addDiscoveryListener(this);
        ((LookupDiscovery)mgt).setGroups(LookupDiscovery.ALL_GROUPS);
    }

    // one or more lookup services have been found
    public synchronized void discovered(DiscoveryEvent de) {
        // get the array of lookup services discovered
        registrars = de.getRegistrars();
        // try to find JavaSpaces
        findSpace(registrars);
    }

    // this method will be called if a lookup service has been
    // removed from the set lookups available
    // You would need to implement the appropriate process
    // to remove the lookup service from your list of available services
    // We simply ignore this event
    public void discarded(DiscoveryEvent de) {}

    // Loop through the lookup services discovered until you find JavaSpaces
    private void findSpace(ServiceRegistrar[] registrars) {
        if(space == null) {
          for(int i=0; i < registrars.length; i++) {
             try {
                space = ServiceFinder.findSpace(registrars[i]);
                if(space != null) {
                    System.out.println("SpaceBean:findSpace - JavaSpaces resolved
➥to: " + space);
                    // notify any caller waiting
                    notifyAll();
                    break;
                }
             } catch (Exception e) { e.printStackTrace(); }
```

LISTING 18.7 continued

```
        }
      }
  }

  // get a reference to JavaSpaces, wait until it is found
  public synchronized JavaSpace getSpace() throws InterruptedException {
    while(space == null) {
      wait();
    }
    return space;
  }

  // additional get and set methods here such as setGroups, setLocators,
  // setSpaceName etc
}
```

The ServiceFinder class (Listing 18.8) is a utility class used by the SpaceBean to build the necessary template to find an instance of JavaSpaces. It builds a generic template and invokes the lookup method on the lookup service. It can also be used to find the registrar by using a supplied template.

LISTING 18.8 The ServiceFinder Class

```
package org.jworkplace.util;
import java.rmi.*;
import net.jini.core.lookup.ServiceTemplate;
import net.jini.core.lookup.ServiceRegistrar;
import net.jini.core.transaction.server.TransactionManager;
import net.jini.space.JavaSpace;
import net.jini.discovery.LookupDiscoveryService;

public class ServiceFinder
  {

    public static JavaSpace findSpace(ServiceRegistrar registrar) {
      JavaSpace space = null;

      ServiceTemplate template;
      Class[] spaceInterface = { JavaSpace.class };
      template = new ServiceTemplate(null, spaceInterface, null);
      return findSpace(registrar, template);
}

    public static JavaSpace findSpace(ServiceRegistrar registrar,
                                      ServiceTemplate template) {
      JavaSpace space = null;
```

LISTING **18.8** continued

```
    try {
        space = (JavaSpace)registrar.lookup(template);
    } catch (Exception e) {
        e.printStackTrace();
        System.out.println("ServiceFinder:findSpace exiting");
    }
    return space;
    }

}
```

Running the Example

The following configuration and services are required to run the portal example.

Configuration

Although defining and deploying WAR files in Tomcat is outside the scope of this chapter, you can use the following Web.xml file to demonstrate the servlet mapping required in the example:

```
<?xml version="1.0" encoding="ISO-8859-1"?>
<web-app>
    <servlet>
      <servlet-name>homeplace</servlet-name>
      <servlet-class>org.jworkplace.homeplace.HomePlace</servlet-class>
    </servlet>
    <servlet-mapping>
        <servlet-name>homeplace</servlet-name>
        <url-pattern>/homeplace</url-pattern>
    </servlet-mapping>
</web-app>
```

Unzip the portal.zip file. The included WAR file can simply be copied to the /webapps directory of your Tomcat installation prior to startup. This file will be expanded to create the Web resources necessary to run the portal.

Starting Services

There are a number of services that will initially be required. These services include Tomcat, reggie, mahalo, and JavaSpaces.

Starting Tomcat

Tomcat has instructions on configuring and starting the Tomcat server. To start the server, go to the \bin directory and invoke the `startup.bat` or `startup.sh` command file. You must set the `JAVA_HOME` environment variable to point to your Java installation prior to startup. Be sure to copy the `homeplace.war` file to the Tomcat \webapps directory prior to starting.

Starting `reggie`

To start `reggie`, the Jini-supplied `ServiceRegistrar`, use the script in Listing 18.9. Simply set the `JINI_HOME` environment variable to your Jini installation, and your `HTTP_ADDRESS` to an accessible Tomcat context, such as /Root and the port Tomcat is using:

```
Set HTTP_ADDRESS=C:\jakarta-tomcat4.0\webapps\Root:8081
```

It is here that you will place all files that must be available for download to clients and services. For instance:

- `reggie-dl.jar`
- `mahalo-dl.jar`
- `outrigger-dl.jar`

LISTING 18.9 The `startReggie.bat` File

```
@echo off
echo must set JINI_HOME and HTTP_ADDRESS
set JINI_HOME=
set HTTP_ADDRESS=
set GROUPS=public

echo Java P2P Unleashed
echo — — — — — — — — — — — — — — — — — — — —.
echo Jini install directory        %JINI_HOME%
echo Tomcat Web server             %HTTP_ADDRESS%
echo Default group                 %GROUPS%
echo — — — — — — — — — — — — — — — — — — — —.
java -jar -Djava.security.policy=%JINI_HOME%\policy\policy.all
➥%JINI_HOME%\lib\reggie.jar http://%HTTP_ADDRESS%/reggie-dl.jar
➥%JINI_HOME%\policy\policy.all .\services\logs\reggie_log %GROUPS%
```

Starting `mahalo`

JavaSpaces requires the transaction service `mahalo`. To start `mahalo`, run the script in Listing 18.10.

18

BUILDING A
PERSONAL PORTAL

LISTING 18.10   The `startMahalo.bat` File

```
@echo off
echo must set JINI_HOME and HTTP_ADDRESS
set JINI_HOME=
set HTTP_ADDRESS=
set GROUPS=public

echo Java P2P Unleashed
echo — — — — — — — — — — — — — — — — — — —·
echo Jini install directory        %JINI_HOME%
echo Web server                    %HTTP_ADDRESS%
echo Default group                 %GROUPS%
echo — — — — — — — — — — — — — — — — — — —·
echo Starting the mahalo transaction service...

java -jar -Djava.security.policy=%JINI_HOME%\example\txn\policy.all -
➥Dcom.sun.jini.mahalo.managerName=TransactionManager %JINI_HOME%\lib\
➥mahalo.jar http://%HTTP_ADDRESS%/mahalo-dl.jar %JINI_HOME%\example\txn\
➥policy.all.\services\logs\txn_log %GROUPS%
```

Starting JavaSpaces

Now start JavaSpaces, using the script in Listing 18.11.

LISTING 18.11   The `startOutrigger.bat` File

```
@echo off

echo must set JINI_HOME and HTTP_ADDRESS
set JINI_HOME=
set HTTP_ADDRESS=
set GROUPS=public
set SPACENAME=JavaSpaces

echo Java P2P Unleasehd
echo — — — — — — — — — — — — — — — — — — —·
echo Jini install directory        %JINI_HOME%
echo Web server                    %HTTP_ADDRESS%
echo Default group                 %GROUPS%
echo Default space name            %SPACENAME%
echo — — — — — — — — — — — — — — — — — — —·
echo Starting the outrigger JavaSpaces service...

java -jar -Djava.security.policy=%JINI_HOME%\policy\policy.all
➥-Dcom.sun.jini.outrigger.spaceName=%SPACENAME% %JINI_HOME%\lib\
➥outrigger.jar  http://%HTTP_ADDRESS%/outrigger-dl.jar
➥%JINI_HOME%\policy\policy.all .\services\logs\js_log %GROUPS%
```

You should now be able to access your portal and begin to add content by starting a Web browser and entering

```
http://hostname:8081/homeplace/homeplace.html
```

Figure 18.5 shows the portal in action.

FIGURE **18.5**

The personal portal.

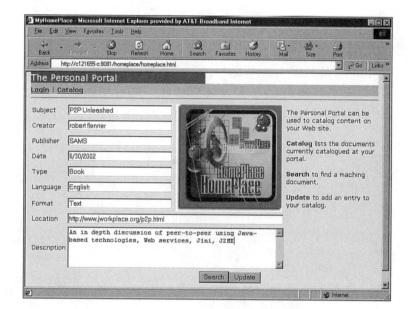

Summary

Many personal portals today are based on individual interests. These sites are primarily informational, and relatively simple in their composition and content.

The personal portals of tomorrow will be the home servers that interface with friends, business colleagues, and the emerging home automation market. Peer-to-peer technologies offer the most promising approach to realizing this vision.

Publishing in your personal content space requires updating the repository with metadata. Our example demonstrated metadefinitions developed by the Dublin Core Metadata Initiative (DMCI).

The major components used in this example include the Tomcat Servlet Engine and the Jini services, including `reggie`, `mahalo`, and JavaSpaces.

By allowing content to remain distributed and providing other users access to your portal, a wide array of peer-to-peer applications become viable. We've only scratched the surface.

18

BUILDING A
PERSONAL PORTAL

The P2P Dashboard

by Rajam Ramamurti

IN THIS CHAPTER

The P2P Dashboard

The P2P Dashboard sample program demonstrates techniques to create communities of peers and groups, and to detect peer presence individually (locally) or within groups (remotely). This program also illustrates the concepts of monitoring and configuration of shared space.

The P2P Dashboard utilizes the following JXTA protocols:

- Peer Membership Protocol
- Peer Discovery Protocol

Community Formation

The P2P Dashboard program provides the capability to create communities by adding new peers and new groups. Peers form groups, and groups form communities. Individual peers can join multiple groups that represent separate communities. You can maintain separate communities by removing peers locally and/or from different groups remotely.

In the P2P Dashboard program, you can add peers or remove them with the exception of the default peer at any time after creation. You can add or remove groups with the exception of the default group in the same manner. You can add peers to one or more groups, and remove peers from one or more groups at any time.

Presence

Discovery services (local and remote) keep peer and group advertisements updated. All advertisements are kept in a local cache for quick lookups. If an advertisement for a peer or group is not found locally, then a remote discovery activity needs to occur to find a given peer and/or group.

The P2P Dashboard provides a mechanism with which you can discover the presence of a peer locally within the group of peers, or remotely in one or more groups.

Monitoring

Monitoring is dependent on the type of peer architecture used. Decentralized, brokered, and centralized architectures utilize various aspects of the concepts of publish-subscribe and point-to-point messaging. Monitoring of shared memory or objects is useful to many peers and/or groups that might depend on such shared resources for information, such as virtual blackboard/scoreboards and shared files.

The P2P Dashboard program provides the capability to monitor local and remote peers. Users can view the current list of local and/or remote peers that have locally cached advertisements. The Dashboard provides widgets, such as a discovery button and local/remote radio buttons, to execute the corresponding peer discovery activity.

Design

The P2P Dashboard is a standalone application designed to have two main components: a graphical user interface (GUI front end), and a JXTA integration (back end), which utilize the latest JXTA platform release. The GUI displays peer and group information for monitoring purposes. The update of such information is handled by the JXTA integration.

When launched from the desktop, the Dashboard appears with two adjacent panels, one for displaying the names of peers, and the other for displaying the groups (see Figure 19.1). For further details, refer to the section "Application Details."

FIGURE 19.1
The P2P Dashboard.

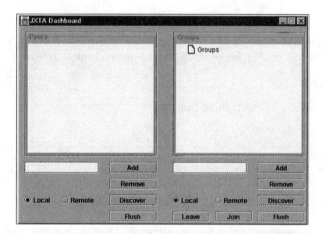

The text fields and buttons on the bottom section of the Dashboard let you perform the following operations:

- Add peers or groups (via the Add buttons).
- Remove peers or groups (via the Remove buttons).
- Monitor the presence of peers or groups (via the Local and Remote buttons).
- Discover the presence of peers or groups (via the Discover buttons).
- Flush the cache storage of names of peers or groups (via the Flush buttons).
- List all the groups a specific peer belongs to (via the Groups check box).

The Tooltip accompanying each action widget describes its purpose.

19

Application Details

The code for the P2P Dashboard application is contained in a zip file. Extract the contents of this zip file to a directory on your local disk. Let's refer to this directory as the installation directory. The readme.txt file in the installation directory contains information for building and running the P2P Dashboard application.

The P2P Dashboard requires a JXTA configuration before it can run. The JXTA Configurator is a part of the JXTA platform. All applications automatically call the JXTA Configurator if no JXTA configuration exists.

First, you must create the default peer using the JXTA Configurator, then you can use the Dashboard for performing several tasks concerning peers and groups as outlined in this section. When you create the default peer, the application creates the default group.

Groups

All the command buttons, text fields, radio buttons, and names that are necessary to add/remove and monitor the peers are displayed in the Groups section of the Dashboard.

To add a new group:

1. Enter a group name in the text field.
2. Click the Add button.

To remove a group:

1. Select a group in the list.
2. Click the Remove button.

Note

If the group contains peers, those peers are also removed.

To perform local group discovery:

1. Select the Local button.
2. Click the Discover button.

To perform remote group discovery:

1. Select the Remote button.
2. Click the Discover button.

To flush local group cache information, click the Flush button.

Peers

All the command buttons, text fields, radio buttons, check boxes, and names that are necessary to add/remove and monitor the peers are displayed in the Peers section of the Dashboard.

To add a new peer:

1. Make sure that the Groups box is unchecked.
2. Select a group to include the peer.
3. Enter the name of the peer in the text field (in the Peers section).
4. Click the Add button (in the Peers section).

To remove a peer:

1. Make sure that the Groups box is unchecked.
2. Select a group from which to remove the peer.
3. Select a peer name in the peer list.
4. Click the Remove button (in the Peers section).

To perform local peer discovery:

1. Select the Local radio button.
2. Click the Discover button.

To perform remote peer discovery:

1. Select the Remote radio button.
2. Click the Discover button.

Note

Note that remote discovery of peers or groups is possible only in a network environment.

To list all the peers in a specific group:

1. Make sure that the Groups box is unchecked.
2. Select a group and see all the peers in that group displayed in the Peers section.

To list all the groups a specific peer belongs to:

1. Make sure that the Groups box is checked.

2. Select a peer and see all the groups for that peer displayed in the Groups section.

To flush local peer cache information, click the Flush button.

Sample Illustrations

This section presents a few samples to illustrate the various features of the P2P Dashboard program.

Creating Peers and Groups (Community Formation)

Let's first create the default peer, peer1, using the JXTA Configurator. The Dashboard application creates the default group to accommodate the default peer.

Follow these steps on the Dashboard:

1. Add three groups: group1, group2, and group3.

2. Make sure that the Groups box is unchecked.

3. Select group1 and add peer1, peer2, and peer3.

4. Select group2 and add peer1 and peer2.

5. Select group3 and add peer1 and peer3.

6. Select the default group.

When you add peers and groups in this manner and select the default group on the Dashboard, the entire Dashboard looks similar to Figure 19.2.

FIGURE 19.2

Newly added peers and groups.

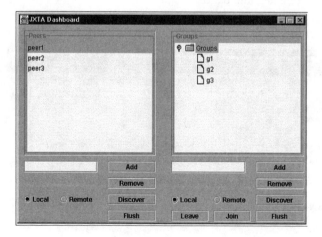

Discovering Peers (Presence)

Now you want to find out how many peers are present in group3. All you need to do is
clear the Groups check box and select group3. The peers in group3 are displayed in the
Peers section, as shown in Figure 19.3.

FIGURE 19.3

Discovering peers
in group3.

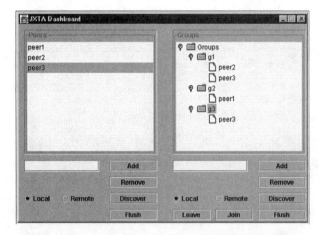

If you want to discover the peers in group1, first make sure that the Groups box is
unchecked, then select group1. The peers in group1 are displayed in the Peers section, as
shown in Figure 19.4.

FIGURE 19.4

Discovering peers
in group1.

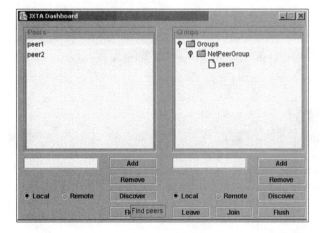

To see where peer2 is located:

1. First perform a local peer discovery by unchecking the Groups box and selecting the Local button, then clicking the Discover button.

2. Select peer2.

The Groups section displays all the groups (group1 and group2) that peer2 belongs to, as shown in Figure 19.5. Also notice that the Groups box is checked.

FIGURE 19.5

Discovering groups for peer2.

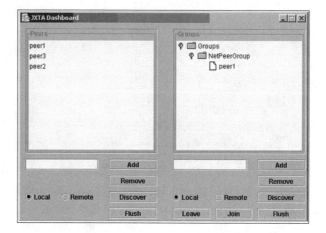

Purpose

The purpose of P2P Dashboard is to illustrate the Peer Membership Protocol and Peer Monitoring/Discovery Protocol of the JXTA technology.

The philosophy behind the design of the P2P dashboard program is to de-couple the graphical user interface from the JXTA platform as much as possible.

Use Cases

A perfect sample use of the P2P Dashboard is in creating, monitoring, and administering various system-level services operating in an enterprise. Other examples are outlined in the following sections.

Chat Room Administrator

Let's suppose that an online site called Oz has administrators that require software to maintain and monitor their online chat rooms. Administrators can add/remove peers in the default Oz group (community). Users of the online chat rooms can add/remove themselves from different user-made-groups that are created based on various chat topics. If a user (a peer) deviates from the Oz online charter, the administrator can remove that user from the online groups by removing the peer definition for that user from the Dashboard. Random chat room monitoring can proceed smoothly while administrators passively participate in various group activities during specified peak activity hours.

Buying Stock

Customers routinely trade stocks online. Brokerage houses (groups) allow their customers (peers) to place orders to buy and sell stock online. Customers can interact with one or more brokerage houses in order to perform such stock trading activities. Real-time stock quotes use the mechanism of publish-subscribe for delivering up-to-date stock quotes for customers who require it. Customers interact with their various groups in order to get stock quotes and conduct stock trades. Brokerage houses maintain their online customers through an administrative software package that allows them to add/delete customers and classify customer investment needs.

Class Design

Four Java classes make up the P2P Dashboard sample program. `P2PDashboard` is the main class that encapsulates all graphical user interface elements and directly interfaces with the JXTA platform. `PeerDiscovery` is the class that handles local/remote peer discovery management. `GroupDiscovery` is the class that handles local/remote group discovery management. `SortedListModel` is a helper class that performs list-related tasks.

Special Details

The current implementation of the graphical user interface depends on a JAR file from the latest version of the integrated development environment NetBeans Version 3.3. The file `AbsoluteLayout.jar` is required to build and run the P2P Dashboard program.

Flushing Peer Information

It is possible for the Dashboard to have stale peer/group information. In order to preempt this occurrence, the discovery feature of the Dashboard provides the capability to manually update this information at any point in time. Before the discovery is done, the flush feature guarantees that all existing peer/group advertisements are cleaned up.

Code Details

This section contains the code for the P2P Dashboard program. Three Java classes make up the P2P Dashboard sample program: `P2PDashboard`, the main class; `PeerDiscovery`, a class that handles local/remote peer discovery management; and `GroupDiscovery`, a class that handles local/remote group discovery management.

Details of the `P2PDashboard` Class

`P2PDashboard.java` is the main class that encapsulates all graphical user interface elements, such as the window frame, command buttons, scroll pane, text fields, radio buttons, tree structure, and button groups for the Dashboard, and it directly interfaces with the JXTA platform.

`P2PdashBoard.java` employs the following methods:

- `main()` to run the program
- `P2PDashboard()` to create the frame for the Dashboard GUI
- `initializeGUIComponents()` to set up GUI objects and their properties
- `configureGroupEvents()` to handle group GUI object events
- `configurePeerEvents()` to handle peer GUI object events
- `exitForm(WindowEvent)` to exit the application
- `handleError(String, String, Exception, boolean)` for error handling
- `checkAddRules(String)` for group validation

`P2PDashboard` utilizes the following JXTA methods:

- `initializeNetPeerGroup()` to initialize the default `NetPeerGroup` to which a local peer belongs
- `initializeDiscovery()` to initialize the peer and group discovery services for handling local and remote discovery events and messages
- `addPeer(String)` to create a peer and publish it locally and remotely
- `removeAdvertisement (String,boolean)` to remove a peer's credentials from the local cache
- `addGroup(String)` to create a new group and publish it locally and remotely

Listing 19.1 presents the code for `P2PDashboard.java`.

LISTING 19.1   `P2PDashboard.java`

```java
import java.awt.Container;
import java.awt.Insets;

import java.awt.event.ActionEvent;
import java.awt.event.ActionListener;
import java.awt.event.ItemEvent;
import java.awt.event.ItemListener;
import java.awt.event.WindowAdapter;
import java.awt.event.WindowEvent;
```

LISTING 19.1 continued

```
import java.io.IOException;
import java.lang.String;

import java.util.Enumeration;
import java.util.Hashtable;
import java.util.Vector;

import javax.swing.ButtonGroup;
import javax.swing.JButton;
import javax.swing.JCheckBox;
import javax.swing.JFrame;
import javax.swing.JList;
import javax.swing.JOptionPane;
import javax.swing.JRadioButton;
import javax.swing.JScrollPane;
import javax.swing.JTextField;
import javax.swing.ListSelectionModel;
import javax.swing.DefaultListSelectionModel;

import javax.swing.border.TitledBorder;

import javax.swing.event.ListSelectionListener;
import javax.swing.event.ListSelectionEvent;


import net.jxta.credential.AuthenticationCredential;

import net.jxta.document.StructuredDocument;
import net.jxta.document.MimeMediaType;

import net.jxta.discovery.DiscoveryService;

import net.jxta.exception.PeerGroupException;

import net.jxta.membership.Authenticator;
import net.jxta.membership.MembershipService;

import net.jxta.peergroup.PeerGroup;
import net.jxta.peergroup.PeerGroupFactory;

import net.jxta.protocol.ModuleImplAdvertisement;
import net.jxta.protocol.PeerGroupAdvertisement;
import net.jxta.protocol.PeerAdvertisement;

import net.jxta.impl.protocol.PeerGroupAdv;
import net.jxta.impl.protocol.PeerAdv;

import net.jxta.impl.id.UUID.PeerID;
import net.jxta.impl.id.UUID.PeerGroupID;
```

LISTING **19.1** continued

```
/*
  P2P Dashboard application
 */

public class P2PDashboard
extends JFrame
{
  // frame reference for JOptionPane message dialogs
  private JFrame frame;


  // group section
  private JScrollPane groupScrollPane;
  private JList groupList;
  private Hashtable groupHT;

  private JTextField groupAddTextField;
  private JButton groupAddButton;

  private JButton groupFlushButton;
  private JButton groupRemoveButton;

  private JRadioButton groupLocalRadioButton;
  private JRadioButton groupRemoteRadioButton;
  private ButtonGroup groupDiscoveryButtonGroup;
  private JButton groupDiscoveryButton;


  // peer section
  private JScrollPane peerScrollPane;
  private JList peerList;

  private JTextField peerAddTextField;
  private JButton peerAddButton;

  private JButton peerFlushButton;
  private JCheckBox peerCheckBox;
  private JButton peerRemoveButton;

  private JRadioButton peerLocalRadioButton;
  private JRadioButton peerRemoteRadioButton;
  private ButtonGroup peerDiscoveryButtonGroup;
  private JButton peerDiscoveryButton;

  private boolean displayPeerGroups;

  // Default NetPeerGroup and discovery service
  private static PeerGroup netPeerGroup;
  private DiscoveryService discovery;
  private String defaultGroupName;
```

LISTING **19.1**   continued

```java
private String defaultPeerName;

// peer and group discovery event handlers
private PeerDiscovery peerDiscovery;
private GroupDiscovery groupDiscovery;



/*********************/
/* Dashboard Methods */
/*********************/

/*
 *Command line arguments
 */
public static void main(String args[])
{
  P2PDashboard p2p = new P2PDashboard();
  p2p.show();

  // setup localPeer in NetPeerGroup
  p2p.initializeNetPeerGroup();

  // prepare peer and group discovery services
  p2p.initializeDiscovery();
}


/*
 *Create a new P2PDashboard frame.
 */
public P2PDashboard()
{
  frame = this;

  // group
  groupScrollPane = new JScrollPane();
  groupList = new JList(new SortedListModel());
  groupHT = new Hashtable();

  groupAddTextField = new JTextField();
  groupAddButton = new JButton();

  groupFlushButton = new JButton();
  groupRemoveButton = new JButton();

  groupLocalRadioButton = new JRadioButton();
  groupRemoteRadioButton = new JRadioButton();
  groupDiscoveryButtonGroup = new ButtonGroup();
  groupDiscoveryButton = new JButton();
```

LISTING **19.1** continued

```java
// peer
peerScrollPane = new JScrollPane();
peerList = new JList(new SortedListModel());

peerAddTextField = new JTextField();
peerAddButton = new JButton();

peerFlushButton = new JButton();
peerCheckBox = new JCheckBox();
peerRemoveButton = new JButton();

peerLocalRadioButton = new JRadioButton();
peerRemoteRadioButton = new JRadioButton();
peerDiscoveryButtonGroup = new ButtonGroup();
peerDiscoveryButton = new JButton();

displayPeerGroups = false;

initializeGUIComponents();
configureGroupEvents();
configurePeerEvents();
}


/*
 *P2PDashboard uses this to setup GUI objects and
 *their properties.
 */
private void initializeGUIComponents()
{
  Container contentPane = getContentPane();
  Insets insets = contentPane.getInsets();

  contentPane.setLayout(null);


  // group section
  groupScrollPane.setViewportBorder
  (new TitledBorder("Groups"));
  groupScrollPane.setViewportView(groupList);

  contentPane.add(groupScrollPane);
  groupScrollPane.setBounds(10+insets.left,
  10+insets.top, 250, 230);


  groupAddTextField.setToolTipText("Add a new group");
  contentPane.add(groupAddTextField);
  groupAddTextField.setBounds(10+insets.left,
  250+insets.top, 140, 20);
```

LISTING 19.1 continued

```
    groupAddButton.setText("Add");
    groupAddButton.setToolTipText("Add a new group");
    contentPane.add(groupAddButton);
    groupAddButton.setBounds(170+insets.left,
➥   250+insets.top, 90, 20);


    groupFlushButton.setText("Flush");
    groupFlushButton.setToolTipText
➥   ("Flush local group cache");
    contentPane.add(groupFlushButton);
    groupFlushButton.setBounds(10+insets.left,
➥ 280+insets.top, 90, 20);

    groupRemoveButton.setText("Remove");
    groupRemoveButton.setToolTipText("Remove a group");
    contentPane.add(groupRemoveButton);
    groupRemoveButton.setBounds(170+insets.left,
➥ 280+insets.top, 90, 20);


    groupLocalRadioButton.setSelected(true);
    groupLocalRadioButton.setText("Local");
    groupLocalRadioButton.setToolTipText
➥   ("Search for local groups");
    contentPane.add(groupLocalRadioButton);
    groupLocalRadioButton.setBounds(10+insets.left,
➥   310+insets.top, 60, 20);

    groupRemoteRadioButton.setText("Remote");
    groupRemoteRadioButton.setToolTipText
➥   ("Search for remote groups");
    contentPane.add(groupRemoteRadioButton);
    groupRemoteRadioButton.setBounds(90+insets.left,
➥   310+insets.top, 70, 20);

    groupDiscoveryButtonGroup.add(groupLocalRadioButton);
    groupDiscoveryButtonGroup.add(groupRemoteRadioButton);

    groupDiscoveryButton.setText("Discover");
    groupDiscoveryButton.setToolTipText("Find groups");
    contentPane.add(groupDiscoveryButton);
    groupDiscoveryButton.setBounds(170+insets.left,
➥   310+insets.top, 90, 20);


    // peer section
    peerScrollPane.setViewportBorder
➥   (new TitledBorder("Peers"));
    peerScrollPane.setViewportView(peerList);
```

LISTING 19.1   continued

```
    contentPane.add(peerScrollPane);
    peerScrollPane.setBounds(290+insets.left,
➥   10+insets.top, 250, 230);


    peerAddTextField.setToolTipText("Add a new peer");
    contentPane.add(peerAddTextField);
    peerAddTextField.setBounds(290+insets.left,
➥   250+insets.top, 140, 20);

    peerAddButton.setText("Add");
    peerAddButton.setToolTipText("Add a new peer");
    contentPane.add(peerAddButton);
    peerAddButton.setBounds(450+insets.left,
➥   250+insets.top, 90, 20);


    peerFlushButton.setText("Flush");
    peerFlushButton.setToolTipText
➥   ("Flush local peer cache");
    contentPane.add(peerFlushButton);
    peerFlushButton.setBounds(290+insets.left,
➥   280+insets.top, 90, 20);

    peerCheckBox.setSelected(false);
    peerCheckBox.setText("Groups");
    peerCheckBox.setToolTipText
➥   ("Display groups peer is in.");
    contentPane.add(peerCheckBox);
    peerCheckBox.setBounds(386+insets.left,
➥   280+insets.top, 60, 20);

    peerRemoveButton.setText("Remove");
    peerRemoveButton.setToolTipText("Remove a peer");
    contentPane.add(peerRemoveButton);
    peerRemoveButton.setBounds(450+insets.left,
➥   280+insets.top, 90, 20);

    peerLocalRadioButton.setSelected(true);
    peerLocalRadioButton.setText("Local");
    peerLocalRadioButton.setToolTipText
➥   ("Search for local peers");
    contentPane.add(peerLocalRadioButton);
    peerLocalRadioButton.setBounds(290+insets.left,
➥   310+insets.top, 60, 20);

    peerRemoteRadioButton.setText("Remote");
    peerRemoteRadioButton.setToolTipText
➥   ("Search for remote peers");
    contentPane.add(peerRemoteRadioButton);
```

LISTING 19.1 continued

```
    peerRemoteRadioButton.setBounds(370+insets.left,
➥ 310+insets.top, 70, 20);

    peerDiscoveryButtonGroup.add(peerLocalRadioButton);
    peerDiscoveryButtonGroup.add(peerRemoteRadioButton);

    peerDiscoveryButton.setText("Discover");
    peerDiscoveryButton.setToolTipText("Find peers");
    contentPane.add(peerDiscoveryButton);
    peerDiscoveryButton.setBounds(450+insets.left,
➥ 310+insets.top, 90, 20);

    pack();
    setTitle("P2P Dashboard");
    setSize(558, 365);
    setResizable(false);

    // JFrame event
    addWindowListener(new WindowAdapter() {
      public void windowClosing(WindowEvent evt)
      {
        exitForm(evt);
      }
    });
  }


  /*
    P2PDashboard uses this to handle GUI object events.
  */
  private void configureGroupEvents()
  {
    // group JList event
    groupList.setSelectionMode
➥ (ListSelectionModel.SINGLE_SELECTION);

    groupList.addListSelectionListener
➥ (new ListSelectionListener() {
      public void valueChanged(ListSelectionEvent e)
      {
        if (e.getValueIsAdjusting()) {
          return;
        }

        JList list = (JList)e.getSource();

        // whenever a group is selected,
        // retrieve its corresponding peer list and
        // display it.
        if (list.isSelectionEmpty() == false) {
```

LISTING 19.1   continued

```
        String group = (String)list.getSelectedValue();
        SortedListModel peers = (SortedListModel)
➡  groupHT.get(group);

        peerList.setModel(peers);
      }
    }
  });

  // group Add JButton event
  groupAddButton.addActionListener(new ActionListener()
➡  {
    public void actionPerformed(ActionEvent e)
    {
      String group = groupAddTextField.getText();
      SortedListModel list = null;

      if (checkAddRules(group) == false) {
        return;
      }

      list = (SortedListModel)groupList.getModel();

      // ensure new group does not already exist
      if (list.contains(group) == false) {
        list.addElement(group);
        addGroup(group);

        SortedListModel slm = new SortedListModel();
        groupHT.put(group, slm);

        groupList.setModel(list);
        groupList.setSelectedValue(group, true);
        peerList.clearSelection();
      }
      else {
        handleError("Group `" + group + "`
➡  already in use.",
                    "Invalid group name", null, false);
      }

      groupAddTextField.setText("");
    }
  });

  // peer Flush JButton event
  groupFlushButton.addActionListener(new ActionListener() {
    public void actionPerformed(ActionEvent e)
    {
      // remove all groups except the netPeerGroup
```

LISTING 19.1   continued

```
        SortedListModel list = (SortedListModel)
➡   groupList.getModel();
        Enumeration enum = list.elements();
        String group = null;

        while (enum.hasMoreElements())
        {
          group = (String)enum.nextElement();

          if (group.equals(defaultGroupName) == false) {
            list.removeElement(group);
            groupHT.remove(group);
          }
        }
        groupList.setModel(list);
        groupList.setSelectedValue(defaultGroupName, true);
        peerList.clearSelection();

        // flush actual local group advertisements
        groupDiscovery.flushGroupInfo();
      }
    });

    // group Remove JButton event
    groupRemoveButton.addActionListener(new ActionListener()
➡   {
      public void actionPerformed(ActionEvent e)
      {
        String group = (String)groupList.getSelectedValue();

        if (group == null || group.equals("") == true ||
            group.equals(defaultGroupName)) {
          return;
        }

        SortedListModel list = (SortedListModel)
➡   groupList.getModel();
        list.removeElement(group);
        groupList.setModel(list);
        groupList.setSelectedValue(defaultGroupName, true);
        peerList.clearSelection();

        removeAdvertisement(group, false);
      }
    });

    // group Discovery JButton event
    groupDiscoveryButton.addActionListener
➡   (new ActionListener() {
      public void actionPerformed(ActionEvent e)
```

LISTING **19.1** continued

```
      {
        // initiate local group discovery
        if (groupLocalRadioButton.isSelected()) {
          groupDiscovery.setLocalDiscovery(true);
          groupDiscovery.run();
        }
        // initiate remote group discovery
        else if (groupRemoteRadioButton.isSelected()) {
          groupDiscovery.setLocalDiscovery(false);
          groupDiscovery.run();
        }
      }
    });
  }


  /*
    P2PDashboard uses this to handle peer GUI object events.
   */
  private void configurePeerEvents()
  {
    // peer JList event
    peerList.setSelectionMode
➥  (ListSelectionModel.SINGLE_SELECTION);

    peerList.addListSelectionListener
➥  (new ListSelectionListener() {
      public void valueChanged(ListSelectionEvent e)
      {
        JList list = (JList)e.getSource();
        String selectedPeer =
➥  (String)list.getSelectedValue();

        if (e.getValueIsAdjusting() ||
➥  displayPeerGroups == false) {
          return;
        }

        // whenever a peer is selected,
        // retrieve its corresponding group list and
        // display it.
        if (list.isSelectionEmpty() == false) {
          SortedListModel peerInGroup =
➥  new SortedListModel();
          SortedListModel peers = null;
          String group = null;

          Enumeration keys = groupHT.keys();
          while (keys.hasMoreElements())
          {
```

LISTING 19.1 continued

```
            group = (String)keys.nextElement();
            peers = (SortedListModel)groupHT.get(group);

            if (peers.contains(selectedPeer) == true) {
             peerInGroup.addElement(group);
            }
          }
        }

        groupList.setModel(peerInGroup);
        groupList.clearSelection();
      }
    }
  });

  // peer Add JButton event
  peerAddButton.addActionListener(new ActionListener() {
    public void actionPerformed(ActionEvent e)
    {
      String peer = peerAddTextField.getText();
      String group = (String)groupList.getSelectedValue();

      // allow defaultPeerName to be added to new groups
      if (peer != null && !peer.equals("") &&
          group != null && !group.equals("") &&
          peer.equals(defaultPeerName) &&
          !group.equals(defaultGroupName)) {
        System.out.println
➡  ("Adding " + peer + " to group '" + group + "'");
      }
      // default peer name checking
      else if (checkAddRules(peer) == false ||
              group == null || group.equals("") == true) {
        handleError("Invalid peer name.",
                    "Invalid peer ", null, false);
        return;
      }

      // do not allow a peer to be the same name as the
      // currently selected group
      if (peer.equals(group)) {
        handleError("Peer cannot be same name as group.",
                    "Invalid peer ", null, false);
        return;
      }


      // retrieve peer list of currently selected group
      SortedListModel list =
➡ (SortedListModel)peerList.getModel();
```

19

THE P2P
DASHBOARD

LISTING 19.1   continued

```
        // ensure new peer does not already exist
        if (list.contains(peer) == false) {
          list.addElement(peer);
          peerList.setModel(list);
          groupHT.put(group, list);

          addPeer(peer);
        }
        else {
          handleError("Peer `" + peer + "`
➥ already in use.",
                        "Invalid peer ", null, false);
        }

        peerAddTextField.setText("");
      }
    });

    // peer Flush JButton event
    peerFlushButton.addActionListener(new ActionListener()
➥ {
        public void actionPerformed(ActionEvent e)
        {
          // remove every peer in every group
          // except defaultPeerName in the netPeerGroup

          Enumeration keys = groupHT.keys();
          Enumeration enum = null;
          SortedListModel peers = null;
          String group = null;
          String peer = null;

          while (keys.hasMoreElements())
          {
            group = (String)keys.nextElement();
            peers = (SortedListModel)groupHT.get(group);

            enum = peers.elements();

            while (enum.hasMoreElements())
            {
              peer = (String)enum.nextElement();

              if (peer.equals(defaultPeerName) == true &&
                  group.equals(defaultGroupName) == true) {
                  System.out.println
➥        (defaultPeerName + " not flushed from " +
➥        defaultGroupName);
              }
```

LISTING 19.1   continued

```
            else peers.removeElement(peer);
            }

        groupHT.put(group, peers);
      }

      groupList.setSelectedValue(defaultGroupName, true);
      peerList.clearSelection();

      // remove all peer advertisements
      peerDiscovery.flushPeerInfo();
    }
});

// peer group display JCheckBox event
peerCheckBox.addItemListener(new ItemListener() {
  public void itemStateChanged(ItemEvent e)
  {
    // display all peers from every group
    // so that when we select a peer, we can
    // show the groups it belongs to.
    if (e.getStateChange() == ItemEvent.SELECTED) {
      displayPeerGroups = true;

      Enumeration keys = groupHT.keys();
      Enumeration enum = null;
      String group = null;
      String peer = null;
      SortedListModel allPeers = new SortedListModel();
      SortedListModel peers = null;

      while (keys.hasMoreElements())
      {
        group = (String)keys.nextElement();
        peers = (SortedListModel)groupHT.get(group);

        enum = peers.elements();

        while (enum.hasMoreElements())
        {
          peer = (String)enum.nextElement();

          if (allPeers.contains(peer) == false) {
            allPeers.addElement(peer);
          }
        }
      }

      peerList.setModel(allPeers);
```

LISTING 19.1 continued

```
          peerList.setSelectedValue(defaultPeerName, true);
          groupList.clearSelection();
        }

      // remove, leave peer might occur now
      // so allow a group and a peer to be selected.
      else {
        displayPeerGroups = false;

        Enumeration keys = groupHT.keys();
        String group = null;
        SortedListModel groups = new SortedListModel();

        while (keys.hasMoreElements())
        {
          group = (String)keys.nextElement();
          groups.addElement(group);
        }

        groupList.setModel(groups);
        groupList.setSelectedValue(defaultGroupName, true);
        peerList.clearSelection();
      }
    }
  });

  // peer Remove JButton event
  peerRemoveButton.addActionListener(new ActionListener()
  {
    public void actionPerformed(ActionEvent e)
    {
      String group = (String)groupList.getSelectedValue();
      String peer = (String)peerList.getSelectedValue();

      if (peer == null || peer.equals("") == true ||
          group == null || group.equals("") == true) {
        handleError("Please unselect
  the `Groups` check box.!",
                    "Remove failed", null, false);
        return;
      }
      if ((peer.equals(defaultPeerName) == true &&
          group.equals(defaultGroupName) == true)) {
        handleError("Cannot remove local peer from
  netPeerGroup!",
                    "Remove failed", null, false);
        return;
      }
```

LISTING **19.1** continued

```
        // retrieve peer list of currently selected group
        SortedListModel list = (SortedListModel)
➥   peerList.getModel();
        list.removeElement(peer);
        peerList.setModel(list);
        groupHT.put(group, list);

      groupList.setSelectedValue(defaultGroupName, true);
      peerList.clearSelection();

        removeAdvertisement(peer, true);
      }
    });

    // peer Discovery JButton event
    peerDiscoveryButton.addActionListener(new ActionListener()
➥   {
      public void actionPerformed(ActionEvent e)
      {
        // initiate local peer discovery
        if (peerLocalRadioButton.isSelected()) {
          peerDiscovery.setLocalDiscovery(true);
          peerDiscovery.run();
        }
        // initiate remote peer discovery
        else if (peerRemoteRadioButton.isSelected()) {
          peerDiscovery.setLocalDiscovery(false);
          peerDiscovery.run();
        }
      }
    });
  }


  /*
   *Exit the application.
   */
  private void exitForm(WindowEvent e)
  {
    System.exit(0);
  }


  private void handleError(String msg, String title,
                           Exception e, boolean exitSystem)
  {
    if (msg == null || title == null ||
        msg.equals("") == true ||
➥   title.equals("") == true) return;
```

LISTING 19.1 continued

```
   if (e != null) e.printStackTrace();
   JOptionPane.showMessageDialog(frame, msg, title,
➡ JOptionPane.ERROR_MESSAGE);

   if (exitSystem) System.exit(1);
 }



 /******************************************/
 /* Peer and Group List Validation Methods */
 /******************************************/

 private boolean checkAddRules(String s)
 {
   boolean check = true;

   if (s == null || s.equals("") == true ||
       s.equals(defaultGroupName) == true||
       s.equals(defaultPeerName) == true) {
     check=false;
   }

   return check;
 }



 /******************/
 /*  JXTA Methods */
 /******************/

 /*
  *Initialize the default NetPeerGroup that our
  *local peer belongs to.
  */
 public void initializeNetPeerGroup()
 {
   try {
     netPeerGroup = PeerGroupFactory.newNetPeerGroup();
     discovery = netPeerGroup.getDiscoveryService();
   }
   catch (PeerGroupException e) {
     handleError("netPeerGroup creation failed!",
➡ "NetPeerGroup", e, true);
   }

   // Print out useful local peer/group information
   System.out.println("JXTA group = " +
➡ netPeerGroup.getPeerGroupName());
```

LISTING 19.1 continued

```
   System.out.println("Group ID = " +
➡ netPeerGroup.getPeerGroupID().toString());
   System.out.println("Peer name = " +
➡ netPeerGroup.getPeerName());
   System.out.println("Peer ID = " +
➡ netPeerGroup.getPeerID().toString());
   System.out.println("\n\n");
 }


 /*
 *Initialize the peer and group discovery services for
 *handling local and remote discovery events and messages.
 */
 public void initializeDiscovery()
 {
   SortedListModel list = null;

   //Save default peer and group name
   defaultGroupName = netPeerGroup.getPeerGroupName();
   defaultPeerName = netPeerGroup.getPeerName();


   //Group Discovery
   groupDiscovery = new GroupDiscovery(netPeerGroup,
➡ discovery, groupList, defaultGroupName);
   groupDiscovery.startJxta();

   // add netPeerGroup to group list in GUI
   list = (SortedListModel)groupList.getModel();
   list.addElement(defaultGroupName);
   groupList.setModel(list);

   // create new peer list for group netPeerGroup
   list = new SortedListModel();
   list.addElement(defaultPeerName);
   groupHT.put(defaultGroupName, list);
   groupList.setSelectedValue(defaultGroupName, true);


   // Peer Discovery
   peerDiscovery = new PeerDiscovery(netPeerGroup,
➡ discovery, peerList, defaultPeerName);
   peerDiscovery.startJxta();

   // Add defaultPeerName to peer list in the GUI
   list = (SortedListModel)peerList.getModel();
   list.addElement(defaultPeerName);
   peerList.setModel(list);
```

19

THE P2P
DASHBOARD

LISTING 19.1   continued

```
    peerList.clearSelection();
  }


  /*
   *Creates a peer and publishes this peer locally
   *and remotely.
   */
  public void addPeer(String peer)
  {
    // create new peer
    PeerAdvertisement peerAdv = new PeerAdv();
    peerAdv.setName(peer);

    // using PeerGroupID.defaultNetPeerGroupID because
    // PeerGroup.getGroupID returns ID and we can't resolve

    // compilation or runtime issues with using
    // new PeerID(PeerGroupID) method.
    // Casting the ID to PeerGroupID will work with new
    // PeerID(PeerGroupID) but causes runtime
    // cast class exception.
    // So we will just default all new peers have
    // the defaultNetPeerGroupID for their group.
    PeerID peerID = new PeerID
➥  (PeerGroupID.defaultNetPeerGroupID);
    peerAdv.setPeerID(peerID);
    peerAdv.setPeerGroupID
➥  (PeerGroupID.defaultNetPeerGroupID);

    //Announce new peer.
    try {
      discovery.publish(peerAdv, DiscoveryService.PEER);
      discovery.remotePublish
➥  (peerAdv, DiscoveryService.PEER);
    }
    catch (IOException e) {
      handleError("Adding peer `" + peer + "` failed!",
➥  "Adding failed", e, false);
    }
  }


  /*
   *Remove a peer's credentials from the local cache.
   */
  public void removeAdvertisement(String s, boolean peer)
  {
    int type = DiscoveryService.PEER;
```

LISTING 19.1 continued

```
      if (peer == false) {
          type = DiscoveryService.GROUP;
      }

      Enumeration enum = null;
      PeerGroupAdvertisement groupAdv = null;
      PeerAdvertisement peerAdv - null;

      try {
        enum = discovery.getLocalAdvertisements
➥ (type, "Name", s);

        if (enum.hasMoreElements()) {
          if (peer == false) {
            groupAdv = (PeerGroupAdvertisement)
➥ enum.nextElement();
            discovery.flushAdvertisements
➥ (groupAdv.getPeerGroupID().toString(), type);
          }
          else {
            peerAdv = (PeerAdvertisement)
➥ enum.nextElement();
            discovery.flushAdvertisements
➥ (peerAdv.getPeerID().toString(), type);
          }
        }
      }
      catch (IOException e) {
        handleError("Remove of peer or group failed!",
➥ "Removal failed", e, false);
      }
  }


  /*
   *Create a new group and publishes this group
   *locally and remotely.
   */
  public PeerGroup addGroup(String group)
  {
    ModuleImplAdvertisement mia = null;
    PeerGroup peerGroup = null;
    PeerGroupAdvertisement pga = null;

    try {
      // create new group
      mia = netPeerGroup.
➥ getAllPurposePeerGroupImplAdvertisement();
      peerGroup = netPeerGroup.newGroup(null, mia, group,
                                     group + " description");
```

19

**THE P2P
DASHBOARD**

LISTING 19.1   continued

```
      // announce new group
      pga = peerGroup.getPeerGroupAdvertisement();
      discovery.publish(pga, DiscoveryService.GROUP);
      discovery.remotePublish(pga, DiscoveryService.GROUP);

      netPeerGroup.newGroup(pga);
    }
    catch (IOException e) {
      handleError("Group `" + group +
➥   "` could not be added!.",
                  "Exception during group add", e, false);
    }
    catch (PeerGroupException e) {
      handleError("Group `" + group +
➥   "` could not be added!.",
                  "Exception during group add", e, false);
    }
    catch (Exception e) {
      handleError("Group `" + group +
➥   "` could not be added!.",
                  "Exception during group add", e, false);
    }

    return peerGroup;
  }
}
```

Details of the `PeerDiscovery` Class

The `PeerDiscovery` class is responsible for the local and remote discovery of peers, as well as for updating the peer information in the GUI. The `PeerDiscovery` class implements the `Runnable` and `DiscoveryListener` interfaces and the following methods:

- The `updateGUI(Boolean stringCast, Enumeration enum)` method updates the peer GUI by adding or removing peers
- The `flushPeerInfo()` method flushes the information in the local peer cache
- The `run()` method uses a thread to discover peers locally or remotely on demand
- The `discoveryEvent(DiscoveryEvent e)` method handles remote discovery messages
- The `setLocalDiscovery(boolean local)` method sets the discovery to be local or remote

- The PeerDiscovery(PeerGroup netPeerGroup, DiscoveryService discovery, Jlist peerList, String defaultPeerName) method creates a new PeerDiscovery object

Listing 19.2 presents the code for PeerDiscovery.java.

LISTING 19.2   PeerDiscovery.java

```java
import java.io.InputStream;
import java.io.IOException;
import java.io.ByteArrayInputStream;

import java.lang.String;

import java.util.Enumeration;

import javax.swing.JList;


import net.jxta.document.Advertisement;
import net.jxta.document.AdvertisementFactory;
import net.jxta.document.MimeMediaType;

import net.jxta.discovery.DiscoveryService;
import net.jxta.discovery.DiscoveryListener;
import net.jxta.discovery.DiscoveryEvent;

import net.jxta.exception.PeerGroupException;

import net.jxta.peergroup.PeerGroup;
import net.jxta.peergroup.PeerGroupFactory;

import net.jxta.protocol.DiscoveryResponseMsg;
import net.jxta.protocol.PeerAdvertisement;


/*
 *PeerDiscovery

 *Responsible for local and remote discovery of peers.
 *Also responsible for updating the peer info in the GUI.
 */
public class PeerDiscovery
implements Runnable, DiscoveryListener
{
  // necessary links to important local peer information
  private PeerGroup netPeerGroup;
  private DiscoveryService discovery;
```

19

THE P2P DASHBOARD

LISTING 19.2 continued

```java
private PeerAdvertisement peerAdv;

// link to peer GUI list
private JList peerList;
private String defaultPeerName;

// link to GUI discovery selection type (local or remote)
private boolean local;



/*
 *Update peer GUI for adding/removing peers
 */
private void updateGUI(boolean stringCast,
➥ Enumeration enum)
{
  String str = null;
  PeerAdvertisement newAdv = null;
  MimeMediaType mmt = new MimeMediaType("text/xml");
  SortedListModel peers =
➥ (SortedListModel)peerList.getModel();

  while (enum.hasMoreElements())
  {
    // Processing String objects
    if (stringCast) {
      str = (String)enum.nextElement();

      try {
        // create an advertisement for each element
        newAdv = (PeerAdvertisement)
➥ AdvertisementFactory.newAdvertisement
➥ (mmt, new ByteArrayInputStream(str.getBytes()));

      }
      catch (IOException ioe) {
        System.out.println
➥ ("Error parsing response element!");
        ioe.printStackTrace();
        continue;
      }
    }

    // Processing PeerAdvertisement objects
    else {
      newAdv = (PeerAdvertisement)enum.nextElement();
    }
```

LISTING 19.2   continued

```
    System.out.println("Discovered peer = " +
➡  newAdv.getName());

    // found a new peer, add them to the peerList
    if (peers.contains(newAdv.getName()) == false) {
      peers.addElement(newAdv.getName());
      System.out.println("Discovered peer = " +
➡  newAdv.getName() + " added");
    }
  }

  // update the GUI
  peerList.setModel(peers);
  peerList.setSelectedValue(defaultPeerName, true);
}


/*
 *Start JXTA method
 */
public void startJxta()
{
  // flush local JXTA cache
  flushPeerInfo();
}


/*
 *Flush local peer cache information
 */
public void flushPeerInfo()
{
  try {
    discovery.flushAdvertisements
➡  (null, DiscoveryService.PEER);
  }
  catch (IOException e) {
    e.printStackTrace();
  }
}


/*
 *On demand, discover peers locally or remotely
 *via a thread.
 */
public void run()
{
  Enumeration enum = null;
```

LISTING 19.2   continued

```
    SortedListModel peers =
➡ (SortedListModel)peerList.getModel();

    try {
      //Add ourselves as a discoverylistener for
      //discovery response events.
      discovery.addDiscoveryListener(this);

      // check local cache for peer
      if (local) {
        enum = discovery.getLocalAdvertisements
➡ (DiscoveryService.PEER, null, null);

        if (enum == null ||
➡ enum.hasMoreElements() == false) {
          System.out.println
➡ ("No local advertisements found");
        }

        System.out.println
➡ ("update GUI peer discovery now");

        //Update peer list in GUI
        updateGUI(false, enum);
      }

      //Wait 10 seconds per remote discovery
      else {
        discovery.getRemoteAdvertisements(null,
➡ DiscoveryService.PEER, null, null, 10, this);

        try {
          Thread.sleep(10 * 1000);
        }
        catch (Exception e) {
        }
      }
    }
    catch (Exception e) {
      e.printStackTrace();
    }
  }


  /*
   *Handle remote discovery messages.
   */
  public void discoveryEvent(DiscoveryEvent e)
  {
```

LISTING 19.2   continued

```
    DiscoveryResponseMsg drm = e.getResponse();
    String response = drm.getPeerAdv();
    InputStream is = null;
    PeerAdvertisement peerAdv = null;
    MimeMediaType mmt = new MimeMediaType("text/xml");

    try {
      // create a peer advertisement
      is = new ByteArrayInputStream(response.getBytes());
      peerAdv = (PeerAdvertisement)
➥ AdvertisementFactory.newAdvertisement(mmt, is);

      System.out.println
➥ ("[ Received discovery response [" +
            drm.getResponseCount() +
            " elements] from peer : " +
              peerAdv.getName() + " ]");
    }
    catch (IOException ioe) {
      System.out.println("Error parsing remote peer's
➥ advertisement!");
      ioe.printStackTrace();
      return;
    }

    // update peers in GUI
    updateGUI(true, drm.getResponses());
  }


  /*
   *set discovery to be local or remote
   *local = true   —> search is local
   *local = false  —> search is remote
   */
  public void setLocalDiscovery(boolean local)
  {
    this.local = local;
  }


  /*
   *Creates new PeerDiscovery object.
   */
  public PeerDiscovery(PeerGroup netPeerGroup,
➥ DiscoveryService discovery, JList peerList,
➥ String defaultPeerName)
  {
    this.netPeerGroup = netPeerGroup;
```

LISTING **19.2**   continued

```
    this.discovery = discovery;
    this.peerList = peerList;
    this.defaultPeerName = defaultPeerName;

    local = true;
  }
}
```

Details of the `GroupDiscovery.java` Class

The `GroupDiscovery` class is responsible for handling local and remote discovery of groups, as well as updating the group information on the GUI.

The `GroupDiscovery` class implements the `Runnable` and `DiscoveryListener` interfaces. It uses the following methods:

- The `updateGUI(boolean stringCast, Enumeration enum)` method updates the GUI for adding and/or removing groups and respective peers under desired groups
- The `startJXTA()` method executes the `flushGroupInfo()` method to flush local group information in the cache
- The `flushGroupInfo()` method flushes local group information in the cache
- The `run()` method uses a thread to discover groups locally or remotely on demand
- The `discoveryEvent(DiscoveryEvent e)` method handles remote discovery messages
- The `setLocalDiscovery(boolean local)` method sets the discovery type to be local or remote

Listing 19.3 presents the code for `GroupDiscovery.java`.

LISTING **19.3**   `GroupDiscovery.java`

```
import java.io.InputStream;
import java.io.IOException;
import java.io.ByteArrayInputStream;

import java.lang.String;

import java.util.Enumeration;

import javax.swing.JList;


import net.jxta.document.Advertisement;
```

LISTING 19.3   continued

```java
import net.jxta.document.AdvertisementFactory;
import net.jxta.document.MimeMediaType;

import net.jxta.discovery.DiscoveryService;
import net.jxta.discovery.DiscoveryListener;
import net.jxta.discovery.DiscoveryEvent;

import net.jxta.exception.PeerGroupException;

import net.jxta.peergroup.PeerGroup;
import net.jxta.peergroup.PeerGroupFactory;

import net.jxta.protocol.DiscoveryResponseMsg;
import net.jxta.protocol.PeerAdvertisement;
import net.jxta.protocol.PeerGroupAdvertisement;

/*
 *GroupDiscovery
 *Responsible for local and remote discovery of groups.
 *Also responsible for updating the group information
 *in the GUI.
 */
public class GroupDiscovery
implements Runnable, DiscoveryListener
{
  // necessary links to important group information
  private PeerGroup netPeerGroup;
  private DiscoveryService discovery;
  private PeerAdvertisement peerAdv;

  // link to group tree GUI
  private JList groupList;
  private String defaultGroupName;

  // link to GUI discovery selection type (local or remote)
  private boolean local;



  /*
   *Update group GUI for adding/removing groups and
   *respective peers under groups.
   */
  private void updateGUI
➥  (boolean stringCast, Enumeration enum)
  {
    String str = null;
    PeerGroupAdvertisement newAdv = null;
    MimeMediaType mmt = new MimeMediaType("text/xml");
    SortedListModel groups =
```

LISTING 19.3   continued

```
(SortedListModel)groupList.getModel();

    while (enum.hasMoreElements())
    {
      // Processing String objects
      if (stringCast) {
        str = (String)enum.nextElement();

      try {
          // create an advertisement from each element
          newAdv = (PeerGroupAdvertisement)
  AdvertisementFactory.newAdvertisement
  (mmt, new ByteArrayInputStream(str.getBytes()));
        }
        catch (IOException ioe) {
          System.out.println
  ("Error parsing response element!");
          ioe.printStackTrace();
          continue;
        }
      }

      // Processing PeerGroupAdvertisement objects
      else {
        newAdv = (PeerGroupAdvertisement)enum.nextElement();
      }

      System.out.println("Discovered group = " +
  newAdv.getName());

      // found a new group, add them to the groupList
      if (groups.contains(newAdv.getName()) == false) {
        groups.addElement(newAdv.getName());
        System.out.println("Discovered group = " +
  newAdv.getName() + " added");
      }
    }

    // update the GUI
    groupList.setModel(groups);
    groupList.setSelectedValue(defaultGroupName, true);
  }


  /*
   *Start JXTA method.
   */
  public void startJxta()
  {
```

LISTING 19.3 continued

```
    // flush local group cache
    flushGroupInfo();
  }


  /*
   *Flush local group cache information.
   */
  public void flushGroupInfo()
  {
    try {
      discovery.flushAdvertisements
➥  (null, DiscoveryService.GROUP);
    }
    catch (IOException e) {
      e.printStackTrace();
    }
  }


  /*
   *On demand, discover groups locally or remotely
   *via a thread.
   */
  public void run()
  {
    Enumeration enum = null;
    PeerGroupAdvertisement pga = null;
    SortedListModel groups =
➥  (SortedListModel)groupList.getModel();

    try {
      //Add ourselves as a discoverylistener for
      //discovery response events.
      discovery.addDiscoveryListener(this);

      // check local cache for peer
      if (local) {
        enum = discovery.getLocalAdvertisements
➥  (DiscoveryService.GROUP, null, null);

        if (enum == null ||
➥  enum.hasMoreElements() == false) {
          System.out.println
➥  ("No local advertisements found");
          return;
        }

        System.out.println
➥  ("update GUI group discovery now");
```

LISTING 19.3 continued

```
            // update group list in GUI
            updateGUI(false, enum);
        }

        // wait 10 seconds per remote discovery
        else {
          discovery.getRemoteAdvertisements
➥ (null, DiscoveryService.GROUP,
➥ null, null, 10, this);

            try {
              Thread.sleep(10 * 1000);
            }
            catch (Exception e) {
            }
        }
    }
    catch (Exception e)
    {
      e.printStackTrace();
    }
}


/*
 *Handle remote discovery messages.
 */
public void discoveryEvent(DiscoveryEvent e)
{
  DiscoveryResponseMsg drm = e.getResponse();
  String response = drm.getPeerAdv();
  InputStream is = null;
  MimeMediaType mmt = new MimeMediaType("text/xml");

  try {
    //Create a group advertisement.
    is = new ByteArrayInputStream(response.getBytes());
    peerAdv = (PeerAdvertisement)
➥ AdvertisementFactory.newAdvertisement(mmt, is);

    System.out.println("[ Received discovery response
➥ [" + drm.getResponseCount() +" elements]
➥ from group: " + peerAdv.getName() + " ]");
  }
  catch (IOException ioe) {
    System.out.println("Error parsing remote peer's
➥ advertisement!");
    ioe.printStackTrace();
    return;
  }
```

LISTING 19.3 continued

```
    // update groups in GUI
    updateGUI(true, drm.getResponses());
  }


  /*
   *Set discovery type
   *local = true   —> search is local
   *local = false  —> search is remote
   */
  public void setLocalDiscovery(boolean local)
  {
    this.local = local;
  }


  /*
   *Creates new GroupDiscovery object.
   */
  public GroupDiscovery(PeerGroup netPeerGroup,
➥   DiscoveryService discovery, JList groupList,
➥   String defaultGroupName)
  {
    this.netPeerGroup = netPeerGroup;
    this.discovery = discovery;
    this.groupList = groupList;
    this.defaultGroupName = defaultGroupName;

    local = true;
  }
}
```

Details of the `SortedListModel` Class

The SortedListModel class is responsible for creating a tree of listmodel objects and storing them in a sorted set. It sorts the listmodel objects that are used to manage either peer or group lists.

The SortedListModel class employs the following methods:

- The getSize() method to obtain the size of the list
- The getElementAt(int index) method to get the desired element at the specified index
- The addElement(Object element) method to add individual elements to the list
- The addAll(Object elements[]) method to add an array of elements to the list

- The `clear` method to clear the list
- The `contains(Object element)` method to check whether the list contains a specific element
- The `elements()` method to obtain an `Enumeration` of the elements in the list
- The `firstElement()` method to obtain the first element in the list
- The `iterator()` method to obtain an `Iterator` for the elements in the list
- The `lastElement()` method to obtain the last element in the list
- The `removeElement(Object element)` method to check whether an element has been removed

Listing 19.4 presents the code for `SortedListModel.java`.

LISTING 19.4 `SortedListModel.java`

```
// Original source from :
//
// Copyright 1999 MageLang Institute
// $Id //depot/main/src/edu/modules/Collections/magercises/Jlist
➥   /Solution/SortedListModel.java#2 $
//
// Source has been modified for JXTA dashboard.
//

import javax.swing.*;
import java.util.*;


public class SortedListModel
extends AbstractListModel
{
  // Define a SortedSet
  SortedSet model;

  public SortedListModel()
  {
    // Create a TreeSet
    // Store it in SortedSet variable
    model = new TreeSet();
  }


  // ListModel methods
  public int getSize()
  {
    // Return the model size
    return model.size();
  }
```

LISTING 19.4   continued

```
public Object getElementAt(int index)
{
  // Return the appropriate element
  return model.toArray()[index];
}


// Other methods
public void addElement(Object element)
{
  if (model.add(element)) {
    fireContentsChanged(this, 0, getSize());
  }
}


public void addAll(Object elements[])
{
  Collection c = Arrays.asList(elements);
  model.addAll(c);
  fireContentsChanged(this, 0, getSize());
}


public void clear()
{
  model.clear();
  fireContentsChanged(this, 0, getSize());
}


public boolean contains(Object element)
{
  return model.contains(element);
}


public Enumeration elements()
{
  // Return the appropriate element
  Vector v = new Vector();
  int size = model.size();

  for (int i = 0; i < size; i++)
  {
   v.addElement(model.toArray()[i]);
  }

  return v.elements();
}
```

LISTING 19.4 continued

```java
public Object firstElement()
{
  // Return the appropriate element
  return model.first();
}


public Iterator iterator()
{
  return model.iterator();
}


public Object lastElement()
{
  // Return the appropriate element
  return model.last();
}


public boolean removeElement(Object element)
{
  boolean removed = model.remove(element);

  if (removed) {
    fireContentsChanged(this, 0, getSize());
  }

  return removed;
}
}
```

Summary

This chapter describes a sample program, the P2P Dashboard, to illustrate the peer membership protocol and peer discovery protocol of the JXTA technology.

The chapter provides illustrations to show how the P2P Dashboard program employs JXTA protocols through activities such as community formation, detecting the presence of peers and groups, and managing peers and groups.

CHAPTER 20

Using SOAP with P2P

by Bilal Siddiqui

IN THIS CHAPTER

In this chapter we will elaborate upon the advantages of implementing Web services over the P2P infrastructure. We will start with a short description of the current Web services model, which mainly relies on the conventional client-server interaction. We will also present the P2P network model, and the concept of operating Web services on P2P networks.

This discussion will eventually lead us to the idea of integrating Web services with P2P through service gateways. We will consider what is common in these two technologies, the manner in which they compete, and how they can cooperate with each other. Taking JXTA as a sample P2P network, we will develop a service gateway application that can work for the benefit of JXTA peers.

What Can We Achieve by Combining Web Services with P2P?

To understand the benefits of operating Web services over a P2P infrastructure, we will first analyze the current Web services model.

The Web Services Usage Model

We introduced the three Web services' interoperability stacks in Chapter 11, "Web Services Explained" (the wire stack, the description stack and the discovery stack). Let's analyze the usage model of the three stacks by considering an example. Suppose you want to find a particular service over the Internet (for example, you want to get the freight charges for sending a packet from source to destination).

Whenever you need a product or a service, you will go through the following three steps:

1. You need to know who is offering the product or service. This is a search, or *discovery*, operation. The result will be a list of service providers. Universal Description, Discovery, and Integration (UDDI) is meant to cover this stack.

2. When you have discovered the service provider, you will need to understand how to talk to the service provider. This is the service *description* stack that is essential in all e-business. If software components don't know what language to speak while talking to other components, they will not be able to communicate. The Web services Description Language (WSDL) covers this description stack.

3. When you know what language to speak, the last step is to talk to the service provider to invoke the service. This is the service *invocation* or *wire* stack, covered by Simple Object Access Protocol (SOAP).

These three stacks are independent of each other, meaning you are not required to follow all three steps. You will use only the step that you think is necessary for you.

For example, if you already know who is offering the freight service, you will not need to do any searching and can move to the service description domain directly. Similarly, if you already know what language to speak while talking to service providers, you can invoke the service directly.

Client-Server Interaction in the Current Web Services Model

Currently, all Web services-related technologies and major implementations depend on the client-server model. An example of client-server interaction in Web service applications is SOAP operating over HTTP. Recall the details of SOAP from Chapters 11 and 12, where we elaborated upon the SOAP structure, as well as the request-response mechanism in SOAP. SOAP clients author SOAP requests to invoke the Web services hosted on SOAP servers. SOAP servers, on the other hand, invoke the Web services and author SOAP responses, which are sent back to the SOAP clients.

This only proves the inequality of communicating parties in SOAP. The responsibilities, and therefore the capabilities, of SOAP servers and clients are different. This is analogous to the well-known client-server interaction between a Web server and a Web browser.

As explained in detail in Chapters 11 and 13, UDDI operates over SOAP. Therefore, UDDI also essentially follows client-server interaction, where UDDI servers are registry operators, and UDDI clients are the Web service publishers or users who want to publish or find Web services.

P2P Messaging Model

Imagine the tons of data being loaded on popular search engines today. UDDI registries provide standard APIs to perform the same publishing and search features that search sites like Yahoo! or MSN offer.

The amount of data that conventional proprietary search engines and standard UDDI registries handle is enormous, and growing. However, it is practically impossible for any search facility to do smart searches related to every subject and every topic.

A better way to manage this enormous amount of data is through *distributed content management*. Content related to any single subject will be handled by the experts of that field. There is really no requirement of central search facilities such as UDDI.

That's one of the ways in which P2P is different from the conventional client-server model. Every peer will manage its own content, search for data of its interest, discover other peers, and respond to search requests. This gives rise to the equality of peers in responsibility and capabilities.

We will use JXTA as a sample P2P infrastructure to demonstrate P2P Web services later in this chapter. As explained in Chapter 16, "JXTA and XML," JXTA has introduced the following major concepts to accomplish a peer-to-peer messaging framework:

- Peers—Everyone taking part in a JXTA network is a peer.

- Peer groups—Peers can join other peers having common interests to form *peer groups*. Every peer is free to join as many peer groups as it wants.

- Rendezvous services—A *rendezvous* is a meeting point for peers. This concept plays a very important role in the JXTA network. Peers can voluntarily chose to act as rendezvous. If you know a few rendezvous points, and some of the rendezvous points know other rendezvous points, you can reach every peer connected to this arrangement. The JXTA infrastructure handles all of this—application developers are not required to handle these core issues.

- Pipes and end points—*Pipes* are logical communication channels capable of routing messages from source to destination. The source and destination are referred to as *end points*.

- Discovery, advertisement, and search services—Peers can advertise their resources (like pipes listening to requests related to particular topics) and search for resources exposed by other peers.

P2P Web Services

We have seen Web services and P2P networks operating independently. We'll now discuss an important architectural model and use case scenarios in which Web services and P2P coexist to provide value-added applications.

SOAP-Over-P2P

The simplest logical model in which Web services can work over a P2P infrastructure is the operation of SOAP over P2P.

The largest number of SOAP deployments today work over HTTP. This means the XML payload of SOAP requests and responses travel over HTTP. To elaborate upon this idea, have a look at the following HTTP request that wraps and transports a SOAP (UDDI) request over the Internet (it's a HTTP request containing a SOAP request that in turn contains a UDDI request):

```
POST /services/uddi/testregistry/inquiryapi HTTP/1.1
Host: www-3.ibm.com
Content-type: text/xml; charset=utf-8
Content-length:509
SOAPAction: ""

<?xml version='1.0' encoding='UTF-8'?>
<SOAP-ENV:Envelope
➡    xmlns:xsi="http://www.w3.org/1999/XMLSchema-instance"
➡    xmlns:SOAP-ENV="http://schemas.xmlsoap.org/soap/envelope/"
➡    xmlns:xsd="http://www.w3.org/1999/XMLSchema"
➡    SOAP-ENV:encodingStyle="http://schemas.xmlsoap.org/soap/encoding">
   <SOAP-ENV:Body>
      <find_business generic="1.0" xmlns="urn:uddi-org:api" maxRows="10">
         <findQualifiers />
         <name>%P2P%</name>
      </find_business>
   </SOAP-ENV:Body>
</SOAP-ENV:Envelope>
```

The only addition to the normal XML payload in SOAP is the inclusion of HTTP headers.

If you want to operate SOAP-over-P2P, you'll transport the SOAP request's XML payload as such, without any headers. If you consider JXTA as an sample P2P network, the transport of SOAP messages will essentially be accomplished through JXTA pipes.

Figure 20.1 shows a SOAP-over-P2P application as a box. This application contains two smaller boxes, each representing a module:

- JXTA peer implementation module
- SOAP client implementation module

FIGURE 20.1
The SOAP-over-P2P architecture.

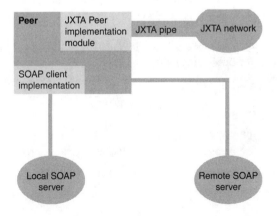

The JXTA peer is connected to the JXTA network through a pipe service. JXTA pipes are capable of receiving any type of data payload. For SOAP requests, this pipe will be used to carry XML payloads.

The SOAP client is responsible for interacting with SOAP servers. We have shown two SOAP servers in Figure 20.1: a local SOAP server, and a remote SOAP server.

The local server can host any applications that this peer would like to host for itself on its own machine. If this application did not have any JXTA module in it, it would be required to own an Internet address (most likely an HTTP URL such as `http://www.mySOAPService.com`), or a static IP address (like `216.23.4.6`) to expose any of its Web services. But with this type of arrangement, it needs neither an HTTP URL nor a static IP address, and it can still host its SOAP services and expose them to the outside world.

If you don't believe what we're suggesting, try the application that we'll develop for this chapter. One of your friends can connect his computer to the Internet through normal dial-up (or any other way) and run the application. You can then access his SOAP services from your PC connected to the Internet!

This is exactly the purpose of P2P. Every peer is responsible to manage its own content (perhaps through SOAP services or by using any means it feels appropriate), and respond to queries from other peers. There is no longer the need to have central data repositories, search engines, and Web servers.

We have also shown a remote SOAP server in Figure 20.1, for the sake of completeness. This remote SOAP server can be any SOAP server over the Internet. Our SOAP-over-P2P application can invoke this remote server through conventional client-server interaction. Other JXTA peers will not know whether the SOAP service being exposed resides locally or remotely.

Use Cases for SOAP-Over-P2P

We will now write two major use cases for our SOAP-over-P2P application. The two use cases involve advertising (or publishing) and service invocation.

The following actors will appear in this use case analysis:

- User—The user of our SOAP-over-P2P application.
- Publishing peer (or publisher)—An instance of our SOAP-over-P2P application that wants to advertise or publish a SOAP service over a JXTA network.
- Requesting peer (or requester)—An instance of our SOAP-over-P2P application that wants to invoke a SOAP service.

- SOAP server—The SOAP server on which there is a SOAP service deployed.
- Rendezvous point—A meeting point in a JXTA network where peers can meet. It is a JXTA service.

Advertising Use Case

While considering this use case, we are assuming that the service that we want to advertise over a JXTA network is already deployed on our local SOAP server. The deployment of services over a SOAP server is an independent process, and depends on which SOAP server you're using. Because our SOAP-over-P2P application is supposed to work with any SOAP server, we will not consider the deployment process in our use cases.

In this use case scenario, the user wants to advertise her SOAP services over a JXTA network. Through a GUI, she will ask the SOAP-over-P2P application to advertise the SOAP service on the JXTA network. The application will ask for the required data (name and description of the SOAP service). The user will provide the required data. The application will create an advertisement according to the data provided, and publish it at all known JXTA rendezvous points. Our SOAP-over-P2P application will also create an input pipe and start listening for service invocation requests.

Service Invocation Use Case

For this use case, we are assuming that you know the name of the SOAP service that you want to invoke. You do not need to know the location of the service implementations (the JXTA network can take care of this, as you'll shortly see), but you still need to know name of the service. The process of finding the name of the service might be part of a UDDI search process, and is not relevant in the present SOAP-over-P2P application.

Here, the user wants to invoke a SOAP service named `P2PCarRentalService` that resides somewhere across the JXTA network. He will ask our SOAP-over-P2P application to find the service. The application will author a search query to find a JXTA pipe service according to the name of the required SOAP service. The application (now acting as a requesting peer) will send the search query to all known JXTA rendezvous points. The rendezvous points will match the pipe services published with them, and also forward the search request to other rendezvous points known to them. If and when the service is found, its advertisement is returned to the requesting peer.

Upon receipt of the pipe (SOAP) service advertisement, our SOAP-over-P2P application will open an output pipe and send the message invocation request to the peer who that's hosting the service.

The requesting peer might receive more than one response. The reason for multiple responses is because there can be any number of publishers hosting the same SOAP service.

Our SOAP-over-P2P implementation will contain both advertising and requesting peers. This will enable the user to use this application for advertising its SOAP services and searching/invoking services from other JXTA peers.

Classes in the SOAP-Over-P2P Application

Based on the preceding use case analysis, we can decide to implement the following classes in the SOAP-over-P2P application:

- JXTAPeer
- Publisher (derived from JXTAPeer)
- Requester (derived from JXTAPeer)
- JxtaGui (graphical user interface)

We'll now see each of these classes in detail.

JXTAPeer

JXTAPeer is the main class that provides all JXTA functionality. We have designed the JXTAPeer class so that other JXTA-related classes will inherit from it for specific purposes. For example, Publisher will extend JXTAPeer and provide specific functionality to act as a publisher of SOAP services.

The JXTAPeer class is responsible for performing the following functions:

1. Make sure that all classes extending JXTAPeer will use the instance of JXTA. This is accomplished in the constructor, where we instantiate the static data member named group (of type PeerGroup). The data member group holds information about the peer group that we will join. While instantiating the group object, we will join the NetPeerGroup, which is the default peer group joined by all peers at startup.

2. Start JXTA. Starting the JXTA service is the responsibility of the startJXTA method, which is called from the constructor. The startJXTA method will instantiate three data members—groupAdvertisement (holds reference to the advertisement service of the peer group), disco (holds reference to the discovery service of the peer group), and pipes (holds reference to the pipe service of the peer group).

3. Create an input pipe to receive incoming messages and advertise it over the JXTA network. The PublishServiceOverJXTAPipe method of JXTAPeer class performs this function.

4. Create an output pipe and send outbound messages. The `JXTAPeer` class contains a method named `CreateOutputPipeAndSendMessage` that performs this function.

These four functions form the major interface of the `JXTAPeer` class. In addition, there are a few small functions that will be described after covering the details of the four methods.

We developed the `JXTAPeer` class by customizing different examples provided at `JXTA.org`. We have copied the licensing information in the `JXTAPeer.java` file.

We'll start with the constructor. Look at the following lines of code from the constructor:

```
public JXTAPeer(){
    if (group==null)
    {
        try {
            group = PeerGroupFactory.newNetPeerGroup();
        } catch (Exception e) {}
        objectCount++;
    }//if (!objectCount)
    startJXTA();
}//constructor
```

This code makes sure that only one JXTA instance exists at a time. We have kept `group` as a static variable, so the `newNetPeerGroup` method will be called only once for all instances of the SOAP-over-P2P application.

The variable `group` is of type `PeerGroup`. Creating a new `PeerGroup` is the first step while instantiating JXTA. The current Java implementation of JXTA that we have used in building our SOAP-over-P2P application provides a class `PeerGroupFactory`, with static methods that can create new peer groups for us. We have used a static method (`newNetPeerGroup`) of this class to create a `NetPeerGroup`.

According to the JXTA specification, every peer at boot-time (while instantiating JXTA) joins the `NetPeerGroup`. Later on, a peer can join other groups as well, and there is no limitation on the number of groups a peer can join.

The next step is to get references to a few services for our `NetPeerGroup`. The following lines of code form the `startJXTA` method that's called from the constructor:

```
groupAdvertisement =
➥    group.getPeerGroupAdvertisement();
disco = group.getDiscoveryService();
pipes = group.getPipeService();
```

We will shortly require discovery and pipe services for this peer group, so we have called the `getDiscoveryService` and `getPipeService` methods of `PeerGroup` class. We will keep a reference to each of these services stored for future use.

20

USING SOAP
WITH P2P

The pipe service will be used whenever an input or outpipe pipe needs to be created. The discovery service is required while performing a search.

This finishes our constructor. We will now have a look at the `publishServiceOverJXTA Pipe()` method of the `JXTAPeer` class.

PublishServiceOverJXTAPipe()

The `publishServiceOverJXTAPipe()` method, as its name implies, will publish our SOAP service over the JXTA network. For this purpose, we will use a JXTA *pipe service*. A pipe service is a mechanism that enables JXTA applications to send and receive messages. If a JXTA application wants to send a message through a pipe service, it will create an output pipe on the service. Similarly, to receive messages, an application will create an input pipe on the pipe service. Think of a JXTA pipe service as a courier service, and the output and input pipes as the sending and receiving ends, respectively.

We will simply create a new pipe service, advertise it on `NetPeerGroup`, create an input pipe on the pipe service, and return a reference to the newly created pipe.

We will use this input pipe to represent our SOAP service. The name of the pipe will be the same as the name of our SOAP service. Other peer applications will search for our pipe service, and when found, create an output pipe to send service invocation messages.

Look at the `publishServiceOverJXTApipe` method signature:

```
protected InputPipe publishServiceOverJXTApipe(
    String ServiceName,
    String ServiceVersion,
    String ServiceDescription,
    String ServiceCreator,
    String SpecURI,
    String PipeAdvFile
    ){
    try{
        // Entire code for this method to be copied in this try block
    }
    catch (Exception ex) {    return null;}

}// publishServiceOverJXTApipe
```

This method takes in six parameters. We will use these parameters in creating the input pipe. `ServiceName` and `ServiceVersion` are the name and version of the SOAP service, respectively. `ServiceDescription` is a textual description of the service being published. `ServiceCreator` is the identification of a company or person advertising this service. `SpecURI` is a URI to a specification (descriptive) document that may reside anywhere (possibly over the Internet).

The last parameter, `PipeAdvFile`, is perhaps the most important. All JXTA services are specified by advertisements. Whether it is a pipe, discovery, or some other service, its details will be specified through XML-based advertisements. You can think about all JXTA services as logical entities that are supposed to function according to their respective advertisements. `PipeAdvFile` is the name of an XML file that we will use to advertise the JXTA pipe so that it can be used to exchange method invocation messages. We will shortly provide a sample of such an XML-based advertisement file.

The `PublishServiceOverJXTAPipe()` method follows three steps to publish a SOAP service as an input pipe. First, it creates a shortform pipe advertisement (an XML file that lets everyone know about the existence of a pipe) and publishes it over the JXTA network. This shortform advertisement only proves the existence of a service, and does not provide its details. In the current implementation of JXTA, the `ModuleClassAdvertisement` class provides the shortform advertisement. The following is the code to create and publish the shortform advertisement:

```
// Step 1: Copy this code in the beginning of try block.
ModuleClassAdvertisement mcadv = (ModuleClassAdvertisement)
➥    AdvertisementFactory.newAdvertisement(
➥    ModuleClassAdvertisement.getAdvertisementType());
mcadv.setName("JXTAMOD:"+ServiceName);
mcadv.setDescription(ServiceDescription);
ModuleClassID mcID = IDFactory.newModuleClassID();
mcadv.setModuleClassID(mcID);
disco.publish(mcadv, DiscoveryService.ADV);
disco.remotePublish(mcadv, DiscoveryService.ADV);
```

All advertisements are created from an `AdvertisementFactory`. After the `AdvertisementFactory` has created a `ModuleClassAdvertisement` object, you can call its set methods to specify its name, description, and ID (unique identification). Although the name and description come from the parameters passed to the `publishServiceOver JXTAPipe()` method, the ID needs to be created by another factory named `IDFactory`. After setting the name, description, and ID, you will use the `DiscoveryService` object created earlier in the constructor to publish this information on the local cache, as well as remotely on the `NetPeerGroup`.

The second step is to create a detailed advertisement for our pipe. This is handled by the `ModuleSpecAdvertisement` class. The purpose of using this advertisement in our application is to enable requesting peers to instantiate our advertisement in the form of a pipe service, so that they can send us method invocation requests through an output pipe. Have a look at the following lines of code that accomplish the creation and publishing of this detailed advertisement:

20

USING SOAP WITH P2P

```
//Step 2, First segment: Copy this code after step 1.
//Create a ModuleSpecAdvertisement and
//call its set methods to specify parameters.
ModuleSpecAdvertisement mdadv =
➥    (ModuleSpecAdvertisement)AdvertisementFactory.newAdvertisement(
➥    ModuleSpecAdvertisement.getAdvertisementType());
mdadv.setName("JXTASPEC:"+ServiceName);
mdadv.setVersion(ServiceVersion);
mdadv.setCreator(ServiceCreator);
mdadv.setDescription(ServiceDescription);
mdadv.setModuleSpecID(IDFactory.newModuleSpecID(mcID));
mdadv.setSpecURI(SpecURI);


//Second segment
//Create a pipe advertisement by reading from an XML file.
//Then copy the pipe advertisement into
//the ModuleSpecAdvertisment created in the first segment.
PipeAdvertisement pipeadv = null;
try {
    FileInputStream is =
➥        new FileInputStream(PipeAdvFile);
    pipeadv = (PipeAdvertisement)
    AdvertisementFactory.newAdvertisement(
➥        new MimeMediaType("text/xml"), is);
    is.close();
} catch (Exception e) {
    receiver.setText(receiver.getText()+"\n"+
➥        "Error reading advert file "+ PipeAdvFile);
    return null;
}//catch

StructuredTextDocument paramDoc =
➥    (StructuredTextDocument)
➥    StructuredDocumentFactory.newStructuredDocument
➥    (new MimeMediaType("text/xml"),"Parm");
StructuredDocumentUtils.copyElements(
➥    paramDoc,
➥    paramDoc,
➥    (Element)pipeadv.getDocument(
➥    new MimeMediaType("text/xml"))
➥    );
mdadv.setParam((StructuredDocument) paramDoc);


//Third segment
//Publish (both locally and remotely) the ModuleSpecAdvertisement,
//which now contains our pipe advertisement.
disco.publish(mdadv, DiscoveryService.ADV);
disco.remotePublish(mdadv, DiscoveryService.ADV);
```

This code is divided into three segments. In the first segment, you will create a `ModuleSpecAdvertisement` and use its set methods in exactly the same way that you created a `ModuleClassAdvertisement` in Step 1.

In the second segment, you will create a pipe advertisement by reading from an XML file specified by `PipeAdvFile`. The XML file will provide an identification (`Id`), type, and the name of the pipe that we want to advertise.

We are going to create a `JxtaUnicast`-type pipe, which means it will be a unidirectional pipe that can have two end points (one transmitter and one receiver). The JXTA set of specifications also specifies a multicast type of pipe that can connect a single transmitter to many receivers.

The following is a simple XML pipe advertisement that can be used for this purpose:

```
<?xml version="1.0"?>
<!DOCTYPE jxta:PipeAdvertisement>
<jxta:PipeAdvertisement xmlns:jxta="http://jxta.org">
    <Id>urn:jxta:uuid-9CCCDF5AD8154D3D87A391210404E59BE4B888209A2241A4A162A109
➡16074A9504
    </Id>
    <Type>JxtaUnicast</Type>
    <Name>JXTA-SOAP-SERVER</Name>
</jxta:PipeAdvertisement>
```

The root element in this advertisement is `PipeAdvertisement`, which belongs to the `jxta` namespace. It contains child elements to specify the ID, type, and name of the pipe being advertised.

After you have created a pipe advertisement, you will add it to the `ModuleSpec-Advertisement` that you created in the first segment. This means our pipe advertisement has to become part of the `ModuleSpecAdvertisement`. For this purpose, you will create a structured text document (a new empty `StructuredTextDocument` object), copy the pipe advertisement into it, then copy the `StructuredTextDocument` into the `ModuleSpecAdvertisement`.

The `StructuredTextDocument` class helps in the marshaling and demarshaling of XML or non-XML structured content. In our case, we want to load our pipe advertisement, which is XML data. Therefore, we have to specify the media type as `text/XML`. After the pipe advertisement has been copied into the `ModuleSpecAdvertisement`, our second segment is finished.

In the third segment of Step 2, you will simply publish the completed `ModuleSpec-Advertisement`, both in the local cache, as well as remotely on the JXTA network.

You are now all set to create an input pipe, which will receive SOAP service method invocation requests.

You will use the `PipeService` object named `pipes` that was created in the `JXTAPeer` constructor. Have a look at the following lines of code:

```
InputPipe ip = pipes.createInputPipe(pipeadv,
➡    ((listener==null)?this:listener));
return ip;
```

You will call the `createInputPipe` method of the `pipes` object and pass on two parameters:

- The pipe advertisement that we created in Step 2.

- A conditional statement to check whether there is a listener object available. The listener object is meant to listen to incoming messages and receive control upon the arrival of a new message.

We have a separate set method available to specify which object should act as a listener for our input pipe. The current JXTA implementation requires every listener to implement the `PipeMsgListener` interface. Our `JXTAPeer` class implements this interface (which is just one method, *pipeMsgEvent*, that will receive control upon the arrival of a new message) so it can act as a listener.

However if the application using our `JXTAPeer` wants to implement its own message receiving logic, it can call the `setMessageReceiver` method of the `JXTAPeer` class to specify the listener. If there is such a listener available, it will be used. If not, the `JXTAPeer` will itself act as the listener.

We will discuss later how to implement application-specific message listening logic (see the discussion on `Publisher` and `Requester` classes later in the chapter).

CreateOutputPipeAndSendMessage()

This method creates an output pipe, and sends a message over it. Our SOAP-over-P2P application needs this functionality for two purposes:

- When a requesting peer wants to send a SOAP service invocation message to the publishing peer

- When a publishing peer wants to send a SOAP response message back to the requesting peer

You'll now see how an output pipe is created and a message sent over it.

First look at the method signature:

```
public void createOutputPipeAndSendMessage(
    String ServiceName,//Name of output pipe service.
    String resBody//Message to be sent.)
{ //Method body ..................... }
```

This method takes two parameters, namely ServiceName and resBody. ServiceName is the name of the input pipe service over which we want to create an output pipe (the input pipe will be the recipient of our message). We will first search for the input pipe advertisement on the JXTA network whose name matches with ServiceName:

```
OutputPipe myOutPipe;//Output pipe to send the message out.
Message msg = null;//The message to be sent.
Enumeration enum = null;
while (true) {
    try {
        enum = disco.getLocalAdvertisements(DiscoveryService.ADV,
            "Name", "JXTASPEC:"+ServiceName);
        if ((enum != null) && enum.hasMoreElements()) break;
        disco.getRemoteAdvertisements(null,
            DiscoveryService.ADV, "Name",
            "JXTASPEC:"+ServiceName, 1, null);
        Thread.sleep(2000);
    } catch (Exception e){    }
}//while
```

The preceding code works on a combination of two methods of the DiscoveryService class: getLocalAdvertisements and getRemoteAdvertisements. The GetLocal-Advertisements method will look for matching advertisements in the local cache. If there are none found, getRemoteAdvertisements will look for matching advertisements remotely on the JXTA network. If found, they will be loaded in the local cache, so that next call to getLocalAdvertisements can find and store them in an enumeration.

Your next task is to read the advertisement from the enumeration:

```
ModuleSpecAdvertisement pipeAdvertisement =
    (ModuleSpecAdvertisement) enum.nextElement();
```

We have read only the first element from the enumeration in order to keep the logic and this explanation simple.

You now have the advertisement stored in an object named moduleAdvertisement. Recall from the discussion of advertising a pipe service (Step 2 of PublishService-OverJXTAPipe method) that we published our pipe service as part of a detailed ModuleSpecAdvertisement. So what you have stored in the moduleAdvertisement object is actually the complete ModuleSpecAdvertisement, from which you will now extract the pipe advertisement. For this purpose, you will use a

StructuredTextDocument (recall that we used the same class in copying a pipe advertisement into a module specification advertisement):

```
try {
    StructuredTextDocument paramDoc =
        (StructuredTextDocument)  mdsadv.getParam();
    String pID = null;
    String pType = null;
    Enumeration elements = paramDoc.getChildren("jxta:PipeAdvertisement");
    elements = ((TextElement) elements.nextElement()).getChildren();
    while (elements.hasMoreElements()) {
        TextElement elem = (TextElement) elements.nextElement();
        String nm = elem.getName();
        if(nm.equals("Id")) {
            pID = elem.getTextValue();
            continue;
        }//if
        if(nm.equals("Type")) {
            pType = elem.getTextValue();
            continue;
        }//if
    }//while
//code blocks A and B should be copied here
} catch (Exception ex) {             }
```

The preceding code reads the Id and Type children of the jxta:PipeAdvertisement element. You will now form a pipe advertisement from the Id and Type values:

```
//code block A
PipeAdvertisement pipeadv = (PipeAdvertisement)
    AdvertisementFactory.newAdvertisement(
    PipeAdvertisement.getAdvertisementType());
    try {
        URL pipeID = new URL(pID );
        pipeadv.setPipeID( (PipeID) IDFactory.fromURL( pipeID ) );
        pipeadv.setType(pType);
    } catch ( MalformedURLException badID ) {             }
```

You are now all set to create an output pipe based on the pipe advertisement that we just formed, then author a message and send it on the output pipe:

```
//code block B
myOutPipe = pipes.createOutputPipe(pipeadv, 11000);
msg = pipes.createMessage();
msg.setString("ServiceName", ServiceName);
msg.setString("SOAPResponse", resBody);
myOutPipe.send (msg);
```

This finishes our discussion of creating an output pipe and sending a message over it. The JXTAPeer class also has three other small methods.

SetInputPipeMessageListener

This method designates an object that will receive all messages destined for the input pipe that we created in the `PublishServiceOverJXTAPipe()` method:

```
public void setInputPipeMessageListener(PipeMsgListener msgListener){
    listener = msgListener;
}
```

PipeMsgEvent

This method is part of the `PipeMsgListener` interface that `JXTAPeer` implements in order to receive pipe messages. This method doesn't do anything, and is meant to be overridden in subclasses:

```
public void pipeMsgEvent ( PipeMsgEvent event ){
}
```

SetMessageReceiver

This method specifies a `JtextArea` object that will display all messages (including the SOAP response message) on the GUI:

```
public void setMessageReceiver(JTextArea msgReceiver){
    receiver = msgReceiver;
}//setMessageReceiver
```

We will now see how our `Publisher` and `Requester` classes will extend the `JXTAPeer` class. Most of the functionality required by the publishing and requesting processes is already covered in the `JXTAPeer` class. Therefore, these two classes only need to implement logic specific to publishing and requesting processes.

Publisher

This class is responsible for performing the following functions:

1. Publish a SOAP service over the JXTA network.
2. Listen for SOAP service invocation messages from requesting peers.
3. Invoke a local SOAP server upon receipt of a service invocation request.
4. Send the SOAP response from the SOAP server back to the requesting peer.

The first and last tasks are already implemented by the `publishServiceOverJXTAPipe` and `createOutputPipeAndSendMessage` methods of the `JXTAPeer` class. Application-level logic (for example, GUI classes) can directly call these methods to publish SOAP services and send responses.

We only need to take care of the middle two points in the `Publisher` class. The interface of the `Publisher` class is very simple. There are only two methods—a constructor and a

20

method named `pipeMsgEvent`. The constructor relies entirely on the methods of the `JXTAPeer` (super) class, while the `pipeMsgEvent` method implements the middle two points.

Publisher **Constructor**

The `Publisher` constructor simply calls the `JXTAPeer` constructor (`super`) and relies on it to check whether a JXTA instance already exists, and to start JXTA accordingly.

```
public Server() {
    super();
    setInputPipeMessageListener(this);
}//constructor
```

After calling the `super`'s constructor, the `Publisher` constructor also sets itself as the listener for receiving all input pipe messages. This is important, because we need to implement comprehensive logic for SOAP service invocation requests. All of this is handled in the `pipeMsgEvent` method.

PipeMsgEvent

This method performs the following tasks:

1. Receive control whenever a SOAP service invocation message is detected over the input pipe.
2. Read the name of the service that is being invoked and author a SOAP request.
3. Send the SOAP request to a local SOAP server.
4. Receive the SOAP response from the SOAP server.
5. Read the name of another input pipe embedded within the SOAP service invocation message. The requesting peer is listening for a SOAP response message on this pipe.
6. Call `createOutputPipeAndSendMessage` to create an output pipe and send the SOAP response back to the requesting peer.

Let's see how all this is accomplished.

As usual, first have a look at the method signature:

```
public void pipeMsgEvent ( PipeMsgEvent event ){
    //method body
}
```

This method takes only one parameter `event`, an object of type `PipeMsgEvent`. The `event` object holds the complete message received from the requesting peer, so your first step should be to extract the message from the `event` object. You will call the `getMessage` method of the `PipeMsgEvent` class that returns the complete message:

```
Message SOAPRequest = event.getMessage();
```

Next you will read the name of the service being invoked from the received message:

```
String SOAPServiceName =
➥      SOAPRequest.getString("ServiceName");
```

Now it's time to author a SOAP request. You will author a very simple hard-coded SOAP request, in which the only dynamic part is the name of the service.

SOAP request authoring requires the creation of an XML file that contains a SOAP enve-lope, a SOAP body, and service-related elements. The following code authors the com-plete XML payload of our simple SOAP request:

```
// SOAP authoring:
StringBuffer sh = new StringBuffer();
sh.append("<?xml version=\'1.0\' encoding=\'UTF-8\'?>\r\n");
sh.append("<SOAP-ENV:Envelope");
sh.append("\r\n");
sh.append("     xmlns:xsi=\"http://www.w3.org/1999/XMLSchema-instance\" ");
sh.append("\r\n");
sh.append("     xmlns:SOAP-ENV=\"http://schemas.xmlsoap.org/soap/envelope/\" ");
sh.append("\r\n");
sh.append("     xmlns:xsd=\"http://www.w3.org/1999/XMLSchema\">");
sh.append("\r\n");
sh.append(
"      SOAP-ENV:encodingStyle=\"http://schemas.xmlsoap.org/soap/encoding\">");
sh.append("\r\n");
sh.append("    <SOAP-ENV:Body>");
sh.append("\r\n");
sh.append("<NS:invoke xmlns:NS='"+SOAPServiceName+"'>");
sh.append("</NS:invoke>");
sh.append("    </SOAP-ENV:Body>\r\n");
sh.append("</SOAP-ENV:Envelope>\r\n");
```

The preceding code simply takes a `StringBuffer` and adds a hard-coded SOAP request to it. The only dynamic part is the name of the service that appears within the SOAP-Env:Body element.

You will now add HTTP headers to this SOAP request and send it to a local SOAP server. We have used a simple HTTP client implementation named `HttpConnection` for this purpose:

```
// HTTP related stuff.
HttpConnection connection;
String response = "";
try{
    connection =
➥          new HttpConnection("http://localhost/soap/servlet/rpcrouter",
➥          8080,
```

```
➥         "text/xml",
➥         "POST",
➥         sh.toString());
   connection.setRequestProperty (
   "SOAPAction:", "\"\"");
   response = connection.call();
} catch(Exception e) {
receiver.setText(receiver.getText()+"\n"+
"Error connecting to SOAP server");
}//catch
```

This is a very simple use of HTTP for SOAP transport between a SOAP client (our SOAP-over-P2P application) and a SOAP server.

The last step is to send the SOAP response back to the requesting peer. You will need to perform the following two steps for this purpose:

1. Get the name of the pipe on which the requesting peer is listening. This name is embedded inside the SOAP service invocation that the peer sent.

2. Call the `createOutputPipeAndSendMessage` and send the SOAP response on the output pipe.

This is accomplished by the following lines of code:

```
String ResponsePipeName = SOAPRequest.getString("SOAPResponse");
createOutputPipeAndSendMessage(ResponsePipeName,response);
```

Requester

The `Requester` class is responsible for performing the following tasks:

1. Search for a given SOAP service on the JXTA network.

2. Create an output pipe and send a service invocation request to the publishing peer.

3. Display the SOAP response message to the user through the GUI classes.

The `Requester` class depends entirely on its parent `JXTAPeer` class for all its functions. GUI classes will create a `Requester` object, and call its methods to perform the first two of the preceding tasks. The third task is handled by the `pipeMsgEvent` method in the following simple lines of code, which are self-explanatory:

```
public void pipeMsgEvent ( PipeMsgEvent event ){
    receiver.setText(receiver.getText()+"Response received:\n");
    Message SOAPMessage = event.getMessage();
    receiver.setText(
        receiver.getText()+SOAPMessage.getString("SOAPResponse")+":\n");
}
```

Graphical User Interface

The GUI class (JxtaGui) is a very simple class that contains the following:

- A set of radio buttons for choosing between publishing and requesting modes.
- Some text fields for data entry. Only two fields must be filled in: the name of the service and the name of the advertisement file. The name of the service is what you will publish as a publisher or search as a requester. As far as the name of the advertisement file is concerned, we have provided two sample advertisement files, `publisher.adv` and `requester.adv`, with the downloads for this chapter on the Web site.
- A button for publishing and requesting. Its caption changes according to the mode selected.
- A message window to display messages and progress.

The GUI can be seen in Figure 20.2.

FIGURE 20.2

The GUI for the SOAP-over-P2P application.

The JxtaGui class has a main method that calls the class constructor. The constructor will instantiate the GUI components, manage their layout, and display them. The JxtaGui constructor also contains handlers for data entry events, such as typing in the text fields and pressing buttons. The event handler for the Publisher/Requester button is the most important one.

When the user presses the Publisher or Requester button (whose caption changes according to the mode selected), the event handler for the button is called:

```
button.addActionListener(new java.awt.event.ActionListener() {
    public void actionPerformed(ActionEvent e) {
        if (button.getText().equals("Publish")){
            publisher.publishServiceOverJXTAPipe(
```

```
                ServiceName,
                ServiceVersion,
                ServiceDescription,
                ServiceCreator,
                ServiceSpecURL,
                ServiceAdvertisementFileName
            );
        } else if (button.getText().equals("Invoke")){
            requester.publishServiceOverJXTAPipe(
                "requester",
                ServiceVersion,
                ServiceDescription,
                ServiceCreator,
                ServiceSpecURL,
                ServiceAdvertisementFileName
            );
            requester.createOutputPipeAndSendMessage(
            ServiceName,"requester");
        }
    }
});
```

In the preceding code, you will first check whether the user wants to publish or request. If the user wants to publish, it calls the `publishServiceOverJXTAPipe` method of the `publisher` object and passes on the values read from the GUI.

If the user wants to send a SOAP service invocation request, the application needs to perform the following two tasks:

1. Publish an input pipe service named `requester`. Technically, this is the same type of input pipe that listens for SOAP service invocation requests, but the requester pipe will act as a return path for a response from the publishing peer.

2. Create an output pipe and send the SOAP service invocation message.

How to Use the SOAP-over-P2P Application

The following are the simple steps for using the SOAP-over-P2P application:.

1. The executable JAR file (`SOAP-over-P2P.jar`) is included in the downloads for this chapter. You can directly execute the JAR file.

2. You can test this application on a single isolated machine, on a LAN, or over the Internet. Upon start-up, JXTA checks for the presence of some configuration files in the current directory. If they're not found, it displays a configuration screen and asks for the following information:

    - Peer name—Any name with which you would like your peer identified for the current SOAP-over-P2P instance.

- Peer TCP and HTTP addresses—You will find this data entry field under the Advanced tab. JXTA will automatically try to detect the IP address of your machine. If you are on a LAN, this will be the address of your machine on the LAN. If you are connected to the Internet, this will be an actual IP address (perhaps the dynamic IP address that changes every time you connect to the Internet).

- Available rendezvous—These are the addresses of volunteer peers that agree to act as meeting points for other peers. If you know a rendezvous point and your friend knows another rendezvous point, and the two rendezvous points know each other (directly or through other rendezvous points), then you can meet your friend over the JXTA network. You can try this type of configuration with the SOAP-over-P2P application, as well.

- Secure user name and password—You will be asked to enter this information every time you start JXTA.

3. You will also have to host a SOAP service, which will be invoked by the requesting peer through a publishing peer. We have hard-coded the address of an Apache SOAP server running on a local machine (`http://localhost:8080/soap/servlet/rpcrouter`, see the earlier discussion on `pipeMsgEvent` method of `Publisher` class). You might have to change it according to your SOAP server.

As a sample setting, we tested this application on a single isolated machine. We started two instances of JXTA Shell (installed on separate locations within the same machine), with each shell acting as a rendezvous service for the other. Each of the two shells were listening at different ports. Next we started two instances of the SOAP-over-P2P application (again, installed on separate locations within the same machine). One SOAP-over-P2P instance had one of the shells in its list of available rendezvous services. Similarly, the other SOAP-over-P2P instance was using the rendezvous service provided by the second shell.

We used one SOAP-over-P2P instance to publish a SOAP service. We had the `publisher.adv` file in the same directory where the `SOAP-over-P2P.jar` was located. This is accomplished by executing the JAR file, selecting the Publish radio button, entering the name of a SOAP service in the Service Name field, and pressing the Publish button. We had a SOAP service with matching name hosted on our Apache SOAP server hosted at `http://localhost:8080/soap/servlet/rpcrouter`.

We used the other SOAP-over-P2P instance as a requester. We had the `requester.adv` file in the same directory where the `SOAP-over-P2P.jar` for the requester instance was located. We selected the Requester radio button, typed the name of the service that we want to invoke on the Publishing peer, and pressed the Request button. We had to wait for a while, in which the following things happened:

1. The requesting peer sends its request to the rendezvous point (one of the two JXTA shells) it knows.

2. The rendezvous point routes the request to the other rendezvous point (the other JXTA shell).

3. The other rendezvous point in turn sends the request to the publishing peer.

4. The publishing peer processes the request, extracts name of the SOAP service and sends a method invocation request to the SOAP server.

5. The SOAP server invokes the SOAP service, prepares the SOAP response and sends it back to the publishing peer.

6. The response takes its route back to the requesting peer.

After all these steps are finished, the SOAP response was displayed on the display text window of the requesting peer.

Proposed Improvements

You might want to incorporate some of the following features to build value-added applications using our simple SOAP-over-P2P idea.

UDDI Support

As discussed earlier, UDDI offers a publish-and-search API similar to JXTA's publish-and-search features. UDDI publishes over server-side data repositories, whereas JXTA publishes over a distributed collection of peers, in which each peer is supposed to manage its own data.

Client-side UDDI implementation can be added to our SOAP-over-P2P application. Users can search for P2P services over UDDI registries, for example, to find what names to search for on the JXTA network.

UDDI offers a comprehensive arrangement of data structures. The parent of all UDDI structures is a business organization that consists of a number of smaller structures called business service structures.

Each service structure in turn consists of a number of binding templates that determine how the service is bound to an implementation. Service-binding detail specifies how and where the service is hosted (for example, the name/address of a SOAP server hosting the service implementation).

We can anticipate that standards will eventually evolve for P2P binding using UDDI binding templates.

For further details on UDDI structures, refer to my article "Using UDDI as a Search Engine" at `WebServicesArchitect.com`.

"Constructing a UDDI Client, Calling the UDDI Registry," another of my articles located at `DevX.com`, provides design and sample implementations of a UDDI client in Java. The integration of such a client into our SOAP-over-P2P application is quite straightforward.

Counting Invocation Requests and Implementing CRM Solutions

We implemented a very simple SOAP request-authoring mechanism within the `pipeMsgEvent` method of the `Publisher` class. This mechanism can be extended to keep a record of the number of invocation requests. A simple database write operation associated with every invocation request can do the job.

Customer Relationship Management (CRM) solutions can also be implemented, based on the data about customers who are interested in a particular service.

Summary

In this chapter, we discussed the operation of Web services over P2P networks. We started with the three Web service domains—discovery, description, and invocation. We then mentioned the advantages of operating Web services over P2P networks. We also proposed a SOAP-over-P2P application architecture and presented a couple of use cases. We then used JXTA as a sample P2P network and provided a skeleton implementation that can advertise Web services over P2P networks, as well as look for and invoke SOAP services published by other peers. Finally, we proposed a few improvements in our sample implementation as food for thought for the readers.

The P2P Game

*by Rajam Ramamurti
and Michael Abbott*

This chapter presents a P2P game example program to illustrate the JXTA techniques of community formation, routing, and message passing.

The P2P Game

The P2P game is a peer-to-peer game that enables players to join and leave the game based on obtaining and passing a Get Out Of Jail token that is circulated among players. This game demonstrates the techniques necessary to form a community of peers, and how to pass messages among the peers of that community.

Community Formation

The P2P game provides the capability to form a community by creating new peers. The community here is the jail. Peers can join the jail, obtain the jail token from the peer who currently has it, and leave the jail by passing the token to a peer.

Routing and Message Passing

The P2P game provides the capability to route the jail token among peers and broadcast a message as to where the token is currently located.

Design

The P2P game is a standalone application designed to have two main components: a user interface (client/front end) and JXTA integration (back end), which utilizes the latest JXTA platform release. The user interface displays peer and group information for monitoring purposes. The updating of such information is handled by the JXTA integration.

The P2P game places players (peers) in a jail community (group). In order to leave this jail community, a player must pass the jail token to a peer, but if that player doesn't have the jail token, she must first obtain the jail token from the peer who has it and then pass it on to another peer. After leaving, the player cannot return to the jail. It is easy to restructure the game to enable players to return to the jail, but after leaving, who in their right mind would want to return?

The first player in the P2P game creates the jail community, enters the jail, and automatically generates the only key (that is, the jail token) that would let anyone leave the jail. Others might join the jail, but they do not yet have the key. The key is not required to enter the jail, but is required to leave.

The P2P game demonstrates how messages are passed from peer to peer using direct connections as well as broadcast methods.

Application Details

This section outlines the highlights of the P2P game. To run this application, you need to have JDK 1.2 or higher installed on your machine.

The code for this application is contained in a zip file. Extract the contents of this zip file to a directory on your local disk. For your convenience, subdirectories for clients, namely the peers participating in this game, are also available in this directory. Each of the client subdirectories has a runCreate.bat file and a runJoin.bat file. The runCreate.bat file launches the application, and the runJoin.bat file lets a participant join the game.

Creating the Jail With One Peer

First you must create the jail with one peer. To create the jail with peer1, run the runCreate.bat application in the client01 subdirectory. The application launches a window for entering the configuration information about this peer. Select the Basics tab, seen in Figure 21.1.

FIGURE 21.1

JXTA Configurator Basic settings panel.

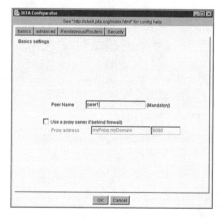

Enter a name for the peer in the Peer Name text field; for example, **peer1**. Click the OK button to proceed and provide other configuration details for this peer.

In the window that pops up, select the Advanced tab (see Figure 21.2).

FIGURE 21.2

JXTA Configurator Advanced settings panel.

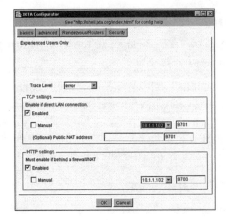

Under the Advanced tab, note the TCP port number, which must be unique for this peer.

Select the Security tab. Under the Security tab, provide a unique username and password for this peer, as shown in Figure 21.3.

FIGURE 21.3

JXTA Configurator Security settings panel.

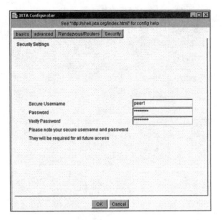

Select the Rendezvous/Routers tab. Make sure that the Use a Gateway box is unchecked, as shown in Figure 21.4.

FIGURE 21.4

*JXTA
Configurator
Rendezvous/
Routers settings
panel.*

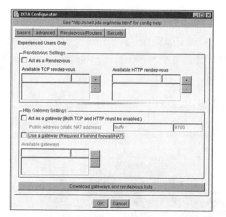

Click the OK button. The program launches a client window for this first peer (peer1), as shown in Figure 21.5.

FIGURE 21.5

Client window for
peer1.

You can perform queries at this point using the Help options, as shown in Figure 21.6. peer1 uses the F option to find out where the jail token is, and discovers that she has the token.

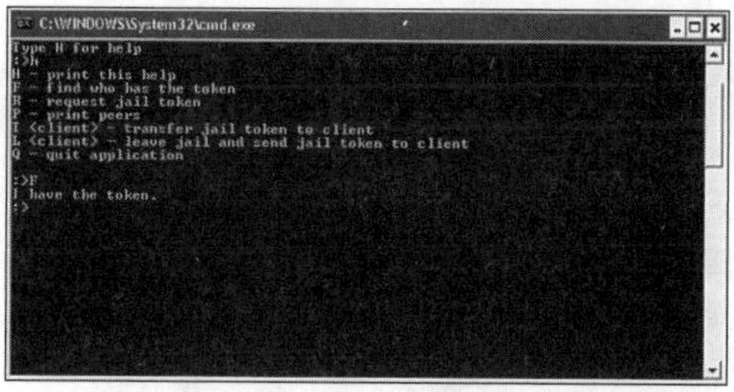

FIGURE 21.6

*Using the Help
options.*

Creating peer2 and Playing the Game

To create the second peer, (peer2), run the runJoin.bat application in the client02 subdirectory. The application launches a window and prompts for information about this peer. Create this peer similarly to peer1, ensuring that this peer has a unique port number, username, and password.

By creating the second peer, the application creates the jail community, and peer2 joins the community, as shown in Figure 21.7.

FIGURE 21.7

peer2 is created and joins the jail community.

peer2 can use the Help options to check for the presence of other peers, check on who has the jail token, and request the token. peer2 uses the R option to request the jail token, and receives it (see Figure 21.8).

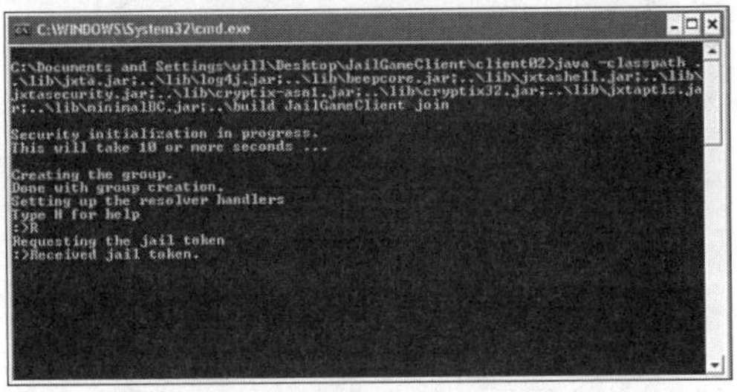

FIGURE 21.8

peer2 requests and receives the token.

The window for peer1 displays the message about sending the token to another peer (peer2 in this case) in Figure 21.9.

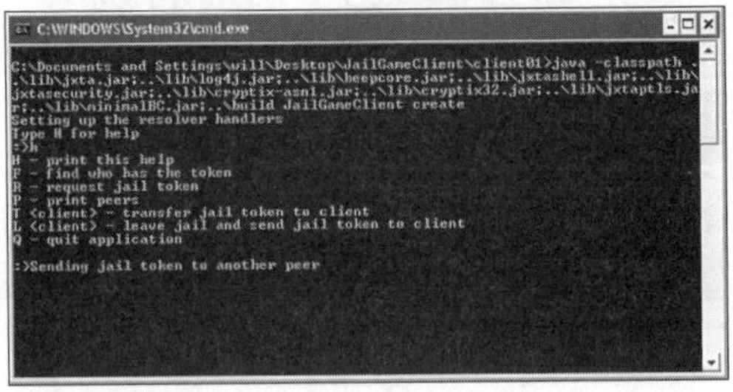

FIGURE 21.9

peer1 sends the token to peer2.

Now peer2 wants to pass the token to another peer. Therefore, peer2 uses the P option to search for peers, and discovers that there is only one other peer, namely peer1 (see Figure 21.10).

FIGURE 21.10

peer2 *searches for peers and discovers only one other peer.*

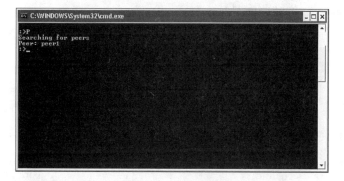

peer2 can transfer the token to peer1 by using the T `<client>` option, as seen in Figure 21.11.

FIGURE 21.11

peer2 *passes the token to* peer1.

Now the jail token is back with peer1. At this point, you can create peer3 to join the jail community.

peer3 Joins the Jail Community

To create the third peer, run the runJoin.bat application in the client03 subdirectory. The application launches a window and prompts for information about this peer. Create this peer similarly to peer1 and peer2, ensuring that this peer has a unique port number, username, and password. Now all the peers are ready to play the game.

peer3 Receives the Key from peer1

peer1 wants to transfer the jail token to peer3, and using the T `<client>` Help option, transfers the token to peer3. (A similar transfer appears in Figure 21.11.)

peer3 receives the jail token from peer1 in Figure 21.12.

FIGURE 21.12

peer3 *receives the token from* peer1.

peer3 Leaves the Jail Community

peer3 wants to leave the jail. In this game, peers have to pass the token to another peer in order to leave. Therefore, peer3 transfers the jail key to peer2 using the L <client> Help option and leaves the jail (see Figure 21.13).

FIGURE 21.13

peer3 *passes the token to* peer2 *and leaves the jail.*

The client window for peer2 broadcasts a message that peer2 received the jail token from peer3 in Figure 21.14.

FIGURE 21.14

peer2 *receives the token from* peer3.

Now the jail token is with peer2.

Transferring the Jail Token

In this game, the player who has the jail token cannot leave the jail without passing the token to a peer. In Figure 21.15, `peer2`, who has the jail token, attempts to leave the jail using the `L <client>` Help option without specifying a peer to receive the token.

FIGURE 21.15

peer2 tries in vain to leave the jail.

Scenarios

A perfect example of the P2P game is in creating a sales proposal document that many peers need to review before having it sent out. There is no specific hierarchy/ordering required, and everyone needs to sign off on the proposal.

Document Passing

Often it is necessary to circulate a document that needs to be edited by several people without using a central repository system. However, if only one person can edit the document, it is necessary to obtain the latest version of the document from the person who has that copy.

To facilitate such an operation, everyone interested in the document must communicate with one another to determine who has the latest version of the document, and there must also be a mechanism to request the document.

Approvals

In a purchase order scenario, several approvals from different supervisors/departments must be acquired before the purchase order is accepted. After a supervisor (peer) gives an approval, the purchase order can be sent to the next supervisor.

In enterprises, typically a purchase order must traverse a certain approval pathway to be converted into a real order. The pathway is often dictated by organizational roles and potential purchasing power. In the jail game, if we imagine that the jail token is a purchase order, we can also imagine multiple peer groups that represent multiple approval levels at a corporation. Each peer is then responsible for perhaps altering a component on the JXTA advertisement ("approve" flag), then publishing to a higher-ranking group for acceptance of the token (purchase order). We might need to extend the logic in each peer for the groups to send the token to a finance group if a "disapprove" flag is set at any level. After the token has traversed to a group that matches the highest approval level on the token (purchase order), the token is returned to the finance department for processing.

In the current jail game example, there is no hierarchy. However, the hierarchy can be implemented by building new peer groups.

Class Design

The `JailGameClient` class is responsible for setting up the jail community, as well as publishing its JXTA group advertisement remotely. If a client wants to join, the client has to search for the jail advertisement and join the group.

The client has the capability to do a broadcast message using the JXTA resolver service to acquire the jail token. The token can also be sent directly to another user.

Code Details

The `JailGameClient` class implements the `Runnable` Interface, and sets up the jail community and publishes its JXTA group advertisement remotely, as well. The `JailGameClient` class employs the following methods:

- `joinPeerGroup(PeerGroup grp)` to let a peer join a group.
- `joinPeerGroup(PeerGroupAdvertisement adv)` for advertising peer groups.
- `createGroup(Stringname)` to create peer groups based on advertisements.
- `createJailUnicastPipeAdv()` to create a pipe advertisement.
- `publishJailAdv(Advertisement adv, int type)` to publish a pipe advertisement for transferring the jail token.

- publishJailAdv(Advertisement adv, int type) to publish advertisements locally or remotely.

- printPeers() to display a list of peers in the jail group.

- refreshPeerSet() to process peer advertisement.

- discoverJailGroup() to synchronize jail group advertisements from peers.

- createPipes() sets up the broadcast and unicast pipes and corresponding listeners.

- setResolverHandler() to handle a listener for the jail token requestor, and another for the jail token locator.

- requestJailToken() to broadcast requests for the jail token by using the resolver service, but not for retrieving the jail token.

- findJailToken() to broadcast to determine the location of the jail token.

- leaveJail(String peerName) to let a peer who has the jail token leave the jail after passing the token to another peer.

- quit() to let a peer who has already handed over the token to another peer and left the jail to quit the program/application.

- transferJailKey(String name) to create an input pipe to the peer with a peer ID and send the jail token to that peer.

- cleanResources() to flush all the resource data, so as to be able to restart from scratch.

- printAdvertisement(Advertisement adv), a utility method, to display the contents of an advertisements on the screen.

- startJxta() to start JXTA techniques.

- run() to discover peers.

- printHelp() to display the help information about running this application onscreen.

Listing 21.1 presents the code for JailGameClient.java.

LISTING 21.1 JailGameClient.java.

```java
import java.util.*;
import java.io.*;

import net.jxta.id.IDFactory;
import net.jxta.pipe.InputPipe;
import net.jxta.pipe.PipeMsgEvent;
import net.jxta.pipe.PipeMsgListener;
import net.jxta.credential.AuthenticationCredential;
import net.jxta.document.StructuredDocument;
```

LISTING 21.1 continued

```java
import net.jxta.document.Document;
import net.jxta.document.StructuredTextDocument;
import net.jxta.document.MimeMediaType;
import net.jxta.membership.Authenticator;
import net.jxta.membership.MembershipService;
import net.jxta.peergroup.PeerGroup;
import net.jxta.peergroup.PeerGroupFactory;
import net.jxta.exception.PeerGroupException;
import net.jxta.exception.ProtocolNotSupportedException;
import net.jxta.document.AdvertisementFactory;
import net.jxta.document.MimeMediaType;
import net.jxta.discovery.DiscoveryService;
import net.jxta.discovery.DiscoveryListener;
import net.jxta.discovery.DiscoveryEvent;
import net.jxta.pipe.PipeService;
import net.jxta.pipe.OutputPipe;
import net.jxta.pipe.OutputPipeListener;
import net.jxta.pipe.OutputPipeEvent;
import net.jxta.protocol.DiscoveryResponseMsg;
import net.jxta.protocol.PipeAdvertisement;
import net.jxta.protocol.PeerGroupAdvertisement;
import net.jxta.protocol.ModuleImplAdvertisement;
import net.jxta.protocol.PeerAdvertisement;
import net.jxta.protocol.ResolverQueryMsg;
import net.jxta.protocol.ResolverResponseMsg;
import net.jxta.resolver.ResolverService;
import net.jxta.resolver.QueryHandler;
import net.jxta.endpoint.Message;
import net.jxta.endpoint.MessageElement;
import net.jxta.document.Advertisement;
import net.jxta.id.ID;

import net.jxta.impl.protocol.ResolverResponse;
import net.jxta.impl.protocol.ResolverQuery;

/**
 * This game places players (peers) in a jail (group).  In order to escape
 * jail, the player must request for the jail token.  Once obtained,
 * the player may leave, but before leaving, the player must leave the
 * token behind with another player.
 *
 * After the player leaves, he can not return.  It would be easy to
 * restructure this game to enable players to return to the jail, but once
 * you leave jail, who in their right mind would want to go back?
 *
 * Whoever creates the jail automatically creates the only key and places
 * himself in jail.  All others may join the jail, but they do not have
 * the key.  The key is not required to enter jail in this game.
 *
```

LISTING 21.1   continued

```
 * The game demonstrates how messages are passed from peer to peer using
 * direct connections as well as broadcast methods using the ResolverService.
 */

public class JailGameClient implements Runnable
{
    public static final String JAIL_GROUP = "JAIL";
    public static final String JAIL_GROUP_DESCRIPTION = "Jail description";
    public static final String JAIL_KEY_QUERY_HANDLER =
➥"jail_key_query_handler";
    public static final String JAIL_KEY_LOCATOR_HANDLER =
➥"jail_key_locator_handler";
    public static final String JAIL_TRANSFER_KEY = "jail_transfer_key";

    public static final int JOIN_GAME = 0;
    public static final int CREATE_GAME = 1;

    private PeerGroup netPeerGroup;
    private PeerGroup jailPeerGroup;
    private DiscoveryService discoverySvc;
    private boolean pipeAdvFound = false;

    private int createOrJoin = -1;
    private boolean groupFound = false;

    private PipeAdvertisement jailUnicastPipeAdv;
    private PipeMsgListener unicastListener;
    private InputPipe inputUnicastPipe;

    private boolean inJail = false;
    private boolean hasJailToken = false;
    private String jailTokenString;
    private Set jailPeerSet = new HashSet();

    public JailGameClient(int createOrJoin)
    {
        this.createOrJoin = createOrJoin;
    }

/**
 * Let a peer join a group.
 */
    private boolean joinPeerGroup(PeerGroup grp)
    {
        StructuredDocument creds = null;

        try {

            AuthenticationCredential authCred =
```

LISTING **21.1**   continued

```
                    new AuthenticationCredential(grp, null, creds);
            MembershipService membershipSvc = grp.getMembershipService();
            Authenticator auth = membershipSvc.apply(authCred);

            if (auth.isReadyForJoin()) {
                membershipSvc.join(auth);
                this.inJail = true;
                return true;
            } else {
                String errMsg = "Unable to join group:" +
➥grp.getPeerGroupName();
                System.out.println(errMsg);
                return false;
            }
        } catch (Exception e) {
            String errMsg = "Unable to join group: " +
➥grp.getPeerGroupName();
            System.out.println(errMsg);
            e.printStackTrace();
            return false;
        }
    }

/**
 * Advertise peer groups.
 */
    private boolean joinPeerGroup(PeerGroupAdvertisement adv)
    {
        try {
            return joinPeerGroup(netPeerGroup.newGroup(adv));
        } catch (Exception e) {
            String errMsg = "Unable to create group from advertisement.";
            System.out.println(errMsg);
            e.printStackTrace();
            return false;
        }
    }

/**
 * Create peer groups based on advertisements.
 */
    private PeerGroup createGroup(String name)
        throws PeerGroupException, Exception
    {
        ModuleImplAdvertisement implAdv =
            netPeerGroup.getAllPurposePeerGroupImplAdvertisement();
        PeerGroup jailGroup =
            netPeerGroup.newGroup(null, implAdv, JAIL_GROUP,
➥JAIL_GROUP_DESCRIPTION);
```

LISTING 21.1   continued

```java
        return jailGroup;
    }

    /**
     * Publishes a pipe advertisement for the transfer of the jail token.
     */
    private void createJailUnicastPipeAdv()
        throws IOException
    {
        PipeAdvertisement pipeAdv = null;

        pipeAdv = (PipeAdvertisement) AdvertisementFactory.
➥newAdvertisement(PipeAdvertisement.getAdvertisementType());
        pipeAdv.setPipeID(IDFactory.newPipeID
➥ (jailPeerGroup.getPeerGroupID()));
        pipeAdv.setName(JailGameClient.JAIL_TRANSFER_KEY + ":" +
➥jailPeerGroup.getPeerName());
        pipeAdv.setType(PipeService.UnicastType);

        this.jailUnicastPipeAdv = pipeAdv;
    }

/**
 * Publish advertisements locally or remotely.
 */
    private void publishJailAdv(Advertisement adv, int type)
        throws IOException
    {
        DiscoveryService jailDiscoverySvc =
➥jailPeerGroup.getDiscoveryService();
        jailDiscoverySvc.publish(adv, type);
        jailDiscoverySvc.remotePublish(adv, type);
    }

    /**
     * Publishes an advertisement locally and remotely with no lifetime.
     */
    private void publish(Advertisement adv, int type)
        throws IOException
    {
        discoverySvc.publish(adv, type);
        discoverySvc.remotePublish(adv, type);
    }

    /**
     * Prints the members of the jail group.
     */
    private void printPeers()
    {
```

LISTING **21.1**   continued

```
        refreshPeerSet();
        try {
            Thread.sleep(10 * 1000); // may want to sleep longer.
        } catch (Exception ignore) { }

        Object [] peers = jailPeerSet.toArray();
        for (int x = 0 ; x < peers.length ; x++) {
            System.out.println("Peer: " +
➡ ((PeerAdvertisement)peers[x]).getName());
        }
    }

    /**
     * This call is asynchronous and uses a DiscoveryListener to process
     * the peer advertisements.
     */
    private void refreshPeerSet()
    {
        jailPeerSet.clear();
        System.out.println("Searching for peers");
        DiscoveryService jailDiscoverySvc =
➡jailPeerGroup.getDiscoveryService();
        try {
            jailDiscoverySvc.flushAdvertisements(null,
➡DiscoveryService.PEER);
            discoverySvc.flushAdvertisements(null, DiscoveryService.PEER);
        } catch (IOException io) {
            System.out.println("Trouble flushing PEER advertisements");
            io.printStackTrace();
        }

        DiscoveryListener listener = new DiscoveryListener() {
                public void discoveryEvent(DiscoveryEvent ev)
                {
                    DiscoveryResponseMsg res = ev.getResponse();
                    String aRes = res.getPeerAdv();
                    PeerAdvertisement peerAdv = null;

                    try {
                        // create a peer advertisement
                        InputStream is = new ByteArrayInputStream
➡ ( (aRes).getBytes() );
                        peerAdv = (PeerAdvertisement)
                            AdvertisementFactory.
                            newAdvertisement(new MimeMediaType
➡ ( "text/xml" ), is);
                        jailPeerSet.add(peerAdv);
                    } catch (Exception e) {
                        e.printStackTrace();
```

LISTING 21.1   continued

```
                    }
                }
            };
        jailDiscoverySvc.getRemoteAdvertisements(null,
➥DiscoveryService.PEER,
➥null, null, 10, listener);
    }

    /**
     * The discovery listener used needs to be synchronized.  It takes
     * a long time to run sometimes.  Furthermore, more than one peer
     * can return the same jail group advertisement.
     */
    private void discoverJailGroup()
        throws IOException
    {
        if (groupFound) {
            String msg = "Already found the jail group";
            System.out.println(msg);
            return;
        }

        while (!groupFound) {
            discoverySvc.getRemoteAdvertisements(null,
➥DiscoveryService.GROUP,
➥"Name",
➥JailGameClient.JAIL_GROUP,
➥1, null);

            try {
                //Wait ten seconds for advertisements to come in.
                Thread.sleep (10 * 1000);
            } catch (Exception ignore) { }

            Enumeration enum = discoverySvc.
                getLocalAdvertisements(DiscoveryService.GROUP, "Name",
➥JailGameClient.JAIL_GROUP);

            //Cycle through all the advertisements cached locally.
            while (enum.hasMoreElements()) {
                //We want to discover the jail group.
                Advertisement ad = (Advertisement) enum.nextElement();
                if (ad instanceof PeerGroupAdvertisement) {

                    try {
                        System.out.println("Creating the group.");
                        jailPeerGroup = netPeerGroup.newGroup(ad);
                        System.out.println("Done with group creation.");
                        groupFound = true;
                        return;
```

LISTING 21.1   continued

```
                          } catch (PeerGroupException e) {
                              e.printStackTrace();
                          }
                      }
                  }
                  System.out.print(".");

          }
      }

      /**
       * Sets up the broadcast and unicast pipe and its listeners.
       */
      private void createPipes()
          throws IOException
      {
          PipeService pipeSvc = jailPeerGroup.getPipeService();

          if (unicastListener == null) {
              //Create a message listener to accept the jail token.
              unicastListener = new PipeMsgListener() {
                      public void pipeMsgEvent(PipeMsgEvent pipeMsgEvent)
                      {
                          //We received a message.
                          Message message = pipeMsgEvent.getMessage();
                          if (message.hasElement("key") &&
➥message.hasElement("sender")) {
                              //Determine the sender and the key.
                              MessageElement element =
➥message.getElement("key");
                              InputStream stream = element.getStream();
                              MessageElement senderElement =
➥message.getElement("sender");
                              InputStream senderStream =
➥senderElement.getStream();

                              try {
                                  byte [] bytes =
➥new byte[stream.available()];
                                  stream.read(bytes);
                                  jailTokenString = new String(bytes);
                                  hasJailToken = true;

                                  bytes = new byte[senderStream.available()];
                                  senderStream.read(bytes);
                                  String sender = new String(bytes);

                                  String msg = "Received key " +
➥jailTokenString +
```

LISTING 21.1 continued

```
                                        " from peer " + sender;
                               System.out.println(msg);

                     } catch (IOException io) {
                         io.printStackTrace();
                     } finally {
                         try {
                             stream.close();
                             senderStream.close();
                         } catch (Exception ignore) { }
                     }
                } else {
                     //Ignore this message.
                }

            }
        };
    }
    //Create the actual pipe based on the advertisement
    //and the listener.
    this.inputUnicastPipe =
➡pipeSvc.createInputPipe(jailUnicastPipeAdv, unicastListener);
    }

    /**
     * Sets up two QueryHandler listeners.
     * One for the jail token requestor.
     * Another for the jail token locator.
     */
    private void setResolverHandler()
    {
        System.out.println("Setting up the resolver handlers");
        ResolverService jailResolverService =
➡jailPeerGroup.getResolverService();
        //Create a handler to process all incoming queries,
        //and process reponses to any queries we send.
        QueryHandler handler = new QueryHandler() {
                /**
                 * Processes any incoming queries. If this client has
                 * the key, we will send it to the requestor.
                 * Otherwise, we will send a "Sorry" response.
                 */
                public ResolverResponseMsg processQuery
➡ (ResolverQueryMsg query)
                {
                    //System.out.println("Key Requestor Query Handler: " +
                    //query.getQuery());
                    if (JailGameClient.this.hasJailToken) {
                        String msg = "Sending jail token to another peer";
```

LISTING 21.1   continued

```
                        System.out.println(msg);
                }
                String response = null;
                //If we have the key, we'll send it.
                //Otherwise, we'll send a "Sorry" response.
                response = (JailGameClient.this.hasJailToken) ?
JailGameClient.this.jailTokenString : "Sorry";
                JailGameClient.this.hasJailToken = false;
                JailGameClient.this.jailTokenString = null;
                //Sending our response.
                return new ResolverResponse
 (JailGameClient.JAIL_KEY_QUERY_HANDLER, "JXTACRED",
query.getQueryId(), response);
            }
            /**
            /* Process responses to our search queries for the
            * jail token. If we receive any non-"Sorry" responses,
            * we receive the token.
            */
            public void processResponse(ResolverResponseMsg responseMsg)
            {
                String response = responseMsg.getResponse();
                //System.out.println
 ("Key Requestor Query Handler: " + response);
                if (!response.equals("Sorry")) {
                    System.out.println("Received jail token.");
                    hasJailToken = true;
                    jailTokenString = response;
                }
            }
        };
        //Register the handler.
        jailResolverService.registerHandler
 (JailGameClient.JAIL_KEY_QUERY_HANDLER, handler);

        //Create a handler to locate the key.
        QueryHandler keyLocatorHandler = new QueryHandler() {
            /**
            * Process queries requesting to see if we have the token.
            * If this peer has the token, respond with the
            * name of this peer.
            */
            public ResolverResponseMsg processQuery
 (ResolverQueryMsg query)
            {
                //System.out.println("Key Locator Query Handler: " +
query.getQuery());
                String response = null;
```

LISTING 21.1 continued

```
                    response = (JailGameClient.this.hasJailToken) ?
➥JailGameClient.this.jailPeerGroup.
➥getPeerName() : "";
                    return new ResolverResponse(JailGameClient.
➥JAIL_KEY_LOCATOR_HANDLER, "JXTACRED",
➥query.getQueryId(), response);
                }
                /**
                 * Process responses to our search queries for the
                 * token. If the response is not a blank string, the
                 * response is  the name of the peer that has the token.
                 */
                public void processResponse(ResolverResponseMsg responseMsg)
                {
                    String response = responseMsg.getResponse();
                    //System.out.println
➥ ("Key Locator Query Handler: " + response);
                    if (!response.equals("")) {
                        System.out.println("Peer: " + response +
➥" has the token");
                    }
                }
            };
        //Register the handler.
        jailResolverService.registerHandler
➥ (JailGameClient.JAIL_KEY_LOCATOR_HANDLER, keyLocatorHandler);

    }

    /**
     * This method uses the resolver service to broadcast a request for
     * the jail token.  It does not do the job of retrieving the token.
     */
    private void requestJailToken()
    {
        if (this.hasJailToken) {
            System.out.println("I already have the token.");
            return;
        }
        System.out.println("Requesting the jail token");
        ResolverService jailResolverService =
➥jailPeerGroup.getResolverService();
        ResolverQueryMsg query = null;
        query = new ResolverQuery(JailGameClient.JAIL_KEY_QUERY_HANDLER,
➥"cred", jailPeerGroup.getPeerID().
➥toString(), "Key request", 1);
        jailResolverService.sendQuery(null, query);
    }
```

LISTING 21.1   continued

```
/**
 * Does a broadcast using the resolver service to determine
 * the location of the jail token.
 */
private void findJailToken()
{
    if (this.hasJailToken) {
        System.out.println("I have the token.");
        return;
    }
    ResolverService jailResolverService =
jailPeerGroup.getResolverService();
    ResolverQueryMsg query = null;
    query = new ResolverQuery(JailGameClient.JAIL_KEY_LOCATOR_HANDLER,
"cred", jailPeerGroup.getPeerID().
toString(), "Key location request", 1);
    jailResolverService.sendQuery(null, query);
}

/**
 * Leaves jail if the peer has the key.  Passes the jail token
 * to peerName.
 * @param peerName The peer name to pass the jail token to.
 */
private void leaveJail(String peerName)
{
    if (!this.inJail) {
        System.out.println("You are not in jail");
        return;
    }

    if (!hasJailToken) {
        System.out.println("You do not have the token");
        return;
    }
    if (!transferJailKey(peerName)) {
        return;
    }
    System.out.println("Leaving Jail");
    MembershipService membershipSvc = this.jailPeerGroup.
getMembershipService();
    //Leave the group and flush all local advertisements.
    try {
        membershipSvc.resign();
        this.jailPeerGroup.stopApp();
        try {
            this.discoverySvc.flushAdvertisements(null,
DiscoveryService.GROUP);
            this.discoverySvc.flushAdvertisements(null,
DiscoveryService.PEER);
```

LISTING 21.1   continued

```
                this.discoverySvc.flushAdvertisements(null,
➥DiscoveryService.ADV);
        } catch (IOException ignore) { ignore.printStackTrace();}

        this.inJail = false;
    } catch (PeerGroupException pge) {
        pge.printStackTraco();
    }
    this.cleanResources();
}

/**
 * Quits the application only if the user has left jail.
 */
private void quit()
{
    if (this.hasJailToken) {
        System.out.println("You have the jail token.   " +
➥"Existing players cannot leave the jail
➥without first having the token and then transferring it.");
    }
    System.out.println("Quitting.");
    System.exit(0);
}

/**
 * Creates an output pipe to the peer indicated by peerID and sends
 * the jail token
 *
 * @return true If the transfer is successful, false otherwise.
 */
private boolean transferJailKey(String peerName)
{
    if (!this.hasJailToken) {
        System.out.println("You do not have the jail token.");
        return false;
    }
    refreshPeerSet();
    try {
        Thread.sleep(5 * 1000);
    } catch (Exception ignore) {}
    // Check to make sure the peer exists.
    Iterator iterator = jailPeerSet.iterator();
    boolean peerExists = false;
    //Find the peer's PeerAdvertisement.
    while (iterator.hasNext()) {
        PeerAdvertisement adv = (PeerAdvertisement) iterator.next();
        if (adv.getName().equals(peerName)) {
            peerExists = true;
```

LISTING 21.1 continued

```
                    break;
                }
        }
        String msg = (!peerExists) ?
➥"Warning:  Peer " + peerName + " may not exist.\n" +
➥"Attempting to transfer anyways." :
➥"Transfering key to peer: " + peerName;
        System.out.println(msg);

        DiscoveryService jailDiscoverySvc =
➥jailPeerGroup.getDiscoveryService();
        DiscoveryListener listener = new DiscoveryListener() {
                /**
                 * Creates the output pipe that connects to the peer we
                 * wish to send the jail token to.  Then sends the jail
                 * token via the "key" element.
                 */
                public void discoveryEvent(DiscoveryEvent ev)
                {

                    DiscoveryResponseMsg res = ev.getResponse();
                    Enumeration enum = res.getResponses();
                    while (enum.hasMoreElements()) {
                        String advString = (String) enum.nextElement();
                        OutputPipe outputPipe = null;
                        try {
                            PipeAdvertisement pipeAdv = (PipeAdvertisement)
➥AdvertisementFactory.newAdvertisement
➥ (new MimeMediaType("text/xml"), new ByteArrayInputStream
➥ (advString.getBytes()));
                            PipeService pipeSvc =
➥jailPeerGroup.getPipeService();
                            outputPipe = pipeSvc.createOutputPipe
➥ (pipeAdv, 1000);

                            //Create the actual message with information
                            //about the token and sender.
                            Message message = pipeSvc.createMessage();
                            MessageElement messageElement =
➥message.newMessageElement("key", new MimeMediaType
➥ ("text/plain"), new ByteArrayInputStream
➥ (jailTokenString.getBytes()));
                            message.addElement(messageElement);
                            MessageElement senderElement =
➥message.newMessageElement("sender", new MimeMediaType
➥ ("text/plain"), new ByteArrayInputStream
➥ (jailPeerGroup.getPeerName().getBytes()));
                            message.addElement(senderElement);
                            outputPipe.send(message);
                            JailGameClient.this.hasJailToken = false;
```

LISTING 21.1   continued

```
                        outputPipe.close();
                        return;
                } catch (Exception e) {
                        e.printStackTrace();
                } finally {
                        if (outputPipe != null) {
                                outputPipe.close();
                        }
                }

            }
        }
    };
    String name = JailGameClient.JAIL_TRANSFER_KEY + ":" + peerName;
    jailDiscoverySvc.getRemoteAdvertisements(null,
➥DiscoveryService.ADV,"name", name, 10, listener);
    // Now sleep for the transfer to finish
    try {
        Thread.sleep(10 * 1000); // we may want to sleep longer
    } catch (Exception ignore) { }

    return !this.hasJailToken;

}

/**
 * This method is used to clean up all the resources so we can start
➥from scratch.
 */
private void cleanResources()
{
    this.inputUnicastPipe.close();
    this.unicastListener = null;

    this.jailPeerSet.clear();
    this.groupFound = false;
    this.inJail = false;
    this.pipeAdvFound = false;
    this.hasJailToken = false;
    this.jailTokenString = null;
    ResolverService resolverSvc = this.jailPeerGroup.
➥getResolverService();
    resolverSvc.unregisterHandler
➥ (JailGameClient.JAIL_KEY_QUERY_HANDLER);
    resolverSvc.unregisterHandler
➥ (JailGameClient.JAIL_KEY_LOCATOR_HANDLER);
    this.jailPeerGroup = null;
}
```

LISTING 21.1 continued

```
    /**
     * A utility method to print out the contents of an advertisement.
     */
    public static void printAdvertisement(Advertisement adv)
    {
        try {
            Document doc = adv.getDocument
➥ (new MimeMediaType("text/plain"));
            ByteArrayOutputStream output = new ByteArrayOutputStream();
            doc.sendToStream(output);
            System.out.println(output.toString());


//              BufferedInputStream stream =
➥new BufferedInputStream(doc.getStream());
//              StringBuffer buffer = new StringBuffer();
//              byte [] bytes = new byte[stream.available()];
//              while ((c = stream.readChar())!= null) {
//                  buffer.append(c);
//              }
//              System.out.println(buffer.toString());
        } catch (Exception ignore) {
            ignore.printStackTrace();
        }
    }

    /**
     * Start up the Net Peer group & get the Discovery Service
➥for that group.
     */
    public void startJxta()
        throws PeerGroupException, IOException
    {
        this.netPeerGroup = PeerGroupFactory.newNetPeerGroup();
        this.discoverySvc = netPeerGroup.getDiscoveryService();
        // Flush all local cache information.
➥We want to start from scratch.
        discoverySvc.flushAdvertisements(null, DiscoveryService.ADV);
        discoverySvc.flushAdvertisements(null, DiscoveryService.PEER);
        discoverySvc.flushAdvertisements(null, DiscoveryService.GROUP);
    }

    public void run()
    {
        try {
            if (createOrJoin == JailGameClient.JOIN_GAME) {

                discoverJailGroup();
```

LISTING 21.1   continued

```
            } else { // Create the group.
➡// Add a propagate PIPE Advertisement to it.

                jailPeerGroup = createGroup(JailGameClient.JAIL_GROUP);
                this.hasJailToken = true;
                // The token is just the current time :)
                this.jailTokenString = "" + System.currentTimeMillis();

                publish(jailPeerGroup.getPeerGroupAdvertisement(),
                        DiscoveryService.GROUP);
            }
            // Publish the unicast pipe used to send the jail token
➡// to others.
            createJailUnicastPipeAdv();
            publishJailAdv(jailUnicastPipeAdv, DiscoveryService.ADV);

        } catch (Exception e) {
            String errMsg = "Unable to start create or join jail group.";
            System.out.println(errMsg);
            e.printStackTrace();

            return;
        }
        if (!joinPeerGroup(jailPeerGroup)) {
            return;
        }

        try {
            this.createPipes();
        } catch (Exception ex) {
            String errMsg = "Unable to create broadcast pipes";
            System.out.println(errMsg);
            ex.printStackTrace();
            return;
        }
        setResolverHandler();
        //The user interface menu.
        for (;;) {
            BufferedReader reader =
                new BufferedReader(new InputStreamReader(System.in));
            String lineToSend = null;
            System.out.print("Type H for help\n:>");
            try {
                while ((lineToSend = reader.readLine()) != null) {
                    lineToSend = lineToSend.trim();
```

LISTING 21.1   continued

```
                    if (lineToSend.equals("")) {
                        System.out.print(":>");
                        continue;
                    }
                    //If the peer is not in the group anymore,
                    //say that to the peer.
                    if (!inJail && !lineToSend.equalsIgnoreCase("Q")) {
                        System.out.println("You are not in jail.
➥You can only quit");
                        System.out.print(":>");
                        continue;
                    }
                    StringTokenizer tokenizer =
                        new StringTokenizer(lineToSend);
                    String command = tokenizer.nextToken();

                    if (command.equalsIgnoreCase("L")) {
                        if (!tokenizer.hasMoreTokens()) {
                            System.out.println("Peer name missing");
                        } else {
                            String peerName = tokenizer.nextToken();
                            leaveJail(peerName);
                        }
                    } else if (command.equalsIgnoreCase("R")) {
                        requestJailToken();
                    } else if (command.equalsIgnoreCase("P")) {
                        printPeers();
                    } else if (command.equalsIgnoreCase("F")) {
                        findJailToken();
                    } else if (command.equalsIgnoreCase("T")) {
                        if (!tokenizer.hasMoreTokens()) {
                            System.out.println("Client name missing");
                        } else {
                            String peerName = tokenizer.nextToken();
                            transferJailKey(peerName);
                        }

                    } else if (command.equalsIgnoreCase("H")) {
                        printHelp();
                    } else if (command.equalsIgnoreCase("Q")) {
                        quit();
                    }

                    System.out.print(":>");
                }
            } catch (Exception io) {
                io.printStackTrace();
            }
```

21

LISTING 21.1 continued

```
        }

    }

    public void printHelp()
    {
        String help = "H - print this help\nF -
find who has the token\nR - request jail token\nP -
print peers\nT <client> -
transfer jail token to client\nL <client> -
leave jail and send jail token to client\nQ -
quit application\n";
        System.out.println(help);
    }

    public static void main (String argc[])
        throws Exception
    {
        if (argc.length < 1) {
            String msg = "Usage: " + JailGameClient.class.getName()
                + " [join/create]";
            System.out.println(msg);
            return;
        }
        int createOrJoin = (argc[0].equals("join")) ?
            JailGameClient.JOIN_GAME : JailGameClient.CREATE_GAME ;

        JailGameClient client = new JailGameClient(createOrJoin);
        client.startJxta();
        Thread thread = new Thread(client);
        thread.start();
    }

}
```

Summary

This chapter describes a sample program that employs the peer membership and peer discovery protocols of the JXTA technology through the techniques of community formation, presence of peers, and the monitoring of peers. The P2P game shows a technique to form a community by creating new peers. The community here is a jail, and a token is needed to leave the jail. The P2P game also shows how to route the jail token among peers and broadcast where the token is located.

CHAPTER 22

Distance Learning

by Rajam Ramamurti and Michael Abbott

IN THIS CHAPTER

This chapter presents the Distance Learning sample program to illustrate the mapping of P2P protocols to agent communication techniques.

Distance Learning

The Distance Learning sample program demonstrates the mapping of P2P protocols to agent communication. A question-answer session is established between a teacher and a student. The teacher creates an agent who records and scores the answers received from the student, and based on the student's exam score, makes recommendations on additional Web sites to research.

Purpose

The purpose of the Distance Learning sample program is to illustrate the discovery protocol and communication protocol of JXTA.

Community Formation

Distance Learning provides the capability to form a community (or group) by creating peers. The community here is the virtual classroom. Students join the classroom by establishing a connection to the application, and leave the classroom by exiting the application at the end of a question-answer session.

Design

Distance Learning is a standalone application with two main components: a user interface (client/front end) and JXTA integration (back end), both of which utilize the latest JXTA platform release. The user interface displays data pertaining to communication among peers, while the JXTA integration handles the update of such data.

This JXTA application is based on a simple peer-to-peer architecture. The teacher is a peer, the agent is a peer, and each student is a peer.

In this program, communication between peers occurs back and forth in the following way:

The teacher receives a request from the student for a question, gets a question from the agent for the student, sends that question to the student, receives an answer from the student, sends that answer to the agent, obtains the next question from the agent, and sends that question to the student. The question-answer session ends when there are no further questions.

Application Details

The code for this application is contained in a zip file. Extract the contents of this zip file to a directory on your local disk. For your convenience, subdirectories for peers participating in this program are also available in this directory. The teacher subdirectory has a runTeacher.bat file, and each student subdirectory has a runStudent.bat file. The runTeacher.bat file launches the program, and the runStudent.bat file lets a peer join the program.

Creating the Classroom with the Teacher

First, you must create the virtual classroom with the teacher as the first peer. To create the teacher, run the runTeacher.bat program. The program launches a window for entering the configuration information about this peer. Then proceed as follows:

1. Select the Basics tab.

2. Enter a name for the peer (say, peer 1) in the Peer Name text field.

3. Click the OK button to proceed and provide other configuration details for this peer.

4. In the window that pops up, select the Advanced tab.

5. Under the Advanced tab, make note of the TCP port number, which must be unique for this peer.

6. Select the Security tab. Under the Security tab, provide a unique username and password for this peer.

7. Select the Rendezvous/Routers tab. Ensure that the Use A Gateway box is unchecked.

8. Click the OK button. The program launches a client window for this peer.

Upon launching the program, the teacher, peer 1, announces the teaching service and waits for students to join the class, as shown in Figure 22.1.

FIGURE 22.1

The teacher's advertisement—ready to teach.

Creating a Student and Running the Program

To create a student as the second peer, run the `runStudent.bat` program in one of the
student subdirectories, `student01` or `student02`, in the installation directory. The program launches a window and prompts for information about this peer. Create this peer
similarly to `peer1`, ensuring that this peer has a unique port number, username, and password. By creating the second peer, the application creates the community. Let's name
this one `peer 2`.

Upon launching, `peer 2` (the student) forms a message requesting `peer 1` (the teacher)
to create a new session (examination), then sends this message to `peer 1`. `peer 2` then
waits indefinitely for an incoming message from `peer 1`.

Upon receiving the message for a new session, the teacher creates an agent that handles
the questions and answers, and also keeps track of the number of correctly answered
questions. The teacher obtains the first question from the agent for the student and sends
that question to the student, as shown in Figure 22.2.

FIGURE 22.2

*The teacher sends
the first question.*

The student responds with an answer. After evaluating the student's answer, the teacher
sends the next question to the student, as shown in Figure 22.3.

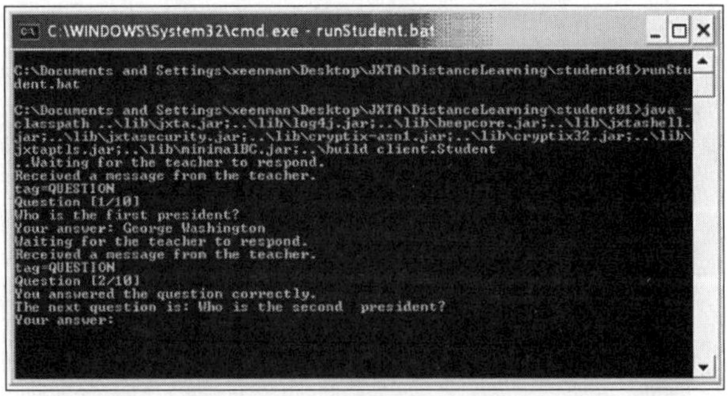

FIGURE 22.3

*The teacher's
response after
evaluating the first
answer.*

Figure 22.4 shows how the teacher receives messages from the student and responds.

FIGURE 22.4

The teacher's screen.

When the student doesn't know the answer to a question and responds with a few question marks, the teacher provides the correct answer before sending the next question, as shown in Figure 22.5.

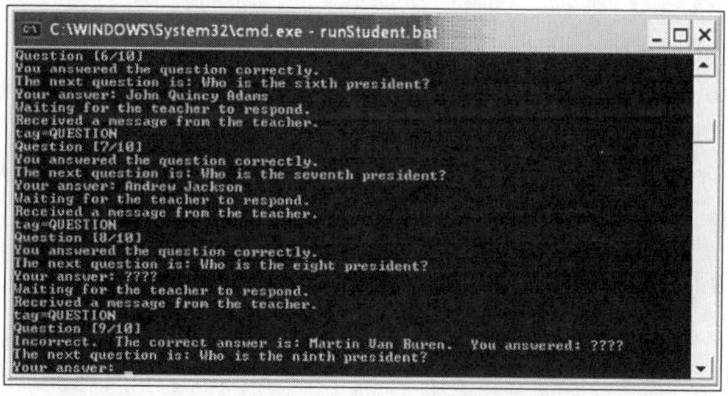

FIGURE 22.5

The student doesn't know the answer to a question.

The teacher and student pass questions and answers back and forth until no more questions remain. The teacher supplies the correct answer if the student's answer is incorrect. When there are no more questions, the teacher returns a suggestion based on the number of questions answered correctly. The student displays the suggestion and then exits the virtual classroom, as shown in Figure 22.6.

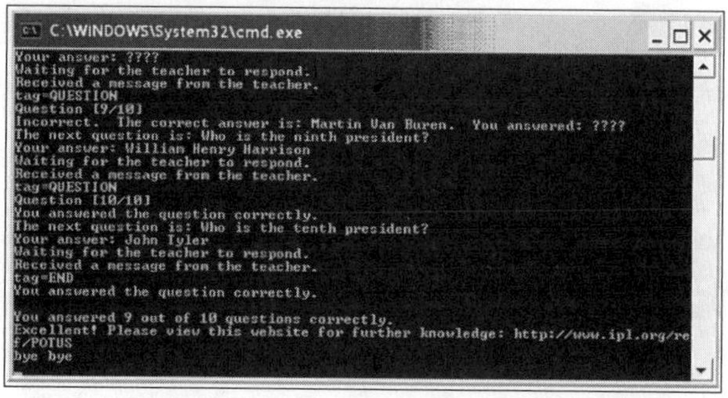

FIGURE 22.6

The teacher provides additional references.

Use Cases

Automation is useful in peer-to-peer communication. One of the use cases for peer-to-peer communication is automating technical support.

Tech Support

In an environment where technical support is necessary, clients needing technical help can type in a topic such as "software installation," and instead of having live people answering phone calls, the server can take over and ask a series of questions. Based on the client's answers, the server can attempt to resolve the problem or point to other resources for further information. Furthermore, the server can be versatile and base its questions on problems encountered by other clients. The server can also formulate questions based on the answers provided. In this sample program, P2P is mainly used to facilitate communication and distribute knowledge.

Class Design

The Distance Learning program uses four classes—Teacher.class, AgentFactory.class, Agent.class, and Student.class—to create the virtual classroom and peers, and provide an environment for communication between peers.

- Teacher—The Teacher class is responsible for setting up the JXTA environment and establishing a communication link to the student.
- AgentFactory—The AgentFactory is a singleton class responsible for constructing the Agent object.
- Agent—The Agent class collects questions and answers. It also responds to the answers the student provides and gives recommendations at the end of the question-answer session.

Special Details

The current implementation of the graphical user interface depends on a JAR file from the latest version of the integrated development environment called NetBeans Version 3.3. The file AbsoluteLayout.jar is required to build and/or run the Distance Learning program.

Code Details

This program uses four classes: Student, Teacher, Agent, and AgentFactory. These classes and their methods are described in the next sections.

Details of the Student Class

The Student class represents the student in the teacher-student relationship in this program. This class creates the JXTA environment for the student. First it connects with the teacher, and accepts the questions sent by the teacher. Then it sends answers to the teacher.

The Student class implements the Runnable interface and employs the following methods:

- discoverTeacherPipeAdv() to discover the teacher's presence
- createTeacherPipes() to create a pipe to connect with the teacher
- publishStudentPipeAdv() to advertise the student's presence
- createStudentInputPipe() to create a channel through which to send the student's answers to the teacher
- accept() for the teacher to acknowledge receipt of the student's answer
- requestNewSession() to trigger a new session of questions and answers
- getUserResponse() to read in the student's input
- sendToTeacher(Map map) to capture and send the student's response to the teacher
- processMessage(Message message) to display a message from the teacher regarding the teacher's question, the student's answer, the teacher's evaluation of the student's answer, and the teacher's subsequent recommendation
- getElementValue(Message *message*, String *key*) to get the literal string value of the message
- startJXTA() to start JXTA techniques
- connect() to connect with the server/teacher
- disconnect() to disconnect from the server/teacher
- run() to request a new session
- main() to run the client/student thread

Listing 22.1 presents the code for Student.java.

LISTING 22.1   Student.java

```
package client;

/**
 * This is the client in the Distance Learning example.  It represents the
 * student in the teacher-student relationship.
 */
```

LISTING 22.1   continued

```java
import server.*;

import net.jxta.id.IDFactory;
import net.jxta.pipe.InputPipe;
import net.jxta.pipe.PipeMsgEvent;
import net.jxta.pipe.PipeMsgListener;
import net.jxta.credential.AuthenticationCredential;
import net.jxta.document.StructuredDocument;
import net.jxta.document.Document;
import net.jxta.document.StructuredTextDocument;
import net.jxta.document.MimeMediaType;
import net.jxta.membership.Authenticator;
import net.jxta.membership.MembershipService;
import net.jxta.peergroup.PeerGroup;
import net.jxta.peergroup.PeerGroupFactory;
import net.jxta.exception.PeerGroupException;
import net.jxta.exception.ProtocolNotSupportedException;
import net.jxta.document.AdvertisementFactory;
import net.jxta.document.MimeMediaType;
import net.jxta.discovery.DiscoveryService;
import net.jxta.discovery.DiscoveryListener;
import net.jxta.discovery.DiscoveryEvent;
import net.jxta.pipe.PipeService;
import net.jxta.pipe.OutputPipe;
import net.jxta.pipe.OutputPipeListener;
import net.jxta.pipe.OutputPipeEvent;
import net.jxta.protocol.DiscoveryResponseMsg;
import net.jxta.protocol.PipeAdvertisement;
import net.jxta.protocol.PeerGroupAdvertisement;
import net.jxta.protocol.ModuleImplAdvertisement;
import net.jxta.protocol.PeerAdvertisement;
import net.jxta.protocol.ResolverQueryMsg;
import net.jxta.protocol.ResolverResponseMsg;
import net.jxta.resolver.ResolverService;
import net.jxta.resolver.QueryHandler;
import net.jxta.endpoint.Message;
import net.jxta.endpoint.MessageElement;
import net.jxta.document.Advertisement;
import net.jxta.id.ID;

import net.jxta.impl.protocol.ResolverResponse;
import net.jxta.impl.protocol.ResolverQuery;

import java.util.*;
import java.io.*;

public class Student implements Runnable
{
    private static final int MAX_TRIES = 5;
```

LISTING 22.1 continued

```java
    private PeerGroup netPeerGroup;
    private DiscoveryService discoverySvc;
    private PipeAdvertisement pipeTeacherAdv;
    private OutputPipe outputTeacherPipe;
    private PipeAdvertisement pipeStudentAdv;
    private InputPipe inputStudentPipe;
    /**
     * Find an advertisement of a Teacher using
     * JXTA discovery services.
     */
    private void discoverTeacherPipeAdv()
        throws IOException
    {
        String name = Teacher.DISTANCE_LEARNING + Teacher.TEACHER_PIPE;
        this.discoverySvc.getRemoteAdvertisements(null,
➥DiscoveryService.ADV, "name", name, 10, null);
        try {
            Thread.sleep(5);
            System.out.print(".");
        } catch (Exception ignore) { }

        Enumeration enum =
            this.discoverySvc.getLocalAdvertisements(DiscoveryService.ADV,
➥"Name", name);
        while (enum.hasMoreElements()) {
            pipeTeacherAdv = (PipeAdvertisement) enum.nextElement();
            break;
        }

    }

    /**
     * Set up the output pipe to the teacher.
     */
    private boolean createTeacherPipes()
        throws IOException
    {
        PipeService pipeSvc = netPeerGroup.getPipeService();
        this.outputTeacherPipe =
➥pipeSvc.createOutputPipe(this.pipeTeacherAdv, 1000);
        return true;
    }

    /**
     * Publish the student advertisement pipes.
     */
    private void publishStudentPipeAdv()
        throws IOException
    {
```

LISTING 22.1 continued

```
        PipeAdvertisement pipeAdv = null;
        String advType = PipeAdvertisement.getAdvertisementType();

        pipeAdv = (PipeAdvertisement) AdvertisementFactory.
➥newAdvertisement(advType);

        pipeAdv.setPipeID(IDFactory.newPipeID(netPeerGroup.
➥getPeerGroupID()));
        String name = "DL:" + netPeerGroup.getPeerName();
        pipeAdv.setName(name);
        pipeAdv.setType(PipeService.UnicastType);

        discoverySvc.publish(pipeAdv, DiscoveryService.ADV);
        discoverySvc.remotePublish(pipeAdv, DiscoveryService.ADV);
        this.pipeStudentAdv = pipeAdv;
    }

    /**
     * Create an input pipe for inbound messages.
     */
    private void createStudentInputPipe()
        throws IOException
    {
        PipeService pipeSvc = netPeerGroup.getPipeService();
        this.inputStudentPipe =
➥pipeSvc.createInputPipe(this.pipeStudentAdv);
    }

    /**
     * Wait indefinitely for the teacher to respond
     * to the message sent.
     */
    public Message accept()
        throws InterruptedException
    {
        System.out.println("Waiting for the teacher to respond.");
        return inputStudentPipe.waitForMessage();
    }

    /**
     * Send to the Teacher a request for a new series of
     * questions and answers.
     */
    public void requestNewSession()
        throws IOException
    {
        Map map = new HashMap();
        map.put("tag", "NEW");
        map.put("course", "whatevers");
```

LISTING 22.1   continued

```
            this.sendToTeacher(map);
    }

/**
    * Get the Student's response from IO.
    */
    private String getUserResponse()
        throws IOException
    {
        BufferedReader reader =
                new BufferedReader(new InputStreamReader(System.in));
        return reader.readLine();
    }

/**
    * Utility method to send a response back to the Teacher.
    *
    * @param map Key/value pair to be sent.
    */
    private void sendToTeacher(Map map)
        throws IOException
    {
        PipeService pipeSvc = netPeerGroup.getPipeService();
        Message message = pipeSvc.createMessage();
        Set keySet = map.keySet();
        Iterator iterator = keySet.iterator();
        while (iterator.hasNext()) {
            String key = (String) iterator.next();
            String value = (String) map.get(key);

            MessageElement element = message.newMessageElement
➥ (key, new MimeMediaType("text/plain"), new ByteArrayInputStream
➥ (value.getBytes()));
            message.addElement(element);
        }
        MessageElement clientElement = message.newMessageElement
➥ ("client", new MimeMediaType("text/plain"),
➥new ByteArrayInputStream(netPeerGroup.getPeerName().getBytes()));
        message.addElement(clientElement);
        this.outputTeacherPipe.send(message);
    }

/**
    * Processes incoming messages from the teacher object.
    * Handles questions and the
    * END signal which signifies the end of the question answer session.
    */
    public void processMessage(Message message)
        throws IOException
```

22

DISTANCE
LEARNING

LISTING 22.1 continued

```java
        {
            String tag = getElementValue(message, "tag");
            System.out.println("Received a message from the teacher.");
            System.out.println("tag=" + tag);

            if (tag.equals("QUESTION")) {
                String question = getElementValue(message, "question");
                String number = getElementValue(message, "number");
                String total = getElementValue(message, "total");

                System.out.println("Question [" + number + "/" + total + "]");
                System.out.println(question);
                System.out.print("Your answer: ");
                String reply = getUserResponse();

// Send back the response to the teacher
                Map map = new HashMap();
                map.put("tag", "ANSWER");
                map.put("ANSWER", reply);
                sendToTeacher(map);

            } else if (tag.equals("END")) {
            // The teacher signals the end of the questions
              // Print out the suggestions
                String suggestions = getElementValue(message, "SUGGESTIONS");
                String response = getElementValue(message, "question");
                System.out.println(response);
                System.out.println(suggestions);
                this.disconnect();
            }
        }

        /**
         * Parses a Message for a specified tag.
         *
         * @param message Contains a message from the Teacher.
         * @param key The key to parse.
         *
         * @returns The value for the key if found.  Null otherwise.
         */
        private String getElementValue(Message message, String key)
            {
                if (!message.hasElement(key)) {
                    return null;
                }
                MessageElement element = message.getElement(key);
                InputStream stream = element.getStream();
                try {
                    byte [] bytes = new byte[stream.available()];
```

LISTING 22.1   continued

```
                stream.read(bytes);
                return new String(bytes);

            } catch (IOException io) {
                io.printStackTrace();
                return null;
            }
        }

    /**
     * Start up the Net Peer group & get the Discovery Service
➥for that group.
     */
    public void startJxta()
        throws PeerGroupException, IOException
    {
        this.netPeerGroup = PeerGroupFactory.newNetPeerGroup();
        this.discoverySvc = netPeerGroup.getDiscoveryService();
        // Flush all local cache information.
➥We want to start from scratch.
        discoverySvc.flushAdvertisements(null, DiscoveryService.ADV);
        discoverySvc.flushAdvertisements(null, DiscoveryService.PEER);
        discoverySvc.flushAdvertisements(null, DiscoveryService.GROUP);

    }

    /**
     * Establish communications with a Teacher instance through JXTA.
     */
    public boolean connect()
        throws Exception
    {
        for (int i = 0 ; this.pipeTeacherAdv ==
➥null && i < MAX_TRIES ; i++) {
            this.discoverTeacherPipeAdv();
            try {
                Thread.sleep(5*1000);
            } catch (Exception ignore) { }
        }
        if (this.pipeTeacherAdv == null) {
            return false;
        }

        try {
            this.createTeacherPipes();
            this.publishStudentPipeAdv();
            this.createStudentInputPipe();
            return true;
        } catch (Exception e) {
```

LISTING 22.1 continued

```
            e.printStackTrace();
            return false;
        }
    }

    /**
     * Exit out of the application.
     */
    public void disconnect()
    {
        System.out.println("bye bye");
        System.exit(0);
    }

    /**
     * Thread to capture the student's responses and
     * process the teacher's messages.
     */
    public void run()
    {
        try {
            requestNewSession();
            for (;;) {
                try {
                    Message message = this.accept();
                    processMessage(message);
                } catch (InterruptedException ie) { }
            }
        } catch (IOException io) {
            io.printStackTrace();
        } catch (Exception e) {
            e.printStackTrace();
        }
    }

    /**
     * Instantiates a Student and launches a thread to allow
     * the student to input answers to
     * questions sent by the Teacher.
     */
    public static void main(String argc[])
        throws Exception
    {
        Student student = new Student();
        student.startJxta();
        if (!student.connect()) {
            System.out.println
        ➥ ("Unable to communicate with the teacher.");
            System.out.println
```

LISTING 22.1   continued

```
➡ ("Make sure the Teacher is ready to teach.");
          System.exit(1);
      }
      Thread thread = new Thread(student);
      thread.start();
   }
}
```

Details of the Teacher Class

The Teacher class represents the teacher in the teacher-student relationship in this program. The Teacher class creates the JXTA environment and establishes a communication with a student. It employs the following methods: netPeerGroup(), discoverySvc(), pipeAdv(), inputPipe(), agentFactory(), sendMessage(), publishPipeAdv(), createInputPipe(), startJXTA(), and main().

The InputPipeMsgListener class in the main() method implements the PipeMsgListener interface to get the pipe message. The InputPipeMsgeListener class employs the following methods:

- getElementValue(Message *message*, String *key*) to receive valid messages
- sendNextQuestions(String *clientName*) to identify the student, evaluate the response, and send the next question
- pipeMsgEvent(PipeMsgEvent *pipeMsgEvent*) to handle messages such as the teacher's action, the student's name, the course name, an evaluation of the student's answer, and subsequent action

Listing 22.2 presents the code for Teacher.java.

LISTING 22.2   Teacher.java

```
package server;

import java.util.*;
import java.io.*;

import net.jxta.id.IDFactory;
import net.jxta.pipe.InputPipe;
import net.jxta.pipe.PipeMsgEvent;
import net.jxta.pipe.PipeMsgListener;
import net.jxta.credential.AuthenticationCredential;
import net.jxta.document.StructuredDocument;
import net.jxta.document.Document;
import net.jxta.document.StructuredTextDocument;
```

LISTING 22.2   continued

```java
import net.jxta.document.MimeMediaType;
import net.jxta.membership.Authenticator;
import net.jxta.membership.MembershipService;
import net.jxta.peergroup.PeerGroup;
import net.jxta.peergroup.PeerGroupFactory;
import net.jxta.exception.PeerGroupException;
import net.jxta.exception.ProtocolNotSupportedException;
import net.jxta.document.AdvertisementFactory;
import net.jxta.document.MimeMediaType;
import net.jxta.discovery.DiscoveryService;
import net.jxta.discovery.DiscoveryListener;
import net.jxta.discovery.DiscoveryEvent;
import net.jxta.pipe.PipeService;
import net.jxta.pipe.OutputPipe;
import net.jxta.pipe.OutputPipeListener;
import net.jxta.pipe.OutputPipeEvent;
import net.jxta.protocol.DiscoveryResponseMsg;
import net.jxta.protocol.PipeAdvertisement;
import net.jxta.protocol.PeerGroupAdvertisement;
import net.jxta.protocol.ModuleImplAdvertisement;
import net.jxta.protocol.PeerAdvertisement;
import net.jxta.protocol.ResolverQueryMsg;
import net.jxta.protocol.ResolverResponseMsg;
import net.jxta.resolver.ResolverService;
import net.jxta.resolver.QueryHandler;
import net.jxta.endpoint.Message;
import net.jxta.endpoint.MessageElement;
import net.jxta.document.Advertisement;
import net.jxta.id.ID;

import net.jxta.impl.protocol.ResolverResponse;
import net.jxta.impl.protocol.ResolverQuery;

/**
 * Encapsulates an Agent framework that handles communication with many
 * Student peers. Sends a series of questions to Student peers, and
 * processes their answers. Once completed, this Teacher peer will
 * recommend additional resources to the student for improvement
 * depending on the exam result.
 */
public class Teacher
{
    public static final String DISTANCE_LEARNING = "DL:";
    public static final String TEACHER_PIPE = "teacher_pipe";
    public static final String ACTION_TAG = "tag";
    public static final String CLIENT_NAME = "client";
    public static final String COURSE_NAME = "course";

    private PeerGroup netPeerGroup;
```

LISTING 22.2   continued

```
    private DiscoveryService discoverySvc;
    private PipeAdvertisement pipeAdv;
    private InputPipe inputPipe;

    private AgentFactory agentFactory = AgentFactory.getInstance();

    // This Hashtable is used to store the agents used
    // for individual students.
    private Hashtable agentTable = new Hashtable();

    private void sendMessage(String clientName, Map map)
        throws IOException
    {
        for (;;) {
            Enumeration enum =
➥discoverySvc.getLocalAdvertisements(DiscoveryService.ADV,
➥ "Name", Teacher.DISTANCE_LEARNING + clientName);

            while (enum.hasMoreElements()) {
                PipeAdvertisement pipeAdv =
➥ (PipeAdvertisement) enum.nextElement();
                PipeService pipeSvc = netPeerGroup.getPipeService();

                OutputPipe outputPipe = null;
                try {
                    outputPipe = pipeSvc.createOutputPipe(pipeAdv, 1000);
                    Message message = pipeSvc.createMessage();

                    Set keySet = map.keySet();
                    Iterator iterator = keySet.iterator();
                    while (iterator.hasNext()) {
                        String key = (String) iterator.next();
                        String value = (String) map.get(key);

                        MessageElement element =
➥message.newMessageElement(key, new MimeMediaType("text/plain"),
➥new ByteArrayInputStream(value.getBytes()));
                        message.addElement(element);
                    }

                    outputPipe.send(message);
                    System.out.println("Sent message");
                    return;
                } catch (IOException io) {
                    io.printStackTrace();
                } finally {
                    if (outputPipe != null) {
                        outputPipe.close();
                    }
```

22

DISTANCE
LEARNING

LISTING 22.2 continued

```
            }
        }

        // Need to look remotely.
        discoverySvc.getRemoteAdvertisements
➥ (null, DiscoveryService.ADV, "Name", Teacher.DISTANCE_LEARNING +
➥clientName, 10, null);
        try {
            Thread.sleep(5 * 1000);
            // 5 sec too short if this is truly distant
            System.out.print(".");
        } catch (Exception ignore) { }
    }
}

/**
 * Publish a pipe advertisement.
 */
public void publishPipeAdv()
    throws IOException
{
    PipeAdvertisement pipeAdv = null;
    String advType = PipeAdvertisement.getAdvertisementType();

    pipeAdv = (PipeAdvertisement)
➥AdvertisementFactory.newAdvertisement(advType);

    pipeAdv.setPipeID(IDFactory.newPipeID
➥ (netPeerGroup.getPeerGroupID()));
    pipeAdv.setName(DISTANCE_LEARNING + TEACHER_PIPE);
    pipeAdv.setType(PipeService.UnicastType);

    discoverySvc.publish(pipeAdv, DiscoveryService.ADV);
    discoverySvc.remotePublish(pipeAdv, DiscoveryService.ADV);
    this.pipeAdv = pipeAdv;
}

 /**
  * Create an input pipe for inbound messages.
  */
public void createInputPipe()
    throws IOException
{
    PipeService pipeSvc = netPeerGroup.getPipeService();
    PipeMsgListener listener = new InputPipeMsgListener();
    this.inputPipe = pipeSvc.createInputPipe(this.pipeAdv, listener);
}

 /**
```

LISTING 22.2 continued

```java
     * Start up the Net Peer group & get the
     * Discovery Service for that group.
     */
    public void startJxta()
        throws PeerGroupException, IOException
    {
        this.netPeerGroup = PeerGroupFactory.newNetPeerGroup();
        this.discoverySvc = netPeerGroup.getDiscoveryService();
        // Flush all local cache information.
        // We want to start from scratch.
        discoverySvc.flushAdvertisements(null, DiscoveryService.ADV);
        discoverySvc.flushAdvertisements(null, DiscoveryService.PEER);
        discoverySvc.flushAdvertisements(null, DiscoveryService.GROUP);
    }

    /**
     * Create the Teacher and initiate the JXTA services.
     */
    public static void main(String argc[])
        throws Exception
    {
        Teacher teacher = new Teacher();
        teacher.startJxta();
        teacher.publishPipeAdv();
        teacher.createInputPipe();
        System.out.println("Ready to teach");
    }

    /**
     * Handles the Student Teacher interactions.
     */
    class InputPipeMsgListener implements PipeMsgListener
    {
        /**
         * Utility method to extract the value of a provided key
         *
         * @param message The Message to parse.
         * @param key The key to search for.
         */
        private String getElementValue(Message message, String key)
        {
            if (!message.hasElement(key)) {
                return null;
            }
            MessageElement element = message.getElement(key);
            InputStream stream = element.getStream();
            try {
                byte [] bytes = new byte[stream.available()];
                stream.read(bytes);
```

LISTING 22.2   continued

```
                    return new String(bytes);

            } catch (IOException io) {
                io.printStackTrace();
                return null;
            }
        }

        /**
         * Get the next question from the Agent and send it
         * to the student.
         */
        private void sendNextQuestion(String clientName)
        {
            Agent agent = (Agent) Teacher.this.agentTable.get(clientName);
            Agent.Problem problem = agent.getNextProblem();
            Map map = new HashMap();

            map.put(Teacher.ACTION_TAG, "QUESTION");
            map.put("question", problem.getQuestion());
            map.put("number", "" + problem.getNumber());
            map.put("total", "" + agent.getTotalNumberOfQuestions());

            try {
                Teacher.this.sendMessage(clientName, map);
            } catch (IOException io) {
                System.out.println("Unable to send a message.  Exiting.");
                io.printStackTrace();
                System.exit(1);
            }
        }

        /**
         * Processes incoming messages from Student objects.
         */
        public void pipeMsgEvent(PipeMsgEvent pipeMsgEvent)
        {
            Message message = pipeMsgEvent.getMessage();
            String messageAction = getElementValue
➥ (message, Teacher.ACTION_TAG);
            String clientName = getElementValue
➥ (message, Teacher.CLIENT_NAME);
            String courseName = getElementValue
➥ (message, Teacher.COURSE_NAME);

            System.out.println("Received a message from " + clientName);
            System.out.println("tag=" + messageAction);

            if (messageAction.equals("NEW")) {
```

LISTING 22.2   continued

```
                // Student requests a new course.
                Agent agent = agentFactory.getAgent(courseName);
                // keep track of the student and agent pair with HashTable
                agentTable.put(clientName, agent);
                sendNextQuestion(clientName);

            } else if (messageAction.equals("ANSWER")) {
                // Process the Student's answer
                Agent agent = (Agent) Teacher.this.agentTable.
get(clientName);
                String answer = getElementValue(message, "ANSWER");
                String nextQuestion = (!agent.processAnswer(answer)) ?
"Incorrect.  The correct answer is: " +
agent.getLastAnswer() + ".  You answered: " + answer + "\n"
: "You answered the question correctly.\n";

                Map map = new HashMap();
                if (agent.hasMoreProblems()) {
                    // Send the next question
                    Agent.Problem problem = agent.getNextProblem();
nextQuestion += "The next question is: " +
                        problem.getQuestion();


                    map.put(Teacher.ACTION_TAG, "QUESTION");
                    map.put("question", nextQuestion);
                    map.put("number", "" + problem.getNumber());
                    map.put("total", "" +
agent.getTotalNumberOfQuestions());

                } else {
                    // no more problems to solve :)
                    map.put("question", nextQuestion);
                    map.put(Teacher.ACTION_TAG, "END");
                    String suggestion = "You answered " +
agent.getTotalAnswersCorrect() + " out of " +
agent.getTotalNumberOfQuestions() +
" questions correctly.\n" +
agent.getSuggestions();
                    map.put("SUGGESTIONS", suggestion);
                    // Remove the agent from the HashMap
                    Teacher.this.agentTable.remove(agent);

                }

                try {
                    // Send the response back to the Student.
                    Teacher.this.sendMessage(clientName, map);
                } catch (IOException io) {
```

LISTING 22.2   continued

```
                        System.out.println
➥ ("Unable to send a message.  Exiting.");
                        io.printStackTrace();
                        System.exit(1);
                }
            }
        }
    } ///:~ InputPipeMsgListener

} ///:~ Teacher
```

Details of the Agent Class

The Agent class collects questions and answers, responds to student answers, and gives recommendations at the end of the question-answer session. This class employs the following methods and a class:

- initProblems() to create a set of questions and answers for the student
- getTotalNumberOfQuestions() to get the total number of questions sent to the student
- getNextProbelm() to get the next question for the student
- processAnswer(String answer) to check whether the answer received from the student for a given question is correct
- getLastAnswer() to get the last answer received from the student
- hasMoreProblems() to check whether all the questions have been sent to the student; lets you know whether the list is exhausted
- getTotalAnswersCorrect() to obtain the number of correct answers received from the student
- getSuggestions() to make recommendations to the student based on the answers received from that student for all the questions posed

The Problem class uses three methods, getNumber(), getQuestion(), and getAnswer(), to get the number of questions, the contents of the questions, and the answers, respectively.

Listing 22.3 presents the code for Agent.java.

LISTING 22.3   Agent.java

```java
package server;

import java.util.*;
import java.io.*;

/**
 * The agent object that encapsulates a series of questions and answers.
 */
public class Agent
{
    private List problems = new Vector();

    private int totalAnswersCorrect;
    private int totalQuestions;
    private String lastAnswer;

    public Agent()
    {
        initProblems();
        this.totalQuestions = problems.size();
    }

    /**
     * Loads the questions and answers.
     */
    private void initProblems()
    {
        Problem problem = null;
        problem = new Problem
        (1, "Who is the first president?", "George Washington");
        problems.add(problem);
        problem = new Problem
        (2, "Who is the second  president?", "John Adams");
        problems.add(problem);
        problem = new Problem
        (3, "Who is the third president?", "Thomas Jefferson");
        problems.add(problem);
        problem = new Problem
        (4, "Who is the fourth president?", "James Madison");
        problems.add(problem);
        problem = new Problem
        (5, "Who is the fifth president?", "James Monroe");
        problems.add(problem);
        problem = new Problem
        (6, "Who is the sixth president?", "John Quincy Adams");
        problems.add(problem);
        problem = new Problem
        (7, "Who is the seventh president?", "Andrew Jackson");
        problems.add(problem);
```

LISTING 22.3   continued

```
        problem = new Problem
➤ (8, "Who is the eight president?", "Martin Van Buren");
        problems.add(problem);
        problem = new Problem
➤ (9, "Who is the ninth president?", "William Henry Harrison");
        problems.add(problem);
        problem = new Problem
➤ (10, "Who is the tenth president?", "John Tyler");
        problems.add(problem);
    }

    /**
     * Gets the total number of questions.
     */
    public int getTotalNumberOfQuestions()
    {
        return this.totalQuestions;
    }

    /**
     * Returns the next question.
     */
    public Problem getNextProblem()
    {
        return (Problem) problems.get(0);
    }

    /**
     * Processes the answer to the current problem.
     *
     * @returns true if answered correctly.
     * @returns false if answered incorrectly.
     */
    public boolean processAnswer(String answer)
    {
        Problem problem = (Problem) problems.remove(0);
        this.lastAnswer = problem.getAnswer();
        if (answer.equals(problem.getAnswer())) {
            totalAnswersCorrect++;
            return true;
        } else {
            return false;
        }
    }

    /**
     * Returns the last answer.
     */
    public String getLastAnswer()
```

LISTING 22.3   continued

```
    {
        return this.lastAnswer;
    }

    /**
     * Returns true if there are more problems left to solve.
     */
    public boolean hasMoreProblems()
    {
        return !problems.isEmpty();
    }

    /**
     * Returns the total number of questions answered correctly so far.
     */
    public int getTotalAnswersCorrect()
    {
        return totalAnswersCorrect;
    }

    /**
     * Returns tips and suggestions to help the student improve his score
     * based on the total number of questions answered correctly.
     */

    public String getSuggestions()
    {
        return (totalAnswersCorrect >= 8) ? "Excellent!
➥Please view this website for further knowledge:
➥http://www.ipl.org/ref/POTUS" : "You need to study harder!
➥Here is a website to help http://www.ipl.org/ref/POTUS";
    }

    /**
     * Encapsulates a problem with a solution.
     */
    class Problem
    {
        private int number;
        private String question;
        private String answer;

        Problem(int number, String question, String answer)
        {
            this.number = number;
            this.question = question;
            this.answer = answer;
        }
```

Listing 22.3 continued

```
        /**
         * Returns the problem number.
         */
        public int getNumber()
        {
            return this.number;
        }

        /**
         * Returns the question.
         */
        public String getQuestion()
        {
            return this.question;
        }

        /**
         * Returns the answer to the problem.
         */
        String getAnswer()
        {
            return answer;
        }
    }///:~ Problem
}///:~ Agent
```

Details of the AgentFactory Class

The AgentFactory class constructs the Agent object. It employs one method, getAgent(String course), to create a new Agent.

Listing 22.4 presents the code for AgentFactory.java.

Listing 22.4 AgentFactory.java

```
package server;

import net.jxta.endpoint.Message;
import net.jxta.endpoint.MessageElement;

import java.util.*;
import java.io.*;

/**
 * A factory to instantiate Agent objects
 */
```

Listing 22.4 continued

```
public final class AgentFactory
{
    private static AgentFactory factory = new AgentFactory();
    /**
     * Get the instance of the AgentFactory
     */
    public static AgentFactory getInstance()
    {
        return factory;
    }

    /**
     * Instantiates an Agent based on the course.
     * Currently returns an Agent object.
     *
     * @param course The course requested.
     */
    public Agent getAgent(String course)
    {
        return new Agent();
    }
}
```

22

DISTANCE LEARNING

Summary

The Distance Learning program illustrates the usage of JXTA community formation, discovery procedures, and peer-to-peer communication protocols. In this program, the teacher is the server and the student is the client. There can be more than one client, but the current sample shows only one client.

Upon launching, the teacher/server sets up a JXTA environment and remotely publishes a JXTA pipe advertisement, announcing the teaching service. The server then creates an input pipe using that advertisement, and waits for the student/client to connect.

Upon launching, the client sets up a JXTA environment, automatically connects to the server, and searches for the server's pipe advertisement. Once it discovers the pipe advertisement using JXTA discovery service, it creates an output pipe using that advertisement to send messages to the server. Subsequently, it creates a JXTA pipe to advertise its own presence, and an input pipe for inbound messages from the server.

Upon receiving the message for a new session from the client, the server creates an agent through an agent factory. The agent handles the session of questions and answers, and keeps track of the number of correctly answered questions. The server obtains questions from the agent, sends the questions to the client, receives answers from the client, and sends the answers to the agent. This communication occurs in a cycle. That is, the server sends the first question to the client and subsequently sends a question after receiving an answer for the previous question. At the end of the session, upon receiving suggestions from the server for further research, the client exits the program.

Future Directions in P2P

by Toufic Boubez

In This Chapter

CHAPTER 23

This is the part of the book where technologists trade in their wireless PDAs for a crystal ball. As such, this chapter will present the personal opinions of where the authors see some trends in P2P and related technologies, with emphasis on *related*. P2P technology does not exist in a vacuum. Several technologies, such as Web services, software agents, wireless devices, and grid computing, have direct relevance to P2P, and all are on a course for either collision or convergence. We obviously hope it's the latter.

Each of these technologies can be (and in some cases has been) the subject of several books. Aside from Web services, which we covered with some detail in this book, we do not hope to give them in-depth coverage in one chapter. We do hope, however, to cover them with enough detail to give an indication of their relevance and generate interest for follow-up reading and investigation. For this purpose, this chapter provides references at the end.

P2P Devices

In a world where every device that has power will also probably have an IP address and some sort of network connectivity, it is a logical expectation that these devices will participate in some sort of peer-to-peer interactions. The concept of Universal Resource Identifiers (URIs), described in Chapter 11, "Web Services Explained," will greatly facilitate these interactions, because URIs can point to any resource on the network, including a networked microwave oven! Devices will participate by either requesting or providing services (or both), combining concepts from the Web services and P2P architectures. This world is almost upon us, and although this was the original vision of Jini, several technical and social hurdles got in the way. A combination of P2P and Web services concepts seems to be the right thing at the right time for enabling this vision.

However, devices bring a host of issues of their own. The term *device* itself encompasses a wide range of computing platforms with widely varying capabilities. You might easily and naturally think of laptops and desktops as devices. PDA devices and cell phones are next in line in this evolution of computing devices. You can even start thinking of traditionally noncomputing devices as peers in P2P networks. As an example, you can easily see how a home entertainment center will communicate with other devices on a home network to schedule some shows according to the owner's calendar, record them, upload or download media files, and so on.

In the device world, however, both hardware capabilities, such as processing power, storage and bandwidth, and software capabilities, such as operating systems and languages, can make for some very diverse environments. On the positive side, the computing power and capacity of devices has been growing in conjunction with the decreasing footprint of embedded Java and other computing platforms. These two lines have already crossed to the point where relatively complex standards-based implementations are possible on some everyday devices. On the other hand, the sheer number of different platform and operating system combinations, along with different capabilities will make interoperability harder.

For example, implementing P2P capabilities on a handheld running Windows CE is a very different proposition from implementing similar (or any) capabilities on a smart phone. This does not even take into account issues of presentation on the client, where work such as the Composite Capability/Preference Profile (CC/PP) from the W3C will be of great value (`http://www.w3.org/Mobile/CCPP/`). This area of interoperability among a large number of platforms is where Web services and P2P are coming into close alignment. Already the concepts of interoperability, capability, profiles, and introspection are being debated in the Web services community. Initiatives like the Web Services Inspection Language (WSIL) and Web Services Interoperability (WS-I) have made significant progress toward eventually solving these issues. A foundation for true interoperability, however, will require some form of semantic representation, possibly through ontologies and a formal framework such as the Resource Definition Framework (RDF). RDF is one of the enabling technologies of the Semantic Web effort, and is already used in CC/PP to represent profiles. The next sections will cover these topics in more detail.

Semantics and Ontologies

P2P technologies utilize the infrastructure of today's Web, which was originally designed for use by humans. The Web is now slowly being extended for use by machines. However, it can be argued that most of the current work in standards, protocols, and interoperability stacks is just facilitating the placement of bits on the wire, with little effort going toward actually understanding the meaning of those bits and the content of the data being transmitted. If the eventual goal of the evolution of the Web is to facilitate integration between human tasks and machine tasks, meaning and context must be taken into account. At a minimum, it is clear that fundamental tasks such as efficient distributed searching, one of the major initial uses for P2P technologies, and task composition in general, would be greatly enhanced if the machines being used for the tasks had some semantic knowledge of the data.

Resource Description Framework

Of course, there have been numerous discussions as to what constitutes *understanding*. Leaving such discussions for the academic types, let us at least agree to require that Web content, and resources in general, be marked up with some structured metadata that can be processed by machines. Metadata is an essential component that facilitates tasks in everyday life, and would be similarly beneficial if introduced into the framework of any Web-based activities, especially distributed computing activities such as P2P computing. XML is the first implementation that makes structured metadata possible, but XML is just a language, and another layer of meaning has to be built on top of it. This layer of meaning is increasingly being exposed through RDF, an application of XML developed under the auspices of the W3C.

RDF, as the name implies, is a framework that enables you to describe resources as structured metadata, and to exchange and reuse these resources in various—possibly unrelated—applications. It is built on the following three concepts:

- *Resource*—A resource is anything that can be uniquely identified by a URI. Resources usually have a reference ID for cross-referencing. Resources also have properties.

- *Property*—A property is a resource that has a name and can be used to describe other resources. A property is defined as a property-type with a corresponding value. The value can either be an atomic value, such as a string, or another resource. A collection of properties that refer to the same resource is called a *description*. RDF is essentially a mechanism to represent resources and their descriptions in a direct labeled graph (DLG). Property-types are namespace qualified, allowing different groups to use the same property-type name to mean different things.

- *Statement*—A statement is a combination of a resource, a property-type, and a value.

A simple RDF example that defines a small subset of the graph shown in Figure 23.1 is as follows:

```
<?xml version="1.0"?>
<rdf:RDF xmlns:rdf="http://www.w3.org/1999/02/22-rdf-syntax-ns#"
   xmlns:books="urn:X-Seriousbooks.com/rdf/books/">
   xmlns:who="urn:X-Seriousbooks.com/rdf/who/">

   <rdf:Description rdf:ID="Book_145"
      rdf:about="http://seriousbooks.com/books/surgery">
      <books:title>DIY Surgery</books:title>
      <books:author rdf:HREF="#Person_213"></books:author>
      <books:author rdf:HREF="#Person_214"></books:author>
      <books:editor rdf:HREF="#Person_014"></books:editor>
   </rdf:Description>

   <rdf:Description rdf:ID="Person_213"
      rdf:about="http://seriousbooks.com/people/terry">
      <who:name>Terry Mitchell</who:name>
      <who:email>tm@seriousbooks.com</who:email>
```

```
    </rdf:Description>

    <rdf:Description rdf:ID="Person_214"
        rdf:about="http://seriousbooks.com/people/joe">
        <who:name>Joe Mitchell</who:name>
        <who:email>jm@seriousbooks.com</who:email>
    </rdf:Description>
</rdf:RDF>
```

FIGURE 23.1

The RDF representation of one of the books introduced in Chapter 11, showing the relationships between the various resources.

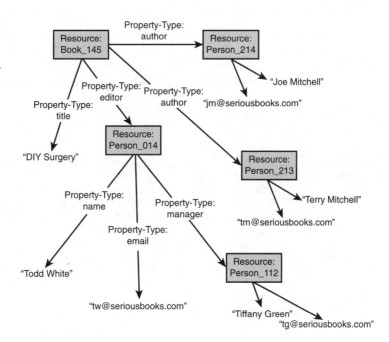

Ontologies

Having a framework to define resources and their relationship is only the first step. What if different applications use different identifiers from different RDF definitions to indicate the same thing? In order for them to interoperate and exchange information, they must reconcile the two terms. This next layer of meaning on top of RDF is provided by *ontologies*. The term *ontology*, originally meaning "concerned with the nature and relations of being" according to Merriam-Webster, has been abused by different communities. In general AI circles, it has come to mean a document containing set of formal definitions of relations among terms. Common ontologies contain a taxonomy of terms and a set of inference rules to make sense of the terms, usually in machine-readable form. For example, this will allow a computer to know that the terms *author* and *creator*, found in two different schemas, actually mean the same thing when applied to a book.

Currently, the most comprehensive and widely accepted effort that extends XML and RDF for specifying and manipulating ontologies is *DAML+OIL*, a joint effort combining a language sponsored by the Defense Advanced Research Projects Agency (DARPA) called *DAML (DARPA Agent Markup Language)*, and a European Union Information Society Technologies-sponsored language called *OIL (Ontology Inference Layer,* or *Ontology Interchange Language)*. The DAML+OIL language defines core resources along with a large number of ontologies, and allows you to express complex classifications and resources (`http://www.daml.org`).

Listing 23.1 shows an example of a DAML document, representing a very simple ontology for the bookstore examples from Chapter 11. The ontology defines a root class (`Item`), some subclasses (`Book` and `Magazine`), an instance of a `Book`, data types such as `SKU` and `price`, and an enumeration of book categories. Much more sophisticated relationships and rules (such as intersections, unions, and transitive relations) can be defined using the language.

LISTING 23.1   Bookstore Ontology

```
<?xml version="1.0" encoding="UTF-8"?>
<rdf:RDF xmlns:rdf="http://www.w3.org/1999/02/22-rdf-syntax-ns#"
         xmlns:rdfs="http://www.w3.org/2000/01/rdf-schema#"
         xmlns:daml="http://www.w3.org/2001/10/daml+oil#"
         xmlns:xsd="http://www.w3.org/2000/10/XMLSchema#"
         xmlns:dt="http://seriousbooks.com/dt"
         xmlns:sbooks="http://seriousbooks.com/metadata/"
         xml:base="http://seriousbooks.com/metadata/">

  <daml:Ontology rdf:about="">
    <daml:versionInfo>1.0</daml:versionInfo>
    <rdfs:comment>
      A very simple bookstore ontology
    </rdfs:comment>
    <daml:imports rdf:resource="http://www.daml.org/2001/03/daml+oil"/>
  </daml:Ontology>

  <daml:Class rdf:ID="Item">
    <rdfs:label>Item</rdfs:label>
    <rdfs:comment>Anything we sell</rdfs:comment>
    <daml:disjointUnionOf parseType="daml:collection">
      <daml:Class rdf:ID="InStock">
        <rdfs:label>In Stock</rdfs:label>
        <rdfs:comment>We have it and can ship it</rdfs:comment>
      </daml:Class>
      <daml:Class rdf:ID="OutOfStock">
        <rdfs:label>Out Of Stock</rdfs:label>
        <rdfs:comment>We don't have it</rdfs:comment>
      </daml:Class>
```

LISTING 23.1 continued

```
  </daml:disjointUnionOf>
</daml:Class>

<!— ****************SIMPLE INHERITANCE**************** —>

<daml:Class rdf:ID="Book">
  <rdfs:label>Book</rdfs:label>
  <rdfs:subClassOf rdf:resource="#Item"/>
</daml:Class>

<daml:Class rdf:ID="Magazine">
  <rdfs:label>Magazine</rdfs:label>
  <rdfs:subClassOf rdf:resource="#Item"/>
</daml:Class>

<!— ****************INSTANCES**************** —>

<sbooks:Book rdf:ID="DIY Surgery">
  <rdfs:label>DIY Surgery</rdfs:label>
  <sbooks:SKU>46540365</sbooks:SKU>
  <sbooks:price>32.49</sbooks:price>
  <sbooks:category rdf:resource="#Medical"/>
</sbooks:BackPack>

<!— ****************DATATYPE PROPERTIES****************—>

<daml:DatatypeProperty rdf:ID="SKU">
  <rdfs:label>SKU</rdfs:label>
  <rdfs:domain rdf:resource="#Item"/>
  <rdfs:range rdf:resource=
      "http://www.w3.org/2000/10/XMLSchema#nonNegativeInteger"/>
  <rdf:type rdf:resource=
      "http://www.daml.org/2001/03/daml+oil#UniqueProperty"/>
</daml:DatatypeProperty>

<daml:DatatypeProperty rdf:ID="price">
  <rdfs:label>price</rdfs:label>
  <rdfs:domain rdf:resource="#Item"/>
  <rdfs:range rdf:resource="http://www.w3.org/2000/10/XMLSchema#float"/>
</daml:DatatypeProperty>

<!— ****************OBJECT PROPERTIES****************—>

<daml:ObjectProperty rdf:ID="category">
  <rdfs:label>category</rdfs:label>
  <daml:domain rdf:resource="#Item"/>
  <daml:range rdf:resource="#BookCategory"/>
</daml:ObjectProperty>
```

LISTING 23.1   continued

```
<!— ****************ENUMERATIONS****************—>

<daml:Class rdf:ID="BookCategory">
  <rdfs:label>BookType</rdfs:label>
  <daml:oneOf rdf:parseType="daml:collection">
    <daml:Thing rdf:ID="Gardening">
      <rdfs:label>Hiking</rdfs:label>
    </daml:Thing>
    <daml:Thing rdf:ID="Medical">
      <rdfs:label>Travel</rdfs:label>
    </daml:Thing>
    <daml:Thing rdf:ID="Fiction">
      <rdfs:label>Camping</rdfs:label>
    </daml:Thing>
    <daml:Thing rdf:ID="NonFiction">
      <rdfs:label>Mountaineering</rdfs:label>
    </daml:Thing>
  </daml:oneOf>
</daml:Class>

</rdf:RDF>
```

Composite Capability/Preference Profiles

CC/PP is an RDF-based framework for describing and managing software and hardware profiles. It is a way to specify what an entity (or a user agent, such as a device, a browser, or a generalized client) is capable of doing, and what its preferences are within that set of capabilities. The framework can be used in a static and dynamic context. In the static context, preset profiles are used to select the appropriate content to send to a requester. In the dynamic case, where content is being generated on the fly, the profiles are used to transform typical XML content into the appropriate representation based on the requester's preferences. This flexibility allows for negotiations between clients and servers or between peer nodes. In the case of Web browsers or PDAs, for example, where displaying information is of major consideration, CC/PP enables the production of optimized markup for display.

One of the advantages of CC/PP is that the framework can be used to generate and provide generic profiles that are accessible on the Web. For example, hardware or software vendors can provide profiles for their various products, eliminating the need for an individual client (whether a device or an application) to transmit their own profile with every transaction. This is an important consideration for devices with limited bandwidth. An excerpt of such a generic profile, in this case for an Ericsson phone, is shown in Listing 23.2. Aside from the significant fact that the profile is represented in RDF, a quick scan through the various components of the document reveals a complete set of definitions for the hardware platform, the software platform, and the network characteristics of the phone. As this is a profile for a mobile phone with well-known, nonchangeable capabilities, it can be found online, in this case at `http://mobileinternet.ericsson.com/UAprof/T68R1.xml`.

LISTING 23.2 Excerpt of CC/PP Profile for an Ericsson T68R1 Mobile Phone

```
<?xml version="1.0"?>
<RDF xmlns="http://www.w3.org/1999/02/22-rdf-syntax-ns#"
    xmlns:rdf="http://www.w3.org/1999/02/22-rdf-syntax-ns#"
    xmlns:prf="http://www.wapforum.org/UAPROF/ccppschema-20000405#">
    <rdf:Description ID="Profile">
        <prf:component>
            <rdf:Description ID="HardwarePlatform">
                <prf:ScreenSize>101x80</prf:ScreenSize>
                <prf:Model>T68R1</prf:Model>
                <prf:InputCharSet>
                    <rdf:Bag>
                        <rdf:li>ISO-8859-1</rdf:li>
                        <rdf:li>US-ASCII</rdf:li>
                        <rdf:li>UTF-8</rdf:li>
                    </rdf:Bag>
                </prf:InputCharSet>
                <prf:ScreenSizeChar>15x6</prf:ScreenSizeChar>
                <prf:BitsPerPixel>8</prf:BitsPerPixel>
                <prf:ColorCapable>Yes</prf:ColorCapable>
                <prf:TextInputCapable>Yes</prf:TextInputCapable>
                <prf:ImageCapable>Yes</prf:ImageCapable>
                <prf:Keyboard>PhoneKeypad</prf:Keyboard>
                <prf:NumberOfSoftKeys>0</prf:NumberOfSoftKeys>
                <prf:Vendor>Ericsson Mobile Communications AB</prf:Vendor>
                <prf:OutputCharSet>
                    <rdf:Bag>
                        <rdf:li>ISO-8859-1</rdf:li>
                        <rdf:li>US-ASCII</rdf:li>
                        <rdf:li>UTF-8</rdf:li>
                        <rdf:li>ISO-10646-UCS-2</rdf:li>
                    </rdf:Bag>
                </prf:OutputCharSet>
                <prf:SoundOutputCapable>Yes</prf:SoundOutputCapable>
                <prf:StandardFontProportional>Yes</prf:StandardFontProportional>
                <prf:PixelsAspectRatio>1x1</prf:PixelsAspectRatio>
            </rdf:Description>
        </prf:component>
        <prf:component>
            <rdf:Description ID="SoftwarePlatform">
```

LISTING 23.2 continued

```
            <prf:AcceptDownloadableSoftware>No</prf:AcceptDownloadableSoftware>
        </rdf:Description>
    </prf:component>
    <prf:component>
        <rdf:Description ID="NetworkCharacteristics">
            <prf:SecuritySupport>WTLS class 1/2/3/signText</prf:SecuritySupport>
            <prf:SupportedBearers>
                <rdf:Bag>
                    <rdf:li>TwoWaySMS</rdf:li>
                    <rdf:li>CSD</rdf:li>
                    <rdf:li>GPRS</rdf:li>
                </rdf:Bag>
            </prf:SupportedBearers>
        </rdf:Description>
    </prf:component>
</rdf:Description>
</RDF>
```

It is clear that P2P technologies could greatly benefit from such a framework in order to describe the capabilities and preferences of heterogeneous distributed nodes in a P2P environment.

Web Services Inspection Language

Discovery mechanisms are another extremely important topic for P2P technologies, and a great candidate for convergence with general Web services technologies. As seen in Chapter 11, UDDI is one of the main discovery mechanisms for Web services. UDDI, however, relies on the concept of a well-known central registry for description information. A more distributed concept for disseminating description information is the Web Services Inspection Language, also known as WS-Inspection (http://www-106.ibm.com/developerworks/webservices/library/ws-wsilspec.html).

Think of how business people exchange contact information. UDDI is the "phone book" model, where you can look up a business in a centralized registry and get complete information about how to access its services. WS-Inspection, on the other hand, is the "business card" model, where an entity such as a business or a node on a P2P network can provide a summary about itself, and pointers to where you can find more information about services it provides. In contrast to the UDDI model, information requests in the WS-Inspection model are made directly to the entity offering the service. WS-Inspection documents are very lightweight, and require very little maintenance because they are indirect references to information contained elsewhere, and they rely on existing standards such as WSDL and UDDI to convey actual descriptions.

An sample WS-Inspection document is shown here:

```
<?xml version="1.0"?>
<inspection xmlns="http://schemas.xmlsoap.org/ws/2001/10/inspection/"
            xmlns:wsiluddi=
               "http://schemas.xmlsoap.org/ws/2001/10/inspection/uddi/">
  <service>
    <abstract>A stock quote service with two descriptions</abstract>
    <description referencedNamespace="http://schemas.xmlsoap.org/wsdl/"
                 location="http://example.com/stockquote.wsdl"/>
    <description referencedNamespace="urn:uddi-org:api">
       <wsiluddi:serviceDescription location=
          "http://www.example.com/uddi/inquiryapi">
         <wsiluddi:serviceKey>4FA28580-5C39-11D5-9FCF-BB3200333F79
            </wsiluddi:serviceKey>
       </wsiluddi:serviceDescription>
    </description>
  </service>
  <service>
    <description referencedNamespace="http://schemas.xmlsoap.org/wsdl/"
                 location="ftp://anotherexample.com/tools/calculator.wsdl"/>
  </service>
  <link referencedNamespace="http://schemas.xmlsoap.org/ws/2001/10/inspection/"
        location="http://example.com/moreservices.wsil"/>
</inspection>
```

Web Services Interoperability

As Web services technologies have matured and adoption has accelerated, several levels and versions of the different specifications like SOAP and UDDI are being produced at accelerated rates. Given the potential to have many necessary interrelated specifications at various versions and schedules of development, it is becoming a very difficult task to determine which products support which levels of the specifications. Thus, even though the industry may have the best intentions to ensure interoperability on a per-specification basis, a user of a Web service product (be it a development tool or the Web service itself) would find it very difficult to match several pieces of software necessary to complete a task or build a solution. To address this issue, the Web Services Interoperability (WS-I) industry group was formed in February 2002. The group proposes to address the issue through the creation and use of profiles.

The WS-I organization has targeted the following set of deliverables, which can also be found at http://www.ws-i.org:

- Profiles—Sets of Web services specifications that work together to support specific types of solutions.

- Sample implementations—With the context of a profile, the teams will work to define a set of Web services that are implemented by multiple team members to identify where interoperability issues are present.

- Implementation guidelines—Recommendations for use of specifications in ways that have been proven to be the most interoperable. These guidelines also provide the set of test cases that the sniffer and analyzer tools detect for compliance verification.

- Sniffer—Tools to monitor and log interactions with a Web service. This tool generates a file that can later be processed by the analyzer.

- Analyzer—Tools that process sniffer logs and verify that the Web service implementation is free from errors.

The first profile, WS-I Basic, has been identified, and consists of the combination of XML Schema 1.0, SOAP 1.1, WSDL 1.1, and UDDI 1.0. The concept of combining different levels of P2P technologies into profiles for interoperability is valuable, and can be a great complement to the CC/PP concept of individual node capabilities and preferences.

Grid Computing

The same trends that brought about P2P computing—cheap computers, bandwidth, and idle processors—also contributed to the emergence of a related concept in distributed computing called *grid computing*. One of the main goals of peer-to-peer computing is to take advantage of computing power at the edge of the network by direct interaction between these devices (without the intermediary of a central server), as exemplified by the typical P2P usage for file searches. This goal emphasizes the concept of individual peers as collaborating computing entities, and the concept of peer independence. Grid computing has some goals similar to P2P, but with an emphasis on large-scale resource sharing for the purpose of high-performance computing.

Whereas the problems tackled by current P2P applications do not require large resource commitments from the peer nodes, grid computing technologies have emerged in response to the so-called "grid problem," in which large-scale computing resources are needed, and those resources cross organizational boundaries. The grid thus refers to an infrastructure that enables the integrated, collaborative use of high-end computers, networks, databases, and scientific instruments owned and managed by multiple organizations. Grid applications often involve large amounts of data and/or computing, and often require secure resource sharing across organizational boundaries that are not easily handled by today's Internet and Web infrastructures. This concept of sharing computing resources across virtual organizations raised a large number of issues that traditional distributed computing did not address, but that were very close to some of the issues that the P2P model faces: how to structure fine-grained access control over resources; taking care of local and global policies; and how to agree on quality of service, scheduling, and co-allocation.

In response, research groups have been developing open architectures and standards to solve some of these problems. One of the most advanced from the viewpoints of acceptance and practicality is the Globus Project (`http://www.globus.org`). The Globus Project is a research and development project focused on enabling the application of grid concepts to scientific and engineering computing. One of the main deliverables of the project has been the Globus Toolkit, a set of services and software libraries that supports the development of computing grids and grid applications. The toolkit has four major components: The Globus Resource Allocation Manager (GRAM) provides resource allocation and process creation, monitoring, and management services; the Grid Security Infrastructure (GSI) provides a single-sign-on, run-anywhere authentication service; the Metacomputing Directory Service (MDS) is an extensible grid information service that combines data discovery mechanisms with the Lightweight Directory Access Protocol (LDAP); and the Global Access to Secondary Storage (GASS) implements a variety of automatic and programmer-managed data movement and data access strategies.

Several large software and hardware companies have now joined the grid computing movement and are contributing to the project. As a result, we have seen the rise of the Open Grid Services Architecture (OGSA) and related technologies for locating and managing grid resources. You can read more at `http://www.globus.org/ogsa`.

Grid Computing Examples

There are currently several good examples of grid computing applications. A well known, if relatively simple, example of shared computing resources is the SETI@home project, managed by the Space Sciences Laboratory of the University of California, Berkeley. SETI, the Search for Extraterrestrial Intelligence, is a scientific effort seeking to determine if there is intelligent life outside Earth (`http://setiathome.ssl.berkeley.edu`).

The SETI@home project is trying to detect signals of extraterrestrial intelligence by scanning a 2.5MHz band of radio frequencies and processing them to look for narrowband signals. The computations involved would overwhelm the largest supercomputers in existence. In order to solve that problem, the project leverages the idle processing power of millions of computers connected to the Internet, whose owners contribute willingly to the project. You can contribute by downloading a client program that runs as a screen-saver and processes data for the project while your computer is idle. On a periodic basis, this client connects to the SETI@home servers to upload results and download new data for the next computation.

Although it is a type of grid computing, the SETI@home computations are well structured and involve all the computers asynchronously running the same client code, making it a relatively simple application of grid computing that does not require the use of complex software such as the Globus Toolkit. Instead, the SETI project handles the data distribution and aggregation from central data and task servers.

More complex and technically significant examples of grid computing include the following:

- The Data Grid Project is a European effort to build the infrastructure to handle large-scale experiments with petabyte-size datasets. The project is intended to address computational challenges similar to the ones that the GriPhyN project faces. Additional information is available at `http://www.eu-datagrid.org`.

- Unlike the previous two projects, the Access Grid project is building the infrastructure and software to enable highly distributed collaborations in conjunction with computational grids. The focus of the project, therefore, is on interactive visualization of data sets and distributed real-time collaboration. Find out more at `http://www-fp.mcs.anl.gov/fl/accessgrid`. Although different in purpose, the project still faces the same kinds of challenges that typical grid computing projects face.

Intelligent Software Agents

Another technology that goes hand in hand with P2P are intelligent software agents. In Chapter 14, "Jini and JavaSpaces," and Chapter 22, "Distance Learning," you saw how agent technology can be combined with P2P technology to improve the user experiences in a distance learning scenario. As the P2P model becomes more prevalent, the complexity of the operating environment will increase significantly. Peer nodes will require more intelligence in order to track, handle, and route requests.

The search problem is a great example of this need. Search bots, a type of intelligent agent software, have existed almost since the inception of the Web. Search bots represent users and their queries, using a certain degree of intelligence (mainly in the form of rules) to streamline and optimize their searches. However, agents need not only represent users.

Software Agents

We can categorize the concepts of intelligent software agents several ways. Over the years, several definitions of *software agent* have evolved amid the discussions of what constitutes intelligence. The two following definitions illustrate the wide spectrum of definitions:

> Intelligent agents are software entities that carry out some set of operations on behalf of a user or another program with some degree of independence or autonomy, and in so doing, employ some knowledge or representation of the user's goals or desires. (IBM Intelligent Agent Definition, 1996)

> An agent is a computational process that implements the autonomous, communicating functionality of an application. (FIPA and OMG architecture, 1999)

As you can see, the first definition includes the concepts of a user and the user's goals, and considers agents to be extensions of users. The second definition, however, considers agents to be a pure functionality embedded within an application or computer program, with no mention or concept of users. Imagine then, a situation in which instead of the traditional pairing of agents to users, each peer node on the network works in conjunction with its own intelligent software agent. The agent can manage the node's resources by filtering incoming requests for relevance and routing outgoing requests based on their type or other learned criteria.

Security, Identity, and Integrity

An essential set of elements to both the agent and P2P concepts are those of security, identity, and integrity. In other words, how can agents prove who they are, how can they communicate information in a secure fashion, and how can they prove the integrity of the information they are delivering? For P2P applications, platforms like JXTA provide the framework for secure communications. On the other hand, the software agent community has recently started adopting the use of digital signatures for authentication and identity. These two technologies, combining security, identity, and integrity, will eventually work hand in hand in a combined P2P/agent platform.

Agent Communications

This leads us to another important topic—agent communications. The important question here is whether agents will use P2P communication protocols, or can agent and peer communications be decoupled? Most of the standards that have emerged in agent communications have come out of DARPA-funded efforts, in this case the DARPA Knowledge Sharing Effort. Traditionally, building knowledge-based systems meant having to construct a new knowledge base from scratch every time. Even if several groups of researchers were working in the same general area, each team has had to develop its own knowledge base. The cost of this duplication of effort has been high, and will only increase as larger and more complex systems are built. The Knowledge Sharing Effort was established by DARPA and other agencies in the early 90s in order to overcome these barriers and advance the state of the art.

Notably, two specifications, one for knowledge representation and the other for knowledge exchange and message passing, have been established:

- Knowledge Interchange Format (KIF)—Used to represent information to be exchanged between agents. KIF is an implementation-independent specification that is a prefix version of first order predicate logic supporting the definition of four types of expressions: terms (objects), sentences (facts), rules (inference), and definitions (constants). KIF knowledge bases are a set of sentences, rules, or definitions that could be used by communicating peers to establish common ground, such as preferences and shared ontologies (`http://www.cs.umbc.edu/kif`).

- Knowledge Query and Manipulation Language (KQML)—An agent communication language. Whereas KIF is used to represent knowledge, KQML is a message format and message-handling protocol used for sharing information between agents at runtime. This is done through an extensible set of constructs that are called *performatives*, because their intent is to cause an agent to perform a specific action (`http://www.cs.umbc.edu/kqml`).

Expressing KIF and KQML in XML for P2P communications should be a relatively straightforward task, and efforts are underway to accomplish that capability.

The Big Picture

It bears repeating that P2P technology does not exist in a vacuum. One of the clear trends to emerge in the last few years is that the technology world is heading toward a model where everything is a service. Computing in general has moved away from being a specialized activity that is the domain of a few experts, and requires specialized, dedicated hardware. It is being slowly transformed into a utility, much like electrical power or cable television. This evolution has spanned the whole spectrum of computing, from personal devices to personal computing to large structured enterprise computing.

To enable this evolution, various technologies will need to interoperate in a seamless manner to provide a rich user experience. We can easily foresee scenarios requiring the interplay of wireless, P2P, intelligent agents, and Web services technologies, as shown in the framework in Figure 23.2.

FIGURE 23.2

The seamless interplay of various technologies.

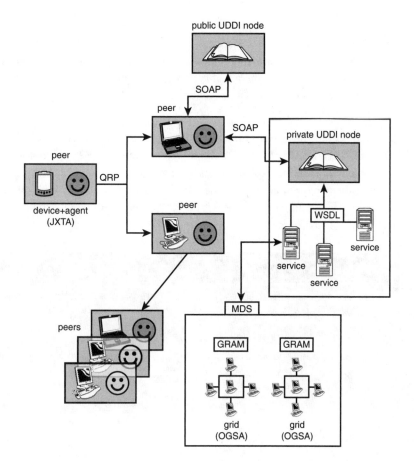

On the personal computing level, imagine going into an airport, to find your flight cancelled. Some current offerings will allow you to manually make new reservations using your PDA. Imagine, however, that your software agent gets notified of the cancellation and takes action. This will trigger a series of transactions and interactions involving a large number of technologies: Using JXTA Search Query Routing Protocol (QRP), your agent will look for another traveler willing to trade their seat for yours, with approval from the airline. Using SOAP to query a public UDDI registry, it will then find a travel agent to reshuffle your travel plans and rebook your itinerary. The travel agent services might in turn involve a combination of several services composed in a particular workflow.

On the enterprise computing level, imagine an engineer walking to the manufacturing floor to examine a prototype that came off the line. Noticing some defect in the design, the engineer can request new computer simulations be performed by having her software agent access her company's private UDDI node and find a relevant computing service by its WSDL description. This service might be a proxy for a computing grid that conforms to OGSA, and computing resources are located through MDS, as defined by the Globus Toolkit. At the same time, the agent is querying other peer nodes for some parameters needed for the computation. Once the simulation is done, the design is updated and downloaded to the manufacturing robots.

It should become clear from these scenarios that standards are an essential requirement for this kind of interoperability. As both Web services and P2P technologies mature, it is inevitable that additional standards and architectures will emerge, blurring the lines between the two types of technologies. In this manner, Web services will be able to act as peer nodes in a P2P environment, and P2P systems will be invoked as services in a Web services environment.

> **Note**
>
> Here are some additional resources for material discussed in this chapter:
>
> - The Global Grid Forum (http://www.gridforum.org)
> - The UMBC Agent Web (http://agents.umbc.edu)
> - S. Franklin and A. Graesser, "Is It an Agent, or Just a Program?: A Taxonomy for Autonomous Agents," http://www.msci.memphis.edu/~franklin/AgentProg.html.

Appendix

J2EE Overview

by Alan Moffet

APPENDIX A

Applications developed for enterprises are difficult to create. The requirements for an enterprise application demand sophisticated technologies and practices. Because of the widespread dependency on enterprise resources, and because those resources are often valuable, quite a bit of care is taken to make sure that they're used efficiently and are protected against failure or abuse. Often, resources must be available for use around the clock, even if they are located in different places. People and machines have to routinely interact between themselves to perform work. Information and knowledge must be created, shared, and persisted as part of ordinary business.

Fortunately, the solutions to problems related to enterprise applications are as old as enterprises themselves. Technology has lent a hand in solving many of the problems, and has also made it possible to create more effective enterprises, while opening up significant opportunities for business. In some cases, it has significantly reduced the complexity of operations that span a country or the globe.

In this appendix, we will briefly explore the Java 2 Platform Enterprise Edition (J2EE). We will become acquainted with some of its key features, review its usefulness in constructing enterprise computing applications, and learn a little more about a few of the technologies that are mentioned earlier in this book, along with some other closely related technologies. Naturally, all of J2EE cannot be covered in an appendix. The platform is comprehensive, and many books have been written about J2EE or its pieces.

> **Tip**
>
> For additional information about J2EE, try one of the following:
> - *J2EE Unleashed* by Paul Allen and Joseph Bambara (Sams)
> - *Sams Teach Yourself J2EE in 21 Days* by Martin Bond, Dan Haywood, Debbie Law, Andy Longshaw, and Peter Roxburgh (Sams)
> - *Special Edition Using Java 2 Enterprise Edition* by Mark Wutka (Que)

J2EE and Enterprise Computing

All enterprise computing applications and systems have similar requirements to support the needs of their users:

- Availability—Users must be able to access an application and use it. The application has to be reliable and resilient, and should resist failure.

- Durability—The application should complete the tasks that it is assigned to perform over a useful application lifetime.

- Quality of service—The application should perform its tasks in a timely manner with results that meet or exceed the needs of its users.

- Adaptability—The application should be able to change to meet new needs. It should be flexible and extensible. Adding new functionality should be relatively easy.

- Scalability—The application should be able to grow so that it can support additional users of functions, while maintaining compliance with user requirements.

- Maintainability—The application should be serviceable.

- Location/Locale independence—The application should be able to support users at multiple locations with transparency.

- Interoperability and portability—The application should work well with other, often heterogeneous, applications and systems. Applications should also be deployable to systems with similar or identical services or functions, without having to change the application.

- Secure—The application should safeguard its users, itself, and other resources.

- Cost effectiveness—The application should provide economic value.

Over the years, vendors have implemented systems to provide enterprise-quality functions to businesses. For the most part, they were successful in delivering high quality solutions. However, the systems were frequently proprietary, thus requiring businesses to "lock-in" to a particular vendor. Because vendors specialized in particular kinds of functions such as data storage or electronic messaging, businesses were required to integrate applications to meet their larger needs. Unfortunately, the systems did not interoperate easily, and often required the custom development of software that tightly coupled the systems. Because of the expense and difficulty, businesses usually only integrated applications for common work functions, or for specific workgroups—resulting in computing "islands" of applications or information.

In 1995 Sun Microsystems introduced the Java programming language. Besides being an interesting and useful programming language, Java promised "write once, run anywhere" portability, and came with a rich platform for building networked applications. This made it possible to easily create applications that were independent of the underlying hardware, operating systems, or networks.

Shortly thereafter in 1996, Sun released the Java Database Connectivity (JDBC) specification, which provided a portable and vendor-neutral standard to access relational databases. A programmer using JDBC can access and manage a database using a well-

A

J2EE OVERVIEW

defined Application Programming Interface (API), without having to consider vendor-specific protocols or functions. Sun continues to produce specifications for enterprise APIs that enable the development of "neutral" applications. In addition, Sun has developed useful frameworks that help developers meet most of the objectives of enterprise computing.

> **Note**
>
> Specifications for APIs and enhancements to the Java platforms are developed and evolved through the Java Community Process (JCP), which includes members from a large number of software and hardware vendors, government and educational organizations, and members of the open source community. The Java community process is described at the community Web site (http://www.jcp.org). There you can also find Java Specification Requests (JSR) for all requests that are under consideration and are publicly available for review.

J2EE is a collection of these enterprise-level APIs and frameworks. Mature enterprise APIs are bundled into a J2EE release. The current specification for J2EE version 1.3, can be found at http://www.javasoft.com/j2ee/download.html. With each release of J2EE, Sun also delivers a reference implementation, a compatibility test suite so that vendors can certify their own implementations, and a BluePrints document that assists developers by providing architectural and design direction for using J2EE technology.

J2EE extends the Java 2 Platform, Standard Edition (J2SE), which includes the Java programming language, support for I/O, networking, and other services and tools.

J2EE Defined

The goal of J2EE is to provide an enterprise-quality platform that is highly available, scalable, flexible, secure, interoperable, portable, and independent of machine or network architecture and vendor-specific software. J2EE also makes it practical to develop and maintain enterprise applications that are significantly less complex or costly than their predecessors. Throughout the remainder of this appendix, you will see how Sun has been able to achieve its objectives.

The Major Components

J2EE applications are made up of components. The J2EE runtime environment defines four types:

- Application clients—Running on a desktop system, these clients look and behave like native applications. As such, they typically have graphical user interfaces (GUI) created using the Swing or Abstract Windowing Toolkit (AWT) APIs, but may also have command-line interfaces. However, unlike applications that do all the work at the desktop, they interact with other enterprise components to do their work.

- Applets—Web browser-based GUI components that are often significantly more "lightweight" than an application client. Applets are written in the Java programming language and execute in a Java Virtual Machine installed in the Web browser. Applets themselves are not installed, but are delivered as part of the content included in a Web page. They usually perform fewer functions than an application, and are often limited to providing a rich user interface while leaving much of the computing work to other enterprise components. Unless the host system explicitly provides permission, applets are restricted from performing operations that may be harmful, such as writing to the filesystem. Applets are frequently designed to limit their use of memory and resources, and are therefore suitable for devices that have limited capacity.

- Web—These components interact with Web servers to respond to HTTP requests from clients. Java Server Pages (JSP) and servlets receive requests from, perform functions for, and often return responses to their clients. JSPs are text files made up of markup and Java code that are compiled into and execute as servlets. JSP provides a more natural way for developers to work with dynamic content. JSPs and servlets often produce HTML pages that are the user interface for an application. They might also produce XML for consumption by their clients. Web components interact with other enterprise components to do their work.

- Enterprise JavaBeans (EJBs)—Enterprise JavaBeans contain the business logic of an enterprise application. A significant amount of support to satisfy enterprise requirements is built into these components and their runtime environment. For example, EJBs and their containers transparently manage transactions, security, and concurrency. EJBs are distributed components—clients can interact with EJBs that do not reside in the same process or machine space. Furthermore, J2EE provides interoperability with EJBs by permitting clients to interface with them in languages other than Java through CORBA. Eventually, clients will also be able to access EJBs through the Simple Object Access Protocol (SOAP). EJBs interact with other EJBs and components to perform their work.

In J2EE, as in other programming models, a component is more than a type for functionally similar pieces of software. Clemens Szyperski defined software components as "binary units of independent production, acquisition, and deployment that interact to

A

J2EE OVERVIEW

form a functioning system." The components of J2EE adhere to this definition. J2EE components are compiled programs written in the Java programming language. They are self-contained software units that can be constructed or purchased independently of other components, assembled to produce a J2EE application, and deployed to J2EE servers. J2EE components implement interfaces defined by the J2EE specification, so they are portable between compliant J2EE servers.

Components help realize some of the goals of enterprise computing by providing high quality interchangeable pieces that are constructed by domain experts. Like pieces of a modern automobile, components can realize the economic benefits of competition or economies of scale, and also benefit from what has been learned from a century of manufacturing practice.

J2EE components consist of one or more class files and an associated file that declaratively defines the extrinsic behavior of the component.

For example, an EJB is comprised of an enterprise bean class, supporting classes, resources, interfaces, and a file (called a deployment descriptor) that defines how the component will be deployed to and then managed by the runtime environment. This is all packaged together into a Java archive (JAR) file, which is then installed into a container that provides the runtime support for the various types of components described previously.

Containers

Containers are an essential part of J2EE. At a bare minimum, containers provide a compatible runtime environment as defined by the J2SE specification. Even this minimal container has an impressive list of features. The environment is platform-neutral, secure, and has been designed from the ground up to support network-aware and mobile components. It provides support for fault tolerance and concurrency, and efficiently manages computing resources such as memory by automatically discarding unused objects.

Each component type has a container that provides support for the unique functions the component performs. In other words, there are containers for application clients, applets, Web components, and Enterprise JavaBeans:

- Application client containers provide J2SE runtime support and access to J2EE APIs.
- Applet containers provide specialized methods for locating and retrieving applets in a system of networked machines, invoking applet methods, interacting with Web browsers, and providing a protected environment for applets to run in.
- Web containers, sometimes called servlet or JSP engines, receive requests and compose and transmit HTTP responses. A Web container determines which

component should receive a request, creates or obtains an instance of that component, and passes control to it. Information about the mapping of a URL to a Web component is contained in a deployment descriptor, as is information about the way sessions should be handled or which error pages to display. Among many other things, Web containers free developers from tracking session states, managing HTTP connections, and creating, destroying, or otherwise managing the lifecycle of component objects.

- EJB containers are the most sophisticated of the containers defined by J2EE, as they perform many advanced functions. Their sophistication also derives from the complexity of the interactions between EJBs and the container. Fortunately, developers are shielded from most of the complexity.

  Because Enterprise JavaBeans can be distributed between processes or machines, the EJB container must provide facilities for clients to remotely access them. The container also manages the creation and destruction of component instances, and often persists instance data to or retrieves it from a database. Among the most valuable functions, EJB containers can guarantee that a sequence of activities occur together, or take corrective action when they do not.

Web and EJB containers perform many of the same functions. These containers extend the basic capabilities of the minimal container defined by J2SE to meet the requirements of enterprise applications. They both perform advanced object lifecycle management, and can pool ready-made instances of components in anticipation of demand. When the demand for a particular kind of component decreases, containers can "throttle back"; reducing the number of available objects and thereby conserving system resources for use by other software. They also manage concurrency by safely permitting multiple clients to use the same bean simultaneously, or by creating instances that are dedicated to serving a particular client. Finally, they perform authentication and authorization, securing components or other resources from unauthorized use.

Much of the functionality described is available without including special code in the components to perform all these useful functions. The *configuration* of the component, as described in the deployment descriptor, determines what behavior supplements the built-in functions of the component.

This greatly simplifies the development of the component, and permits the developer to focus on the business logic of the component. As a result, enterprise applications using J2EE can be less costly to produce, and have higher quality—all the container functions have already been well tested.

You might have noticed that clients interact with components through containers. For example, HTTP requests are passed to the container for delivery to a Web component.

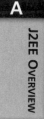

A

J2EE OVERVIEW

Clients of Enterprise JavaBeans find the beans they are interested in and invoke methods that "pass through" the EJB container, so that the container can manage transactions or concurrency. When one thinks of all the support that a container lends a component, it is easy to see why a container is so intimately involved with its components.

By design, containers have well-defined and standard open interfaces for interacting with components and component clients. The behavior of containers is also openly documented. Containers improve interoperability, and because they support a Java-based run-time environment, they also satisfy portability requirements.

As you can see, J2EE containers and components provide many of the functions required to deliver enterprise-quality applications.

J2EE-compatible containers also provide APIs that components use to access a standard set of services.

> **Note**
>
> As mentioned earlier, it is not possible to provide a detailed look at each of the components mentioned in this section. However, there are a number of good books about Java, applets, JSPs, servlets, and Enterprise JavaBeans that can help you get up to speed. Also, Sun hosts several Web sites for Java developers. Specifications, reference implementations, tutorials, and white papers are all available without cost. See `http://www.javasoft.com` and `http://developer.java.sun.com`.

The Services Provided

Over years of development, Sun has produced specifications and implementations of APIs for a number of useful enterprise-level services. The current J2EE specification defines which APIs are required as standard services for a J2EE-compatible platform implementation. These services support the application components reviewed earlier:

- HTTP/HTTPS—Clients that want to communicate using HTTP or HTTPS use the J2SE `java.net` package and the `javax.net.ssl` extension package. These APIs permit one to establish connections, receive requests, and produce responses. Using HTTPS adds the capability of performing secure communication using the Secure Sockets Layer (SSL), or the newer Transport Layer Security (TLS). The servlet and JSP component APIs define the server-side interface.

- Java Transaction API (JTA)—This application programming interface provides support for demarcating boundaries around methods. The boundaries signify the beginning and end of a series of operations that must be completed together. Collectively, the series of operations are called a *transaction*. Components can manage transactions themselves by using this API, but often designers permit containers to manage transactions on behalf of the component. The API provides the interface between a transaction manager, which has the low-level responsibilities for transactions, and a resource manager that handles resources available to the application that are transactionable. A database server or messaging system is an example of a resource manager. Transaction managers work with applications and one or more resource managers to extend the transaction capabilities of a resource manager to the application in a portable way.

- RMI-IIOP—The APIs that compose this subsystem permit components or other software to communicate with objects that are not part of the local execution context. RMI (Remote Method Invocation) enables a programmer to use an object as though it were locally created without having to understand complex protocols, or difficult programming. Java programmers can quickly build distributed applications using RMI, without having to learn an Interface Definition Language (IDL) or its mappings. "Native" RMI for J2SE is based on the RMI Transport Protocol, which uses a combination of HTTP and object serialization to invoke methods and return data. Naturally, this kind of communication depends on features that are present in the Java runtime environment—as such, it is proprietary. To meet the interoperability goals for enterprise applications, RMI can also be used with the Internet Inter-ORB Protocol (IIOP) as the underlying transport. IIOP is a part of the Object Management Group's (OMG) CORBA family of specifications and is based on open standards defined with the participation of hundreds of vendors and users. The use of IIOP and RMI-IIOP makes it possible for J2EE applications to access CORBA services that are external, or for external CORBA objects to use EJBs. Because CORBA is language-neutral, application components written in C, C++, Smalltalk, or other languages that provide CORBA bindings can communicate with J2EE applications.

- Java IDL—J2EE applications use Java IDL to act as clients of CORBA services. Like RMI-IIOP, Java IDL allows Java applications to invoke methods on remote objects. Java-IDL adds CORBA-capability to the Java platform using the industry standard OMG IDL and IIOP. Programmers develop applications using CORBA IDL to define interfaces and an IDL compiler to produce Java versions of the interfaces. On the other hand, the APIs for RMI-IIOP, while permitting interaction with CORBA services, permit developers to work completely in the Java programming language.

- Java Database Connectivity (JDBC)—This API is used to connect to and work with relational database systems. J2EE applications can make connections to systems and query, update, or manage data. JDBC applications can use SQL to perform queries. A Service Provider Interface (SPI) enables the J2EE platform to make use of drivers that are designed to access vendor-specific RDBMS.

- Java Message Service (JMS)—Supporting interfaces to enterprise messaging via message-oriented middleware (MOM) products, JMS enables J2EE clients and applications to send messages to other systems and each other. You can think of this as email for applications. Chapter 11, "Developing P2P Applications using J2EE, J2SE, and J2ME," introduced you to the concepts of JMS and presented an example of a simple JMS application.

- Java Naming and Directory Interface (JNDI)—Enterprise computing applications and resources are frequently distributed across machines and can be separated geographically. Naming and directory services are used to associate user-friendly names and attributes with objects so that it is easier to locate them. By going to one of these services, a client can provide the service with a name and obtain a reference to an object, or an object itself. Directory services are typically more capable than naming services. Directory services can associate attributes, in addition to names, to objects and also support sophisticated searches. JNDI provides a standard API for naming and directory service access. JNDI is independent of any specific naming or directory service implementation. A service provider interface attaches a provider, which keeps track of the names, attributes, and objects, to the API. JNDI service providers give access to many different kinds of systems, including filesystems and a variety of existing naming and directory services, such as LDAP, DNS, NDS, and NIS, and the Windows Registry.

- JavaMail—Most enterprise applications interact with people. In some cases, a client or application will need to send email to a person to notify her about status, or perhaps to invite her to perform a step that cannot be done by the application itself. The JavaMail APIs provide a platform- and protocol-independent means to send and receive email. An SPI is defined so that vendors can integrate their products as providers to JavaMail's vendor-neutral API.

- JavaBeans Activation Framework (JAF)—The JavaBeans activation framework is used by the JavaMail API to provide dynamic handling of mail content. MIME types identify the content type(s) associated with a particular piece of mail. JAF identifies and creates objects to process different content types.

- Java API for XML Parsing (JAXP)—Although there are several useful standards and implementations for processing XML documents, each implementation has unique methods for instantiating parsers, processors, or documents. Parsers also vary in how processing options are set or retrieved. JAXP provides a well-defined API that works with the SAX and DOM APIs to standardize parser and document creation. Similarly, JAXP standardizes the methods to create and invoke XSL processors. JAXP provides facilities for developers to plug in implementations of their choice. The reference implementation provides Apache's Crimson Parser and Xalan XSLT processor.

- Java Authentication and Authorization Service (JAAS)—J2EE applications can use JAAS to authenticate users and implement access controls. JAAS performs security-related functions, such as authentication by password validation, independent of the underlying authentication technology. Security providers create implementations of authentication services that are "plugged into" the JAAS framework. Applications using JAAS can reuse enterprise-wide authentication services such as Kerberos, or an NT Domain.

- J2EE Connector Architecture—Frequently, a company has already made or will make a significant investment into Enterprise Information Systems (EIS) that are integral to their business. To accommodate the integration of data and functions of those systems into J2EE applications, Sun has defined the connector architecture. The connector architecture defines system-level interfaces and behaviors (called *system contracts*) between a J2EE application server and a *resource adapter*, which acts as an intermediary for the EIS. These contracts provide support for the underlying mechanisms that enable transactions, security, and connection management, including resource pooling, in the J2EE environment. The connector architecture also defines a *Common Client Interface* (CCI) that is used for clients to programmatically interact with an EIS through a resource adapter, using a generic function-call/return-results model. Once a resource adapter has been written, the functionality offered by the EIS is treated as a natural extension to the standard services offered by a J2EE application server.

As you can see, J2EE provides a rich set of standard services that avoid vendor lock-in through useful, open APIs.

The J2EE Application Server

J2EE application servers provide important support for enterprise applications. Besides hosting the various server-side containers, J2EE servers make it possible to easily deploy and manage components and applications. J2EE servers manage global resources, such as database and network connections and naming services. Finally, they also provide a secure operating environment.

Although not required by the J2EE specification, most are capable of distributing their work to balance the load or provide fail-over support through clusters of servers.

J2EE's features make it possible to develop capable networked enterprise applications with only the addition of a database to store persistent business data. Yet, J2EE strives for

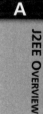

A

J2EE OVERVIEW

interoperability with other enterprise applications by adopting standards for communicating with other systems (TCP/IP, HTTP, and HTTPS), for interacting with other applications (CORBA, including IIOP), and for exchanging information (HTML, XML). Through the use of the connector architecture, it invites other enterprise information systems to participate in presenting a federated view of information and services to applications. With J2EE, Sun has raised the standard for enterprise-capable platforms.

J2EE Application Tiers

Up to this point, we have spent time discussing the J2EE platform for developing enterprise applications. In defining J2EE, Sun has also produced a recommended application architecture. The application architecture is documented as part of the "Java Enterprise Blueprints" program.

Applications designed for the enterprise are frequently divided into pieces that work together to achieve the overall goals of the application. This modular approach at an architectural level simplifies the construction and enhances the flexibility of complex applications.

By now, most software developers are acquainted with the idea of grouping functionality into layers, or *tiers*. Layering enables clients of a service within a layer to be independent of the underlying implementation or mechanisms. One of the significant ideas associated with layers is that there are well-defined boundaries and interfaces. Well-defined layers can be substituted, making it possible to build systems that are easily modified or extended. Demands for change in one layer might not require changes in other layers, and more often than not do not require rebuilding an entire application. Layers also offer the potential of reuse.

The term *layers* implies that there are a series of individual pieces that are built one upon the other. Although the application is layered, it exists as a series of composite layers. The outermost layer cannot function without all the underlying layers. When we want to speak of layers that can aggregate to perform functions, yet still exist to provide services independently, we use the term *tier*.

J2EE partitions functionality into tiers. Tiers provide services through well-defined access points, and consist of the technologies required to deliver the functionality with the quality expected by its clients. In providing a service, a tier might become a client of another tier, or access other resources such as a database. In any case, J2EE refers to anything that a tier might use to perform its work as a resource. Consequently, any of the defined tiers become resources to other tiers. Within the context of a tier, clients access tier services with client protocols. Similarly, tiers use resource protocols to access the resources in other tiers. Applications are not required to use every tier.

J2EE components such as servlets or Enterprise JavaBeans, along with their containers and J2EE resources that are exposed through JDBC or via Java Connectors, provide the services offered by a tier.

Tiers are defined wholly by their responsibilities and the kind of services they offer. As would be expected, the functionality of the tiers reflects the capabilities of the J2EE components they embody. Now let's look at the tiers. Figure A.1 will help you visualize the tiers and their components as they are presented.

> **Note**
>
> Tiers are logical entities that encapsulate functionality. Tiers can be distributed across multiple machines, or they may coexist on a single machine. The decision to divide tiers along physical lines is usually made to optimize performance or provide increased security. It should never be made for the sake of making architecture visible in a data center.

FIGURE A.1

J2EE application tiers.

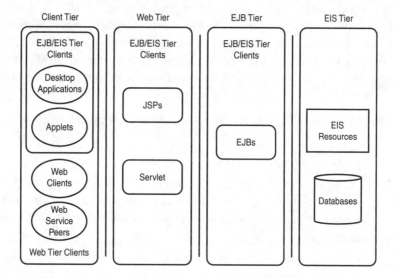

The Client Tier

The client tier is responsible for interacting with users. Through it, users direct the activity of an application, input data, and retrieve results. Programs in this tier can make use of all the other tiers. The J2EE application Programming Model defines these types of clients:

- Web clients—These clients interact with the Web tier by using HTTP or HTTPS to access content.

- Web Service peers—Web service peers also access the Web tier using HTTP or HTTPS. However, they can request services from the Web tier using higher-level protocols such as SOAP or ebXML. Web service peers often represent other computing devices that might not be interacting with a user at the moment, if they do at all. As such, they fall outside of the strict definition given at the start of this section, but they are nonetheless a client in the client tier.

- EJB clients—These clients interact directly with Enterprise JavaBeans in the EJB tier. Their client access protocol is RMI-IIOP, pure IIOP, or RMI over the RMI Transport Protocol. They can also use JMS to communicate with Message-Driven Beans.

- EIS clients—These clients access databases or other resources that expose their functionality through JDBC or Java Connectors in the EIS Tier. They may also use proprietary or other client protocols.

Clients can make use of nearly any of the technologies available for use in the J2SE runtime environment. This means that there are quite a few possibilities for defining client types. Earlier, we learned about the two client components that J2EE defined—applets and application clients. Applets, because they are hosted in a Web browser, are suitable only as Web clients. On the other hand, application clients can be any of the client types just described. All the client protocols are available to application clients through the rich set of APIs provided by the Java platforms.

The J2EE application Programming Model adds a few more types:

- Web browsers (a Web Client) interact with the Web tier to provide user interaction via HTTP/HTTPS and HTML or xHTML.

- Rich clients are similar to application clients, but can only interact as Web service peers. In addition, because rich clients do not have to be written in the Java programming language, they are not defined as J2EE components by the J2EE specification.

- Finally, although they do not have a special name given to them, the model also recognizes those clients that are written in programming languages other than Java, which can "speak" a client protocol and interface directly to any of the defined tiers to use their services.

The Web Tier

The Web tier is composed of services that interact with clients using the HTTP and HTTPS protocols. In turn, services make use of J2EE Web components and their containers, along with the J2SE and J2EE technologies and APIs to build application functionality. Using servlets and JavaServer Pages, the Web tier is capable of providing all the logic necessary to host applications that are accessible to the World Wide Web. In most cases, however, applications will require the services of a database and will use the EIS tier as a resource. For enterprise applications, the Web tier will leverage the features of both the EJB and EIS tiers.

The Web tier can interact with any of the other tiers, and may also interact on a peer-to-peer basis with other systems that support a Web services interface.

The EJB Tier

This tier provides applications and other tiers with access to the sophisticated capabilities of Enterprise JavaBeans. As we learned earlier, EJBs and their containers take care of many of the system-level details for handling resource pooling, concurrency, security, persistence, and transactions. Programmers can then concentrate on implementing business processes. Because of its usefulness, the EJB tier is the most accessible tier—clients can access EJBs using native RMI, RMI-IIOP, or CORBA. In addition, with the addition of the Message-Driven Bean in EJB 2.0, clients can communicate with services in the EJB tier using the Java Message Service (JMS). Although Enterprise JavaBeans interact universally, they frequently use resources from the EIS Tier.

The EIS Tier

Data and services implemented by external Enterprise Information Systems are part of the EIS tier. Databases, enterprise resource planning sytems, and legacy applications are all part of the EIS tier. J2EE applications access these resources using technologies such as JDBC and Java Connectors. Use of these technologies insures a complete integration into the J2EE environment. EIS systems can also implement proprietary client protocols or provide access using CORBA. However, they will not realize many of the benefits of J2EE. Any tier can access the EIS tier.

Peer-to-Peer and J2EE

Peer-to-peer computing is a powerful way to build systems. In Chapter 1, "What is P2P?," you learned that P2P is a system in which peers participate as equals in producing or consuming services. You also saw that networks of peer-to-peer devices can already meet many of the requirements to support enterprise applications. One can easily imagine that the applications being developed for the peer-to-peer model would be very useful to businesses. What business wouldn't be interested in collaborative technologies, file or document sharing, and distributed searching?

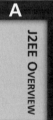

In this appendix, you learned that J2EE has been designed from the beginning to support networked enterprise applications. Its components offer services using standard and open protocols such as CORBA to access them. It will provide access to services using HTTP and SOAP in the near future. J2EE also defines a flexible application architecture that does not require interaction between *n*-tiers—applications can decide how to best use J2EE resources themselves. It offers a full suite of proven technologies for doing everything from supporting code mobility to handling distributed transactions. The platform is extensible and interoperable, making it possible to create bridged or hybrid solutions. Although J2EE does not solve all the problems left in peer-to-peer computing, it is an attractive platform for the development of peer-to-peer services.

Additional Resources

Sun is the preeminent source for information about Java and J2EE. However, there are many Web sites that are helpful to developers—a few of them connected with the development of the specifications and reference implementations are noted here:

- Java 2 platform specifications—The specifications for Java 2 platforms and technologies can be found at http://java.sun.com/products/.

- Java Enterprise Blueprints—The prescribed architecture for J2EE applications, best practices, and guidelines for using J2EE technologies are published in a book, *Designing Enterprise Applications with the Java 2 Platform, Enterprise Edition* by Nicholas Kassem, et al. An online copy of the book, along with the source code for the reference applications is located at http://java.sun.com/j2ee/download.html#blueprints.

- Java 2 Platform source code—The source code for the standard edition of the Java 2 APIs is included in the distribution of the Java 2 Software Developers Kit. For the truly adventurous, the source code for the rest of the J2SE platform, along with the source for the J2EE platform and other Java technologies, can be found at http://www.sun.com/software/communitysource/.

- Java Developer Connection—Offering support for developers, the Java Developers Connection (http://developer.java.sun.com/developer/) provides tutorials, examples, access to early versions of emerging specifications and products, and forums for discussion.

- Open source implementations of Java specifications—Working closely with Sun, the Apache organization implements Java specifications using an open source model. Several of their projects are used in Sun's official reference implementations. Tomcat (http://jakarta.apache.org/) is used in the servlet and JavaServer Pages reference implementation, and Crimson and Xalan (http://xml.apache.org/) are used in the reference implementation of JAXP.

INDEX

XML
JAXB. See JAXB, XML
authoring/processing
SOAP messages, 296-297
authoritative servers, 86
authorization, 46, 116, 200-201, 222
confidentiality, 211-212
integrity, 211
Kerberos, 201
Kerberos v.5, 202-203
.NET Passport, 207-211
architecture, 209
attributes, 207-210
cookies, 209-210
Kerberos interoperability, 210
nonrepudiation, 213-215
PKI, 203
SAML, 205-207
tokens, 324
autonomy
networks, 82
nodes, 21
availability (J2EE), 676-677
Avaki, 79
Axis, 256

B

B2B (business-to-business) model, 423
B2C (business-to-consumer) model, 423
bags, 410
balancing loads, 78, 139
bandwidth, 78, 138-139
Basic settings panel (JXTA Configurator), 599
Bday Precision attribute (.NET Passport), 207

beans
MetaBean, 506
MetaDataEntry, 506
MetaDataEntryBean, 506
ReceivingServlet, 320
SendingServlet, 319
SpaceBean, 506
BEEP (Blocks Extensible Exchange Protocol), 145-147
APEX, 155
channels, 146
continuous, 147
management awareness, 151
future, 155
incoming messages, 152
initial tuning channels, 146
initiators, 146
Java binding
initiating peer example, 152-155
installing, 147
listening peer example, 147-152
Web site, 147
listeners, 146
management channels, 146
peers, 145
initiating, 152-155
listening to, 147-151
profiles, 146
sessions, 146, 154
TCP-based sessions, 151
behaviors (local), 449
big-endian architectures, 109
bind() method, 369
bindings
JXTA, 437
late, 430
popes, 28
schemas, 308-309

bindingTemplate data type, 269
bindingTemplate structures, 328-330
Birthdate attribute (.NET Passport), 207
Block Cipher Rijndael Web site, 234
Blocks Extensible Exchange Protocol. *See* BEEP
bodyMethod attribute, 296
BPSS (Business Process Specification Schema), 338
bridges, 134
broadcast messages, 123-124
adaptive broadcast, 20, 123, 130
frequency, 127-128
multicast vs. unicast, 124-126
radius, 126
selective, 19, 123, 129
simple, 19
virtual spaces, 131-132
brokering techniques, 104
browsers
creating, 45
J2EE client, 688
brute-force attacks, 190
BSD sockets, 172
buddies, 221
building
RDF metadata standard, 170
SOAP messages, 257-258
W3C RDF metadata standard, 169
WSDL documents, 261, 263-264
abstract operations, 263
data type definitions, 262-263
element definitions, 263
invocation addresses, 264
operation implementation, 263-264

InetAddress, 102
InputPipeMsgListener, 641
InternationalString, 357
JailGameClient, 606
  code listing, 607-625
  methods, 606-607
JAXB, 310 311
JiniAgentService, 383-386
JiniUserAgent, 387-390
JoinManager, 383
JxtaGui, 591-592
JXTAPeer, 578-580
  CreateOutputPipeAndSend
    Message() method,
    584-586
  PipeMsgEvent() method,
    587
  publishServiceOverJXTA
    Pipe() method, 580-584
  SetInputPipeMessage
    Listener() method, 587
  SetMessageReceiver()
    method, 587
LeaseRenewalManager,
  422-423
Message, 402
MessageConsumer, 285-290
MessageProducer, 288-290
MetaBean, 508, 511-515
MetaDataEntry, 508-510
MetaDataEntryBean, 461,
  508, 515-517
ModuleSpecAdvertisement,
  461-463, 581
Monitor, 44
Naming, 369
Organization, 356
P2PDashboard, code listing,
  535-556
PeerDiscovery, 535, 556-561
PeerGroupFactory, 579
PersonName, 357
PhoneNumber, 357

PostalAddress, 357
Publisher, 587-590
Query, 309
Request, 309
Requester, 590
Service, 357
ServiceFinder, 521-522
SOAP-over-P2P, 578
  JxtaGui, 591-592
  JXTAPeer, 578-580
  Publisher, 587-588
  Requester, 590
SOAPEnvelope, 314
SOAPMessage, 313
SOAPRequest
  function, 297
  listing of, 293-295
SOAPResponse, listing,
  300-301
SortedListModel, 535,
  567-570
SpaceAccessor, 413-414
SpaceBean, 508, 519-521
StructuredTextDocument, 583
Student, 633-641
Teacher, 641
  code, 641-648
  Distance Learning appli-
    cation, 632
  methods, 641
TextListener, 290
Trial, 415
trusted, 36
UnicastRemoteObject,
  369-372
untrusted, 36
classification trees, 348-349
ClassificationNodeFilter ele-
ment, 355
classifications
  publishing, 347
  trees, 348-349

classified entries, searching,
  350-352
classpaths, 310
classrooms (virtual), 629
ClassServer class, 367
Clause element, 354
CLDC (Connected Limited
  Device Configuration), 50
cleanResources() method,
  607
clear() method, 568
client tier (J2EE), 687-688
Client-Server Exchange, 202
client-server model, 573
clients
  EIS, 688
  EJB, 688
  invoking, 367
  J2EE, 688
  J2EE applications, 679
  Jabber, 68
  JAXM SOAP, 316
  Jini-P2P, 387-390
  JMS, 281, 285-289
  messaging, 279-280
  prime number cruncher appli-
    cation, 465-469
  SOAP, 297-298, 313-316
  SOAP implementation model,
    576
  Web, 688
clusters, 71-72, 138
CMS (Content Management
  Systems), 74
code. *See* listings
code mobility (Jini), 90
collaboration, 73
  Consilient, Inc., 76
  file/resource sharing, 70
  Groove, 75-76
  Ikimbo, 76
  KM, 75
  shared spaces, 74
  workflow management, 75

S

Object Query Management, 347

classification trees, discovering, 348-349

classified entries, searching, 350-352

entry criteria, searching, 352-354

outrigger, 411-412

peer group, 449

personal portals, 522-525

pipe, 580

Property, 182

Query, 170, 182

registering, 381-383

remote discovery, 468

rendezvous, 574

replication, 170

security, 188

Time, 182

transaction, 392-393

unicast, 369-372

W3C RDF metadata standard, 170

Web. *See* Web services

services layer (JXTA), 93

ServiceVersion attribute, 580

session keys, 193

sessions

BEEP, 146, 154

TCP-based BEEP, 151

setBodyMethod(), 296

setDescription() method, 361

SETI@home project, 667

SetInputPipeMessage Listener() method, 587

setLocalDiscovery() method, 556

SetMessageReceiver() method, 584, 587

setQuery() method, 309

setResolverHandler() method, 607

sets, 469

SGML (Standard Markup Language), 160

SHA (Secure Hash Algorithm), 195

shared spaces (collaboration), 74

shared variables, 408-409

shares, 221

sharing

files, 71-72

information, 502-504

resources, 69-72

shells, 476

commands, 477

connecting, 494-495

message compression, 494

piping output into input, 477

redirecting output/input, 477

standard input/output streams, 477

JXTA, 478

commands, writing, 489-490

environment variables, 479-484

extending, 488-489

man command, 478

messages, creating, 484-487

responses, 487

starting, 478

Unix, compared, 479

pipes, 477

remote peer interaction, 484-488

SHS (Secure Hash Specification), 195

Sieve of Eratosthenes, 455

signatures (digital), 117, 194

silos (information), 70

simple agent frameworks, 424

Simple API for XML, 277

simple broadcasts, 19

Simple CORBA Object Access Protocol (SCOAP), 114

Simple Mail Transfer Protocol (SMTP), 85, 144

Simple Object Access Protocol. *See* SOAP

simple peers, 122

SimpleClause element, 355

sites (Web)

Access Grid project, 668

AES Algorithm (Rijndael), 234

ALPINE Network, 130

Apache, 506

Apache Axis, 256

Avaki, 79

BEEP Java binding, 147

Block Cipher Rijndael, 234

CC/PP profile, 657, 663

Consilient, 76

Cytaq Distributed Resource Network , 79

Data Grid Project, 668

DMCI, 505

Edutella, 169

Free Haven, 235

Free Riding on Gnutella, 235

geektimes, 216

Global Grid Forum, 672

Globus Project, 667

Gnutella, 72

Groove, 75

GSS-API, 235

Hive, 112

IBM UDDI Business Test Registry, 271

IETF, 64, 203

Ikimbo, 76

IMPP, 65

U

Related Titles from Sams Publishing